Too Proud to Fight

WOODROW WILSON'S
NEUTRALITY

1917. Woodrow Wilson, President of the United States, and Colonel
Edward Mandell House

Too Proud to Fight

WOODROW WILSON'S NEUTRALITY

———

PATRICK DEVLIN

———

The example of America must be a special example. The
example of America must be the example not merely of peace
because it will not fight, but of peace because peace is the
healing and elevating influence of the world and strife is not.
There is such a thing as a man being too proud to fight. There
is such a thing as a nation being so right that it does not need
to convince others by force that it is right.

Woodrow Wilson, 10 May 1915

OXFORD UNIVERSITY PRESS
NEW YORK and LONDON
1975

© *Patrick Devlin 1974*
Library of Congress Catalogue Card Number: 74–14284 2-27-76

Printed in the United States of America

DEDICATION

When Woodrow Wilson was a young man he was ambitious to 'write something that men might delight to read and which they would not readily let die'. Many would like to do that but not many who have not given their whole life to writing get the chance to try. I get it because I was young enough to miss the Great War of 1914 and so to speed to early attainment through the gaps it blasted out of the classes above me. The chance was bought for me by the dead: my gain is what they lost. I write about life in the office and not on the battlefield, but beneath the text there is the insistent drumming of the fight, of wounds and death. The death of the unripe. All through the writing I have been pricked by that. So I dedicate this book for what it is worth to the Unfulfilled and in particular

TO THE MEMORY OF

JOHN DUNCAN ABEL

CAPTAIN OF UPPINGHAM SCHOOL

SCHOLAR OF CORPUS CHRISTI COLLEGE, OXFORD

SECOND LIEUTENANT SEAFORTH HIGHLANDERS

KILLED IN ACTION NEAR DERNANCOURT

26 MARCH 1918

AGED TWENTY

This book is relevant to that death and not only because, if it could have been written differently, my cousin would not have died. The splendid achievements of the twentieth century, the probing of matter, the conquest of space, the care of the body, cannot stop these deaths. Their cause lies deep in the mind of man. To examine just a speck of history is to take a tiny part in the work of discernment and eradication. History is a tale of progress from an uncertain beginning to an uncertain end; and the historian, unable to extract from it more than a moment infinitesimal in the measure of time, searches this moment for a clue which, added to others in a laboratory of all the arts and sciences, may some day make known to man out of what his mind comes and into what it is to go.

PREFACE

THE plot of this story is the emergence of the United States into the international world with her entry in April 1917 into what was then called the Great War. It cannot be unfolded in a single narrative for there were different influences at work. America's effort to save her neutrality by restoring the peace of the world is, together with its deviation into the House–Grey Memorandum of February 1916, one narrative. Britain's effort to starve Germany by her blockade without allowing it to alienate America and how near that came to disaster is another. Germany's effort to starve Britain by the use of the submarine to destroy all shipping, neutral as well as belligerent, and how in the end that did come to disaster is another. These narratives are intertwined. Within them we see the dying of the nineteenth-century hope, expressed in so many Hague Conventions, that war could be tamed and civilized; and we see being born the hope that by covenant war could be outlawed.

The chief character in the story is Woodrow Wilson. Colonel House, Sir Edward Grey, Secretaries of State Bryan and Lansing, the ambassadors Page, Spring Rice, and von Bernstorff have large parts in it; and there is a host of others. But as the story unwinds, while the others in it play according to their natures the roles that events assign to them, Wilson reveals himself as more than the leading character. His character becomes a part of the story itself. Events no longer matter only objectively. It becomes relevant to see how they appeared to Wilson, how they mixed with the sort of man he was, and how in the chemistry of his thoughts the future was precipitated. As Winston Churchill wrote in *The World Crisis*:

It seems no exaggeration to pronounce that the action of the United States with its repercussions on the history of the world depended, during the awful period of Armageddon, upon the workings of this man's mind and spirit to the exclusion of almost every other factor; and that he played a part in the fate of nations incomparably more direct and personal than any other man.[1]

The United States was not in April 1917 swept into war. She was not dragged into it by treaties she had to honour. She was not directly threatened. She made no calculation of probable gains and losses. Why then did she go to war? In this book I reach the conclusion that it was because Wilson so decided. This is a simple conclusion which depends for its validity on the weight of evidence. But when it is reached it raises inescapably a question far more complex. Why did Wilson go to war: what made the man who was 'too proud to fight' descend into the arena?

The answer to this question requires as a first step a searching analysis of Wilson's character. For this purpose a list of qualities and defects will not do. Such a list tells as much about a man's character as a list of features tells about his face; and even the most skilful portrait tells infinitely less about a man's face than a few seconds of seeing it in mobility. To know a man's character one must see him in action.

It is a peculiarity of Wilson's character that it does not fully exhibit itself in any segment of his career, such as the one studied in this book, the period of American neutrality 1914 to 1917. His is not a life story that one can jump into easily at any point, journeying along until one wishes to take leave. This is because the material on which he worked he impressed with a pattern that repeats itself constantly, not with exactitude but with similarity enough to make it necessary to examine all the manifestations in order to completely understand one of them. A conspicuous example of this is in his diplomatic method: if indeed in 1914 his European contemporaries could have amassed and computerized all the data to be got from his early handling of Mexico, they could have foretold much of what he was to say on a world platform during the next four years. But the picture is wider than that. His eight years as President of Princeton University foreshadowed in a remarkable way, as has often been pointed out, the eight he served as President of the United States—the early successes, the subsequent despondencies, and the final defeat. There is more than an over-all resemblance. There is the lead into the first reform and then the outdistancing leap; he turns but not to narrow the gap, only to firm his stance and get a better purchase for the tug and heave of his effort to haul his followers up to where he stands.

So it appears to his admirers. But his detractors point to backslidings. The most notorious of them, the compromises to secure the Treaty of Versailles, occurred after neutrality was over. One that occurred before neutrality began is to be found in his abandonment in the exercise of presidential patronage of the rule with which he started—'the best man for the job'. Within the period of neutrality there is chronicled in detail in this book the stages of his descent from the high principle with which he first challenged Germany over the sinking of the *Lusitania*. Then there is the dramatic turnover whereby the candidate who in November 1916 was returned to office as the man who kept the nation out of war, five months later threw her into it. Why at times did he yield and at other times stand fast? When seeking the answer to this question the two last incidents have to be considered with the others.

Some may see in these incidents and in others like them nothing more than the concessions that a practical man has to make to the facts of life: let them be taken piecemeal as they come and without trying to fit them into a pattern. But then how does one fuse the conceding Wilson with the unconceding, the man who bowed to events with the man who went down in defiance? Surely if there was any malleability in the man he would not have insisted on the whole and nothing but the whole of his Princeton plans in 1908 and again in 1910. And how does one reconcile the notorious compromise in Paris on the terms of the Treaty with the equally notorious refusal in the face of certain defeat to accept a compromise on the covenant of the League? This conflict gets to the heart of Woodrow Wilson. Was he the conventional statesman, one, to be sure, with high ideals but always practising the art of the possible? Or was he a man who could not be budged from what he thought was right? A man who always does what he believes to be right does not inevitably disqualify himself from holding a high place in the world of affairs. What is right and what is expedient may go together; and with some men for whom the conjunction is favourable, they may travel in unison for a long way. So it was with Wilson. This is not the story of how they clashed in 1910 and again in 1919. It is the story, so far as Wilson is concerned, of how and why and at what cost in 1917 the clash was avoided.

I do not think it was avoided because Wilson compromised in 1917 with his beliefs of 1916. I know that Wilson in the days when he was a political scientist wrote of the part played in statesmanship by compromise and expediency, but I do not believe that a quarter of a century later he found himself able to translate theory into practice. When sometimes he had to force marriage on rightness and expediency he was under the painful necessity of first having to convince himself that the ceremony was lawful; and he lacked altogether the negotiating ability which sweetens the uses of compromise. What he did was not to compromise but to jettison. He made no abatements: he trimmed nothing off: he would not take half or even 90 per cent of a loaf: he disdained the second best. But what he would do on the rare occasions when he reached an impasse was to make a total sacrifice of the lesser in order to save the greater. It was the logical thing to do and he did it, as he did most things, quietly and without fuss. He accepted political jobbery because only thus could he get his measures through Congress and the measures mattered more. In the case of the *Lusitania* he abandoned the thesis in his first Note of 13 May 1915 when he saw that the price of enforcement would be war. By then he was beginning to have a vision of a higher peak: the duty of purging maritime warfare of inhumanity was of a lower order than that to which belonged America's duty to remain outside the conflict so that thus detached she could offer to both sides not only mediation, but to them and to the world the gift of permanent and universal peace. The day came, 31 January 1917, when it appeared that the price of permanent and universal peace was war itself. When Wilson realized that by avoiding war he would lose his power to make the peace, he threw overboard schemes and hopes to which he had committed himself in speech as well as in thought. It was his greatest sacrifice to that date and it seems almost as if he jettisoned a part of himself that he never fully replaced.

But when there was no lesser object to jettison, what then? Then Wilson sailed ahead heedless of the perils of the seas. He would not make for any port other than the one he had determined on. Then it was all or nothing. At Princeton the only peak he saw was Princeton as he wanted it to be. In Paris he sacrificed much to secure the Covenant of the League of Nations, but he preferred to lose the Covenant itself rather than to let it be diminished.

Thus it happened that while I was writing the story that forms four-fifths of this book—Part II, 'American Neutrality 1914–1917'—there emanated from it the theme of Woodrow Wilson's personality and its interaction with the events I was recording; and this, though it was implicit where the others were explicit, became as much a part of the story as the other intertwining narratives which I have mentioned. It also became apparent that it was not a theme which could be developed entirely within the period. One reason for this I have already given—that it is only by a study of different imprints of the same stamp that the pattern becomes clear. There are others equally important.

By many of his contemporaries Wilson was thought to be an ambitious and hypocritical opportunist. There are at least two occasions in the period I cover from which material can be taken to support the charge. The first is his devious behaviour at the time of the House–Grey Memorandum. The second, which is crucial to his reputation, is his conversion to warmaking. As to this, I have just advanced one hypothesis; another is that he was simply a purchaser of a seat in history who used the currency that was needed for it, turning from peace to war as easily as one exchanges dollars for sterling. I doubt if the charge can be satisfactorily rebutted without putting his whole character in issue; and certainly it cannot be disposed of without mention of an earlier count in the indictment. This relates to his move from one political foothold to another as he transferred in 1911 from the right to the left wing of the Democratic party in his climb to the top.

Another reason is Wilson's temperament. It is easy to follow the workings of his mind when it was, as it usually was, moving quietly and rationally. Its characteristic then was caution. But sometimes it jumped impetuously; to understand the workings of it then it is necessary to know that Wilson was contrary to appearances a highly emotional man. Loves and hates he had in excess. Manifestations of the hates are scattered through his life. There were Princeton enemies and political enemies, not Americans only but men like Huerta in Mexico whom Wilson never met; as bugbears they all seem much the same. The fear that his emotions might take control may have been one reason why Wilson tended to avoid discussions that could turn into confrontations. There is for comparison one such with the Princeton Board of Trustees on 13 January 1910 and another in Washington with Congressional rebels on 21 February 1916. At both there was on Wilson's part what was at best maladroitness and at worst an appearance of duplicity. On the other side of the coin there was the love and affection which Wilson had for Colonel House. It cannot be appreciated without at least a glance at his feeling for Professor Hibben. It was perhaps the major inducement which led the champion of open diplomacy into the twistiness of the House–Grey Memorandum. It is certain that throughout his life Wilson was abnormally reliant on those few who provided him with what he called 'sympathy and close support of heart'. A psychiatrist might be able to tell to what extent this was due to his early family life which to a layman seems to have been a forcing house for emotional dependence.

Finally, there is a question which faces the reader from the start. At the beginning of the story of American neutrality he finds Wilson ensconced in the White House, a politician of only four years' experience, nearly half of it gained as chief executive, firmly in control of the presidency and uttering sentiments apparently of the highest nobility and the purest disinterestedness. The question which, unless it be answered will tease him throughout the rest of the story, is—how on earth did Wilson get there? What prompted him to start in politics? How did he get past the bosses? How did he survive a party convention?

I have thought it best not to handle in fragments all the various matters that I have touched on in this preface but to supply in the brief and selective biography in Part I what I think the reader will want to know about Wilson's life before 1914. I have included almost everything that seems to me to illuminate his character and omitted almost everything that is not significant to his career as a world statesman. So there is no account of his American achievement in the years 1912 to 1914—only, I hope, enough allusion to it to prevent the reader from forgetting that Wilson was not only an international figure. Agreeing as I do with Churchill that a knowledge of the workings of Wilson's mind is essential to an understanding of his times, I have titled Part I with words taken from the passage I have quoted—'This Man's Mind and Spirit'.

CONTENTS

PLATES

PART ONE

THIS MAN'S MIND
AND SPIRIT

I

EARLY LIFE

Birth, 1856 — student at Princeton, 1875-9 — at University of Virginia, 1880 — law practice in Atlanta, 1882-3 — student and fellow at Johns Hopkins, 1883-5 — publication of *Congressional Government*, 1883 — marriage, 1885 — associate at Bryn Mawr, 1885-7 — professor at Wesleyan, 1887-9 — professor at Princeton, 1890-1902 — President of Princeton, 1902

His religion — observance of proprieties — influence of his parents — too proud to fight — falling in love and marriage: Ellen Axson — family and intimates: Mrs. Peck — health; and stroke in 1905 — trips to Britain — ambition — elocution and style — the will to lead

THOMAS WOODROW WILSON—not until he was twenty-five did Tommy Wilson become for ever Woodrow—was born on 28 December 1856. Or so it was always supposed until the researchers discovered that it was in fact forty-five minutes after midnight and so on 29 December.

His paternal grandparents migrated to America from Ulster in 1807. They moved west to Ohio and Woodrow's father, Joseph Ruggles Wilson, was born there in 1822. Joseph Wilson married in 1849 Jessie Woodrow. The Woodrows were a Scottish family; Thomas Woodrow, the President's maternal grandfather, crossed the English border in 1820 to be minister of a congregational church in Carlisle. Then in 1835 he went to America and in 1837 became pastor of the First Presbyterian Church at Chillicothe, Ohio. The President's father was also a Presbyterian Minister and was pastor of the first Presbyterian Church of Staunton, Virginia, when Woodrow Wilson was born. Soon after that event the Revd. Dr. Wilson moved to Augusta, Georgia, a pastorate which he held until Woodrow was thirteen. Thus they were newcomers to the South but they always liked to think of themselves as Southerners. After Georgia there were four years in South Carolina and after that eleven years in Wilmington, North Carolina. Dr. Wilson's influence on his church extended beyond his pastorate. He was one of the leaders of the Southern Presbyterians after they had broken with the North in 1861.

Woodrow was brought up in a comfortable home in which there was enough money but never too much. He was a solitary boy, though not an only child. He had two elder sisters and a brother, Joseph, ten years younger than himself. The Wilsons constituted an aloof family, intensely devoted to itself: 'there were in the community', Wilson wrote later, 'almost no companionable people for us'.[1]

Tommy wore spectacles from an early age and was considered delicate. Mrs. Wilson disbelieved in schooling, so Tommy did not learn to read until he was nine or ten and did not go to school until he was twelve. He was, Wilson recalled, 'a laughed-at Mamma's boy until I was a great big fellow'.[2] He went to Princeton in 1875 graduating in 1879, thirty-eighth out of 105 ranked. It would be unwise to take the grading as an assessment of his talents. His early schooling had not been first class; he always, as he said later, cut a sorry figure in examinations and indeed he never took another one; his reading, though intensive, had been largely extracurricular. He did badly in scientific subjects and poorly in political economy; throughout his life he never succeeded in interesting himself in any scientific or economic subject. History and politics he read a good deal of, chiefly works by authors who wrote well. In the summer of 1876, for example, he was reading Macaulay with great relish and also Gibbon. At the same time he was reading Shakespeare's plays systematically; he read and re-read *King Lear*. He read also Dante's *Inferno*. He had *Half-Hours with the Best Authors* in six volumes.

He was not wasting his time at Princeton. He was editor of *The Princetonian* and a prominent member of the debating society. He got a lot out of the life, earned the respect and liking of his classmates, and the intimate friendship of a few. The class of 1879 had a strong and long-lived class feeling from which Wilson was to benefit. Quite a few became wealthy and influential citizens; six became in due course members of the Board of Trustees, the governing body of the college. Three of the class were 'the real friends whom college life gave me for an inspiring possession'.[3] These three, all of them rather younger than Wilson, were Bobby Bridges, Charlie Talcott, and Hiram Woods. None of them attained any exceptional distinction. Woods went into medicine and finished a professor. The other two shared Wilson's interest in politics. In a letter to Bridges in February 1880 Wilson wrote of 'my brightest dream that you and I will someday be co-laborers in the great work of disseminating political truth and purifying the politics of our own country'.[4] Bridges became a journalist and ended up as editor of *Scribner's Magazine*. Talcott became a lawyer and was in Congress from 1911 to 1915 and again in 1920.

Almost immediately after he left Princeton Wilson won a mark of distinction that rejoiced his friends. He had an article entitled 'Cabinet Government in the United States' (signed Thomas W. Wilson) published in the *International Review*. The editor who accepted it and thus opened for the future

President the first gate on his road to fame was the future Senator Henry Cabot Lodge.

Dr. and Mrs. Wilson hoped that their son would choose the Ministry for his profession, but he chose the law: or rather he chose politics and the law because it was the way to politics. So in the fall of 1879 he entered the University of Virginia to read law. He found it 'terribly boring'.[5] In the letter to Bridges in which he wrote of his 'brightest dream' he called the law 'a treadmill'. He seems never to have settled down happily there. He had a continuous cold, the climate did not suit him, and the food gave him indigestion. As early as April 1880 his parents, who were always wanting him with them, were suggesting that he should quit and study at home; the suggestions becoming more urgent, he left the university at Christmas 1880. He saw his doctor who told him, so he wrote, that if he did not have systematic medical treatment, he would become a confirmed dyspeptic.[6]

Wilson was satisfied that he could qualify himself for practice by home study and he and his family began looking for a place where he could earn his living. By August 1881 he had decided on Atlanta, Georgia. But an unhappy love affair caused his work, as he said, to be 'considerably broken in upon',[7] and he did not get to Atlanta until May 1882. There he started up an office with a young partner called Renick. Through Renick he met casually the first of the men who were to be with him in public life, Walter Hines Page, then a young reporter, who was struck by his talents. But these talents did not bring him swift success. There was 'just enough business to do to keep me in spirits'[8] he wrote to Bobby Bridges: not too much to disallow the expenditure of his afternoons on writing and 'reading on old and loved topics, history and political science'. The business was definitely not a loved topic. Already by August 1882 Dr. Wilson, who was subsidizing him with $50 a month, was urging him to stick to it. 'It is hardly like you, my brave boy, to show a white feather before the battle is well joined.'[9] But by February 1883 Wilson had made up his mind to quit. It was not really because of the lack of immediate success. Atlanta was a growing city and there was a living to be made there. A contemporary practitioner, Hoke Smith, got on fast and moved into politics as a Democrat as Wilson had hoped to do; he was in Cleveland's administration in 1893, Governor of Georgia in 1907, and in the Senate during the whole of Wilson's two administrations. When he got his first Cabinet appointment in 1893 Wilson as a professorial critic wrote:

Mr. Hoke Smith is not suspected of knowing more than enough law to serve the practical purpose of his professional engagements. . . . Once admitted to practice he made an eager, astute, unremitting and successful effort to get business.[10]

This was an echo of what he had written to Bridges ten years before.

A man must become a mere lawyer to succeed at the Bar; and must, moreover, acquire a most ignoble shrewdness at overcoming the unprofessional tricks and underhand competition of sneaking pettifoggers.[11]

It was not his wish, he went on, to become a mere lawyer.

My natural, and therefore predominant, tastes every day allure me from my law books; I throw away law reports for histories, and my mind runs after the solution of political, rather than of legal problems, as if its keenest scent drew it after them by an unalterable instinct. My appetite is for general literature and my ambition is for writing. Small as has been my success in writing, I feel as if, after a thorough and undiscourageable disciplining of my faculties, and an ample storing of my mind, I could write something that men might delight to read, and which they would not readily let die.[12]

More sententiously he wrote a month later to Dabney, a friend he had made at the University of Virginia: 'The practice of the law, when conducted for purposes of gain, is antagonistic to the best interests of the intellectual life.'[13] And Dabney, who was a professor of history, replied with equal virtue:

Law is a subject which by its very nature precludes the possibility of a man's becoming great—a benefactor of the human race as a whole. The greatest lawyer upon earth is still no great man.[14]

Thus Wilson left the direct road to political power and returned to his studies. But he did not intend to become a mere academic any more than a mere lawyer. His plan, as it will be seen to take shape, was to make of himself an outside force, an expounder of practical politics, an interpreter of theory to men of action. He tried for a fellowship at Johns Hopkins University at Baltimore; and when he failed to get it, he went there as a graduate student in September 1883. After a year he got a fellowship, bringing in $500 which his father supplemented. The fruit of his first year at Johns Hopkins was his book *Congressional Government* which was published in January 1885. It attracted favourable notice and the offer of several appointments. In September 1885 he went to Bryn Mawr, the recently founded Quaker College for women near Philadelphia, to teach history and political economy.

So Wilson was twenty-eight before he began to earn a living and then it was a modest one, $1,500 a year, just enough to marry on; and in June 1885 on the strength of his appointment he had in fact married Ellen Axson, a girl from the South and a daughter and granddaughter of the manse. Apart from his book (then a *succès d'estime*, now in its fifteenth edition), he was still on the lowest rung of the ladder. His immediate goal was a chair at

Princeton. The appointment was by election of the Board of Trustees, the governing body of the university, which had on it the pick of the alumni; so he gladly accepted an invitation to propose one of the toasts at the annual dinner of the New York Alumni in March 1886. It offered him a chance to make a mark, but for almost the only time in his life a speech by Wilson was a flop. He used the occasion, which was highly festive, to give the alumni half an hour or more of earnest disquisition on a theme in which he was hardly disinterested, namely, that 'in every college there is missing a professor of politics'.[15] *The Princetonian*, perhaps out of kindness to a former editor, described it as 'the solid fare of the evening'. Wilson himself five years later—with perhaps some exaggeration in the other direction—described it as the occasion on which he emptied a very large dinner hall by an after-dinner speech.[16] In April 1886 he began work on his second book which was to be a textbook of political science called *The State: Elements of Historical and Practical Politics*. It needed three years' painstaking research conducted in his usual methodical way with the help of an extensive card index. 'A fact book', Wilson called it, 'a plebeian among books.'[17] It was a description of government in different countries, ancient and modern. He consoled himself with the thought that it was a necessary drudgery for the Novum Organon of politics which he intended to be his magnum opus. Renick, his partner in Atlanta, had also quit the practice of the law and had gone into government service. Wilson asked him to keep an eye open for a suitable government position. In November 1887 Renick had the wild idea that Wilson might be considered for an assistant secretaryship of state, a $4,500 a year job. Wilson ('my old political longings set throbbing again')[18] clutched at it but naturally in vain. He tried his hand at a short story and a couple of literary essays, but nothing came of them either. This was the perigee of his star.

His fortunes began to change when after two years at Bryn Mawr he was offered and accepted a professorship of history and political economy at Wesleyan University, Middleton, Connecticut. This was not a startling promotion, but it eased his finances. The stipend of the professorship was $2,500 and he was beginning to get an income from other sources, notably a course of lectures at Johns Hopkins. In the fall of 1889 *The State* was published. It was soon successful as a textbook (ten years later while Wilson was still only a professor the revised edition was published in England). He found himself in demand for miscellaneous lectures and articles. But what was more important was that he began to find himself. His letters often show him to be an accurate observer of himself; and this to his wife in March 1889 after a year at Wesleyan is worth quoting:

Have I told you that latterly—since I have been here, a distinct feeling of maturity—or rather of maturing—has come over me? The *boyish* feeling that I have so long had and cherished is giving place, consciously to another feeling—the feeling that I am no longer young (though not old quite!) and that I need no longer hesitate (as I have so long and sensitively done) to assert myself and my opinions in the presence of and against the selves and opinions of old men, 'my elders'. It may be all imagination, but these are the facts of consciousness at the present moment in one Woodrow Wilson—always a slow fellow in mental development— long a child, longer a diffident youth, now at last, perhaps, becoming a self-confident (mayhap a self-assertive) man. I find I look older, my former (Princeton) college friends here being the witnesses.[19]

Some of Wilson's 'former (Princeton) college friends' were already as alumni influential in the affairs of the college; one of them was already a trustee. In 1889 Bobby Bridges was actively canvassing on his behalf. Embryonically he was the first of Wilson's campaign managers; and likewise Wilson foreshadowed his own special method of non-fighting in elections, that is to say, as he told Bridges, that although 'profoundly averse from assuming the attitude of a candidate' he would not 'hesitate to say anything not undignified that would secure me an election I so much desire'.[20] In 1890 he was elected Professor of Jurisprudence and Political Economy at $3,000 a year. So at thirty-three he had a chair at Princeton and two books to his credit. He wrote to his father: 'Congratulations pour in from all sides; evidently I am "writ down" in the category of "successful men".'[21] But his first success left him—as all of them always did—thinking not of the place he was to occupy, but of the work he was to do.

He soon made himself a popular and effective member of the faculty. Also, 'hungry for reputation and influence', as he describes himself,[22] he continued to make his mark outside. By now a practised orator he was willing to speak anywhere he could make himself felt—the World's Fair at Chicago, a gathering of Ethical Culturists at Plymouth, Mass. (where in 1894 he first met Mrs. Toy*), a women's club in Denver. 'He was a man who could talk about potatoes', a fellow historian said, 'and make it sound like holy writ.'[23] He knew his increasing value and made businesslike bargains about his fees. In 1898 his earnings from lectures alone were $1,760, equal to half his salary as professor. Topics such as 'Religion and Patriotism', 'Patriotic Citizenship', and 'Leaders of Men', when well turned over in the lecture halls, could be turned into essays for publication. 'Democracy' was with some revisions delivered thirteen times in just over seven years, three times gratis, twice at $50, and eight times at $100. He was frequently reported in the local press and by 1900 he had qualified for its purposes to be 'The Famous Princetonian'.[24]

---

* See p. 23 below.

In 1897 Walter Page, by now editor of the *Atlantic Monthly*, tried to get him to write the history of the Civil War. But Wilson was out for bigger game. He had three well-known publishing houses competing for a *History of the American People*. The contract went to Harpers in 1900, the work to be serialized for $12,000 and then published in book form with an expected sale of 100,000. It was not a work of scholarship but a putting together of material, much of it used before, 'a giltedged potboiler'[25] a Princeton colleague called it. When Wilson ended his academic career in 1910 it had earned him $40,000.

In 1896 his Princeton reputation was markedly advanced by the striking success of a speech he made during the Sesquicentennial Celebration when Princeton declared herself a university. The address came on the second day after Dr. Henry van Dyke had, as the Memorial Book records, 'recited with refinement and deep feeling'[26] an academic ode composed by himself on behalf of the Cliosophic Society. A letter from Mrs. Wilson gives a loving account:

It was the most brilliant,—*dazzling*,—success from first to last. And *such* an ovation as Woodrow received! I never imagined anything like it. And think of *so* delighting *such* an audience, the most distinguished, everyone says, that has ever been assembled in America.[27]

The peroration is a good example of the style in which Wilson dressed elevating thoughts. His power as an orator, even over less-cultivated audiences, was due not at all to turgidity nor much to the pungent phrase but to the diction and beautiful delivery of lofty ideas in a manner, a contemporary critic wrote, 'giving to the average man a vague sense that he was being admitted to the inner shrine of a high intellectualism'.[28] Here is the peroration:

I have had a sight of a perfect place of learning in my thought—a free place, and a various—where no man could be and not know with how great a destiny learning had come into the world; itself a little world, but not perplexed, living with a singleness of aim not known without; the home of sagacious men, hard headed and with a will to know; debaters of the world's questions every day, and used to the rough ways of democracy; and yet a place removed; calm Science seated there, recluse, ascetic, like a nun; not knowing that the world passes—not caring, if the truth but come in answer to her prayer; and Literature walking within her open doors in quiet chambers with men of olden times,—storied walls about her, and calm voices infinitely sweet . . . Who shall show us the way to this place?[29]

During the next six years Wilson grew in standing with the faculty, especially with the younger members. He was sympathetic to reform and yet his manner and sobriety of outlook seemed a guarantee that he would always act judiciously. In 1892 he had refused the presidency of the University of Illinois and as a consequence his salary had been raised to $3,500. He was then the highest paid member of the faculty after the president. In 1897 he was offered the presidency of Virginia. He was very tempted; it would probably be the highest honour of his life, he wrote. But he put Princeton one higher. So did a wealthy group of his classmates more of whom were now Princeton trustees. With a promise, as definite as they dared to make it, of things to come, they coupled an annual retainer of $2,500 privately paid as an addition to his salary so long as he remained at Princeton. Five years later in 1902 he mounted the throne.

Temporarily he felt satisfied. He wrote to his wife:

It has settled the future for me and given me a sense of *position*, and of definite, tangible tasks which takes the *flutter* and restlessness from my spirits.[30]

But, showing that the itch was still troublesome, he wrote at the time he was preparing his inaugural address:

I feel like a new Prime Minister getting ready to address his constituents. I trust I shall seem less like a philosophical dreamer than Mr. Balfour does.[31]

These are the bare bones of a career which at the age of forty-five brought Woodrow Wilson to the top of the profession he had chosen, while that which he had but dreamt of was still to come. There must now be added to the bones the flesh which amplified them—his religion, his love of family, his love of words, his friends, the habits he formed and the characteristics he displayed and which determined so much of what he did thereafter.

Woodrow Wilson was born and bred in the Presbyterian faith. The faith remained with him unquestioned all his life and gave him the deep religious sense from which the principles of his conduct sprang. Thus he had the first requirement of a man of action—that he should not have a questing mind on fundamentals. For such a man thought must be settled so as to leave time and energy for action; perturbation must be only on the surface. This perhaps is why philosophers are rarely kings or kings philosophers. Wilson never debated about religion, within himself or with others, for he held it to be a matter of faith and not of understanding. 'So far as religion is concerned, argument is adjourned',[32] he once said. And again:

There are people who believe only in so far as they understand—that seems to me presumptuous and sets their understanding as the standard of the universe. I am sorry for such people.[33]

The practice of his religion meant much to him. 'I do not see', he said, 'how any one can sustain himself in any enterprise in life without prayer.'[34] It was his daily habit to read a chapter of the Bible. During most of his time at Princeton he kept in the shorthand he had taught himself a diary in which he ended every entry: 'Thank God for health and strength': and once with the prayer: 'The blessings of another day are added to my load of gratitude to God.'[35] He wrote in February 1884 to the woman he was to marry:

It does give me such unspeakable comfort, as my thoughts turn, during these quiet Sabbaths, these grave pauses before a new week's work, to the greatest subjects of life, diligence and duty and Christian love and faith, to think that you and I love and confide in and seek to serve the same Saviour, that we are one in these greatest things, as in all things else.[36]

It was not a narrow doctrine he was taught. His uncle, Dr. James Woodrow, whom the nephew greatly admired, was one of the leaders of modernist thought in his church. Dr. Woodrow was a geologist and a chemist as well as a theologian and for many years taught at the Columbia Theological Seminary where he was Perkins Professor of Natural Science in Connection with Revelation. The time came in the eighties when he found difficulties with the 'connection' and became unable to reconcile his geology and his chemistry with his theology in a manner that won the approval of the seminary authorities. It got about that he was unsound on evolution; and his response to an invitation from the Board of Directors to clear his character was to proclaim in 1884 his belief in the Darwinian hypothesis. This was the beginning of a battle which rocked the Presbyterian world and in which the Wilson family was on his side.

As well as being given a broad view of his own faith, Wilson was brought up to be tolerant of others, including even Roman Catholicism. He did not believe in everlasting torment; hell was no more than a frame of mind. But while there was no bigotry about him, there was no softness either. His real God was Jehovah, author of the moral law which was supreme, inflexible, and to be obeyed. Stockton Axson, his brother-in-law and close friend, wrote of him: 'The idea of an all merciful God was . . . to him a piece of soft sentimentality.'[37]

He was stern about the proprieties. He would not listen to any jesting about sex and that included any allusion to the natural functions. One of his complaints against a professor whom as President of Princeton he eventually got rid of, was that he made in class risqué remarks, such as that women were good for raising bread, babies, and hell. He would have got on well with Mr. Bowdler; after reading *Othello* he noted in his Princeton diary: 'The pleasure of its perusal is somewhat marred by the many improper passages which occur in the course of the play.'[38] An editorial which he wrote in

The Princetonian in 1879 sounds excessively straitlaced even for the day and age. It was about his inability to take lady visitors into the galleries of the gymnasium because of sights disgusting even to the hardened male eye. Bare arms could not be objected to: 'but the armholes take the form of a long opening which discloses no small portion of the wearer's side'.[39] As President of the United States in 1915 he appointed the notorious Comstock,* then just ending his career of prudery and entering his metamorphosis into a figure of fun, to represent the United States at an International Purity Congress.*

Wilson's religious belief went hand in hand with his belief in and reverence for his father. Dr. Wilson was a remarkable man—handsome, attractive, a commanding figure in the pulpit. His aim, which he achieved, was to be a friend and companion to his son as well as a father. Wilson in his thirties was still seeking his father's advice. Their affection for each other never diminished. In 1889 the father wrote:

> Ah, my son, this old heart—you fill it and with a charm that is quite unspeakable: —so that I am made to feel that after all I can never be lonely, were everything else stricken from my grasp, and you alone were to remain. Of course I am not forgetting —and do always remember—the other children, who are very close to my sympathies. But you were my companion more entirely than they; and are now not merely my child to whom consanguinity attaches by a tie of natural regard, but my *friend* to whom community of thought binds by ligatures which are thicker than blood. I am sure that we are the two who thoroughly—most thoroughly— comprehend each other. You satisfy my intellect as I believe I am able to content yours.[40]

The following year the son—notwithstanding the home of his own and the family he adored—wrote of the 'heart-sickness' from which he suffered because of his separation from his father and younger brother.

> It seems to me that the older I get the more I need you: for the older I get the more I appreciate the debt I owe you, and the more I long to increase it. It seems to me that my separation from you, instead of becoming a thing of wont, becomes more and more unendurable.[41]

In the beginning the father perceived in the son the latent powers that were so long in surfacing and he was the son's constant support throughout the early years of little achievement. He was his son's tutor in the arts in which Wilson later excelled and especially in the use of language. His definition of oratory—Wilson copied the whole of it out (this was in January 1878 when he was at Princeton) marking it 'from one of Father's excellent letters'—gave Woodrow the pattern that thereafter he applied. Dr. Wilson was dealing with the distinction between oratory and writing and answering

---

* Craig, *Banned Books of England*, Allen & Unwin, London, 1937, p. 107.

perhaps a query from his 'beloved Thomas' about the place in both of 'imaginative illustration'; his Thomas always liked a bit of adornment. Dr. Wilson wrote:

The soul of oratory is thought, the *body* of oratory is the suitable expression of this thought:—and usually the simplest words give this expression the best. To a lawyer—to a judicial mind—*the logic is everything*—and the true oratory, whether of the bar or the pulpit or the hustings, consists in the statement of connected thought (i.e. logical statement) uttered with energy and courage of *conviction*. If the speaker be in earnest, he will set fire to his logic as he proceeds; and out of this fire will spring the very illustrations he most needs.[42]

By example the Doctor taught him also the thoroughness which left no subject alone until penetration was thought to be complete. When he was a child, the two of them would take a passage from a favourite author, such as Charles Lamb, and then 'set to work to pick it apart and see whether the concepts it contained could be better expressed in some other way'.[43] This is the sort of teaching that shapes a man's mind. If in the pulpit his father hesitated for a word, the son would try in his own mind to supply it and be overjoyed if the event proved his choice. This was the beginning of his mastery over words and also perhaps of his belief in their efficacy.

Dr. Wilson could be critical but always in a friendly, sometimes even apologetic, way. He could be reproving too, as he was when Woodrow—it seems to be the only time he deviated from the straight and narrow path— cut his 'recitations' at the University of Virginia and got a bad report.[44] But on the whole the father tended to be too lavish in praise and support. He shared his son's 'surprise and indignation' at a Princeton grading in December 1878: no doubt, he wrote, it was because he had failed to 'cringe the pliant knee . . . Be assured though that we accept of your report rather than that of the faculty.'[45] Perhaps it was right with a sensitive boy in adolescence; and the father seems to have feared a lack of confidence in Woodrow rather than over-complacency. He felt too that his own life had been 'too much one of self depreciation' and urged his son—'to think as highly of yourself as possible'.[46]

This was an imbalance which was greatly aggravated by Woodrow's mother. She was a quiet and reserved woman, said by the neighbours to have 'English ways'. She doted on Woodrow, fussed over him and coddled him, assured him that he was always right, and constantly entreated him to take care of his health and not to catch cold. 'Miserably unjust'[47] was her comment on the 1878 grading; and when from the University of Virginia Wilson wrote of a tiff with a professor, while she was careful to caution him not to incur the professorial ill-will, she did not 'hesitate to say that his conduct in the matter is simply contemptible'.[48]

No doubt emotional starvation can warp the character but overfeeding chokes the natural growth of independence. Emotionally Woodrow was never taught to feed himself. The family was reserved towards outsiders and contained all its lovingness within itself. Their separation from each other was a continuous pain. In the family correspondence assurances and repetitions of love and affection are like water-lilies in a stagnant pool. 'Our peace of mind depends upon our hearing frequently from you',[49] his mother wrote him in 1876. And in 1877 in answer to a letter in which Wilson had evidently asked whether his letters were of the sort his mother wanted, she replied:

> The more we hear of each other this way, the less painful—more endurable—our separation—don't you think so, dear? Of course the essential points to be treated in your letters are, your health and happiness—and the assurance of continued love for us—who love you so dearly.[50]

In these surroundings Wilson never grew out of emotional dependence, as he himself realized. 'I tell you one thing, Bobby,' he wrote to Bridges in September 1880, 'I am absolutely dependent upon sympathy.'[51] He said the same thing during their engagement to his future wife: 'never forget that I am *absolutely dependent* upon your love and sympathy.'[52] Mrs. Reid* wrote of him that, while he was coldly objective when an intellectual problem was under consideration, he was 'almost weakly sensitive to praise or blame and to a sympathetic and affectionate personal atmosphere'.[53] He himself wrote of 'the almost feminine sensibility I have with regard to the feeling others may have for me'.[54]

There is no record that as a boy or a young man Wilson was ever in a fight. The nearest thing to it is a diary entry of 12 October 1876 about a fracas between the Princeton students and the 'townies'; 'I escaped without any hurt as I did not go into the fight but merely stood on the defensive'.[55] High feelings were aroused that year over the Hayes–Tilden election. Wilson followed it closely and on 10 November wrote in his diary that the suspense was almost insupportable. The suspense was due to the closeness of the electoral vote; eventually an electoral commission declared elected Hayes, whom Wilson called 'that weak instrument of the corrupt Republicans' and who was known to the party bosses as Granny Hayes because of his old-fashioned ideas on honesty. Wilson in a letter to his mother may have talked of the possibility of high political words leading to blows. At any rate he received in return the following motherly advice.

> The fear that you may be provoked beyond endurance during these anxious days, by those Radical companions of yours, has crept into my heart. I know

---

* See p. 23 below.

your self-control—or I would be miserable—but it is so hard to bear their ignorant thrusts quietly—and yet that is the only thing to be done—for one's own self respects sake. I trust you have been brave enough to disregard their insolence. Tommy dear don't talk about knocking any body down—no matter what they do or say—or rather don't *think* of doing such a thing. Such people are beneath your notice.[56]

There is a foreshadowing here of the great neutrality speeches and in particular of the most notorious of them. 'There is such a thing', President Wilson said nearly forty years later, 'as being too proud to fight.' He meant that a man might be proud enough to ignore provocation, too convinced of the justice of his cause to feel the need of proving it in battle, too proud to use his fists. No natural politician could have said it. The words themselves, as well as the utterance of them, tell much about Wilson. He hated the dust of the arena. He liked to talk of his Irish blood and to describe himself as a good fighter. So he was in his own way, and he enjoyed fighting in his own way; everyone gets some pleasure out of fighting with weapons in whose use he is adept. There are different sorts of fighting; a man who manipulates the buttons of modern warfare may lack the gusto for wielding a caveman's club. Wilson was a long-range fighter. His weapons were impersonal—the book, the article, the public speech—used to move the forces of righteousness by which his opponents would be overwhelmed, submerged in the waters, their death-cries stifled in their throats without letting of blood. But when men talk of fighting they are thinking of closer grips than that and most politicians are practised in the grapple of human personalities. Many of them in all countries are temperamentally pugnacious. Theodore Roosevelt was and Henry Cabot Lodge, Wilson's two deadliest enemies in the United States. So were Clemenceau and Lloyd George, Wilson's two great contemporaries in Europe, both masters of invective who never left an insult unrepaid. Men of this sort who have, as Lloyd George put it, 'fought their way to the top, giving and taking on the way the blows that hammer character',[57] disliked Wilson's methods as much as he disliked theirs. They had rubbed shoulders with their fellows, quarrelled with them and made it up, and learnt their quality. Wilson never fought on a personal issue, he never openly quarrelled with anyone, he never answered back and he never made anything up. It was thus that he made enemies, or rather kept the enemies he made. The scratches lightly inflicted when paths are crossed in public life become festering sores when treated with silence and contempt.

Wilson's mother died in April 1888. His father lived on for another fifteen years, dying in 1903 when he was nearly eighty-one. He spent his last years with Woodrow and Ellen at Princeton, and lived just long enough to see his son installed as president of the college. After which he told his granddaughter:

'Never forget what I tell you. Your father is the greatest man I have ever known.'[58]

Wilson was not a man who could live alone. When he outgrew his home he had to find a mate; and when he found one he was dissatisfied away from her. His wife was to be, not only his comfort and delight, 'but my *safety* also—against all the morbid tendencies which gather in me when I am compelled to live alone'.[59] When he found her she was 'the only person in the world,—except the dear ones at home,—with whom I do *not* have to act a part'.[60]

He began his search in 1881. During the two years when his career was in the doldrums at the University of Virginia and then in Atlanta his emotions were in turbulence. Maybe there was some connection between his unsatisfied longings and his inability to settle down. 'Hungry for a sweetheart',[61] as he afterwards described it, he courted his cousin Hattie Woodrow. 'I never knew a handsomer, more intelligent, noble or loveable girl', he wrote to Bobby Bridges;[62] her rendering of 'The Last Rose of Summer'[63] he thought equal to the great Patti's. In December 1880 he told his parents of his love for Hattie. He did not, however, propose until 25 September 1881 and then he was firmly refused. (Many years later Hattie's grandson made amends by marrying Wilson's granddaughter.) Wilson was deeply distressed and it took him a year to recover. When he was telling Bridges 'the painful story' in March 1882 he said that he was unable to speak of it without a rush of feeling. And his father wrote to him in August 1882:

I admire your unselfishness in still loving where you cannot secure, and in wishing for her happiness even though she may not care for yours in the way you desired.[64]

At first he salved the wound by persuading himself that she was as much in love with him as he was with her and refused him only because they were first cousins; as he put it in his letter to Bridges, 'she rejected me only because of a prejudice which made her regard it as her duty to do so'. But after he had succeeded with Ellen Axson so that his pride needed no further solace, he said that he had been mistaken in thinking Hattie capable of loving; she had no heart to give.

When he went to Rome, Atlanta in the fall of 1882 he met a young lady, the niece of the woman in whose house he boarded, in whom he became interested and she perhaps rather more than interested in him; a 'one-time intimacy, with its romps and its energetic correspondence'[65] he called it two years later. But in the following spring his eye alighted on a greater, more enduring attraction. It was when he was finishing up in Atlanta. One of the small pieces of legal business he had to deal with was about some property in Nebraska of his mother, land valued at about $20,000 and entrusted to the mismanagement of her brother-in-law, James Bones. Mr. Bones was a former Sunday-school superintendent with a face that shows mournful incapacities flowing down into a drooping moustache. Fortunately for Woodrow the rescuing of the estate proved to be quite a prolonged operation. On the first Sunday of the visit Woodrow of course went to church and there he spied Ellen. He described it to her six months later:

I remember thinking 'what a bright, pretty face; what splendid, mischievous laughing eyes! I'll lay a wager that this demure little lady has lots of life and fun in her!'[66]

He asked who she was and, on being told that she was the daughter of the Revd. Mr. Axson, a friend of his father, took an early opportunity of calling at the manse. After some conversation with the minister on such topics as the diminishment of night congregations, he inquired after the health of Miss Axson, who was accordingly summoned to the parlour to meet him. This was the beginning of a courtship that followed with outward sedateness and increasing inward excitement the centuries-old pattern from which the twentieth has been the first to break away. There were boating parties, picnics and walks in which they discussed poetry and books; she was at least as well read as he. They talked about Shakespeare and Wordsworth; she wanted him to enjoy the Brownings as she did and introduced him to *Middlemarch* which at once he started to read, fancying himself as Lydgate. After a fortnight he knew he was in love. She was just the woman for him— three years younger, very pretty in a simple unworldly way, a bright and sunny look reflecting her disposition, a 'little lady',[67] 5 ft. 3 in. tall and weighing 115 lbs., undeniably attractive with numerous admirers. After a second visit to Rome Wilson told his mother on 1 June that he was in love. Then there was a third visit during which Wilson advanced by the customary stages. There were verses copied out and given to her to read, the contents selected not so much for their literary merit as to indicate indirectly the state of the donor's heart. This was followed up by the offer of an opportunity to the lady to indicate indirectly the state of *her* heart. Woodrow spoke of what he called his 'needs and embarrassments as regarded her sex' and told her of the 'very foolish love affair' with Hattie 'sometime before exploded'.[68] Was a man such as he, he inquired, a future professor with uncertain prospects and narrow means, entitled to ask any woman such as he could love to make the sacrifice of marrying him? He himself thought not.

This was on 25 June 1883 when they were strolling in the dusk along the river bank. How should the nineteenth-century lady answer? As Ellen wrote him later:

> I couldn't say frankly and simply what I really thought,—what *any* woman with the smallest claim to the name would think—on the points proposed; yet I couldn't lie and say that I thought your position correct, that it would be both unjust and ungenerous for you to ask any woman to share your dreary lot![69]

So, as she said, she 'managed to slip out' with a reference to Mrs. Carlyle.

But by then he had touched her heart. She had had, as she told him later, 'that first glimpse of your aims in life . . . to be an enobling, inspiring, influence in the world'.[70] Thus the affair moved into its next stage and Woodrow, while they were sitting together on a hammock, was given the 'privilege' of correspondence.[71] In a long letter which he wrote her on 4 July, he took the opportunity to overreach any rumours that might come her way about the young lady in Atlanta. 'Miss Katie, though most attractive and companionable in holiday hours' and 'having that keen sense of the subtler forms of humour which is never given to coarse minds' was not, he might say, 'without even hinting the least abatement of praise . . . a woman of the sort most attractive to me'. The correspondence flourished. Then at an unexpected encounter on 16 September 1883 Wilson took the citadel by storm. She had resolved to make him wait until he was sure. He was sure, he insisted,[72] and uncertainty would interfere with his work and spoil his year at Johns Hopkins. So they engaged themselves and sealed the betrothal with the first kiss and later with a lock of hair. The engagement lasted for a year and three-quarters during which they saw very little of each other. It was an age in which desires were subordinated to duties. Ellen's mother had died in 1881; and until her father died in May 1884 it was Ellen's duty to look after him. Woodrow's duty to his parents meant that he must spend much time with them in Wilmington. Indeed, Ellen's first visit to Wilmington was almost frustrated by her duty to her grandmother. In the Georgia of the old lady's youth it was not etiquette for the bride-to-be to visit the home of her future parents-in-law, at any rate if the prospective groom was there. At a time when Ellen thought that her father's illness would put a visit out of the question anyway, the old lady made her promise that she would not go. So Ellen wrote sadly in July 1884:

> Even if I had not promised I could not think of going when she is so violently opposed to it . . . her opposition is the *only* thing *now* which prevents my doing as you wish; but of course you see yourself that it would be impossible under the circumstances to go.[73]

Woodrow saw it just as she did. He replied:

It would not have been becoming in you to disregard your grandmother's wishes, so expressed and urged. Unless her opposition can be overcome, the visit must, of course, be foregone.[74]

At the same time Woodrow manœuvred to overcome the grandmaternal opposition and a tactful letter from Mrs. Wilson succeeded in doing so.

The near contretemps would not be worth relating if it were not an almost bizarre application of the tenets which ruled the couple's lives and a proof that they honoured in their deeds as on their lips the virtues they had both been bred to respect. Love, duty, service, and acceptance of the will of God: these are the themes that run through their letters. The love they pledged each other, they said, was but an aspect of their love of God. Service and duty were burdens to be welcomed; Ellen's idea of heaven was not as a place of rest but as one of 'perpetual service without weariness'.[75] For her the art of living, as she once wrote to Woodrow, was not to neglect the duties that lie at the foundation of all joys.[76] Beneath it all there was the firm belief in a divine providence. A few days after her father's death Ellen wrote almost passionately:

Oh, how can people presume as they do, to pry into the providence of God! They call this a 'judgement', and that a 'reward', and the other 'a special answer to prayer', as calmly as confidently as if they were omniscient themselves, or had been present at His counsels. *I know* it is all right, and I not only know it but *feel* it with all my heart. Not for a moment would I wish it other than as He wills. Sometimes when I think what it means to be in God's hands, under His direction I scarcely dare to ask for any earthly good, lest taking me at my word, He should give me *my* will rather than His. Is it not better to trust Him altogether,—to wait quietly and let Him decide? But I don't trust because I understand; I know that 'The end will tell, the dear Lord ordereth all things well'.[77]

Ellen had a talent for drawing and painting at which she was able to make a little money in Georgia. After her father's death she spent a year in New York studying with the Arts Students' League. She heard there a lot of talk about 'a woman's right to live her own life'.[78] It meant nothing to her at all. In answer to a letter from Woodrow in March 1885, in which he said that he felt 'guiltily selfish' about the interference of love with her profession and the sacrifice it might involve, she began by giving him a matter-of-fact assessment of her talent.

My experience and observation since I have been here have driven me to the conclusion that I *have* talent, above the average among the art-students. It is barely possible that my talent for art combined with my talent for work *might*, after many years win me a place in the first rank among American artists,—who don't amount to much *anyhow* you know! But 'art is long';—it would take years of steady effort to do any *really* (not just *comparatively*) good—to say nothing of 'great' work.[79]

This she followed with one of the most beautiful of her many declarations of love.

As compared with the privilege of loving and serving you and the blessedness of being loved by you, the praise and admiration of all the world and generations yet unborn would be lighter than vanity. If *now* I held such *greatness* in my hand I should toss it away without a second thought that the hand might be free to clasp yours. Indeed I should probably drop it without even the *first* thought simply because, having something better to think of, I had forgotten all about it,—had forgotten to hold it. My darling, it would not be a sacrifice to die for you, how then can it be one to live for you?[80]

Naturally Ellen embraced with enthusiasm Woodrow's conception of the ideal wife, a woman of feminine charm entering into the husband's intellectual labours with keen sympathy and appreciation. Sympathy was what was wanted from her, not co-operation: 'not such a woman as John Stuart Mill married and doted on, who expels sentiment from life, knows as much as her husband of the matters of his special study and furnishes him with opinions, ministering not to his love but to his logical faculty.'[81] She must be ready to beguile his lighter moments, to strengthen his graver moods by a womanly love of wisdom, and to turn with eager enjoyment to the music and the greater thoughts of poetry. There was to be a workroom in which she would sit while he was studying, because it was then that he most needed sympathy and the presence of someone to whom he could speak from time to time of what he was writing or reading and who would volunteer a caress or a kiss when she learnt that she could rest and delight him in that way in the intervals of his work.

To this Ellen responded: 'You are *very* good love, to let me *live* by your side. You could not grant me a privilege which I shall prize more.'[82]

They were married on 25 June 1885, as soon as he had an income; indeed, his ardent desire for marriage was the strongest inducement to him to take the job at Bryn Mawr. He felt it was a little undignified to be teaching females; and for him to serve under a woman was, Ellen thought, 'jarring to one's sense of the fitness of things'.[83]

They were then and for ever in love. Their first child was born ten months after the wedding and then two more, all girls, in 1887 and 1889. Their love still rises freshly from the hundreds of letters they wrote each other for they wrote almost every day they were apart. His sometimes seem contrived, but his craft was in words and the contrivance is that of the jeweller setting gems for his beloved, and giving her the best of his talent. The twentieth-century reader may want to brush aside the cobwebs—the adjectives which are no longer in the mode, 'winsome', 'arch', 'womanly', the studied quotations, the raillery of the 'Sir' and 'Miss' type—but he should remember that there was a time when these held charms which they may hold again if the future were to find the twentieth-century style depressingly nude. If he is cloyed by the surfeit of repetitions, he must remember that for lovers apart love's protestations cannot too often be repeated. Taken in this way, he will find them as touching a lot of love letters as any in the lives of the famous. They were paid for by sacrifice—for it was a real sacrifice to these two to be apart and, as he said, under bondage to pen and ink—and posterity is now the beneficiary of their payment.

In 1892 when they had been seven years married Ellen went south with the children on a round of family visits. Such visits in those days were never short and she was away for two months most of which Woodrow spent in the Nassau Hotel at Princeton. Each daily letter was half filled with what they called 'love passages', his with an accompaniment of poetry varying from the pretty simplicity of Burns to the classic beauty of

> Nor shines the silver moon one half so bright
> Through the transparent bosom of the deep,
> As doth thy face through tears of mine give light:
> Thou shinest in every tear that I do weep;
> No drop but as a coach doth carry thee.[84]

Woodrow was highly sexed, a quality which he wrote of as 'the riotous element in my blood' or 'my intensely passionate nature'[85] and once in apologetic recollection of my rude demonstration of my man-like love'; and once after fifteen years of married life of 'all the sweet passionate secrets of married love' which 'do not stop short of complete and exquisite satisfaction'.[86] Ellen was inevitably more reticent in her replies but often she wrote that she loved him passionately. Chiefly she dwelt upon the irresistible compound of greatness and sweetness that fed her adoration, even now 'among the foremost thinkers of his age'[87] and yet 'with such ineffable tenderness, such unselfishness and thoughtfulness in things great and small'. She repaid him by making his home and herself within it the place of his delight. He wrote to her in July 1899:

If any authentic piece of literature should ever come out of my home, it will be a thing explained, provoked, shaped in some deliberate and unconscious way by you.[88]

She was a wise and constant counsellor, knowing how to give him the advice which he would heed. She was an equal partner in all the decisions of his career. She was the woman of the Proverbs, her price above rubies.

The outer family included many cousins on both sides who stayed with them for long periods. The Wilsons were always extremely generous to relatives and friends. At a time when his income was at its lowest for what it had to do—that is, when he was still at Wesleyan and after the birth of the second baby—and he himself was borrowing from his father and others, Wilson responded at once to a plea by his former partner, Renick, for a loan of $100. Their house was nearly always filled with young cousins and their generosity did not stop at having them to stay; they sometimes paid their college fees as well. At Princeton their household was usually around ten, exclusive of the cook and housemaid they kept. Their second house at Princeton was the one they liked best and which they returned to in sentiment when they were living in much grander residences. It was designed by Wilson himself[89] who had, his family felt, a flair for architecture. His taste was that of his time, which decorated in the Gothic the happy Georgian of the old Princeton. 'By the very simple device', he once said, 'of building our new buildings in the Tudor Gothic style we seem to have added to Princeton the age of Oxford and of Cambridge.'[90] At 50 Library Place the Tudor for the most part overcame the Gothic.

Immediately outside the family there was a small circle of intimates, women as well as men. Wilson does not seem to have been interested in girls until he was at the University of Virginia and well into his twenties; but from the time he started on his quest for a mate until well into middle age he had an eye for a pretty woman. He always told Ellen all about it. During their engagement he told her about an encounter with the 'young lady in the next seat' on the ride from Bryn Mawr to Philadelphia and Ellen in reply chaffed him about his ravings over the Misses Bingham and Miss Hall. More seriously, he wrote her on 14 February 1889 by way of a Valentine·

I am peculiarly susceptible to feminine beauty, as you know, and to all feminine attractions. A pretty girl is my chief pleasure, a winsome girl my chief delight: girls of all degrees of beauty and grace have a charm for me which almost amounts to a spell . . . Only one woman is or could be the pivot of my life . . . *She* knows—for she knows me—that other women may play upon the surface of my susceptibilities, but that she is part of me and that I look at them, as it were, *through her*.[91]

During his first marriage he was on terms of platonic friendship, which Ellen sensibly encouraged, with half-a-dozen women. They had to be, to use his own words, 'cultivated and conversable',[92] neither merely pretty nor merely intellectual. There were Mrs. Peck, Mrs. Reid, and Mrs. Toy; and he managed even during his busiest days to write them long and affectionate letters. The two latter, wives of professors, he met first when he was away lecturing in 1894. In Baltimore, Mrs. Reid, 'so bright, so whimsical, so sweet, so pretty',[93] immediately eclipsed a Miss Duer who only the week before had been found 'thoroughly intellectual and thoroughly feminine' as well as 'very attractive in person'. These and other lavish praises are all contained in his letters to Ellen and he always followed them with 'love passages' exalting her; of Mrs. Reid he wrote, 'while she delights me, you enslave me'.

Mrs. Peck was the prima donna. In 1906 Wilson had something like a stroke and one of the conditions made by his doctors to his resumption of work was that he should take regular and restful vacations. On one of these he went to Bermuda. Mrs. Peck had a house there and was evidently the local lionhunter. Wilson wrote:

Mark Twain arrived on the boat this morning, and Mrs. Peck at once took possession of him. They are old friends. Indeed, she seems to know everybody that is worth knowing.[94]

By the time Wilson left Mrs. Peck and he had become close friends and thereafter they corresponded regularly; in seven years he wrote her two hundred letters. She came to stay at Princeton. 'Gay and entertaining', Wilson's sister-in-law wrote of her, 'a woman of the world, not beautiful but giving the effect of beauty, . . . nothing if not smart.'[95] No one met Mr. Peck. He was her second husband and understood to be a successful New England manufacturer. When Wilson was a public figure, Mrs. Peck came into the limelight and there was a great deal of gossip. It is impossible to believe there was anything in it. Dean West, Wilson's bitterest enemy at Princeton, said: 'Heaven knows I hated Wilson like poison, but there is not one word of truth in this nonsense. It is simply not in character.'[96] Theodore Roosevelt also dismissed the stories, guffawing that Wilson would be better cast as the Apothecary than as Romeo.

Among men, Wilson was not a natural mixer. Even when young he had a reserve and stiffness which put off those who might otherwise have become casual acquaintances. Broad chaff—or unrefined wit, as he called it—was not at all to his taste.

I have always regarded teasing as of doubtful gentility when ventured by any but one's nearest relatives and dearest intimates: and I am quite sure that some people who have teased me have thought me curt and disagreeable.[97]

But for those who got past the stiffness there was a charm which he never lost. Lloyd George speaks of it in Paris in 1919 as 'the charm which emanates from a fine intelligence, integrity of purpose and a complete absence of querulousness or cantankerousness'.[98]

Mrs. Reid described him as a

tall young man with a formal, over-sensitive manner . . . His friendships were more like those among English men than among Americans. A gathering of his friends would usually be in quiet home surroundings, and good talk would be their recreation.[99]

The good talk was not always serious. Woodrow wrote to his wife after one gay occasion:

Mr. Babcock and I capped each other's stories all through the dinner, keeping the table in a roar—and Mrs. Babcock listened to his stories almost as well as you listen to mine.[100]

If he could be criticized at all as a general talker, one of his friends said, 'it might be that he seems more interested in what he was saying than in what you were saying'.[101] He knew about this little failing and spoke of it engagingly; 'a very interesting fellow,—a capital listener' he said of another fellow guest. He once wrote to his wife:

I suppose that it is for the best that I should be dragged out thus from my den to see people: my tendency is too much towards shutting myself up. I love to talk, but only when I can keep the floor much in sympathetic company—isn't that true?[102]

Ellen told him some time later that he was not as unsocial as he thought he was: 'you *do* enjoy meeting interesting people, and it does you good.'[103]

So they had a number of friendships though within a narrow circle, but the only really intimate one, beginning about 1899, was with the Hibbens—the 'dear Hibbens' as Wilson always called them in his letters, 'the dear friends whom I carry always in my heart'.[104] When Wilson left on a trip to Europe in June 1899, he wrote to Mrs. Hibben—the men were, uniquely, Jack and Woodrow to each other, but she of course was Mrs. Hibben—of his distress at having 'to miss this summer of closer-drawn friendship and intimacy'. In reply she told him that 'Jack is lost without you';[105] and Ellen wrote that he 'seems quite lovesick for you'.[106] 'Our love for you both has put you beyond the reach of competition',[107] Woodrow wrote to Jack on his return. When the next year he heard the news that the Hibbens were to go to Europe for nine months and realized that when they got back the Wilsons themselves would be away he wrote to Ellen, 'we shall have only five months with them out of two years and four months'.[108] 'What shall we do without them?' he underlined; and went on: 'That's the worst of having friends whom one really loves,—the pain of the inevitable separations.'

Hibben was the Stuart Professor of Logic and much respected at Princeton. When Wilson went on vacation in 1906 he left Hibben to act as president in his place.

Religion, family, health, and ambition: these were the four lines that squared Wilson's life. Health was a subject always on his mind; he was brought up by his parents to worry about it and his correspondence is full of it. It must be remembered that the ideas of the nineteenth century about health are, like its ideas about courtship, romance, duty, and providence, much more easily apprehensible by the generations that preceded it than by the present. Change of air, exercise, and purgative doses are no longer the standard prescriptions for those who are feeling out of sorts. The antibiotic and the injection have proved revolutionary. There was then no saying what catching cold might not lead to, but now strong men no longer get pneumonia and die within days. Appendicitis, of which Wilson had a 'haunting dread',[109] is now no great menace. It was not so much fear of suffering that deterred as the fear that health undermined might result in a woman becoming a permanent invalid (two-thirds of the women she knew, Ellen wrote in 1885,[110] were invalids to a greater or less degree) or unfit a man for his task in life. Health and strength were, as in Wilson's diurnal prayer, closely connected. 'One must not be spendthrift of strength.'[111] 'Do *do do* guard your health' is a typical ending to a letter from father to son. And again in 1890:

Let me beg of you, my darling son, that you will so arrange your affairs as that overwork may not pull down your constitution and shake the foundations of your health.[112]

Ellen on 7 April 1885 told Woodrow that she had long ago realized 'that my darling's health is not *poor* exactly, was what might be called "uncertain" —not very strong; that his constitution is one with which he must not dare take any liberties'.[113] Woodrow agreed that it was 'precarious'.[114] The following year he told a correspondent of having 'had a long tug with ill-health these last two months'.[115] His afflictions in youth were mainly digestive and gastric; he suffered also from nervous headaches. The trouble that led to his leaving the University of Virginia, where, as he subsequently wrote, he had 'gotten his system out of order',[116] was of this sort. The sovereign remedy was regular exercise; he kept a set of Indian clubs. The occasional games he played in his youth were presumably for the sake of exercise; at any rate he never writes of any enjoyment he got out of them. Later on he took to dosing and dieting himself and was always on the lookout for new remedies. In 1901 he was attracted by a magazine article on the moral value of hypnotic suggestion; the author must have been genuine, else he would hardly have practised as Dr. Quackenbos. But later in the year Wilson fell for a quack and paid $20 for 'The Swoboda System of Physiological Exercise' after Mr. Swoboda had diagnosed his troubles as 'due to lack of blood and nervous force'.[117]

As Wilson moved towards his forties his health was threatened in a more serious way. This manifested itself in 1896 in the form of neuritis. He had been overworking—all his writing and lecturing on top of his teaching; and there was the financial strain of paying for 50 Library Place. The neuritis in his right arm was so severe that for a considerable time he could not use it to write. It is a remarkable proof of determination that he taught himself to write with his left hand. His doctors ordered him to take a complete rest and thus it was that in the summer of 1896 he took his first trip abroad. Fortunately for his health he was the type of man who could relax; perhaps because of his trust in divine providence, he was able to leave all his anxieties behind and so recuperate very quickly. It was on his return in the fall of 1896 that he delivered his celebrated Sesquicentennial Oration.

Ten years later something much more serious happened. In 1905 he had an operation for hernia and after that he spent five weeks in hospital with phlebitis. The neuritis in his arm became acute. Then one day in May 1906 he awoke to find that he could not see out of his left eye. The Philadelphia doctors made a grim diagnosis; it was a hardening of the arteries causing a stroke of some sort and they thought that his active career was at an end. But again his exceptional power of recuperation pulled him through. After a long summer in England, during which he hardly read or wrote at all, he was back at work again in the fall. The only permanent result was some restriction of vision in the left eye. After this grave warning, he was far more careful than before, schooling himself to take regular recreation and to avoid overstrain. The attack in 1906 was the last serious one before the historic stroke in 1919.

Wilson's relaxing trips abroad usually took him to Britain. Before he landed at Brest at the end of 1918 he had only once been on the continent of Europe, a visit of a few weeks in 1903. Always he returned to Britain, making five trips in all between 1896 and 1908. His admiration for Britain's institutions was a point whispered against him by 'the philistines'[118] when he was being considered for the chair at Princeton. He even preferred her spelling as more 'classical'—the 'u' in 'labour' and so on[119]—and abandoned it reluctantly in 1902 when it was vetoed by his publishers. Once in an address in 1894 he referred to her as 'the old country'.[120] There is a surprising dichotomy between all this and his distrust and dislike of the British character. He made only one real English friend and he was an artist whom he met at Rydal in the Wordsworth country. Wilson felt that he liked the company of 'a jolly, irresponsible lot of artists'[121] and Fred Yates tickled his fancy from their first meeting on Pelter Bridge across the Rothay when he introduced himself as 'poor, but thank God, not respectable'.[122] They became warm friends. But until 1917, when the United States and Britain were together in the war, Wilson had hardly met any British public figure. Had Wilson himself been in politics before 1910, no doubt on these trips to Britain he would have met some opposite numbers. As it was, and apart from Bryce, who was an academic as well as a statesman, the only British public figure whom Wilson had met was Lord Morley. On paper this sounds an interesting encounter, since Morley was the nearest thing (though still some distance removed) to a Wilson in British politics. He was the intellectual in action, the disciple of John Stuart Mill, who became one of the leading figures in Gladstone's last cabinet. 'Attractive-minded man—something like a young John Morley',[123] Beatrice Webb had noted in her diary after she had met Professor Wilson at Princeton. Wilson met Morley in 1908 at the Scottish castle of Andrew Carnegie, the American steel magnate, where he was fund-raising as President of Princeton. Morley was then seventy and in the Cabinet. Wilson was shocked to find him 'old and bent and a bit feeble'[124] but enjoyed very much what he heard of his talk. The acquaintance ended there. Wilson did not even ask him about Gladstone. This was surprising, since Gladstone was Wilson's boyhood hero as Disraeli (the 'old fox'[125] Wilson called him) was the villain. Burke, Brougham, Bright, Cobden, and Macaulay were others whom he admired and read. Bagehot was the acknowledged creditor of *Congressional Government*. Green's *Short History of the English People* was Wilson's model for his history of the American people. He was at least as familiar with British political thought in the nineteenth century as with American.

In the summer of 1896 Wilson did Britain on a bicycle. His energy seems prodigious and he went everywhere. His letters brim over with his delight in the English countryside and in the treasures of her cathedral towns; and the nostalgic can distil from them all the joy of a highway free of motors. It was also a literary pilgrimage. He plucked grass from Adam Smith's grave in Edinburgh; turned aside to see the cottage where Burns was born; visited Hartley Coleridge's Nab Cottage and Dr. Arnold's Foxe How, Wordsworth's grave, of course, and Dove Cottage, which yielded a tiny flower and some ivy leaves; the Shakspere (he preferred to spell it that way) country from the Woolpack at Warwick; Burke's grave from the Rose and Crown at Tring; a ride of twenty miles beside the Wye with a pause at Tintern Abbey to read the 'Lines'; Bagehot's grave (a leaf enclosed to be pressed and kept) near Wells, whose cathedral he thought the most beautiful of all, and he had seen York, Durham, and Lincoln and half a dozen others. He revelled in it all, even in the 'neat and cheerful village'[126] of Slough which, as he told Ellen, has nothing to do with the Despond of the *Pilgrim's Progress*. He went to Cambridge where he talked with the great jurist, F. W. Maitland. Oxford he found the hardest place to leave: 'a mere glance at Oxford is enough to take one's heart by storm.'[127]

Three years later in 1899 he took another midsummer bicycle trip but this time in company with Ellen's younger brother Stockton. Stockton was devoted to Woodrow. When he was fourteen and going off to school, his father told him that there was 'no better model to follow than the son of my friend Dr. J. R. Wilson'.[128] Stockton never married and spent a lot of his time with the Wilsons; he suffered from ill-health and melancholia and had rather an owlish face. It was the same sort of trip as before, through the Burns country to the Lakes which Wilson loved almost as his own. From the White Lion at Patterdale he wrote of the road that runs by Ullswater:

Close to the water, in full command of every view, and yet busy, not with that, but with taking you by the easiest slopes first through one park and then through another, past quiet fields and neat barnyards, quite like any other neighbourhood road, whose business it is to find a man the way home, regarding very much as if they were accidents the cool avenues of ancient trees it must go through and the shining water just beyond one of its hedges. It is all the more perfect a road because its perfect beauty seems, not deliberate, but inevitable. We seem infinitely far away from *all* the world here in this tiny sequestered village this evening,—from the world of England as well from the world across the sea that holds our treasures. An unspeakable peace rests upon this place, and our spirits cannot escape the spell it casts.[129]

Thence they went by rail across to Durham, where they attended the Assizes, and down to Cambridge, encountering only one setback at Peterborough, 'a wretched hostelry: dirty, crowded, hardly respectable,—if we may judge by the too free manners and conversation of the young women who waited on us'.[130] They resolved to write to the Cyclists' Touring Club to have it 'stricken from the list'. Otherwise all was joy at the Bell at Ely and the Bull at Cambridge and the like. Wilson loved Cambridge and described it at length: 'but I know of no place in the Kingdom more to be desired than Oxford.' At Oxford he met A. V. Dicey the famous Vinerian Professor of

English Law. Each evening Stockton and he walked to New College garden and sat and chatted under a beech tree until it grew dark. But after Oxford Stockton found the exertions of bicycling too much and withdrew to a friend Snyder's cottage in Surrey. Wilson went on by himself to the West Country, Wells again ('where take it all in all, I should rather be than anywhere else in England')[131] and visiting Clovelly where inevitably he ran into a party of old friends from Middletown. After that there was a week in Ireland and then the boat to Glasgow and thence home.

Wilson found the English friendly.

It's always the same story; stiff and ungracious in manner when first approached, but kindly, helpful, interesting, communicative when once your need or question is stated.[132]

But here Wilson was referring to the people he met at 'very humble and unpretentious inns'. He does not seem to have taken to those higher in the world, as is shown by a comment made on a later trip in 1908.

It is not exactly an attitude of condescension but it is an attitude of tolerant curiosity: as if they would *like* to know what Americans are like and what they think and how they talk and act and feel about the ordinary things of existence, but are not very *keen* about it,—do not regard it as *very* interesting, and would, on the whole, rather talk to their own kind and about their own things.[133]

When youthful admiration goes unrequited it can turn, if not into hostility, at least into irritation.

When Wilson became President of Princeton he appeared to be stepping into his niche in the world. It is true that he was not a scholar in the full sense. He was well aware that he had not an original mind. He wrote in his journal of 1889: 'I *receive* the opinions of *others* of the day. I do not *conceive* them.'[134] He was not erudite. He did not thirst for knowledge for its own sake; he learnt what he wanted for a particular purpose,—an article, a book or a set of lectures,—and expressed what he had learnt clearly and gracefully. But his talents fitted him well for the roll of scholar-administrator. He had, as his later career proved, a great gift for administration. He looked the part too—a clean angular face and a presence; though, as Keynes was later to observe, like Odysseus he looked wiser when seated. His manner was affable and dignified—perhaps a little too much dignity expressing itself in 'an old world habit of utterance and demeanour'.[135] If to the public generally he showed a little too much reserve and aloofness, these attributes are not unbecoming in the academy. He drew respect from everyone and deep

affection from those few who got to know him well. He was popular alike
with the students and with the faculty. He had already some reputation
with the public and clearly it would grow, for his devotion to Princeton
never blocked his vision of the widths beyond. 'Princeton for the Nation's
Service' was the title of his inaugural address. The American university
presidency has been likened by M. Halévy to a medieval bishopric:[136]
Wilson seemed now destined to occupy for life one of the great sees.

But in truth for Wilson the presidency of Princeton was more an assuage-
ment than an achievement. It did not take from him the restlessness that
simmers on the top of power confined. He was not a professor accidentally
diverted into public life. When he got his hands on the control of government,
he would not have learnt so quickly how to move the levers if the thought
that he might some day move them had left him altogether. It was part of his
ambition at an early age and left him only on fulfilment. To begin with, he
had the usual juvenile daydreams of deeds of derring-do. (It is curious that
in nearly all the heroic parts he played in boyish fantasy he was an Englishman with an English title and decorations.) He had perhaps also the usual
hankering of youth after success in games. Being himself no athlete (he
lacked, a friend says, the physical qualification for manly sports), he encouraged from the sidelines, was known as a 'magnetic cheerleader',[137] and
was fond of theorization and exhortation in the columns of *The Princetonian*.
But he yearned to be a real leader. Early in his Princeton days he had read
Carlyle's *Heroes* and summarized in a commonplace book—Index Rerum
he called it[138]—the passage in 'The Hero as King' in which the author con-
trasts two sorts of ambition—'the selfish wish to shine over others' to be
accounted 'poor and miserable'; and 'the irrepressible tendency in every
man to develop himself according to the magnitude which Nature has made
of him; to speak-out, to act-out, what Nature has laid in him'. Wilson had
'the irrepressible tendency'; and the ambition for leadership, as it came out
of the nebula of boyhood, took concrete form as an ambition to lead by the
power of words and towards a high moral purpose. The idealization of this
is the great democratic statesman. So he made Gladstone his living hero
and at the age of fifteen hung his picture over his desk. So too he strove with
all his might to make himself proficient in the composition and utterance of
words. As a student at Princeton he made a 'solemn covenant' which he
described five years later:

I remember forming with Charlie Talcott (a classmate and very intimate friend
of mine) a solemn covenant that we would school all our powers and passions for
the work of establishing the principles we held in common; and that we would
acquire knowledge that we might have power; and that we would drill ourselves
in all the arts of persuasion, but especially in oratory (for he was a born orator if

any man was), that we might have facility in leading others into our ways of thinking and enlisting them in our purposes.[139]

In May 1881 when he was at home, he wrote to Bridges that he was practising elocution for about an hour a day.

I took some lessons from a very capital instructor some months ago, and now I am my own tutor, with the guidance of a very excellent textbook prepared by an experienced teacher. In addition to the vocal exercises I make frequent extemporaneous addresses to the empty benches of my father's church in order to get a mastery of easy and correct and elegant expression in preparation for the future. My topics are most of them political. . . .[140]

He had a youthful contempt for the idea of reading a speech. 'Oratory is persuasion,' he wrote in *The Princetonian*, 'not the declamation of essays.'[141] But except for casual occasions his speeches were well prepared, textually for a great speech and for others by means of notes. The notes were not an aid to delivery; he used then the words that came to him. The notes were food for thought; or, it might be, the metal of the speech not to be transmuted by a stroke of alchemy but to be illumined as the light in a long evening changes a summer moon from silver to gold.

'Wilson,' said a reader of one of his articles in 1884, 'you have picked up a capital literary style somewhere.' 'Picked up, indeed!' Wilson commented when he reported this to Ellen. 'Has'nt my dear father been drilling me in style these ten years past?'[142]

It was in those days a great thing to have style. De Buffon's apophthegm, 'le style est l'homme même', was thought worth anglicizing and quoted by many (including Wilson himself).[143] Every writer worth his salt must have a style of his own. Wilson thought a lot about his and talked about it too. A girl student at Bryn Mawr—the women there were no more appreciative of Wilson than he was of them—said that

it sometimes seemed to me that it played the same part in his conversation that the weather did with others. Lamb, Burke, Bagehot were his literary ideals and it seemed as if he were really more interested in their manner of expression than he was in the thoughts and ideals expressed.[144]

In July 1877 Wilson made a note in his diary about his friend McCarter.

I wish I could find some agreeable way of hinting to him that his use of words is extremely loose and careless. He is getting into very bad habits through mere carelessness and thus threatening to ruin his diction.[145]

McCarter went into the law where, perhaps because of ruined diction, he rose no higher than Attorney-General of New Jersey. An even less distinguished fate befell a Mr. Brown to whom Wilson began a letter in September 1898: 'My dear Sir, I cannot say that I think your article on the Philippines shows style.'[146] Mr. Brown also took to the practice of the law but did not rise out of his home town of Woonsocket, R.I.

Certainly Wilson himself had a beautiful style, easy and graceful, rising sometimes to the heights and never dull. He acquired it by practising style as he practised oratory. He suggested to a friend whose writing he thought effective that they should write to each other twice a week each criticizing the other's letters. When he began his *History of the American People* he wrote to Mrs. Reid:

> I must cultivate a new style for the new venture: a quick and perfectly pellucid narrative as clear as the air and coloured with nothing but the sun, stopped in its current here and there, and yet almost imperceptibly, for the setting in of small pictures of men and manners, coloured variously, as life is. It must be a work of art or nothing, and I must study the art.[147]

Wilson liked to refer to himself as 'a literary fellow'[148] and to be thought of as a writer rather than a scholar, at any rate the sort of scholar whose chief concern was the collection and scientific arrangement of facts. Reviewing a book by a rival political scientist, he criticized him for writing not 'in the language of literature, but in the language of science' and for constructing his sentences 'upon the homeliest principles of grammatical joinery'.[149]

Oratory and writing were for him two manifestations of one art. His spoken and written prose were much the same. Diction was the greatest strength of his oratory. What he wrote can be read aloud and what he spoke taken down and published with little or no correction. The amalgamation benefited his speeches rather than his writings. Decorations of language that enter the mind through the ear and leave without coming to rest can with a light impression give a pleasure which perusal in print does not confirm. Floridities that are imposing when delivered become tiresome when read. *Per contra*, concision that is appreciated by the eye can carry the thought too rapidly past the ear. Composed always for the ear rather than for the eye, Wilson's prose was slacker than he could have made it and the lucidity is sometimes only on the surface. It is not that he is generally obscure. The editor of the *Political Science Quarterly* made in 1889 this comment on the original draft of Wilson's review (a review which observed that the author's style, 'while lacking distinction, is eminently straightforward and clear')[150] of Bryce's *American Commonwealth*:

> I hope you will not mind my saying that some of the sentences are not as lucid as your sentences regularly are. You generally have the knack of saying the thing

so that it is understood at first glance—but in reading some of the sentences in this article, I found myself running back to see just what you meant. Of course I could always find out, but it was a surprise to me to be obliged to look back at all.[151]

The criticism is fair, if not perhaps very helpful to an author since, as Wilson pointed out in reply, 'the very obtuseness which made me write obscurely has prevented my seeing the obscurities'.[152] Wilson never resented professional criticism.

By his self-training in speaking and writing Wilson very soon made himself a highly accomplished performer. His set oration on John Bright, given when he was only twenty-three at the University of Virginia, is a magnificent example of prose written for delivery;[153] and he soon learnt how to rouse and hold an audience as well as how to catch interest on paper. This was the weapon that took him to the top and it was not until he got there that it showed its flaw. It was only then that it began seriously to matter when rhetoric befogged clarity. Wilson was always afraid lest what he wrote for the public to read should sound dull and uncoloured. The first of the Fourteen Points affords a celebrated example of this. 'Open Covenants of Peace openly arrived at.' What Wilson meant to say was that international agreements should be published; he did not mean that they should be negotiated in public. Of course the phrase as written has a swing lacking in the simple sentence that covenants should be open; and a bare but precise statement that treaties when made should be published, doubtless sounds quite flat.

As well as his oratory and his style, Wilson practised, as best he could within the small polities available in college, the art of constitutional government. In his schooldays and wherever he went thereafter, he started or invigorated a debating club and usually wrote a constitution for it—at Princeton, at the University of Virginia, in Atlanta, at Johns Hopkins, and at Wesleyan. They all copied parliamentary procedure and the last of them he called the Wesleyan House of Commons.

Thus he acquired painstakingly the tools he needed. Needed for what? Certainly not for teaching. As a professor he was, as hindsight would presume, a superb lecturer. The many tributes from his pupils that his biographers have collected are paid to his power of lucid and exciting exposition, not to his tutoring. He was not really interested in teaching; his delight was not in getting another to learn but in his own power of expression. Whether at a desk, on a rostrum, or in a chair, he spoke as from a platform. He said to Ellen in 1884: 'I have a sense of power in dealing with men collectively which I do not feel always in dealing with them singly.'[154]

'After all it's my writing, not my teaching, that must win me reputation,'[155] he told her when she wondered whether Bryn Mawr was a good enough place for him. This explains his insistence on 'style'. He would not be a 'mere student'.

> I want to write books which will be read by the great hosts who don't wear spectacles—whose eyes are young and unlearned! I don't care how much contempt may look upon my pages through professors' glasses![156]

As a way into politics, teaching jurisprudence and political economy offered a route more congenial to him than a practice in Atlanta. But he never thought of either otherwise than as a route. When he left Atlanta he changed the avenue of entry and the point of arrival but not the ultimate destination. The destination was a place of political influence. The point of arrival had to be different. He no longer saw himself as a party leader. One of his lectures repeatedly delivered and first written in 1889 was called 'Leaders of Men'. In it he set out and illustrated the qualifications for leadership. It seems—though the point merits close examination*—that he thought the capacity to compromise must be one. The leader must also be a good mixer or, in Wilsonian language, a man 'open at all points to all men', to which he added, 'ready to break into coarse laughter with the Rabelaisian vulgar'.[157] It is just possible that in 1889 Wilson thought that he himself might make a successful compromiser; but he could never have persuaded himself that he would be ready to break into coarse laughter with or without the Rabelaisian vulgar. It is clear that at this time he had written himself off as a political leader of the ordinary sort.

He told Ellen in the early days that, since he was shut out from realizing his first ambition of active participation in the direction of affairs, he wanted to become 'one of the guides of public thought'.[158] Was it still, she asked in February 1885, his dearest ambition? Did he regret being shut out? Even if, she thought, one were obliged to choose strictly between two careers, for her there would be no hesitation. 'Of all the world's workers, those which to my mind take by far the highest rank are the writers of noble books.'

Wilson's answer to this is a revelation of his mind.

> I do feel a very real regret that I have been shut out from my heart's *first-primary-*ambition and purpose, which was, to take an active, if possible, a leading part in public life, and strike out for myself, if I had the ability, a *Statesman's* career. That is my heart's—or rather, my *mind's*—deepest secret, little lady. But don't mistake the feeling for more than it is. It is nothing more than a regret; and the more I study the conditions of public service in this country the less *personal* does the regret become. My disappointment is in the fact that there is no room for such a career in this country for *anybody*, rather than in the fact that

---

* See the discussion in the Preface, p. ix above.

there is no chance for *me*. Had I had independent means of support, even of the most modest proportions, I should doubtless have sought an entrance into politics *anyhow*, and have tried to fight my way to predominant influence even amidst the hurly-burly and helter-skelter of Congress. I have a strong instinct of leadership, an unmistakably oratorical temperament, and the keenest possible delight in affairs; and it has required very constant and stringent schooling to content me with the sober methods of the scholar and the man of letters. I have no patience for the tedious toil of what is known as 'research'; I have a passion for interpreting great thoughts to the world; I should be complete if I could inspire a great movement of opinion, if I could read the experiences of the past into the practical life of the men of to-day and so communicate the thought to the minds of the great mass of the people as to impel them to great political achievements.[159]

He agreed with her about the writing of noble books.

But my feeling has been that such literary talents as I have are *secondary* to my equipment for other things: that my power to write was meant to be a handmaiden to my power to speak and organise action.[159]

But he accepted the providential ordering of his life as conclusive on that point.

Certainly I have taken the course which will, with God's favour, enable me to realise *most* of what I had first proposed to myself.[159]

Congressional Government had given him a start. It was read by practising politicians as well as by theorists. In November 1886 he wrote to Talcott to remind him of the 'compact'.[160] He suggested getting together 'a band of young fellows' so that he might meet men who were not 'book politicians'. In an article in the *New Princeton Review* he made the same point.[161] He referred there to the example of Bryce and Morley, the professor and the writer, who both became cabinet ministers. Did he himself hope for a call? In February 1898 he paid a visit to Washington and found it 'an idle society of rich people';[162] but when he went to watch the Congress, 'the old longing for public life comes upon me in a flood as I watch'.[163] If he was resolute in thrusting back the thought from the forefront of his mind, he never lost the ambition that impelled it. Nor his belief that he had the power to lead. As with every man there were times, especially when he was lonely, when he had doubts, but they were rare. He had 'the irrepressible tendency' and even by the age of twenty-three he knew how to recognize it for what it was, and how to describe it—'a sort of calm confidence of great things to be accomplished'.[164]

II
INTO POLITICS

MRS. REID says that during the first months of his presidency at Princeton Wilson 'was happier, gayer, than he had ever been in his life, or than he was ever to be again'.[1] The first four years of his presidency were triumphant. He reorganized the curriculum upon a plan which has been permanently successful and which was soon adopted by other universities. He devised and in 1905 introduced the 'preceptorial system', based on the principle of Oxford tutorials. As the preceptors or tutors which the system required he found—most of them personally and by the power of the enthusiasm which an interview with him could inspire in a young man—fifty of the best young scholars in the country, thirty-seven of them from other universities. One of them, who came from Yale and who consented only rather reluctantly to an interview, recalls:

Before the talk was over my loyalties were entirely committed to him. Had Woodrow Wilson asked me to go with him and work under him while he inaugurated a new university in Kamchatka or Senegambia I would have said 'yes' without further question.[2]

In 1906 he was held in admiration by all and thought of as Princeton's greatest asset. Such universal popularity did not come again until 1918.

There was harmony in the faculty. One of the most powerful men on it was Andrew Fleming West, Dean of the Graduate School and Giger Professor of Latin. He was about five years older than Wilson, also a graduate of Princeton, genial and charming, an 'arm-round-the-shoulder' man, popular with students. Wilson and he got on well enough together in the early days; once when during Ellen's absence in 1892 they dined together, West succeeded in making Wilson drink some Californian claret which gave him a raging headache the next day.

West drew his power as much from his connections as from his position in the university. He was on easy terms with the wealthiest alumni. He persuaded President Cleveland to attend the Sesquicentennial in 1896. The two men became very friendly, and when Cleveland's term of office was over he bought a home in Princeton and became a trustee of the university. Like Wilson, West was an improver and naturally the object of his schemes was his own graduate school. He wanted a building for it, a college in the Oxford and Cambridge style.

Dean West's dreams were seriously disturbed by a competing project which Wilson evolved in 1906. At Princeton, as at several other universities, the majority of the students lived in clubs, some of which were expensive and luxurious. Wilson disapproved of this as undemocratic and as forcing undesirable social distinctions; the competition for membership of the best clubs distracted students from the real business of a university. He wanted the pattern of the university to be like that of the colleges at Oxford which he so much admired. So he proposed the revolutionary step of abolishing the clubs and replacing them by halls of residence built around quadrangles. Thus his plan came to be called the Quads Plan.

It was in May 1906 that Wilson had the stroke which affected his left eye. Jack Hibben came over at once and took him to Philadelphia to see the doctors. They said he must have at least three months complete rest. This was the summer that he spent at Rydal when he first met Yates. Quite possibly the new friendship helped towards his recovery. As he wrote to Yates after his return to America: 'It would be hard to say now what a mere summer in the dear Lake District would have done for me if I had got mere rest and recreation. It is always affection that heals me, and the dear friendships I made were my real tonic.'[3]

The enforced idleness gave him time for thought and enabled him to bring to maturity the plan which had been in the back of his mind for a long time. The Quads Plan was ready to be laid before the Board of Trustees on 13 December 1906. The reception was favourable and a committee, with Wilson as chairman, was appointed to examine the plan and report. The report, written by Wilson himself, was unanimously adopted by the Board on 10 June 1907 and then published. Early in July Wilson went on vacation. Then the controversy began. The younger members of the faculty, most of whom had been chosen by Wilson, were in favour of the plan. But among the elder members there was strong opposition, led by Dr. Van Dyke (the reciter of the academic ode) and Dean West; they disapproved in principle and thought it high-handed of Wilson to have acted without consultation with the faculty. But their disapproval was unimportant compared with the indignation of the alumni, many of whom were deeply attached to their former clubs. By the end of the summer it became clear that at least three-quarters of the alumni were hostile. Had they been no worse than apathetic it would have been as bad, since the scheme needed their active support. It was they who made up the university's annual deficit. It was they who in effect had paid for the new preceptorial system, which with its great increase in the size of the faculty had more than doubled the budget. When Wilson took office the annual deficit was $27,000; four years later it had increased to $113,000. The Quads Plan was estimated to cost $2,000,000 and the alumni must be the chief source of the money. Not all the opposition to the scheme was uncompromising. There was much support for some measure of reform which would make the clubs less exclusive and bring them under closer control. But Wilson, while he maintained that he intended 'the freest possible discussion . . . in order that every element of common counsel may contribute to the final decision',[4] was going to insist on his plan or nothing.

Jack Hibben felt that, while Wilson was theoretically right, he was pushing his ideas too hard and too fast and risking a disastrous split. On 8 July 1907 he wrote to Wilson to tell him so and to say that he could not support him. Wilson replied that each must do his duty as he saw it.

Your friendship, by which I have lived, in which I have drawn some of the most refreshing, most renewing breath of my life, is to be as little affected by our difference of opinion as is everything permanent and of the law of our hearts.[5]

During the vacation Van Dyke and Hibben journeyed to the 'somewhat remote retreat . . . 24 miles from the railway'[6] where the Wilson family was holidaying in the Adirondacks and tried in vain to persuade Wilson to compromise.

On 26 September 1907 the first formal faculty meeting to discuss the Quads Plan was held. Van Dyke moved the resolution against the plan and Hibben with the courage of his convictions seconded it. Wilson had doubtless supposed that Hibben's withdrawal of support meant no more than non-belligerency and he was obviously shocked by the intervention. 'Do I understand', he asked, 'that Professor Hibben seconds the motion?'[7] At the adjourned meeting Wilson made a tremendous speech. The faculty actually cheered; and, as a Wilsonian records, even Dean West, 'good sport that he was',[8] joined heartily in the applause. When the vote was taken Wilson was victorious by 80 to 23. It is true that among the 80 there were 49 out of the 50 preceptors; of the old faculty Wilson carried 60 per cent. But while the support of the faculty was soothing, the opposition of the alumni was deadly. On 17 October 1907 the Board of Trustees went back on their decision and withdrew their approval of the plan. Wilson wrote of his 'complete defeat' and 'mortification'[9] and started to draft a letter of resignation. Then he resolved to fight on and to 'go to the country'—that is to say, he revealed for the first time, and as it were in embryo, the way in which he was always to meet opposition. He determined to hold meetings of the alumni and to present his case directly to them. At a series of meetings he made some headway but not so much as he hoped for and needed. In the spring of 1908 he dropped the plan.

The great friendship with Hibben was not immediately destroyed. When in the following June Wilson, troubled again with neuritis, went back once more to the Lake District for rest and solace, Jack Hibben saw him off. But Wilson spoke to Yates of Hibben's 'disloyalty' and the sore began to fester. Bare opposition he could stomach; he remained friendly with Van Dyke whom he later appointed Minister to Holland, where, being a rather fussy and pedantic man, he became a thorn in the flesh of the future President Hoover who in 1914 was in charge of Belgian relief.

But by Hibben whom Wilson had loved he felt himself betrayed. When Hibben took the wrong side in the next Princeton controversy, he was finished and cast out. His election three years later to succeed Wilson as President of Princeton was felt as a terrible blow. Although Wilson was, as Governor of New Jersey, almost bound by precedent to attend the inauguration, he absented himself conspicuously. On the same day he poured out his feelings in a letter to Mrs. Peck:

Alas! my dear friend, it is a hard world to live in! I dare say no man is so humble as not to feel the jolts and jars and clashes of it. And who shall set an estimate in such circumstances upon real, tested friendship,—friendship with insight and comprehending sympathy, that understands before the case is stated and sees as much as your own heart does? It is *that* that makes life noble and beautiful and good to live.[10]

In February 1911 he wrote to her of an unhealed wound, reproaching himself for his blindness and stupidity in loving the people who proved false to him.[11] Mrs. Wilson spoke of 'the loss of the friend he took to his bosom'.[12] The ending of the friendship, Stockton thought, 'left a permanent scar on Mr. Wilson's spirit'.[12] Years after his death one of his daughters wrote: 'The two major tragedies in Father's life were his failure to carry over the League of Nations and his break with Mr Hibben.'[13] Stockton, whom Wilson had brought in to the Princeton faculty, left on Hibben's election, and so did his brother-in-law who had married Ellen's younger sister, Margaret.

The presidency of the United States was to make no difference to Wilson's loves nor to his hates. When among his few old friends any reminder of it made him uncomfortable: 'how I hate the office, when it holds me off from the people I want to get close to.'[14] Conversely, it put him on no height from which to drop old enmities. After a visit to Princeton in September 1913 he wrote: 'Unfortunately I ran across Hibben just before leaving. Stock says that I behaved pretty well and did not freeze him.'[15] The encounter left Hibben warm enough to send a cordial letter. He understood, he wrote on 10 October that the President would be coming to Princeton to vote in the midterm elections on 4 November and he would like him and all his party to lunch at Prospect. The invitation received no personal acknowledgement.

Margaret in a memoir gives a more animated version of the snub, doubtless as it was spoken in the family lore. A student, she says, thought it would be a good joke—for the breach was notorious—to tell Hibben that the President was at the station and wanted to see him. The old friend hurried down. One can imagine his thought: at last perhaps the reconciliation: at least there was the duty he owed to pay his respects to the President of the United States in Princeton. He arrived in haste and breathless. Wilson was surrounded by a group of townspeople and friends on the faculty.

'Mr. President,' he said, 'one of the students told me that you were asking for me.'[16] Woodrow, his manner perfectly courteous and unbelievably remote, looked at him and said just one word 'No.'

Wilson's friendships with women never foundered in this manner. Naturally as a matter of propriety he would not have allowed his emotions to become engaged. Perhaps because with men they were more heavily engaged or perhaps because the men were not so prolific as the women of uncritical sympathy or perhaps because discussion with him of his plans and policies gave them the greater opportunity of committing offence, none of the men (except in the old college friendships that absence pickled) endured to the end. Jack Hibben, the intimate from his fellows on the faculty; Walter Hines Page, almost the earliest political disciple; Edward Mandell House, 'my second personality'; Joe Tumulty, the devoted secretary; all these were warmly brought in and irretrievably put out. It is perhaps unlikely that a man whose emotions cut such deep outlets would have for ever rested content with academic life when his talents fitted him for something more demanding. Still, the presidency of Princeton is no mean office. Perhaps the place or another like it would have contented him; perhaps, as most men do, when they reach their fifties and feel that it is time to jettison, he would have looked back a little regretfully upon the young ambition unfulfilled, but not in dissatisfaction with the freight he was to carry to the journey's end. But it chanced that a signal was given and Wilson hoisted sail.

If one man was responsible for bringing Wilson along Wilson's own way and on his own terms and within the span of a few years to the leadership of his country and then of the world, it was Colonel George Harvey. The colonelcy, like that of the more celebrated Colonel House, was in House's words a geographical and not a military appointment. It was a 'gilt-braid' honour given by the governor of a state as a reward for political service. Harvey got his at the age of twenty-four from the Democratic Governor of New Jersey. By nature Harvey was a Republican, being most comfortably at home in the world of big business, and only by upbringing a Democrat. His father was an aggressive Democrat in Vermont, that impenetrably Republican state, and christened his son George Brinton McClellan after the General who was the Democratic candidate in 1864, the year of his son's birth. Devotion to his father's memory perhaps, or perhaps the string of names, kept the son nominally a Democrat almost to the end.

He became one of the most successful journalists of his day. At twenty he caught the fancy of the famous Joseph Pulitzer, proprietor and editor of the *New York World*, the leading Democratic newspaper, and at twenty-seven he became editor of it under Pulitzer.

It was during this period that Harvey performed his political services. In the 1892 election he worked hard for Cleveland and in the course of it made the acquaintance of a number of Democratic magnates, in particular of Thomas Fortune Ryan who had made his money out of public utilities in New York. At the end of 1893 Harvey resigned from the *World*, went into Ryan's line of business, and did well for himself. By 1899 he had made enough money to buy an estate at Deal on the New Jersey coast and to go back into journalism, owning and editing his own paper, the *North American Review*. Two years later he became president of Harper and Brothers and editor of *Harper's Weekly*, a concern which had got into difficulties and had been rescued by Pierpont Morgan, with whom Harvey was *persona grata*. The man whom Harvey succeeded as editor was Walter Page and by a curious chance Harvey was destined to succeed him again as ambassador to Britain.

Harvey was a rather tall man with a thatch of hair, parted in the middle, that he kept into old age, and prominent rimmed spectacles. He liked being original, and a little mysterious. He went in for the startling prediction (some came true and no-one bothers to remember for long predictions which do not) and the enigmatic smile. He did not parade his originalities:

he preferred them to be discovered. Once upon a transatlantic trip, his biographer records, sitting with a group of friends on deck, he did not join in their vivacious conversation but spent an hour or more poring intently upon the pages of a book. At last he rose and strolled away 'with thoughtful mien',[17] and a friend to relieve his curiosity picked up the book which Harvey had not forgotten to leave on his chair: it was the Bible.

As a journalist he had a pungent style: one of his eulogists called him 'the master creator of ungloved literature'.[18] It was always a sadness to him that he had not had a college education and he was gratified by honorary degrees and smaller attentions from universities. It was said of him that he spoke three languages—academic, commercial, and political. So he was well qualified to be an antenna for the group of highly placed Democrats who after the turn of the century were on the look-out for a new type of presidential candidate. For an understanding of their difficulties it is necessary to summarize what had been happening in party politics during the time that Wilson had been walking his scholastic way.

The one Democrat to have been President since the Civil War was Grover Cleveland in 1884, though Tilden, as we have seen,* had a very near miss in 1876. Cleveland won the election only with the aid of Republican defections and even then only by the narrowest majority and because of the New York electoral vote. The victorious Democrats hungered for office. Cleveland disliked the spoils system and earned Wilson's 'respect and admiration'[19] by his determined effort to fill the higher offices on merit. But in the matter of postmasterships, which were the current coin for the remuneration of the lower ranks of the faithful on both sides, Cleveland had to submit; and by the end of his first year 15,000 postmasterships had changed hands.

Cleveland was nominated again in 1888 as a matter of course. This time he achieved a bare majority of the popular vote but lost New York which turned the vote in the electoral college in favour of the Republican Harrison. By the end of President Harrison's first year 30,000 postmasterships had changed hands. Thus Rehoboam chastised with scorpions where Solomon had chastised with whips.

It was during Harrison's administration that the Populist revolt began and led to the reformation of the Democratic party into the shape it had when Wilson entered politics. William Jennings Bryan of Nebraska was the chief instrument of the change. 'The Great Commoner' was four years younger than Wilson and was elected to Congress in 1890, the year that Wilson became a professor at Princeton. Almost at once he became the dominating force of the left wing of the party. He was one of the greatest of popular

* See p. 14 above.

orators and a shrewd politician and party manager; but no intellectual and no statesman.

It was his qualities of character rather than of mind that won for him such loyalty as no other leader of his generation could command. Irreproachable in private and in professional life, his career was characterised by utter sincerity, passionate conviction, courage, audacity, genuine faith in the wisdom of the plain people and the process of democracy, religious belief in the identity of morals and politics, and an unalterable assurance that the right must eventually triumph over the wrong.[20]

The two springs of the Populist movement were industrial unrest and the distress of the farming states. The increasing number of immigrants threatened to depress wages; in 1890 there were more strikes than in any other year of the century. But the Populists were not primarily a party of the city; their main strength was in the West. The land boom of the eighties, during which farms expanded on credit secured by mortgages, came to an end with the disastrous harvest of 1887, and that set in motion a train of foreclosures. In the terminology of today a period of inflation was succeeded by a sharp deflation. The sufferers felt that the cure for their malady was a less rigid control of the currency. As always, the debtors wanted cheap money; and the creditors, that is, the banks and investors generally, wanted dear money. That conflict was not new. The orthodox monetary theory, accepted by the banking and business community generally, was the bullion theory. It meant that the currency in circulation was tied to gold and therefore limited by the quantity of gold bullion held in the country. The alternatives were either to detach the currency from bullion or to increase the bullion basis by adding another metal, namely, silver. The latter course commended itself as being the less revolutionary of the two and had already many adherents before the time of Populism. So the Populists put in the front of their programme the free and unlimited coinage of silver, pre-ambled by a declaration that 'the fruits of the toil of millions are boldly stolen to build up colossal fortunes for a few';[21] and battle was joined dramatically between poor and rich, silver and gold.

The Populists began by making local alliances with the Democrats. But the core of the Democratic party was almost as difficult to penetrate as the Republican. So for the election of 1892 the Populists had their own con-vention and candidate. For the major parties Cleveland and Harrison fought again. Cleveland won with 46 per cent of the popular vote while Harrison had 43 per cent; the Populists had over 8 per cent and gained 22 votes in the electoral college.

Cleveland's second administration was cautious and unprogressive. Many of the discontented who had voted Democrat rather than Populist in the belief that the greater party could do more for them, were disappointed. In the midterm election of 1894 the Populists increased their popular vote by nearly a half. Many of the left wing of the Democrats were silver men. There was a danger of a split, a secession and the formation of a great third party under the Populist banner. The peril would be averted only if the Democrats opened their ranks and admitted the Populists.

That was what the Democrats did in 1896; and that they did it was Bryan's achievement. He created the Democratic party of Franklin Roosevelt and the twentieth century. Till then it was primarily the party of Tammany and the Southern states; for Bryan it was always the party of the under-privileged. So he declaimed:

On the one hand stand the corporate interests of the United States, the moneyed interests, aggregated wealth and capital, imperious, arrogant, compassionless. . . . On the other side stand an unnumbered throng, those who gave to the Demo-cratic party a name and for whom it has assumed to speak. Work-worn and dust-begrimed, they make their mute appeal.[22]

Bryan was for silver, of course, and he devoted the two years from 1894 to 1896 to organizing the silver forces in the party. The Republican convention met first and came out for gold; twenty-two silver delegates left the hall. The Democrats would have gone silver, no doubt, even if it had not been for Bryan's great speech and the peroration that made him famous:

We will answer their demand for a gold standard by saying to them:—'You shall not press down upon the brow of labor this crown of thorns; you shall not crucify mankind upon a cross of gold'.[23]

That speech gave him too the Presidential nomination. He was then thirty-six. He was adopted with enthusiasm by the Populists. He exchanged the support of some gold Democrats for that of the silver Republicans. The line was drawn between the business East and the agrarian South and West. Bryan's tremendous fight earned the unstinted admiration of his opponents. Mrs. Henry Cabot Lodge wrote to a friend:

The great fight is won and a fight conducted by trained and experienced and organised forces, with both hands full of money, with the full power of the press— and of prestige—on one side; on the other, a disorganised mob at first, out of which burst into sight, hearing, and force—one man, but such a man! Alone, penniless, without backing, without money, with scarce a paper, without speakers, that man fought such a fight that even those in the East can call him a Crusader, an inspired fanatic—a prophet![24]

Wilson voted as a gold Democrat; he thought the 'cross of gold' speech ridiculous. Bryan fought again in 1900 but with rather less success.

President McKinley, selected by the omnipotent Boss Hanna of Ohio, was the successful Republican candidate at both these elections. He died six months after his second inauguration, shot by an anarchist. Thus unexpectedly and to the outspoken distress of Boss Hanna the Vice-President, Theodore Roosevelt, became the twenty-sixth and up to that date the youngest President of the United States; he was then forty-three and Wilson forty-five.

Much of Roosevelt's character can be stated in the fact that he was a short-sighted and rather puny child beglamoured, as many such are, by an excessive admiration of physical prowess, but also, as few are, endowed with a power of will that drove him to overcome his frailties. He learnt to box, ride, and shoot and to live rough; and he made himself corporally what from his birth he had been mentally—a strong and lively person. He was a new type in American politics. Though not himself a rich man, he came from the aristocracy of inherited wealth. In politics he was a progressive, belonging to the left and minority wing of the Republican party. He was no friend to big business and it was during his Presidency that the anti-trust laws first began to bite. His interests and abilities went far beyond the field of politics. He was widely read and could hold his own in talk in any company—on some subjects with authority; he was for example, a first-class naturalist. He made himself a rancher and a soldier. He became nationally famous with the Rough Riders whom he organized and fought with in the Spanish-American War. On his return from the war in 1898 he was elected Governor of New York. His governorship did not please the bosses, and his nomination for the vice-presidency was due to a wish to sidetrack an awkward character as well as to cater for the progressive vote. Surprisingly he agreed to go down the alley with the gate at the end that only Atropos could then unlock and he passed through it to the Presidency. As President he stormed the imagination of the public, and his personality—full-blooded, boisterous, vital—was magnified to heroic proportions. In 1904 he was nominated as presidential candidate with the lukewarm support of the old guard; he was by then far too popular a figure in the country for the party to put on the shelf. The Democrats, hunting for the votes of big business which disliked Roosevelt's anti-trust policies, nominated Judge Parker, an Eastern conservative who did not qualify as one of Bryan's 'workworn and dust-begrimed'. The election was a resounding Roosevelt victory.

The twenty-sixth and the twenty-eighth Presidents of the United States first met on 3 March 1896 on the platform at a municipal reform meeting in Baltimore. Roosevelt had been in politics for fourteen years; starting in the New York Assembly at the age of twenty-three he was now a police commissioner of New York City. Wilson was in Baltimore for his course of lectures at Johns Hopkins which were so successful that this year they had been thrown open to the public. After this meeting the two men became quite friendly. When Roosevelt was Governor of New York Wilson sought his help in finding a job for Renick. Also he drew him into the circle of advice, as he put it, about a chair of Politics at Princeton. But Wilson was not even then an impassioned admirer. Forwarding to Ellen a note from Roosevelt about the chair he commented that it showed 'a very sane, *academic* side of him . . . constituting his hope of real and lasting eminence'.[25] Wilson's first visit to the White House was when Roosevelt was in occupation; they talked and he spent the night. Roosevelt was delighted when Wilson became president of Princeton. He went there for the inauguration but failed to charm the Wilson ladies with his jocularities. The early cordiality did not survive Wilson's rise to power. Each man had a confidence in the righteousness of his own judgements and an intolerance of opposition that bred an antipathy to those who opposed. But with Roosevelt it was all extroverted; he exploded where Wilson repressed. They were men destined to mutual enmity.

    This then was the position in the early years of the century; both the great parties were expanding outwards and in each a right and a left group was solidifying. These were the men, Roosevelt and Bryan, Wilson's contemporaries, who were running into fame and glory in the race he had dropped out of so soon. But although he did not practise politics, the eloquent addresses he gave all over the country made him a man to be noted. In 1901 he refused a Democratic nomination for the New Jersey Senate, but not unconditionally. He declared his lack of interest until the party had 'regained its balance';[26] he did not, he wrote, sympathize with its general attitude on 'many of the chief articles of its creed'. In May 1902 'Old-Fashioned Democrat' wrote to the *Indianapolis News* to say that he was 'tired of politicians and so-called statesmen' and to ask if a man of the type of 'Prof. Woodrow Wilson, of Princeton University, who lectured in this city a few days ago' would not be the best man for the Democratic ticket in 1904.[27] Old-fashioned Democrats who write to the newspapers are not often such early birds.

    Wilson was president of Princeton before he made his first significant political speech. It was made to the Society of Virginians in New York in November 1904 three weeks after the election in which Bryan, though not the candidate, had played a conspicuous and unrestrained part. Wilson had never met Bryan but in his early feelings about him some envy must have struggled with contempt. The party, to whose leadership Wilson had suppressed his aspirations, had been captivated by a man four years his junior, 'the boy orator' as he was called, who was intellectually negligible. Bryan had all the adulation which the youthful Wilson might have dreamt of for himself; Wilson, the thinker, was comparatively unknown. Bryan was certainly not a political scientist. His uncooked ideas were offensive to Wilson's stomach and Wilson was indignant at the recent exhibition of them in the Democratic campaign. He regarded Bryan as a doctor looks down upon a quack and denounced him in these terms:

It is now high time that the South, which has endured most by way of humiliation at the hands of this faction, should demand that it be utterly and once for all thrust out of Democratic counsels.[28]

There were also references to 'reform without loss of stability' and to 'thoughtful moderation in affairs' which were highly pleasing to his audience. Theoretically Wilson never was a radical. He liked what he once called 'spirited and confident, but conservative, progress'.[29]

Harpers had published Wilson's *History* and in this way Colonel Harvey came to know Wilson. The first time he saw him in action, as it were, was when he attended his inauguration as president of Princeton; and he was impressed. In February 1906 Wilson was the guest of honour at a dinner of the Lotos Club in New York. Harvey delivered the eulogy and concluded:

As one of a considerable number of Democrats who have become tired of voting Republican tickets, it is with a sense almost of rapture that I contemplate even the remotest possibility of casting a ballot for the president of Princeton University to become President of the United States.[30]

The speech was reported. It was the sort of compliment that might be paid to dozens of guests of honour without anything more being heard of it. But it evoked a response which Harvey found surprising. It came at a time when the thoughts of those concerned were beginning to turn to the Democratic nomination for 1908; was it to be Bryan again or the colourless Judge Parker? Roosevelt had proved that big business was not safe with the Republicans; a moderate Democrat was a temptation to Harvey's Wall Street friends. Harvey, nourishing the hope that he had picked a winner, followed up the line in the columns of *Harper's Weekly*. The idea was talked about and praised as a wonderful thing that was not likely to happen. Wilson himself gave it no overt encouragement. He did not want to allow the notion that he was running after a will-o'-the-wisp to interfere with his work at Princeton; and he did not want to be made a fool of. 'Delightful to have such things uttered about me, whether they were deserved or not'[31] he wrote to Harvey after the Lotos Club dinner. He viewed with some alarm an approach made at Harvey's instigation by the *Brooklyn Eagle* in March 1906: 'nothing could be further from my thoughts than the possibility or the desirability of holding high political office'[32] he wrote to the editor. But he did not go so far as to say that his name should be dropped. If, however, it should be taken up, it should not be in order to obtain the nomination for him but merely to see 'what the country was willing to think of . . . by way of organising an opposition with which conservative men could without apprehension ally themselves'. He regarded himself, he wrote, as the personification of 'views which would hold liberal and reforming programmes to conservative and strictly constitutional lines of action to the discrediting of rash and revolutionary proposals'. Sentiments of this kind would of course be well received by the right wing of the Democratic party; and Wilson prepared with exceptional care the address which he delivered at the Jefferson Day dinner of the National Democratic Club on 16 April 1906 where the bigwigs of the right were assembled.

In October 1906 Harvey got a chance to step out. There was a vacancy for a United States senator from New Jersey. The Democratic progressives in the state, restive under boss control, wanted to nominate Edwin A. Stevens, a former classmate of Wilson. It was only a titular honour as the Republicans had already got a majority in the New Jersey legislature which was the electoral body. Harvey thought the nomination would be a useful mark for Wilson and persuaded the New Jersey bosses that it would be a good way of heading off Stevens. Stevens remonstrated and Wilson eventually withdrew his name, while being careful on Harvey's advice not to support Stevens' candidacy. He found the affair rather embarrassing and it showed him his ignorance of the ins-and-outs of politics.

Harvey, who to the end was like a gambler fascinated by the lure of the dark horse, continued to thrust Wilson's name into the ears of Democrats powerful in the party machine. Wilson asked Harvey who the men were who wanted him for President and got a list of them. They were all of the right wing, the two most active being Ryan, the Wall Street operator who had got Harvey into business, and Laffan, owner of the *New York Sun* which led the Democratic press opposition to Bryan. On 15 March 1907 there was a 'little dinner'[33] at Delmonico's for Laffan and Ryan to have a look at Wilson. Everybody seemed satisfied and Wilson incidentally secured a subscription from Ryan for the endowment of the preceptorial system.

Meanwhile Wilson's position and the high ideals he professed attracted others besides the reactionaries. Page wrote in January 1907 of the gossip that he might be a presidential candidate: 'What if a political miracle should happen and the long lost old party should find itself by nominating such a man?'[34]

Harvey attended the Democratic convention in 1908 with the idea that Wilson might be used to defeat Bryan for the nomination. It was never more than a bare possibility (Bryan was in fact nominated on the first ballot) and Wilson did not for the sake of it postpone his trip to Europe though he agreed to be in Edinburgh at the critical time where he could be cabled. By November 1908 he was taking it all sufficiently seriously to tell Mrs. Peck that he did not want the presidency.[35]

In the election of 1908 Roosevelt decided not to stand again. He was in a position to choose his successor and he named his friend Taft who had been his Secretary of War. Bryan fought and lost again, polling the smallest popular vote of his three elections. Taft was a large, genial, and likeable man and an able lawyer. He had been an excellent judge. His ambition was to become a Justice of the Supreme Court; he achieved it, but only after the presidency, when in 1921 he was appointed Chief Justice. Like many good judges he was not a man of action. As a politician he was sincere but with a sincerity too cautious to frighten the party regulars. There are Presidents, as Roosevelt had been and Wilson became, who treat it as their business to do all that the President is not constitutionally forbidden to do: and there are those, like Taft, who think it right to do only what the President is expressly empowered to do. Roosevelt went off to hunt big game and leave his successor free of apron strings. The Administration drifted back.

The gathering forces of reform turned to the Democrats. The year 1912 was looking good for them if they could find the right candidate. Bryan had lost three times and had proved that a radical, however great his power over the party, could not carry the country. Parker's failure had shown that a conservative nominee could do no better. What was needed was someone acceptable to the East and yet sounding sufficiently advanced to get the support of the left, and with enough of a personality to compete with Bryan within the party. Harvey and his friends thought that Wilson would fill the bill. He was not, they had every reason to think, at all friendly to progressive measures, but his reputation as a man of ideals and his dissertations on uplifting subjects should be attractive to liberal opinion.

But Wilson's political ideas had begun to change since Harvey and he had first met. It would be truer to say that they had begun to form, for at the start he had done no thinking at all outside his own subject. He was a political scientist, not an economist; he was interested in the machinery of government, not in measures. He was drawn to politics, not because there was any great measure which he passionately wanted to see enacted, but because he thought he knew how to govern. He had the mechanic's desire to get his hands on an engine which he understood how to work and to drive for the sake of driving. He had at first no particular destination. His political science was nourished chiefly on his reading of the English nineteenth-century political philosophers and that made him naturally a supporter of *laissez-faire*.

Not that he was unconscious of social evils. He recognized that there were men at the top of big business who had achieved positions of power from which they could control the welfare of the millions and that some were abusing their power. He never, as a real reactionary might, defended such men in his heart while condemning them with his lips. But he believed that the remedy lay not in government regulation of all business but in directing the law against the individual malefactor. To demand wholesale interference, as the progressives did, was to employ the panic measures which Wilson up till at least 1908 vigorously denounced.

But Wilson was by instinct an improver. He did not have to be very long in the driver's seat before he conceived very definite ideas about the route. That became apparent as soon as he was in control at Princeton. Naturally his own ideas about reform did not strike him as 'rash and revolutionary proposals'. Not many men are so detached as to feel that *laissez-faire* can be applied as beneficently to their own plans as to those of others; the mighty weapon of government action is too tempting. As Wilson began to give more thought to political measures, he grew less conservative in his outlook. It was a gradual change. Professor Link traces its beginnings back to December 1909, just after Taft's election.[36]

It is reasonable to think that this change of mind was caused to some extent by Wilson's experiences at Princeton in 1908 and 1909. He found himself increasingly contending against wealth and privilege and in the end thwarted. His final defeat in 1910 not only made him available for a political career but left him rebuffed, angry, mortified, and willing to believe that the influences, which seemed to him to be corrupting Princeton life, were at work also in the nation. It may not be insignificant that ex-President Cleveland, who personified the right wing of the Democratic party, was now a strong opponent of the Quads Plan. Up to 1908 Wilson could be happily conservative about other people's reforms, for the society in which he lived was accepting his; when he found himself obstructed, his emotions, from whose influence he so erroneously believed himself to be immune, as much as his intellect, forced a change.

The battle over the Princeton clubs was succeeded by another and even fiercer one over the graduate college. It will be remembered that the dream of Dean West's life was a college wherein to house his graduate school, a Gothic building with a stately dining hall and a high table where he would sit as master. The idea appealed to Wilson and was specifically endorsed by him when he became president. In January 1903 West put his scheme on paper and it was published in the form of a booklet with the idea of raising money; Wilson contributed an enthusiastic preface. West hoped to raise $3,000,000 for the school of which $600,000 was wanted for buildings. In September 1905 the school was opened at a temporary residence. In March 1906 a legacy of $250,000 made it practical to begin thinking of building. In October 1906 West was offered the presidency of the Massachusetts Institute of Technology. Before he declined the promotion he obtained an assurance from Wilson of support for his plans for the graduate college.

This was just after Wilson had returned from the vacation in the Lake District during which he had matured his Quads Plan. When that plan was published in June 1907 West's conservatism would have sent him into opposition anyway. But it was also a severe blow to the plan for the graduate college. Both plans needed money; and appeals for the Quads would be likely to postpone indefinitely the financing of the graduate school. Instead of giving him the support which he expected for his project, the president had set up a rival. The dean considered Wilson guilty of bad faith and both he and Cleveland said so. When Cleveland died in June 1908, Wilson, his former admirer, did not order a memorial service and made no public reference to his death. It was thought at the time that Cleveland had left behind him a damaging letter addressed to Van Dyke in which he described Wilson as a man of ungovernable temper and lacking in intellectual integrity. The possibility of its publication four years later during the 1912 election campaign was serious enough to frighten Wilson's supporters, and to cause Wilson to compose a cool and effective reply. But Van Dyke would not allow the letter to be used.

When the Quads Plan came to grief in the spring of 1908 West's project revived. West wanted a site for the college off the campus. Wilson had from the first advocated that it should be in the midst of the campus, an integral part of the university. The issue was not simply topographical. The site might tilt the balance between dependence and a measure of autonomy. Whether or not Wilson had that in mind from the start, he had not after the Quads controversy any idea of giving West, his declared opponent and a man of that forthright, outspoken, aggressive type he never could get on with, any more freedom than he could help.

Once again Wilson scored the opening victories. On 9 April 1908 the Board of Trustees approved the proposal that the college should be built in the grounds of Prospect, the president's house. Not content with that, Wilson during the rest of the year rallied his friends on the faculty and endeavoured to secure the deposition of the dean. That was beyond him, but in February 1909 he obtained a resolution of the Board that the powers of the dean should be transferred to a committee of the faculty, and Wilson's party had a majority on this committee.

If Wilson hoped that this would make West resign, he mistook his man.

West had a card up his sleeve and in May 1909 he played it. There was a Mr. Procter, a wealthy soap manufacturer, a friend of West and one of his first pupils. Through West he made an offer of $500,000; one of the conditions was that the college should not be built at Prospect, that site being in his opinion unsuitable. In spite of argument throughout the summer, Procter would not budge from this term. In October 1909 the Board voted by 14 to 10 to accept the gift, thus in effect reversing the decision it had given in favour of Wilson a year and a half before. It was a heavy blow to Wilson's prestige. He more than toyed with an offer of the presidency of the University of Minnesota, but in the end decided to stay on at Princeton. There were a few months of uneasy truce. Then in December Wilson determined to force the issue. He prefaced his next step with the curious suggestion that the project, like the baby submitted to Solomon, should be cut in half and one part of the college built at Prospect with the original money and the other at West's site with Procter's money. When Procter rejected this, Wilson delivered an ultimatum to the Board in a letter written on Christmas Day 1909. The guidance of the university was being taken out of his hands, he said; he could not permit educational policy to be dictated by money-givers; either the gift was refused or he resigned.

The Board met on 13 January 1910. The struggle had reached the crisis. Each side had its passionate adherents on the Board but there was a large floating vote and none knew how the decision would go. In this situation the West party had resolved upon a clever move to reduce to its proper size the geographical quarrel over the site and bring out the real dispute. They produced a letter from Procter in which he said that while he could not approve the president's proposal of two colleges, in the interests of harmony he was prepared to accept it. Wilson, as he later said, was completely taken aback. In fact he lost his head. He declared that the site was quite unimportant: if the school was based on proper ideals, he said, it would be a success anywhere in Mercer County.

Why then had he ever opposed the acceptance of Procter's offer?

Because, he said, Procter was putting his money behind West's ideals and West's ideals were radically wrong. Holding up West's booklet of 1903, he exclaimed: 'They are his personal ideals; they are not the ideals of Princeton University.'

Why then had he written a preface praising the book?

He had not, he said, read the book when he wrote the preface. A lot of ink has since been spilt over the question whether this was true or untrue. But, whichever it was, it did not sound convincing.

The interrogation reverted to Procter's letter. Why did Wilson now reject Procter's acceptance of the plan which he had himself suggested?

Because, Wilson said, after making the suggestion he had discussed it with his friends on the faculty who had convinced him that it was unwise.

Why then in his Christmas Day ultimatum had he referred to the plan and said: 'This suggestion meets with the hearty concurrence of my colleagues here'?

Wilson had no answer to this. It was clear that he had put forward the suggestion in the expectation that it would be rejected and that he would be credited with a willingness to go halfway. 'It was the kind of dickering', Mr. Baker, the official biographer, says, 'a dickering he intensely disliked and should never have attempted,—in which his opponents were far cleverer than he.'[37] In fact he was outmanœuvred in the game he had begun and made to look a fool. He had allowed himself to get very excited. Indeed, he himself said afterwards that he did not feel at all sure that he had acted with self-control and propriety. To his opponents his conduct appeared as final and indisputable proof of his mental dishonesty.

Though Wilson got much the worse of the encounter, the verbal exchanges hardly touched the real question. Was the Board ready to face Wilson's resignation? As is the way of Boards the world over, they adjourned the matter for a month and appointed a committee of five to reach a settlement.

Thus by the beginning of 1910 Wilson's mood was no longer *laissez-faire*. During 1909 he had been giving much thought to questions of national as well as educational policy, and in both he was developing along the same lines. In an address at Princeton in June 1909 he declared that businessmen were unprofitable servants, keeping their legal obligations but piling up wealth which they had forgotten how to use honourably (Procter?) and coming near to debauching the nation. In another address on 10 January 1910 he said that social ambitions were invading colleges from outside so that they were ceasing to be centres of democratic regeneration. At a dinner of New York bankers on 17 January he talked in terms that Pierpont Morgan, who was there, thought personally offensive. On 21 January he spoke to a crowded meeting of progressives in the great ballroom of the Hotel Astor in New York. It was the occasion on which Wilson acquired an evangelist, Ray Stannard Baker, who recorded it as a 'truly determinative' experience, writing of the orator's 'fire-like sincerity and conviction' and of 'the man who in a chaotic world, plagued with evil spirits, knew what to do'.[38]

Mr. Baker was an American journalist about fifteen years younger than Wilson. His picture shows a serious, kindly face with rimless spectacles and a small moustache. What marks his nationality distinctively as an American of his period is an expression of suspended disapproval. He was one of those Americans who went to Europe in the same mood as upper-class Victorian Englishmen had gone to the Continent half a century before. He thought rightly that European standards could be much improved and came to believe as fervently as Wilson himself that his country's example could show how that ought to be done.

When the Paris Peace Conference of 1919 was over, Mr. Baker wrote a hasty history of it in three volumes and during the work became a devoted friend to his hero. Wilson wrote no autobiography or memoir, no defence to his critics. The last letter he wrote—it was on 25 January 1924, nine days before his death—was an offer to Baker of access to all his papers: 'I would rather have your interpretation of them than that of anybody else I know.'[39] So gathering together all the documents—which (Wilson was a methodical filer of every scrap of paper), Mr. Baker says, weighed eleven tons in all—and helped by three research assistants and a secretary, Baker laboured for eighteen years on the official biography, sustained by the thought that he was making a memorial to a great American whose life was in the great American tradition. He had in eight volumes reached the end of the First World War by the time the Second broke out. He left untouched the last years—the fight with the Senate, paralysis, and death. To his researches numerous subsequent biographers of Wilson are indebted.

Meanwhile, stories of the row at Princeton were getting about. On 31 January the *New York Times*, preparing a pro-Wilson editorial, wrote to him offering to make the facts known and asking for 'guidance'. By return of post Wilson sent back an unbridled letter. Procter's offer must be refused, he said, because he was insisting on demoralizing ideals; the issue was social exclusiveness against genuine democracy, whether there should flourish in Princeton the bad elements of social ambition and unrest or sober ideals and sound scholarship. He would be glad in a confidential way, he said, to go into further details if wanted.[40] On 3 February the editorial appeared, beginning with a resounding fanfare:

AT PRINCETON, the scene of a battle fought a century and a third ago for the establishment of American democracy, is in progress today a struggle not less significant for the future of American youth, and of Government in the United States. It is the more significant, though pitched in Academic halls, because it will decide the issue whether Americans shall henceforth fall short of their democratic mission. . . .[41]

The writer went on to elaborate the theme in a highly coloured reproduction of Wilson's letter. There were references to the invasions of the dilettanti, and the principles of sound scholarship were contrasted with exclusive social cliques devoted to the smatterings of culture.

The editorial caused a sensation. Some suspected but none could prove that it was inspired by Wilson. But the crisis was already passing. On 6 February Procter withdrew the gift either because he and his friends were satisfied that they could not get a majority on the Board or perhaps because he was disgusted by the course of events. So on 10 February 1910 the Board had nothing to do except record a victory for Wilson.

Thus Wilson became known to a wide public as the university president who in the cause of democracy and true education had turned down $500,000. Whether or not Harvey approved of this, it did not seem to affect his plans which in January 1910 were reaching maturity. In May 1909 *Harper's Weekly* had proclaimed: 'We now expect to see *Woodrow Wilson* elected Governor of the State of New Jersey in 1910 and nominated for President in 1912.'[42]

It was time to take the first step. On two Saturdays running in January Harvey gave lunch at Delmonico's to former Senator James Smith and convinced him that, if Smith could hold the Democrats in line, Wilson was the man who could get enough votes from liberal Republicans to turn the scale in the gubernatorial election. The prospect was attractive to Smith: a long period of Democratic rule in New Jersey had ended in 1896 and since then the Republicans had been entrenched in office. Smith was known as the 'Big Boss'; he had a half-share in the control of New Jersey. He and Harvey were old friends; Harvey had worked on his newspaper for a short time twenty-two years before. Smith was an Irish Catholic, the suave type of city boss, well-groomed and usually silk-hatted, generous and likeable, six feet tall, with a rich, musical voice. He had been in the United States Senate from 1893 to 1899, having got in with some help from Harvey (for which he was duly grateful) and got out with some aspersions on his integrity; the proximity of a purchase of sugar shares to a vote on the sugar tariff had got him a shattering reprimand from Cleveland. He knew Wilson—he had had three sons at Princeton—and admired him. Indeed, the Big Boss was to the end carried away by Wilson's oratory, even when it was directed against the bosses. One of Wilson's perorations against privilege—'men are not put into the world to go the path of ease; they are put into the world to go the path of pain and struggle'—brought tears into the big man's eyes. 'That is a great man, Mr. Tumulty,' he said in a choked voice, 'he is destined for great things.'[43]

Wilson was overwrought and needed a holiday. On 14 February he sailed for Bermuda and returned on 5 March. Either just before he left or just after he returned, Colonel and Mrs. Harvey spent the night at Prospect, and Wilson and the Colonel sat late in the library after dinner. Harvey asked:

If I can handle the matter so that the nomination for governor shall be tendered to you on a silver platter, without you turning a hand to obtain it, and without any requirement or suggestion of any pledge whatsoever, what do you think would be your attitude?[44]

Wilson was not unprepared. Six months earlier he had written to a friend that if such an invitation came, 'it would be my duty to give very careful consideration to the question where I could be of the most service'.[45] He walked up and down the room for several minutes. He had to think carefully, not so much about the move itself as about its timing, since it might be treated as a flight from his Princeton foes. At last he answered: 'If the nomination for governor should come to me in that way, I should regard it as my duty to give the matter very serious consideration.'[46] Harvey had to be content with that. It was agreed that the matter should be left there while Harvey was away on his annual trip to England.

The war with West was still on and being fought in a rage that tore up social life in Princeton. Now that it had come out in the press, letters, articles, and pamphlets were being put out on both sides. The Battle of Procter was apparently won but West with his demoralizing ideals remained at Princeton and was still dean of the graduate school. Wilson had been surprised and a little alarmed by the effect of the editorial and did not wish to add fuel to the flames. He gave out his opinion that the editorial was highly exaggerated. The West party pressed him to repudiate it but he would not do that; the foundation of it, he said, was true. But Wilson did not relax. Before he left for Bermuda he suggested to various members of the faculty that they should tell the Board they could not work with West and that he should be made to resign. On his return he resolved to campaign among the alumni, using his favourite weapon of public address. A vacancy on the Board gave him a battlefield; the West party put up a Mr. Adrian Joline as an anti-administration candidate, and the rival parties were near enough in numbers to make the election vital.

The issue was now very confused. No one really knew whether the site mattered or not. West's choice was perhaps to be regarded as a symbol of social exclusiveness. There was something like a revival of the dispute on the Quads Plan and the parties were similarly aligned. Wilson began his meetings on 11 March 1910 with some very conciliatory speeches and in the end he did in fact defeat Joline.

He broke off to keep an important political engagement, a Democratic Dollar Dinner on 29 March. He spoke on 'The Living Principles of Democracy'. He did not condescend much to detail, but he was definite that the power of the trusts should be curbed—not by direct management by the

Government, he said, but by 'legal regulation'. In such terms did he begin in his public addresses to edge away from *laissez-faire*. The speech was enthusiastically received and the other principal speaker, the senator from Oklahoma, was cheered when he implored Wilson to run for governor of New Jersey.

But for the moment this was just an interlude in the Princeton fight which Wilson resumed with an address to the New York alumni on 7 April. It was very coldly received, and this setback was followed by a more serious one from the Board of Trustees a week later. Wilson had hoped to confront the Board meeting on 14 April with a demand from the faculty for West's resignation. But even the most devoted of his supporters refused to follow him thus far, so he tendered a more moderate request that there should be an official faculty poll on the graduate college question. The Board refused it. These rebuffs angered Wilson and at a meeting of the Pittsburgh alumni on 16 April he let loose an unrestrained denunciation. The future was for state universities, he said, and not for privately endowed institutions.

The American college must become saturated in the same sympathies as the common people. The colleges of this country must be reconstructed from the top to the bottom. . . .

The great voice of America does not come from seats of learning. It comes in a murmur from the hills and woods and the farms and factories and the mills, rolling on and gaining volume until it comes to us from the homes of common men. Do these murmurs echo in the corridors of universities? I have not heard them.

He did not spare the churches which he said were as bad as the colleges, 'having more regard to their pew rents than to the souls of men'.

What we cry out against is that a handful of conspicuous men have thrust cruel hands among the heart-strings of the masses of men upon whose blood and energy they are subsisting.[47]

What of the 'calm voices infinitely sweet'* of the great Sesquicentennial Oration? They had receded into the soundless past. The Pittsburgh speech was as near as Wilson ever got to mob oratory. It made the headlines: 'Princeton President's Fiery Speech.'[48]

There were those on the Board who felt that this open warfare must be stopped if Princeton was not to get an incurable wound. A settlement was prepared that commended itself to the moderates on both sides. Wilson was displeased because it did not provide for the elimination of West, but the terms were hard enough for him. While the college was to be built on his chosen site, he was to retire as dean of the school and to be no more than resident master of the college. West saw himself put out of place and

* See p. 9 above.

authority, his life's ambition frustrated, the work of ten years and more almost unrewarded. West thought it no compromise but surrender and he resolved to fight. The proposal was to come before the May meeting of the Board which was expected to adopt it.

Within a minute of the twelfth hour there was a most dramatic stroke. Isaac C. Wyman of Salem, Mass., was an old Princetonian of the class of 1848 and reputedly a very wealthy man. Just after his election as President of Princeton Wilson planned to visit Mr. Wyman to invite him to his inauguration; he got as far as Boston but there he missed his connection and lost his opportunity. Thereafter West ploughed the neglected soil. The old man travelled unhastily into his eighties, giving no signal of the journey's end, till on 18 May 1910 West was summoned to the funeral. There he learnt that almost the whole of the Wyman estate, estimated at three or four million dollars (in fact it produced for Princeton only $660,000, but at the time it was the estimate that mattered), was left to him and another trustee to build the graduate college. '*Te deum laudamus*', West exulted from the graveside.

Thus were the jaws of defeat prised apart and down the monster's gullet went the mixture as before, but this time in a lethal dose. Wilson could fight half a million, he said, but not two or three; he could argue with the living but not with the dead. Procter's offer was renewed and on 9 June the Wyman bequest and the Procter gift were unanimously accepted. A mile from the campus, on the very site of General Washington's victory, there stand now the memorials of Dean West's doughty though less bloody triumph. There is Wyman House; there is Procter Hall, the dining hall of the dean's dreams; there is a larger-than-life bronze statue of the dean himself; over all the Cleveland Tower raises its Gothic head. Wilson's 'Princeton enemies', as later he used to call them, had won. For years afterwards when his mind was restless he saw them in his dreams; and in these nightmares there hung the fear, he confided three and a half years later to his greatest friend, that once again before the end the sweets of success might moulder into dust.

He never forgave nor forgot. When on 22 October 1913 the graduate college was opened, President Wilson did not attend; it was left to the former President Taft to sing the praises of the former President Cleveland. When in the following year the President invited the class of 1879 to dine with him in the White House he excluded two who had been active on the victorious side. Only a few months before his death he referred contemptuously to the 'Ivory Soap money' that had bought the soul of Princeton.

But all this was after the wound had festered. At the time of its infliction he behaved with a dignity that contrasted well with the offensive jubilation of his opponents. He attended the celebration dinner at West's house and said all that was necessary. There was not then any further talk of resigning. But if, one might ask, half a million dollars' worth of demoralization was intolerable to Wilson, how could he now face four or five times that amount? Wilson gave out that this great gift had altered the whole perspective; there would now be a large graduate faculty; the virus would be, as it were, diluted.

Undoubtedly the situation was different. It is one thing to use the weapon of threatened resignation when it can be counted on to give a good chance of victory and another thing to splinter it on a brick wall. Wilson did not hang on because he had no comfortable alternatives. He had several quite attractive offers from other universities to consider as well as his political prospects.

These events provided Colonel Harvey with an admirable opportunity for renewing his overtures when he returned from England. He seemed not at all put out by the fiery speech at Pittsburgh or by Wilson's other castigations of privilege. He may have thought it all no more than an academic tempest from which his man would bring home to the serious business of politics a countenance attractively weathered to the progressive colour that was now beginning to be quite the fashion.

The Princeton defeat did not, however, cause Wilson to solicit Harvey. On 20 June 1910 he took his family off to Lyme in Connecticut for the summer vacation and Harvey returned to find Boss Smith demanding a decision. Harvey arranged for Wilson and Smith to meet on Sunday, 26 June and was dismayed to receive a telegram from Wilson regretting his inability to attend because there was no Sunday train from Lyme. Harvey sent a car. The dinner was a great success; Smith had been on a trip to the Middle West and had satisfied himself that he could get support for Wilson as a presidential candidate; he saw himself as the maker of presidents, the master boss of his time. Colonel Henry Watterson, a tempestuous political figure from Kentucky known as 'Marse Henry', a veteran of seventy-one who was Harvey's friend and liked to think he was his mentor, made the fourth at dinner. He too was enthusiastic, and it was delightful to find that Mrs. Watterson and Mrs. Wilson were distant cousins. The politicians offered Wilson the New Jersey governorship and a fair chance of the White House. Wilson still refused to commit himself; he must consult his Princeton allies as he did not wish to desert them in the hour of defeat. But he promised a definite answer by the end of the week.

The next day he wrote to his friends on the Princeton Board setting out his prospects—the governorship and the 1912 nomination: 'the opportunity really seems most unusual' he commented mildly.[49] But he was not out of the Princeton fight; it would be necessary, he wrote, to agree upon concerted action in the matter of a successor in order that no reactionary be chosen. The response was cordial and on 12 July Wilson met a number of New Jersey politicians at a luncheon at the Lawyers' Club at 115 Broadway arranged by Harvey and gave his answer. He still made no concessions. On the liquor question he declared himself in favour of local option; and when told that the party had been fighting it for years, replied: 'Well, that is my attitude and my conviction. I cannot change it.'[50]

Three days later he publicly announced that, though not a candidate, he would accept the gubernatorial nomination if it were 'the wish and hope of a decided majority of the thoughtful Democrats of the State'.[51] On 15 September the thoughtful Democrats gathered together in a noisy convention and Wilson was nominated by 749 votes to 667. This slender majority was the best that could be got by the crack of Smith's whip. Wilson was unknown to the rank and file of the party and unwanted by the progressives who had their own candidates. But after the vote the progressives were converted almost in a body by Wilson's speech accepting the nomination which swept the meeting. Straightway he began his campaign. He tendered his resignation as President of Princeton while hoping that the Board might await the result of the election before deciding to accept it. But the trustees thought it too good a chance to end the strife and made it plain that they expected him to go. On 20 October his presidency ended and on 8 November 1910 he was elected Governor of New Jersey.

III
THE 1912 ELECTION

THE *New York Times* predicted that Wilson would win the New Jersey election with a majority of 7,000: Boss Smith was much more hopeful and put the majority at 25,000: the ever optimistic Harvey put it at 40,000: in fact it was just over 49,000. There was a Democratic landslide in many States that year but Wilson's victory was an outstanding triumph.

By a stroke of the fairy wand this man of fifty-four had in six months been transformed from a humiliated university president into a national figure, governor of a great state and presidential timber. After twenty-five years in the chrysalis Wilson the leader of men had suddenly emerged. The astonishing change of fortune left his poise unaltered. In October 1910 there had appeared in the *American Magazine* Kipling's poem 'If', which begins:

> If you can dream—and not make dreams your master;
> If you can think—and not make thoughts your aim,
> If you can meet with Triumph and Disaster
> And treat those two impostors just the same

Wilson cut it out, carried it for months in his pocket, and had a framed copy of the poem in his study at the White House. He kept it till the day he died.

At first Wilson hoped and expected to be able to pay all his personal campaign expenses out of his own pocket; for this purpose he had arranged to deliver three lectures to earn $500 which he thought would be quite sufficient. Indeed, on 25 September 1910 he returned contributions sent him by the brothers David and Thomas Jones who were in succession pro-Wilson trustees. Later he was glad to accept the $3,500 raised by his Princeton friends which went towards meeting a total campaign expenditure of well over $100,000. Harvey raised $10,000 from among those who, he told

Wilson, considered it a favour to be permitted to help along a movement for better government; among them was Ryan, 'who always responds generously to anything in which I am personally interested'.[1]

How did Wilson and the New Jersey bosses, even with Harvey's skilled brokerage, come to form their victorious partnership? In June 1910, before he had committed himself, Smith asked about Wilson's attitude to the Democratic organization and Wilson returned an oracular answer.

> So long as the existing Democratic organisation was willing to work with thorough heartiness for such policies as would re-establish the reputation of the State and the credit of the Democratic party in serving the State, I should deem myself inexcusable for antagonising it, so long as I was left absolutely free in the matter of measures and men.[2]

Smith professed himself satisfied. Men often find it difficult to believe that ideas quite unrecognizable in their own spheres of thought can be sincerely held by others. The bosses were so accustomed to lofty ideals being kept within the bounds of campaign oratory that they could hardly believe that any intelligent man could think them fit for anything else. To show gratitude to the men who put you in office was part of their code, and surely, they thought, as good an ideal as any that Wilson preached about. If gratitude did not move him, they could if necessary make him see which side his bread was buttered; a semi-political professor should be tender to the touch. Meanwhile, his notions were a most valuable asset. 'How the hell do I know whether he'll make a good governor?' one of them said in reply to a natural question. 'He'll make a good candidate and that is the only thing that interests me.'[3]

Wilson, of course, was bound to ask himself why the bosses selected him. He did not ask *them*: 'too great a knowledge of their motives might conceivably have embarrassed me' he said frankly in a campaign speech.[4] But whatever he might think about *their* corruption, he could not believe that they would regard *him* as capable of practising their arts or of not meaning exactly what he said. 'I concluded on the whole', he explained later to his friends, 'that these gentlemen had been driven to recognize that a new day had come in American politics, and that they would have to conduct themselves henceforth after a new fashion.'[5] The fact is that each man believed what he wanted to believe. Wilson at any rate could tell himself that, unless words were thought to signify nothing, he had made his position perfectly clear. In his speech accepting the nomination he emphasized again that he had given no pledges and had been asked for none, that he would serve the State with singleness of purpose. In the course of the campaign he went much further than that. He denounced the boss system; and, asked how he proposed to abolish it, he replied: 'By the election to office of men who will refuse to submit to it and bend all their energies to break it up, and by pitiless publicity.'[6] If elected, he said, he would deem himself for ever disgraced if he submitted to political influence or control in the matter of appointments to office or assent to legislation. 'Pitiless publicity' was the first of those hammer-blow phrases that struck the American public.

Two days after the election the Big Boss came to tender his formal congratulations and to remark that his friends were urging him to become a candidate for the United States Senate; he hoped the legislature would offer him the seat. Now, Smith had not presented himself as a candidate for the Senate at the Democratic primaries in September, perhaps because he did not anticipate that the Democratic victory would be extensive enough to win control of the legislature or perhaps because he thought that the candidature of the Big Boss was better kept concealed until after the *vox populi* had spoken. Furthermore, he had allowed Harvey to give Wilson to understand that he would not be a candidate. The party had chosen in the primaries a Mr. Martine, a Bryan Democrat, an amiable hack who liked to be known as the Farmer Orator. Senators were then elected not as now by direct popular vote (that was the result of the Seventeenth Amendment in 1913) but by the vote of the newly elected State legislature. In law the legislature could name whom they would but the choice of the primaries was recognized in the Democratic party platform as expressing the will of the people. No one— certainly not Wilson—thought that the Farmer Orator would make a very worthy senator; the contest in the primaries had not aroused much interest and Martine's vote was less than a quarter of the number of Democrats who had elected the legislature. By contrast Smith had held the party together and largely financed it since the defeat in 1896; he had personally contributed $50,000 to Wilson's own campaign; by all current political standards he was entitled to his reward in the hour of victory. Wilson could hardly oppose him on personal grounds though he expressed his approval backhandedly: 'I have very little doubt', he wrote to Harvey, 'that he would acquit himself with honor and do a great deal to correct the impressions of his former term.'[7] But the pith of the matter was that to substitute for Martine the party boss would be a bit of jobbery of the sort Wilson had so clearly and repeatedly condemned.

Technically Wilson could have avoided the issue. As governor he had no part to play in the choice of a senator; in law he had no duty even to advise. But Smith's proposal challenged the principles he had been proclaiming and he could not in conscience remain silent. Nor was it, if he saw his own future rightly, in his interest that he should; acquiescence would give him a quiet governorship but would make him nationally a nonentity. When Wilson made up his mind to fight, he took the first of two important decisions which gained him the presidency and in which he appeared to disdain the easy and immoral solution; but where in fact principle happily coincided with political interest in the long view. Nevertheless, for a man who was scarcely blooded in politics it was a bold decision to give battle to Smith on his own pitch. Wilson did not take the decision hastily or lightly and he first tested the ground.

He found that he would not have to fight single-handed nor without some practised assistants. At the first murmur of Smith's candidature the indignation of the progressives was aroused. In fact Wilson did not have to take the initiative; he had to decide whether to join the fray and take command. There were those in the organization whom the machine chafed and who resented the power of Smith and (ironically) the way in which he had two months before forced Wilson down their throats; they could form a nucleus of professional politicians to staff his campaign. One of the first of these on whom Wilson called was Joseph Patrick Tumulty. This young Irishman started in politics as a ward worker and in 1907 was rewarded by the organization with a place in the Assembly. He was now thirty-one: 'bright blue eyes in a round pink face' is how one of Wilson's daughters describes him.[8] But he was not then or ever simply a starry-eyed idealist; youthful fervour started him out on the progressive side but did not prevent him from learning all the tricks of the trade. He had bitterly denounced Wilson and was one of the Sauls who were caught on the road to Damascus when on 15 September 1910 they heard his speech accepting the nomination. He has described the scene.

Men stood about me with tears streaming from their eyes. Realizing that they had just stood in the presence of greatness, it seemed as if they had been lifted out of the selfish miasma of politics, and, in the spirit of the Crusaders, were ready to dedicate themselves to the cause of liberating their state from the bondage of special interests.[9]

When Wilson called on him on 25 November Tumulty urged him to fight and offered his aid: 'one of the ablest of the young Democratic politicians of the State,'[9] Wilson wrote about him, 'a guide at my elbow in matters of which I know almost nothing'.[10] A few weeks later Tumulty became his secretary. He was one of those who devote themselves to a person rather than to a cause. He soon conceived a boundless admiration for Wilson and thenceforward struggled after the vision, giving all that was in him. Anyone who was not prepared to do likewise was a damned crook: 'another of Tumulty's damned crooks' became a Wilson family joke.[11]

As Tumulty puts it, certain things in the way of accommodation were necessary to be done before a definite step was taken. One of the earliest of these was in Hudson County, Tumulty's own. There were thirteen key votes there which 'belonged' to Boss Davis who was under a gentleman's agreement to deliver them to his overlord Smith. It was Davis who had found Tumulty his place in the Assembly. He was, Tumulty says, a fine old fellow with an engaging human side; his orders to his 'working force' in the legislature to support this or that bill were always 'clean' and without a threat of any kind. This meant in practice that he would allow them their progressive flutters provided that they stood pat on the liquor question and on patronage. In this instance Davis went so far as to say that he would not 'feel hurt' if his orders were not followed. Davis was ill, dying of cancer, and at the critical moment his affairs were in the hands of James Hennessy, 'a fine clean-cut wholesome Irish-American'—again the description is Tumulty's.[12] Hennessy was sent for, and Wilson and Tumulty both talked to him about Wilson's 'unselfish purposes' and the expediency of his getting on the band wagon before it was too late. We do not know which of these reasons Hennessy took to be the more cogent, but he did eventually deliver the goods. These and other reconnaissances of a like character satisfied Wilson that he could fight and probably win; and that he must fight or abdicate. He had to be tough to fight the man to whom he owed his place and to listen to reproaches of ingratitude. He made a final attempt to deflect Smith, and, that failing, on 9 December 1910 he threw down the gage in a public statement. He took his stand on the vote in the primaries which he said was conclusive.

Absolute good faith in dealing with the people, an unhesitating fidelity to every principle avowed, is the highest law of political morality under a constitutional government.[13]

In these terms Wilson declared war on his patron. On 9 December 1909, twelve months before, he had been about to throw down the gage at Princeton and pondering an ultimatum to his Board of Trustees. The year 1909 was indeed as closely packed with events momentous to himself as any other yet to come.

Out in the open Wilson's aim was to arouse public opinion to such an extent that it would impress itself irresistibly on the legislature. At public meetings he did not pull his punches; the bosses, he said, were 'warts upon the body politic'.[14] As well as speeches there were personal letters to and nightly talks with assemblymen at the University Club in New York and at the Collingwood Hotel. The election was held on 24 January 1911. On the first ballot Martine got 40 votes to Smith's 10, only 1 vote less than the necessary majority, and the end came on the following day. Wilson wrote to Mrs. Peck:

> I pitied Smith at the last . . . He wept, they say, as he admitted himself utterly beaten . . . It is a pitiless game, in which, it would seem, one takes one's life in one's hands,—and for me it has only begun![15]

It was just seven months since one of the anti-Wilson trustees at Princeton, commenting on Wilson's entry into politics, had written to a friend that Wilson's head had been turned by dinner-table applause and that he would be 'a child, a dear delightful infant, left to the tender care of James Smith'.[16]

It is a curious thing that Franklin D. Roosevelt, then twenty-eight and an admirer but not a follower of his cousin Theodore, made his political debut in the same year as Wilson and, though in a smaller field, in much the same way. His victory is another example of the swing over to the Democrats and of the surge of national feeling that gave such momentum to Wilson's initial triumphs. Roosevelt stood for the New York Senate at Poughkeepsie, a seat kept safe for Republicans since 1856, declaring his independence of the interests. He won by a narrow margin and his first act was to fight the Tammany boss Murphy. He led an insurrection against the Tammany nominee for the United States Senate and defeated him on the sixty-fourth ballot.

So Wilson's successful challenge to the machine was not unique, but it was widely publicized and won him a national reputation. What is more significant is that it confirmed him in his belief in 'the people' and in the rightness of his political method. 'The people of the United States', he said when he started his campaign for the presidential nomination, 'are just like the people of New Jersey. If they believe in an issue, once it is stated to them in terms they understand, they will force their leaders to adopt it.'[17] This is too simple a view of his victory over Smith. It is not recorded that he held more than two public meetings. It is possible that the evening conferences with senators and assemblymen and the little talks, of which the one with Hennessy does as an example, were much more effective. Very likely, as his campaign biographer was to write it up, that the Governor 'merely told them to follow their consciences and tried to assure them that they would suffer no harm if they did so'.[18] Wilson's greatest asset throughout the New Jersey period was that no politician believed that he meant what he said. Anyway it is not necessary to say anything very explicit to recall to an assemblyman's mind the advantages of attending to a governor's wishes. Not the whole of the campaign was conducted on Wilson's high level; Tumulty made use of one or two tricks which he had learnt, he says, 'in the rough school of practical politics'[19] and of which he later confessed he was not proud.

Wilson was inaugurated as Governor on 17 January 1911. He was determined to be not merely the chief executive of the state but also the leader of his party and the initiator of legislative reform. He had not worked out any measures of his own and the day before his inauguration he called a conference of progressive legislators of both parties; they resolved to concentrate upon four bills—election reform, corrupt practices, public utilities, and employers' liability.

Wilson's methods of leadership were a mixture of the new and the old. Old-fashioned legislators were startled by offers from the Governor, which none accepted, to debate the issues with them publicly in their own districts. Then there were announcements of the type in which the headmaster expresses his hope that he will not have to name the boys who are letting the school down. But there were also get-together meetings arranged by Tumulty: at one of them the Governor danced a Virginia reel: 'after all', as Tumulty says, 'men are just boys'.[20]

The first bill to be introduced was the Election Reform Bill. It struck directly and hard at the boss-controlled nomination (such as Wilson's own); and Smith and Nugent, his nephew and aide, resolved to test again their power and influence over Democratic assemblymen by trying to kill the Bill. They summoned a caucus meeting for 13 March 1911. Wilson heard of it and asked to come. This was unprecedented but difficult to refuse. He went with a copy of the state constitution in his pocket, anticipating the objection of a machine assemblyman who wanted to know what right Wilson thought he had to interfere in legislative matters; the Governor's right under Section 6, Article 5, Wilson retorted, to 'recommend such measures as he may deem expedient'.[21]

This descent on the bosses' sheepfold was typical of Wilson's direct approach and of his belief in his power of persuasion. In a speech that lasted three hours and was admitted by all to be a masterpiece of effectiveness he converted the caucus. The Bill, he said, was not as the bosses urged a plan to destroy the party but to revitalize it and 'arm it for the war to which the swelling voice of a people called it in an hour of palpitant expectancy'.[22]

There was more wrestling of this sort. There was a dramatic occasion when Nugent rose to propose a toast to the Governor of New Jersey—'an ingrate and a liar';[23] and several of the company dashed their glasses to the ground. Anyone who enjoys a rousing yarn in which the fresh hero tackles the villains in fair fight, scorning trickery, and they slink away like whipped curs, can read a technicoloured account in the 1912 campaign biography written up by William Bayard Hale. It made excellent propaganda in a country which was getting sick of the boss pestilence.

There was indeed a reality of great achievement. Wilson had broken the machine in a boss-ridden state and by the end of the legislative session all his four measures had been enacted. He was entitled to write to Mrs. Peck:

I got absolutely everything I strove for . . . I wrote the platform, I had the measures formulated to my mind, I kept the pressure of opinion constantly on the legislature, and the programme was carried out to its last detail . . . I feel a great reaction today, for I am, of course, exceedingly tired, but I am quietly and deeply happy that I should have been of just the kind of service that I wished to be to those who elected and trusted me. I can look them in the face, like a servant who has kept faith and done all that was in him, given every power he possessed, to them and their affairs. There could be no deeper source of satisfaction and contentment!

There is no telling what deep waters may be ahead of me. The forces of greed and the forces of justice and humanity are about to grapple for a bout in which men will spend all the life that is in them. God grant I may have strength enough to count, to tip the balance in the unequal and tremendous struggle![24]

It was with this sense of dedication that Wilson inspired his New Jersey followers in 1911. They witnessed reforms which had been talked about for years made law in a few months and they felt intensely the impact of the dynamic personality that had so suddenly come among them to do these mighty deeds. He generated once again the same glowing enthusiasm as in the early days at Princeton. But this too did not last. The bosses could no longer steer the boat but they could wreck it. The election of November 1911 resulted, in spite of a vigorous campaign by Wilson, in a Republican majority in both houses: Smith and Nugent deliberately let the Republicans in for Essex County. Wilson was not good at working with those who were not subject to him and he would not try by persuasion to lead his Republican opponents. He took a particular dislike to the Republican majority leader in the Senate who was a professor at Columbia University. Moreover, he was distracted by the coming presidential election. So the 1912 session was a dismal record of conflict and veto. His report to Mrs. Peck was in a bitterly different tone:

This has been a petty and barren legislature. It has done nothing worth mentioning except try to amend and mar the wonderful things we accomplished last year . . . And what shall we say when we find the leader of the petty partisan band a learned and distinguished Professor in a great University with plenty of independent means and plenty of brains, of a kind, but without a single moral principle to his name! I have never despised any other man quite so heartily, — tho.

there are others whom I have found worthier of hate and utter reprobation—in *another* university![25]

The great Democratic victories in the mid-term elections of 1910 filled the party with a new hope of the presidency and set the arena for new contenders. Bryan was still the party leader and of immense power with the rank and file; but there was now a feeling—which in some measure perhaps he shared for he made no effort to fight off his rivals for the headship of the pack—that he had passed his zenith, that Bryanism had worn thin and that the times called for fresh blood. So one by one the new braves stepped out. First came the two governors. Governor Harmon of Ohio was a safe, solid, pompous figure—'hasn't had a new political thought since Cleveland's administration', Wilson said.[26] Then Governor Wilson: the continuous thrumming of Harvey had now been taken up all over the country and the boom was swollen by the New Jersey triumphs in the spring of 1911. Soon the governors were joined by two congressmen of long experience in the House who had attained office for the first time after the Democratic victory in the 1910 mid-term election. The first was Underwood of Alabama, Chairman of the Ways and Means Committee. He was comparatively young, fifty, a quiet, effective man, whom Bryan disliked as a conservative. Wilson admired his abilities and even spoke of standing down in his favour, but after meeting him in June 1911 was not satisfied that he had 'a genuine grasp of progressive principles'.[27] The other was James Beauchamp—known as Champ—Clark of Missouri, in Congress since 1892; he had led the party in the House since 1909 and was elected Speaker in 1911. He was a friend of Bryan, an old political hand and a sound party man 'whose breast is covered with the scars of honor', as his nominator was to say:[28] 'a sort of elephantine smart Aleck' Wilson thought.[29] He was the last to emerge. By the beginning of 1912 the lists were virtually closed and the fight was on between these four men.

By then the nominating convention, which was to be held at Baltimore in June 1912, was only a few months off, and long before this, even before the first New Jersey session was over, Wilson was making or permitting tentative moves. In March 1911 Page got together an informal committee to discuss strategy and a rudimentary publicity organization was formed. 'I am not to be put forward as a candidate', Wilson said. 'Confine your activities to answering requests for information.'[30] William F. McCombs was put in charge; he was a former Princeton pupil, a New York lawyer with some experience of Tammany politics. It was as early as 9 March that Governor Wilson made his first political speech outside his own state, and that, appropriately enough, was at Atlanta, where he had unsuccessfully tried his hand at law thirty years before; he had nothing in particular to say, he told Mrs. Peck, but was going 'because I thought it wise (which, being translated, means politic) to go'.[31] He had a long conference with Governor Hoke Smith and found something in particular to say to him, for on 6 April 1911 Hoke Smith announced that he would support Wilson for the presidency. This was the first important political figure to declare for Wilson. But there must be, the committee decided, a campaign in the West. Wilson was well enough known in the East and had family ties with the South. It was in the West, in Bryan's strongholds, that he had to be tested out. And before that there was the problem of Bryan himself: was he to be fought or conciliated?

If Bryan had ever heard of Wilson as President of Princeton it may well have been in connection with an incident when he was campaigning in September 1908. Two of Wilson's former students arranged a meeting for him in Alexander Hall on the Princeton campus. Wilson talked to them of Bryan's 'vacuity' and inability to think clearly;[32] he asked them not to embarrass him by holding the meeting in Princeton and so Bryan was banished to Princeton Junction. This, if he knew of it, would not have rankled long with him. He was stirred by Wilson's New Jersey victory, and immediately sent him a telegram of good wishes. This led to correspondence and in February 1911 Bryan wrote enthusiastically about Wilson in his paper *The Commoner*. Bryan may or may not have wanted the nomination if it came his way; he kept his counsel. He was a great-hearted man and the cause meant more to him than personal triumph. The two men first met on 12 March 1911. Bryan, an active Presbyterian, was visiting Princeton to address the Theological Seminary on 'Faith'. This time Alexander Hall was available. Wilson was hurriedly summoned back from Atlanta by his wife to entertain him at dinner. The meeting was a success on both sides: Wilson confessed himself captivated by Bryan's sincerity and charm. It was not an unusual reaction. The Republican Elihu Root, who regarded the presidential candidate of 1900 as 'a disgusting, dishonest fakir', became 'awfully chummy'[33] when he met him as Secretary of State in 1913, and the two often took their early morning rides together.

Bryan did not disapprove of the projected speaking tour in the West. It took place in May and June, as soon as the 1911 New Jersey session was over, and Wilson was able to please his radical audiences by announcing his conversion to the Initiative, Referendum, and Recall, one of their favourite nostrums which Wilson as a political scientist had always condemned. The change of mind, while convenient, may well have been genuine, for Wilson's experiences in New Jersey had convinced him of the value of direct contact with the people. He hedged a little later by means of a device which he used for meeting several prickly questions; he said that it was a matter for each state to decide for itself; thus ardour in states which liked it could be mixed with coolness in those which did not, and Wilson did not thereafter press the reform.

Oratorically the tour was triumphant. But nomination depends on delegates and they do not solidify from the evanescent applause of audiences. Wilson was wont to say in his speeches that he was 'not thinking about the presidency' till his wife told him tactfully to stop it as the newspapers were getting sarcastic about it. Still Wilson was disposed, as Mr. Baker says, to rely on 'the call of the people'. He did not like the idea of a campaign manager which would mean, he thought, a descent into the arena and 'would create some very unfavourable impressions'.[34] He consented to the information bureau being formalized with the opening of an office at 42 Broadway. In June the group was joined by William G. McAdoo, a successful businessman forty-seven years old, who later became Secretary to the Treasury and then married Wilson's daughter Eleanor. At last in October McCombs was officially designated manager. He had the responsibility of raising money and spending it in trying to secure the election of Wilson men by the state conventions which sent delegates to Baltimore. He raised just over $193,000, of which almost half was contributed by Wilson's Princeton friends.

But where in all this was Colonel Harvey? Where was the first Wilson man who had arranged his nomination as governor and was so much at home in electoral approaches? Although Harvey had given no signs, he cannot have been happy about his protégé. He had not protested against Wilson's progressive tirades. In the matter of the senatorial election he had given no comfort to his old friend Smith; his attitude was in effect that business was business and he was not going to do anything to impair Wilson's chances of the presidential nomination. After Smith had been beaten, *Harper's Weekly* proclaimed Wilson's decision to fight the boss as the most daring act ever performed in American politics and hailed him as the Knight Errant of the New Democracy.

Harvey was a very clever man and he was playing a well-considered game for very high stakes. He had never been interested in doing the ordinary thing—backing at short odds a horse from a well-known stable. He had picked himself a most unlikely winner; it was a shrewd choice and events proved his judgement to be absolutely right. He made another vital calculation that also turned out to be right in theory. While he realized that he might not get from Wilson much in the way of conventional rewards, he foresaw that Wilson was bound to need a sagacious political adviser who could handle men while Wilson handled measures. The role of *éminence grise* has a great temptation for ambitious men who do not look their best in floodlight. If Harvey could obtain that place, it would not matter much if Wilson's goings-on did displease men like Ryan and Morgan, so long as it helped to get him elected. What went wrong with the calculation was something that Harvey could not be expected to provide for. There was indeed a vacancy for the sort of man Harvey aspired to be, but Wilson could not work in that way with any man, except one or two for whom he conceived a strong affection; and Harvey never penetrated the armour of his indifference. The vacancy was filled but not, in spite of all his claims, by Harvey. The two men met for the last time (if there is excepted an almost formal call by Harvey at the White House in 1914) on 7 December 1911. On 24 November 1911 Wilson had his first meeting with another colonel, Edward M. House. It was Harvey who first mentioned House's name to Wilson and his last benefaction was to commend him to Wilson for his sound political views.

During some months before that it was being made plainer and plainer to Harvey that he was not wanted as the trusted counsellor. In the New Jersey election Wilson had constantly turned to him for guidance but after the victory he seemed to go his own way. He let Harvey know what he was doing about Smith but that was all; and that was because he hoped that Harvey could persuade Smith to stand down. For the presidential nomination for which Harvey had worked so hard Wilson was setting up an organization without even asking Harvey to help. If Harvey now wanted an interview he had to ask for it, and on an occasion about the end of October 1911 the request was quite firmly put off—a temporary loss of perspective, Harvey called the rebuff. Still he did not give up. The Republican victory in the New Jersey elections on 7 November 1911 was a setback to Wilson's presidential campaign and *Harper's Weekly* rushed to his relief. Harvey put at the head of the editorial columns the legend 'For President Woodrow Wilson', and, his biographer says,

filled those columns with some of the most brilliant and convincing articles the famous old paper had ever contained. . . . Casting ancient friendships into the discard for the sake of the cause he had at heart, he excoriated Smith with every conceivable resource of burning irony and stinging sarcasm.[35]

But pressure was being brought upon Harvey to oppose Wilson. He said so to Colonel House, whom he had to lunch on 5 December 1911, and added that he had told his friends that he had an open mind and would oppose Wilson if convinced that he was dangerous. Wall Street's approval of Wilson had not survived the amplification of his views; and Harvey's friends, whose support he had enlisted for Wilson, were becoming understandably restive at what they termed his Bryanism. One of the most shocking things was Wilson's conversion, to the Initiative, Referendum, and Recall. These words were regarded by conservatives with the horror attracted by an evil incantation; the thing was not merely a measure to be discussed and disapproved, it was not merely radicalism, it was almost socialism; it was a proposal to 'lynch representative government'. Perorations against privilege were the current coin of campaign speeches, the customary largesse demanded by the voters, but the positive endorsement of the I., R., & C. branded Wilson with the mark of the apostate. The *New York Sun*, which since Harvey's cultivation of Laffan had consistently supported Wilson, turned right round and led an attack on him by the conservative press.

It would not do for Harvey to lose the favour of the magnates if he was not to be compensated by his position with Wilson. He had to find out definitely from Wilson where he stood. His method of doing this was characteristic: he did not stage a melodramatic showdown or ask Wilson straight out; he arranged to subject him to the test of a question or two that would induce revelation. On 7 December 1911 Wilson came by invitation to 'Marse Henry' Watterson's apartment at the Manhattan Club, New York, to discuss campaign expenses. Waterson suggested that the burden was getting too heavy for the Princeton friends who were the main contributors and offered a handsome contribution from Ryan. Wilson could hardly accept without tying himself nor refuse without showing his hand. He made it plain that he disliked the idea and said some 'uncivil things' about Ryan. Then Harvey put a question to which he said he wanted a frank answer. Was there anything left of the cheap talk that he was advocating Wilson on behalf of The Interests? Was the support of *Harper's* embarrassing his campaign? Wilson answered that some of his friends told him that it was not doing him any good in the West. Harvey suggested that he should 'sing low' and Wilson assented only too readily. It did not occur to him that the moment would be a happy one for expressing a sense of his obligation to Harvey for his support in the past. Thereby he illustrated not only the slow reaction of his personal touch but also his ingrained belief that political support was not a personal matter at all. It told Harvey as plainly as he needed to be told that he was not wanted and had nothing to hope for. It also gave him—and doubtless the question was framed to achieve this end as well—the chance of a strategic retreat without incurring the odium of desertion.

It was not until after *Harper's* had removed Wilson's name from the top of the editorial columns and someone (Tumulty claims that it was he: 'I immediately scented the danger of the situation and . . .')[35] asked Wilson what he had done that it was brought home to Wilson that he might not have said all that was to be said. Thereupon on 21 December he wrote to Harvey:

Every day I am confirmed in my judgment that my mind is a one-track road and can run only one train of thought at a time! A long time after that interview with you and Marse Henry at the Manhattan Club it came over me that when (at the close of the interview) you asked me that question about the Weekly, I answered it simply as a matter of fact, and of business, and said never a word of my sincere gratitude to you for all your generous support, or of my hope that it might be continued. Forgive me, and forget my manners![37]

Harvey answered pleasantly and ended his letter:

Whatever little hurt I may have felt as a consequence of the unexpected peremptoriness of your attitude toward me is, of course, wholly eliminated by your gracious words.[38]

But Marse Henry with old ideas of Southern courtesy was horrified at the curt acceptance of his friend's sacrifice. After Christmas he went on a tour to lecture on World Peace, and, perhaps as a relief from a subject which could hardly have appealed to his natural bellicosity, he worked himself up into a fury over Wilson and laid plans to expose him before the electorate. At each stopping place he spread among his journalist friends the tale of Wilson's ingratitude. Rumours of a break began to get about. On 17 January 1912 Harvey issued a statement that *Harper's* had ceased to advocate Wilson's nomination in response to a statement made directly by him that their support was affecting his candidacy injuriously. This was unjust, since it made it look as if Wilson had required him to withdraw. Watterson followed up with a full account of the interview with angry comment:

I am not sure that I had not said as much [i.e. that his support was injurious] to Colonel Harvey himself, but that Governor Wilson, without the least show of compunction, would express or yield to such an opinion, and permit Colonel Harvey to consider himself discharged from the position of trusted intimacy he had up to this moment held, left me little room to doubt that Governor Wilson is not a man who makes common cause with his political associates or is deeply sensible of his political obligations; because it is but true and fair to say that, except for Colonel Harvey, he would not be in the running at all.[39]

Tumulty describes the affair with the zest of a sporting journalist:

The story of the Manhattan Club incident broke about the Princetonian's head . . . charges of ingratitude to 'the original Wilson man' flew thick and fast . . . soon the stock of the New Jersey man began to fall. . . .[40]

As Tumulty says, 'this unfortunate episode did not sit well on the stomachs of the American people'.[41] But in the end it did Wilson politically much more good than harm. It persuaded the Western progressives more potently than speeches could do that Wilson was not a Wall Street nominee, and it did not displease those who disliked the boss system: as the *New York Times* wrote tartly: 'Ingratitude is one of the rarest virtues in public life.'[42] Bryan was strongly impressed. 'The venom of his adversaries', he wrote, 'removes all doubt as to the reality of the change.'[43]

Harvey was a good loser. Six years constant advocacy, much work, and some money had gone for nothing. He did not make things easy for Wilson, and he did not discourage, if indeed he did not abet,* Marse Henry's fulmination; but it would have needed an angel to rise above some natural bitterness. After the hubbub had died down he dropped quietly out of the fight without doing anything spiteful. He did not transfer his support to any other candidate and after Wilson's nomination *Harper's* campaigned strongly for his election; he remained on friendly terms with Wilson. When Wilson was President with patronage Harvey would have taken the London embassy, but it was given to Page, greatly to Marse Henry's indignation, who wrote of 'the punctuation of this slight by the appointment of another New York publisher'.[44] There was a suggestion of the Paris embassy but Harvey did not want it much and Wilson did not press it.

Wilson sent for Harvey once to come to the White House on 4 October 1914. The interview was arranged by Tumulty who perhaps had his eye on the coming mid-term congressional elections. According to the White House press statement the two men discussed 'the general situation': the interview must have been very different from those for which Harvey had hoped and striven. When Harvey left the White House after the colourless talk, it might have been his exit from the Wilson drama after a great part in the first act. But events, which sometimes can shape themselves with as much neatness as any dramatist can contrive, brought him back before the curtain fell.

Before the storm over the Harvey affair burst, Wilson had been given another awkward situation to deal with. This was at the Jackson Day Dinner of 8 January 1912, the greatest of the party pre-nomination events and the occasion for a parade of presidential starters. A minor misfortune was that Nugent had cunningly bought up all the dinner tickets assigned to New Jersey so that none of Wilson's state supporters could be there. Nevertheless, Wilson had a magnificent reception, surpassing that of any other candidate, and this in the presence of all the bosses. Among them was the one who was in the end the most effective in the fight for the nomination. This was Roger Sullivan of Illinois. He was then engaged in a desperate struggle for his bossdom against Chicago rebels and in spite of Boss Smith's experience in

---

* Professor Link considers that Harvey instigated it and behaved hypocritically; Link 1.365.

New Jersey he did not appear hostile to Wilson. He had a son called Boetius who, whether because of his name or his nature, was a Wilson devotee; and Tumulty believed that the son and Wilson's Jackson Day speech were the ultimate influences which caused Sullivan to desert Clark.

What might have been a more serious misfortune at the Jackson Day Dinner was that two days before the dinner Adrian Joline, whose candidature Wilson had defeated for the Princeton Board of Trustees,* permitted (while 'hoping that it would not be inferred that he had any ill-feeling toward Wilson')[45] the *New York Sun* to publish a private letter written to him five years before in which Wilson had expressed the wish that they 'could do something, at once dignified and effective, to knock Mr Bryan once for all into a cocked hat'.[46] But Bryan was too big a man to be antagonized and he behaved generously, acknowledging Wilson's deft apology by putting his hand affectionately on his shoulder.

These were not the whole of Wilson's campaign troubles. He had rejected almost contemptuously an offer of support from Hearst's yellow press, refusing even to meet the man, and so the mighty dungsplasher attacked him venomously. All the anti-Wilson press found material in his application in October 1910 after his retirement from Princeton for a distinguished service pension from the Carnegie Foundation and in a number of very uncomplimentary things he had said in his *History* about foreign immigrants. Champ Clark got the support of the Hearst journals (together with a sizeable campaign contribution) which Wilson had rejected, just as Harmon and Underwood got Ryan's money.

The Jackson Day Dinner was the official opening of the contest for the nomination. From then on Wilson was up and down the country speaking incessantly. The state conventions began making their returns in February and as the weeks went by it became manifest that while Wilson at meeting after meeting had been attracting vast applause and while Clark had not ventured far beyond an occasional recitation entitled 'The Signs of the Times', it was Clark who had been collecting the delegates. He was an amiable and popular figure and his long service had given him many valuable contacts with local politicians. Moreover, he stood well with the progressives. He was not a crusader like Bryan and he was far from being a powerful personality like Wilson, but he had been, as Bryan put it, 'on the right side of all the reform questions'. The Hearst press had proved very useful to him.

Harmon of Ohio had been persistently attacked by Bryan and was now almost annihilated. In the Ohio primary he got 100,099 votes to 89,116 for Wilson, and a man who could carry his own state only by such a narrow majority stood no chance of nomination. By contrast Wilson had a heartening

* See p. 56 above.

victory in New Jersey on 28 May 1912 which by then he badly needed. Smith fought hard for Champ Clark but Wilson carried by enormous majorities 20 out of the 21 counties and Smith only just held his stronghold of Essex County. That gave him only 4 out of the 28 delegates, so Smith, Nugent, and two other cronies were submerged by 24 jubilant Wilsonians.

The state of opinion in the country and the power of Bryan made it likely that a progressive would be nominated; Underwood had to rely upon the chance that the convention might after all turn to a conservative. Subject to this the issue lay between Clark and Wilson. Bryan displayed himself as equally favourable to both; both, he thought, were to be trusted. The Nebraska delegation which Bryan led was by the vote of the state convention pledged to Clark as first choice.

When all the 1,088 delegates had been chosen, every political punter was putting his money on Clark. Some 436 delegates were pledged to him, compared with 248 to Wilson; 224 were unpledged and in the hands of various bosses and 180 pledged to Underwood and minor candidates. No doubt Wilson had more devoted and enthusiastic support; Franklin Roosevelt, though unable to get on to the New York delegation, was present throughout the convention and working indefatigably for him. But Clark was much more acceptable to the party organization, and the probability was that the 224 unpledged votes would move under their bosses towards him rather than Wilson. Thus Wilson's figure seemed to be near his limit while Clark had a lot in reserve. The powerful New York delegation ninety strong, under the leadership of Charlie Murphy, the boss whom Franklin Roosevelt had flouted, was among those uncommitted; its swing, well timed, would carry much else with it.

It looked then as if all the hope centred on Wilson was but a bubble to be pricked by these hard figures. Wilson himself wrote to Mrs. Peck on 9 June:

Just between you and me, I have not the least idea of being nominated, because the make of the convention is such, the balance and confusion of forces, that the outcome is in the hands of the professional, case-hardened politicians who serve only their own interests and who know that I will not serve them except as I might serve the party in general. I am well and in the best of spirits. I have no deep stakes involved in this game.[47]

The Governor of New Jersey had a mansion at Sea Girt. Wilson went there to get what quiet he could; newspaper correspondents were encamped in tents around and there was a private wire to the convention. Wilson appointed McCombs as leader of his managers 'on the ground' at Baltimore; McAdoo and Burleson of Texas, both to become members of his cabinet, were in the team.

Clark waited in the Speaker's Office in the Capitol at Washington. His chief manager was Senator William J. Stone of Missouri, a formidable and experienced politician, an ardent admirer of Bryan and one of his managers in previous campaigns. From 1914 to 1918 Stone sat in the chair of the crucially important Foreign Relations Committee, so it is worth saying who and what he was. In 1912 he was aged sixty-four, had been governor of his state before the turn of the century, and senator since 1903. He was a great man in Missouri and there is now in Nevada a statue of him, lifesize in bronze, in which a downfall of benevolence from the forehead and through the nose contends for the control of his features with an upthrust of shrewdness from the chin and mouth. He was a man of ideals and principles, but as a biographer says, 'few equalled and probably none excelled Stone as a practical politician'.[43] It was not an age in which it was easy to be a practical politician and remain unstained; and Stone got the sobriquet of Gum-Shoe Bill as a tribute to his adroitness in avoiding charges of political corruption.

The first session of the convention was due to begin on the afternoon of Tuesday, 25 June 1912, in the Fifth Regiment Armory, a factory-like building which had been adorned with bunting and multi-coloured draperies and a huge picture of Jefferson; and for two days before the delegates were assembling with banners and brass bands in the crowded hotels. 'Noble city!' Marse Henry soliloquized in the *Louisville Courier*, 'In deep reflection the spirit of democracy walks thy streets this day; broods amid thy solitudes.'[49] But the real struggle had begun before this and Wilson had already taken a vital decision. The cause of it was the proposal by the 'Committee on arrangements' to make Judge Parker, the conservative candidate of 1904, temporary chairman. Bryan was outraged. Ignoring Harmon and Underwood as hopelessly reactionary, he telegraphed to the other candidates protesting against the offence to 'Members of a Convention overwhelmingly progressive by naming a reactionary to sound the keynote of the campaign'[50] and inviting them to join with him in opposing the appointment.

Parker's selection had the full support of Tammany so that the problem for convention strategists was how to keep the support of Bryan without losing the Tammany vote; if the risk had to be taken of giving up one, which should it be? Clark's answer could not really be in doubt. Though it was disagreeable to have to lift so early a foot from one camp or the other, his course was dictated by the fact that Tammany paid in votes and Bryan did not. If Clark could add Tammany's 90 to the 436 already pledged to him, it gave him 526 votes or only 19 short of a majority. It was true that it needed a two-thirds majority to secure the nomination, but not since 1844 had a candidate who had got a bare majority failed to go on and win the necessary two-thirds, and it was almost as securely established that no candidate could be nominated who was not supported by Tammany. It was impossible for Clark to reject the opportunity of making sure of Tammany's support; so he returned an evasive answer to Bryan and made a secret pact with Boss Murphy that Clark delegates would support Tammany over the chairmanship and at the right strategic moment Murphy would declare for Clark.

For Wilson's managers the problem was agonizing. How could he possibly succeed unless he won votes from the unpledged and how could he hope to do that if he began by affronting the most powerful among them? If the 90 Tammany votes were invaluable to Clark, they were essential to Wilson to save him from defeat. The best solution, McCombs thought, was to be non-committal and to try not to offend either side. Wilson hesitated. Then he decided on clean and unqualified support for Bryan. He telegraphed his reply: 'You are quite right. . . . The Baltimore convention is to be a convention of progressives—of men who are progressives on principle and by conviction.'[51]

As in the case of Smith in New Jersey, Wilson could have remained aloof. He could, as at first he thought of doing, have replied that he was not a member of the convention and had no right to direct its organization. But to sit legalistically on the fence would get him nowhere. If he was not going to support Bryan, then he should woo Tammany: if he was not going to woo Tammany, then he had better support Bryan wholeheartedly. Morally he could not woo Tammany; the act would be a denial of his principles. But here again the right moral decision was in the long view also the right political decision. It was difficult for those whose eyes were focused on the numerals of pledged and unpledged to see it. To McCombs this defiance hurled at Tammany seemed to invite certain disaster and he moaned that all his work was gone for nothing. But what chance in fact had Wilson of getting the Tammany vote in competition with Champ Clark? The attempt would lead to almost certain failure and quite certain ignominy. Just as the occasion gave Clark his opportunity of clinching Tammany, so it offered to Wilson the moment to proclaim himself in contrast with Clark the only true progressive, to lay claim to the Bryan inheritance and to put his frailer hope of victory upon the chance that a swelling wave of popular approval would overwhelm all calculations.

At first it seemed that Bryan had already worn his mantle threadbare. He made a long speech at the opening session but his style of oratory was going out of fashion and a biblical peroration about pillars of fire by night and of cloud by day called up no emotion. The Clark managers delivered enough votes to get Parker elected by 579 to 508. Bryan was now in a rumbustious mood. Ryan had slipped into the convention as a delegate from

Virginia and Bryan introduced a resolution that he and other Wall Street figures should be expelled. This resolution in a curtailed form, the penalty of expulsion being omitted, was carried by 883 to $201\frac{1}{2}$. The size of this majority and the size of the minority vote on the chairmanship (it must have included a number of Clark delegates who would not toe the line) were significant. These and other preliminaries occupied the time of the convention until nearly midnight on Thursday 27 June, when the nominating began.

Before that there had been the usual list of disputed elections brought before the credentials committee. The committee was a market for the exchange of commodities, not a tribunal for the administration of justice. Among the bargains made was one between the Wilson managers and Boss Sullivan which had far-reaching consequences. There had been in the Illinois primaries a bitter struggle for mastery between the Boss, who led the conservative wing, and Mayor Harrison of Chicago who led the progressive. The Mayor, who as a progressive should have been Wilson's natural ally, took a dislike to him and in association with Hearst gave his support to Clark; Sullivan did not commit himself. Clark got a handsome majority over Wilson in the primaries so that the Illinois delegation of fifty-eight arrived in Baltimore pledged to him. But it was still uncertain whether it was controlled by Sullivan or by Harrison; that depended upon a disputed election in Cook County, and whether the Sullivan or the Harrison slate for the county was deemed to have succeeded. Another dispute on credentials came from South Dakota, where there were Wilson and Clark delegations, each claiming to have been lawfully elected.

The latter dispute came first before the credentials committee. Clark's man on the committee succeeded in seating the Clark delegation and the Wilson managers proposed to challenge the decision on the floor of the convention. While that appeal was still pending, the Cook County dispute came before the committee. If the committee decided in Sullivan's favour, his nominees would be installed as the rightful delegates unless and until the convention set the decision aside. Wilson's managers made a bargain with Sullivan that they would support him in the committee if he used the 58 votes of his delegation in their favour on the floor. The deal came off; Sullivan got control of the Illinois delegation and the Wilson delegation from South Dakota was seated.

It was a very good bargain for Wilson. It added 10 to his votes and it established good relations with Boss Sullivan. Wilson had nothing to hope for from the Hearst–Harrison combination and Sullivan was at least preferable to that. It was also, though Wilson personally had no part in it, a rather discreditable bargain. There is little doubt that Sullivan was not entitled to the Cook County seats and there is evidence that Wilson's managers had first tried to do a deal with Harrison.

At seven o'clock in the morning of Friday, 28 June, after a night of nominating speeches (Wilson was nominated as 'the seer and philosopher of Princeton'), the first ballot was cast. The result was:

Clark	$440\frac{1}{2}$
Wilson	324
Harmon	148
Underwood	$117\frac{1}{2}$

The remaining 56 votes went to minor candidates, the only significant one being Governor Marshall of Indiana who had 31. Wilson profited by the withdrawal in his favour of the Governor of North Dakota. Harmon's figure was inflated by New York's 90 which Murphy had temporarily deposited there for safe custody. After the first ballot the convention adjourned till the afternoon.

Everyone expected that when the balloting was resumed Murphy would declare for Clark. It was thought that it would be on the third or fourth ballot but in fact it was not till the tenth. Clark's men were trying to make doubly sure that the declaration let slip a landslide; they attempted to get the Underwood vote by offering him the vice-presidency. Meanwhile, Wilson's managers were doing their best to meet the coming blow. Their plan was an alliance with Underwood on the basis of their mutual interest in stemming the rush to Clark. Fortunately Underwood was not interested in the vice-presidency and preferred a promise that if for any reason Wilson dropped out, his managers would release his delegates to Underwood.

The afternoon of Friday 28 June passed sultrily away in eight ballots in which Clark picked up 14 votes and Wilson 24. These were but raindrops before the storm. It was late in the evening when the tenth ballot began. When Murphy declared, Clark's men went wild, sang and danced for an hour, and shouted for victory. Wilson's managers made use of the time to exhort the Underwood delegations to keep faith. As the states polled in alphabetical order, the next after New York was North Dakota. This state was almost the newest of Wilson's adherents and the atmosphere was tense as the leader called: 'Ten for Wilson.' The Wilson men let out a yell of relief. Next came Oklahoma, another Wilson state. An Oklahoman shouted that Clark was the convention's choice; another, a picturesque character called 'Alfalfa Bill', hallooed out against Tammany, waving a red bandanna handkerchief, amid cheers and counter-cheers. Oklahoma stood firm, and then the Wilson men demonstrated for an hour. When the noise had subsided and the ballot was finished, it was early in the morning of Saturday, 29 June, and the figures stood:

Clark	556
Wilson	$350\frac{1}{2}$
Underwood	$117\frac{1}{2}$

The remaining 64 were split between Marshall and Harmon.

The next ballot would show whether Clark was to have that day the victory he expected. Would the Underwood delegations, who had polled in the tenth ballot before New York, stand fast? They did. The eleventh ballot showed no change and the convention adjourned at four o'clock in the morning of Saturday, 29 June.

So the Wilson managers had succeeded in preventing immediate victory, but when they had time to consider the position in the depressing light of Saturday's early hours, it looked as though they had only postponed inevitable defeat. Clark's 556 was 11 over the half, and time and precedent were almost bound to turn it into the required two-thirds. Wilson took the news calmly. 'So, McCombs, you feel it is hopeless?'[52] Hearing Wilson say this down the telephone was how the tentered Tumulty learnt the news. Mrs. Wilson shed a tear or two for her husband's disappointment, but Wilson's personal fortunes never seemed to excite him. While the convention was on, he had been playing golf in the afternoons and in the evenings reading aloud to the family from Morley's *Life of Gladstone*. Now he sent Tumulty for a pencil and pad so that he might prepare a message of congratulation for Champ Clark. Clark at the same time in Washington was composing a telegram of acceptance.

But someone decided that the fight should go on. There has been much argument since about who did not lose his nerve and when: probably McAdoo remained the staunchest. At all events the fight went on. The delegates re-assembled later on Saturday morning and the twelfth and thirteenth ballots were cast without any significant change. Senator Stone indignantly sent a telegram to Wilson demanding that he should withdraw in accordance with traditional practice and 'in vindication of the democratic principle of majority rule'.[53] This was an awkward request, for Wilson held strongly that the two-thirds rule was 'a most undemocratic regulation' and had said a year before, though luckily not in public, that he refrained from urging a change 'because it would be so manifestly in my interest'.[54]

These two inconclusive ballots showed at least that the landslide Clark was counting on was not going to happen. The checking of an impetus means a swing back, for the thought and emotion of a thousand men must always be in flow. There was no doubt that the meeting was predominantly progressive in temper, at least in things that were not matters of hard business; the voting on Bryan's initial resolutions proved that. Bryan was now satisfied that Clark had put himself under obligations to Tammany that would cripple any administration over which he presided, and other Clark delegates besides Bryan felt any alliance with Tammany to be unpalatable and thought it quite intolerable that in this great year of Democratic revival Tammany should dictate the nomination. After the thirteenth ballot Senator Hitchcock of Nebraska asked that the Nebraskan delegation be polled and it was found that 13 out of 19 were for a change of vote. Bryan then decided to act. On the fourteenth ballot he rose and amid interruptions asked leave to explain his vote. 'As long as Mr. Ryan's agent—as long as New York's 90 votes were recorded for Mr. Clark, I withhold my vote from him and cast it. . . .'[55] The rest was drowned in the uproar. When Bryan got a hearing again, he said that the vote of New York represented the will of one man, Charles Murphy; that he would vote for no candidate who would be subservient to him and to Morgan and to Ryan; and that he would give his vote to Wilson with the understanding that he would withdraw it if New York cast her vote for him.

The news of Bryan's defection came as a terrible blow to Clark, already agitated by the prolonged balloting. He never forgave Bryan and to the end of his days believed that he had been cheated out of the presidency by a dishonest and hypocritical attempt by Bryan to grab the nomination for himself. He hurried down to Baltimore to assume direct command of his forces but by the time he got there the convention had adjourned after the twenty-sixth ballot. The twelve ballots that followed Bryan's declaration brought no sensational change in the figures but a gradual diminishing of Clark's strength. Nebraska gave Wilson 13 of its votes. The Kansas delegation had a peculiar instruction to vote for Clark till his nomination became impossible and then for Wilson; they changed on the twentieth ballot and gave their 20 votes to Wilson. Massachusetts moved its vote into neutrality by transferring it from Clark to her own Governor Foss, or perhaps she planned to give him a status as a possible compromise candidate. When the session ended, the voting stood:

Clark	$463\frac{1}{2}$
Wilson	$407\frac{1}{2}$
Underwood	$112\frac{1}{2}$
Foss	43
Marshall	30
Harmon	29
Bryan	1

These were the immediate results of Bryan's dramatic intervention. He did not give Wilson the nomination. In palpable figures he gave him only 13 votes and these were not pro-Wilson votes but anti-Tammany. But his attitude was perhaps the biggest of the several factors that made for Wilson's victory. For Wilson could not win unless Tammany was beaten and it was Bryan's self-appointed task, beginning with his introductory resolutions and ending with his change of vote, to beat Tammany. He had concentrated progressive sentiment in such a way as to ensure that only a progressive could be nominated and with Clark now badly compromised that meant that out of the four original candidates only Wilson qualified. From then on the issue really lay between Wilson and some eleventh-hour contender if one could be found. Clark survived in the figures but he had not the personality to make a come-back. If he could not deliver the delegates, he could arouse no popular support. Champ as a convention candidate and Clark as an all-but-president were two different pictures. He was after all only a country politician in a broad-brimmed black slouch hat and, as his opponents unkindly recalled, had once advertised a patent medicine: he had about utterly collapsed, he testified, from overwork and nervous tension, 'but three bottles of Electric Bitters made me all right'.[56]

On the Sunday the sober Democratic press came out strongly in favour of Wilson. Clark was fighting mad; he may have been sipping electric bitters but gossip debited him with a preference for stronger liquor in greater quantity than was good for him. He conferred all that Sunday with Senator Stone, his manager, and Hearst and Murphy (he might have been wiser if he had had a word with Sullivan who, it was reported, was not too pleased at being ignored) and threatened to stay in Baltimore all summer if necessary to stop Wilson and Bryan. But Boss Murphy was already looking in other directions. Wilson's backbone was composed of Pennsylvania with 76 votes and Texas with 40. Murphy offered the nomination to the leader of each of these delegations in turn if he would desert Wilson; and each refused his help. McCombs, too, was not idle and his sabbath dealings were more successful; he sold the vice-presidency to Marshall of Indiana for 29 votes.

Indiana's shift became effective on the twenty-eighth ballot, the second to be taken on Monday, 1 July. Iowa under the influence of Bryan followed on the thirtieth ballot with the result that Wilson just passed Clark—460 to 455. All the rest of that day the voting dragged on over twelve more ballots with only slight gains for Wilson; 'at the present rate', he told the reporters humorously, 'I will be nominated in 175 more ballots'.[57] But bosses and delegates are practical men and, however Clark might rage, they had no intention of staying in Baltimore all summer. On the first ballot on Tuesday, 2 July, the forty-third in the series, there was a dramatic change. Boss Sullivan moved his 58 votes from Clark to Wilson. That broke the deadlock and began the end. On the forty-sixth ballot Wilson was nominated. At a signal from Tumulty a brass band of forty pieces emerged from behind a clump and blared its way to Sea Girt with 'Hail to the Chief'.

The choice of Wilson is one among many illustrations of the curious way in which the machinery of an American convention, which seems to be almost deliberately designed to produce the worst man, so often ends up by way of a combination of factors difficult to evaluate in selecting the best. Wilson's character and personality and his proclamation of progressive views formed the essential material that was brought to Baltimore and processed by Bryan's anti-Tammany strategy, by Wilson's own bold decision to cleave to Bryan, and by skilful and determined management on the floor of the convention. Something of course was done by trafficking. Wilson declared in the Baltimore *Sun* his belief that his managers' 'only means of getting support is argument'[58] and his determination that no vote should be obtained by means of any promise. After his nomination Wilson, who knew nothing of the pact with Marshall of Indiana, insisted on the vice-presidency being offered to Underwood. Fortunately Underwood refused it, so that McCombs without having to make any embarrassing disclosures was able to keep his bargain with Marshall—'a small-calibre man', Wilson lamented.[59] On the whole Wilson's managers showed moderation, and there was at least one respectable precedent for turning a deaf ear to their principal's declarations. In the Republican convention of 1860 which nominated Lincoln Indiana's vote was secured with the Secretaryship of the Interior. 'I authorise no bargains and will be bound by none', Lincoln said; but his manager thought that that must be meant for the record.

With the nomination there came to Wilson the undisputed leadership of the Democratic party. At the close of the convention Bryan made a little speech which Wilson called a noble valedictory:

Tonight I come with joy to surrender into the hands of the one chosen by this convention a standard which I have carried in three campaigns, and I challenge my enemies to declare that it has ever been lowered in the face of the enemy.[60]

Those who were convention-minded thought that Bryan had looked to a deadlock between Clark and Wilson to bring the nomination to himself. Doubtless he would have accepted it, but he did not stir to get it, and he took up the second fiddle with the utmost grace. In the election campaign he spoke every day ten times a day for seven weeks; and said to his Nebraskans:

Let me ask you to do twice as much for Wilson as you ever did for Bryan. For I have as much as stake in this fight as he has, and you have as much as I have.[61]

Underwood pledged his allegiance with warmth and admiration. Champ Clark was sulky but submissive; he issued a loser's statement pointing out that he had beaten Wilson in the primaries and led on thirty ballots and attributing his downfall to his not having enough money to pay for postage stamps, his being tied down in Washington by the duties of the speakership, and to the 'vile and malicious slanders'[62] of Bryan. But for the two-thirds rule, 'my father would have been elected in 1912 . . . this country would not have gone into the World War': so spoke Senator Bennett Champ Clark in 1936 when 'with all the energy of an avenging fury'[63] he brought to a successful conclusion his fight to abolish the two-thirds rule.

Tammany professed enthusiasm, but Wilson did not allow it to be left in doubt where victory lay. It will be remembered that when Wilson was fighting with Boss Smith over the New Jersey senatorship Franklin Roosevelt was waging a similar battle with Boss Murphy over the senatorship from New York. In this battle the newly elected Governor Dix did as Smith wanted Wilson to do; he stood aside. Murphy now proposed to give him his reward in the form of a re-nomination for the governorship. This was stoutly opposed by the Franklin Roosevelt progressives, and Wilson intervened with such effect that Murphy dropped Dix.

Two days after the nomination Nugent surrendered and enrolled himself as a supporter of the ingrate and the liar. Only the Big Boss went down to perpetual darkness with his colours flying. Audaciously he proffered himself once again for the Senate. Wilson turned aside from his presidential campaign to swoop on him and chastise him so severely that he was beaten in the primaries by so crushing a vote that he retired from public life for ever. That was in September 1912, just two years after James Smith, the Big Boss, with his silk hat and his rich, musical voice, 'handsome, cool and dignified',[64] as Tumulty pictures him, had taken Wilson by the hand and led him to the top of the mountain and together they had looked down on the promised land: he had walked long in the wilderness and he had found the leader who was to bring his comrades, all the Murphies, big and little, the Sullivans, the Tumulties and the hungry Hennessies, into the places of milk and honey; but for Big Boss Smith the ashes of humiliation and the bitter bread of exile.

Three days before the Democrats began their work at Baltimore the Republican machine at Chicago had forced the nomination of Taft, the retiring president, through the convention and left Theodore Roosevelt indignant and not impotent. Roosevelt had returned to the States in June 1910 and was bitter in his disappointment with the weakness of his legatee: a wit defined Taft as 'a large body surrounded by men who know exactly what they want'.[65] Soon Roosevelt was countering Wilson's New Freedom with a New Nationalism and a Square Deal. By February 1912 he had as good as said that he would be a candidate for the nomination; and Taft had said that supporters of the New Nationalism were political emotionalists and neurotics. The party machine was on Taft's side and it never lost its control of the convention. The credentials of 200 delegates were in dispute and the places were nearly all awarded to Taft men. Roosevelt withdrew his followers in disgust; they met on 5 August in Chicago and, as the new Progressive party, nominated Roosevelt in opposition to Taft.

The Republican split made a Democratic victory certain, and Wilson, preaching what Roosevelt called 'an ardent and diffuse progressiveness',[66] was elected on 5 November 1912. He had 42 per cent of the vote, Roosevelt 27 per cent, and Taft 23 per cent. So strong was the swing to the left that, even with 69 per cent divided between Wilson and Roosevelt, 6 per cent of the vote went to a Socialist candidate. Wilson's majority in the electoral college was overwhelming, and the Democrats won control of the House with 290 to 145 and of the Senate with 51 to 45. The New Freedom had received an impressive endorsement.

IV
THE PRESIDENCY: 1912–1914

The family in the White House — Colonel House — Cary Grayson — Tumulty — Wilson as Party Leader — the Cuban and the Boer Wars — Panama tolls controversy — Mexico — Senator Root — Wilson's political and diplomatic method

---

THE simplicity of Woodrow Wilson's religious faith suggests that, if he had been a Roman Catholic, he would have been one of those who get comfort from the use of relics and petitionary formulae. Since the Presbyterian creed does not countenance such methods of protection against temporal or spiritual misfortune, he had to make do with lucky charms in which he had a curious belief. There was a large horse-chestnut which he invariably carried in his pocket and polished ritually every day. As some sort of a compromise with scepticism he insisted that 13 was a lucky number. There were 13 letters in his name, he was the 13th President of Princeton, and it was during his 13th year on the faculty that he became so. It was doubtless a matter of some satisfaction to him that it was in the 13th year of the century that he was made President of the United States; and perhaps of some regret that his inauguration did not take place on the 13th day of the month. It is said that on the door of his bedroom at the Shoreham Hotel where he spent the night before the ceremony, there was hung a silver 13.

When on 4 March 1913 he became the twenty-eighth President, Wilson was two months past his fifty-sixth birthday, a trim and alert figure, a little above medium height, a little below medium weight, light brown hair beginning to turn grey. Five years before, in the last book he published, *Constitutional Government*, written in 1908 as an up-to-date edition of his *Congressional Government*, in speaking of the presidential office he had said that it demanded 'an inexhaustible vitality'.[1] He knew that he could answer the demand—his performance as governor and candidate had not lacked vigour—but only, he believed, if he guarded himself against all unnecessary strain. He had been trying to do this since his stroke in 1906. He had then got himself for the first time in his life a full-time secretary. He had begun to take an extra vacation in winter, usually in Bermuda. Since strenuous walks and bicycle rides were no longer as feasible as in youth, he had taken up golf to replace them. He was even on medical advice sipping Scotch occasionally. He retained his enviable facility for dropping into sleep, even if only for a brief nap.

It is possible that the stroke did some slight damage to the brain. Certainly the severe stroke in 1919 did and they were both arteriosclerotic. A physical change of this sort in the brain can affect the quality of the mind, blinkering a man's outlook, making him intolerant of opposition, suspicious of those he sees as thwarting him and exaggerating his emotional responses. That Wilson displayed these defects after 1906 to a greater degree than he had before then this narrative has shown. But then before 1906 he had had things very much his own way. Undoubtedly there was some change, not a personality change or anything that was marked enough to be noticed at the time, between the Wilson of, say, 1900 and the Wilson of 1912. The latter was tougher than the former, more unyielding, less approachable. In the present state of our knowledge of mental processes no one can say whether Wilson's mind was affected by a physical change in the brain or by the impact of a new situation calling for a new type of response; or if the former, how far the change was by a natural process of ageing and how far affected by the stroke. Whatever its origin, the change was doubly a cause of a narrowing in Wilson's social life, first, because it increased his disinclination for it and, secondly, because it induced him to avoid all dissipation of his strength.

The home that the Wilsons left for the White House was cultivated middle-class. There must have been many of its type, serious, scholastic, consciously refined, in every university town in America and Britain; book-lined walls, carefully chosen furniture, a head of Hermes, a statue of Apollo Belvedere and a Winged Victory (it was a good joke when the man who came to mend a wing offered to put the head on too if they could find it), crayon enlargements by Mrs. Wilson of Woodrow's political heroes, English and American, and 'volumes of poetry scattered about on small tables'.[2] There was nothing of the absent-minded professor; all papers were filed away in an orderly fashion; the typewriter was kept covered and the rolltop desk locked when not in use. Punctuality was a household rule.

Mrs. Wilson had grown from a pretty and petite girl into a sweet careful little woman who was afraid of lightning and dogs and never allowed her children to sit on the grass. Her days were spent on household tasks. She made all the children's clothes as well as her own, the latter being very simple and hardly varying from a brown dress and hat. She had her water-colours—when she was at the White House three pictures, sent in anonymously, were accepted by the New York Academy—and a passion for gardens; outside her family these were her interests. She continued to adore Woodrow and to think him the greatest man in the world but she was never frightened of making suggestions; and when he consulted her as he often did, she did not hesitate to give advice, which she knew exactly how to do. When it was a question of sticking to principle, she was as unyielding as he: 'there must be no hedging',[3] said she when Woodrow discussed what his answer should be to Bryan's crucial telegram at the beginning of the Baltimore Convention.*

Withal she was a very understanding woman in the way she could send Woodrow off for a holiday on his own and let him have his little fling with Mrs. Peck without a qualm. She had Mrs. Peck to stay at Sea Girt, the imposing summer mansion on the coast which New Jersey provided for its governor; it had been part of the state's exhibition at the Chicago World's Fair in 1893 whence it had been removed and put together again. Situated between the National Guard parade ground and the railway line, it was not beloved of the Wilsons but its air of grandeur may have suited Mrs. Peck. Anyway she was a great success. It was allowed that she could smoke without shocking. Wilson himself did not smoke at all though he kept a box of cigars for his male company. Mrs. Wilson could never really approve of women smoking. And before the end Mrs. Peck had made too many suggestions about improving the appearance of the daughters and changing Mrs. Wilson's style in hats.

There was in the family the same intense love and outspoken affection, devotion by the parents and reverence by the children, as there had been in the Wilson and Axson families the generation before. To the three girls their parents were always 'Father' and 'Mother'. They were in their twenties when he became President and had each been brought up with a talent to cultivate. Margaret the eldest had a voice; she sang professionally and never married. Jessie, the second, had the dreamy beauty of the Axsons; she often had to refuse proposals of marriage and 'wept softly and steadily throughout the ordeal'.[4] She wanted to be a missionary but took up social work instead; and eventually was secured, Nell says,[5] by a charming old lady for a favourite nephew. They were married from the White House in November 1913. Eleanor or Nell was the youngest and the sprightliest; she studied art, married McAdoo as his second wife in May 1914, and with the help of a lady journalist wrote a book about the Wilsons.

The entourage to the family was also almost exclusively female. There was his sister Annie, more or less his contemporary, who was now a widow and used to come for long visits. The cousins whom the Wilsons educated

* See p. 78 above.

and largely supported, starting with Mary Hoyt at Bryn Mawr, were mostly female. Then there was Margaret Axson, sister to Mrs. Wilson but twenty years younger, not much older than her nieces; her parents died when she was young and for most of the Princeton period until she married she lived with the Wilsons. Then there were some honorary cousins, Lucy and Mary Smith, daughters of a Presbyterian minister. The Wilson family had first met them on a summer vacation in the Princeton days; and when it was discovered that they were distantly related, they became, as Margaret Axson says, 'almost a recognized part of the family',[6] visiting for long periods at least once a year. There was a genuine cousin, Helen, daughter of the incompetent uncle Bones, whom Nell or the lady journalist describes as 'a lovely little creature with blue-black hair and great gold-flecked eyes'.[7] She was a special favourite of Woodrow's. Indeed, she was almost a daughter. She came to live at the White House as Mrs. Wilson's secretary. The only close male relative was Stockton and he looked up at Wilson from below. True, McAdoo was a relative on the same level, but the relationship was cordial rather than intimate, that of a Cabinet officer rather than that of a son-in-law. Woodrow now saw little or nothing of his young brother. Though family relationship meant much to the Wilsons, he and Josie had nothing but it to share. Josie was, Woodrow wrote in 1892, 'not an intellectual or literary man, but simply a fine sensible fellow . . . not always wise and prudent',[8] while Joseph felt that Woodrow underestimated him. There were of course no sons to bring in their friends to join the family table. Beaux for the girls had not been encouraged. Wilson adopted a rather 'young whipper-snapper!' attitude towards them and particularly disliked their use of the telephone; they should take the trouble to ask at the door, 'like gentlemen'. He once observed: 'I can imagine no worse fate for a girl than to marry a man of coarser spiritual fibre than herself.'[9] Margaret Axson, who was herself very fond of Wilson, wrote of the Princeton days:

Naturally I had no prevision of what future critics were to say, but as I saw the two rows of smiling women at the dinner table and Woodrow, the lone man, at the head, it somehow seemed to me not quite normal, and I often said to myself, 'There are entirely too many women around this place!'[10]

Wilson joked about himself as 'submerged in petticoats'[11] but he never tried to float clear. The body of women had the temperature thermostatically controlled at the degree he wanted. They were responsive, uncritical, protective, and kept out the draughts. They all testified to his sweet temper.

Wilson had never cared much for general company, whether male or female. In the early days at Princeton he used to drop in to the Nassau Club for a game of billiards or for general talk; and he enjoyed the simple entertainment of his friends at Library Place, as well as of intellectual visitors from Europe such as Lowes Dickinson and the Sidney Webbs.* But really what he enjoyed was just his family, varied occasionally by a few intimates. He not only enjoyed it: he needed it. He was not—outside his work and in his pleasures—a self-sufficient man, either intellectually or emotionally. He was no lover of solitude and by now he had no solitary occupations. He had brought his scholarship to an end. He had not since his youth enlarged his literary tastes. He read very little fiction, detective stories excepted. He would look through *Punch*: no laughs but full of smiles, he said. He would pick up familiar books and read bits from them. Certainly he enjoyed Jane Austen and felt all the attraction of Elizabeth Bennet. In fact his mode of life and his manners were much nearer to that period than to the present; the recreations he enjoyed were the sort that Jane Austen has immortalized— the pleasures of the restricted circle, polite conversation, reading aloud after dinner, and songs around the piano with Woodrow's light tenor joining in, 'Sweet and Low' or 'Annie Laurie' with an argument about the pronunciation of Maxwelton. Many of his moralizations that sound priggish today, like the one about 'no worse fate for a girl', might have been heard at any time at Mansfield Park. Besides much conversation, serious and light, there were charades sometimes and an occasional game of whist played rather heavily. But mostly talk, Nell says:

. . . interesting abstract discussions that rambled off into delightful arguments. . . . Nearly every evening, and often at meals, there were heated arguments or long discussions about the meaning or derivation of some word or the exact significance of some phrase and, before these questions were settled to the satisfaction of everyone, there were sometimes eight or nine books of reference on the floor beside his chair.[12]

The character of the home was not changed by the move to the White House. The White House is not lived in as a palace. It is true that on the first floor there are the State Rooms opening into each other through double doors—the great East Room at one end, used for the big receptions, the Green Room, the Blue Room, and the Red Room and the State Dining-room on the west side. The family lived, as it still does, on the second floor, reached by a continuation of the grand staircase that leads from the ground floor up to the public rooms, or by an elevator. A long corridor runs from east to west with perhaps half a dozen rooms, some of them spacious, on each side of it for the President, his family, and his guests. Until in Theodore

* When after dinner Mrs. Wilson invited Mrs. Webb to leave the men to smoke, the lady indicated that she preferred to remain and smoke with them. This may have done something to prepare the astounded Mrs. Wilson for the habits of Mrs. Peck later on.

Roosevelt's time the west wing was built as executive offices, the second floor had to provide the President's offices as well; and the Cabinet met in the President's study, as it still did sometimes under Wilson.

The nicest room, which the Wilsons used as their living-room, was the Yellow Oval Room—yellow to distinguish it from the Blue Oval Room below. Both these rooms were on the south side over the portico, beautifully light with a bay window looking over the gardens and the trees of the Ellipse to the Washington Monument beyond. The President's study was next door to the Yellow Oval Room. The west end of the corridor was made into a sort of sitting-room where Mrs. Wilson's social secretary had her desk. These were their only sitting-rooms. They ate in the family dining-room on the State floor.

Of course the presidency made a material change in their way of life. After years of economy there was affluence. They found themselves also— they who, as Nell says, had been taught to be close-mouthed about their family affairs—exposed to publicity and relentless personal questioning by the Press. It was Wilson's characteristic reaction to this which, his daughter feels plausibly enough, helped to give him from the start the reputation for aloofness and unfriendliness which stuck. Wilson had to raise an overdraft of $5,000 for the expenses of the move to the White House, the first big sum he had ever borrowed. He bought for his wife a diamond pendant, known in the family as 'the Crown Jewel'; and the girls had their first jewellery too as inauguration presents. It was before this that there took place a small but revealing incident which Nell records:

I was sitting with Mother when one particularly persistent women reporter asked why we never wore jewels. 'Have you some sort of moral prejudice against jewellery, Mrs Wilson?' Mother smiled, and, as I looked at the hard-faced, sharp-eyed woman, I realised how impossible it would be for her to understand why Mother had no jewellery. Mother, who had sacrificed for us, so that Father might have the books he needed, the vacations; that we might study art and singing; that there might always be room in the house for relatives and friends. I thought of her rigid economy, her perennial brown dress and hat, and I felt a wave of dislike for the woman who stubbornly repeated, 'But why, Mrs Wilson?' Mother said, 'No, I have no prejudice against it; we just haven't any'. The simplicity and gentleness of that answer was a great lesson to me, and brought quick tears to my eyes.[13]

Behaviour inside or outside the White House was judged chiefly by the standard of 'gentlemanliness', a term which everyone at that time thought he understood, the basis of the understanding being that one was a gentleman oneself. Wilson himself was much concerned with this.

After all, if a man is a gentleman before he becomes President, he should not cease to be one afterwards.[14] No, my dear Senator, the President of the United States must always do the gentlemanly thing.[15]

The first of these was apropos the custom by which the President goes through a door before a lady, and the second is an excerpt from Tumulty. Wilson could also, his daughter says[16] (perhaps with memories of a beau who had not taken the trouble to call at the door), use the word with a shade of stress, a subtle emphasis, that made it the most cutting insult in the world. He made it a rule never to give unnecessary trouble to a servant; consequently he was thought of respectfully by the White House staff but not overliked. Both the Wilsons were scrupulously tidy. Until he became President, Wilson always polished his own shoes with great care. He was always quietly and neatly dressed. 'The President was dressed in a very becoming sack suit of grey with a light grey silk tie' is quite a typical entry in Colonel House's diary.[17]

The Wilson family and their friends in their reminiscences of the President all speak of his capacity for fun; and in their anxiety to portray the obverse of the public picture of the austere professor with the pince-nez and the wintry smile, perhaps exaggerate it. They tell how he could play the fool, and dance a jig or waggle his ears if required. They say he was a good mimic and that his imitations of the society lady or the monocled Englishman were very droll. He was acknowledged to have a good repertoire of stories and he could tell them well; there were many about imaginary Irishmen and darkies which must here be left untold since like most such stories they mortify in print. There was much ritualistic teasing with the twinkle in the eye and paterfamilias jocosity. Whenever Mrs. Wilson said 'Oh Woodrow', the family looked expectantly at him and were never disappointed.

'Oh, Woodrow, you know you don't mean that'. Then father always said with the utmost gravity, 'Madam, I was venturing to think that I meant that until I was corrected'.[18]

Which was the true Wilson, the family man or the public figure? The answer is that both were true, and the sharpness of the contrast is explained by the curious fact that there was nothing in between. Most men have a circle of casual acquaintances for whom they have a manner that is neither for their intimates nor for the public, a manner for those who see them, as it were, in the half-and-half. Wilson had not. There was no outer circle of friends: friendship meant to him he told Mrs. Reid, 'sympathy and close support of heart':[19] it was that or nothing. When he met outsiders, as of course he had to do, he could be very agreeable with his stories and his limericks if he made the effort. If he did not, an encounter could shatter the dreams of the most ardent worshipper. William Allen White, a leading Republican progressive who had his first meeting after he had become a fervent admirer of Wilson on paper and declared his support, records how he was given a hand that 'felt very much like a five-cent mackerel'.[20] His experience with Wilson may be contrasted with Mr. Baker's with Taft.

He had a frank, free, whole-hearted way of greeting his visitors, giving one that impression of joy of living which is one of the most beguiling of human traits. Once or twice he threw one of his great arms over the shoulder of a congressman and led him off into a corner to talk over some especially private matter. He asked me to remain to the last.[21]

The fact was that Wilson got for himself nothing from such contacts. From the inner circle he got the sustenance he needed, and he got it too from the response his oratory obtained from people in the mass. But the territory in between was a desert which he did not know how to cultivate for his own enjoyment. He would labour in it and often fruitfully for those who talked to him, but not for himself. He found no relaxation in it and so naturally avoided it except in the way of duty. He thought that he understood the masses and certainly he could speak to them but he did not truly think of them as individuals. The girl student at Bryn Mawr, who said of him that he liked lecturing but not teaching, was perceptive.[22]

Such was the social habit that Wilson brought with him to the White House. He startled Washington by the unprecedented austerity of dispensing with the inaugural ball, till then regarded as an established institution, and he would not hold the customary New Year's receptions. This was not due to parsimony, for all the other official entertainment which he gave was done generously and with quiet distinction. His decision to reduce the number of these functions arose as much out of his dislike of flummery as out of his distaste for society. But he made the latter equally manifest. He refused to join the Chevy Chase Country Club to which hitherto the President had belonged as a matter of course; he simply had no interest in Washington society or in meeting smart or rich or even distinguished people. Other than formally he never entertained outside his own small circle. An old friend like Page might come to an occasional meal: no politics were ever talked. The extent to which he excluded politicians from his society is shown in the case of Houston. Houston served the full two terms in Wilson's cabinet and of all its members he was the nearest to Wilson in character and background; he was not a professional politician and gave up the presidency of a university at Wilson's request to serve the state. His social relationship with Wilson during the whole eight years was comprehended within the span of one uneasy game of golf.

On this point Wilson's conscience found in favour of his inclinations. If he asked one politician, he thought, he would have to ask all, lest he should be thought to be favouring one rather than another. So he had perforce to remain isolated. Thus he was delivered from temptation.

> I will not permit my home to be used for political purposes. If I make an intimate of a man in politics, it isn't long before he wants me to do something which I ought not to do.[23]

There was one exception to this golden rule and one man whom Wilson did make his intimate who never seemed to want him to do something which he ought not to do. Colonel House was the last and the most influential of those friendships which Wilson formed emotionally and impulsively; and the penultimate entrant into the ring of those who gave Wilson 'sympathy and close support of heart'.

The delegation from Texas had been among those which supported Wilson through the thick and the thin of the Democratic convention. Its composition was the result of a defeat inflicted by Wilson supporters on the party machine at the state primaries. Among the men who helped to bring about the victory were Burleson and Gregory; they were included in the delegation, were active in the convention, and later became members of Wilson's cabinet. But there was one helper who was not included in the delegation or later in the cabinet. Colonel House had no wish to be a delegate to or member of any body, not even of a cabinet. Neither was he active in the convention or indeed present at it, because he did not care for any gatherings where the talk rose above the level of conversation.

Edward Mandell House was then fifty-four, a man of means and leisure (an income from investments of $25,000 a year) with a reputation for work behind the scenes in Texan politics; that was how he had got his 'gilt-braid' colonelcy. Like Wilson he was born with a consuming interest in politics and a distaste for the ordinary channels of political advancement; moreover, he thought his poor health made political office impossible for him. Therefore like Wilson he chose an unusual route to power; but while Wilson's talent was for the expression of ideas, House's was in the handling of men. He had not Wilson's air; in fact he looked rather insignificant. He was no orator as Wilson was, but he was a master of the *ad captandum*. A proposition formulated by Wilson was no more mobile than a public monument. But for House it was: 'Have a word with Smith on those lines': 'Put it in that light for Jones': 'Tell Robinson what Smith thinks about it'. 'Just between you and me and the angels' was a favourite expression.[24] He was a small man with a small moustache, ears that stuck out just a little and a receding chin—a rather mouse-like face. Indeed, the temptation to call him Colonel Mouse would be irresistible if it were not for the little touches of the feline, not the claws or the cat's eyes but the soft pad and the purr. He was married to an unobtrusive wife. He had also an unobtrusive daughter; but many years later the son-in-law obtruded in a way that contributed to House's downfall.

House had grown weary of local politics but at first would not take the plunge into the national counsels of the Democrats; his views were liberal, but he thought Bryan, whom he liked as a friend, 'wildly impracticable'.[25] In 1910 the Democratic success in the state and congressional elections came as a foretaste of presidential victory and set House among others in the party searching for the right candidate. He came to the conclusion on paper that Wilson was the man best fitted for the job. After some correspondence they met in New York at 4 p.m. on 24 November 1911 when Wilson called at the Hotel Gotham where House was staying. House recorded his first impression the next day in a letter to his brother-in-law:

He is not the biggest man I have ever met, but he is one of the pleasantest and I would rather play with him than any prospective candidate I have seen. . . . it is just such a chance as I have always wanted for never before have I found both the man and the opportunity.[26]

Within a short time his feeling grew much warmer and the two men became intimate friends. This means that House was a real person. A man who was only a wirepuller would never have attracted Wilson. But House combined with his gift of manipulation and his love of the shadows a personality that, although subdued, was capable of giving and receiving great affection; and the exceptional thing about him was that he could put talents of the sort that are so often used only for personal intrigue to the service of ideals which he strongly and sincerely believed in. They were Wilson's ideals also and the two men came together in a rush. House wrote of their early meetings:

A few weeks after we had met and after we had exchanged confidences which men usually do not exchange except after years of friendship, I asked him if he realised that we had only known one another for so short a time. He replied, 'My dear friend, we have known one another always'. And I think this is true.[27]

They never called each other by their Christian names. House called Wilson 'Governor' and continued to do so after he had become President. Wilson wrote to House as 'My dear friend'.

House's first service to Wilson was to commend him to Bryan. There was nothing so crude as a direct recommendation; there was a careful planting of bits of information, selected to show up Wilson indirectly as the sort of man Bryan would approve of.[28] For example, Bryan might be interested to know that a friend of Mr. Hearst's had told House that the Hearst press would be against Wilson: Harvey had told House that the bankers were putting $250,000 into New Jersey to defeat Wilson delegates there; on one matter about which he was writing to Bryan Wilson 'had replied in almost the exact terms you used to me'; on another, 'I think you are both wrong there': and so on. He sailed for Europe the day the Baltimore convention began; it was his custom to spend the summer in Europe and anyway his talents were not suited to the hurly-burly. But he was back before the election and already preparing to advise Wilson on the business of Cabinet-making. He wrote in his diary in October 1912:

> I am on constant watch for good material from which to select a Cabinet and other important places. I wish to be well informed if Governor Wilson should consult me.[29]

Wilson did consult him; indeed, he hardly consulted anyone else. House did not want public recognition (he resisted Wilson's pressure to take any cabinet office he chose except the State Department which had to be reserved for Bryan) and he shared Wilson's political ideas. Wilson had no interest in men except as instruments for executing his policies. 'What are men as compared with the standards of righteousness?'[30] he had exclaimed during the election campaign. He wanted to devote much of the time between election and inauguration to preparing his mind for the great work he had to do, and he was delighted to be relieved of what he thought of as presidential chores by a man he could trust absolutely. So House did most of the interviewing. If the callers were applicants for office, he examined their qualifications; if purveyors of information, he sifted the facts from their opinions; if makers of requests he tested their good faith. He was Wilson's contact man. With House at his elbow Wilson escaped the sort of mistake he had made in the Harvey episode. 'If I were you', House would write, 'I would send him a line indicating that you appreciated his interest and had found his suggestions helpful.'[31] Ellen had done the same sort of thing for her husband in the pre-political days but with a lighter touch.

> He seems to be a good sort of goose, and being a Southerner to boot, perhaps you might write him an amiable little letter and refrain from telling him what an ass he is.[32]

House did not conceal his function as joint Cabinet-maker. 'I informed him of what we had in mind for him' is the way he noted the opening of his interview with the future Secretary of the Interior.[33] Important offices, if below cabinet rank, might be awarded on his say-so. He recorded on 4 March 1913:

The President had never met Marble and had made no enquiries concerning him further than mine. He said he would send his name in tomorrow, along with the names of his Cabinet.[34]

Very occasionally this sort of thing happened without House's advice and then he was a little nettled. He noted on 24 February:

The thing that impresses me most is the casual way in which the President-elect is making up his Cabinet. I can see no end of trouble for him in the future unless he proceeds with more care.[35]

This was apropos the appointment of Garrison as Secretary of War which certainly happened in an odd way. House's nominee had refused the place; Wilson spoke about it to Tumulty who said he would like to see a New Jersey man in the Cabinet and would suggest a name within a few hours. Tumulty's source of inspiration was a lawyer's diary where he ran across the name of Vice-Chancellor Garrison who had heard a few of Tumulty's cases and 'made a deep impression on me as a high type of equity judge'.[36] Only a few hours after House was told of the name and before he had time to look him up, Wilson had sent for Garrison, was very much pleased with him and had appointed him.

Inauguration Day ran its usual course on 4 March. Before he spoke, Wilson made a slightly theatrical gesture of a sort that he did not often employ. 'Let the people come forward', he said,[37] beckoning them up to the Inauguration stand. Then he spoke in the style that was to become very familiar, of dedication, the forces of humanity, the great trust, and his need for counsel and sustenance from forward-looking men. He had invited Colonel House and his wife to be of the presidential party. Mrs. House went but the Colonel preferred to loaf in the Metropolitan Club: 'functions of this sort do not appeal to me and I never go'.[38] It was much more important to House that he should be at the Executive Offices at 9 a.m. on 8 March to hear the President's impression of his first cabinet meeting and to arrange a cipher for their confidential correspondence.

In a surprisingly short while—but applicants for office must have sharp eyes and ears—House became universally known as the channel through which the President was most easily reached. In April 1913 *Harper's Weekly* called him Assistant President House; and after that the press generally referred to him as the Silent Partner. It was in truth a partnership that Wilson formed with him. They were complementary to each other. Wilson described him as 'my second personality; my independent self: his thoughts and mine are one'.[39] Not that House, or anyone else for that matter, profoundly influenced Wilson in the conclusions which he reached. House was a sympathizer as much as a consultant; he rarely argued directly with anyone and met opposition, if he thought it worth meeting, by retreat followed by infiltration, apparently accepting what was said to him. 'That's true, that's true', he would say. 'He had a way of saying "I know it"', the British Foreign Secretary was to write, 'in a tone and manner that carried conviction both of his sympathy with and understanding of what was said to him.'[40] The President and his second personality did their business socially. House made trips to Washington and stayed at the White House, and the President stayed at House's apartment whenever he came to New York. There would be a family dinner, followed by family pursuits; Wilson might read aloud for an hour or so or amuse himself and the company with his limericks. Then House would get out his budget of political items.

What was House's reward for this unstinted service? He never took a salary and at first would not take even the expenses of his trips to Europe. His greatest reward was that he was leading exactly the life he wanted. High office meant pomp and publicity which he disliked and an irksome routine which he felt his health would not stand. His association with Wilson gave him the sweets of office without any of its stodginess. 'The life I am leading', he wrote in 1916, 'transcends in interest and excitement any romance.'[41] There was too the satisfaction of a real devotion to Wilson and belief in his leadership. At moments their deep affection for each other came to the surface. Of one of such moments House wrote:

I asked if he remembered the first day we met, some three and a half years ago. He replied, 'Yes, but we had known each other always, and merely came in touch then, for our purposes and thoughts were as one'. I told him how much he had been to me; how I had tried all my life to find someone with whom I could work out the things I had so deeply at heart, and I had begun to despair, believing my life would be more or less a failure, when he came into it, giving me the opportunity for which I had been longing.[42]

There were also the pleasing moments when his position was delicately recognized by fellow connoisseurs. Here is House's account in his diary of an interview with Tyrrell of the British Foreign Office concerning the proposed visit by House to Germany in 1913:

He did not think it necessary for me to take any credentials. He advised having our Ambassador in Germany whisper to the Kaiser that I was 'the power behind the throne' in the United States. That if this were done, I would have to warn our Ambassador to tell official Berlin I did not care for 'fuss and feathers'; otherwise I would have red carpets laid for me all over Berlin.[43]

'It is hard to estimate the effect of flattery and politeness upon Europeans.

. . . they value such things far beyond our conception' House wrote complacently to the President in 1915.[44] Flattery, when properly cooked and served to taste, is appreciated by most men, and House was no exception.

There were also satisfactory little jokes to be made, such as calling up Walter Page and saying, 'Good Morning, Your Excellency', and then relieving Page's agitation by asking him if he would accept the Ambassadorship to the Court of St. James.[45] Finally, there was his diary. He began it in September 1912 at the start of the election campaign. It was the mirror in which he looked at himself daily and could not help being quite pleased at what he saw. It was the monument he wanted to himself and of his deeds. He did not want a Roman column round which the vulgar could crowd and gape, but he wanted the record to be there for the discerning to seek out. He preserved in it the compliments he received, some of them most extravagant. The dictation to his secretary was a satisfying ritual. Mr. Baker, who did not like him much, once watched it: 'He spoke in a smooth, even voice, bringing his hands together softly from time to time; sometimes just touching the fingertips, sometimes the whole palms.'[46]

There were times when he thought of himself as a lot more effective than he was. There were indeed times when he thought of himself as the maker rather than the chosen of his master. He had in fact no serious claim to be a President-maker. He helped considerably with Bryan (though hardly enough to justify his opinion that he thereby 'probably caused Wilson's nomination by bringing Bryan round')[47] and he was one of several at work in Texas: that was the sum of his service. In the fall of 1911 when Wilson's prospects were good and it looked as though the two-thirds rule might be used to block his nomination, House made some efforts to get it abolished; luckily they failed. After Clark's rise in April and May 1912 House had his eye on alternatives to Wilson and he left for England the day the convention began when Wilson's fortunes were at their lowest. He wrote regretfully that he was 'physically unequal to the effort';[48] and he included in the same letter a prognostication, neither more nor less wise than anybody else's, to the effect that if Clark's strength crumbled Wilson would be nominated. A few days earlier, he had written to Mrs. Bryan pledging his support for her husband if he were again nominated. But after the event he seems to have persuaded himself that his recognition of Wilson as the best man for the office was as good as the conferment of the office upon him. Lloyd George sums it up thus:

Wilson was his idol, but his in the sense that it was House who had picked him out, shaped him as a politician, built the altar for him and placed him there above it to be worshipped.[49]

The presidency brought with it two additions to the inner ring. The other man besides the Colonel, and the only man besides Wilson himself to live in the White House, was Cary Grayson. He was a young lieutenant from Virginia in the medical corps of the Navy who had been assigned as one of President Taft's medical advisers. It was a stroke of luck for him that at Wilson's inaugural reception the new President's sister Annie fell on the marble staircase and cut her forehead, and he had his equipment handy. When he came to report on the patient's condition, he delighted the family, Nell wrote, with his handsome aristocratic face, a soft attractive voice, and (the simile being perhaps another contribution from the lady journalist) 'a chuckle that sounded like tearing silk'.[50] Wilson took an immediate liking to him and gave him an official appointment as medical adviser to the White House. He became an intimate friend and remained in attendance upon Wilson until his death. There is not much to say about him; he never seems to emerge from underneath Wilson. He refused to use his intimacy for any political purpose, or indeed for any purpose of his own except to serve his only ambition, which was to become a rear-admiral. The result of that was one of the rare occasions on which Wilson defeated his conscience. In January 1917 he gave Grayson the rank, the highest in the Medical Naval Service, the only other holder of it being the Surgeon-General.

Undoubtedly Grayson rendered very fine personal service to the President. Throughout the strain of nearly seven years of office, that is, right up to the point when Wilson himself decided that he must put his health and everything else that was in him to the hazard, Grayson kept him fit and equal to his work. Very soon after he came to the White House he found Wilson in bed with a headache and indigestion. From that moment Dr. Grayson took over. He banished the patent medicines, controlled the stomach pump, and prescribed a diet. He insisted on regular exercise and himself was Wilson's usual golfing companion. He insisted also on relaxation—daily motor rides which Wilson restricted to a few routes ('one cannot', Grayson writes, 'too often emphasize his preference for doing the same thing repeatedly')[51] and occasional trips in the *Mayflower*, the presidential yacht. After a while he persuaded the Wilsons, who had never been theatregoers, that the regime should include a weekly visit to the theatre. It was always the same theatre—at first Poli's in Washington and then Keith's—and Wilson took whatever was going, drama, comedy, variety, or a musical show, and enjoyed it all, but especially vaudeville.

There was one other man within the ring, Joseph P. Tumulty. Wilson had to override some strong objections to taking him with him to the White House. The position of secretary to the President is after all a very important one; and Tumulty was only thirty-two and untried and had, Wilson had to concede, 'an interest in the mechanism of small politics'.[52] He was, moreover, an ardent Catholic, a thought which in some caused considerable consternation: 'the secrets of state will always be made known by him to his Priest and thence to the Papal Delegate' an adviser warned.[53] But Mrs. Wilson, having no son of her own, was very fond of him and very much wanted him to come; and House and McAdoo both backed him for the job. So after considering other possibilities, Wilson gave it to him.

As Private Secretary Tumulty was in charge of the Executive Office. He had under him two assistant secretaries and the necessary clerical staff. The President of course had his personal stenographer, Charles L. Swem. In addition to routine duties Tumulty was the President's main liaison with congressmen and the press and party officials; he had to be ready to advise Wilson on public feeling. He had a considerable voice in patronage. With few exceptions no caller got an interview with the President except through Tumulty. He himself of course had ready access to Wilson; his room in the Executive Office was next to the President's. But even with him Wilson liked to do business in writing. Tumulty would put up memoranda which Wilson would mark 'Okeh' (which Wilson believed to be the correct term to use) or 'No'.

Wilson took with him also to the White House his portable typewriter. The searchlight on men in high places usually discloses some idiosyncrasy consciously or unconsciously acquired; the public like a great man to have some mark of individuality, even of eccentricity. So the typewriter became Wilson's personal insignia. It was installed in his study where it was noticed —almost recognized—by every caller. It went with him to Paris and on one occasion was borne to him majestically as he sat in conference in the Salle des Cloches. Journalists were quick to invest it with great age and a battered case. It symbolized Wilson accurately enough as the man who had been trained to think on paper, as the man of letters who tapped out his ideas rather than the big executive behind the telephones.

Wilson's dazzling rise so late in life from comparative obscurity to one of the great positions in the world did not turn his head. He never in his own mind invested himself, as a lesser man might do, with the panoply of his office. He wrote:

Everything is persistently *impersonal*. I am administering a great office,—no doubt the greatest in the world,—but I do not seem to be identified with it: it is not me, and I am not it. I am only a commissioner, in charge of its apparatus, living in its offices, and taking upon myself its functions. This impersonality of my life is a very odd thing, and perhaps robs it of intensity, as it certainly does of pride and self-consciousness (and, maybe, of enjoyment) but at least prevents me from becoming a fool, and thinking myself IT![54]

His sudden emergence was hailed as little short of a miracle by those who, believing that there was a seed of goodness in the American way of life, had hardly dared to hope that it would ever flower in American politics. But there were some, equally high-minded but with a natural disbelief in miracles, who thought that Wilson had thrust his way up as much by the exercise of his own adroitness as by the leverage of events. They did not altogether believe in the lucky moment at which the politicians had caught Wilson on the rebound from the loss of his Princeton love and lured him out of his academic groves. They pointed out that Wilson had been toying with politics for some time before that. They wondered whether, fearing that he might be swept out of Princeton by a swift current of resentment, he had set his sails some time before 1910; fighting luxury and privilege and turning down half a million dollars for the sake of principle is a good way to enter politics. They marvelled at the superb audacity of his double-cross of the bosses. He had not deceived them with words. He had loudly proclaimed that he would destroy them, well knowing that they would be caught in the trap of their own disbelief that any political campaigner ever said what he really meant. At first he professed sound and conservative politics so as to get his start in New Jersey; then he played radical politics so as to get Bryan and the West—Bryan whom he first despised and then found captivating. When he was quite satisfied that the East had served all his purposes except the final one of being publicly disowned, he cleverly staged a dramatic quarrel with Colonel Harvey, his chief benefactor. After that he played the usual game of stopping away and leaving his friends to make the promises he did not intend to keep. There is matter for thought in all this, but one must be careful not to credit Wilson with superhuman foresight and skill. Those who like to find for every event a commonplace explanation have sometimes to endow mere human agency with such uncanny powers that they let in the supernatural by the back door.

It is at any rate certain that as President he learnt the practical side of his job quickly; he had after all studied the theory of it very thoroughly. It was not merely that of being the chief executive. It was not enough for him that he should be, as in fact he proved to be, a capable and firm administrator. It was essential to his conception of the presidency that he should take part in legislation. He had always admired the British system of cabinet government in which the Prime Minister sits in the Commons, and he was resolved to be not merely the Prime Executive but also, as he had been in New Jersey, the Prime Initiator of legislation. He succeeded in this. In his first two years he got through Congress a big programme of reforming legislation, notably on tariffs and banking. He had no doubt the powerful aid of a favourable public opinion; those who opposed his reforms dared not fight in the last ditch, for they knew that in principle he was doing what the great majority of the country as manifested in the 1912 election wanted him to do. He achieved much too by his own tremendous power of will; he got things done by the sheer force of his resolution to have them done. But he could not have succeeded if he had not learnt how to use the party as an instrument. A British Prime Minister by virtue of his office leads in the legislature as well as in the executive; the President cannot lead in the legislature and can work only indirectly with tools, the powers of persuasion and patronage, unspecified in the Constitution. Wilson had to master these and he adapted himself to them surprisingly well. But also he got as near to Congress as he could. In 1800 President Jefferson had abandoned the custom of speaking to Congress in person on the ground that it looked too much like a speech from the Throne; he put his messages and addresses on paper and had them read by the clerk. Defying precedent and in spite of adverse criticism— 'cheap and tawdry imitation of English royalty', the senator from Mississippi called it[55]—Wilson reversed the practice. He began a new practice too in the holding of regular press conferences. But here he was less successful and he abandoned them in June 1915. Professor Link has written:

Few presidents in American history have better understood the importance of good press relations and failed more miserably to get on with newspapermen.[56]

He considered that journalists were not 'accurate-minded'.[57] He said that he prepared for conferences as carefully as for any lecture; but to his dismay he discovered that journalistic interest was 'in the personal and trivial rather than in principles and policies'.

He used the more conventional tools as well as his own inventions. He applied himself assiduously to contacts with senators and congressmen. Much was done by correspondence and he wrote a charming and effective letter. But much was also done by interviews—rather formal, but not so freezing as the communicant had feared. This was not the sort of work he enjoyed. 'I am discouraged by the eternal talk with senators one by one' he once said; he wanted to be 'heard in debate fully'.[58]

What was most surprising was that he learnt quite quickly the value of the political machine and the need for keeping it greased by the use of patronage. In the novitiate there was the ideal from which he started—the best man in the right place. At the end of the lesson, though he never got quite to that point, there were the notions of a man like Bryan who combined idealism with jobbery in a way that could be found nowhere outside America.

Bryan was himself incorrupt; but he was steeped in the old ways, treating party patronage as in the natural order of things. 'Can you let me know what positions you have at your disposal with which to reward deserving Democrats?' he wrote[59] to one who had already got his place: for the waters of patronage must flow down the rivers and flood the creeks. So many were the deserving and so few the places that Bryan evolved the idea of temporary diplomatic appointments to give everyone a turn. This modification was not always as saleable as the real thing. 'I think you have a little daughter' one senator, to whom Bryan had offered the disposal of the embassy at St. Petersburg, wrote to a doubtful client. 'Think what it would mean to her all the remainder of her life to say that her father had been Minister to Russia. . . . No diplomatic matters will be taken up during your service. . . . But if you accept the position it must be with the understanding that you will resign October 1, 1914.'[60] The diplomatic matters not to be taken up would thus have included the outbreak of a European war. It was lucky for Britain that London was not served in that way. But Bryan did not see it in that light. 'Would you like', he wrote to Wilson, 'to have me look about for a good Democrat who would like a winter's stay in Greece?' He had the good of the party as a whole in mind as well as of individuals. 'We have been quite short of prefixes', he told Wilson; Democrats were going about as Misters or at best as Honorables while the Republicans had been able to introduce Secretary or Ambassador So-and-so.

The first tussle came over the Post Office. There were 56,000 appointments to be made. Wilson had made Burleson his postmaster-general, an upright, old-fashioned Texan gentleman with sixteen years in Congress behind him. He had the benign face of an archdeacon and the collar of a stage butler, a combination which Wilson christened the Cardinal. 'Now, Burleson,' Wilson said at his first interview, 'I am going to appoint forward-looking men and I am going to satisfy myself that they are honest and capable.'[61] Burleson was shrewd and patient; he argued for two hours and he chose the right argument. 'It doesn't amount to a damn who is post-master at Paducah, Kentucky,' he said, 'but if you turn down the congress-man who recommended him, he'll get into bitter trouble at home; he'll hate you and he won't vote for anything you want.' He convinced Wilson that it was the price he must pay for getting the big things done; it was the argument of principle, the lesser yielding to the greater, that appealed to Wilson. He soon came to realize the practical truth of it as he grew more and more absorbed in pushing through his measures. As he confessed to Burleson and Tumulty, it was the 'standpatters' and the 'old guard' upon whom he leant for support. 'You know, Wilson never appreciated politicians', Burleson remarked long afterwards: 'he used them, and knew he needed them, but he never appreciated them.'[62] He did not regard them as men with whom he worked; they were men who had votes, and as such were pieces, more or less valuable, whom he had to move on the board in order to gain the positions he wanted.

Sometimes Wilson could invoke another sort of principle. The voice of the primaries was the voice of the people; and if an old guardsman was elected in the primaries he was entitled to Wilson's support even against a progressive. That was the line he took in endorsing Boss Sullivan for election to the Senate. By the time the midterm elections came round in 1914 Wilson was concerned above all things to keep the Democratic majority in Congress. He did so (although it was reduced in the House from 73 to 25), but only by the use of the machine as well as by appeal to the people. The New Jersey machine, his earliest opponents, came over to his side; one of the organization had been made a judge. For the New York primaries Wilson wrote cordially endorsing the Tammany candidates against two progressives, one of them Franklin D. Roosevelt. In the minds of most men there is a curtain which can be dropped between the present and the inconsistent past, opaque enough to blur the facts if not to hide them. If Wilson had looked back with clear vision to the fight with Tammany two years before, would he have been shocked? Probably he did not shock F. D. R.

Nor would he care to remember the times when he had to wriggle and shift nor how he bore his share of the politician's misfortune, the half-promise which he cannot perform. Abraham Lincoln, as Professor Harbaugh has written, 'appointed a string of inferior men to high office in order to secure the success and promote the great objects of his administration'.[63] A leader must have followers who will obey him if he is to obtain the sort of moral victory that Wilson won in the Panama tolls controversy.* The need for obedience was his justification for the use of patronage and influence. At least he could claim that he never used it in fear or ill-will and rarely indeed for favour or affection. Here is a letter he wrote on 22 April 1913:

> My dear, dear brother:
> I never in my life had anything quite so hard to do as this that I must do about the Nashville Post Office. Knowing as I do that a better man could not possibly be found for the place, and sure though I am that it would meet with the general approval of the citizens of Nashville, I yet feel that it would be a very serious mistake both for you and for me if I were to appoint you to the Postmastership there. I cannot tell you how I have worried about this or how much I have had to struggle against affection and temptation, but I am clear in the conviction that

---

* See p. 116 below.

I am sure that in the long run, if not now, you will agree with me that I am deciding rightly.

I can't write any more just now, because I feel too deeply.

With deepest love, I remain
Your affectionate brother,
Woodrow Wilson.[64]

Contrast the depth of feeling with the trifling prize, one of 56,000, and one must be hard not to be touched. Perhaps it was Ellen who kept him firm. Ten years before she had not let him appoint his nephew to a place at Princeton.

The triumphs of Wilson's first term were in the domestic field. Talking to a friend at Princeton shortly before he left for the White House, he remarked that it would be 'the irony of fate' if his administration had to deal chiefly with foreign affairs. Fate did not become supremely ironical until August 1914. Before that the President had only the usual small clutter of foreign problems, the two outstanding ones arising from the Panama tolls controversy and the troubles in Mexico. The solution of either could have led to a nasty British–American clash. The dexterity required to avoid a collision gave the statesmen on either side a better understanding of each other; this gave Britain a helpful start in the inevitable quarrels between belligerency and neutrality. In these two incidents there is also to be seen the first display by Wilson of his diplomatic method and on the international stage of his devotion to principle.

Wilson's remark about the irony of fate was not an indication of insularity. To be sure he did not belong to the tiny band of Americans with an interest in European affairs. But a process of thought started by the Spanish-American War had led him to a firm and clear conclusion of principle about the role which the United States should play in the world. The war with Spain was begun and ended in 1898. The Boer War began in 1899 and was not so brief. They were wars of conquest in the nineteenth-century imperialist style. One was started by America without anything that even then could decently be called an excuse and the other, in substance if not in form, by Britain. They are worth a brief mention as a preface to 1914 and thereafter: it is fair to remind the reader that both nations entered the century as warmongers.

The island of Cuba is on the doorstep of the American Continent. Together with the island of Puerto Rico it was the vestige of the great Spanish transatlantic empire which had ended in South America when Spain was driven out in 1824. Through the rest of the century Spain retained over Cuba a difficult ascendancy disturbed by several rebellions: the sympathies of the whole Continent were with the rebels. In 1895 there was an insurrection which Spain determined to suppress with the utmost force. The cruelty with which she did so, unadorned by efficiency and uncrowned by success, stirred the American public to high indignation. Atrocity stories exaggerated to the point of invention when not in themselves sufficiently inflammatory, were spread by all the newspapers, particularly those of Hearst. In that generation in which the power of the British and American Press was as great as it was ever to be, the most notorious of the men who exercised it were either nasty or unstable: William Randolph Hearst was both.

In October 1897 a new ministry in Madrid promised a change of men and measures in Cuba accompanied by some degree of home rule. President McKinley thought that the new Spanish Government ought to be given a chance and said so in his Message to Congress in December 1897. On 15 February 1898 the U.S. battleship *Maine*, which had been sent to Havana despite the misgivings of the Spanish Government, was blown up in the harbour by a mine with the loss of 260 of her crew. On 28 March the U.S. Naval Court of Inquiry reported that there was no evidence to show who was responsible: history has not improved upon that verdict.

Mr. Hearst heard the news of the explosion when he rang up the editor of his principal paper, the *New York Journal*. Where have you put the story, he asked: on the front page of course, he was told. Anything else on the front page? Only the other big news, the editor replied. Hearst said: 'There is not any other big news. Please spread the story all over the page. This means war.'[65] From then on he laboured mightily to make his prediction come true. The hysteria created by the yellow press with Hearst in the van made the difference between peace and war. No financial or industrial interest wanted war, nor the party bosses, nor any of the men in power, except Theodore Roosevelt and he was then only Assistant Secretary of the Navy. Madrid bent backwards to conciliate: on 10 April the American Minister cabled from Madrid that if nothing were done to humiliate Spain he hoped to obtain a settlement on the basis of Cuban autonomy or independence or cession to the United States. The next day the President sent the matter to Congress, he having, so he said, 'exhausted every effort to relieve the intolerable condition of affairs which is at our doors'. On 20 April 1898 Congress resolved that it was the duty of the United States to demand 'that the Government of Spain at once relinquish its authority and government in the island of Cuba'. Three days were allowed for compliance.

Spain, declaring that the resolution was equivalent to a declaration of war, broke off relations. The United States at once began hostilities.

President McKinley, who a year later blamed it all on 'the inflamed state of public opinion and the fact that Congress could no longer be held in check', had been afraid that if he resisted the clamour, the Republican party would be broken; Elihu Root, whom next year he made his Secretary of War, told him that an attempt to retard the momentum would destroy the presidential power and influence. Thus the President put it up to Congress. The House voted 310 to 6 for war, though the Senate, less pervious to the press, divided quite narrowly by 42 to 35.

Professor Morison brilliantly describes the national sentiment:

No one who lived through them will forget those gay days of 1898. With what generous ardour the young men rushed to the colours to free Cuba, while the bands crashed out the chords of Sousa's 'Stars and Stripes Forever!' And what a comfortable feeling of unity the country obtained at last, when Democrats vied in patriotism with Republicans, when the South proved equally ardent for the fight, and Joe Wheeler, the gallant cavalry leader of the Confederacy, became the actual commander of the United States Army in Cuba. It was more close and personal to Americans than the Great War; it was their own little show for independence, fair play, and hip-hurrah democracy, against all that was tyrannical, treacherous, and fetid in the Old World. How they enjoyed the discomfiture of Germany, France, Italy, and Russia, and how they appreciated the hearty goodwill of England! Every ship of the smart little navy from the powerful *Oregon*, steaming at full speed round the Horn to be in time for the big fight, to the absurd 'dynamite cruiser' *Vesuvius*, was known by picture and reputation to every American boy. And what heroes the war correspondents created—Hobson who sunk the *Merrimac*, Lieutenant Rowan who delivered the message to Garcia, Commodore Dewey ('You may fire when ready, Gridley'), blaspheming Bob Evans of the *Iowa*, Captain Philip of the *Texas* ('Don't cheer, boys, the poor fellows are dying!'), and Teddy Roosevelt with his horseless Rough Riders. It was not a war of waiting and endurance, of fruitless loss and hope deferred. On the first day of May, one week after the declaration, Dewey steams into Manila Bay with the Pacific Squadron, and without losing a single man reduces the Spanish fleet to old junk. The Fifth Army Corps safely lands in Cuba, and wins three battles in quick succession. Admiral Cervera's fleet issues from Santiago Bay, and in a few hours' running fight is completely smashed, with the loss of a single American sailor. Ten weeks' fighting and the United States had wrested an empire from Spain.[66]

Included in the empire wrested from Spain there were the Philippines. as President McKinley put it:

There was nothing left for us to do but to take them all, and to educate the Filipinos, and uplift and civilize and Christianize them.

Colonel George Harvey, President of Harper and Brothers and editor of *Harper's Weekly*

Jack Hibben, Stuart Professor of Logic at Princeton, and President of Princeton after Wilson

1913. The Wilsons at Cornish, New Hampshire
From the left: Wilson, Jessie, Eleanor, Mrs. Wilson, and Margaret

1913. Wilson at his desk in the White House

Doubtless he had in mind, since he was addressing a group of Methodists, that the Christianity available from 'Her Most Catholic Majesty of Spain' would not be as beneficial as the homespun variety.

Puerto Rico, Guam, and the Hawaiian Islands were all annexed. Cuba itself retained a precarious independence; Congress in its resolution had disclaimed any intention to take it over. Professor Morison has said of the war that 'it was imperialist in result, but not in motive'. There is no doubt that most Americans were for the war because they thought it noble and uplifting to rescue the Cubans from the oppression of the old world. Even Hearst probably believed quite a bit of what his paper printed. Roosevelt was passionate for the cause. He wrote to his friend Brooks Adams:

The blood of the murdered men of the Maine calls not for indemnity but for the full measure of atonement which can only come by driving the Spaniard from the New World.[67]

Bryan volunteered for service and organized the Third Nebraska Volunteer Regiment but it did not get further than Florida. He supported the annexation of the Philippines. Mr. Baker, the biographer, who as late as March 1898 was hoping that 'the sober judgement of the American people will prevail',[68] by May was writing of 'the sly Spanish who would not stand up and take their medicine'.

If you are going to wage a war of aggression, it is important to get it over as quickly as you can, if possible before the world is given time to mutter. Britain's Boer War lasted nearly three years. This may be one reason why it came in for more contemporary criticism than the Cuban War. Another reason undoubtedly was that it looked worse. While the United States was tackling an old empire so as to free a small nation from its grip, Britain was tackling a small nation so as to add to her own enormous dominions. Her marked lack of success in the early stages gave time for ridicule as well as odium to accumulate.

In South Africa the Cape of Good Hope and Natal had been British colonies since the Napoleonic War. In 1836 the considerable Dutch population in the Cape Colony made the Great Trek north and in due course founded the Boer Republics of the Transvaal and the Orange Free State. In 1885 gold was discovered in the Transvaal and the city of Johannesburg arose on the site. It attracted many exploiters, mainly British. They came in swamping numbers and in a surprisingly short time formed the majority of the population, engendering great prosperity for the Transvaal. Nevertheless, these Uitlanders, as they were called, were regarded by the Transvaal

Boers under the leadership of their President, Paul Kruger, as destroyers of the ancient Dutch ways and infiltrators of British imperialism. Indeed, the two little Republics with their tiny Afrikaner population were beleaguered by the might of Britain. To the south there was the empire-builder Cecil Rhodes, Prime Minister of the Cape, and to the north the territories of Rhodesia which he had acquired. Beyond them lay British East Africa (now Kenya), Nyasaland (now Malawi), and Uganda, the two latter recently declared British protectorates. Coming down to meet them in 1898 was the army of Kitchener, conqueror of the Sudan.

The Uitlanders were treated politically as second-class citizens, taxed without representation. This was something that in that age imperial Britain, who had a vague claim to suzerainty over the Transvaal, could not be expected to tolerate. Eventually in April 1899 a monster petition was presented to the Queen beseeching 'Your Most Gracious Majesty to extend your Majesty's protection to your Majesty's loyal subjects resident in this State'.[69] It was accompanied by a dispatch from Sir Alfred Milner, the British High Commissioner, which referred to 'thousands of British subjects kept permanently in the position of helots'. The Conservative Government in Britain accepted his recommendation that 'the case for intervention was overwhelming'. The Boers, when driven to it, were willing to make concessions. In July 1899 they prepared a Franchise Bill which went a long way towards remedying the Uitlanders' grievances. The British Government demanded that the Bill should be submitted to a joint inquiry. To accept that would be tantamount to an admission by the Boers that they were not masters in their own house. This, indeed, was the real issue: would the Boers accept the paramountcy of Britain in South Africa? Milner, the man who was considered by anti-imperialists in and out of Britain to have engineered the war, certainly wanted war if he could not get that degree of submission. President Kruger had for long believed that Britain wanted a war with or without a cause. Jan Smuts, the State Attorney who had drafted the Franchise Bill, believed that England would not dare 'to venture into the ring with Afrikanerdom without a formally good excuse'. But if she did, the sooner the better.

Our people throughout South Africa must be baptised with the baptism of blood and fire before they can be admitted among the other great peoples of the world.

Unfortunately for his cause Kruger did not saddle the British with the need to find the 'formally good excuse'. On 9 October 1899 he delivered an ultimatum and forthwith invaded Natal and Cape Colony: if he had waited a little longer he would doubtless have received an ultimatum from Britain.

This was not an issue on which all Britain was united and the fact that she was put on the defensive made the British Government's case much easier to get across. Certainly it made no difference to the imperialists but not all Britons were imperialists. Those who were imperialists, men like Milner, were not unprincipled. Their dream of a British Africa from the Cape of Good Hope to the Nile was not an unworthy one. They believed that the British knew better than others how to bring good order, justice, health, and humanity to backward races. They believed firmly that the Boers with their narrow outlook, their hidebound institutions, and their repressive, even cruel, attitude to Africans had no idea at all how to do this. Subsequent events have not so far disproved this opinion.

These two episodes in Cuba and in the Transvaal illustrate the fundamental similarity in British and American imperial ventures as well as the contrast in method. Wilson himself appreciated the former. In the *Atlantic Monthly* of March 1901 he wrote:

It is our peculiar duty, as it is also England's . . . to impart to the people thus driven out upon the road of change, so far as we have opportunity, or can make it, our own principles of self-help; teach them order and self-control in the midst of change; impart to them, if it be possible, by contact and sympathy, and example, the drill and habit of law and obedience which we long ago got out of the strenuous processes of English history.[70]

Britain and the United States were each quite convinced that she would bring superior benefits to the country she took over. The Americans believed that little nations should under a suitable mentor be allowed to control their own destinies, but they felt sure that the little one could very easily be persuaded to believe that their mentor was right. The British took a more robust view: they did what they thought was good for their pupils and did not care whether they liked it or not. Fundamentally both nations thought of themselves as guardians or trustees; the Americans believed— or, some would say, kidded themselves—that they were giving their services free; the British saw no reason why they should not take a commission in the form of strategic and economic advantages.

The American motive in the Cuban War was purer than the British motive in the Boer War. But each operation dirtied some linen and it is to the credit of Englishmen that many of them insisted on it being washed in public. In the United States not a voice was raised at the time to condemn the way in which she went to war. In Britain the Liberal party in opposition was split into three parts; and since several of the men affected were in power when Wilson was President, it is worth seeing who they were and what their attitude was to the war.

Campbell-Bannerman, the party leader, was where party leaders ought to be—in the centre. This section disliked the war and felt that the Conservative Government was in the main responsible for it; on the other hand, Kruger was a reactionary and the Boers no better than they should be, and it was difficult in wartime for the patriotic to say anything which would discourage the armies in the field, especially when they were sustaining reverses. The more venerable Liberals, such as Morley and Bryce, were of this way of thinking; so was Reid who as Lord Loreburn supported the peace movements in 1916 and 1917. The younger leaders-to-be were either right or left of centre.

But this posture of the centre had solid support in the country. In October 1900 the Government, believing (erroneously, as it turned out) that the war was as good as won and seeking to take advantage of the Liberal disarray, held a general election. It was known as the 'khaki' election and was fought by the Conservatives on the slogan that 'a seat lost to the Government is a seat gained by the Boers'. Had there been no war and no disarray, the swing of the pendulum after five years of Tory rule might well have brought the Liberals back. That of course did not happen but the Conservatives gained little. Their majority of 130 at the time of the dissolution of Parliament was increased to 134; their popular vote was 2,400,000 against the Liberal 2,100,000. In June 1901 Campbell-Bannerman produced an echoing phrase. 'Methods of barbarism.' He applied it to Kitchener's methods. The Boers with no army left continued to resist from fortified farmhouses; Kitchener destroyed the farms and put the non-combatants into concentration camps.

The three outstanding men on the right wing of the Liberal party were Asquith, Grey, and Haldane. In 1914 the first was Prime Minister, the second Foreign Secretary, and the third Lord Chancellor. Sir Edward Grey plays so large a part in this narrative that he must be described more fully later. Asquith and Haldane were lawyers by profession. Each had a powerful mind; and Asquith added to his an integrity of character and a commanding personality that made him one of the great Englishmen of the century. Haldane had a wider intellect, a more devious way of thought, and a brain that could grasp a philosophic concept as easily as an administrative detail. He was Secretary for War from 1906 to 1911, and his reputation as one of the best Britain has ever had has survived until today without even a temporary slump. All three men were Whigs rather than Liberals with patrician minds bedded securely but unjingoistically in the greatness of Britain. They were all three close friends. Asquith was also very friendly with Milner, a Balliol contemporary at Oxford. The three men with their followers were known as the Liberal Imperialists, though as imperialists they were regarded by the extreme conservatives as lacking in guts. Grey became depressed about the war. He admitted the necessity for it and that it must be carried on, but 'it has no business to be popular'.[71] Asquith and he were critical of pre-war British diplomacy but believed that Kruger was in the wrong. They accepted the eventual annexation of the Boer Republics; and, indeed, even the central group were reconciled to the fact that it would be the inevitable outcome of the war.

Not so David Lloyd George. He was the chief of the Radicals on the left: 'Little Englanders' was the kindest name their opponents gave them. For Lloyd George the English were the oppressors as for years they had been the oppressors of his native Wales. Three weeks before the war he wrote: 'If I have the courage I shall protest with all the vehemence at my command against the outrage which is perpetrated in the name of human freedom.'[72] He had the courage. The vehemence at his command was very considerable and he expressed it with compelling oratory and in biting phrase. His sustained opposition to the war brought him at the time hatred, obloquy, and suffering; but left him at the end of a life, not thereafter marked by a sacrificial devotion to unpopular causes, with a badge of honour which his detractors have never tried to take from him.

There is no evidence of what Wilson thought about the morality of the Boer War. His attitude towards the Cuban War was much the same as Mr. Baker's and perhaps of most American liberals in its conversion from initial distrust to pride in American arms and thence to a glow of approval. He was not roused by the destruction of the *Maine*. He wrote of it at the time as very likely an accident and Mrs. Wilson expressed her contempt for those senators who were failing to 'set the example of self-control to the nation'.[73] He became enthusiastic about American exploits but he also thought deeply about the whole thing. In August 1898, when the three months' war was just over, he wrote a memorandum apparently only for his own use. It was mildly apologetic in tone. If there was no positive proof, he said in effect, that the Spanish had blown up the *Maine*, nevertheless they were just the sort of people who might have done.

It may be that we were a trifle too hasty in some of the things that followed . . . the processes of our modern life are swift: we cannot stay them by regrets.

The question now, he went on, was what ought America to do. She had been brought suddenly into the midst of those nations who sought to possess the world, 'England, Russia, Germany, France, these are the rivals in the new spoliation'. The question was not simply one of expediency but also of moral obligation.

In his *History of the American People* he wrote approvingly of the venture and of the annexation of the Philippines. Speaking as President in January 1916 he said:

The world sneered when we set out on the liberation of Cuba, but the world sneers no longer. The world now knows, what it was then loath to believe, that a nation can sacrifice its own interests and its own blood for the sake of liberty and happiness of another people.[74]

This was the spirit in which in 1913 Wilson approached the problems created by disorders in Mexico. Mexican problems and the controversy over the Panama Canal tolls were the first occasions in his administration in which British and American diplomacies intertwined.

The Panama Canal was expected to be opened to traffic in 1914 and one of the last measures of President Taft's administration was an act to provide for its operation. The canal was to be open to ships of all nations; but in return for the American capital and labour that had gone into its construction, it was enacted that American coastal shipping should be free of toll. This exemption would have been most fair and reasonable if Congress had been a free agent. But under the Hay–Pauncefote Treaty with Britain of 1901 it was expressly provided that the canal should be open 'on terms of entire equality, so that there shall be no discrimination . . . in respect of . . . charges of traffic or otherwise'. It was by this treaty, and in consideration of this provision, that Britain had given up her interest in the building of the canal and permitted the United States to have the exclusive control of it. She therefore objected to the exemption of American shipping as a breach of treaty. On 17 January 1913 President Taft rejected Britain's protest and her offer of arbitration.

This was the situation when Wilson came into power. The country as a whole approved Taft's attitude. The Democratic platform at Baltimore— of course with Wilson's assent—had endorsed it, and so had the Roosevelt progressives. But a number of leading Republicans, including the two influential senators Root and Lodge, were shocked by Taft's disregard of the treaty obligation. Wilson himself, as he began to appreciate the point, began also to change his mind. On 17 January 1913 he met at the Round Table, a dining club in New York, a group of the dissenting Republicans. Root expounded the issue and told him that the good faith of the United States was at stake. At the end of what he said was an illuminating discussion, Wilson declared: 'I think I now understand it and the principles which are involved. When the time comes for me to act you can count upon my taking the right stand.'[75] Thereby Wilson took on a formidable task. He had to reverse a decision recently and deliberately enacted and in the process convert his own party as well as the country. But it was the sort of straightforward moral issue on which Wilson was at his best. He waited for a suitable moment and then on 5 February 1914 came out for repeal. The emotions of the powerful Irish element in the Democratic party were roused by talk of concessions to England. At one time it looked as if the party might split and Wilson was pushed to the point where he talked of resigning and 'going to the country'. Burleson and Tumulty made heroic efforts, in one case even arranging for the construction of a branch post office so as to place an applicant for favours. By this means or that Wilson succeeded in converting his party, Root and Lodge carried enough Republicans with them, and on 11 June 1914 the repeal became law. It was a great achievement: 'a controversy which the President settled to the lasting glory of honest diplomacy' as House said to Sir Edward Grey when they reminisced in November 1917.[76]

The other inheritance in foreign policy which President Taft left as an immediate bequest to his successor was an eruption in Mexico. In 1910 Mexico celebrated the centenary of her independence from Spain, the eightieth birthday of her President Porfirio Diaz and the thirtieth year of his reign, which had brought stability, if hardly freedom, to his country. Next year the long suppression was brought to an end. Diaz was ousted by Francisco Madero, a liberal-minded young man whose intentions were infinitely better than his capacities. There followed an uneasy fifteen months during which factions diversified and army generals came into their own. Madero trusted the most efficient of them, Victoriano Huerta, who in return betrayed, imprisoned, and killed him (shot while attempting to escape), got himself appointed provisional president, and informed all interested governments, including the American, that from now on peace and prosperity would reign. This happened on 13 February 1913, a fortnight before Wilson's inauguration.

The European powers with interests in Mexico thought that Huerta was more likely than anyone else to restore the torpidity of the days of Diaz. Henry Lane Wilson, the American ambassador, who had taken a dislike to Madero, agreed. He joined with the other ambassadors in recommending that after a decent interval the Huerta Government should be given *de facto* recognition. Such was the usual practice, as John Bassett Moore advised the President, pointing out that *de facto* recognition was not concerned with law or morals but only with the fact. Moore was a great authority on international law whom Wilson had persuaded to leave his chair at Columbia University to become Counselor of the State Department. But Wilson rejected his advice; it was, he felt, his duty to scrutinize the character of the new government.

No government dominated by Huerta—an unattractive figure, squat, bald, and spectacled, whose cunning was only slightly impaired by his addiction to the brandy bottle—was likely to stand up well to Wilsonian scrutiny. Wilson soon came to see the question of recognition as an issue between the oil interests, especially the British, who were prepared to purchase by expenditure of principle the stability which they believed the Huerta regime would give, and those who thought Huerta was a bloody and tyrannous man, striving to rule the Mexican people without their consent. Moreover, by the end of March 1913 it was clear that Huerta's promise of peace and prosperity would not be speedily fulfilled. His power was challenged by a party calling itself the Constitutionalists under General Carranza—a patriarchal figure, but not as guileless as his long white beard and simple blue eyes suggested—and something like civil war developed.

Wilson and Bryan advanced hand in hand towards their goal. They shared a distrust of diplomats and lawyers intense enough to embrace their own ambassador; Lane Wilson certainly seems to have dabbled too much in Mexican politics. They selected William Bayard Hale, the journalist who had written Wilson's campaign biography, to investigate and report. Hale advised having nothing to do with Huerta. He did not doubt that Huerta would yield to the threat of force any more than he doubted that the European governments which supported Huerta would yield to eloquence. Then there would be free elections and a government which the United States could recognize.

The plan was beautifully simple. Wilson and Bryan decided to recall Lane Wilson and to send out as the President's representative John Lind, a former governor of Minnesota. Mr. Lind was a progressive Democrat, anti-imperialist, and a friend of Bryan; these qualifications outweighed his lack of diplomatic experience and of any acquaintance with Mexico and the Spanish language. He was provided with a letter of instructions not intended for publication but which got into the newspapers of 5 August 1913, the day after he left on his mission. It made unusual reading for diplomats. The United States, Mr. Lind was to say, was not as other governments; it was 'expected by the powers of the world to act as Mexico's nearest friend'; it sought 'to counsel Mexico for its own good' and, indeed, 'would deem itself discredited if it had any selfish or ulterior purpose' in transactions where the peace, happiness, and prosperity of a whole people were involved; it called for 'a definite armistice solemnly entered into and scrupulously observed'. In conclusion Mr. Lind was to inquire whether Mexico could 'give the civilized world a satisfactory reason for rejecting our good offices'. If so, and she had any better suggestions to make, the President would be more than willing to consider them.

But all the good offices with their solemn entries and scrupulous observances were contemptuously rejected, as was also the sweetener, the offer of a loan, which accompanied them; and Huerta was palpably unwilling to give the civilized world any reason for doing so other than several variants of the notion that the President should mind his own business. Mr. Lind retired baffled. Wilson told Congress on 27 August 1913 that there was nothing to do but wait patiently and watch developments—a policy of 'watchful waiting', as the newspapers christened it, and one which went on for so long that it became, as the *New York Times* said reprovingly a year later, 'the joke of the shallow-minded'.[77] Meanwhile, Wilson declared: 'We can afford to exercise the self-restraint of a really great nation which realises its strength and scorns to misuse it.'[78]

Hopes were raised when Huerta said that he would agree to hold elections. But before they took place Huerta on 26 October 1913 fell upon the Chamber of Deputies, composed mainly of his opponents, and imprisoned 110 of them; after that he naturally got himself elected. Wilson was very angry and especially indignant with Britain; he felt sure that Huerta would not have dared this stroke without British support and he believed that British policy was being dictated by Lord Cowdray's oil interests. He told Colonel House that he was going to 'build a fire back of the British Ministry through the British public'.[79] Bryan and he drafted a Note for circulation among the European powers in which all the powers, but chiefly Britain, were charged with antagonizing and thwarting the United States and encouraging Huerta in return for commercial concessions, and the Note demanded that the powers 'withdraw that recognition which has exerted so baneful an influence'. This was an unprecedented demand in language almost insulting. Bassett Moore had the courage to tell Wilson so, and Wilson accepted it from him that the diplomatic consequences would be serious. On 7 November a more moderate circular was issued in which Wilson said that it was

his clear judgment that it is his immediate duty to require Huerta's retirement from the Mexican Government, and that the Government of the United States must now proceed to employ such means as may be necessary to secure this result.[80]

After this Moore gave up his turbulent clients and in the spring of 1914 retired from the State Department. His successor as Counselor was Robert Lansing, a man of no great attainments who within hardly more than a year was to be raised to the exalted position of Secretary of State.

Ambassador Page, who warmly supported Wilson's Mexican policy, wrote to House on 2 November 1913:

> The Englishman has a mania for order, order for order's sake, and for—trade. . . . Talk to him about character as a basis for government or about moral basis of government in any outlying country, he'll think you daft. Bah! what matter who governs or how, so long as he keeps order. He won't see anything else.[81]

Wilson exhorted Page to continue 'pounding elementary doctrine into them'.[82] The British realized that it would not do to quarrel with the United States over a matter of this sort. Sir William Tyrrell, the Foreign Secretary's private secretary but then in Washington acting for the ambassador who was ill, was told to patch things up. He first saw Bryan who handled the matter with gusto, touching on the wickedness of the British in Egypt and India and declaring that Cowdray was the paymaster of the British Cabinet. Tyrrell replied—with mock solemnity—that Cowdray had not enough money; the price of the Cabinet would be very high. 'Then you admit the charge', said Bryan.[83]

A conversation with the President on 13 November, arranged through House, was more productive. Tyrrell promised that Britain would withdraw support from Huerta. The matter of the Panama tolls was still then unsettled: there was no bargain—both sides vigorously denied that—but there was perhaps an exchange of unconnected donations. At the end of the interview Tyrrell asked Wilson for a statement of his policy which he could explain to the British people. 'I am going to teach the South American republics to elect good men', Wilson said.[84] What he wanted, as he later said,[85] was order for the mass of the people and not merely for the benefit of the old-time regime and the vested interests. That was the old order and the old order was dead. Under the new order it was the duty and privilege of a big country to look after a small one and teach her the right way of living. He seemed to be announcing a policy of spiritual colonization.

Wilson was surprised and hurt that his policy found no greater favour with Huerta's opponent, Carranza, than it had with Huerta himself. Carranza rejected Wilson's overtures and refused to admit the right of any nation to interfere in the affairs of Mexico. Wilson had committed himself to the elimination of Huerta by 'such means as may be necessary'; if Carranza would not co-operate there might in the end be no alternative to blatant intervention.

The period of watchful waiting was not disturbed when in February 1914 a British resident was executed by the anti-Huerta faction. This roused a Britain in which Palmerston was still a living memory. 'Kill an Englishman at home', wrote Page, 'and there is no undue excitement. But kill one abroad and gunboats and armies and reparations are at once thought about.'[86] Wilson counselled 'infinite patience and infinite firmness': 'a country the size and power of the United States can afford to wait just as long as it pleases.'[87] But he sang a very different song when an incident involving America occurred on 9 April 1914. Some American sailors, landing at Tampico without permission to load supplies, were arrested; and an hour or so later, as soon as the local general was informed, were released with profuse apologies. This was not good enough for Admiral Mayo, who demanded a formal apology and the hoisting on shore of the Stars and Stripes with a salute of twenty-one guns to be rendered to it. The General was given until 6 p.m. on the following day to comply. Incredible though it may seem, his action was immediately endorsed. The American chargé in Mexico was instructed to support the application with the utmost firmness. Before he got these instructions, he had already called on Huerta and obtained a written expression of regret and a request that the ultimatum be withdrawn. Bryan and Daniels, the Secretary of the Navy and an uncritical sympathizer with Wilson who was very fond of him, thought this sufficient. But Wilson did not; and the exchanges went on. This was the sort of old-fashioned stuff that Victoriano Huerta knew how to handle. He questioned the legality of the landing; he raised difficulties about firing salutes in Holy Week; if he fired the salute how could he be sure that it would be returned? Would it not be better to fire simultaneous salutes? Should not the matter go to The Hague? Finally, and quite unanswerably, who was *he* to give a salute? If he was the Government of Mexico, why did not the United States recognize him? If he was not, what was the value of his salute?

The time limit for the salute, thrice extended, was passed on 19 April 1914. The next day Wilson went to Congress to ask for authority 'to use the armed forces of the United States in such ways and to such an extent as may be necessary to obtain from General Huerta and his adherents the fullest recognition of the rights and dignity of the United States'.[88] He mentioned the Tampico affair as one count only in the indictment against Huerta. For the rest he dredged up two trivial incidents* without even, as Mr. Baker says, giving the explanations that mitigated them.[89] On 21 April an American detachment about 1,000 strong entered the port of Vera Cruz and seized the customs-house and the next day the main Atlantic fleet arrived and landed another 3,000 men. The Mexicans resisted and were routed: 126 of them were killed and 185 wounded, American casualties

---

* The incidents are set out in Link 2: 398. The author condemns Wilson's speech as a misrepresentation of the facts; Huerta and his subordinates, he says, had acted with studied courtesy to the United States.

being 19 dead and 71 wounded. Wilson had not believed that the Mexicans would resist so great a display of force and he was unnerved and deeply distressed by the bloodshed. On 25 April he thankfully accepted an offer of mediation from the Argentine, Brazil, and Chile; and Huerta under pressure from Britain, France, and Germany accepted also.

The Mediation Conference met in May 1914. Wilson did not abate his demands which went far beyond any issue in which the United States was materially interested. He still required the elimination of Huerta and the setting up of a provisional government acceptable to all parties. The Government could hardly in the circumstances be acceptable to Huerta; what Wilson wanted, he later explained, was the transfer of political power from Huerta to 'those who represent the interests and aspirations of the people'. Wilson did not submit to the Conference the question whether Huerta or his opponents best represented the popular interests; on this sort of matter he preferred to rest on his own judgement. Nor was he content to regulate Mexico's behaviour to her neighbours; he demanded domestic measures such as land reform. A compromise was reached on 24 June 1914 which fell far short of Wilson's hopes. Huerta was not proscribed, though events caused him to flee in the following month. Nothing more was heard of the salute. Nothing was said of internal reforms. Carranza, as the representative of 'the interests and aspirations of the people', turned out to be disappointing. He had resented the Vera Cruz landing just as much as Huerta did, and he said that he would be no party to proceedings which placed the election of the President of Mexico in the hands of the Washington government. Wilson had thought of Carranza as 'honest', 'very narrow and rather dull', but to be 'counted upon no doubt to try to do the right thing'.[90] It was one of the few occasions upon which Wilson admitted a mistake. Eighteen months later in talk with House he laughingly referred to Carranza as the man who 'once or twice put it over us in a very skilful way'.[91]

Thus ended, but only for the time being, the Mexican imbroglio. Before trying to assess what Wilson's handling of it portended for his European policy, there is one incident in it—the Tampico débâcle—which deserves a closer look. What made Wilson wave the flag, play the bully, and present to Congress a tendentious account of petty complaints? This sort of abasement happened when, as at Princeton, he was thwarted, especially if there was some contending personality, 'that scoundrel Huerta' as he called him, 'so false, so sly' and 'seldom sober',[92] to arouse emotion. Pride then took charge of him: the thing was right because it was he who did it. But it is doubtful if the image of Huerta, like those of the bad men at Princeton, remained to plague him. Because he was able to regard Huerta as a different sort of animal—'a diverting brute' he called him and wrote to Mrs. Peck of a 'sneaking admiration'[93]—he was able to turn the bogy into a figure of fun.

It is noteworthy that Wilson never again behaved in the same way. Whether or not he admitted it to himself, he had learnt the lesson that any display of force could lead to bloodshed. That thought must have come back many times when he hesitated and half turned on the road to the war in Europe.

The Tampico affair has yet another significance. It sowed the seed of the antagonism between Wilson and Root and this is important because Root was—certainly if Roosevelt is taken as disqualifying himself by his unorthodoxy (and many would say whether or not)—the ablest Republican of his time and more than any other the repository of the party conscience. Elihu Root's career bears many superficial resemblances to Wilson's whose lifetime he spanned with a decade or more to spare at either end. He was the son of a professor of mathematics. He was fifty-four before he went into national politics and then it was because the office sought him; in July 1899, just after the Cuban War, President McKinley invited him to become Secretary of War. But while Wilson spent his pre-political years in academic life, Root spent his at the New York Bar where his talents took him rapidly to the top; he was a corporation lawyer with the pervasive Thomas F. Ryan as one of his best clients. As Secretary of War he was brilliantly successful. Haldane, who did the same job in Britain a few years later, regarded Root's five annual reports as 'the very last word concerning the organization and place of an army in a democracy'.[94] In July 1905 he became Roosevelt's Secretary of State. Taft, a fellow-lawyer whom McKinley and he had made Governor-General of the Philippines, succeeded him as Secretary of War. Roosevelt, Root, Taft, and Lodge. These were the years when the four men who were to be the pillars of the Republican opposition to Wilson were closest together in friendship and in work, three in the Administration while Lodge co-operated in the Senate. The bond was shattered beyond repair by the 1912 split. After that Taft and Root never even spoke to Roosevelt until 1916; Lodge, though like Root he sided with Taft, managed to keep the peace with Theodore. While during Wilson's Administration Roosevelt went his own way, the other three were broadly in harmony with each other, though at some points, as will be seen, they took divergent action.

When Taft formed his Administration in 1909 he would have liked Root to carry on in the State Department but Root preferred the Senate. At the end of his six-year term there he did not stand for re-election. Yet his stature was such that, though he never again held office, he remained at least for the next five years the outstanding figure in the party. He was talked of for the presidency but the path to the White House was then as the eye of the needle for the corporation lawyer, and anyway Root had neither the great ambition nor the gift of self-projection that inspires. He achieved instead the high reputation for sagacity that is rarely conferred on a man who reveals much of himself.

Like Wilson Root presented a cold aspect to the world at large but was loved by his intimates who formed for him a circle far less restricted than Wilson's. He had the same astringent and unmalicious humour. He had the same general reputation for integrity traversed by specific charges of dishonesty, such as those that arose from his ruthless handling of the 1912 Republican convention in order to secure Taft's nomination. In this respect both men had the insensitivity produced by taking a narrow view, Root because of his bent towards political orthodoxy and Wilson because of his one-track mind. Men who have minds like headlights and drive hard on them turn their judgement of what is right and wrong on what they see in front of them and do not pause to consider how the path they cut may look to those around them who see it in a diffuse light.

Wilson and Root could never have run in harness. Root was essentially conservative, not reactionary but certainly not what Wilson called 'forward-looking'. But they could have worked in combination on projects where they happened to agree. They also could have made contacts at points on which they differed; and if Wilson had been the sort of man who could talk about particulars without demanding sympathy in general, he might have gained a lot from contact with Root. In short they might have gone on as they did in fact begin. They were in alliance over the Panama tolls. Root in August 1913 went out of his way to support Wilson's Mexican policy at that stage when it was under attack by Republicans, including Lodge, and thereby earned a note of thanks from the White House. It was largely on Root's recommendation that Lansing got his appointment as Counselor, though Root was acting out of friendship for John W. Foster, Lansing's father-in-law and a former Secretary of State, rather than out of a high opinion of the candidate's abilities and powers of judgement. But when after Tampico Wilson sought the approval of Congress for his action, Root and Lodge led the opposition in the Senate. Root was careful to express his admiration for Wilson generally and his confidence in his devotion to peace. But he used words that would cut Wilson to the quick:

American children will go through life fatherless because of the action that we are to approve tonight, and when these children grow to manhood, turn back the page to learn in what cause their fathers died, are they to find that it was about a quarrel as to the number of guns and the form and ceremony of a salute, and nothing else?[95]

As a comment on what was one of the silliest and least defensible actions in Wilson's political life, the words are not too harsh. But they were the sort of words that Wilson could not swallow. It was not long before Root was put into the gaol for 'contemptibles' where with brief absences on ticket-of-leave he thereafter remained.

Wilson by his Mexican policy injected some new ideas into international thought. They were high-minded ideas and the attempt to apply them failed so completely as to make Wilson look ridiculous. To be able to laugh gently and a little maliciously at the misfortunes of the very good is most refreshing for the not so good. But it does not mean that the very good are not the better of the two. Wilson proceeded from the basis that self-interest should not be the only motive of foreign policy: there was a morality which must govern the deeds of nations as of individuals. This was derived from Gladstone. Morley, Gladstone's biographer, wrote:

> At nearly every page of Mr Gladstone's active career the vital problem stares us in the face, of the correspondence between the rule of private morals and of public. Is the rule one and the same for individual and for state? From these early years onwards Mr Gladstone's whole language and the moods that it reproduces— his vivid denunciations, his sanguine expectations, his rolling epithets, his aspects and appeals and points of view—all take for granted that right and wrong depend on the same set of maxims in public life and private.[96]

Since Gladstone's time, if not before, English-speaking communities have in general accepted that there is a morality to which governments should conform in their dealings with other governments. They reject the Machiavellian doctrine that the pursuit of national interest is on a level above the law, though they compromise by allowing certain types of national interests, usually designated as 'vital interests', to justify actions which, if done by individuals, they would think wrong. But is international morality restricted in its operation to one government's dealings with another: or can it be used as a source of standards to which governments should conform in their dealings with their own subjects if they wish to be accepted without reserve as fit members of the society of nations? Different answers are likely to be given to this question not only by English-speaking communities as against European communities but also by liberal sentiment in English-speaking communities against conservative. Here again there is an English tendency to compromise, to accept as a general principle that the way a government treats its own subjects is its own affair while acknowledging that there may be circumstances so outrageous as to call for reproof, especially if the ill-treatment impinges on the convenience of the reproving government.

The society of nations is run in much the same manner as a primitive settlement of huts. If your neighbour is beating his wife, it is his own affair up to the point that her screams awaken your baby. Then you are entitled to intervene. And then—so at any rate advanced thinkers would say—you are not bound to concentrate upon the screams as the sole offence. Some observations upon the impropriety of wife-beating are then admissible: the conservative view would be that they should be restrained, but from the Gladstonian Liberal there would issue the 'vivid denunciations' and the 'rolling epithets'. Wilson, of course, would belong to the rolling epithet school. But he went to the limit or beyond in substance as well as in form. What he asserted in effect was that there was a *duty* upon you to stop your neighbour beating his wife, not merely a right contingent upon the awakening of the baby. Indeed, if you waited until then, you risked the charge of not being disinterested. So in the case of Mexico the standard practice of *de facto* recognition was repugnant to him. The question was not whether the government to be recognized was one that it was possible to deal with effectively nor even whether it was a lawful government, that is, constituted *de jure* as well as *de facto*: but whether it was a government that ought to be dealt with.

Non-recognition was not the limit of Wilson's Mexican policy. There was, as he saw it, a right and a duty not only to withhold recognition from a bad government but also to intervene actively to promote good government and in particular to ensure that the government represented the will of the people. This was the 'new order' that Wilson announced in his speech of June 1914[97] based upon the duty of a big country to teach a small one the right way of living and to do it without thought of gain for itself. So Wilson expressed it in the Fourth of July oration that followed.

My dream is that as the years go on and the world knows more and more of America, it will also drink at these fountains of youth and renewal; and it also will turn to America for those moral inspirations which lie at the basis of all freedom; that the world will never fear America unless it feels that it is engaged in some enterprise which is inconsistent with the rights of humanity; and that America will come into the full light of the day when all shall know that she puts human rights above all other rights and that her flag is the flag not only of America but of humanity. What other great people has devoted itself to this exalted ideal?[98]

What other ventures into international paternalism Wilson might have undertaken and where they would have led him no one can say. For the war in Europe diverted America's duty to counsel and inspire and the 'exalted ideal' was transposed into the ambition to restore peace. But anyone who read these utterances again after America had come into the war and victory had conferred on her an unchallengeable right of participation in the resettlement could have been left in doubt about what Wilson's objectives would be.

It is possible now to attempt an analysis of the Wilsonian political and diplomatic method.

The attempted analysis will be blown off the ground by an initial blast of incredulity unless it is moored to the fact that the second half of the nineteenth century and the beginning of the twentieth were for Western civilization a period of unparallelled optimism. The world was becoming a better place and there was no reason why it should not better itself indefinitely. All that it had to do was to progress. Reason produced enlightenment and enlightenment improvement; and these were the powers at work. Democracy ensured the beneficent use of power. Belief in the virtue of the democratic process was then at the flood. The great nations of the West were emerging from a long period in which power had been abused by the few and did not yet foresee the possibilities of exploitation when it was dispersed among the many. To be democratic was to be enlightened and rational and progressive: to be autocratic was to be obscurantist and reactionary. The nations of Europe were thought to be moving at varying speeds towards the ideal democracy which the United States of America had in her own opinion already attained. Had she no duty to share the wealth of her ideals? It was an age in which the upper classes were supposed to do good works to improve the lot of those less fortunate; in which the rich were taught not to feel happy unless they were doing something useful; in which earnestness, sacrifice, and charity were not only virtues but duties. When Wilson told Americans in his Fourth of July oration that they ought to go slumming—or, put more delicately, take up some international social work—he was only giving them the sort of advice that was then frequently given to the well-to-do with advantage both to themselves and others.

There was also an enthusiastic belief in the power of public opinion. The voice of the people was transmitted to the government not merely from time to time through the electoral machinery but also constantly through public opinion. Disapproval as so expressed was in a well-knit and responsive community through whose members it could speedily travel a force in itself. There can be no doubt that men like Wilson, able both to influence public opinion in the making and to give it what appeared to be authoritative expression, were correspondingly powerful. When moral standards were uniform and social conventions greatly respected, public opinion regulated behaviour without the need of any physical sanction. John Stuart Mill, Morley's master in philosophy and chief begetter of the permissive age, in his treatise on Liberty in 1859 was far more concerned with public opinion as the enemy of nonconformity than he was with the law.

There was therefore nothing curious in Wilson's belief that the essence of political leadership lay in the power to mobilize public opinion. What was unique was his belief that a politician needed no other skill; the man who knew how to blow the bugle need not bother about other weapons. For him the whole art of politics was the art of presenting an issue to the public clearly and forcefully and so that they could understand it aright. He excelled in that art and it is very human to appraise highly the weapon whose use we best understand. He could practise the art on groups and even on individuals, but only as if they were minor public meetings. The tune was not varied and neither were the instruments, though where the theatre was confined the full orchestra need not be employed; the brass could be left out and an adaptation for strings performed. But these are not the ordinary politician's skills. The canvassing of influential men and the exchanging of support, which form so large a part of political management, were things which Wilson did not understand and which, if they could not be dispensed with, he left to others. He did not essay the social touch: conversation across the lunch-table is not a medium well adapted to the exposition of eternal verities. To speak so that his voice was echoed by the voice of the people seemed to him to be the only skill a leader needed.

Was his a skill that would avail him just as well when he was calling to all nations as to one? Before we examine his belief that it was, we must look more closely at what was meant for him by the voice of the people. His most successful lecture in the nineties was on Democracy.[99] It was very fully thought out; in fact he delivered it thirteen times and it was spread over more than seven years. It expresses his belief in representative government, not in direct. The people were not 'our masters'. He valued public opinion not because it was the 'average judgment' or 'an unstudied or instinctive opinion' but because it was the opinion of 'a people, not self-directed, but directed by its boldest, most prevalent minds': as he put it in a lecture note, 'formed by the concert and prevalence of commanding minds, not commanding numbers'.[100] 'There is no apparent contradiction', he wrote, 'between democracy and the concentration of authority or command in the hands of one or a few.'[101]

> The freedom of the democratic nation consists not in governing itself: for that it cannot do: but in making undictated choice of the things it will accept and of the men it will follow.[102]

These themes remained in his mind and perhaps became even more influential when the ideas which he had evolved in the laboratory were tested by the involvement of his own personality and emotions. Every door must be open, he wrote in an address on Lincoln in 1916, 'for the ruler to emerge when he will and claim his leadership in the free life'.[103]

The sovereign power of the people was released through two channels. In addition to the great power of election they had the power of decisive moral judgement. The justification for that, Wilson thought, was that passions which would overcome the individual's sense of right would not overbear the people's.[104] Though he never quite said so in terms, he came near to the sentiment that *vox populi* was *vox Dei*. After all American ideals were for him undoubtedly right and these were American people applying American ideals. In his Fourth of July oration in 1914 he said:

If I did not believe that the moral judgment would be the last judgment, the final judgment in the minds of men as well as at the tribunal of God, I could not believe in popular government.[105]

After his rejection and not long before he died he said:

In spite of all that has happened, I have not lost one iota of my great faith in the people. They act too quickly or too slowly, but you can depend upon them ultimately; you can depend upon their search for the truth and for what is right.[106]

This led to an idiosyncrasy. He also was an American impregnated with American ideals. Could *he* be wrong? On practical matters possibly. But on questions of faith and morals, as for him most questions were, surely not if he listened to the voice of the people. Of course on a mundane level he listened to reports on popular attitudes; and he believed, quite erroneously, that he had rubbed shoulders with all sorts and conditions of people.[107] But he talked also in a general way of refreshing at fountains,[108] drinking at sources, and so on, which, put less allegorically, doubtless means that he thought his mind tuned in to the popular mind. He had thought so even in his academic days. In the passage in his journal in which he conceded that he was not an original thinker, he set himself

a task not of origination, but of interpretation. Interpret the age: i.e. interpret myself. Account for the creed I hold in politics. Institutions have their rootage in the common thought and only those who share the common thought can rightly interpret them. . . . Why may not the present age write, *through* me, its political *autobiography*?[109]

What he had then felt instinctively was seemingly confirmed by the evidence of his political success. The extraordinary way in which, beginning in New Jersey only three years before, he, a novice, had obtained so speedily and largely popular approval for himself and his measures may well have persuaded him that he knew intuitively what the people wanted. After all, what the people wanted was what was morally right and that was what he wanted too. So that when he talked of 'going to the country' or appealing to the people, he was not thinking of recourse to a tribunal where the issue was uncertain. He simply wanted to silence doubts by obtaining an endorsement in solemn form.

Thus it would mean to him a great deal that in international affairs he could feel that his voice was that of the American people; and that since the American people could decide better than any other between right and wrong, he could speak almost *ex cathedra*. He did not find it difficult to persuade himself that he could influence public opinion in other countries as he did in America. 'This is an age', he said in October 1914, 'in which the principles of men who utter public opinion dominate the world.'[110] And again: 'The opinion of the world is the mistress of the world.'[111]

To be sure, he was often talking to countries such as Mexico where popular opinion was hardly allowed expression, let alone admitted to any say in policy. As to that, he assumed that the Mexican people were receptive and were only waiting for someone to order a free election.

They say the Mexicans are not fitted for self-government; to this I reply that, when properly directed, there is no people not fitted for self-government.[112]

The idea that there was a world public opinion which even autocracies would not defy was not in 1914 peculiar. Without some such belief all the Hague Conventions that proliferated into international law at the beginning of the century could hardly have been taken seriously. In Britain even the most hard-headed statesmen of the old order believed so firmly that Germany would not dare to torpedo a peaceful merchantman that they would not have it discussed as practical politics.* No doubt Wilson's belief was more profound than most and, like all the rest of his beliefs, exceptionally difficult, if not impossible, to dislodge. Anyway, since he had never studied international statecraft and had not in his formative years foreseen for himself a role in international politics, he had not at his command any method other than the one which he believed would work in American affairs, that is, to seek what is right and pursue it to the uttermost. But when all is said on the subject that can be, he had no rational ground for thinking his methods in Mexico likely to be any more successful in other parts of the world. Persistence in them must have been primarily a matter of faith in the essential goodness of mankind and in the wonders that it could be made to work. Certainly he did persist. Implicitly if not in terms he put over and over again the question he had put to Mexico of how she thought she would stand in the opinion of the civilized world if she did not, etc. All his personal communications to other governments on the affairs of the world were

---

* See p. 191 below.

written for reading by the world. He continued to believe in the efficacy of 'building fires back of governments'. He acted on the presumption of a world opinion as effective as if the world were at one.

The pattern of Wilson's mind was thus clearly revealed to the world some years before he became its chief arbiter. There was nothing left to be learnt about his method except the fact that it was quite inflexible and was to be repeated almost with exactitude in the issues that arose out of the European war. There were notes and protests and measures short of war; exhortations and pronouncements of principle. Wilson knew of course that the ultimate sanction was the use of force. He pointed towards it, when he had to, with a wave of non-committal circumlocutions. The employment of such means as might be necessary to secure the result: this was the phraseology used in his Note of 7 November 1913* and it was to be frequently repeated. He was like a physician who detests surgery and has such faith in the treatment he prescribes that he can go on telling the patient that the operation will not be necessary almost up to the point when he is being wheeled off to the theatre. In the same way Wilson had difficulty in bringing himself to believe that force would ever really be needed, that words would not be enough, that the proclamation and constant repetition of true principles would not in the end, and after perhaps much watchful waiting, win recognition of what was right. 'The steady pressure of moral force', he called it.[113] His strategy was limited to the frontal attack and the war of attrition which were to be so much criticized when practised by Allied generalship on the western front. When that failed his personal resources were at an end. He understood, no one better, the language of exposition, but not the language of manœuvre.

* See p. 119 above.

PART TWO

AMERICAN NEUTRALITY
1914–1917

V

NEUTRALITY IN THOUGHT

Armageddon — international morality — the invasion of Belgium — neutrality: the American attitude — Wilson's neutrality and its objectives — the Foreign Ministers: Bryan and Grey — the ambassadors: Page, Gerard, Bernstorff, and Spring Rice

IN 1914 everyone thought that war would come sometime but no one expected it when it came. From the beginning of the century Europe had been divided into two armed camps. On the one side was the Triple Alliance, the empires of Germany and Austria and the kingdom of Italy; when the hour came, Italy remained neutral and later was bribed over to the other side. France, struck down by the young Germany in 1870 and knowing that she was too weak to fight her again single-handed, had allied herself with the Russian Empire. Britain, alarmed by Germany's increasing navy and pursuing her traditional policy of maintaining the balance of power on the Continent by siding against the strongest nation, had bound herself loosely to France by the Entente Cordiale. There had been war scares in 1908 and 1912, but in July of 1914 even after the murder by a Serbian assassin of the Austrian Archduke Franz Ferdinand, heir to the Imperial Throne, all seemed calm. 'Berlin is as quiet as the grave', the American ambassador wrote on 7 July. On 23 July Lloyd George, the Chancellor of the Exchequer, told the House of Commons that British relations with Germany were better than they had been for years.

Ten days later most of Europe was at war. Austria, rightly indignant at the Archduke's murder, thought the time had come to teach the Serbs a lesson. She sent a crushing ultimatum which Russia thought went too far. Germany, who had given her ally Austria at the very least too free a hand with the terms of the ultimatum, would not leave her unsupported. France refused to desert her ally Russia. By 2 August all these great powers were belligerent.

Britain hesitated for a few days. Though not bound by the Entente to go to the help of France, it was the understanding that she should not remain indifferent and as a matter of policy she would not wish to see a German triumph. But policy was not enough and almost to the last the Cabinet was divided. The German plan to destroy France had as a military requirement the passage through Belgium whose neutrality in the event of a European war had been guaranteed by the great powers including Germany herself, France, and Britain. Belgium resisted and the German invasion roused the British nation. The treaty of guarantee bound Britain to go to her aid if she was attacked and on 4 August Great Britain declared war.

Switzerland of course kept neutral and so did Holland. So did Spain at the extremity of Europe; and Denmark, Norway, and Sweden at the other end. The rest of the Continent was engulfed into the war. In October 1914 Turkey with justifiable suspicion of Russian intentions against her joined the Central Powers, that is, Germany and Austria. Portugal adhered to her ancient alliance with England. Italy, Bulgaria, and Roumania were out for booty. In 1915 Bulgaria cast her lot with the Central Powers; Italy in 1915 and Roumania in 1916 went with the Allies, as Britain, France, and Russia, the powers of the Entente, called themselves. By the end of 1915 Greece also was involved. These were all the sovereignties of Europe at that time. Hungary was then united with Austria and their empire included what is now Czechoslovakia and, except for Serbia, what is now Yugoslavia. Poland was then partitioned between her imperial neighbours and the whole of Ireland was an integral part of the British Isles.

Great Britain brought with her into the war her dominions, colonies, and protectorates which were spread all over the globe. Canada, Australia, New Zealand, South Africa, India, and what are now Pakistan and Bangladesh were all in the fight. So was almost the whole of the African Continent since there was not much of it unattached to a European power at war. Japan in the expectation of pickings from the German possessions in the Far East did not hesitate to honour her alliance with Britain. Of all the great powers in the world only the United States, who a century before had decreed her own exclusion from the entanglements of Europe, remained aloof.

At the beginning of the twentieth century hardly anyone was deeply distressed by the idea of war. Nevertheless, the sudden precipitation of so many nations into what was called the Great War created a shock, strongly accentuated by the brutality with which the first blow was struck. The sixty years that had passed since the close of the Crimean War had seen a remarkable blossoming of international law and detailed developments in the rules for the waging of war. We are inclined today to regard national wars as lawless and consequently to see something absurd about the laws of war. But international morality did not before the twentieth century condemn war. It accepted it as one of the facts of life and as our ancestors accepted trial by battle. Pious men like Oliver Cromwell believed that victory proved that God was on their side. But to be morally acceptable the war must be a just war, that is, it must be waged for a just cause and fought fairly and humanely. On this basis the good man could fight and thereby win increase of virtue.

Whether or not the end was just was a matter that had to be left to conscience. Had there been a tribunal to determine the justice of the cause there would have been no need to resort to war. So international law could regulate only the mode of fighting and for this purpose there were established two great principles. The first was that the fighting must be confined to the combatants, meaning thereby not only the combatant nations but those men whom those nations put forward to fight. Neutral nations and civilians in the warring nations were exempt from attack provided they kept clear of the fight. The second principle outlawed cruelty (such as the killing of prisoners or of the wounded) which either played no part in overcoming the resistance of the enemy or inflicted suffering on the individual disproportionate to the advantage gained. These were the objects of the laws of war and of neutrality which were codified in the Declaration of Paris 1856, in the numerous conventions made at The Hague in the first decade of the twentieth century, and in the Declaration of London in 1909.

It can be argued that if a war is being fought for a just end, defeat will result in injustice; and that it is better that the means should be foul than that the end should be unjust, that is, that the end justifies the means. There were before 1914 a number of German writers who maintained that modes of warfare must be governed by 'necessity'. Since every nation can claim to be the sole judge of what is necessary in order that it should achieve victory, this means in truth the negation of law, but it sounds more respectable to say that principle must be modified to accommodate necessity than to say that it must be destroyed.

Machiavelli is mercilessly clear. 'Where the very safety of the country depends upon the resolution to be taken, no consideration of justice or injustice, humanity or cruelty, nor of glory or of shame, should be allowed to prevail.' Germany did not go as far as that. She never claimed that necessity should overrule the second of the two great principles, the prevention of cruelty to individuals: no civilized nation yet has. She claimed only that in her own interests she could disregard the safety of non-combatants and override the rights of neutrals. Although her claim was denounced at the time the twentieth century has admitted it. The history of international law in the twentieth century has been and will be the history of the withering away of neutrality. Civilization no longer demands that combatants and non-combatants be distinguished. Both may be slaughtered; and neutrals are only non-combatant nations. Germany can take the credit for perceiving that modern methods of waging war would not permit discrimination. In this respect her practitioners were in advance of her theorists. With the bombardment of the civil population of Strasbourg and Paris in 1870 they took the first steps on the path which led to Hiroshima and beyond. Before the end of the Great War all the warring nations—with Germany always in the lead—had made great strides forward in the new warfare.

In 1914, however, not even Germany dared do more than plead 'necessity' as dispensing from rules still generally accepted. On the plea of necessity she did what she had long planned to do in a war with enemies on two fronts. In such a situation she believed it essential to her safety that she should smash the enemy on the western front before turning her main force east. The belief was wrong as events turned out, for she failed to smash France with her initial blow and did not lose the war because of that. But her belief made it imperative, so she thought, for her to take the cheapest and easiest way to victory in the west; and it lay across Belgium. Although by the treaty of 1839 the independence and permanent neutrality of Belgium had been guaranteed by the five powers of whom Prussia was one, the treaty must yield to 'necessity'.

Because the rulers of Germany had no serious belief in international law, it did not occur to them that it could have value for others. It did not strike them that the violation of Belgium would in the end present them with a bill which they could not meet, just as later they did not realize the full extent of the price they would have to pay for their illegal use of the submarine. Yet if Britain had not joined in the fight against her in 1914, Germany would probably have won the war; and if the United States had not joined in 1917, she would not have lost it. There was undoubtedly a powerful body of opinion in Britain which thought that Germany would have to be fought anyway; and there was a substantial body in the United States which thought the same in 1917. But both were democracies whose peoples had a say in matters of war and peace and neither could have been brought in for purely strategic reasons. It was the invasion of Belgium that united Britain and which was both the substantial and the formal cause of her entry into the war. Her conditional ultimatum demanded withdrawal from Belgium and nothing else. Germany was in the end defeated by the forces behind international morality. Her grand mistake of strategy was not in the field of military operations but in that of morality whose strength she knew not how to measure.

Her plain belief that international morality was a negligible force and her incredulity that anybody could possibly set any store by it made the thing appear much worse than it need have done. Defiant in a cloak of righteousness she dinned her misdeeds into every ear and stamped her convictions into every detail of the subjugation of Belgium. The German Chancellor's blood boiled at 'this hypocritical harping on Belgium'.[2] Was England, he asked the British ambassador, going to stab a kindred nation in the back when she was fighting for her life against two assailants 'just for a scrap of paper'? To this sort of mentality resistance by Belgians appeared as needless, almost provocative, folly. 'Our advance in Belgium certainly is brutal', the German Chief of Staff wrote to the Austrian on 5 August 1914, 'but for us it is a matter of life and death and whoever stands in our way must take the consequences. . . . I am sorry that blood should flow but Belgium has rudely rebuffed all our most far-reaching assurances.'[3]

The spectacle of the German Empire crashing through a weak and tiny nation was repulsive enough. She made it quite nauseating when with sanctimonious reliance upon the letter of international law German generals shot in cold blood civilians who were alleged to have fired on their troops or obstructed their advance. The reprisals she took, shooting hostages and burning towns and villages, culminated in the sack of Louvain which began on 25 August and lasted for six days. A sudden Belgian attack flung the Germans back in disorder upon Louvain. In the confusion German soldiers were shot in the town. Belgium said that they had fired on each other in the dark; Germany said that they had been fired on by Belgian civilians, alternatively that civilians had fired from rooftops as signals to the Belgian army. Following a perfidious attack by Belgian civilians, the Wilhelmstrasse announced to the world, Louvain was punished by destruction. The heart of the city was given to the flames. The fourteenth-century Clothworkers Hall and the superb library with its collection of 650 medieval manuscripts were utterly consumed. 'The entire responsibility for these events', Germany proclaimed, 'rests with the Belgian Government.'[4]

This then was how Germany began the war in August 1914. The stench of it is not yet dissipated by time nor put out of memory by the dreadful deeds of Hitler.

The impact of these events was as strong in the United States as in the rest of the civilized world. They were made known to her by Brand Whitlock, her ambassador in Brussels, and by a team of brilliant newspaper correspondents. Wilson was among those deeply moved though he did not say so in public. He expressed to House his indignation at the 'scrap of paper' comment[5] and he felt strongly the destruction of Louvain. He spoke to the French ambassador with 'an emotion that he did not attempt to hide'[6] and left M. Jusserand feeling that he had a real sympathy for France. Spring Rice, the British ambassador, reported to Grey, the Foreign Secretary, on a conversation in September 1914:

> He is a great student of Wordsworth and when I alluded to the sonnets at the time of the great war, especially 'It is not to be thought of that the flood' and 'We must be free or die who speak the tongue'—he said he knew them by heart, and had them in his mind all the time. I said, 'You and Grey are fed on the same food and I think you understand'. There were tears in his eyes, and I am sure we can, at the right moment, depend on an understanding heart here.[7]

It was one of the rare moments when president and ambassador were *en rapport*. But in the Wilsonian constitution the heart was not recognized as a chamber with executive power. When on the outbreak of the war the President proclaimed America's neutrality, he called for it 'in fact as well as in name':[8] the United States must be 'impartial in thought as well as in action'. Except for these one or two occasions in the beginning, he was even in private (unless he was talking with his 'second personality' Colonel House) himself the most rigorous observant of his precept. In his memoirs Count von Bernstorff, the German ambassador in Washington, wrote:

> No unneutral remark of Mr. Wilson, even in private, has ever reached my ears. He always resisted the pressure of the Entente party in spite of the fact that he was almost entirely surrounded by anti-Germans.[9]

International lawyers define neutrality as the attitude of impartiality adopted by third states towards belligerents. But such impartiality was not—outside the textbooks, at any rate—generally held to exclude sympathy for one side or the other: the idea of neutrality in thought was a novel one. Britons in particular were disturbed by Wilson's coldness. They were, they conceived, fighting the evil things which America too detested—military despotism, the breaking of treaties and the bullying of smaller nations. Did neutrality require Americans to control their thoughts about this? But British critics, when objecting to what Wilson called 'the cooler assessment of the elements engaged', forgot that the Allied cause had to be judged as a whole and that the aspirations of their Allies were not all as noble as they thought their own. Moreover, in their own motives they tended to ignore the mundane. Even House, who before the end of 1915 had become active for intervention, sometimes got impatient at what he called the cant and hypocrisy indulged in by the British over Belgium. If the French army had marched through Belgium, he once asked, would Britain have been found on Germany's side?[10]

Yet undoubtedly there was a moral issue and the complete disregard of it by a man who was so fond of moralizing was a constant source of bewilderment to the British. They could never make out what Wilson was about or solve the puzzle behind 'his deportment of studious unpleasantness to both sides', as Lloyd George put it after the war.[11] They felt that he must be speaking for the record. But he was not. In the first place, his thoughts soon became quite impartial about the underlying causes of the war, though he could not bring himself entirely to overlook Germany's methods of conducting it. In the second place, impartiality was not for him a negative based on indifference but a positive policy which would lead to great and noble things.

Wilson's personal attitude must be considered against the background of the American attitude to the war. There was in 1914 no sentiment at all for intervention. All Americans of both parties, even Theodore Roosevelt, Senator Lodge, and their friends who later became ardent advocates of intervention, approved the proclamation of neutrality. Neutrality in action seemed to be assured. Neutrality in thought was secured in the nation partly by indifference and partly by a clash of sympathies. On the one side there were those who were attached to Britain or France or distressed by the German treatment of Belgium. On the other side there were over 8,000,000 German-Americans and over 4,500,000 Irish-Americans for whom England could do no right: there were over 4,000,000 Jews, many of whom were strongly anti-Russian: there were 2,000,000 Swedish-Americans who were historically anti-Russian and friendly to Germany. In the middle there were those who did not care enough to be embroiled or who, if they were disposed to care, did not see the war as America's business. Walter Lippmann, recording the unpreparedness of a young American for the age he was destined to live in, relates how he spent most of July in the English Lakes at the feet of Bernard Shaw and the Webbs, then in the last week crossed the Channel to Belgium, loitered in Brussels and, taking a ticket to Germany, was surprised to find himself stopped at the railway station. 'For two years thereafter', he says, 'I struggled with misgiving and reluctance to grasp our interest in the war.'[12]

The belligerents on both sides set to work to propagate their cause. In this struggle the Allies had every advantage and were in the long run much more successful. But the Germans were first in the field. Dr. Dernburg, a former minister, was at once dispatched to New York to set up an information office. There were plenty of articulate German-Americans such as Professor Munsterberg of Harvard to help him; and also pro-German American journalists such as William Bayard Hale, the man who had written Wilson's campaign biography. As the shock of the Belgian invasion wore off the case for the Central Powers began to make headway. It was strong enough to obtain to a wide extent suspension of judgement about the causes of the war. Czarist Russia was cast as the villain, a role which in American eyes she was well fitted to play: Servia had put herself quite in the wrong: Austria's natural desire to exact condign punishment was, it was said, suitably moderated by Germany: it was Russia who turned a manageable affair into a world war, thereby creating a situation not unwelcome to France who wanted revenge for 1870 and the recovery of Alsace-Lorraine. In truth, if Germany had not invaded Belgium, there would have been, superficially at least, little to choose between the belligerents. There would have been a political crisis in Britain and a fierce battle between those who favoured war and those who favoured neutrality. If the former had won, Britain would have gone to war for the simple reason that in her own interests she was not willing to see France defeated a second time and there would have been no moral issue for the world to take notice of. Of course Germany did invade Belgium but even that could be explained. In the debate in the Reichstag which took place before he made his agitated reference to a scrap of paper, the German Chancellor had attempted a more statesmanlike justification.

Gentlemen, we are in a state of necessity, and necessity knows no law. Our troops have occupied Luxembourg and perhaps are already on Belgian soil. That is contrary to international law. The wrong we thus commit we will endeavour to repair directly our military aim is achieved.[13]

This utterance at the time annoyed most of the Chancellor's compatriots (a gallant few protested against the invasion) who felt that no apology was needed. But it gave reassurance to Germany's friends abroad and enabled them to argue that even on this point judgement ought to await further elucidation of the circumstances in which Germany had acted.

All this made its impression on Wilson. At first he had condemned Germany even more strongly, House noted on 30 August 1914, than the Colonel himself.[14] Then with time for reflection and animated by the prospect of becoming the good shepherd who when the time was ripe would descend uncommitted into the arena and lead the foolish nations back into the ways of peace, his mind soon moved easily on the track of complete neutrality of thought. In October 1914, discussing the war with two family friends, 'he so obviously felt', one of them said, 'that all the wrong was not on one side'.[15] In December 1914 he gave an off-the-record interview to a reporter from the *New York Times*. 'It will be found before long', he said, 'that Germany is not alone responsible for the war, and that some other

15 November 1913. Wilson with his Private Secretary, Joseph P. Tumulty

Senator Elihu Root

Senator William J. Stone, Chairman of Foreign Relations Committee 1914-18

William Howard Taft, Wilson's predecessor as President

Senator Henry Cabot Lodge

nations will have to bear a portion of the blame in our eyes.'[16] Not even for the invasion of Belgium should she be finally judged. He did not want to see an outright victory for either side. Evidently he hoped that the 'trial at arms' might be found futile and a decision reached by the forces of reason. If the war had to end in a dictated peace, he had no very pronounced views about which side he would like to see victorious. Victory by the Central Powers would not be 'the ideal solution': victory by the Allies would not 'hurt greatly the interests of the United States': Britain was 'safe' because 'satiated'.

This was perhaps an extreme statement of disinterest. From time to time he would oscillate; and when he did, which was usually when he was talking to House, it was towards the Entente. On 25 November 1914 House mentioned the possibility of Italy and Roumania joining the Allies.[17] Wilson expressed pleasure at this, House recorded, and hoped that the two countries would not delay too long. This was a diary entry and one might wonder whether House made too much of the remark. But one finds on 9 February 1915 the Colonel reporting in the same sense on the discussions he was then having with Grey and earning no rebuke for unneutrality of thought. He had been told by Grey frankly, House wrote, 'the position the Allies were in, their difficulties, their resources, and their expectations. That part of it is not as encouraging as I had hoped, particularly in regard to Italy and Roumania.'[18]

Whatever he might say at this time or that, what kept Wilson on an even keel was his thought about the part which his country and himself could play in bringing peace out of war. He did not distinguish between his country and himself for he always believed that the American people thought as he did. 'Some of their passions', he said in his annual message to Congress on 8 December 1914, 'are in my own heart.'[19]

From the very first he had spoken of his hopes. He said to reporters on 3 August 1914:

I want to have the pride of feeling that America, if nobody else, has her self-possession and stands ready with calmness of thought and steadiness of purpose to help the rest of the world.[20]

He returned to the theme in his message to Congress. The character and reputation which America had as the champions of peace and of concord, he said, 'may presently, in God's providence, bring us an opportunity such as has seldom been vouchsafed any nation, the opportunity to counsel and obtain peace in the world and reconciliation and a healing settlement'.[21] In this speech he gave his first public indication of his indifference to the moral issue when he referred to the war as 'one with which we have nothing to do, whose causes cannot touch us'. Again in a speech in January 1915 he said:

Do you not think it likely that the world will sometime turn to America and say, 'you were right and we were wrong. You kept your head when we lost ours . . . now, in your self-possession, in your coolness, in your strength, may we not turn to you for counsel and assistance?' May we not look forward to the time when we shall be called blessed among the nations because we succoured the nations of the world in their time of distress and dismay? I for one pray God that that solemn hour may come . . . I know the high principle with which the American people will respond to the call of the world for this service, and I thank God that those who believe in America, who try to serve her people, are likely to be also what America herself from the first intended to be—the servant of mankind.[22]

The President's objectives were therefore to preserve neutrality and to be ready to mediate. At first the two were kept separate. Neutrality was preserved through the ordinary machinery of the State Department; mediation was first conceived by Wilson as a passive operation in which he awaited a summons to give counsel and assistance. The two began to interact when neutrality became so difficult to practise that America found herself with a direct interest in ending the war by mediation. Then, following the initiative of House and in accordance with his methods, mediation began beneath the surface. It rose above the surface in 1916 when Wilson took matters into his own hands.

American diplomacy in pursuit of both objectives was conducted with Britain on the one hand and with Germany on the other. The preservation of neutrality was threatened only by naval warfare and Britain and Germany were the two naval powers. The secret diplomacy in pursuit of mediation was likewise conducted between Germany and Britain because Germany was indisputably the leader of the Central Powers and Britain the one amongst the Allies with whom it was easiest for America to talk confidentially.

On the American side Wilson was always in direct command. Bryan was no diplomatist either above or below the surface. He was made Secretary of State because his services to the party gave him the right to what was regarded politically as the top job after the presidency and he could not see that he was unfitted for it. Indeed, the only one of his disqualifications for the office which occurred to him when he was being appointed as 'possibly an insurmountable objection' was 'the exclusion of intoxicating liquors from our table'.[23] He had no regard for the dignity of the office and made it look ridiculous by combining its duties with Chautauqua lecturing. Abroad he was regarded as a figure of fun and House on his visits to foreign capitals gave up the attempt to defend or explain him. Even in domestic affairs, about which he might claim to know something, his *naïveté* was extreme. 'Any man with real goodness of heart', he is quoted as saying, 'could write a good currency law.'[24] He was happily ignorant of everything outside the United States and had no wish to be enlightened. Bryce wrote of him that he was 'unable to *think* in the sense that you and I would use that word'.[25]

Bryan had not sought his position because he wanted place and pomp— that would be quite foreign to his character—nor even because it was the natural place for the second-in-command, but because he thought of himself as an apostle of peace. He was sure that war could be abolished if someone like himself set about the task. Those in the old world who looked upon Wilson as a visionary might have reflected that by comparison with Bryan—and there were many Americans who thought like Bryan—he was hard-headed. Bryan's pet project, which Wilson encouraged and Senator Stone enthusiastically helped, was a forerunner of the idea elaborated in the League of Nations, a set of 'cooling off' treaties, whereby the signatories bound themselves not to go to war until a specified period had elapsed after a dispute had broken out. It was a gallant attempt to bring out a new age. Bryan was very proud of his achievement in this field which he thought would give him a place in world history. Most of the European nations regarded the proposal as harmless and Bryan was busy collecting signatures from them even after the war had broken out. Germany was one of the few who refused on the ground that if she signed with the United States she would be asked to sign by some European nation and thus would throw away her advantage of being the readiest of nations for an immediate and decisive blow in war. Bryan made great efforts to bring Germany in, pointing out on 17 August 1914 that the treaty would cover any disputes that might arise between the United States and European governments during the war. But Germany, although she was by then at war with all the European nations she wanted to fight and could hardly hope to strike an immediate and decisive blow at the United States, persisted in her refusal and so lost a cooling-off period of nine months that would have come in handy in 1917.

Bryan was not without influence. Wilson respected his opinions as one respects the opinions of a man who has gone further along the path of virtue than one can go oneself. And in the end the methods of peacemaking which Bryan advised and which Wilson was led by House to reject were those which he came to adopt. Yet Bryan's influence was that of an outsider rather than that of the head of the diplomatic service. In the formal exchanges Wilson looked for help to Lansing, who as Counselor was second in command at the State Department (there were no under-secretaries in those days) a lawyer through and through; he used him, as it were, as the head of his legal department. Unofficially he relied upon Colonel House whom he used as his minister for foreign affairs.

In Britain the Foreign Secretary, Sir Edward Grey, conducted foreign affairs in fact as well as in name. The Cabinet gave him a free hand; Asquith, the Prime Minister, was one of his oldest friends and anyway not the man to subject his colleagues to supervision.

The Foreign Secretary had a striking appearance with his 'well-cut, hawk-like visage' (the words are Asquith's)[26] and his athletic build. He played real tennis and was amateur champion in 1896. But primarily he was an out-of-doors man; fishing was his sport and he was a great walker. He was a politician of a type then not uncommon in England but rare elsewhere because the product of a well-settled order. He came of a class that was born to govern. His great-great-grandfather fought in George III's war against Washington less unsuccessfully than most and was given an earldom; the second Earl Grey was the Prime Minister of the Reform Bill; Edward Grey's grandfather, the man who influenced his childhood most, was Home Secretary in Victoria's reign. Edward went to Winchester and then to Balliol and then straight into political life. In 1885 at twenty-three he was the youngest member of Parliament. The cast of his mind as well as his ancestry took him into the Liberal party. He was interested in social questions and not initially in foreign affairs: he was essentially an Englishman with a love of England, never in his life went abroad for pleasure, and after he was Foreign Secretary only twice on duty. But parliamentary under-secretaryships are not always allotted according to qualifications. When the Liberals came to power and Gladstone, for no known reason except that his son had just declined it, offered the one at the Foreign Office to Grey, Grey accepted it with surprise. He made a very good job of it. Rosebery, his former chief and now Prime Minister, wrote in 1895: 'He is one of the most important members of the Govt. . . . persona gratissima to the H. of C., popular, admired and respected.'[27]

The House of Lords was considered in those days to be the proper forum for the discussion of foreign affairs: no Foreign Secretary had been in the Commons since 1868. But apart from the minor blemish of his commoner status, Grey was the obvious candidate for the Foreign Secretaryship after the great Liberal victory of 1905. He entered the office at the age of forty-three and held it for exactly eleven years from 1905 to 1916 beginning and ending on Monday, 5 December, the longest continuous period in English history. In foreign affairs he was always the Liberal Imperialist and on the right of his party. But on other issues—votes for women, social insurance, trade unionism and so on—he was well to the left. This combination resulted in his keeping the respect of the whole party. He was a clear, persuasive, and sincere speaker, but not a powerful orator in an age when oratory wielded power. A colleague applied to him Emerson's dictum on Chatham: 'those who listened to him felt that there was something finer in the man than anything which he said.'[28] His policies might be criticized but the man himself until the war came got little but praise from his contemporaries. Prudent suavity, breadth of judgement, stainless honour, sound, temperate, and strong—these were the sort of epithets continually used about him.

His grandfather left him a baronetcy and a sufficient income for a life of leisure. Leisure for him meant time at his beloved Fallodon, the family home in Northumberland; 'leisure for books', he wrote, 'endless opportunities for observing the natural life of birds and beasts, the beauty of trees, the delights of a garden, the ever-varying and ever-recurring seasons, leisure for sport and exercise'.[29] Of all his books he liked best his Wordsworth and this gave him a link with Wilson and with Ambassador Page. He thought more deeply about the poetry than either of them; he delivered a careful disquisition on *The Prelude* in his presidential address to the English-Speaking Association in 1923. But the thought did not lead him to stray from home even as far as the Lakes. For weekends he had a cottage in Hampshire ('Thank goodness,' he wrote to a friend, 'with all their inventions, anyone who wishes to reach this cottage on wheels can still do it only in a wheelbarrow')[30] where he fished the Itchen and watched birds. When he could get away for longer he went always to Fallodon. All this he contrasted in his book *Fly Fishing*, published in 1899, with the hot June days he was forced to spend in London: 'the aggressive stiffness of the buildings, the brutal hardness of the pavement, the smell of the streets festering in the sun, the glare of the light all day striking upon hard substances, and the stuffiness of the heat from which there is no relief at night—for no coolness comes with the evening air.'[31]

Being free to choose between leisure and service to the State, he chose service. He knew with his intellect, he wrote to Haldane in 1890, that a life of pleasure gave no satisfaction, 'but I dare neither look nor listen for fear I should not be able to resist'.[32] Still he would not completely commit himself. When his first term of office ended in 1895, he declined the Prime Minister's unusual offer to an under-secretary of a privy councillorship, because it would be regarded, he wrote, 'as an undoubted pledge and earnest of future public work'.[33] His willingness to cut loose at any moment was genuine as well as frequently proclaimed, but could always be curbed by an appeal to duty.

Duty drives from behind and not from within. Grey had no inner propulsion as Wilson had or Lloyd George, no fire that raged, no wish for immortality, no talent that he dared not bury. He gave to history without seeking from history anything in return: such men contribute to history but they do not make it. He was not a weak man, but steadiness not vigour was his hallmark. A sexless marriage to a handsome, difficult, and frigid woman did not damage him. Her death only two months after he took office as Secretary of State struck him grievously. Life and work, his biographer has written, 'degenerated into a routine without expectation'.[34] He remained a widower until 1922, sustained by what he called 'an unusual gift of solitude, the power to enjoy being alone'.[35] For his age—he was fifty-two in 1914—he was remarkably fit. But in that year he found that he could not see the ball quite accurately when playing squash nor could he identify with his usual ease the stars in their constellations. In May 1914 his oculist told him that he was slowly but incurably going blind. He shouldered this burden as he went towards his encounter with his most testing time. Office clung to him, not he to office.

Grey had proclaimed just before he took office, and he always maintained thereafter, that friendship with the United States was a cardinal feature of British policy.

Ambassador Page in London has been mentioned as one of Wilson's early friends and an ardent admirer. He was a good scholar, a brilliant journalist, and a most attractive man, original, alert, positive, outspoken. Herbert Hoover, the future President, wrote of him that he was 'one of those blossoms of American life which justify our civilization'.[36] Page wrote superb letters: the volumes published in 1922 were best sellers. Wilson loved getting them and often read them to his family. But Page was no diplomat. It was not England who suffered in consequence but Wilson. Page could be stiff enough when he had to deal with the high-handedness of the British Admiralty and vigorous enough in pressing individual claims. But he so detested the evil in Germany that he was useless as an instrument of moral neutrality. The war was hardly a month old when he was telling Grey about an American general, 'very careful both in speech and observation', who was in Germany when the war broke out and had reached the conclusion on evidence undetailed that 'there was no conceivable barbarity of which the Germans were not capable in this war. It was quite probable that they would drop bombs on London.'[37] Page saw the Germans always as bullies and barbarians. As for the British, he said simply to House in September 1914: 'I thank Heaven I'm of their race and blood.'[38]

Before the war the President and his ambassador got on famously. In July 1914 Wilson described him as

an indispensable man in the right management of our foreign relations . . . speaks my mind and my point of view to the ministers over there as I am sure no one else could speak them.[39]

But the war began to drive their views apart. As early as October 1914 Wilson was writing to House that he was a little disturbed by Page's recent messages; he hoped that he would not get into an unsympathetic attitude and 'forget the temper of the folks at home'.[40] At the same time he wrote a long letter to Page—'not a sermon' but 'a message of friendship and sympathy'— hinting delicately at the ambassadorial duty to 'present and emphasize our neutral point of view'.[41] Neither this tender rebuke nor a much stronger one[42] that he caused House to send in December 1914 had the slightest effect. 'I'm immensely proud', Page wrote to an American friend in May 1916, 'to be of what service I can to these heroic people.'[43]

Page was quickly moved to sentiment and credulous of anything that awakened it. He poured out his heart to Wilson in his letters: 'this volcanic outburst of fundamental emotions' he called a long letter he wrote in January 1915.[44] He got very angry with the State Department. Bryan he regarded as a crank; and Lansing as a 'law-book precedent man . . . if England were blotted out, the world would be the same to him . . . What a shame to have this manikin in that place now!'[45] His exasperation brought Page into alliance with the British Foreign Office. On one occasion he read out to Grey the communication from the State Department which he had been instructed to deliver, said he disagreed with it, and sat down to help write the answer. It is small wonder that Grey referred in his memoirs to the 'comfort, support, and encouragement that his presence was to the Secretary of Foreign Affairs in London'.[46] Page loved the British though their pomp and circumstance irritated him at times: the British loved Page without reservation. When he died they put up a tablet, unveiled by Grey, in Westminster Abbey to 'the friend of Britain in her direst need'. This ought not to happen to an ambassador.

Gerard, the American ambassador in Berlin, was a Tammany politician whose place had been given to him for party services including a handsome subscription to the 1912 campaign. Wilson had thought first of Henry B. Fine,[47] Dean of the Faculty at Princeton, who had been one of his leading supporters there. He pictured Fine as languishing in the reign of Hibben; and since there would be no diplomatic problems with Germany that could not be left to subordinates (as Mrs. Wilson put it to Mrs. Fine), it would be a great opportunity both to escape Hibben and to browse around German universities. But Fine refused. He was in fact getting on very well with Hibben who had revealed himself as a skilled healer of wounds.

House thought well of Gerard but Wilson did not care for him much. He was the sort of bustling and pushful man who was not at his best on paper which was almost the only place that Wilson ever met him. Near the end of his embassy Wilson characterized his letters very fairly. 'It is odd how his information seems never to point to any conclusions whatever; but in spite of that his letters are worth reading and do leave a certain impression.'[48] Hoover, who liked 'real punch',[49] found him very good with the Germans over Belgian relief.

All negotiations between America and Germany passed through Count Johann von Bernstorff, the German ambassador in Washington. Germany has not produced many notable envoys and the Count ranks as one of the few. He was appointed to Washington in 1908; and his business from 1914 onwards was to put the German case before Americans and to keep America out of the war. In both these tasks he was fighting against increasing odds and in an atmosphere of hostility. Sentiment in the East was anti-German, and Washington society, except for a handful of hostesses known as the Rhine Maidens,[50] virtually boycotted the Count. In the country at large the British had every advantage in the battle of propaganda because of the common language and the more appealing case. In the long and disheartening fight Bernstorff never wavered. 'If it had not been for his patience, good sense and untiring effort, we should now be at war with Germany', House wrote in October 1915;[51] and again in April 1916: 'Bernstorff keeps his temper and his courage and it is impossible not to admire these qualities in him.'[52]

He was not a conventional diplomat; his methods were nearer to those of the not too scrupulous business negotiator; he was wily beyond the call of diplomatic duty; concealment, bluff, and a little bit of deception here and there were for him permissible means to his end. This single end was the keeping of the peace between Germany and America because he was utterly convinced that, if America came into the war, it meant defeat for the Fatherland. He always regarded American mediation as the only way out. Wilson and Lansing distrusted him. House had a soft spot for him: each man flattered himself that he could handle the other and so they conducted their conversations with equal zest. In this battle of wits the Colonel was the victor; to the very end Bernstorff believed that House was the only one of the President's advisers who was 'always definitely neutral'.[53]

Sir Cecil Spring Rice, the British ambassador in Washington, was a career diplomat, scholarly and experienced but also tense and emotional. A journalist's description of him is of 'a small grey figure, neat grizzled beard, metal-rimmed spectacles, delicate sensitive face'.[54] Like Page he was a prolific and very readable letterwriter. His letters, except towards the end when he wearied and at times when spotted by touches of prejudice, were lucid and informative; Grey frequently circulated them to the Cabinet. They were wittily sarcastic too: and his staff, with whom he was very popular, used, as his First Secretary records, 'to crowd round them and chortle over them'[55] before they were dispatched. No doubt the chortlers sent some at least of these jests on their Washington rounds where they did not always increase good will.

Sir Cecil's frame of reference was White-Anglo-Saxon-Protestant. He specially disliked Jews and Jesuits. While Catholics were on the whole not unfavourable to the Allied cause, he wrote in November 1914, 'the Jesuits as one man are on the side of Prussia'.[56] His intense patriotism made him unable to comprehend that an American could be anti-British without being pro-German. McAdoo, the Secretary of the Treasury, had a Yankee dislike of the British; the ambassador's reports on his supposed pro-Germanism seriously misled the British Government. McAdoo was a very able man indeed, by far the ablest of Wilson's Cabinet, and he was also very ambitious. He made no great secret of his desire to succeed his father-in-law. The combination of high ability and high ambition rarely attracts affection and anyway McAdoo was not altogether a likeable character; although one of Wilson's family there was never any intimacy between them. Spring Rice knew him well and found him, so he reported to Grey on 22 September 1914, honest and capable.[57] But a fortnight later he changed his mind. McAdoo, he discovered, had had business relations with the Jewish banking firm of Kuhn Loeb who had financed his bills. It was 'perfectly fair and honourable', Spring Rice said,[58] but one of the partners in Kuhn Loeb was Paul M. Warburg.

This Mr. Warburg had been nominated by Wilson to the Federal Reserve Board in May 1914 and his appointment was confirmed on 7 August. On the outbreak of war he made himself one of the few vocal pro-Germans in Wall Street. The appointment, Spring Rice felt, had been forced on McAdoo by the Jewish banks. The situation gave him, he told Grey on 5 October 1914, 'considerable cause for anxiety . . . a coterie of German-Jews seems to have control of the financial policy of the Government'.[59] Thus the Jews had by the 'simple expedient' of financing the Secretary's bills 'captured the Treasury Department'—this to be added to their capture one by one of the principal newspapers. By April 1915 Spring Rice was describing McAdoo as the 'German agent in the Cabinet'.[60] By May he was being labelled in Whitehall as 'notoriously pro-German so that perhaps too much reliance should not be placed on what he says'.[61] By September 1916 he had become 'the one dishonest and probably hostile member of the Administration'.[62] There was not a grain of truth in all this as will be seen on almost every page hereafter on which McAdoo's name is mentioned.

As a young man Spring Rice served in the Washington embassy in the eighties and nineties when he had made firm friends of the Roosevelts (he was Theodore's best man at his second marriage in 1886) and the Lodges and others in their circle. He was the friend to whom Mrs. Lodge wrote the letter already quoted* about Bryan's fight in the 1896 election. When Roosevelt was President he had asked in vain for Spring Rice's appointment. It was not made till 1913. It was then a sad mischance that removed Lord Bryce—who was respected by Wilson as a political scientist and might therefore have been one of the precious few to get some sort of entrée to the White House—and substituted for him the intimate of two leaders of the opposition who were to become Wilson's chief antagonists on the issue of neutrality. Hardly a day passed when he did not visit Lodge to 'unpack his heart with words'.[63] There can be no doubt about the type of words he unpacked. Spring Rice was passionate for the utter defeat of Germany. He was one of those who at the end of July 1914 had trembled at the thought that England might shirk. There was an awful moment, he wrote to his old tutor at Eton, when it seemed that both political parties were 'indifferent to all calls of honour'.[64] His Republican associations must have coloured his feeling for the President and they made both Wilson and House feel that he was antipathetic.

In the beginning the ambassador's task seemed a very easy one as he basked in the approval of the pro-Allied East. The President, whom in February 1914 he had called a 'hardened saint',[65] six months later had melted at the Wordsworth Sonnet interview, when he spoke also of the long trial of the Civil War and with deep emotion of his certainty that England likewise would show her power of endurance for a high cause. During September and October the President and the ambassador corresponded pleasantly.[66] The ambassador sent copies of Grey's telegrams and the President acknowledged them effusively (Wilson was inclined to effusiveness on paper), saying how highly he valued such frank confidence, how

* See p. 44 above.

he felt afresh the ambassador's generous spirit of friendship and the fine spirit of Sir Edward Grey. Later in the year the President was a little less cordial though still friendly. 'If things get tangled, we must patiently disentangle', he wrote to the ambassador on 23 December.[67]

Spring Rice felt that his embassy was sustained by popular opinion. 'Almost unanimous in our favour', he exulted in September 1914, 'except among Germans who raise a continual shriek.'[68] On 6 October he noted 'signs of a change of feeling' due, he thought, to the Japanese incursions in the Pacific, British censorship and 'the various questions connected with the seizure of contraband'.[69] But he was not much disturbed; 90 per cent of the English-speaking people, he wrote on 21 October, and half the Irish were on the side of the Allies.[70]

The process of disillusionment was as sharp as the crunch of the British blockade. At first Sir Cecil could hardly believe, as he wrote to Grey on 3 November,

that this Government would be ready to incur the undying indelible disgrace of insisting for small and selfish interests on measures which would destroy the efficiency of our defence and thus taking sides for the meanest motives against those who were fighting for the principles on which the American republic was founded.[71]

Ten days later he was still sticking to his estimate of 90 per cent.[72] Eleven weeks after that he swung right over to the opposite view. Do not, he wrote to the Prime Minister of Canada on 2 February 1915, be 'misled by statements to the effect that 80% or 90% of the American people wish success to the Allies: put no reliance whatever upon American help or sympathy'.[73]

This drastic reappraisal was the result of increasing friction. While Germany's battleships reposed in Kiel and her submarines were as yet inactive, the Allied navies swept the oceans of the world. The first British Orders-in-Council brought back unhappy memories of the war of 1812. Indeed, the President sent through House a personal message to the ambassador on 28 September 1914 on the danger of letting it be thought that

England is reviving old claims hostile to trade between neutrals. Great interests are involved which will affect many sections of the country but what will arouse most sentiment would be the idea that England intends to cripple all trade except her own and to do so is going back on principles enunciated by herself and confirmed at London Conference 1909.[74]

The last piece is a reference to the British volte-face over the Declaration of London.* The idea that she had 'repudiated' it was so strong and persisted for so long that when in March 1917 the United States was about to

* See p. 165 et seq. below.

enter the war and the British Government asked the Washington embassy for an appreciation of Anglo-American relations, the resulting statement, seen and approved by the President, included the sentence:

There are serious Americans who hold that the violation of Belgium has been to some extent balanced by the repudiation of the doctrine of the Declaration of London.[75]

Suspicion on one side of the Atlantic bred resentment on the other and the affair of the *Dacia** in January 1915 produced an outburst in Britain of anti-American feeling.

Spring Rice's disillusionment coincided obversely with the President's. He, as we have seen, was beginning in the autumn of 1914 to question the Allied motives. His initial fondness was replaced first by the patient effort to disentangle and then by some degree of suspicion and irritation. Moreover, the President was 'very sensitive',[76] so Spring Rice thought in April 1915, to British criticism in the quality press he liked to read, such as the *Spectator*. St. Loe Strachey, the *Spectator*'s editor, had lost his good opinion of Wilson. In a letter to Grey on 19 March 1915 he wrote: 'If there had been no war he might have passed for a great President. As it is, history will judge him as the man who was too small for the part for which Fate cast him.'[77] Fate's casting turned out not to be quite the same as Mr. Strachey's. But it was a view widely held in 1914 that Wilson had irretrievably diminished himself by his failure to speak out for the right, that he had lost his charisma.

Spring Rice's estimate of House accorded with the general opinion. 'House is absolutely unselfish and quite devoted to the President. He has no political aim of his own, is endlessly patient as a listener and very clear as an informant.'[78] But House found the ambassador nervy and excitable, even 'irrational' and eventually wanted him recalled. He is the only person so far as is recorded, who ever caused House to lose his temper and to declare warmly that he had been insulted. The truth was that Spring Rice was never in good health; he was also a natural pessimist, emotionally involved in the fighting and often a worried irritable man. In January 1918 he was abruptly superseded and died within weeks. House said of him that at his best no man could be more charming and recognized the deep devotion to duty that strained a worn mind: 'he gave his life for his country as surely as though he had been slain on the field of battle', House wrote.[79] Spring Rice was a poet and there is one of his poems that is in many anthologies. It begins

I vow to thee, my country—all earthly things above—
Entire and whole and perfect, the service of my love.

* See p. 187 below.

A month before his death he sent it to Bryan as a tribute of affection inspired, he said, by reading Bryan's 'Heart to Heart Appeals'.[80] For that 'lovable but elusive troubadour of politics', as a junior member of the embassy staff called Bryan, most men seem in the end to have exchanged exasperation for affection.[81]

VI

THE LEGAL BATTLEFIELD

The battle for Wilson's mind — the Law of the Seas — Prize Law and its defects — the Declaration of London and the British volte-face — the British Order-in-Council of 20 August 1914 — the setting for the Economic Blockades: British and German problems

AFTER the first terrific onslaught on France had been checked at the Battle of the Marne in September 1914 and the great German armies turned back almost from the threshold of Paris, the war settled into a shape which lasted until the end. Germany, nearly always outnumbered, with all her proven skill and efficiency matching and serving the arrogance of her military caste, defended the centre of Europe against France and Britain on the west, Italy on the south, and Russia on the east. Austria-Hungary, vast and slack, and Turkey, a decaying empire and not yet a nation, were subordinate: Berlin was the nerve-centre.

The heart of the war beat on the western front where the three foremost powers met. It was there that the final decision would have to be made. The opposing armies stretched out against each other in a long thin line that began on the Belgian coast just west of Ostend and twisted and curled its way south and then east to the frontier of Switzerland. For three and a half years the armies fought about this line. It was a trench which ran as near as no matter along one of the great divides of Europe that had lain there for at least a thousand years and is only now in the second half of the twentieth century being filled in: 'the line which separated the speakers of the various vernacular forms of Latin from the speakers of German dialects'.[1]

During the thirty months or so that elapsed between the Battle of the Marne and the entry of the United States into the war a prescient man would have transferred his interest from the daily reports of yards gained and lost on the western front to the arguments tautening and slackening between Washington and London and Washington and Berlin. Bernstorff as a commander in the diplomatic field would have seemed to him more important than General von Falkenhayn and the actions of Grey more significant than those of General Joffre. These men—Bernstorff under the control of his

superiors in Berlin and Grey in direct contact with House—were fighting
for the goodwill of the United States on which, as it happened, all in the
end depended; and in the course of this fight each side was forging the
weapon of blockade which proved the most powerful of all, Germany's
blockade bringing her in the spring of 1917 as close as she ever came to
victory and the British blockade sapping the German will to fight. The
British objective in this fight was put simply and cogently by Grey when
he wrote:

Blockade of Germany was essential to the victory of the Allies, but the ill-will
of the United States meant their certain defeat . . . The object of diplomacy,
therefore, was to secure the maximum of blockade that could be enforced without
a rupture with the United States.[2]

The ill-will of the United States would be a reflection from the mind of
Wilson. The battle for the mind of Wilson was fought with moral and legal
forces and by two wings, as it were, of the same army, the hottest fighting
being sometimes on one wing and sometimes on the other. The British,
who began by supposing that their opponents would be morally routed,
gradually became reconciled to hearing their own denunciations of Prussian
militarism matched by reproaches about British navalism and their slogans
about freedom from despotism countered by slogans about freedom of the
seas. On the moral wing neither side triumphed; on the legal the British
never captured the mind of Wilson but Germany eventually lost it altogether.
The reason for this curious state of affairs—curious in that in the mind
of Wilson the law should even have the appearance of mattering more than
morality—lay in Wilson's conviction that the Great War, until America
came into it, produced no moral issue except the observance or breach of
the law. It was Germany's deliberate flouting of the law that lost her the
battle but only after a long struggle in which at times Britain came within
sight of defeat. There were thus two battles in progress and interacting—
the battle of the blockades and the battle for Wilson's mind. The interaction
between them made the legalities of blockade more important than the naval
encounters, since the loss of the legalities spelt defeat even more surely
than the failure of the blockade. International law came to life when the
sanction for breach of it was not just the disapproval of the powerless but
the hostility of the most powerful neutral in the world. For the United
States, although without an army and unready for war, had in 1914 a navy
that in size came next after those of Britain and Germany and an industrial
plant equal to that of all Europe.
The reader, if he accepts that the struggle for Wilson's mind was more
important than anything else that was going on in these two and a half years

and if he wants to follow its ups and downs, must be as willing to be told
about the legalities as he would be about the marches and countermarches
and the manœuvres and logistics of armies in the field. What he has to study
is not the advance of an army demonstrable with pins on a map but the
sweep of events driving Wilson from one position to another until his own
logic forced him into war. The terrain which was fought over and which
it is necessary to begin by describing is the antiquated law of the seas. The
rules now seem almost as unreal as the rules of jousting and very much
less precise.

The high seas belong to all nations, being at once a right of way and a vast
common: so vast that two enemies could fight one another on it without
interfering at all with peaceful traffic. Provided, that is, that they fight each
other in pitched battle or with weapons, such as the torpedo, aimed at
a target. Aimless and concealed weapons, such as the underwater mine,
could interfere with the right of way, but until the close of the nineteenth
century such weapons were unknown. The merchantmen of the warring
nations, who might well be carrying neutral goods, were non–combatants.
An enemy merchantman, if encountered on the high seas, could be captured, but, unless she resisted, could not be fought. Neutral merchantmen
could use the high seas for passage or for trade as freely as they would in
peacetime provided that they complied with two conditions. The rules for
applying in detail these two conditions made up the greater part of the
international law of the seas.

The first was that the neutral ship lost her immunity if she interfered in
legitimate naval operations such as a blockade of a port. A blockade-runner
could be dealt with as a combatant, but the blockade must not be used as
an excuse for casual interception of a neutral ship simply because she was
on her way to a port which the belligerent had declared to be blockaded.
The practice of fictitious or 'paper' blockades was condemned by the
Declaration of Paris in 1856. The blockade must be an effective one capable
of keeping out any intruder who was not prepared to run the gauntlet. This
sort of blockade, the only one recognized by international law, has come to
be called the close blockade. In fact in the wars of the twentieth century
there were no close blockades of any importance. What became important
was the long–distance or economic blockade. This was a so-called blockade
not of a single port but of a whole country or at least of a whole coastline.
To call this a blockade was for an international lawyer a misuse of the term.
What the economic blockader had to claim was precisely that which the
law of close blockade denied, namely, the right to intercept a ship anywhere

on the ground that if she was proceeding to the enemy country she was running the blockade.

The second condition was that the neutral ship should not assist the enemy by bringing in military supplies. This was the foundation of the law of contraband. Contraband is by definition neutral cargo which is by its nature capable of being used to assist in and which is in fact on its way to assist in the naval or military operations of the enemy. By this definition the law drew the lines between peacetime and wartime trading. Trading in peacetime commodities must be allowed to continue; trading in war material could be stopped. Carrying contraband was not considered to be a hostile act. Any neutral ship could try it and get away with it if she could, but she must be prepared to observe the rules and to pay the penalty of failure. The rules allowed a belligerent to stop and inspect a neutral ship. This was the right of visit and search, an operation closely controlled by international law. Every neutral ship must be prepared to submit to it. The penalty, if contraband was found, was capture of the cargo and maybe of the ship as prize of war, that is, seizure and confiscation.

What could be captured was enemy property and contraband—nothing else. Thus if an enemy ship was intercepted, she was subject to capture together with any enemy property on board her and any neutral cargo that was contraband. Neutral cargo that was not contraband must be restored to its owner. The same rule applied if a neutral ship was intercepted, except that the neutral ship was not herself subject to capture unless she was carrying more than a certain percentage of contraband. In that event she was deemed to have assumed the character of an enemy ship and could herself be captured as prize. Otherwise, relieved of her contraband, she must be allowed to continue on her voyage, even though her destination was an enemy port. It followed, of course, that all subjects of a neutral nation could travel freely where they wanted, whether on a belligerent or a neutral ship, though they had to put up with any inconvenience that might be caused by visit and search or the capture of the ship.

So stated, these principles may seem to embody a neat set of rules capable of being used to run the war on the high seas to the satisfaction of all concerned. But in truth they suffered from three grave defects which made them very nearly unworkable.

The first was that each nation made its own rules and administered them in its own prize court. This body of rules was known as prize law and French prize law, for example, might be quite different from British prize law. A nation's prize law was basically a statement of the conditions under which it would permit neutrals to trade with its enemies. It was saved from being nothing more than this by the belief that it was international law, that is to say, that it was based on treaties, customs, or practices which were (or which in the opinion of the prize court hearing the case ought to be) adopted by all maritime nations. The prize courts of most countries, including the United States, Germany,* and France, accepted from their governments modifications by decree of the law they administered; others held themselves independent, saying that they were bound only by international law. The British belonged in theory to the latter class, but with their customary aplomb before 1914 they got the best of both worlds by refusing to contemplate the possibility of a divergence or to proceed to what Lord Stowell, the great Admiralty judge, described in 1811 as 'the extreme indecency' of supposing that an Order-in-Council could run counter to the law of nations.[3] The court, he said, was bound to enforce the law of nations and bound also to enforce the Order-in-Council; there was no inconsistency in this since the Order was presumed to conform to the law. In 1916 the Privy Council, whose Judicial Committee constituted the highest prize court in Britain, put the matter on a footing more readily comprehensible by neutrals by deciding that the court was not bound by an Order-in-Council, but would give 'the utmost weight and importance to every such Order short of treating it as an authentic and binding declaration of law'.[4] Before that, in July 1915, the Foreign Office had assured the State Department that if any Order-in-Council was upheld in the British Court as complying with international law and the United States wished to contend that it did not, Britain would agree to a review by an international tribunal.[5]

There was not so much difference in practice between the decisions of a prize court which was formally bound by its government's decrees and one which was not. The latter might keep its government from overstepping the mark in details, but it would be asking too much of even the most conscientious judicial mind that it should condemn generally as illegal the measures which its government considered it necessary to take for the successful prosecution of a war in which the nation's life was at stake. It is not so much that on such issues a conflict of duty arises in the judge's mind; it is more that he is predisposed to find the same sort of reasons for justifying the measure as his government has found. The decisions of the British prize courts in the Great War were, like those of other countries, as much distinguished for their patriotism as for their impartiality; and there is no instance of their rejection of an Order-in-Council.

---

* Consequently, the legality of unrestricted submarine warfare was never considered by the German Prize Court; cf. C. John Colombos, *International Law of the Sea*, Longmans, London, 5th edition, 1962, p. 701.

The second great defect in the system, which would have persisted even if there had been a unified law, was the fact that there was no authority with power to amend it. In the absence of such an authority it was always possible for a nation to declare in good faith that the law was no longer applicable. Methods of warfare were changing more rapidly in the twentieth century than ever before. The introduction of submarine warfare was one of the great changes. The submarine could not stop and search a ship on the high seas as an ordinary warship could. Must a submarine therefore allow enemy ships and neutral ships probably carrying contraband to proceed unhindered? Even for an ordinary warship the search of a large modern merchant ship with a multiplicity of cargoes had become a much lengthier task. Was the ship still to be searched on the high seas with the added danger that the warship would be an easy target for torpedoes? In such circumstances was there a right to bring a neutral vessel into port to be searched there?

Then by 1914 there was already perceptible a profound change in the character of war from a limited operation between combatants to a total war in which the whole strength of the nation was engaged. By 1916 the change had taken the life out of the laws of contraband and blockade and left only a few bones for the lawyers to pick. It destroyed the distinction between contraband and non-contraband; any supplies that helped to keep the nation alive, whether they had anything to do with military operations or not, increased its power to resist. The 'close blockade' expanded into the economic blockade and the role of the navies on both sides was reduced to that of being the most active of the several weapons employed in the waging of economic warfare.

The third great defect arose out of the point we have just been considering. The lack of authority capable of administering and enforcing the law made room for the doctrine of reprisals. If a belligerent committed grave and persistent violations of the rules of warfare, its opponent might retaliate by itself committing a breach, the retaliation to be proportioned to the offence initiating it and not to be continued after the enemy had been brought back to rectitude. As between belligerents the doctrine is sound enough. It is unreasonable to expect one belligerent to obey a law which the other can successfully disregard; and where no sanction can be imposed the best way of ensuring respect for the law is by tit-for-tat. If the enemy burns your villages, then you burn his, so as to teach him that there is no point in flouting the law. In this form the doctrine was a recognized part of international law and no more difficult to apply than the doctrine of self-help in ordinary law.

The difficulty arises when the measure taken in retaliation injures incidentally a neutral nation or encroaches on her sovereignty. When, for example, in 1914 Germany, so as to gain a military advantage against France, invaded Belgium, would the law have permitted France against the wishes of Belgium to cross the border to meet her foe or must she allow the buffer state to fall totally under the dominion of the enemy? In land warfare the problem rarely arises; and then usually, as in 1914, the victim will be thrust into the war and invite help against the aggressor. But in maritime warfare it is hardly possible to retaliate at all without injury to neutral trade. War of its nature diminishes by the ordinary law of contraband the scope for trade; and so a reprisal, being an extraordinary measure, must of its nature diminish the scope still further. The belligerent must of course accept that there is a limit to what the neutral can be called upon to suffer by what a combatant calls inconvenience and a non-combatant injury. But since, if the neutral will put up with no inconvenience at all, there can be no effective reprisal, he must put up with some; and this will have the additional effect, so the belligerent may hope, of inducing the neutral to put pressure on the enemy to desist from his originating misconduct. Soon the effect hoped for will be transmuted into the purpose intended. When during the Napoleonic War the British in November 1807 issued an Order-in-Council as a reprisal for Napoleon's Berlin Decree, the Order recited that the earlier Order-in-Council of January 1807 had not 'answered the desired purpose, either of compelling the enemy to recall those orders [i.e. the Berlin Decree] or of inducing neutral nations to interpose, with effect, to obtain their revocation'.[6] As a result it came to be argued that it was not permissible to injure by a retaliatory measure a neutral who was unaffected by the originating offence since, if unaffected, he had no cause for protest.

But this sort of argument was put up only by neutrals who had gone halfway towards submission. Those who could afford to make the attempt sought to reject entirely the doctrine of reprisals. From the point of view of the neutral the doctrine had nothing to be said for it. It meant simply that the hardship caused to him by an offence on one side could be increased by a breach of the law on the other side. One belligerent would begin by selecting the rule of law which he regarded as the most irksome and by contending, plausibly or not, that under changed conditions it no longer applied. The other belligerent would contend that it certainly did apply and, denouncing his opponent's action as a violation of international law, would select the rule which *he* found most irksome and by way of reprisal get rid of it. Why should the neutral be made to adjudicate on the merits of the belligerents' dispute? If he did, he would be bound to offend one side or the other and be lucky if he did not tumble into the war. The neutral's contention was summed up in the proposition stated in argument in the

British Prize Court (it was not until 1918 that the point was finally decided in British prize law) as follows:

> A belligerent cannot, by measures in reprisal against an enemy, interfere with the commercial rights of neutrals in a manner which extends the recognised modes of interference, namely, blockade and the prevention of unneutral services and contraband trade.[7]

In truth the conflict of view was insoluble in logical terms. The belligerent asked whether it was just to permit a lawless enemy to obtain unfair advantages over a law-abiding opponent; and could get no satisfactory answer to his question. The neutral asked whether reprisal was to be piled upon reprisal *ad infinitum* until the law expired; and he too could get no satisfactory answer. The lack of sanction vitiated the law. As a leading international lawyer put it in 1935:

> The truth seems to be that the problem of reprisals in naval warfare is one that defies a satisfactory solution by judicial methods; it may even be that it marks the vanishing point of law as a means of regulating the conduct of war.[8]

There was, however, a political if not a legal solution and it was one to which America was beginning to find her way. Belligerence which could not be contained within the law destroyed the foundation upon which rested the disinterestedness of neutrals. Neutrals would then be justified in saying that nations who could not fight according to the rules must stop fighting and be made to settle; and in intervening to bring about that result. The plan which House conceived in the autumn of 1915 was for a forced settlement upon reasonable terms. Wilson a year later elevated this into a principle: neutrals, he said, could not stand aside when a great war caused so great a disturbance.

But these developments were yet to come. At the start in 1914 Britain and Germany both adopted the belligerent doctrine while the neutrals, including America, were firm in denial of it.[9] No international lawyer could say which was right. History gave half-hearted support to the belligerent view and took its precedents from a similar situation a century before. Then too Britain had with the sympathy of many Americans been fighting against a continental aggressor and then too both sides were interfering with neutral rights at sea. All that most Americans remembered about it was that in 1812 it was against Britain and not against Napoleon that the United States had gone to war: not, however, on the exact point. The United States then admitted, by implication if not expressly, that reprisals could abridge neutral rights (only Denmark among the neutrals in 1807 stood pat), her complaint being that Britain went too far. The British Orders-in-Council of January and November 1807 were the forerunners of the economic blockade of the 1914 war, the latter declaring that French controlled ports should be subject to the same restrictions 'as if the same were actually blockaded by His Majesty's naval forces in the most strict and rigorous manner'.[10] They were expressed as retaliatory to the Berlin decree of November 1806 which required the seizure of British goods wherever found. The American objection to the Orders-in-Council was based on the contention that they hurt American trade much more than the Berlin decree did or was intended to do and so were out of proportion. Secretary Madison said in March 1808:

> A declaration of a belligerent, which he is known to be either not in a situation, or not to intend to carry but partially into execution against a neutral, to the injury of another belligerent, could never give more than a right to a commensurate redress against the neutral.[11]

In 1810 Napoleon offered to revoke the Berlin Decree and the Milan Decree which had followed it if Britain revoked the Orders-in-Council or America 'caused her rights to be respected by the English'.[12] This destroyed the justification for the reprisal but Britain failed to respond. This was the burden of the President's—Madison was by then the President—message to Congress in November 1811 and the point which led to war.

Thus the nineteenth-century argument between Britain and the United States was conducted on the footing that fundamentally the retaliatory orders were unobjectionable. Their validity was neither challenged nor conceded in the British Prize Court. The Treaty of Ghent, which in 1814 concluded the war between Britain and the United States, was silent on the subject, which thereafter with an exactitude rare in history slumbered for one hundred years. When in 1914 it was roused by the kiss of another great maritime war, there was nothing in the legal textbooks to tell the diplomats what the law was or should be. Indeed, the subject was not mentioned at all. Yet it was crucial: for it soon became apparent that neither Germany nor Britain was minded to keep her naval measures within the confines of the ordinary law.

These then were the three great defects in the international law of the seas: the first, that each nation made its own prize law; the second, that there was no international authority to unify, amend, and modernize the law; and the third, that the whole structure was at the mercy of the doctrine of reprisals. The first was not in practice quite as bad as it sounds. Various influences were at work which tended to uniformity. A maritime nation might be a belligerent in one war and a neutral in the next; her own interest therefore suggested that she should hold a fair balance between belligerency and neutrality; she would not desire to have the decisions of her own prize courts cited against her. Another factor working for uniformity was that nations, when allies in war, found it convenient to adjust their prize laws to correspond. But what the international lawyers wanted was an acceptable code to cover not only prize law but all the laws of war. The Declaration of Paris, made in 1856 after the Crimean War, was the first in a great series of attempts to create a real common law by which all nations would be bound. The last great attempt began at the second Hague Peace Conference in 1907. This conference was concerned chiefly with the law of contraband and with the difficulty of deciding how to classify commodities that were capable of being used to assist in military operations and how to determine whether they were in fact destined for that use. A distinction was drawn between absolute contraband and conditional contraband. Some goods, such as arms and ammunition, must obviously be intended for military use; they were absolute contraband and could be condemned out of hand. Goods which might or might not be used to assist in military operations were conditional contraband. Food, for example, might be used either for feeding the army or for feeding civilians. On proof that it was intended for the former use it could be condemned, otherwise not. There was also suggested what was a novelty in the law of contraband, namely a 'free list'. Up till then it had been left open to the belligerent to declare his own list of contraband. This right was to be modified so that he could not declare as contraband anything that was on the free list, which covered commodities such as cotton (which came to be greatly used in the manufacture of munitions), wool, rubber, and fertilizers. No final agreement was reached on any of these points but many of them were adopted in the Declaration of London two years later. The concrete achievement of this conference in prize law was the Twelfth Hague Convention establishing an international prize court as a court of appeal from the national prize courts.

But it was felt by the British that it was not much use establishing a court while there was still so much uncertainty about the law which it would have to administer. Consequently in 1908 Sir Edward Grey called the conference of naval powers which in the following year produced the Declaration of London. The object of the Declaration was to codify the law. Probably no nation went to the conference table anxious only to produce a code which would be fairest to all. Certainly Britain did not. By this time she foresaw as more than a possibility a naval war with Germany in which she would use her superior navy as a weapon of aggression. But since she had no clear idea of how such a war should be waged, she had likewise no idea of the sort of legal system she would like to wage it under.

It must be remembered that in the major wars which occurred after the Crimean War—the American Civil War, the Franco-Prussian War of 1870, and the Russo-Japanese War of 1904—Britain had remained neutral and her trade had profited by it. There was much attraction for Britain in the argument (which if she had not had a superior navy would have been compelling) that in wartime her interest lay in securing supplies for herself rather than in seeking to cut off supplies from other more self-sufficient nations which had land as well as sea access. For this purpose the less contraband the better. The British delegation at the conference went so far as to advocate its total abolition. But this proposal, they reported, had 'so unfavourable a reception' that they

decided to concentrate our efforts on obtaining as strict as possible a limitation and definition of the term contraband and on securing the adoption of provisions for the exaction of rigorous proof by the captor for the establishment of the contraband character of the goods seized.[13]

In the pursuit of this objective they were very successful indeed. The proposal for the 'free list' was adopted, the delegation describing it as a 'welcome guarantee of security to valuable branches of British Commerce'; and formidable difficulties were placed in the way of proving the enemy destination of conditional contraband.

At the conference a compromise was reached on the doctrine of 'continuous voyage'. This doctrine, which came to play an important part in the 1914 war, was invented by the English Prize Court during the Seven Years War and worked up by the American Prize Court in the Civil War. A ship whose ultimate destination was an enemy port might call at several neutral ports on the way. If at her first port of loading she shipped cargo for the ultimate enemy port, could she be intercepted in the earlier stages or must the interceptor wait until the last leg of the voyage? The American Prize Courts amid protests from foreign writers decided that the interceptor need not wait. The doctrine was then expanded to cover the case where the ship's final destination was a neutral port but where arrangements had been made, whether or not the ship was aware of them, for on-carriage of the goods by land or sea to an enemy destination. The Declaration of London applied the doctrine of continuous voyage to absolute contraband but not to conditional.

All the great powers including Britain signed the Declaration. Under the British constitution a treaty which involves an alteration in the law of the land cannot be effective until the necessary legislation has been enacted by Parliament. So in 1911 the Government introduced the Naval Prize Bill.

The Bill was strenuously fought. It hardly needs the advantage of hindsight to see that its opponents had a much more realistic idea than its supporters of the sort of war Britain was likely to fight in the future, especially against Germany. The Government case minimized the value of intercepting contraband and stressed the importance of the close blockade. The Opposition contended that the value of the close blockade had been greatly diminished by modern developments. It would no longer need a naval battle in the old style to disperse a blockading fleet; it could be harassed by submarine and torpedo and subjected to the greater range of modern coastal artillery. The idea that Germany would either have to submit to the blockade or risk a battle with a superior force was a thing of the past. Moreover, the great improvements in railway communications made a continental nation much less dependent than before upon access to its own ports. Germany could obtain goods almost as conveniently through Dutch, Danish, and Scandinavian ports as through her own. In short, the only way of effectively denying supplies to the Germans would be through the interception of imports as contraband. The Government forced the Bill through the House of Commons, but in the House of Lords it was defeated, so that Britain never became a party to the Declaration. Nevertheless, the Declaration could fairly be described as the latest summary of the best thought on the law of the seas. Accompanied by a full commentary it found a place in the leading textbooks. It was indeed included in the *Prize Manual*, the book which was issued to British naval officers to instruct them in their duties in time of war.

It was upon this quaking surface that neutrals had to take their stand in 1914. In the State Department Bryan left the legalities to Counselor Lansing. Lansing did not personally consider the Declaration of London 'standing alone, as the best and most equitable code of naval warfare',[14] but he wanted to get some firm ground under his feet. The State Department on 6 August asked the belligerents whether they intended to apply the Declaration.[15] Germany answered that she did provided that her enemies did likewise. In the meantime British naval strategy had been revolutionized. Even before the Naval Prize Bill had passed the Commons Winston Churchill had become First Lord of the Admiralty and had set up a naval staff (none had existed before) which revised all war plans and scrapped the close blockade. The new policy of the distant blockade was laid down in the Admiralty War Orders of 1912. So to Lansing's inquiry Britain replied, in effect though not in terms, that she would accept the parts of the Declaration which she liked.[16]

The Order-in-Council of 20 August 1914[17] was in the form of applying the Declaration with some amendments, thus traversing the Declaration itself which by Article 65 provided that it must be accepted as a whole. The Order enacted that conditional contraband consigned to a 'merchant under the control of the authorities of the enemy state' could be seized regardless of the port, whether enemy or neutral, to which the vessel was bound: this applied to conditional contraband the doctrine of continuous voyage contrary to Articles 34 and 35 of the Declaration. Further, the Order provided that 'any sufficient evidence' could be used to prove destination: this was contrary to Articles 32 and 35 which said that the ship's papers were conclusive proof of her destination unless she was clearly off course.

Lansing prepared on 26 September a lengthy protest which he took to the point of saying that the British attitude would 'awaken memories of controversies which it is the earnest desire of the United States to forget or to pass over in silence'.[18] Since Britain was not bound by the Declaration of London (neither for that matter was the United States, for though in April 1912 the Senate advised ratification, the President, after Britain had backed out, took no further action) the Counselor could do no more than register his 'keen disappointment' at the way in which it was being treated. But on any view, he said, the proposed modifications were 'wholly unacceptable'. The 'reversion to the doctrine of continuous voyage' made 'neutral trade between neutral ports dependent upon the pleasure of belligerents'. The effect of this strong language was inevitably diminished by the fact that it was that of poacher turned gamekeeper. The main support for the doctrine of continuous voyage in international law came from decisions of the American Prize Courts.

But anyway the protest got no further than Page to whom it was sent for information only. For when the President saw Lansing's draft House was with him and obtained permission to talk to Spring Rice so as to 'get at the bottom of the controversy'.[19]* The ambassador was shown the draft and 'was really astonished at the tone in one or two of the sentences'.[20] The upshot was that Wilson himself settled a brief, firm, and friendly telegram as a basis for an informal and confidential talk; and Lansing went round after dinner on 29 September to see Spring Rice and to discuss with him ways and means of giving Britain what she wanted within the framework of the Declaration.

In this more relaxed atmosphere Britain prepared a new Order-in-Council and sent the draft to Washington for discussion.[21] By this Order a number of commodities, such as copper, oil, and rubber, were to be raised to the

---

* It was when he saw Spring Rice on this occasion, 28 September, that House conveyed also the President's personal warning of American ill-feeling if Britain was really trying to cripple trade: see p. 153 above.

status of absolute contraband as used 'exclusively for war'. But foodstuffs could not by any stretch of the definition be brought within it. On this point the British proposed a modification of their earlier Order. They would still intercept foodstuffs and other conditional contraband destined for a neutral port but they would seize and condemn them only if they were addressed 'to order' of the shipper and not to a named consignee. Thus the British would abandon their claim to regard any neutral consignee on 'any sufficient evidence' as an agent of the enemy government and would replace it with the presumption that cargo 'to order', i.e. for which the shipper reserved his right to name the consignee, was intended for shipment to the enemy. This compromise served neither legal purity nor effective action. In strict international law it was just as objectionable as the one it replaced while its effect could easily be evaded by naming dummy neutral consignees. The really drastic provision of the draft was in Section 4 whereunder Britain could name any neutral port as one through which the enemy was drawing supplies for its armed forces; and thereupon all conditional contraband consigned to that port would be regarded as having an enemy destination. This clause was intended for use against neutral countries which refused to lay an embargo on the passage of contraband or failed to enforce it.

Page commended the draft in a telegram to the President that began his splendid career of total unneutrality.[22] This was not just a war, he said, it was the world clash of systems of government, a matter of life and death for English-speaking civilization, not an academic discussion. Precedents had gone to the scrapheap. The English simply could not admit raw materials, such as rubber and copper and oil, into Germany. They would risk a serious quarrel, even war, rather than yield: and they would be right.

On 16 October Lansing dispatched his objections to the draft.[23] Section 4 he rightly described as a new doctrine without precedent. But he was so desperately anxious to get the Declaration accepted in form that he was ready to resort to almost any expedient. He sent on the same day another telegram with a plan that Page could put to Grey, 'stating very explicitly that it is your personal suggestion and not one for which your government is responsible'.[24] The plan was for Britain to issue an Order-in-Council accepting the Declaration while making, as the Declaration permitted, additions to the list of absolute contraband; and then to follow it with another order, 'of which the United States need not be previously advised', enacting the obnoxious Section 4. True, Section 4 was 'a new principle', but the excuse would be that the Declaration had failed to provide for exceptional conditions. This, Lansing was convinced, 'would meet with liberal consideration by this government and not be the subject of serious objection'. A few hours later the President himself telegraphed to Page. He begged him not to regard the matter as academic; contact with American opinion would alter his views. He urged him to use his 'utmost persuasive efforts to effect an understanding, which we earnestly desire, by the method we have gone out of our way to suggest, which will put the whole case in unimpeachable form'.[25]

'Do you mean', Grey asked Page when he presented the proposal on 19 October, 'that we should accept the Declaration and then issue a proclamation to get round it?'[26] Page thought, though he did not say quite as much to Grey, that it was the Declaration of London with the addition of a dishonest reservation. Page had completely ignored the direction to present the proposal as his own and he let Wilson (whom he supposed could not have understood it) know that he thought such a subterfuge unnecessary: 'my relations with Sir Edward have not been built upon this basis and could not survive this method of dealing long'.[27] At the same time he wrote to House that he had now tried four times to get Grey to accept the Declaration of London and that if Lansing brought it up again he would resign.[28]

On 22 October Lansing gave up. The United States declared that in future she would define her rights and duties in accordance with the existing rules of international law. The British issued their Order-in-Council on 29 October 1914 and the State Department, as Grey had suggested, reserved its rights.

So the stage was set for the development of the economic blockades. To understand the methods employed it is best to begin by considering how the method could have been used by each side if it was prepared to disregard altogether the rules of international law.

The British naval power was strong enough to prevent access to the North Sea at either end, north or south. The south entrance by the English Channel was easily controlled. A minefield laid across the Straits of Dover, completed in February 1915, compelled every ship to go through the Downs, that is, the narrow passage between the Goodwin Sands and the coast of Kent, where she could be conveniently searched while at anchor. The north end was more difficult. The distance between the Orkneys and the coast of Norway is 200 miles but since Norway was neutral a ship could cross the line unmolested by keeping within Norwegian territorial waters. To prevent access to Norwegian waters, the British Navy had to patrol a line of over 600 miles running north from the Shetlands to Iceland and Greenland. So the Northern Patrol was a considerable naval operation. But with the British Grand Fleet based on Scapa Flow in the Orkneys, and the weaker German fleet unwilling to risk a pitched battle, the control would succeed.

Thus the North Sea could be made a British lake and the entrance to every port in Germany could be blocked.

So, however, could the entrance to every port in Holland, Denmark, and Scandinavia. But unless these powers (the Northern Neutrals as they can conveniently be called) were to be forced into opposition, their ports could not be controlled without allowing them some supplies and some vestiges at least of peacetime trade. Holland and Norway and Denmark had no weapon to retaliate with except the extreme one of joining the enemy camp. Sweden was in a less vulnerable position since during a large part of the year the only way of getting supplies to Russia from her allies was by the use of the Swedish railways. Moreover, Sweden was not so dependent on imported food and forage as were the others. Britain would have to consider also the hostility of other neutrals outside the area whose trade through the North Sea ports was affected. The only one of these who was in a position to retaliate was the United States. Britain was herself so dependent on supplies from that country that the United States without resort to force had the means of backing her demands.

The problems confronting Germany if she embarked upon a blockade were entirely different. Britain was far less self-sufficient than Germany and entirely dependent for imported supplies on her own ports. A successful blockade of those ports could bring her to heel without affecting the supplies of any other country. Germany's problem was how to effect that blockade in the face of what by a later generation would have been called Britain's superiority in conventional naval forces. The only answer to them was the submarine. But the use of the submarine meant something far more serious than the confiscation of goods as prize, for which if necessary compensation could be paid. It meant the sinking of ships and the loss of life. Thus the danger of retaliation by neutrals was much greater. What were their potentialities for harming Germany? Any hostility by the Northern Neutrals could be answered by the threat of invasion and occupation. What Germany had to fear came from those outside countries whose trade with Britain would be affected and chief among these was the United States. The United States would have no economic weapons to use against Germany because her trade with Germany would be cut off by the British. She could do nothing except go to war.

Thus Germany's problem involved the single calculation of whether or not an effective blockade by submarines would bring America into the war. Would she be provoked to fight simply to maintain her trade with the Entente? Would she be provoked to fight—and this was the factor which Germany was always disposed to underrate—because the measures taken to attack her trade involved the loss of civilian life and the rejection of the fundamental idea, still dominant at the beginning of the twentieth century, that civilian life, whether belligerent or neutral, was sacred? The risk of bringing America into the war could be contemplated only if there was a corresponding likelihood that a submarine blockade would defeat Britain. The submarine was an untried weapon. It was uncertain both how effectively it could be used and what measures might be devised against it.

Neither side had before the outbreak of war made any comprehensive plans for blockading the other because neither side had realized what an effective weapon the blockade would turn out to be. It was of course a weapon that took time to take effect and both sides thought that a great war would be short. After the Battle of the Marne had resulted in a military stalemate they had to think again.

Under the doctrine of reprisals it was comparatively easy for either side to take the first step and give it a colour of legality. The build-up of the blockades will be described in the next chapter.

VII

NEUTRALITY IN ACTION

Neutrality and non-involvement — submarine parts and private loans — German merchantmen in American ports — arms embargo — the British blockade; division of opinion between sailors and diplomats — Hankey — economic warfare; black list, interception, navicert, rationing, control of cables, delay — the Ship Purchase Bill and the *Dacia* — Germany's blockade; her constitution; division of opinion between sailors and diplomats — the emergence of the submarine — the start of the starvation policy — minelaying and reprisals — the German Submarine Declaration of 4 February 1915 — the British Order-in-Council of 11 March 1915 — the *Wilhelmina* — Bryan's *modus vivendi* — the *Falaba* — the sinking of the *Lusitania*

IN 1914 it would have taken a very percipient American to see that neutrality might not be enough and that neutrality and 'non-involvement', as it came to be called, meant different things. The area of neutrality can be no larger than both belligerents will permit or, in default of such permission, than what neutrals are prepared to fight for. To fight is to be involved; and so the area that is common both to neutrality and non-involvement is what belligerents will permit. The object of international law is to define the area which belligerents will permit and with which neutrals will be content. Where that object is achieved neutrals are able to trade with either belligerent without getting involved and so in theory neutrality and non-involvement are the same.

Such was the theory, but it could very easily be distorted. From the beginning there were two factors pulling it out of shape; and a third was added in the spring of 1915. In the first place the theory desiderates that at the start of the war the neutral has a more or less equal volume of trade with each belligerent. 'More or less' can be wide enough to allow for a considerable difference but not for a huge preponderance, for then the neutral is bound to begin with some degree of economic involvement. American pre-war trade with the Allies was ten times as much as with the Central Powers. In the second place the theory desiderates that the interference with trade which war occasions will be felt equally by both belligerents. But in practice this is not usually so. What is affected by the war is not trade in contraband but trade in intercepted contraband. Both sides are equal in the eyes of the law of contraband but they have not usually equal powers of interception. In 1914 there was, if the law was observed, a gross disparity between the two sides in their ability to intercept. Under the existing law, which banned the unrestricted use of the submarine, Germany had virtually no power of interception. The British power, even if it had been diminished by a more scrupulous observance of the rules, was very considerable. Thirdly, the theory presupposes that there will always be room for a substantial trade in non-contraband with both sides. This was altogether upset when early in 1915 each side made it its aim to stop trade with the other in every sort of commodity.

In this aim neither side completely succeeded. Certainly British control of the Atlantic meant that all direct trade with Germany was cut off. But in spite of all that the British could do, trade did continue indirectly through the ports of the Northern Neutrals. American exports to Norway, for example, had by 1917 increased ninefold. Still on balance there was a very heavy loss of trade. On the other hand, United States trade with the Allies was enormously increased, it has been estimated by 184 per cent. It was the trebling of a volume of trade which had started by being ten times greater, rather than the grave diminution of American trade with Germany, that made the significant difference. If Germany's power of interception by means of the unrestricted use of the submarine had succeeded in cutting down this trade to the extent that would have been necessary to impair the war effort of the Allies, the American economy would have been seriously affected.

So as the war went on and it became apparent that America could not have both non-involvement and neutrality according to the law, she had to make up her mind which should be the major objective. If she chose the former, she would be hurt certainly in pocket and perhaps also in pride. In pocket she would be hurt by the loss of foreign trade. This was what she accepted in 1939 when she limited her trade to what was paid for and taken away, the 'cash and carry' provisions grafted on to the Neutrality Act of 1936. In pride she would be hurt by being forced to submit to decisions in which she had no say. When the belligerents decided to stop all trade with the enemy and not merely, as the law allowed, trade in contraband, America had either to submit or to risk involvement. She could save her pride only in dubious ways. She could pretend to be convinced by the argument, which would undoubtedly be put forward, that the measures were justified as reprisals. She could accept the other arguments, which would also undoubtedly be put forward, that the changed conditions of warfare required a change in the law. But then the whole concept of neutrality of which as

London, 24 May 1913. Walter Page, the new American ambassador, arrives at Euston Station

Berlin, 1916. James Watson Gerard, the American ambassador to Germany

Washington, July 1915. Robert Lansing, the American Secretary of State
(*right*) with his predecessor William Jennings Bryan

Rear-Admiral Cary T.
Grayson, the President's
doctor, with Wilson

the leading neutral she was proud to be the custodian would be unsettled by changes made to order and not by treaty.

Americans in 1914 certainly wanted non-involvement but had no idea at all of making any sacrifices in pride or in pocket in order to secure it. Ought Wilson to have clarified the issue for them and either driven or led them to one solution or the other? The issue did not emerge as one that had to be faced until the spring of 1915 with the declaration of the two blockades. It did not push itself to the forefront as something urgently demanding a solution until the submarine began to take its toll of American lives. The alternatives were then starkly presented to the President by Bryan, the peacekeeper, in favour of non-involvement and by Lansing, the lawyer, who spoke for neutrality under the law. By June 1915 the President had come down definitely on the side of neutrality under the law and had rejected non-involvement with the consequence that Bryan resigned.

Wilson's decision was made only after a hesitation that lasted through the month of April and beyond. After the outrageous sinking of the *Lusitania* in May 1915, it would have been difficult for him politically to have made any other choice. But it was also the decision that suited his conception of America's role. To proclaim her non-involvement would be to detach her not only from the struggle but from her position of influence during and after the struggle. It would have meant the practice of a sterile neutrality and Wilson intended to fertilize American neutrality with America's duty to serve the world. This was the irresistible attraction: not the safe-guarding of American prosperity—there is no evidence that in this connection Wilson ever thought of that—nor, if one may judge from his subsequent attitude at the various times when war impended, primarily the maintenance of American pride, though to this he was never indifferent. The prime attraction was that America's neutrality should be fruitful.

But the fruits of American wisdom and high-mindedness which Wilson wanted to dispense would not be acceptable unless the nations invited to partake of them could be seated at an impartial table. To be recognized as impartial America had to follow the law because there was no other test of impartiality. She could not surrender her rights without incidentally acting to the advantage of one side or the other. If she ceased to trade with the Allies to the extent that her neutrality permitted her to do, she would give an advantage to the Central Powers and thus be said to be adopting an unneutral attitude. The man who acts strictly according to law can blame the law if his decisions please one side rather than the other. The man who leaves the law and makes his own decisions, even if in substance they may be just, loses the appearance of impartiality; and when a man comes to tender his good offices, the appearance is even more important than the reality.

Nevertheless, until Wilson was brought hard up against the fact that the price of impartiality was strict adherence to the law, he followed his natural bent in eschewing 'mere legalism'.[1] He had no fondness for precedents amassed from past incidents which between wars lay neglected on undusted shelves; and when the lawyers in the State Department got down the bones and started to reconstruct the skeleton, Wilson was all for breathing into it the spirit of justice. In the first months of the war he and Bryan were breathing together, discomfiting the lawyers and also the British.

Early on there were two anti-British decisions in which Wilson was neutral in spirit but not in the letter. Two American corporations had signed contracts to build submarines to be delivered in sections for the British Government. Wilson was advised that in law the sale of assembled submarines would be unneutral but that the delivery of submarine parts would be proper. Under the influence of Bryan, Wilson declined to draw this distinction which he regarded as 'a violation of the spirit of neutrality'.[2]

Another and more important anti-British decision was over loans. Private loans to belligerent governments were not deemed to be unneutral. The French Government requested J. P. Morgan & Co. to float a loan on its behalf in the United States. Bryan argued against it; preservation of neutrality would be impossible if powerful financial interests were concerned on one side or the other. So with Wilson's approval he announced on 15 August 1914 that 'in the judgement of this Government loans by American bankers to any foreign nation which is at war are inconsistent with the true spirit of neutrality'.[3] But almost immediately increasing trade with the Allies made it impossible to maintain in all its clarity Bryan's idea that 'money is the worst of all contrabands because it commands everything else'.[4] By 23 October 1914 the President had observed a decided difference between an issue of government bonds and 'an arrangement for easy exchange in meeting debts incurred in trade'.[5]

This enabled the Allied Governments to get what they wanted until the summer of 1915 when their purchases had become so huge that the flotation of a loan was the only alternative to the sale of the American securities they held or the shipment of gold. Britain needed both the securities and the gold and in a large measure if she was to maintain the credit of sterling in the markets of the world. A loan was then proposed and Bryan's pronouncement was allowed to lapse.*

These two early decisions against Britain and against the letter of the law began the destruction of the British illusion that the spirit of neutrality

* See p. 356 below.

might be persuaded to move towards them because their cause was just. The fact that the existing law favoured them enormously over Germany and that in matters much more crucial than assemblage of submarines Wilson gave decisions to their advantage was not put to his credit. For example, there were in August 1914 a number of German merchantmen cooped up in American ports. They could have been converted into auxiliary cruisers and made themselves very effective on the Atlantic routes. It was a great though not unexpected relief to Britain when the United States ruled that no armed ships would be allowed to leave an American port. But the British then went on to take the point that the ruling should not be applied so stringently as to prevent Allied merchantmen, armed for defensive purposes only, from trading in American ports, and the ruling was modified accordingly. There was undoubtedly a recognized distinction in international law between the offensive and defensive armament of ships, but it was one that was hard to apply in practice (much more was to be heard of it before the war was over) and might have been brushed aside by a hostile adjudicator.

Then the United States did not challenge the British action in laying a large minefield in the North Sea in October and in subsequently declaring the whole of the North Sea to be a war zone. It is true that American shipping was not likely to be much affected by these measures. But they were of doubtful validity. American silence indicated at least a desire not to make things unnecessarily difficult.

Finally, there was the supply of arms, as to which the United States made no concessions at all to German feelings. Germany saw the United States as a country supplying the Allies with all they wanted, munitions of war as well as food, while acquiescing in the British effort to starve Germany. By November 1914 the German-Americans were demanding an arms embargo. Embargo Bills were introduced into Congress. There was an attraction, which at first drew Wilson, in the idea that it was wrong to prolong the war by selling arms to either of the belligerents. But would not an embargo benefit the side that had made ready for war? Argument and counter-argument on this point have since become familiar. Wilson was advised by Lansing that for a government to take power to prohibit private sales of arms would be unneutral, the more so when the power could be used effectively only against one side. Bryan, who might have been expected to take the sentimental view, in fact shared Lansing's opinion. So Wilson followed the law. Without formal pronouncement he made known his views in January and February 1915 and the Bills perished.

Both in Britain and in Germany from the beginning of the war there were two parties, one for taking the hard line and the other the soft, one for pressing the blockade regardless of consequences and the other for cautious handling of neutral protests. In each country, as was to be expected, the Admiralty led the former party and the Foreign Office the latter. Not that all those concerned in the Foreign Office in London saw things exactly alike. Beneath Grey there were two under-secretaries, one political, Lord Robert Cecil, who sat in the House of Commons, the other a civil servant and the permanent head of the office. Lord Robert inclined to the 'stand-no-nonsense-from-America' school but was quite sensible and restrained about it. Nicolson, the permanent under-secretary until June 1916, played little part in blockade matters; Grey had not much use for him anyway. The permanent official who counted for most (and who but for his domineering manner might well have succeeded Nicolson) was the head of the contraband department, Sir Eyre Crowe. Crowe was a formidable man in his early fifties with a long experience behind him and his most important jobs still to come. He had a German mother, a German wife, and German schooling, attributes which touched off the Northcliffe press in the autumn of 1915: Grey firmly and successfully resisted the agitation. In fact Crowe had been for years an implacable opponent of German ambitions; he wrote a powerful memorandum on the subject in 1907.* Of those under Crowe the ablest was Lord Eustace Percy, a prodigy from the ducal house of Northumberland, a young man of high intelligence who was to become a Cabinet minister in 1924 at the age of 37 but to storm no further heights. Then there was Cecil Hurst, the legal adviser, who after the war and the treaty became the British judge at the International Court of Justice.

These men communed with each other in the old style, that is, by putting handwritten minutes on a file that began at the bottom of the scale of authority and ended at the top. In the very highest echelons the minutes were terse; below they tended to the loose and conversational, were full of 'venturing to think' and the like, and sometimes dilated on general topics. Sometimes Crowe would explode, as in January 1916, 'We must always be conciliatory, America may always be offensive',[6] and then Cecil added placidly: 'Hard words break no bones.'

Crowe was anti-American. He had no sympathy with the American mind and obviously disliked what he knew of President Wilson's. Like a number of other Englishmen, the British ambassador in Paris especially, he thought that Americans were interested only in their own politics. Trust the United States with nothing, he minuted during the 1916 election: everything would be decided 'solely and shamelessly according to the exigencies of the party game'.[7] Percy also was for being tough with the Americans but for quite

* See p. 241 below.

a different reason. He had been at the Washington embassy as an attaché from 1910 to 1914 and consequently fancied himself as 'a fairly good judge of American politics'.[8] He was very optimistic about the degree of strain which Anglo-American friendship could take; and he saw it as an asset which Britain should exploit. Quite a typical minute of his in February 1916 says: 'We can, I believe, so far as America is concerned, adopt any naval policy that we please.'[9]

So there was within the Foreign Office plenty of antidote to Grey's pro-Americanism and some stimulus to aggressive action. But Grey, who had after all been Foreign Secretary for nine years when the blockade began, had his team well in hand; and within the office no one but himself decided policy. Outside it he had to contend with the young Winston Churchill at the Admiralty, thrusting impatiently. Grey had not the abilities of Churchill, but in the Cabinet where the crucial decisions were taken steadiness of character counted for more than talent. Churchill was argumentative and wearied his colleagues with monologues. Grey commanded great respect where Churchill aroused slight suspicion, being a recent recruit not only to Liberalism but also to the importance of sea power. Before he went to the Admiralty he had opposed increases in naval armament. His enemies thought him hare-brained, his friends thought him brilliant, and those in between thought neither quality to be a recommendation. Asquith treated him with amused indulgence tempered by respect for his genius.

Outside the Cabinet the Admiralty had greater support. Members of Parliament kept prodding at Grey in the House of Commons and the British public was on their side. The public did not know and could not be told, as Hankey (himself on this point keenly on the Admiralty side) very fairly observed,[10] how much material the Allies were getting from the United States and how important it was to avoid upsetting her.

Maurice Hankey was then in the early stages of the career which made him one of the great civil servants of the century. He was in his late thirties and officially only a captain in the marines. After rapid advancement in that branch of the service he was chosen in 1909 to be assistant secretary to the Committee of Imperial Defence. This was a body started by Balfour when he was Prime Minister in 1904 as a Cabinet Committee to concern itself with defence or with what less kindly people might term warmaking. In 1912 Hankey became the secretary. In November 1914 the committee merged imperceptibly with the War Council which later in 1916 became the War Cabinet. Hankey was the secretary of the War Cabinet and then of the Big Four of the Peace Conference. Thus he founded the Cabinet Secretariat which is now a permanent feature of our constitution, and lived long enough to teach those who ran the second war and made the peace of

1945 some of the lessons to be derived from the first war and the peace of 1919.

He was a passionate believer in the naval might of Britain. He believed that in any war with Germany the function of the British Navy would be to surround Germany as an army surrounds an impregnable fortress and to reduce her by starvation. Thus he foresaw the importance of the economic blockade at the time when the Admiralty was still dithering over ideas of the close blockade. He was horrified by the proceedings that led up to the Declaration of London. The idea of an international prize court he regarded as 'merely a trick to clip the wings of our sea power'.[11] Although the secretary to the Committee of Imperial Defence who was his chief, he being then assistant secretary, had been a member of the delegation that accepted the Declaration, Hankey disagreed so violently that he got his chief's permission to prepare a cogent memorandum of his views. The memorandum was rejected by the Foreign Office 'somewhat contemptuously',[12] but better received in the Admiralty where the First Sea Lord told him not to worry since the Declaration would tumble down as soon as the guns went off. Hankey claims also that in both Houses of Parliament the speeches in opposition were based to some extent on his views. It was one of the secrets of his power that as a servant he could hold and express strong views and yet retain the confidence of the masters with whom he disagreed. Where there is more than one master such a servant often wields more power than any of them individually because he has the ear of them all.

Cajolery was what made the British blockade work so well. The British used their economic power as much as the legal power which prize law gave them. They exploited ingeniously the uncertainties of the law. Sometimes they stretched it almost to breaking point, but they never pulled it out of recognizable shape as the Germans had to do to justify the submarine. They behaved as litigants who preferred to settle. The chief weapon of economic power was the Black List, and of legal power the interception and search of neutral vessels. The system grew in strength as the war progressed. In the spring of 1915 it was still in its infancy, but it is convenient at this point to look forward a little and describe its nature and development.

In 1914 Britain was the greatest trading nation in the world. Two-thirds of the world's steam tonnage (excluding that owned by the Central Powers, which the British Navy from the first immobilized in enemy or neutral ports) was under Allied flags. The Allies could and did refuse to carry the goods of traders they suspected of trading with the enemy. Britain controlled the supply of much important raw material, such as rubber, and she could and did prevent its sale to manufacturers who traded with her enemies. This power of the Black List was used against traders, American and others, who sought to bring goods into the North Sea. It avoided the need for any formal proof that the goods had an enemy destination. The Northern Neutrals had to weigh the fact that Britain was a main supplier as well as their best customer.

The Black List was in two parts. The first part, the 'statutory list' as it was called, was a public document being part of the British trading with the enemy legislation. It contained the names of those neutral concerns connected with the Central Powers with whom under the legislation British subjects were forbidden to trade. The second list, List B, was secret. It contained the names of all those traders who were regarded with suspicion. Cargoes consigned to them would probably be intercepted as having a suspected enemy destination and British concerns were advised not to trade with them. 'His Majesty's Government', the American Consul-General was informed when he inquired about one such name, 'are unable to contemplate the possibility of such advice being disregarded by any British firm'.[13]

There was also a White List and for a neutral shipowner it was almost as important to be on the White List as off the Black. In those days Britain was a large exporter of the best quality bunker coal and she also controlled many of the coaling stations on the main trade routes. There were as yet few oil-burning merchantmen. A neutral ship would find great difficulty in getting bunkers if she was not on the British White List. To get on this list the shipowner had to give an undertaking that none of his ships would be chartered to an enemy or other person 'specially notified', that they would not trade in enemy ports, and that when bound for a neutral port, they would call in at a British port for examination. No cargo was to be carried which was consigned 'to order' or which it was known would 'expose steamers to detention by British authorities'. These were the express requirements.[14] A ship on the White List was also expected to be obliging about carrying British cargoes when required. In brief, only good ships got bunkers.

The Black List and the White List were the chief economic weapons. The legal weapon was the examination of cargo to which every ship going in or out of the North Sea had to submit. Outgoing ships had to present certificates of neutral origin for their cargoes; it was important to stop German exports so as to prevent her from obtaining credits abroad. But the main concern of the blockade was with incoming ships. A ship going through the Channel would have to call at the Downs if she had not already been cleared at a more westerly port. The naval examination service there would make an analysis of her cargo and send it by telegraph to the War Trade Intelligence

Department in London. There it would be considered in the light of all the accumulated data and a report made to the Contraband Committee which decided whether the cargo should be released or held. If all was well, the ship would be given a green card without which she would not be allowed to proceed to her destination. A ship coming in from the north would be similarly dealt with though not so easily. The nearest point at which she could be searched was Kirkwall in the Orkneys, maybe several hundred miles from the point of interception. The practice, which was of doubtful legality, was for the intercepting cruiser to divert the ship to a port where she could be properly examined and if necessary to put an armed guard on board her to make sure that she went there. Later in the war this process was much simplified and delays incidental to examination greatly reduced by means of the navicert, an invention which enabled the well-behaved ship to obtain the equivalent of a green card before she set out on her voyage. But this was not in full working order until the latter half of 1916.

The doctrine of continuous voyage was the British warranty in law for seizing goods consigned to a Northern Neutral port but destined to go on into Germany. The difficulty was to identify such goods. At an early stage in the war the British began the solution of this by negotiating agreements with the neutral governments concerned; they promised the speedy release of intercepted cargoes against a guarantee that they would not be re-exported into Germany. But while this might prevent the importation into Germany of cargoes covered by the guarantee, it would not stop the importation of a corresponding amount of home-produced goods. This danger could be avoided only by restricting the importation into the neutral country of any commodity to the amount required for home consumption. A general agreement with Holland was negotiated which accepted this principle while it left room for argument about amounts. A similar agreement was concluded with Denmark in November 1915 but only on the terms that some exchange trade with Germany was permitted. Negotiations with Norway and Sweden for a comprehensive agreement were unsuccessful though agreement was reached covering specific commodities, such as cotton.

Towards the end of 1915 a growing body of opinion in Britain was reaching the conclusion that what was called 'forcible rationing' was the only solution. This would involve the British Government in estimating for itself the quantity required by the neutral for its own consumption and seizing the excess on the presumption that it was destined for export to the enemy. The Cabinet was advised in November 1915 that it was highly doubtful whether the British Prize Court would accept this presumption as by itself proof of enemy destination.[15] Certainly there was no principle of international law which allowed belligerents to ration neutrals. Nevertheless, in the summer of 1916 the decision was taken to do so. No announcement of policy was made. The British Government simply issued a press notice as occasion arose that no more facilities would be accorded for the importation into a specified country of specified goods for a specified length of time. The point was never fully tested in the Prize Court.

By 1916 the British had a huge library of information about every aspect of neutral trading which enabled them to detect the enemy interest behind the innocent façade and to estimate the point at which there would probably be in a neutral country such an excess of any commodity as might overflow into the outstretched hands of the enemy. Some of the information came through ordinary commercial routes; the British Government and the big trading concerns had of course their agents in neutral countries. But most of it was extracted by the use of belligerent power. The statistics accumulated through the examination of cargoes at British ports were very valuable. Interception of mail was another source which became prolific in 1915. From the outset the British were able to oversee everything that went by transatlantic cable. The German cables, which all ran through the Channel, were at once cut. The British cables which ran from Penzance and the French from Brest were in wartime subject to censorship. The American cables had at least one terminal, Penzance or Waterville, in Britain, so that messages going through them could be read.

The loss of the cables was, as we shall see, a great handicap to Germany, not only in the trade war but in the conduct of her diplomacy. Radio was not a satisfactory alternative. Wireless messages could of course be read by anyone who picked them up. Unlike cables they were, if sent from a neutral station, subject to neutral censorship. The reason for the distinction was that a radio message could be sent to a ship at sea and thus used to direct naval operations from neutral territory; the distinction was drawn in the Hague Convention of 1907 on neutral rights and duties. Pursuant to this the American Government would not allow any radio message to be transmitted that was not 'strictly neutral in character'.[16] All messages were censored: translations had to be supplied of any in a foreign language and also the key to any message in code.

Britain's system of blockade was not operated without a great deal of friction. The power behind the British demands was not so much the threat to seize with or without compensation consignments which they could show to have an enemy destination as the threat to behave in a way which would utterly dislocate the neutral's trade. The deadliest weapon, which the British did not scruple to use, was the weapon of delay applied to all cargoes, whether innocent or not; and after delay there was the prospect of protracted proceedings in the British Prize Court, which had early laid down the rule that it was for the cargo owner to prove his innocence and not for the Government to prove guilt. As an alternative to this the British offered comparatively smooth and regular trade of fixed quantities; if the neutral businessman did not get enough, at least he knew what he was going to get and when. Uncertainty is the bugbear of business and to remove it the Northern Neutrals were prepared to sacrifice a great deal.

Continuous voyage, extension of contraband lists, and the validity of reprisals were points at which the law was stretched. Where it was strained to breaking point was in the diversion of ships and their detention. This derived from the power of visit and search. The traditional method of exercising this power was to require the vessel to heave to and then to send a party on board her, examine her papers, and inspect her cargo. In the days when contraband consisted of easily recognizable raw materials and when the port of discharge was accepted as the final destination, this was doubtless effective enough. The British claimed that changed conditions of commerce, the increased size of vessels, and the ease with which cargo could be disguised made search at sea impossible. Diversion and detention in port for the purpose of search was, they claimed, a necessary adaptation of existing rights to modern conditions of commerce and navigation. The difficulty about this argument was the close resemblance it bore to the argument which Germany used to justify the total abandonment of visit and search by the submarine. The British had to be careful to stress changed conditions of commerce rather than changed methods of war. Nor did they stress the fact that during a search at sea the warship would be a sitting target for an enemy submarine.

The fact was that diversion and detention had become the cornerstone of the whole British system of blockade and they had to keep it. It was the touch of the whip without which the cajolery would not have worked. The whip was applied with care and discrimination. In March 1915 detailed recommendations were put before the Cabinet for the treatment of detained vessels. They are full of references to 'leniency' and 'liberality' on the one hand and 'severity' on the other. Here is the opening paragraph of the section which covers vessels on their way to Northern Neutral ports:

> The object aimed at should be to induce vessels not to carry goods for Germany. Vessels should therefore be detained long enough to make them feel the inconvenience of carrying such goods, and the advantage of not doing so, but they should be given the benefit of the doubt when the case is not clear. The treatment should gradually grow stricter. Ships of owners who show no indication of conforming to the desires of His Majesty's Government should be dealt with more severely.[17]

Initially the United States protested against the practice of diverting ships for the purpose of searching them. But, having taken the point generally, she put individual complaints on the ground of undue delay. Tacitly she accepted the system. If she had wanted to destroy it, she could have combined with the Northern Neutrals in forging weapons to fight it. In spite of broad hints from the Northern Neutrals she did not offer to co-operate. She regarded herself, as Wilson put it, as 'the chief custodian of neutral rights'[18] and her concern was to preserve them pending mediation. In the issues raised appearances counted for a lot. If British activities were reconcilable with what was at least a possible view of the law and could be represented as disputable breaches rather than as calculated defiance, United States policy was to grumble and protest but not to quarrel.

The grumblings did, however, create an unhappy atmosphere. Copper, cotton, and rubber were all commodities capable of being used in the manufacture of ammunition, but they could of course also be used for civilian purposes. By nature they were obviously conditional contraband, but the British Admiralty ('the Admiralty are more and more in command of the Government' Page alleged on 14 November 1914)[19] wanted to put them all on the list of absolute contraband. Grey persuaded the Cabinet that this would be too much for America to stomach; and cotton, because it so greatly affected the trade of the Southern states, was the one selected for omission.

This was certainly wise, for the ban on copper was enough to cause great irritation. The United States produced over half the world's supply and the Senate passed a resolution about it. Complaints from exporters streamed into the State Department. These and complaints about the treatment of foodstuffs and about the long delays stimulated the Department into a series of protests. They culminated in a lengthy Note presented on 28 December 1914 which went so far as to say that, if nothing was done, 'it may arouse a feeling contrary to that which has so long existed between the American and British peoples'.[20] Lansing's original language was much stronger. Bad and incomprehensible English as well as offensive, Wilson thought when he sent it back for softening. He was still determined, as in his reaction to Lansing's first protest,* to avoid open provocation and keep the pressure below the surface.

Page called the softened version 'an admirable paper, and it is a pleasure to present it. It takes the English action at its weakest—its lack of a consistent plan.'[21] From the opposite viewpoint Spring Rice wrote sarcastically home about the equanimity of an Administration which had survived the subjugation of Belgium and the ruin of Mexico now being completely upset

---

* See p. 168 above.

by the capture of a cargo of copper owned by Mr. Guggenheim. 'It is rather hard to conduct a reasoned and specific argument between a nation which is making war and a nation which is making money.'[22]

The first outburst came over the fate of German merchantmen interned in American ports. The war was making plain the extent to which American trade was dependent on foreign shipping and the shortage of ships was causing a great increase in freight rates. The object of the Ship Purchase Bill, introduced on behalf of the Administration into the Senate by Senator Stone (one of Spring Rice's 'notorious pro-Germans';[23] certainly there were many German-Americans in his state of Missouri), was the creation of a federally owned and operated merchant marine. Senator Root called it 'a measure of state socialism which, if established, will inevitably destroy individual liberty',[24] and on this ground alone it was bound to encounter widespread opposition. There was other cause for alarm. The ships most obviously available for purchase by the Administration were German ships lying idle in American ports where they had taken refuge from the British Navy. According to the Declaration of London, which in Article 56 gave effect to the British and American practice, the transfer of an enemy vessel to a neutral flag after the outbreak of hostilities was invalid unless the owner could prove that the transfer was not made in order to avoid capture. An inquiry by an Allied prize court into the good faith of the American Government as buyer could hardly fail to cause international complications.

Republican opposition in the Senate was strong and Democratic support lukewarm. Senator Lodge introduced an amendment prohibiting the new shipping board from purchasing ships owned by belligerents. This and the challenge to his leadership by dissident Democrats led Wilson to make the thing a personal issue. He wrote to Mrs. Toy:

You cannot know to what lengths men like Root and Lodge are going, who I once thought had consciences but now know have none. We must not suffer ourselves to forget or twist the truth as they do, or use their insincere and contemptible methods of fighting; we must hit them and hit them straight in the face, and not mind if the blood comes.[25]

As it turned out, the faces that had to be hit were those of seven rebellious Democratic senators. Wilson tried to outmanœuvre them; at one stage he even called at the home of his old foe Speaker Champ Clark to obtain advice and support. But in the end the opposition of the seven rebels, whom Wilson felt to be guilty of 'grievous disloyalty',[26] was decisive. On 17 February 1915 the Bill was dropped and Wilson made the best of his defeat.

The prospect of Germany getting a good price for the ships which the British Navy had bottled up and of their taking to sea again under the American flag naturally caused a great stir in Britain. If Wilson's motives were clear, it was said, why did he not accept the Lodge amendment? Wilson would never have pushed things to extremes by sending the ex-German ships across the Atlantic; he would probably have used them in trade with South America. But he would not accept the amendment, partly because it was Lodge's amendment and so a matter of prestige, partly because it would hamstring the speedy creation of a merchant fleet, and partly because the United States, he said, as 'the chief custodian of neutral rights' must not appear even temporarily to be renouncing rights which he believed to be 'susceptible of clear establishment in any impartial tribunal'.[27]

While the fight was raging in Washington and indignation was at its height in London, a Mr. Breitung of Marquette, Michigan, took a hand in the game. He foresaw a small fortune by buying up German ships and using them to carry cotton to the Central Powers. He made a beginning with the *Dacia* which he had transferred to the American registry on 4 January 1915. He secured a cargo of cotton for her and asked the State Department to clear the voyage to Rotterdam. On 14 January the Department asked the British Foreign Office to allow the projected voyage without prejudice to subsequent voyages. This request crossed a message from Grey that he was much concerned with the situation: Britain must seize the ship but would pay for the cotton at the price ruling in Germany. Further consideration did not alter his view; it was a test case and he could not compromise. The French ambassador in Washington joined in with a Note to say that the purchase of German ships 'in their present tied-up condition' would be an act of assistance to the enemies of France.[28]

This was the first occasion on which British resentment of American neutrality boiled over. The press was in full cry. Page telegraphed on 18 January: 'For the first time I have felt a distinctly unfriendly atmosphere. It has the quality of the atmosphere just before an earthquake.'[29] Grey brought pressure to bear through several channels. He had more than an hour's talk with Page on 18 January which resulted in the telegram from which the above excerpt is taken and was followed by another of the same tenor on 19 January. On the same day as he saw Page Grey telegraphed to Spring Rice a comprehensive indictment of American hostility which he preambled by saying that public opinion was becoming deeply and unfavourably impressed by the attitude of the United States Government.[30] The indictment was in four counts: the prohibition on the publication of ship's manifests which hampered the interception of contraband, the prohibition on the export of submarine parts, the Ship Purchase Bill, and the movement to embargo munitions. While Germany was the aggressor and had inflicted great misery and wrong on occupied territory, 'the only act of the United States Government on record is a protest singling out Great Britain as the only Power of all those at war whose conduct is open to reproach'.

Spring Rice decided to load both barrels of his gun. He asked Bryan on 21 January whether he would like to know what the British papers were saying and followed the Secretary's incautious reply that he would with a long letter based on Grey's telegram, particularizing all four counts and adorning the general sentiments. He prepared also an edited version of the telegram, stronger rather than weaker, and delivered it to House on 22 January. Both recipients, as was doubtless intended, placed these offerings before the President.

The President caused a soothing message to be sent in return. But with the struggle over the Ships Purchase Bill at its height he would not yield over the *Dacia*. Neither would the British. They would not even, as Page and other wellwishers urged, take advantage of what Root called the 'profound feeling of affection for France as well as the hereditary aversion for England'[31] by suggesting to the French that they should make the capture. But, as it happened, the *Dacia* herself gave the British the relief they were too proud to seek by sailing into a French cruiser off Brest. She was seized on 27 February 1915 and duly condemned in a French prize court. After the defeat of the Ships Purchase Bill the agitation died away.

For the first six months of the war Germany did nothing on the high seas to upset the United States whose indignation was accordingly directed against Britain. With the institution of the German economic blockade in February 1915 this situation began to change.

The division of opinion in official Germany over the extent to which the submarine blockade should be pushed was much sharper than that in Britain over the surface blockade. The division began as one between the sailors and the diplomats and it developed, as the significance of submarine warfare was grasped, into a division between the armed forces both military and naval, and the civil side of the Government. To understand the conflict one must know something, though it need not be much, of the working of the German constitution. One can for this limited purpose ignore the fact that the German Empire was a federation of states, with Prussia by far the most powerful, and consider it as a unitary government. It was an autocracy ruled by the Kaiser with the Imperial Chancellor as his principal servant and head of the civilian government. All other ministers were subordinate to the Chancellor. The Reichstag was an elected body of about 400 members. It was an organ of public opinion and had some rudimentary powers over the budget and legislation, sufficient to make it necessary that the Chancellor should retain its confidence. But the Chancellor, though he could address it, was not a member of it or in any way responsible to it; he was appointed and dismissed by the Kaiser. A special feature of the constitution was that the Kaiser was Supreme War Lord not only in name but in power. The direction of the Army and Navy was completely outside the Chancellor's competence. There was a Navy minister who operated within the political sphere but the Kaiser had his own military and naval cabinets, each with its own chiefs. In addition the Army and the Navy had their own heads who had direct access to the Kaiser. The head of the Army was the Chief of the Great General Staff who was also throughout the war Commander-in-Chief in the West. The Navy had a Chief of the Naval Staff separate from the Commander-in-Chief of the High Seas Fleet.

Thus whereas in Britain conflicts of opinion between the civil and military arms were resolved by the collective wisdom of the Cabinet, in Germany they were resolved by the Kaiser as Emperor and Supreme War Lord. Kaiser Wilhelm II was not, however, capable of giving the German system any of the advantages which might be supposed to flow from autocracy in wartime. His mind was not powerful enough to make it other than fortunate for Germany that he suffered from an inability to make it up. Flamboyant, peevish, and uncertain of himself, the All-Highest swung from one opinion to another according to the fears and hopes of the day and the persuasiveness of his ministers.

Of these the most important by virtue of his office was Theobald von Bethmann Hollweg, the Imperial Chancellor since 1909. He came from no political party; his career had been in the civil service. One might·call him the Brahms type of German (he played the piano and was very fond of that composer), in his late fifties, bearded and urbane, not an impressive public personality but perhaps less unremarkable as a statesman than history has yet allowed. It is at any rate generally agreed that within the primary area of his operations, which was not the Reichstag (that was secondary) but the Kaiser and his entourage, he was a very skilful politician. Von Jagow at the Foreign Office was very much his subordinate, an ugly little man but intelligent and rather nice, shy and a reluctant minister.

The one army figure who counted was General Erich von Falkenhayn who had been Minister of War and who after the Battle of the Marne succeeded von Moltke as Chief of the General Staff. Falkenhayn was an able soldier, young as ranking generals go, only fifty-two, far from tongue-tied, indeed fluent in presenting a case, and with a manner very acceptable to the Kaiser. The strength of his position was that physically he was the closest to the throne. The Army General Headquarters were at Charleville on the Meuse behind the line, 50 miles or so from Verdun. The Kaiser liked to be there. He had nothing to do with warlike operations, but it gave him the feel of warlordship; and the proximity of Sedan, where he would sometimes walk, may have promoted happy meditation. Falkenhayn did not abuse his position. He worked agreeably with Bethmann (who after a few months at the Kaiser's side returned to the Chancellery at Berlin), each respecting the other's sphere. But his proximity to the fountain-head barred any other voice on military affairs and the Chief of the Kaiser's Military Cabinet hardly mattered.

It was not so in the Navy, where there were at least three figures of equal importance. The Secretary of State for Naval Affairs, who if he had had to rely only on his position might not have emerged from under the Chancellor, mattered a great deal when he was Grand Admiral von Tirpitz. A gigantic Neptune of a man with a forked beard and an almost pathological hatred of the British, he was the bogyman for all good English children in 1914. He had been Minister since 1897 and was called the Father of the German Navy. Although in his capacity as Secretary Tirpitz was not concerned with naval operations, because of his renown a special decree on 30 July 1914 granted him the right to give his opinion on them to the Kaiser.[32] Admiral von Pohl was the Chief of the Naval General Staff and Admiral von Muller was Chief of the Kaiser's Naval Cabinet. Since Tirpitz was one of the earliest and most vocal supporters of unrestricted U-boat war, it was fortunate for Bethmann that he had not got the Kaiser's ear and that the man who had it, Muller, shared Bethmann's view of the diplomatic dangers. The Kaiser, in whose reign the German Navy began, regarded it as his pet and disliked Tirpitz's pretensions. Once in 1916, when Tirpitz was too pressing in the exercise of his special rights, the Kaiser wrote: 'What I do with my Navy is my business only.'[33] The Kaiser disliked also the methods, especially the manipulation of the press bureau in the Navy Ministry, by which Tirpitz sought to get his way.

Considering the achievements of the submarine as a commerce destroyer in the first German War, it is astonishing to find that, with one exception, no naval brain on either side had an inkling of what the submarine was going to mean. The exception was Fisher, the erratic genius who was First Sea Lord from 1904 to 1910 (the year in which he predicted that war with Germany would break out in the autumn of 1914) and again at the age of seventy-four for six months from November 1914 and who was not at all inactive in between. In June 1912 and again at the end of 1913 Fisher sent memoranda to Churchill full of true prophecy about the submarine and the use to which Germany would put it. In the latter he said: 'This submarine menace is a terrible one for British commerce and Great Britain alike, for no means can be suggested at present of meeting it except by reprisals.'[34] The basis of the general British disbelief in the menace was the fact that the submarine would be unable to effect a capture under the rules of prize law coupled with the assumption that the torpedoing of unarmed merchantmen would be universally regarded as a barbarism that no civilized nation would dare commit. The Whewell Professor of International Law said so firmly in lectures on the subject at the War Course in 1914. Churchill replied to Lord Fisher by comparing the sinking of merchant vessels with such outrages as the spreading of pestilence and the assassination of individuals.[35] It was frankly unthinkable, he said, and added that the excellence of the paper was marred by the prominence assigned to it. The bit about 'marring' he had got from the then First Sea Lord who had made that comment on Fisher's memorandum. No one in the Admiralty thought differently. The paper was shown to the Prime Minister but not to the Cabinet; and thereafter was not seen again until it was proved true.

In Germany the submarine was thought of mainly as an auxiliary in naval operations and there was no great belief in its value as an independent arm. An expedition of 10 out of the 28 submarines in commission, which set out on 6 August 1914, returned without any catch and with one loss by ramming. Then on 5 September a British cruiser was torpedoed; and this was followed shortly afterwards by a tremendous success. On 22 September the U9 sank with huge loss of life three aged cruisers which had been rashly sent on patrol without destroyer protection in the Broad Fourteens off the Dutch coast. The idea that merchantmen could be dealt with in the same way and even more easily and that their destruction on a large scale could be far more useful than that of aged cruisers, once it arose, spread rapidly. The feeling that Germany had for her enemies had by now reached a degree of indignation, if not hatred, hot enough to consume scruples; and between the belligerents reprisal and counter-reprisal were succeeding each other swiftly.

In the first month of the war both sides had independently committed serious breaches of international law, the British by the institution of the starvation policy and the Germans by minelaying.

The starvation policy was initiated on 14 August 1914 when the Cabinet discussed 'the best means of bringing economic pressure to bear upon

Germany by cutting off her supplies of imported food'.[36] It noted the main difficulty, which was that the principal base of supply was the neutral port of Rotterdam, and decided to approach the Dutch Government with the offer of a deal, coal from Britain in exchange for a Dutch prohibition on the export to Germany of imported food. But Britain did not wait for the result of this before taking action. The Navy had already intercepted cargoes of grain bound for Rotterdam and believed to be destined for Germany; and the legality of what it was doing had come under examination. On 14 August Hurst advised that food could be seized only if Britain excluded Article 35 of the Declaration of London (he was of course writing before the Order-in-Council of 20 August which did just that)* and if she could prove that the food was intended for the armed forces of the enemy.[37] The Attorney-General was equally firm.[38] He was Sir John Simon whom Asquith called 'The Impeccable', a man of clear and supple mind, one of the Cabinet who opposed Britain's entry into the war but went not quite all the way with Morley. His decision to remain was hardened by a hint of promotion, and in May 1915 he became Home Secretary. Sir John, while pointing out that the fact that the food was going to Germany was not by itself enough, drew attention to the words in Article 31 of the Declaration: 'destined for the use of the fleets or armies of the enemy or *of a Government Department of the enemy State*'. These last words were novel. The old law was as stated by Hurst. The extension of it to consignments to any government department had not been favoured by the British delegation at the London Conference.

On 19 August a high-powered conference was held at the Foreign Office with Grey in the chair.[39] Churchill and the First Sea Lord were there to speak for the Navy and the Lord Chancellor and the Attorney-General to speak for the law. The Home Secretary, McKenna, was also there and he said that there were 'reliable reports' that the German Government had taken over the whole of the foodstuffs in Germany. On this the conference gladly invoked Article 31 of the Declaration; it was agreed that where the Declaration embodied provisions 'wider than those which had previously been recognised by British Prize Courts and therefore in Great Britain's interests' they should be adopted. So it was 'agreed that all possible steps should be taken to prevent foodstuffs in particular from being imported into Germany in neutral vessels, whether directly or through Dutch ports'. This conclusion was endorsed by the Cabinet the next day. The invocation of Article 31 was helped by the fact that its gist had been reproduced by the State Department in its circular of advice on neutrality issued on 15 August.[40]

There followed a period of confusion. The Cabinet of course had other matters to attend to. It was the eve of the Battle of the Marne: the French

* See p. 168 above.

Army was in terrible danger of defeat: from 27 to 31 August the Cabinet was preoccupied with the fear that the British Army was not giving the help it should. The civil servants, who were working well below the level of the military crisis, lamented in copious minutes[41] the lack of attention from above to the problems of blockade as well as the multiplicity of committees that were sitting upon it. The Admiralty was diverting neutral vessels on their way to neutral ports and British ports were being choked with grain without any thought being given to consequential problems. Moreover, the interception of neutrals was not being matched by the control of Allied vessels bound on similar errands. 'Absolutely chaotic', Crowe said.

The War Orders given by the Admiralty on 26 August were clear enough.[42] All food consigned to Germany through neutral ports was to be captured and all food consigned to Rotterdam was to be presumed to be consigned to Germany. Mr. McKenna's reliable reports had not as yet (and indeed have never) seen the light of day. Clouds of doubt began to form before August 1914 was ended. The Netherlands Government was of course greatly concerned. The Dutch Minister of Marine had on 10 August expressed his fear that within a very few months hunger would drive Germans over the Dutch frontier.[43] The more realistic fear was that the British Navy by intercepting all food going into Rotterdam would starve the Dutch as well as the Germans. Britain met this with her offer to allow food into Rotterdam against a guarantee by the Dutch Government that it would not get into Germany.[44] On 25 August the Netherlands Minister called at the Foreign Office to see Mr. Hurst, bringing with him a business adviser.[45] The adviser thought it 'not inherently impossible' that the German Government might be controlling rye, oats, and barley, but not wheat, which, he said, was not of much importance to the Army or the mass of the population. Hurst could only offer the consolation that in that case the captured wheat would probably be released by the Prize Court.

All that the Admiralty was concerned about was capture; if in the fullness of time the foolishness of lawyers released the grain, that was not their affair. What Grey was concerned about was neutral reaction. He had no wish to exact the penalty for contraband. The ideal would be to seize the food but also to pay for it instead of treating it as prize. This solution, which he proposed on 29 August for what he naïvely called 'comparatively innocent contraband such as foodstuffs',[46] was soon to become the cornerstone of British blockade strategy. The French did not like the idea of paying. They wanted to invoke a Hague Convention which made it an unneutral act to permit a belligerent to move troops or convoys of munitions or supplies across neutral territory, but the British would not swallow that.

The British position, however, was very shaky. It rested on two planks.

The first was the assumption that there was in Germany some measure of government control; the second was the hope that, whatever the measure might be, it would be strong enough to label imports of food as 'destined for the use . . . of a Government Department'. As to the first, the Foreign Office noted on 29 August that doubt had already been cast on the assumption and that there was no concrete evidence for it.[47] The search for evidence did not begin in earnest until after the hypothesis had been acted upon for almost two months. On 29 September 1914 Grey wrote to the Procurator General (the official who represented the Crown in prize matters) that he had information but no evidence good enough for the Prize Court.[48] On the same day he circulated British attachés and agents abroad. One of the principal British aims, he said, was to prevent all foodstuffs from reaching Germany. Orders had been given for the arrest of all neutral vessels carrying food directly or ultimately destined for Germany on the ground that the Government had assumed control of all food: 'it is necessary that all possible evidence should be secured to support this contention'.[49]

The appeal was unsuccessful. The Hague on 19 October and Copenhagen on 21 October replied not just that there was no evidence but that the evidence was to the contrary. The best that could eventually be produced was a German decree of 28 October fixing maximum prices for cereals and providing that they should also be the prices to be paid by the Government if the grain was requisitioned. On 11 November Hurst advised that this was not an assumption of control.[50] The Attorney-General on 29 October had advised: 'I don't see how we can on existing materials claim condemnation of foodstuffs merely because they are passing via neutral ports to Germany.'[51] The Foreign Office had to struggle with the conscience of their lawyers on the one side and with the French as well as the Admiralty on the other. The French in October expressed serious alarm and disappointment at the idea that food to Germany might not be intercepted,[52] even though Crowe warned them of the risk of incurring war with the United States. They appreciated that it would be contrary to the rules, they said, but they stressed the misbehaviour of Germany in the territory she had occupied and the destruction she had done there.

The British, however, found the fiction of German control more serviceable than the claim of eye for eye and tooth for tooth. They did not expose the fiction to the scrutiny of their own Prize Court. The *Miramichi* was a British ship bound for Rotterdam and loaded with a cargo of wheat consigned without subterfuge (for it had been shipped before the outbreak of war) to German merchants in Colmar and Mannheim.[53] The British skipper dutifully inquired from the Admiralty whether he could go to Rotterdam and was told that he could not. He put in to a British port where the cargo was seized on 1 September 1914. With a speed that was not to be repeated when the queue grew longer, the case came before the Court on 3 November 1914. The Attorney-General himself appeared and did not even raise the question of contraband; instead he argued unsuccessfully that the German interest in the goods was sufficient to justify the condemnation as enemy property.

The British were determined on the starvation policy, whether or not it was lawful. The fiction helped them to evade an admission of illegality, and it also gave them room for manœuvre. By 30 September British pressure on Holland (which without the fiction would have been open blackmail) for an embargo on exports to Germany had gone far enough to enable Grey to tell Page that soon American food could go to Holland without interference; Page was sufficiently bewitched to describe this as 'an important concession in our favor'.[54] The only other way in which Britain could, while paying lip-service to the law, have achieved this object would have been by declaring food to be absolute contraband. This she would not do. She would not mobilize such scanty authority as was available in support of a minority view and declare roundly that starvation was in itself a legitimate weapon. Curiously enough Wilson himself, though he could hardly be expected to remember it, in the brief acquaintance he made with the subject in Professor Southall's lectures at the University of Virginia, had taken the following note:

Contraband is whatever is termed useful in war. It therefore varies from time to time as the arts of war change. Agricultural products, it is said, may become contraband when the purpose of one belligerent is to reduce his adversary by starvation.[55]

But this was not the general opinion and the British Government would not go as far as this for publication. It would have looked far too like the German 'frightfulness' they wanted to condemn. Moreover, they were handicapped by previous utterances made when Britain was seen in the role of the starved rather than the starver. They dug up some precedents for the proposition, such as what Bismarck had said in 1885 about the rice trade in Chinese waters:[56] but they referred to them only for the purpose of getting such credit as was going for resisting temptation.

So when they had to meet American criticism of their policy, they stated firmly in a Note of 10 February 1915:

The most difficult questions in connection with conditional contraband arise with reference to the shipment of foodstuffs. No country has maintained more stoutly than Great Britain in modern times the principle that a belligerent should abstain from interference with foodstuffs intended for the civilian population.[57]

Abstention from interference with food for civilians had not in the past been regarded as raising questions of exceptional difficulty. The principle of the law was clear and its application to the type of warfare for which it was designed did not raise more than the usual quota of nice cases. Military operations were then confined both in time and in place; they were conducted expeditiously and within a limited area. In so far as an army did not live off the surrounding country, it would probably, transport overland being rudimentary, be supplied by sea, its base of supply being the nearest port to which food and equipment could conveniently be consigned. Thus the first distinctive mark of contraband, and one essential to its character, was derived from the place of consignment. If the place was a military base, there was some presumption, the strength of it varying according to the nature of the commodity and the character of the consignee, that the cargo was destined for military use. As to the nature of the cargo, if it was like food, which could have both civil and military uses, the Prize Court would have to act on such indications as the circumstances afforded. Quality, for example, could be a guide. The cheaper and the rougher it was, the more likely to be intended for soldierly consumption: *per contra*, 'luxuries for the use of domestic tables'.[58]

Such was the old law. But was it part of a realistic picture of modern warfare? In 1914 huge armies were continually in operation and were being fed from sources remote from the battlefields. No longer could any particular port be labelled as a base of supply. For a nation totally committed to war every port was a base. The British put the point in their Note of 10 February:

In any country in which there exists such tremendous organization for war as now obtains in Germany, there is no clear division between those whom the Government is responsible for feeding and those whom it is not. Experience shows that the power to requisition will be used to the fullest extent in order to make sure that the wants of the military are supplied, and however much goods may be imported for civil use, it is by the military that they will be consumed if military exigencies require it, especially now that the German Government have taken control of all the foodstuffs in the country.[59]

The argument, even without the addendum on government control, flows easily from the extension to Article 31 of the Declaration. Indeed, it echoed the commentary appended to the Article, the work of the celebrated international lawyer, M. Renault. He wrote:

If a civil department may freely receive foodstuffs or money, that department is not the only gainer, but the entire State, including its military administration, gains also, since the general resources of the State are thereby increased.[60]

The peril that lurks in the path of all moderate reformers is this: that in the course of making what seem to them reasonable adjustments to modern conditions, inadvertently they pull out the linchpin of the old structure. When M. Renault brought within the principles of contraband anything that increased the general resources of the State, he obliterated the distinction between military and civilian uses and between combatants and non-combatants and thereby made way for the concept of total war. The lawyers were to talk for many months to come of 'adaptation'. But the law was just not adaptable. 'Total war' was then an unfamiliar expression but, though unmentioned by name, it was what Article 31 foreshadowed and what the British Note was talking about. 'The general resources of the State' would not in time of war be used for feeding civilians while the Army went without. If it was permissible not to increase the general resources of the State, it must also be permissible to weaken them and thus was begun the argument for the long-range bomber; if resources could not be weakened without bombing or starving women and children, then women and children must suffer.

The man of 1914 scrupled to make use of such words. It was what followed logically from the argument in the British Note but the draftsman left it to logic to project the line. And if it could be left as a dotted line, so much the better. For any extension of the new road that was being cut must lead straight to the realization that a civilian at sea could demand no greater protection from the peril of the torpedo than one on land from the peril of famine.

Under the pressure of war the winds of change were to blow so fiercely that the law of contraband, so meticulously constructed during a century and a half, bent, buckled, and finally collapsed; and the velocity was such as to blow into irrelevance, even as they were emerging, the words from lawyers' mouths. Phenomenally rapid though it was by the measurement of lawyers' time, nevertheless the whole process took about two years. The starvation policy received legal recognition in Britain in a decision of the Privy Council given in October 1917.[61] The scarcity of food in Germany, the court said, 'made the victualling of the civilian population a war problem': salted herrings—this was the cargo that was seized—if fed to civilians, would release bread and meat for the armed forces.

In 1914 the law, put at its most favourable for the British on the footing that they could pick and choose from the Declaration of London, stopped halfway between the old and the new. It permitted the interception of food for civilians but only if consigned to the use of the Government. The seizure of food on the rumour that it was under government control—a seizure which was not casual or accidental but part of a deliberate policy for which a pretext was being sought—was a breach of the law beside which

Germany's offences in the autumn of 1914, which we must now consider, were venial.

Germany began the war with a belief, which the British did not share, in the efficacy of the mine and with the intention of using it aggressively. The control of minelaying by international law was derived from the principle that belligerents had no right to pitch their battles on any land or water that they chose or to make all civilian activity subordinate to their measures. Perhaps this idea now seems ridiculous. In 1945, when the belligerents abandoned the battlefield they had made of Egypt and Libya, they left behind them minefields in which thereafter a huge number of Egyptians were killed or maimed without marking the conscience of mankind. The trickle that began in 1914 had become, as the wars of the century succeeded one another, a swollen river of indifference to civilian life. But until 1914 the safety of non-combatants was paramount. It had to be recognized that the mine was a legitimate weapon of war and could be used as such, for example, in a minefield to protect your own naval bases or, if you were daring enough, to hamper the enemy from emerging from his. The Eighth Hague Convention of 1907 dealt with the subject. To some extent it had to be hortatory—'every possible precaution must be taken for the security of peaceful shipping'—but it contained also specific provisions about giving notice of where mines were laid and ensuring that any floating mines were rendered harmless after an hour.

On the first day of the war Germany laid mines 30 miles off the coast of Suffolk; the cruiser *Amphion* struck one on 6 August and sank with the loss of 151 lives. On 7 August Germany gave notice of minelaying in very vague terms. She then proceeded to lay mines indiscriminately in the North Sea. Two merchantmen were sunk on trade routes. Germany denied that she had done anything improper. In any event, she said, although she had herself signed the Convention (indeed her delegate had spoken eloquently at the Hague Conference about the inhumanity of mining), it had not been signed by all the belligerents (Russia was the only non-signatory) and so by its own terms was inapplicable.

The British bore all this with seeming patience. The Cabinet on 17 August discussed retaliation and decided that it should only be done in the last resort.[62] A resounding protest was prepared against the German behaviour whose 'manifest inhumanity must call down upon its authors the censure and reprobation of all civilized peoples'.[63] The British reluctance to retaliate was not, however, entirely due to fear of censure and reprobation. The Admiralty did not believe in the value of aggressive mining. The Royal Navy was the dominant fleet in the North Sea and regarded minefields, whether its own or the enemy's, as a hindrance to its operations. It was Churchill who fought the demand for countermeasures[64] and Asquith who pressed for them, writing to the First Lord on 29 September that the time had come to start mining 'if necessary on a Napoleonic scale'. The sinkings on 22 September* may have helped the argument. The office of the three aged cruisers had been to act as an outpost against enemy warships. The success of the submarine made it clear that the outpost could not be replaced and a minefield would be a useful alternative. At any rate the 'manifest inhumanity' protest, which was issued only on 26 September, was still reverberating when on 2 October Britain announced that she would herself lay mines. She was more considerate than Germany in that she specified the danger area, but blurred the effect by adding: 'Although these limits are assigned to the danger area it must not be supposed that navigation is safe in any part of the southern waters of the North Sea.'[65]

But the British minelaying was comparatively slight. It was not after all the right weapon for the superior naval force. So when later in October Britain discovered a German minefield north of Ireland on the Atlantic route, she was not tempted to retaliate further in kind. She resorted instead to a measure which initiated a startling development in the war at sea. It was felt necessary, an Admiralty notice said on 2 November 1914, 'to adopt measures appropriate to the novel conditions under which this war is being waged'. The whole of the North Sea was declared to be a military area, or 'war zone' as it came to be called. This was a new practice (there was a very limited precedent for it in the Russo-Japanese War when Japan had declared certain waters closely adjacent to her coast as 'defence sea areas') and, unless it could be justified as a reprisal, an illegal one. The effect of making the sea a war zone was to subject peaceful traffic to the hazards of naval operations. Merchant ships sailed in the zone at the risk of damage, for which they would get no redress, from warships searching for suspicious craft. If they wanted to be safe, they must keep to the safety lanes provided, thus incidentally facilitating interception by the British Navy. 'Any straying, even for a few miles, from the course', the notice said, 'may be followed by serious consequences.' The Admiralty notice aroused strong protests from the Northern Neutrals. Norway invited the United States to join in but, whether from indifference or from goodwill to Britain, she declined to do so. On 21 November 1914 Tirpitz gave a bellicose interview for publication in America in which he said: 'What will America say if Germany declares submarine war on all the enemy's merchant ships? Why not? England wants to starve us. We can play the same game.'[66] But in fact he was more

* See p. 191 above.

cautious than he sounded, doubting whether Germany had enough submarines for an effective blockade of England. Bethmann feared the antagonism of the neutrals, especially the United States; they would not declare
war, he thought, but they might aid actively the British blockade. The chief
campaigner for the submarine was von Pohl. The commander of the submarine fleet advised him that a blockade could be made effective if there was
no need to warn enemy merchantmen before sinking them nor to take undue
pains about sparing neutrals. Armed with that report Pohl appealed to the
Kaiser. The Kaiser on 9 January 1915 upheld Bethmann, telling Pohl in
effect to continue his preparations and to apply again later. But Pohl continued to argue with Bethmann. He argued that neutral shipping would not
be in peril since it would avoid the war zone; and he stressed the political
danger of resisting the public demand, which had been fanned by Tirpitz's
speech, for retaliation against the starvation policy. Moreover, if Britain
could declare a 'war zone', why could not Germany also? A third ground
for retaliation seemed to be offered by an Admiralty order of 31 January
1915 authorizing British merchant vessels to hoist a neutral flag as a device
for escaping attack. This was one of the *ruses de guerre* conditionally permitted under international law, but a somewhat irritating one both for the
neutral and the enemy. On 2 February the Chancellor gave in. Pohl lost
no time at all. He drafted the proclamation at once, gave it to the Kaiser the
next day, told him that the Chancellor no longer opposed it, and had it signed
and issued on 4 February 1915.

The historic declaration was as follows:

> The waters around Great Britain, including the whole of the English Channel,
> are declared hereby to be included within the zone of war, & after the 18th inst.
> all enemy merchant vessels encountered in these waters will be destroyed, even
> if it may not be possible always to save their crews and passengers. Within this
> war zone neutral vessels are exposed to danger since, in view of the misuse of the
> neutral flags ordered by the government of Great Britain on the 31st ult. and of
> the hazards of naval warfare, neutral vessels cannot always be prevented from
> suffering from the attacks intended for enemy ships.[67]

The initiation of the policy which two years later brought the United
States into the war was not taken very seriously in Washington where it was
treated as just another move against Allied shipping. The German Foreign
Office hastened to get out an explanatory memorandum justifying the new
measure as a reprisal.[68] This impressed Lansing as a strong presentation of
the German case and made him wonder whether any sharp protest, or indeed
any protest at all, was advisable.[69] When Bernstorff delivered the German

Note at the State Department he asked Bryan to warn Americans of the danger of travelling in belligerent ships and to recommend American shipping to keep clear of the war zone. Bryan seemed incredulous and to regard a submarine campaign of that sort as unthinkable. The effect of the German Note in Washington was to make the German pot about as black as the British kettle, but not any blacker. On 10 February Wilson sent off plaintive Notes to both sides and recorded his impartiality in a letter on 14 February to Mrs. Peck: 'Together England and Germany are likely to drive us crazy.'[70]

The Note to Britain expressed 'grave concern' at the use of the American flag.[71] Occasional use under the stress of immediate pursuit was, it suggested, very different from a settled policy. The German Declaration had made the point that the belligerent use of the American flag put American shipping in danger. This point made a greater appeal to the American public than the British plea, legally correct, that it was a legitimate *ruse de guerre*; tricks of the game which imperilled American ships could not be looked upon indulgently. Spring Rice referred to

the rather surprising fact that the feeling against England for authorising the use of the flag is almost as strong, at least on the surface, as the feeling against Germany for the Berlin proclamation.[72]

The Note to Germany did not censure her departure from the laws of war or her threat to non-combatant lives.[73] It simply expressed the American Government's reluctance to believe that such an 'unprecedented' act would be allowed to affect Americans. The phrase 'strict accountability' was dredged up from the diplomatic language of the nineteenth century. If a submarine should destroy an American vessel or the lives of American citizens the American Government would be constrained to hold the German Government to a strict accountability; and, the Note then went on with greater precision, 'to take any steps it might be necessary to take to safeguard American lives and property and to secure to American citizens the full enjoyment of their acknowledged rights on the high seas'.

The German Declaration of 4 February 1915 was just what the Admiralty were waiting for. They were not perturbed by the threat. In fact Germany had by then only twenty-two submarines in service. Moreover, the Admiralty had set up a drifter net barrage across the Straits of Dover; and to avoid it (and fortunately Germany overestimated its efficacy) added 1,400 miles, or an extra seven days, to the submarine's journey to its chief hunting ground in the Western Approaches, i.e. the approaches from the Atlantic to the Channel and the Irish Sea. Germany's first submarine campaign, which lasted until the end of September 1915, although more effective than the British expected, destroyed a tonnage little more than half the new construction during the period.

So at the outset the Admiralty regarded the German Declaration joyfully as providing an occasion for reprisal. On 6 February 1915 Churchill submitted to the Cabinet the draft of an Admiralty notice to be issued without delay.[74] After a forceful preamble, 'the German declaration substitutes indiscriminate destruction for regulated capture' being the theme developed, it announced the consequences as 'special measures' which might 'in some respects involve a departure from previous practice'. The suggestion of a departure was an understatement. All ships carrying goods of presumed enemy destination, ownership, or origin were to be detained and taken into port. Ships and cargoes would not, however, be confiscated unless condemned on other grounds.

This was a drastic proposal. As a retaliation for the submarine blockade, which no one outside Germany then took very seriously, the British would delete the word 'contraband' from the dictionary of international law and throttle all trade with Germany. The supporters of the all-out economic blockade rejoiced in the pretext (Hankey's word)[75] afforded by the German Declaration. Others were nervous about the effect on neutrals, and the Cabinet was divided. The French, who had earlier pressed for a more rigorous blockade, now got cold feet.[76] This was a procedure so damaging to neutrals, they said, as to encounter the most extreme protest: the suggestion that cargoes would be purchased might involve an enormous outlay and who was going to pay? They advocated instead an invitation to neutrals to co-operate in framing measures to put an end to the German use of submarines; if neutrals maintained an attitude of detachment on the above modes of warfare, the Allied governments would take measures which might 'involve a departure from the lines upon which they have acted hitherto'. As an earnest of what was to come, 'a blockade of the German North Sea coast would be at once announced'. 'The announcement', the Attorney-General, Sir John Simon, said mysteriously in presenting these proposals to the Cabinet, 'is unobjectionable, though the enforcement of it will not be found ultimately to comply with international rules.'

The Cabinet met on 16 February. Churchill strongly urged the original version and his view prevailed, the Prime Minister, Grey, and Lord Crewe (always close to Asquith) being in the minority. The minority considered, the Prime Minister reported to the King, the proposed reprisal to be 'obviously much more injurious to neutral commerce and interests than the more or less illusory German threat',[77] and urged the importance of not alienating and embittering neutral and particularly American opinion.

The Cabinet met again on 23 February and it was decided that the French should be asked to give way. They did give way, and on 1 March 1915 the Prime Minister announced the terms of the reprisal in the House of Commons. 'A red letter day for the development of our policy of economic pressure', Hankey said.[78] The Order-in-Council was formally issued on 11 March.[79] Its object was bluntly stated: 'to prevent commodities of any kind from reaching or leaving Germany'. Asquith, whose doubts were either overcome or kept concealed, said in the House on 1 March that there was 'no form of economic pressure to which we do not consider ourselves entitled to resort'.[80] He pointed out that in his statement the words 'blockade' and 'contraband' were not used nor other terms of international law.

In dealing with an opponent who has openly repudiated all the restraints, both of law and of humanity, we are not going to allow our efforts to be strangled in a network of juridical niceties.

Naturally this was not good enough for Lansing who wanted to cut and dry the legal element; Britain, he felt, ought to be made to assert whether she was or was not setting up a blockade. So with the President's permission, and in language which the President himself rendered rather less abrupt, he sent to London on 5 March a demand to know the answer.[81] But there was no chance of Britain meeting head on a 'confirm-or-deny' attack; she wanted to keep all lines of argument open, those that attracted the lay as well as those that attracted the legal mind. The Foreign Office lawyers knew quite well that it was not a good blockade under existing law. They knew that it would be hopeless to try to convince any prize court that it was and in fact they never did try. The layman's view, on the other hand, was expressed by Churchill who wrote a powerful note for the Cabinet, contending that it was 'not a case of a paper blockade, but of a blockade as real and as efficient as any that has ever been established'.[87] So it was: and the fact that it was a blockade of a range of ports and not only of a single port was but a reflection of an increase in naval power. But there was no precedent for a blockade of *neutral* ports and their inclusion in the range was something that no lawyer could justify.

So the Foreign Office line was to suggest everything and to press nothing too hard. The suggestion of a blockade could not be pressed very far without resort to the argument that the old law should be adapted to modern conditions; and how far could that argument be taken without strengthening the German case for much more radical reform? Retaliation, which was the strongest argument legally, was, even if acceptable to them as a matter of law, naturally repulsive to neutrals. Moreover, its validity was dependent on German policy; it was subject to the danger—very real, as was already

being made manifest*—that Germany might desist, or at least pretend to
desist, from the measures provoking the reprisal.

So the reply to Lansing's interrogatory was as vague as could be.[83] It
was sent on 15 March 1915 together with a copy of the Order-in-Council
just issued. The Order was entitled 'Reprisals restricting German Commerce', it did not use anywhere the word 'blockade', and the accompanying
Note did not give formally the notification necessary to constitute a valid
blockade. The effect of the Order, the Note said with bland simplicity, was
'to confer certain powers upon the executive officers of His Majesty's
Government'. True, the object was 'succinctly stated, to establish a blockade',
but Britain, desiring to alleviate the burden, would not exact the normal
penalty of confiscation imposed upon a blockade-runner. The Note implied
that well-behaved neutrals had little to fear. The extent to which the
'certain powers' would be actually exercised and the degree of severity with
which they would be operated would depend on administrative orders and
each case would be dealt with on its own merits; moreover, 'a wide discretion is afforded to the prize court in dealing with the trade of neutrals in
such manner as may in the circumstances be deemed just'.

'Very adroit', was Lansing's comment.[84] If the Order-in-Council itself
had described the measure as a blockade, it would have contradicted the
Order-in-Council of 29 October 1914† which adopted the Declaration of
London without excluding Article 18; and that Article prescribed that 'the
blockading forces must not bar access to neutral ports or coasts'. So the
accompanying Note, when it talked of a 'blockade', was quite inconsistent.
The President had the matter discussed in Cabinet on 19 March or at least
he told the Cabinet that he thought the Note should be answered, and he then
put his thought into draft.[85] The draft was as vague as the Note it was
answering: it could have been condensed into an expression of belief that
Britain would comply with international law, avoid upsetting America, and
make reparation if she did so. Lansing went to the other extreme with a draft
of detailed refutation.[86] He examined the phraseology of the two documents and demonstrated their lack of harmonization. He dealt also with
retaliation and set out the American position as follows:

> The right of a nation to retaliate upon an enemy, when the enemy has violated
> the established rules of war, is not contested so long as the injury is inflicted
> directly upon the enemy, but when the retaliation seeks to make neutral nations
> its agents and at the same time to deprive those nations of rights which they are
> legally entitled to enjoy, the retaliating power invites the condemnation and
> protest of the nations, which it has so grievously injured.

Bryan sent Lansing's draft to the President with a common-sense letter.

        * See p. 207 below.   † See p. 170 above.

Doubtless the Secretary's mind lacked subtlety but he could go straight to a blunt point as fast as any man. Why fuss about the word 'blockade'? Britain was asserting a right to stop non-contraband goods going to and from neutral ports. Unless all merchandise could be declared contraband, which he understood it could not be, she was wrong. So much for Lansing. As for Wilson's draft, he suggested that it might be unwise to assume that Britain did not intend to act in accordance with the clear language of the Order.

All this was material for the President's second thoughts which turned out much better than his first. On 2 March he received from Page, who was still influential with him, his comments on the Order. The ambassador advised complaints about concrete cases rather than general communications.

They quietly laugh at our effort to regulate sea warfare under new conditions by what they regard as lawyers' disquisitions out of textbooks. . . . They care nothing for our definitions or general protests but are willing to do us every practical favor and will under no conditions either take our advice or offend us.[88]

Page also made the point, which the President noted and which the British thereafter took every opportunity of rubbing in, that on balance the war was far from doing American trade any harm.

Personally Wilson was as allergic as Asquith could wish to 'juridical niceties'. Inconsistencies, he wrote to Bryan, were neither here nor there. 'We are face to face with *something they are going to do.*'[89] They were not going to be argued out of it; and what the American answer should do was to state firmly and clearly the American attitude and then wait for the facts to show whether the British intended to violate American rights.

The British unwillingness to plant either leg firmly on legal ground left the draftsman in reply a wide field of manœuvre. In the reply which was finally settled and dispatched on 30 March 1915,[90] the President, choosing to regard the British Note as a notification of blockade, parried it in Bryan's way; forms of blockade, however they might be adapted to fit modern conditions, must still 'comply with the well-recognized and reasonable prohibition of international law against the blockading of neutral ports'. As to reprisal, ignoring the legal aspect, he treated the British references to the German measures they were retaliating against 'as merely a reason for certain extraordinary activities on the part of His Majesty's naval forces and not as an excuse for or prelude to any unlawful action'. But really what he did—very astutely, since essentially what he wanted to do was to preserve American rights without a clash on the law—was to seize on all the protestations in the British Note about discretion, administrative powers, and willingness to show consideration, and say that everything depended on the way the British executed the Order, and that America reserved her rights.

In view of these assurances formally given to this Government, it is confidently expected that the extensive powers conferred by the order in council on the executive officers of the Crown will be restricted by 'orders issued by the Government' directing the exercise of their discretionary powers in such a manner as to modify in practical application those provisions of the order in council which, if strictly enforced, would violate neutral rights and interrupt legitimate trade.

There was, however, a very significant difference between the official American attitude towards Britain and that towards Germany which arose out of the nature of the case rather than from goodwill. It was, to put it in legal language, that for Britain 'accountability' meant a claim for damages while for Germany it carried with it also the threat of an injunction. The former could wait for settlement until after the war; the latter could be made effective only by immediate intervention.

It would be tedious to pursue in detail the British-American controversy over the blockade as it developed in notes and counternotes over the next eighteen months. The argument on principle boomed in undertone to the shriller complaints of malpractice. On principle the Americans had decidedly the better of it. Indeed, Grey set his advocates an impossible task. He disliked their only real argument based on reprisal because he thought that it would be resented. In this he was probably right; and he never lost sight of his paramount object which was not to win an argument but to retain goodwill. The faint hope of sustaining the Order-in-Council as a blockade lay in the argument of changed conditions; and at the same time as he was cutting out the plea of reprisal, Grey was saying 'how careful we must be in using this argument lest we should thereby justify Germany's use of the submarine against the merchant ships'.[91]

When the time came for the Crown to justify the Order-in-Council before its own prize court, it pleaded only that it was a legitimate reprisal. By that time it was plain that the submarine campaign was far more than an 'illusory threat' and so the chief legal objection to the argument of reprisal, that it was out of proportion, had been removed. The court held that the Order was lawful as not entailing on neutrals a degree of inconvenience unreasonable considering all the circumstances of the case.[92]

While the terms of the Order-in-Council were still under discussion in London, there occurred a diversion which might have affected, though it did

Sir Cecil Spring Rice, British ambassador in Washington

1916. Count Johann von Bernstorff, German ambassador to the U.S.A.

not in fact affect, the Allied course of action. The German Foreign Office made a determined attempt to present the Declaration of 4 February 1915 as a reprisal in the true sense and not an independent measure of war by offering to abandon it if Britain abandoned the starvation policy.[93] They began on 7 February, three days after the date of the Declaration, by talking to the American ambassador about a formal assurance that imported food would not be used by the military and offering to leave its distribution to American organizations. They followed this up with a hint, given to Gerard and also in a communication through Bernstorff, that if Britain allowed in food on these terms, Germany would withdraw the Declaration. Then on 16 February in the Note in which he answered the American Note of 10 February Jagow made the point more formal. 'If England invoked the powers of famine', he wrote, Germany must 'appeal to the same grim ally.'[94] But if America would find a way of ensuring the observance of the Declaration of London and thereby render possible for Germany 'the legitimate supply of foodstuffs and industrial raw materials', Germany would 'gladly draw necessary conclusions from the new situation thus created'.

Counselor Lansing was sceptical.[95] If Germany could make her submarine blockade effective, Britain would suffer from it more than Germany from the British blockade since she was so much more dependent on food imports: Germany must, he noted on 18 February, expect the plan to fail. But Bryan had acted on the first hints.[96] The British position, he suggested to Wilson on 15 February, was without justification. So he bade Page tell Grey of the proposal to distribute through American organizations and inquire whether this did not remove British reasons for stopping food imports. Page was also to suggest the probability of the withdrawal of the submarine Declaration if the food question could be adjusted. As it happened, there was a concrete case on food imports awaiting decision. In January 1915, with intent to show up the British starvation policy, German agents or sympathizers in the United States chartered an American ship, the *Wilhelmina*, loaded her with food, and consigned her to Hamburg. The shippers sent their manager to Europe with instructions to see that the cargo was sold only to civilians. The State Department was kept well informed and, when the *Wilhelmina* was intercepted, Page was sent to inquire. This was towards the end of January and the British apparently did not like to say unequivocally that they were stopping all food anyway. So they gave two particular reasons. One was a German decree which was said to be coming into effect on 1 February 1915 and which, so the British alleged, empowered the German Government to seize all foodstuffs. The other one was that Hamburg, to which the ship was consigned, was a fortified place. The latter was a tit-for-tat for Germany rather than an argument to convince

America. The fortifications of Hamburg could hardly be such as to raise the presumption that food sent there went only into military stomachs. But in November 1914, at a time when the Royal Navy had quitted Scapa Flow until it was made submarine-proof, Germany had seized the chance to make a couple of raids on the East coast of England, shelling Scarborough and other towns and killing women and children. She sought to justify this wanton bit of bravado with the claim that these towns were fortified: so if Scarborough, why not Hamburg, was what the British said. On 15 February 1915, the day before Page was instructed to take up the question of food imports generally, Bryan had written to ask for the release of the *Wilhelmina*, stating, as was the fact, that the new German decree did not apply to imported food and that anyway it applied only to grain which made up no more than 15 per cent of the cargo in question.

The cargo of the *Wilhelmina* was eventually taken by the British and paid for and the case itself was now submerged in the larger question. Bryan in his message of 16 February had observed that 'a policy which seeks to keep food from non-combatants, from the civil population of a whole nation, will create a very unfavorable impression throughout the world'.[97] This put the matter strongly indeed and the situation was canvassed at luncheon on 17 February between Asquith, Grey, Page, and House who was then in London.[98] All that emerged, however, was a tentative suggestion that if Germany abandoned the whole of her submarine and mining policy, Britain might refrain from taking the further (and illegal) step of making food absolute contraband. Even this was seized upon in Washington as 'a ray of hope' and Page was told to press for a deal, the controlled admission of food against 'concessions of equal importance'.[99] Page hastily denied any perception of the ray; he was spending the weekend with the Prime Minister at Walmer Castle and would follow it up, but he had little hope; the Germans, he wrote, had bungled the matter.

But Bryan, with Wilson's approval, was not going to let go so long as he saw any possibility of the submarine and starvation policies cancelling each other out, thus relieving America of a double embarrassment. So when Page got back from a very uncomfortable weekend—the castle had no central heating and the meals were not at all to his vegetarian taste—he found waiting for him to deliver a Note, dated 20 February and identical with one sent to Germany, proposing a *modus vivendi* 'based upon expediency rather than legal right'.[100] It was a comprehensive proposal covering minelaying and the use of the neutral flag as well as the use of the submarine. The pith of the bargain was that in exchange for Germany's abandonment of the under-water attack Britain would not interfere with food consigned to American agencies in Germany for distribution to non-combatants only.

While Page found Grey personally sympathetic though non-committal, the proposal was angrily received in the British Foreign Office. They had just pointed out in their Note of 10 February,* which Bryan could hardly have had time to digest before being caught up in the excitement of the German opening, the hopelessness of trying to separate military and civilian food. Even if none of the imported food found its way to the military, the importation would release for them a corresponding quantity of home-grown food. The Admiralty reaction, expressed in a memorandum circulated by Churchill to the Cabinet on 28 February, was much fiercer.[101] It opened with a reference to the 'strongly unneutral character' of the proposal: 'an unblushing attempt to assist our enemy'. It would be as well, the author said, to see what were the causes that had produced such a note; it was probably inspired by the strong German element in the Administration. In its quieter parts the memorandum put forward the argument that this was a new sort of war in which the old distinction between the civil and military population could not be maintained. It did not of course extend that argument on to the decks of merchant ships.

Hankey also entered the fray on 25 February with a minute to the Prime Minister.[102] It is of the utmost importance, he wrote, 'not to take any action which would fetter the use of the weapon of starving Germany unless over-whelming advantages are to be gained thereby'. The advantages, which plainly Hankey did not consider overwhelming, were exemption from sub-marine attack and American friendliness.

In framing his proposal in the *modus vivendi* Bryan ignored the indica-tion in Jagow's Note of 16 February that 'industrial raw materials' as well as food must be part of the deal. From Gerard's reports it became clear that the military arm of the German Government would require substantially more than the admission of food in exchange for the abandonment of sub-marine war.[103] Germany's formal reply to the *modus vivendi*, made on 28 February 1915, was a cautiously worded document.[104] She shied away from the American superintendence of food distribution and talked vaguely of guarantees of that nature. She suggested that all conditional contraband should be treated in the same way as food and that all raw materials on the free list of the Declaration of London should be admitted without question.

Britain's announcement on 1 March of her blockade boded ill for fruitful discussion of the *modus vivendi*, even though it was accompanied by a brief note to say that the latter was 'under careful consideration'.[105] The result of the consideration appeared in a memorandum dated 13 March.[106] It did not concentrate on—it did not even mention—the argument that military and civilian supplies could not be effectively separated. Perhaps it

* See p. 196 above.

was thought unwise to do more than, as had already been done in the Note of 10 February 1915, skirt the point that the inevitable result of the policy was national famine and that famine could not be alleviated in part without alleviating the whole. At any rate the purport of the memorandum was the justification of the food blockade as a retaliatory measure for German misdeeds which were set out at great length, stretching from the ill-treatment of prisoners of war to the bombardment of Scarborough. It quite ignored the point of the *modus vivendi*, which was that each side should cease from wrongdoing and thereby eliminate the cause for retaliation, and concluded by declaring that the food blockade was 'a natural and necessary consequence of the unprecedented methods, repugnant to all law and morality, which have been described above'. Thus the food blockade, started in the first week of war, was made to follow 'the unprecedented methods' as convincingly as the horse the cart. In fact in the week before they were announced, on 28 January 1915, the merits of the British starvation policy were being discussed at a London luncheon table.[107] An American attaché, 'very strongly pro-German', asked whether it was fair to starve women and children, to which an Englishwoman retorted that Germany would do the same to England if she could. This degree of wisdom was the percolation from the doctrine of reprisals that reached the ordinary citizen: doubtless the same simplicity of thought prevailed at the luncheon tables of Berlin.

What resounded through Britain's Note of 13 March was her resolution not to bargain with Germany. This was the point that pierced, for Germany after 1914 stood exposed as one whose word was not to be taken.

The *modus vivendi* was dropped. Certainly the German Note sought concessions which Britain could justifiably refuse; she could not by this means be forced to adopt the Declaration of London. But it would not have been unreasonable for Germany to ask for some limit to Britain's liberty to make up her contraband lists in any way she pleased. When in October 1915 she issued a new list, it contained forty-two items of absolute contraband (including for example, paraffin wax, barbed wire, motor vehicles, and lubricants) and only fourteen of conditional. She was beginning to make all contraband absolute.

While the German Note had been carefully worded to show willingness to deal, Britain's was a flat refusal to talk to the point. Her diplomatic language was smooth, but she could rely on Page to convey unofficially the fierceness of her rejection. He told the State Department on 6 March that the British feeling was that 'our pacific intentions and our lack of appreciation of what the war means have led us to play into Germany's hands'; they thought it 'well-intentioned meddling' and it 'lessens their respect for our judgement'.[108]

The United States would advance no further. If she had seized upon Germany's willingness to negotiate and pressed it upon Britain, the result could only be to expose the fact that Britain was determined on her starvation policy, whether or not it was justified as a reprisal. President Wilson was not at this stage of the war willing to bring that about.

The announcement on 1 March 1915 of the British blockade, because it was seemingly aimed against American trade, created much greater indignation in the United States than the German Declaration of submarine blockade, which was at first thought of only as a move affecting the belligerents. Even the pro-Allied press denounced the British. The *Tribune*, usually favourable, called it 'a piece of arrogance for any one nation to hold that international understandings must yield in an emergency to its temporary self-interest'.[109] The offer to buy rather than to seize cargoes was not well received. 'The financial side of this arrangement', another newspaper said, 'is so obviously designed to placate Americans that it amounts to an insult.'

These were angry cries, but in the result the German blockade beat the British in bringing American temper to the boil. The American reply of 10 February to the German Submarine Declaration had been drafted in less than a week. Underrating the menace in it Wilson had taken up an ill-considered position. He missed the crucial distinction between American ships and American lives and allowed his warning to apply in the same terms to both. An American ship could be identified and action avoided, but no submarine commander could detect the presence of an American on an Allied ship. For Germany to agree to spare American ships would be a hindrance to the campaign; an agreement to spare American lives would make it impossible.

Wilson missed the distinction unless he was privy to an extraordinary product of Lansing's second-class legal mind. Lansing appreciated the point, he said, and intended that American lives should be covered, but realized the difficulty facing a submarine commander who did not know whether or not an American was aboard a British ship.[110] The solution Lansing thought of for this was that a British ship should notify the presence of an American on board by flying the American flag. This solution, however, he said, could not be proposed since America was at the same time sending a Note to Britain protesting against the use of the American flag and the two Notes would have been inconsistent! So the crucial point in the Note to Germany had to be left ambiguous. It was just as well that it was, if clarity could have revealed only Lansing's solution. The idea that an American citizen planted on every British ship could secure for her immunity from the torpedo was not a very practical one.

It is more likely, however, that Wilson concerned himself simply with the undoubted fact that in international law an American citizen was entitled to travel in safety on a belligerent merchantman. The immediate American response to the German threat, made the more easily perhaps because the threat was taken lightly, was simply to assert all American rights. But, as it happened, one of the very early casualties of the submarine blockade brought the issue out into the open and confronted Wilson with it almost before he had finished dealing with the British. The *Falaba* was the first of those ships whose tombstones are set along the American road to war. She was a small British liner outward bound from Liverpool to West Africa and she had among her passengers a Mr. Thrasher, an American engineer returning to his job on the Gold Coast. On 28 March 1915 she was torpedoed in the Irish Channel and Mr. Thrasher was one of the killed. The passengers and crew were given ten (in the German version twenty-three) minutes in which to abandon ship and she was torpedoed while the lifeboats were still being lowered. The same submarine had sunk another British liner the day before and had opened fire on the passengers and crew as they were taking to the boats, killing eight. These facts were not lost in the telling and perhaps for the first time America realized what the submarine campaign might mean.

'I do not like this case. It is full of disturbing possibilities.'[111] Thus Wilson wrote to Bryan on 3 April 1915. The issue raised by the *Falaba* began an intense debate within the State Department. Lansing, though feeling the gravest anxiety about the result, put forward the stern view. Bryan was for non-involvement. Both belligerents, he said, were waging a bitter war and both had warned off neutrals. If an American citizen lost his life by ignoring the warnings, was there not, as Bryan put it, 'contributory negligence' on his part? Was 'one man, acting purely for himself and his own interests, and without consulting his government, to involve the entire nation in difficulty?' Chandler Anderson, an international lawyer who was a special assistant in the State Department and whose *métier* it was to make all allowances for both sides, supported Bryan at least to the extent of saying that as the sinking of the *Falaba* was not a deliberate affront to the United States, the case could be met by an indemnity. Each side, as is usual in such disputes, was confident that its view was that of the public generally. American public opinion, Lansing wrote to Bryan, 'would never stand for a colorless or timid presentation of a case in which an American had been killed by an atrocious act of lawlessness'.[112] 'Our people will be slow to admit', Bryan wrote to Wilson, 'the right of a citizen to involve his country in war when by ordinary care he could have avoided danger.'[113]

Bryan played fair, submitting Lansing's views to the President as well as his own; but his own he pressed ardently. His contemporary reputation for woolliness of mind must have been due to unwillingness when making his judgements to detach his reason from his feelings. When they ran well together there was no lack of incisiveness in argument. Commenting on a journalist's report on opinion in Berlin he wrote to Wilson on 19 April:

There is no doubt as to the sentiment in Germany and the view they take is a natural one. 1st, They have warned Americans not to travel on British ships. Why do Americans take the risk? Not an unreasonable question. 2nd, If we allow the use of our flag, how can we complain, if in the confusion one of our boats is sunk by mistake? 3rd, Why be shocked at the drowning of a few people, if there is no objection to starving a nation? Of course Germany insists that by careful use she will have enough food, but if Great Britain cannot succeed in starving the noncombatants, why does she excite retaliation by threatening to do so?[114]

Then he urged another sort of solution, a proposal for a conference to discuss terms, not a secret proposal, but a public appeal strongly worded. '*You* are the one to act', he wrote. Then he quoted: 'Who knoweth whether thou art come to the kingdom for such a time as this?'

Wilson thought carefully, realizing the full gravity of the issue; it must end either in acquiescence in the new warfare or in opposition, perhaps deadly. By 22 April he had come to the conclusion that it must be opposition. The incident could not be dealt with by itself. Germany must be persuaded that it arose 'out of her mistake in employing an instrument against her enemies' commerce which it is impossible to employ in that use in accordance with any rules that the world is likely to be willing to accept'.[115] This he wrote to Bryan; and he asked for a Note to be drafted accordingly, 'a very moderately worded but none the less solemn and emphatic protest', put on very high grounds, not on 'the loss of this single man's life but on the interests of mankind' and 'on the manifest impropriety of a single nation's essaying to alter the understandings of nations'.

Bryan replied frankly that he disagreed.[116] The proposed Note was likely, he wrote in his own hand on 23 April, to bring on a crisis. The alternative was the open appeal for peace. Wilson was deeply impressed by the strength of Bryan's convictions. He was no longer confident that he had put the thing rightly, he wrote to Bryan on 28 April. He even went so far as to say that perhaps it was not necessary to make formal representations at all. Then he added:

What I have been thinking about most is your alternative proposition, that we publicly call upon the belligerents to end the war. I wish I could see it as you do. But in view of what House writes me I cannot. . . . We would lose such influence as we have for peace.[117]

Two new incidents excited Lansing. They were the first to involve American ships. The *Cushing* on 29 April was bombed in the North Sea by a German aeroplane; there was little damage and no loss of life. The tanker *Gulflight* on 1 May was torpedoed without warning in the Irish Sea; the captain died of heart failure and two sailors were drowned. Then on that same day there appeared in the American press a notice issued by the German embassy. Travellers were reminded that there was a state of war, that the war zone included the waters adjacent to Britain, and that vessels flying the British flag were liable to destruction in these waters; they sailed at their own risk. The warning had been prepared by Bernstorff a fortnight before because he thought that Americans still underestimated the dangers of the situation. As it happened the notice was published on the day that the *Lusitania*, Britain's Cunard liner and the largest ship in the North Atlantic service, was due to begin the crossing from New York. She was carrying 1,257 passengers, of whom many were American. One of them heeded the warning.

Lansing considered the case of the *Cushing* to be a more flagrant violation than the case of the *Falaba*.[118] The warning to travellers was, he thought, an impertinent act, 'a most improper proceeding diplomatically'.[119] The Government must uphold the American citizen's right to take passage on a British vessel. Everything seemed to point, he wrote to Bryan on 3 May, to a determined effort to affront the American Government and force it to an open rupture.[120]

Bryan passed this on to Wilson, but he himself, he wrote, thought the warning a fortunate thing, evidence of a friendly desire to evade an awkward situation.[121] The President and the Secretary discussed the case of the *Gulflight* on 3 May. It looked as if Wilson would accept Bryan's view. He began to talk in terms of an interim representation with final settlement postponed until the end of the war. Thus the reaction to the German blockade seemed to be falling into line with the reaction to the British. Wrath against Britain waxed. On 5 May Franklin K. Lane, the Secretary of the Interior and strongly pro-Entente, was writing to House in London about his resentment of German insults but adding that the English were not behaving well: 'each day that we meet', he wrote of the Cabinet, 'we boil over somewhat at the foolish manner in which England acts'.[122] America's great asset, he thought, was the confidence of the people in Wilson; they did not love him because he appeared to them 'as a man of the cloister' but they respected him as a wise, sane leader who would keep them out of trouble. Everything was being blamed on Bryan, which Lane thought gravely unjust.

I am growing more and more in my admiration for Bryan each day. He is too good a Christian to run a naughty world and he does'nt hate hard enough, but he certainly is a noble and high-minded man and loyal to the President to the last hair.

On the same day Wilson was telling House to emphasize to Grey the serious change in public sentiment 'because of the needless delays and many willful interferences in dealing with our neutral cargoes'.[123] The suggestion of an embargo might grow, he wrote, and when Congress assembled in December it might be difficult for him to prevent action.

Was Bryan going to win over the President? America could still without much loss of face withdraw to a policy of non-involvement, the policy which she was to adopt so easily and immediately in 1939. The question hung in the air.

In the first days of May there was a pause in history as if to give the men who made it a little time to settle their own affairs. The sinking of the *Falaba* was five weeks old and still the United States said nothing. A part of Wilson's mind was elsewhere; for him there was another question hanging in the air. On 4 May, sitting with the beautiful Mrs. Galt in the warm evening on the south portico of the White House, he, a widower of nine months, had offered marriage; and she had said neither yes nor no. In London on that same evening, as he walked back to Downing Street, Asquith was full of gloom, sensing the emotional catastrophe that came upon him a week later, when the young Venetia Stanley ('To see you again, and be with you, and hear your voice . . .', he had written to her a week before, 'has made a new creature of me. You are the best and richest of lifegivers')[124] announced her engagement to Edwin Montagu. In London too House dallied. He had been in Europe for three months, achieving nothing, but seemingly unable to tear himself away from the intimate dinners, the cosy talks, the summons to the Palace, the word here and the word there, all the delights which were to him what money and titles are to other men. On 5 May he lunched quietly with Lord Northcliffe, the press magnate, who criticized Asquith and his government for lack of determination: an early sign of the storm that drove Asquith a fortnight later into the shelter of a coalition. The next evening House was dining with Lady Paget, one of London's most indefatigable lion-hunters. He broke in upon the usual British self-deprecating talk to say that of all the belligerents Great Britain had performed her part best. He catalogued her achievements and ended by saying that Germany had the fear of God in her heart. There were 'hear-hears' and Mr. Balfour said* it was the most eloquent speech he had ever heard.

There were curious premonitions. On 2 May Page wrote: 'If a British liner full of American passengers be blown up, what will Uncle Sam do? That's what's going to happen.'[125]

---

* See p. 274 below.

'A lovely spring with sparkling air and wonderful blossom and the whole world looking like paradise':[126] so in May 1940 the head of the Foreign Office described Kew Gardens when he sought a respite from war while the future of Britain was hanging on the Battle of France. House and Grey walked together in the gardens on the morning of 7 May 1915 and talked among other things of the probability sooner or later of an ocean liner being sunk by a submarine. Perhaps all this tempted the gods. Or perhaps some god as in the Homeric age thought it was time to meddle again in the doings of men and looking around for a warrior to use saw Herr Kapitan-Leutnant Walter Schwieger in his submarine U20. At 1 p.m. on 7 May Schwieger sighted 'a great passenger liner' 15 miles off the Old Head of Kinsale on the south coast of Ireland. At 2.10 he fired one of his three remaining torpedoes. At 2.28 the *Lusitania* sank. Schwieger submerged and ran out to sea and out of history. Two-thirds of the passengers and crew, 1,201 in all, perished. They included 270 women and 94 children. They included, too, 124 American citizens.

The sinking of the *Lusitania* was the second milestone on America's road to war and marks the most decisive turning point. It lit, as House had told Grey that morning that it would, a flame of indignation that swept across America. But the flame did no more than lick the hard core of neutrality. It did not, as House had told Grey it probably would, carry America into the war. Yet it did two things. First, it consolidated pro-Allied and anti-German sentiment. It shattered the universal approval of neutrality, in action at least if not in thought, which was the mood of the nation on the outbreak of war. Theodore Roosevelt came out with an article proclaiming 'Piracy on the High Seas', and the right wing of the Republican party began gradually to follow him. Secondly, and more significantly, Schwieger's torpedo hit a bigger target than the *Lusitania*; it sank Bryan's policy of non-involvement. A single death could be eluded but not a massacre. On 7 May an issue was drawn up whose settlement diplomacy could only postpone. Either Germany crippled her blockade or the United States ate the dust.

VIII

PEACEMAKING BEGINS

DURING the winter after he first met Wilson, House wrote a novel which he published anonymously. It was called *Philip Dru: Administrator*. The hero had the panache which House lacked. He was a handsome graduate of West Point, incapacitated for military service by his health, who joined a rebellion against a stupid and reactionary government. He became dictator, put the country in order, brought it out into a world that was based on Anglo-Saxon dominance—and then, his task completed, handed back the powers he had taken.

There was no limit to House's belief in his power to put things in order and no territorial limit to his ambition. What came to fascinate him was the world of nations and the lack of order among them that led to the futile extravagance of war. He had a simple nostrum to administer. It was that there should be a code of morals between nations as between individuals governing their conduct. He talked of this many times. We get a glimpse of him through his diary talking it out with a friend over lunch at the Century Club in September 1914:

We fell to philosophising upon international morals and governmental affairs. I did most of the talking, trying to point out the fundamental error in international morals, in as much as they are upon a different level from individual morals. No high-minded man would think of doing as an individual what he seems perfectly ready to do as representative of a state. It has been thought entirely legitimate to lie, deceive, and be cruel in the name of patriotism. I endeavoured to point out that we could not get very far toward a proper international understanding until one nation treated another as individuals treat one another.[1]

The Colonel probably did not mean by this attack on Machiavellianism

to exclude from international affairs the stratagems and ruses which are
to be found in business dealings between individuals. If he did, the deception of Germany involved in the House-Grey Memorandum to which we
shall come was a sad lapse. But in his general idea was he not right? Order
depends on law and law grows out of morals. So the basis of an orderly
international society, as of any other, is the moral sense. The difficulty is
the age-old one of transforming ideas into institutions.

But while House could create in fiction a Philip Dru who could tackle
this sort of job single-handed, he knew that in real life he must act through
another man who had what he had not, the personality to command the
multitude and the willingness and the physical constitution to handle the
chores of government. 'I was like a disembodied spirit', House wrote in
a memoir, 'seeking a corporeal form.'[2] The man he had chosen for his
incarnation was Wilson. On the surface of things Wilson was the master
and House the servant. Wilson could speak of House as his other self,
thereby emphasizing the very special nature of his service. House could
not speak to others of Wilson in such terms of partnership. But that, as
he saw it, was the reality; and at the peak of their friendship and in a moment
of emotion, he did not hold back the thought from Wilson, telling him how
he had tried all his life to find someone with whom he could work out the
things he had at heart.

There were two conditions essential to this partnership. The first was
that House should in fact give loyal service and the second that he should
appear to be giving nothing more. The relationship of trust and affection
between the two men imposed the first condition. The proposed combination of talents imposed the second. If House's other half was to be a man
of commanding personality, he could not also be a man who admitted his
advisers to equality. House's influence must not be overt and it must not
be suspected by Wilson to be greater than he allowed.

The first condition required that Wilson and House should have the
same objects. 'Nine times out of ten we reached the same conclusions',
House wrote. 'When we did, neither he nor I felt it necessary to counsel
with the other.'[3] On the great matter of a new and peaceful international
order, the matter which soon came to absorb House to the exclusion of
almost everything else, undoubtedly they shared the object. Where they
differed was in method. They were both very American in their confidence
that new methods would succeed where the old had failed and in their
belief that success would come from the American way of doing things.
They were both idealists. Wilson believed—and this was one expression
of the American soul—that ideals were best served by preaching, that the
peoples of the world could be persuaded to respond and roused to push

their representatives into acting accordingly. House believed—and this was another expression of the American soul—that to get things done you must put something into a nation's pocket as in a business deal. His method of accomplishing results, he once explained, was 'not to take it up from a sentimental or purely ethical viewpoint, but to try to prove that it would be of material advantage to Germany'.[4] He kept his ideals mostly to himself and talked about them only to those Americans and Englishmen whom he knew to share his moral sense.

There was then this difference between them which the two men never argued out. House did not deceive Wilson except in the sense that extreme tact can sometimes come to the border of deception. There was no need for outright deceit since their objects were the same: and no reason to think that, had there been a need, House would have satisfied it. He did give loyal service: he never used his position to further ends which he knew Wilson would have disapproved of; he never completely concealed from Wilson what he was doing though he sometimes held back news of his activities until he felt the time was ripe for putting them across persuasively. He did consciously handle Wilson so as to get the decisions on method that he wanted. He thought his methods superior to Wilson's. Although he often believed that Wilson was setting about things the wrong way, he never suggested it in so many words. Only *in extremis* did he allow himself to get into argument. Usually they would talk until Wilson perhaps revealed a shadow of a doubt and then House would encourage it. He was not blunt with Wilson, but if that was wrong the fault was in Wilson's nature as much as in his. To keep his partnership he had to study his approaches.

The fulfilment of the second condition was a matter of appearances. House was not ambitious to rob Wilson of any of his power. He accepted that Wilson must make all the decisions and that he, House, could only do his best to see that they were right. But what was required was not only that Wilson's sphere of power should not be invaded but that Wilson should never be allowed to fancy that there was any threat of invasion; and the latter requirement meant that it should not be generally thought that House had invaded it, since Wilson could accept neither the fact nor the appearance of invasion. In all this House exercised great care. He never thrust himself on Wilson. He preferred to live away from Washington and to wait until he was sent for. He avoided blatant publicity not only because it was not what he cared for but also because he knew that it was dangerous. He must never be known as the man behind the throne. He was always anxious about this. When he was talked of as 'assistant president', he wrote to his brother-in-law: 'I do not know how much of this kind of thing Woodrow Wilson can stand.'[5]

This meant of course a severe restraint. Very occasionally we shall find House yielding to a natural temptation and talking big. But this was rare. Nearly all the men of power with whom House dealt thought of Wilson as the mind and House the voice. Lloyd George wrote of him that he was 'essentially a salesman and not a producer'[6] and that he could have put across just as deftly the theories of any other man. In this Lloyd George was wrong, but it was the impression that House wanted to give. For he was astute enough to see that it was because he was thought of as his master's voice that men like Lloyd George listened to him. If they had thought of him only as the man who had the master's ear, they would have wondered how long the ear would be his and to the extent of their doubts discounted what he said.

No man with House's sense of his own capacity could hold himself in for ever and House did not. But for a long time he did. For a long time Wilson thought of him as he wrote to Josephus Daniels: 'What I like about House is that he is the most self-effacing man that ever lived. All he wants to do is to serve the common cause and to help me and others.'[7]

The big programme of legislation initiated by the President at the beginning of his Administration threw out problems for House as for all his advisers. But as soon as he could give the time, House turned his attention to the state of Europe. He recognized the danger to peace as being the rivalry between Britain and Germany, or, as he put it, Germany's aspirations for expansion and English intolerance of them. The answer, he thought, might be to encourage Germany to exploit South America in a legitimate way, and the impact of this on the Monroe Doctrine did not in the least deter him. In April 1913 he was asked to lunch downtown in New York to meet Bernstorff, the German ambassador. It is an illustration of his little peculiarities that he declined on the ground that he never went downtown and of his importance that two days later he was asked to lunch uptown. The lunch was at Delmonico's on 9 May and after lunch the two men walked away together. Bernstorff, who never lost an opportunity of showing goodwill, appeared sympathetic and House was pleasantly surprised.

The next month House was in London and he put his ideas to Page.[8] Page was most enthusiastic. He also had been thinking of 'some great constructive forward idea', great world forces to combine to clean up the tropics, 'gradually forget the fighting idea'. House had been charged to tell the Foreign Secretary about Wilson's attitude on the Panama tolls controversy, so Page invited the two men to a quiet lunch at the Coburg

Hotel* on 3 July: this was how Grey and House first met. Page's letter of invitation sang the praises of the 'silent partner'; 'I cannot get him far outside his hotel, for he cares to see few people, but he is very eager to meet you'.[9] House took the opportunity of telling Grey of his conversation with Bernstorff and felt that he had planted 'the seeds of peace'.

But nothing crystallized in House's mind until after he had talked to Tyrrell, Grey's private secretary, at the end of the year. It was when Tyrrell was in Washington on the Panama business and it was perhaps Tyrrell who turned House's mind away from the development of South America to the more lively question of disarmament. Tyrrell thought that House had 'a good sporting chance of success' of bringing about an understanding between France, Germany, England, and the United States regarding a reduction of armaments.[10] It seems plain from the conversation, however, that the sporting chance depended upon House's ability to convince Germany that she had an extravagant navy and should curtail militarism generally. In March 1913 and then again in October Churchill as First Lord of the Admiralty had made his proposals for a moratorium in naval building. Tyrrell suggested that House should see the Kaiser first and promised to give him all the papers 'in order that I might see how entirely right Great Britain had been in her position'.[11]

This was on 2 December 1913. Ten days later House saw Wilson who thoroughly approved of the proposed expedition. On 1 January 1914 House wrote to Gerard to put matters in train for his visit and they decided that the best time to get the Kaiser would be in late May on his return from Corfu. In the interval House learnt all he could about the personality and thoughts of the Kaiser and the other men he would have to tackle. He knew that the odds were heavily against him. He called his journey 'the great adventure'.[12]

House arrived in Berlin towards the end of May and on 29 May he reported to Wilson on what he had done so far. The chief event was an hour's talk with Tirpitz, whom House found very anti-English and unsympathetic to disarmament talk; he said that all Germany wanted was peace but that the way to maintain it was to put fear into the hearts of her enemies. It was not easy for Gerard to arrange for House to see the Kaiser alone since protocol required that an official of the Foreign Office should be present. But House insisted and Gerard succeeded. The two men were invited to the Whit Monday *Schrippenfest* at Potsdam and it was arranged that after the luncheon House should speak with the Kaiser alone, that is standing on the terrace, with Gerard and Zimmermann, the Under-Secretary at the Foreign Office, in attendance, but out of hearing. In this

---

* Now the Connaught Hotel.

fashion they spoke together for a full half hour.[13] The Kaiser evidently thought it important or else he got carried away, for he kept his special train waiting. Everyone of course was agog to know what high secrets were being exchanged, but in fact nothing more was said than what usually passes between great men on such occasions. House asked politely why the Kaiser was increasing his navy and how long it would go on for. The Kaiser replied that he must have a large navy to protect Germany's commerce and one that was commensurate with her growing power and importance; the increase would stop when the present building policy was concluded. House asked why Germany had refused to sign Bryan's cooling off treaty and the Kaiser said it was because Germany was always ready for war and would not give her enemies time to prepare. House said that he would now take the matter up with the British Government; and would the Kaiser like to be kept informed? The Kaiser said he would and that letters would reach him through Zimmermann. Really what was accomplished was that House had got the ear of the Kaiser and the opportunity of writing to him further.

House left for Paris the same evening, 1 June 1914. He wrote to Wilson that he had been as successful as he anticipated and was very happy over what had been accomplished. Wilson replied warmly:

Your letter from Paris, written just after coming from Berlin, gives me a thrill of deep pleasure. You have, I hope and believe, begun a great thing and I rejoice with all my heart. You are doing it, too, in just the right way with your characteristic tact and quietness and I wish you God speed in what follows. I could not have done the thing nearly so well.[14]

Paris was in a Cabinet crisis. Madame Caillaux, the wife of the Minister of Finance, had shot the editor of *Figaro*. House felt he could do nothing there, so he spent a quiet week, declining all invitations to dinner and luncheon, 'my most arduous duty being to dodge Americans and others wanting to see me'.[15] This did not restrain him from writing to Wilson that in France he had not found the war spirit dominant and that her statesmen dreamt no longer of the recovery of Alsace and Lorraine.[16] House did not like to be found without news and views, ostensibly first hand; and if he had heard nothing, he did the best he could. Wilson wrote again with undiminished enthusiasm:

I cannot tell you how constantly my thoughts follow you and how deeply interested I am and thankful besides to have a friend who so thoroughly understands me to interpret me to those whom it is most important we should inform and enlighten with regard to what we are really seeking to accomplish. It is a great source of strength and relief to me and I thank you from the bottom of my heart . . . remember that I always think of you with deep gratitude and affection.[17]

On 9 June House took the boat train to London and on 12 June he lunched with Page to discuss plans. They found it slow work getting conversations going. London was enjoying what is now nostalgically remembered as the last season of the old world. Page reported to Wilson that they were keeping House's ball rolling slowly. 'You can't talk with them except at luncheon or dinner,—food with talk every time.'[18] 'Everything cluttered up with social affairs, and it is impossible to work quickly', House reported.[19] So it took nearly a week to arrange lunch with House and Tyrrell on 17 June. Grey was visibly impressed, House thought, and the British Government seemed eager to carry on the discussion. House felt that his visit was justified even if nothing more was accomplished and that his dream was beginning to come true. 'It is hard to realise', he wrote, 'that every government in the world may be more or less affected by the moves we are making and every human being may be concerned in the decisions reached from day to day.'[20]

But what moves and what decisions? The Kaiser had gone to Kiel for the regatta and House suggested that Grey and he might meet him there in some way, 'but this was not gone into further'. House suggested that Germany might be permitted to aid in the development of Persia, but Grey thought that the Germans were so aggressive that that might be dangerous. On 26 June there was another lunch with Grey and Tyrrell, Lords Haldane and Crewe being additional guests. The conversation lasted two hours. House expounded his doctrine that international matters could be worked out as individuals worked out their private affairs. 'The general idea was accepted; that is, that a frank and open policy should be pursued between all the parties at interest.'[21] That morning there had been breakfast with Lloyd George. House recorded that there was fried sole, sausage, ham, eggs, fruit, coffee, and tea; that George ate a very hearty breakfast and was peculiarly ill-informed regarding America.[22] On 2 July House went to lunch with the Prime Minister and had a quarter of an hour's earnest talk with him. But the talking was done by House and was on general subjects.

Mr. Asquith cast the usual slur upon Mr. Bryan . . . they do not do Mr. Bryan justice, but it is absolutely useless to fight his battles, because in doing so you discredit the purpose you are striving for.[23]

So the days passed. House's reports continued to be rapturously received in Washington. On 26 June Wilson wrote:

Your letters give me a peculiar pleasure whenever they come. They bring with them an air of sincere thought and constant endeavour for the right thing, which is just what I need to sustain the energies in me. I thank you with all my heart

for your report of your meeting with Sir Edward Grey with regard to the matter
we have so much at heart . . . I hope you are getting a lot of fun and pleasure out
of these things, and all my little circle here join me in the warmest messages.[24]

House did not push his idea of a meeting at Kiel. But Gerard went there
and missed a race on the Kaiser's yacht because of 'the murder in Bosnia'.
He returned to Berlin to celebrate the Fourth of July with the American
colony and found it as 'quiet as the grave'. House in London brought up
his plan again of developing 'the waste spaces of the earth' and on this
softer ground made some progress. He thought he might get a plan which
Wilson could put to the governments concerned.

On the harder ground it is difficult to know what House was hoping for.
Something presumably which he could take back to the Kaiser and thus
keep the contact alive. On 3 July he got it in the vaguest possible form.
Grey sent word through Tyrrell that he 'would like me to convey to the
Kaiser the impressions I have obtained from my several discussions with
this government, in regard to a better understanding between the nations
of Europe, and to try and get a reply'.[25] Grey would not send anything
official or in writing for fear of offending Russian and French sensibilities.
House did the best he could with this. He composed a long, flattering,
and platitudinous letter to the Kaiser which he sent off on 7 July.[26] He
had tried to read the thought of the French people, he said, and found that
her statesmen had given over all thought of revenge. He had found Sir
Edward Grey 'sympathetic to the last degree'. He was convinced that the
British Government desired an understanding and hoped for a response
from the Kaiser that might permit another step forward.

'So you see things are moving in the right direction as rapidly as we
could hope', House wrote to Wilson.[27] But he was too close to the hour
and events outpaced his project. He left for America on 21 July and the
day before he sailed Tyrrell brought him another message from Grey 'that
he wished me to know before I sailed that the Austro-Serbian situation
was giving him grave concern'.[28] On 23 July Austria sent her ultimatum to
Serbia and when House arrived at Boston the world was on the brink of
war.

The Kaiser in exile is reported to have said of House's visit that it 'almost
prevented the World War'.[29] The Kaiser's contemporaneous judgements
are not reliable and those made retrospectively are worth less. House himself, both at the time and later, tended to blame 'the conservative delay of
Sir Edward and his confrères'[30] which made it impossible for him to go
back to Germany and see the Kaiser. But the thin answer he had to take
back could hardly have justified him in trying to see the Kaiser at Kiel
or pursuing him on his Norwegian cruise where he was until the crisis

came. House's plan was one for the long term. He had not, and could not be expected to have, any solution for a crisis.

But surely the great adventure was worth while if only as a demonstration of the spirit of a man who stood up to fight events. Alone in America, and among very few in Europe, House foresaw the crisis and its significance for his own country with sufficient clarity to throw himself heart and soul into an attempt to avert it. The words with which Page greeted the attempt when he first heard of it are also its best epitaph.

. . . The big thing is to go confidently to work on a task, the results of which nobody can possibly foresee—a task so vague and improbable of definite results that small men hesitate. It is in this spirit that very many of the biggest things in history have been done.[31]

When House landed in the United States on 29 July Mrs. Wilson had barely a week to live. She had not been really well for some time past. She was in fact suffering from Bright's disease and tuberculosis of the kidney and the diagnosis was made about the middle of July. Her life ran out with the last days of European peace. Tragedy and crisis came together and Wilson as best he could divided his time between them. Either he was not told of the disease and of its swift and inevitable end or he did not take it in. On 2 August he wrote to Mrs. Peck, not entirely without hope, of his wife 'as struggling through the deep waters of utter nervous prostration'.[32] She died on 6 August.

Her death ended a union of 'wedded sweethearts' as he called it in a letter to her just a year before: 'it seems to me that I have never loved you as I do now!'[33] He counted on her being with him; she let him go away when it was for his work or when she thought it good for him, but the previous summer of 1913 was almost the first time that she herself had left his side. They had leased in Cornish, New Hampshire, for the summer a house in Victorian-tinctured-by-Georgian style, built by the other Winston Churchill, the novelist; and when Wilson found that he could not leave Washington he insisted on the family going without him. He wrote to her every day and she would read the letters to the children, leaving out 'the sacred parts'.[34] She did not believe that anyone else could look after him as she could. But that he should be looked after was the last thought in her mind when she died.

It was more than the ending of a marriage, it was the shattering of a way of life. His complete dependence on his family and his craving for feminine support left him utterly exposed to grief and desolation. He was as one suffering from lack of nourishment, for there was no other comparable source on which he could draw. There was still one unmarried daughter, Margaret, but she was twenty-eight now, disliked Washington, and had her singing to keep her busy. Nell, newly married to McAdoo, was in Washington and the two could come in for lunch or dinner. There was Helen Bones, the favourite cousin, who when they moved to the White House had come to help Mrs. Wilson; she stayed on to help Margaret with her duties as the official hostess. So the family was still there but in bits and pieces. It was Ellen who had held it all together. She was the house in which Wilson lived and took shelter and the others only the furniture. She was the supreme confidante, the listener, the comforter, the unfailing reassurance. Once in the black period when he had thought that he might be cast out by Princeton and there was then nowhere else to go, he had bade her, if she wanted to know what he owed her, to read the twenty-ninth sonnet that begins

> When in disgrace with Fortune and men's eyes

and ends

> for thy sweet love remembered such wealth brings,
> that then I scorn to change my state with kings.

She was his wealth and now he was impoverished.

He insisted on Dr. Grayson and Tumulty taking their usual vacation and on the family going to the house in Cornish. Washington in August before the days of air-conditioning was a place to be avoided. House, who had gone straight to Pride's Crossing, his summer house on the north shore of Massachusetts, wrote on 1 August: 'If I thought I could live through the heat, I would go to Washington to see you; but I am afraid if I reached there, I would be utterly helpless.'[35] Helen Bones stayed behind and his brother-in-law Stockton came to see him through the worst part.

Towards the end of August he got away to Cornish and House came to stay. 'Reminds one of an English place',[36] he commented, and found the view superb and the furnishings comfortable and artistic. The President gave him the room that Mrs. Wilson used to have, next to his, with a common bathroom between them. It was a wing of the house in which they were quite to themselves, a small stairway leading down to the study. House reported all the details of his mission and they shared the feeling that it had only just failed.

He talked also to House about his loss. 'Tears came into his eyes, and he said he felt like a machine that had run down, and there was nothing left in him worth while.'[37] He did not see how he could go through the next two and a half years. According to the convention of the time the bereaved did not speak intimately of their loss and their friends did not allude to it lest recollection might make sorrow harder to bear. So House was surprised. But Wilson was writing freely to all his friends pouring out his grief and demanding their sympathy in his struggle to keep going. 'The day's work must be done . . . it matters little how much life is left in him when the day is over.'[38] And to Mrs. Peck: 'It is amazing how one can continue to function in all ordinary, and some extraordinary, matters with a broken heart.'[39]

Back in the White House Grayson became his closest companion. The two men would meet at meals and often eat alone. In the evening Grayson would sit reading on one side of the study table while Wilson worked on the other; and then when the work was over Wilson would talk about his childhood, his family, and especially his married life. He would read to Grayson some of the letters he had received that day, as he had been used to read them to his wife, especially Page's letters. Page, he said, was the best letter-writer he knew. They went for walks together and automobile rides.

Sometimes he filled the house with family and old friends and sometimes he paid short family visits. He wrote constantly to all his women friends. It was as if he was trying to collect from a diversity of sources the abundance that had flowed from her.

He made unexpected visits to House in New York. One evening he said suddenly that he wanted to go out for a walk and refused to have the secret service men following him. House slipped his revolver into his pocket (it seems an odd thing for him to have handy till one remembers that he was brought up in Texas) and went with him. When they got back, he said that he wished that someone would have killed him, telling House again that he was broken in spirit and not fit to be President. House wondered that he remained sane.

This was the background to his life when he was struggling with the early problems of neutrality. Outwardly, and except to his intimates, he appeared as usual. Mr. Baker, who saw him on 17 September, just after his return from Cornish, found him looking very well, clear-eyed, confident, cheerful, a black band on his left arm, a dark tie with a gold ornament.[40] At Christmas there was a family gathering and the President decorated the Christmas tree for his little great-niece. Not long after, his first grandchild, Jessie's son, was born. At a party in January 1915 Mrs. Toy was staying at the White House and thought him looking better than she had ever seen him physically. She missed, she thought, 'the old buoyancy' but he said he had never felt better in his life.[41] There were moments when he seemed very sad. After dinner he enjoyed his usual pleasure of reading aloud. 'Let's read my chapter on the President', he said. 'I haven't read these lectures since I delivered them.'[42]

One day when the President and Grayson were on a drive together, Grayson bowed to a friend. 'Who is that beautiful lady?' the President asked and was told that it was a Mrs. Galt.[43]

Within six weeks of the outbreak of war the great battles of the Marne, of Tannenberg, and of Lemberg had been won and lost and the combination of victories and defeats had resulted in deadlock. Winston Churchill thus states the position in his great history:

By the middle of September what may be called the first round of the World War was over. The Battle of the Marne was decided, and the great thrust on Paris, embodied in the Schlieffen Plan had definitely failed. The expulsion of Rennenkampf from East Prussia had ended the Russian invasion of Germany. Almost simultaneously the Battle of Lemberg had resulted in a Russian victory. France had survived the onslaught; Germany had destroyed the Russian invasion; and the whole Austrian Army had suffered defeat. The slaughter of these battles, in which all the best trained troops of the warring nations had been desperately engaged, had exceeded anything which history records of the past and was destined to surpass any month even of the Great War itself.[44]

The ending of the first round showed that there was to be no quick and easy victory for either side. Neither side had committed itself to any objective in terms from which it could not withdraw without loss of face. This was the opportunity for a peacemaker. Germany was in occupation of Belgium and North-Eastern France but in the territory beyond that she would have to fight for every inch. If what had caused the war was in Germany the fear of encirclement and among the Allies the fear of German aggression, might not each side be secretly feeling that it had done enough to deter its enemy, Germany by the infliction of devastating blows which had brought her territorial conquest and the Allies by halting the advance a long way short of total victory? As the alternative to a long and exhausting struggle, could not both sides make with honour a peace of accommodation?

House thought the opportunity well worth stretching out for, while he appreciated that what might look promising on paper might well founder on mutual distrust. Each side believed that the other's objective was total destruction and if it was found that this belief gripped strongly enough, a peace of accommodation would seem to each to be only a postponement. As early as 17 August 1914 House sent a feeler to Gerard. On 5 September with Wilson's approval he wrote to Zimmermann asking if he could serve as a confidential medium. He had received an acknowledgement from Zimmermann of his letter to the Kaiser and had treated this as giving him the opportunity to write. On the same day he dined out to meet Baron Dumba the Austrian ambassador. He wrote in his diary:

I am laying plans to make myself persona grata to all the nations involved in this European War, so that my services may be utilised to advantage and without objection in the event a proper opportunity arises.

That evening the German ambassador was dining in New York with an American sympathizer with whom he met a former American ambassador to Turkey, a Mr. Oscar Straus. A not unhelpful response by Bernstorff to Straus's inquiry whether the Kaiser would consider a mediation offer from the President so excited Straus that he took the midnight train to Washington and went straight to see Bryan. Bryan was equally excited, and after consultation with the President instructed Gerard in Berlin to make immediate advances. Then without waiting for any reply he summoned the British and French ambassadors to the State Department and told them they must state their terms. The whole affair was conducted in a blaze of publicity which accorded with Bryan's horror of secret diplomacy and wrecked any chance of success that the negotiations might have had. Bryan's objective was to initiate not a negotiation but a public debate on what each side was fighting about and what it wanted. Both sides answered cautiously. Bernstorff insisted that the approach had come from Straus who was an Allied sympathizer. But he wanted, as he put it in his report home, 'to leave the odium of rejection to our enemies'.[45]

There followed a series of odium-shifting manœuvres by both sides. Spring Rice ended his telegram of 7 September, in which he reported the incident, with the advice that Britain should emphasize her 'desire not only to end this war but all wars by a thoroughly satisfactory settlement'. Grey telegraphed back that any proposal from the United States Government to accomplish this would doubtless be welcomed, but that he had no reason to suppose that Germany would 'accept just terms, for instance with regard to Belgium'. The Foreign Secretary was a little more specific on 9 September when he told Page that any settlement 'must provide for an end of militarism for ever and for reparation to ruined Belgium'. Meanwhile, Bernstorff put it about in the American press that Germany was ready to make peace on moderate terms but England was not. To counter this Spring Rice was furnished with another telegram from Grey, sent on 18 September and obviously intended for transmission to the President (it was one of those which Wilson warmly acknowledged),* elaborating

* See p. 152 above.

on what he had said to Page. Grey's messages were private. So ostensibly was Germany's reply to Gerard's advances. War had been forced upon her, the Chancellor said: 'it is up to the United States to get their enemies to make peace proposals'. This message, doubtless through the good offices of Bryan on behalf of open diplomacy, appeared almost verbatim in the *New York Times* of 18 September.

This apparently brought the Straus affair to an end; and anyway Bryan took himself out of the picture on 18 September by going off on a vacation to be followed by a bout of campaigning in the mid-term elections. He was away until mid November. He left Lansing in charge, whom Spring Rice, reporting the event, described as 'a lawyer of no great importance personally or politically, and accustomed to conduct matters of smaller importance like claims commissions'.[46] From behind the smokescreen of these interchanges there emerged two men who meant business. Whatever Bernstorff might say, and he was always ready to say whatever might be suited to the occasion, he was constant in a firm belief in peace by settlement. Colonel House had a firm belief in his own capacity to settle anything. Both were men ready to make the most of any opportunity. They met in the Colonel's New York apartment on 18 September. House proposed that the German and British ambassadors should get together at his dinner table. This was so contrary to protocol, which required belligerent ambassadors in neutral countries, if by accident they met, to eye each other coldly from a distance, that even Bernstorff was startled. Eventually he agreed provided it was done in the utmost secrecy. House promised that, if anything came out of the ambassadorial conference, he would get permission for Bernstorff to radio his government in code without disclosing the key. Strictly, this was a breach of neutrality,* the first step on the path that led to the celebrated affair of the Zimmermann telegram.

The next thing for House to do was to get the go ahead from Wilson. He wrote him a letter the same day which he ended by tolling the bell he rang only for the high summons.

> The world expects you to play the big part in this tragedy—and so indeed you will, for God has given you the power to see things as they are.
>
> Your faithful and affectionate
> E. M. House[47]

Losing no time and anticipating the commission which he at once received, House wrote to Spring Rice asking him to come urgently to New York. On the telephone on 19 September Spring Rice demurred but House persuaded him on to the midnight train. He met him early next morning at

---

* See p. 183 above.

the Pennsylvania station, remaining concealed in his car so that their meeting might not be observed, and permitting the ambassador to make a call on the British consul-general so as to baffle any sleuth. Spring Rice was understandably nervous; he had to think of the Allies, for it was only a fortnight since they had publicly bound themselves not to consider a separate peace.

'He was extremely sympathetic', Spring Rice reported to Grey, 'and showed that he fully understood and admired our policy.'[48] But House warned the ambassador that American sympathy, at present strongly with the Allies, would be modified if the Allies appeared unresponsive to peace moves and determined on the elimination of Germany. He spoke of his visit to Berlin and of his conviction that if the military party received a check the Kaiser would be able to exercise his influence for peace. Bernstorff, he said, shared this view. Would Spring Rice meet Bernstorff? Spring Rice flatly refused; apart from protocol, he disliked and distrusted the man. But he produced the telegram from Grey which he had just sent to the President and House was delighted with it. The two *sine qua non* conditions, the restoration of Belgium and a permanent settlement, would, House said, 'at once win the sympathy of the whole world'.[49] Spring Rice cautiously replied that, while the conditions were indispensable, they were not an enunciation of policy; and no terms could be discussed which were not acceptable to Britain's allies. This seems to have led House into some speculation about what these allies might want and to put forward what he was careful to call only his own peace programme. He thought that Germany might hand back Alsace to France but keep Lorraine and he visualized an independent Poland, the formation of a Balkan Federation at the expense of part of the Austro-Hungarian empire, and the neutralization of the Dardanelles. This was the first time that House had indulged his taste for replanning Europe. Nothing more was heard of it for the time being, since the ambassador evidently regarded it as expressing only House's personal view and did not report it to London.

The Colonel had met Sir Cecil briefly over the Panama tolls affair but this was his first important negotiating contact with the ambassador. He found him 'frank and honest' and 'a high-minded scholarly gentleman'.[50] The ambassador evidently found the initial impact of House very persuasive, for he went with him further along the road to mediation than he could ever again be tempted to go. They composed together a cable for the ambassador to send to Grey. It suggested that the moment was propitious for negotiations, which the President might facilitate, on the basis of Grey's two conditions (which later came to be called 'the two-point programme'); and warned against a *non possumus* attitude.

On 22 September Bernstorff called on House to find out what was happening. He was told that Spring Rice was asking for instructions and he thought this reasonable, though for his part, he said, his instructions warranted him in taking up negotiations of this sort. Three days later he furthered the good work by buttonholing a friend of House whom he found lunching alone at the Ritz-Carlton, the Count's headquarters in New York, and putting out the idea that something might be done if House went first to London and then to Berlin. For Germany he promised co-operation and a favourable reception. Bernstorff believed in making contacts and starting talks. His method, then and thereafter, was to invite talk by exaggerations in Washington of his government's approachability which could, if necessary, be repudiated if they boomeranged from Berlin.

Wilson, whom House saw on 28 September, would not sanction the visit until some word came from London. This may have come as a disappointment to House who wrote in his diary that evening:

I find the President singularly lacking in appreciation of the importance of this European crisis. He seems more interested in domestic affairs, and I find it difficult to get his attention centred upon the one big question.[51]

The next day House saw Spring Rice and tried to push him into saying what was happening in London, but all he got was the expectation that it would be some time before anything was heard, which he took to mean that the British would do nothing until they thought the moment propitious for a peace move. He added to his diary:

I could see that Sir Cecil was thoroughly of the opinion that Germany should be badly punished before peace was made. There was something of resentment and almost of vindictiveness in his attitude.[52]

Page in London was saying the same sort of thing in a letter of 15 September which House would have received about then. 'You needn't fool yourself', he wrote, 'they are going to knock Germany out, and nothing will be allowed to stand in their way.'[53] And he implored House not to let the notion get afloat 'that we can or ought to stop it before the Kaiser is put out of business'.

House persevered. He replied to Page in a letter written 'with the President's knowledge and consent and with the thought that it will be conveyed to Sir Edward'. He expounded once again his approval of Grey's two conditions, his feeling that Germany would soon be willing to discuss terms, his disagreement with the view that she should be completely crushed, and his fear that, if she were, Russia would become dominant. He ended:

There is a growing impatience in this country because of this war and there is constant pressure upon the President to use his influence to bring about normal conditions. He does not wish to do anything to irritate or offend any one of the belligerent nations, but he has an abiding faith in the efficacy of open and frank discussions between those that are now at war.[54]

This produced no reaction from Grey, some diminution of interest by Wilson ('I am sorry to say, as I have said before', House put in his diary for 22 October, 'that the President does not seem to have a proper sense of proportion as between domestic and foreign affairs')[55] and no news from Page until six weeks later, when he wrote:

A long luncheon talk to-day with Sir Edward Grey revealed the state of mind of the government, namely that peace cannot be thought of and will not be discussed until Germany will agree to pay for the full restoration of Belgium, and he does not think that Germany will agree to this till she is thoroughly exhausted.[56]

This diagnosis of the German mind was only too true. House began to come round to the same view and to think that discussions would do no good until Germany had been pushed back into her own territory. So much he said to Wilson on 3 December in a significant conversation.

The conversation began with the President reading a letter of 1 December from Bryan suggesting that he, Wilson, move boldly by calling upon the belligerents to state their war aims. Bryan had first put forward this idea in a long letter of 19 September written just after he had gone on vacation. Then he became absorbed in the election campaign. By mid November he was back in Washington and trying out the idea unsuccessfully on Spring Rice. Then he renewed his appeal to Wilson to 'discharge this nation's duty as the leading exponent of Christianity and as the foremost advocate of worldwide peace'.[57] 'I was certain', House wrote in his diary, 'it would be entirely footless to do this, for the Allies would consider it an unfriendly act, and further it was not good for the United States to have peace brought about until Germany was sufficiently beaten to cause her to consent to a fundamental change in her military policy.'[58] When that time came, House would go to Germany and try to get the Kaiser to accept the two-point programme. Wilson agreed but doubted whether the Kaiser would be allowed to consent to such terms. Then the diary continues:

The President said that he, Mr. Bryan, did not know that he, the President, was working for peace wholly through me, and he was afraid to mention this fact for fear it would offend him. He said Mr. Bryan might accept it gracefully, but not being certain, he hesitated to tell him . . . The President had a feeling that I could do more to initiate peace unofficially than anyone could do in an official capacity, for the reason I could talk and be talked to without it being binding upon anyone.

As a result of this talk House tried Page again with a letter written on 4 December.[59] Would Page convey delicately to Sir Edward Grey the thought that America was becoming restless, that the President therefore wanted to start peace parleys at the very earliest moment; would the Allies consider parleys upon the basis of the two-point programme? He was ready to go to Germany at any moment and then to England. Ten days later he decided to give up and cabled Page to ignore the letter. He had become convinced, he recorded, that the British were determined to make a complete job of it and he felt in his heart that that was best.

Before he got the cable Page had answered the letter robustly. 'You say the Americans are becoming restless. The plain fact is that the English people, and especially the English military and naval people, don't care a fig what the Americans think and feel.'[60] Page gave also a straightforward answer to the question whether the Allies would talk peace.

Now if anybody could fix a basis for the complete restoration of Belgium, so far as restoration is possible, and for the elimination of militarism, I am sure the *English* would talk on that basis. But there are two difficulties—Russia would not talk until she has Constantinople, and I haven't found anybody who can say exactly what you mean by the elimination of militarism.

It was now mid December 1914 and the psychological moment for peace-making had slipped away. The hope had vanished that the fighters might have second thoughts before beginning the second round. Both sides were preparing for a struggle to the end; and on the Allied side the preparations contemplated the purchase of new supporters by commitments which destroyed the prospect of a simple peace of restoration and disarmament. From now on a peace that was not based on the total defeat of one side or the other became increasingly difficult.

But neither Wilson nor House was ready to give up. The moment at which they were pausing in their efforts is a good moment to examine a little more closely what their efforts were directed to and to look again at their surprising conversation on 3 December. What is so surprising about it is Wilson's rejection of the Bryan method of peacemaking in favour of the House method. Bryan was truly neutral and House was not. Bryan was for open diplomacy and House was not. Bryan had no thought except to stop the war somehow or, if that could not be done, to keep America out of it. Wilson was not quite as neutral as that and he thought of a more positive role for America to play. But on all the evidence, if one excludes the evidence of what passed between himself and House, he was far closer in thought to the neutrality of Bryan than he was to the partiality of House. House had by this time formed a clear view of what the American objective should be and he did not thereafter radically depart from it. The worst thing that could happen would be a German victory, wide or narrow. The next worst thing would be the crushing defeat of Germany. The best thing would be a moderate victory for the Entente, enough to destroy the German military spirit but no more. His views of what degree of victory was necessary for this purpose fluctuated; and just at this moment on 3 December, he is shown as feeling that it might not be obtainable while the Germans were on foreign soil. But, whatever the fluctuations, House always wanted to see the Entente victorious in some measure, and this is not impartiality. His object called not for a policy of neutrality but for the friendly and restraining hand. It meant keeping the goodwill of the Allies; they must not, as House was saying on this occasion, be upset by offers which they might construe as unhelpful. Above all, the policy might mean war. House, if he had not realized that by 3 December 1914, soon did and was not horrified.

Then as to method. Bryan's method was the Wilsonian method as it had been practised in the past in Mexico and as it was to be practised again when, after the failure of House's policy, Wilson, though not dispensing with House, became his own foreign minister. Wilson himself did not believe in conversations with envoys; he hardly ever saw them; he believed in the efficacy of the diplomatic note. Yet he chose House as his instrument, and he turned down Bryan's policy, as he frankly told Bryan,* on the ground that open diplomacy would clash with what House was doing. What is the explanation? It is not that House concealed his object. It is certainly possible that he did not generate as much enthusiasm in Wilson as he thought he did. There is a number of occasions in which it is clear that House was not obtaining from those he talked to the whole-hearted agreement which his diary records. He was often too confident about the effect of his persuasive talent. But that House said the sort of thing his diary records and that he was left thinking that it was acceptable—in other words, that his diary is not fabrication—cannot be disputed. As the story unfolds, there will appear ample corroboration in the letters which Wilson received from House that he knew House's sentiments, knew what he was doing, and did not dissent.

The reader may by this time have in his mind a picture of Wilson as a man utterly impervious to outside influence, who shaped his policies in his own mind and personally directed their execution. Yet if there is to be an exception to the general statement that Wilson was never decisively influenced by anyone, House would be the natural choice. Wilson had for him, more than he had for any other man, affection, trust, and admiration.

* See p. 213 above.

Moreover, he believed him to have talents which he himself had not got. He could believe this without envy because they were not the sort of talents that Wilson wanted to have—the talent for 'dickering', as Mr. Baker called it, which, put more politely, is the talent for negotiation. Wilson cannot have been unaware that negotiation is the method by which diplomatic results have from time immemorial been obtained. He needed the help of someone whose negotiating talent could put him in a position to use his own talent for proclamation. Once in that position he would know exactly what to do. But how to get to it? If House could get him there, why not let him try, on the basis that, as House recorded in his account of the conversation of 3 December, he 'could talk and be talked to without it being binding upon anyone'. But it often happens that the loose threads of talk are woven into ropes and that the ropes begin to bind.

There are two further things about their relationship that should be considered, one that needs no explanation and one that does. What needs no explanation is that if Wilson was using House in this way, he should have given him a free hand. He did in fact leave House to his own devices, never giving him any detailed instructions and commenting on House's reports only in terms of wide and warm approval. He used House as an architect uses a craftsman; there is nothing surprising in that. But what will be found to be so odd is the way in which Wilson seems to dissociate a part of himself from what House was doing. Since House worked in secret, the public image of Wilson as a man of peace, a disinterested friend of humanity above the conflict, looking with equal favour or disfavour on the good and the bad in the strugglers below, was kept untouched. But the curious thing is that, while House as Wilson's agent was moving into alliance with Britain and bringing America up to the point of war, the image seems to have remained untouched in Wilson's own mind. It was as if House was the mechanic employed by Wilson to hoist the image to the mountain top where the proclamation of peace and the laying down of the law was to begin. Wilson saw separately the mountain top and the route to it, as if he were looking at each at different times through a telescope and did not relate the one vision to the other.

Mr. Baker, the biographer, was a Bryanist at heart ('broad, sound thought, with constructive ideas which Wilson was afterwards to profit by' he says of Bryan's letter of 19 September)[61] and he thought that House's activities were mischievous. If Wilson thought so, why did he permit them? Did House influence him against his better judgement? But is Wilson then to be presented to posterity as the man whom House led into mischief? No hero-worshipper could stomach that. The picture that emerges from Mr. Baker's chapters[62] is that of a wise king, whose only fault was too great an affection for a favourite prince, allowing him to burn his fingers in affairs of state, indulgent to his fantasies but intervening every now and again to bring him back to reality, reality usually being the bad behaviour of the British. Perhaps the picture is true. Other biographers and historians have painted other pictures; in most of them the lines are blurred. But it is idle to speculate further until the reader has seen how House's policy developed and the situations which it produced.

As it happened, 3 December 1914, the very day on which Wilson and House had all but decided to shelve their hopes, was also the day on which Herr Zimmermann in Berlin was flying a kite.

Zimmermann, the Under-Secretary at the Foreign Office, was not only the man whom the Kaiser had appointed as his channel of communication with House but also the German whom House liked best and with whom he considered that he had established the best relations. House had not yet met Bethmann; when House was in Berlin in July 1914 the Chancellor was away; his wife had just died. Von Jagow, the Foreign Minister, had just married; and though House did meet him at dinner, he was on his honeymoon on the occasion of the Potsdam feast on 1 June 1914, which was why Zimmermann had been in attendance. Gerard also liked Zimmermann and treated him as a personal friend. 'A very jolly sort of large German', Gerard told House, 'plain and hearty manners and a democratic air.'[63] Zimmermann was in fact of bourgeois origin, quite a surprising thing to find in any foreign office at that time. He had begun in the colonial service, transferred to the Foreign Office in 1902, and become Under-Secretary in his early fifties in 1911. Gerard much preferred him to the aristocratic von Jagow, whom he thought looked down on him. But appearances were deceptive. Zimmermann was the outsider who wanted to get in. He was not in the least likely to do anything that would put him in bad standing with the military. 'He was in his heart always pro-U Boat', Bernstorff wrote in his memoirs, 'that is, he always swam with the stream and with those who shouted loudest.'[64] Gerard was unpleasantly surprised in 1917 to hear that Zimmermann said that 'he had been compelled, from motives of policy, to keep on friendly terms with me'.[65]

The decision was not Zimmermann's to fly the kite but Bethmann's. House's letter of 5 September 1914 to Zimmerman had not been ignored. It had not arrived in Berlin until 20 October, but it had after that been seriously studied by Bethmann himself. In order to understand how his mind was moving, it is necessary to consider in greater detail than hitherto what had brought Germany into the war and what she hoped to get out of it.

Germany was the youngest of the great European powers. By two short wars—indeed, by two battles, Königgrätz in 1866 and Sedan in 1870— she had beaten Austria and France and won her place on the Continent. If Bismarck had had his way, she would have left it at that. But she was possessed by greater ambitions. She foresaw that in twentieth-century power politics nations would count for little; she desired to be more than the first nation in Europe; she wanted, using Europe as her base, to become one of the world powers. This was not a dream only of the soldiers. It was shared by her industrialists; also by her academics whose thoughts in the eighties and nineties were the food for action in 1914. One of the most influential of them wrote of the man who was

perceptive enough to realise that the course of world history in the twentieth century will be determined by the competition between the Russian, English, American and perhaps the Chinese world empires, and by their aspirations to reduce all the other, smaller, states to dependence on them, will also see in a central European customs federation the nucleus of something which may save from destruction not only the political independence of those states, but Europe's higher, ancient culture itself.[66]

The Central European Customs Federation was the most persuasive form of the Mitteleuropa which Germany wished to create and dominate. She was not thinking of an old style Napoleonic Empire laid on top of restless nationalities struggling for release. She wanted the economic mastery and political leadership of Europe as the base of an overseas empire which would put her on a par with Britain. For this she must have a navy which could at least look Britain's in the face. The accession to the throne of Kaiser Wilhelm II in 1888 and the dismissal of Bismarck in 1890 initiated the new policy of expansion which the Kaiser described as Germany's entitlement to 'a place in the sun'. But in order to get it she had to disturb a number of suspicious occupants. There were vacant squares on the chessboard, but if she moved on to one, it was seen as a threat to somebody else's position—Britain's trade route to India or Russia's sphere of influence in Persia. Germany was by no means the only pike in the pond. All the European nations, big and small, were engaged in shifting alliances and continual jockeying. But Germany distinguished herself by her determination to show that she was taking her place in the sun by no man's leave but by the strength of her own right arm. The Kaiser especially enjoyed the jostling and the shouting and the treading on toes. The exhaustion of German patience, the phrase with which the world became so familiar in Hitler's thirties, began with the Kaiser in 1911.

By the end of the nineteenth century the groupings between the great powers were beginning to settle. Germany had made in 1879 the alliance with Austria which was the basis of Mitteleuropa. The treaty with Italy in 1891 began the Triple Alliance. Meanwhile, the nations that Germany was alarming were drawing together. The Russo-French military alliance began in 1893, the Anglo-French Entente in 1904, and the Anglo-Russian Entente in 1907. This, Germany said, was 'encirclement', the hoop of iron intended to keep her for ever in her place.

The responsibility for the Great War is not something to be settled by a 'war guilt' clause; and in the revulsion that set in among Germany's former enemies against the manner of its imposition by the Treaty of Versailles in 1919 it became popular to think and say that the war was really nobody's fault at all—or rather as much anybody's fault as anybody else's. On this view the precipitating cause of the war was that Austria pushed too hard against Serbia; the mechanism of control which was governed by the balance of power was too finely adjusted to allow for a gross mis-judgement; the impetus of the Austrian ultimatum to Serbia set things going too fast to be checked and within eleven days of it the five great powers were at war. At worst there was negligence but no malice aforethought: 'manslaughter, not murder' was Lloyd George's verdict in 1933[67] and he was prepared to bring it in against everybody, including Grey with whom at that time he was quarrelling over the remains of the Liberal party. Grey was then dead: 'a mean man', Lloyd George told his mistress, 'I am glad I trampled upon his carcase'.[68]

Most historians would now agree that the mechanical theory lets Germany, and perhaps Russia as well, off too lightly. The murder of the Arch-duke was the sort of incident that was continually occurring and which depended for its effect on the way it was handled by the great powers. Austria would have risked nothing without German approval. Germany's attitude was that the sharp chastisement of Serbia was necessary to Austria's 'political rehabilitation',[69] as Jagow put it in a letter to the German ambas-sador in London, and that this could be accomplished only by a puni-tive war; if this led to a general war, a showdown between the two groups was inevitable sooner or later and now was as good a time as any, if not better. So Germany approved the ultimatum which Austria delivered to Serbia on 23 July 1914 and which was designed to make submission impossible.

Thereafter the question whether the war would be general or local depended on Russia. It would be too complicated here to describe Russia's interest in Serbian independence: partly it was based on Pan-Slavism with Russia as the protector of the smaller Slav nationalities, but there was also a long history of Russo-Austrian rivalry in the Balkans. It is

sufficient to say that the Russian interest was generally recognized. Bethmann had observed eighteen months before that it was 'almost impossible
for Russia to look on inactive in case of a military operation of Austria-
Hungary against Serbia'.[70] Germany's hope or expectation that Russia
would not intervene was based on a belief not in her indifference but in
her lack of readiness. Germany knew for certain that if Russia did intervene, France would be brought in. This was not merely because of the
Franco-Russian alliance but because of Germany's war plan. The Schlieffen
Plan for a war on two fronts required Germany to defeat France within a
few weeks (as in fact she nearly did) before she dealt with Russia who was
a slow starter. Thus it was Germany's intention if she went to war with
Russia to make (as in fact she did) a demand for French neutrality in terms
so humiliating that they could only be refused. Serbia, within a time limit
of forty-eight hours, gave Austria a highly conciliatory reply. Nevertheless,
on 28 July Austria declared war on her. On 30 July Russia ordered general
mobilization. This according to the conventions of the time was equivalent
to a declaration of war on all whom it might concern. Thereafter there was
no looking back.

This sparse account does not do justice to an issue to which immense
study has been devoted. Its purpose here is not to apportion degrees of
blame but, first, to explain how it was that each side passionately believed
itself to be in the right and secondly, why it was that neither side when it
went to war had (if one excepts the Austrian intent to crush Serbia) any
definite and limited objectives. Each side thought simply that the time
had come to break the other. Germany's conduct was on any view so reckless that, taken in conjunction with her constantly proclaimed willingness
to fight, it provides abundant material for a charge of aggression whose
object was the domination of Europe and of which her callous invasion
of Belgium could be alleged as the final proof.

In British eyes there was in addition the deliberate challenge to her
naval supremacy. Britain had no army to speak of and depended for her
security solely on her fleet. Germany had the best army in Europe and
needed no navy to defeat any continental foe. Why then was she building
a navy to compare with Britain's and designed for action in the North Sea?
As the century moved through its first decade there were few Englishmen
unready with an answer to that question. In April 1902 Spring Rice, then
at home, wrote: 'Everyone in the office and out talks as if we had but one
enemy in the world, and that Germany.'[71] Grey as usual put a plain point
plainly when he wrote in July 1908:

If the German Fleet ever becomes superior to ours, the German army can
conquer this country. There is no corresponding risk of this kind to Germany:

for however superior our Fleet was, no naval victory would bring us any nearer to Berlin.[72]

Balfour, Prime Minister until 1905, wrote in 1908 that he had brought himself reluctantly to believe in the 'German scare': and Eyre Crowe, in a memorandum that has become a classic, wrote in 1907 that 'the union of the greatest military with the greatest Naval Power in one State would compel the world to combine for the riddance of such an incubus'. Compel the world? There were indeed a very few in the United States, notably a minor diplomatist writing anonymously in January 1913,* who thought that the destruction of the balance of power in Europe and of the British Navy would threaten the security of the United States.

The German citizen, not merely the German military mind, saw it all quite differently. 'We are innocent of the outbreak of the war; it was imposed on us.'[73] Thus wrote the German Roman Catholic bishops in a pastoral letter in December 1914. In politics right and left shared a common viewpoint. The Social Democrats were the party of the left and in 1912 became the largest single party in the Reichstag with 110 seats out of 391. They were so much to the left that before 1914 the Kaiser had never received one of them into his presence. They subscribed to the doctrine of international socialism that the workers would oppose all war and in particular refuse to vote war credits. Yet when the time came the German Socialists, like their comrades all over Europe, went over *en masse* to the warmakers. 'We are threatened by the horror of hostile invasion. Today it is not for us to decide for or against war but to consider the means necessary for the defence of our country.'[74] So all but one voted for the credits for which on 14 August Bethmann asked. They joined the deputation from the Reichstag and were received by the Kaiser: 'I no longer recognize parties', he said, 'only Germans!'

For the German citizen the prime cause of the war was the provocative interference by Russia in what would otherwise have been a local dispute. This interference, he believed, was by no means casual or unpremeditated but reflected the considered decision of the 'encircling' powers, envious of German virility and of her industrial prowess and determined to thwart her legitimate aim to expand by tightening the constraining hoop until she was squeezed to death. But it was Britain that became the chief object of hatred; so much so that in August Gerard in Berlin was advising Americans to wear small American flags in their buttonholes to ensure that they were not mistaken for English.[75] A German could hardly fail to realize that what he regarded as legitimate expansion would involve the dispossession of France and Russia and so it was in accordance with the law of nature

* Lewis Einstein in the *National Review*, lx. 736.

that they should fight. But surely there was room in the world for Britain and Germany together? The German Navy was but the natural concomitant of her increasing maritime trade and her reasonable colonial aspirations. All that she wanted was to take her place side by side with Britain as a world power. Jealousy and greed could be the only motives for the British stab in the back when Germany was already engaged with two foes; and Britain's hypocritical attempt to use the regrettable necessity for the invasion of Belgium as a justification for her conduct made it all the worse. These were the thoughts of Bethmann, who was the man in charge of Germany's foreign policy and whose mind was fairly representative of middle-of-the-road civilian thought. This was the way too in which the situation, at first but not for long, presented itself to Joseph Grew, second-in-command at the American embassy in Berlin, a career diplomat with a considerable future to be made available for posterity in a voluminous diary. On 8 August 1914 he wrote: 'We all believe here that this war was carefully cooked up by Russia, England and France.'[76]

As a result of the Oscar Straus affair* Gerard was instructed on 7 September 1914 to find out whether it was true that the Kaiser would accept mediation if the other side would. This was at the time when the German Army was daily expected to enter Paris. Gerard talked to Zimmermann 'in an informal manner', as he said, which appears to have covered the suggestion, as Zimmermann recorded it, that Germany, after she had taken Paris, could 'impose an immensely high indemnity on France and take as many of her colonies as we wanted'.[77] Zimmermann with Bethmann's approval turned it down flat. After the defeat of France, he said, Germany would still have to face England and Russia. The war had been forced on Germany and she could only accept a real and lasting peace that would protect her from new attack. 'It is therefore up to the United States to get our enemies to make peace proposals.'[78]

But naturally Bethmann in the expectation of victory over France had had to consider what terms Germany would demand. They would not necessarily be the final terms since Britain still had to be beaten and French co-operation was desirable for that, but they must provide at least the basis for the permanent peace. In this spirit on 9 September Bethmann put down on paper what he described as 'provisional notes on the direction of our policy on the conclusion of peace' and what has since come to be called the September Programme.[79] The 'general aim of the war', stated by way of introduction, was the reduction of France to the status of a second-rate

---

* See p. 229 above.

power and the thrusting back of Russia to a position where she could no longer meddle with Mitteleuropa, so as to give Germany security in west and east 'for all imaginable time'. Furthermore, a 'continuous central African colonial empire' was to be created by means of colonial acquisitions. The aims in the east and in Africa were left for future delineation and the concrete part of the programme was confined to the west.

The keystone in the west was the plan for Mitteleuropa. Bethmann rejected proposals from the right wing for wholesale annexations. He evaded the Kaiser's pet idea (which he described as 'beguiling' and worth consideration 'up to a certain point') whereunder 'deserving N.C.O.'s and men' (one is reminded of Bryan's 'deserving Democrats'*) should be rewarded as were Roman legionaries of old by settlement of land on conquered territory specially cleared for the purpose. In the programme annexations were quite moderate. From Belgium Liege and Verviers would have been taken and possibly Antwerp; Bethmann had already let it be known that his word of honour to evacuate Belgium immediately after the war had been vitiated by Britain's entry into it. France must yield the enormously valuable ore field of Longwy-Briey on the Franco-German border. Its acquisition would double Germany's reserves of iron and enable her, the industrialist August Thyssen calculated, to catch up with America and pass her: as a corollary it would cut France's production by 80 per cent so that, a German report concluded, it would end her large-scale iron industry. Apart from this great prize, it would be left to the military to decide what annexations were necessary for their purposes on the borderlands of the Vosges and, as an anti-British measure, on the coast-line from Dunkirk to Boulogne. The tiny independent duchy of Luxembourg at the southern end of Belgium, which had been invaded as a matter of course, could be made into a German Federal State with a little extra territory added from France and Belgium.

The kernel of the programme was economic.

We must create a *central European economic association* through common customs treaties, to include France, Belgium, Holland, Denmark, Austria-Hungary, Poland, and perhaps Italy, Sweden and Norway. This association will not have any common constitutional supreme authority and all its members will be formally equal, but in practice will be under German leadership and must stabilise Germany's economic dominance over Mitteleuropa.

More detailed provisions to secure economic dominance were made for France, Belgium, and Holland. There was to be a commercial treaty with France which would exclude British commerce and secure for Germany

---

* See p. 106 above.

'financial and industrial freedom of movement'. France was to pay an indemnity high enough to prevent rearmament. Although it was not mentioned in the programme, Belgium also was to pay an indemnity, presumably as a consequence of her impudence in offering resistance; and on 26 August Bethmann had given instructions for the amount to be calculated. He had rejected as 'Utopian' the complete annexation of Belgium. But the September Programme got as near to Utopia as it could.

> Belgium, even if allowed to continue to exist as a state, must be reduced to a vassal state, must allow us to occupy any military important ports, must place her coast at our disposal in military respects, must become economically a German province. Given such a solution, which offers the advantages of annexation without its inescapable domestic political disadvantages, French Flanders with Dunkirk, Calais and Boulogne, where most of the population is Flemish, can without danger be attached to this unaltered Belgium.

As to Holland, the Dutch dislike of compulsion must be borne in mind, so she 'must be left independent in externals, but made internally dependent on us'.

House's letter to Zimmermann arrived, as has been said, on 20 October 1914. Something of House's conversation with Dumba, the Austrian ambassador in Washington, also came through to Berlin in the form of a suggestion from the Austrian Foreign Minister that it would be a mistake to reject in principle an offer of mediation and that Austria and Germany should agree upon their 'relatively moderate' war aims. The setback on the Marne was in any event causing Bethmann to reconsider the September Programme. On 10 November 1914 he had a long conversation with Falkenhayn, the Commander-in-Chief in the west. The General had come to the conclusion that Germany was not strong enough to get the peace she wanted on both fronts. The two men decided that the war aims in the west were the more important and that the right solution was a separate peace with Russia. Bethmann summed it up:

> Thus for the price of having our relations with Russia remain in essentials what they were before the war, we would create what conditions we liked in the west. At the same time, this would end the Triple Entente.[80]

So Bethmann held to the September Programme in the west. Perhaps he would himself have relaxed a little if it came to the crunch. His personal minimum was Longwy-Briey from France and the military and economic domination of Belgium, whether or not she remained independent in name. But relaxation was difficult in the existing climate of opinion. Obviously the public could not be told that complete victory was now at least doubtful, and so the autumn saw no withdrawal from the extreme demands for large annexations both west and east as essential to the future security of the Fatherland. These were the views of the War Aims Majority, a group in the Reichstag which was drawn from the right and centre parties and represented nearly three-quarters of its membership. The Social Democrats were officially opposed to annexation. When in the beginning they gave their support to the war they had demanded that 'as soon as the aim of security has been achieved and our opponents are disposed to make peace this war shall be brought to an end'.[81] But many individuals among them would have accepted as an 'aim of security' as much as was visualized by the September Programme.

Bethmann's reorientation after his talk with Falkenhayn on 10 November was not something which could even be hinted in Austria. It was in the east that Austria hoped for profit and she would not be interested in German acquisitions from France and Belgium. Accordingly, Jagow, in his answer to the Austrian approach, passed over the suggestion that the two nations should formulate joint war aims. In his discouraging reply, which voiced Bethmann's views, Jagow expressed the attitude which then and thereafter the German Government maintained on the value of the American approach.[82] First, any idea of permanent peace through an international order was pure *schwarmerei*. Secondly, Germany would not make peace by conference: which would mean, Bethmann wrote to Jagow on 23 November 1914,

Mr. Wilson's and Mr. Bryan's known do-good tendencies and the injection of a lot of questions (disarmament, arbitration and world peace) which, the more Utopian they are, the more they make practical negotiations difficult.[83]

Thirdly, in any negotiations Germany did not want Wilson's mediation, since this for the sake of American commercial interests would be likely to favour England.

This left Germany with only two objects to serve in conversation with the President or his emissaries. The first was appearances: it would not look well for a nation forced into a war of defence to spurn all suggestion of peace; 'the impression of a sympathetic reception', as Bethmann put it, was what was needed. The second was that conversation of this sort might extract some proposal from the other side. Even if the subject-matter of the proposal was of no interest, it would be useful to put the other side in the position of taking the initiative.

So the letter which House received on 15 December 1914, ostensibly from Zimmermann but actually drafted by Bethmann, while it did not depart in essence from the attitude expressed to the earlier American approach, was in its language more enticing.

The war has been forced upon us by our enemies . . . this makes it impossible for us to take the first step towards making peace. The situation might be different if such overtures came from the other side . . . worthwhile trying to see where the land lies in the other camp.[84]

Optimistically House took this as an acceptance of the view that Germany could not do better than a drawn peace with nothing given or received. He read into the letter what he wanted to be in it—an indication that she would give up Belgium. He hurried to the White House where Wilson agreed with him on immediate action. On 17 December he saw Bernstorff, who corroborated all his hopes. When House told him it would mean the evacuation and indemnity of Belgium and drastic disarmament, he received the glib assurance: 'No obstacle in that direction.'[85] He asked the ambassador to get confirmation of this from Berlin, noting in his diary that he might 'have difficulty in holding him to any verbal agreements'.[86] Then the Colonel got to work on Spring Rice, telling him that the Austrian and German ambassadors were pressing him, that they had been told that before negotiations began a formal pledge must be given about the evacuation and indemnity of Belgium, and that he was ready to advise the President to take action as soon as Britain agreed.[87] Sir Cecil telegraphed this to the Foreign Office on 18 December.

Grey could not afford, any more than Bethmann could, to turn down this sort of approach, but he did not like having to deal with it. First, he doubted that Germany would really accept such terms; and in this he was entirely right. Secondly, while he himself would not ask for more, he knew of many in Britain and more still in France and Russia who would not be so easily satisfied. Thirdly, he was already beginning to make promises to allies, actual or potential, which could only be fulfilled out of the proceeds of total victory. Lastly, these negotiations with potential allies would be seriously affected if they heard that Britain was talking about peace.

Grey tackled his problems in a direct way. First, he made it clear that what he was going to say represented his personal views. He could not speak for the Allies. They would have to state their own conditions for themselves 'and what they will be', he wrote frankly, 'will largely depend on the progress of the war'.[88] Secondly, he guarded against leakage by saying nothing must on any account be told to the State Department; it was for Wilson and House only. On this basis, he said that the two main objects to be secured were the evacuation of Belgium with compensation and a durable peace. As to the first, Britain would fight for it if she had to fight alone: it was the absolute minimum. But if Germany agreed to it, 'the barrier to peace discussions as far as we are concerned would be removed'. As to the second, a durable peace was not to be obtained by crushing Germany. What was wanted was an agreement between the Great

Powers with the object of mutual security and preservation of peace. This 'might have stability if the United States would become a party to it and were prepared to join in repressing by force whoever broke the Treaty'.

All this Grey put into a cable for Spring Rice which he sent on 22 December 1914. He must, however, have given some earlier indication of his attitude, for on 20 December the ambassador sought urgently an interview with House to tell him that Grey had sent word that he personally did not think it would be a good thing for the Allies to stand out against a proposal which embraced indemnity to Belgium and a satisfactory plan for disarmament. House reported at once to the President who was much elated and talked of House going to Europe forthwith.

For secrecy's sake Spring Rice and House usually met at the home of William Phillips, Third Assistant Secretary of State, who enjoyed the special confidence of the President and the Colonel. In the course of the Mexican embroilment in January 1914 he had been selected, probably by House, for a delicate piece of negotiation; in his memoir he gives an interesting glimpse of Wilson's direct and informal way of dealing with minor emissaries.

> I would be conducted to the President's library on the second floor. There Mr. Wilson would examine my report of the exchanges which I had had with Cabrera during the day. He would discuss them with me and would then sit down at his typewriter and, with his back to me, type out instructions for the following day.[89]

After receiving Grey's cable of 22 December the ambassador had another talk with House at this rendezvous. Sir Cecil did not show House the cable but communicated to him what he had learnt by heart. In particular he stressed the point that Grey had not yet taken up the proposal with his own Cabinet, much less with the Allies. Sir Cecil himself was anxious to probe House's ideas about the permanent settlement. House, it will be remembered,* had already aired his notions and Spring Rice tried to pin him down on the French part of Lorraine for France and Constantinople for Russia. House said all this could be thrashed out later and that they must begin on broad lines. He agreed with Spring Rice that the military party in Germany would try to prevent parleys being brought to a satisfactory conclusion and that the people as a whole were with them. But House thought that the Kaiser, the Chancellor, and the Foreign Secretary knew that the war was already a failure and would like to get out of it.

On this the ambassador cabled Grey on 24 December expressing House's conviction that both German and Austrian ambassadors desired peace

---

* See p. 231 above.

and had been instructed by their governments to say so. 'He assured me most positively that the German Ambassador said in clear terms that his Government would agree to evacuation and compensation of Belgium, and to security against renewed attack in future.'[90] But he had nothing encouraging to report about Grey's idea of a postwar treaty with American participation. House, he said, 'pointed out that the United States could never become an active party to an agreement to join in repressing by force whoever broke it'.

After the interview the Colonel went back to the White House where he found the President anxiously awaiting him. They decided to go no further with Bernstorff until House had heard something more from Grey. 'Then we could put the question squarely up to Bernstorff by telling him I was ready to go to London, but he must not let me go only to find Germany repudiating what he had said.'[91]

No confirmation came from Berlin, which was not surprising since Bernstorff had not asked for any and almost certainly knew that he would not have got it if he had. He was always the middleman, prepared to say anything to get the parties together in the hope that, if they got talking, a bargain might emerge. Later he denied that he had ever said anything about conditions of peace, telling the German Foreign Office that all he had said to House was that he would be well received in Berlin.[92] On 3 January House wrote direct to Zimmermann saying that on an indication that Germany would discuss the two points he would leave immediately for England where he had reason to believe he would get a sympathetic hearing.

No word came from Grey either. So on 4 January House took it up with Page ('I have not been able to get from Spring Rice any expression from his government') and asked him to see Sir Edward.

Grey in fact was still on the fence. Perhaps he was influenced by Asquith, who had seen Spring Rice's cable of 24 December; the Prime Minister treated Germany's reported assent to the two-point programme as 'significant as showing how the wind is blowing' but of course not 'good enough either for France or Russia'.[93] So Grey cabled Spring Rice on 2 January with yet another reminder that France and Russia had to be consulted. Once again he pointed out that there had been no confirmation from Berlin and said that he could not open discussions unless very sure of the ground respecting Germany's real disposition. Moreover, the thing that Grey was now putting first was his idea that the war would have been fought in vain if at the end of it there was not a guarantee against future aggression; and he had been rather chilled by the way House had turned down all idea of American participation. So in his cable he said:

I gather that the President's friend considers there is no chance of the United

States Government countersigning any agreement for preservation of future peace. If this is so it is difficult to see how a durable peace can be secured without complete exhaustion of one side or the other.[94]

He went on to ask how a durable peace was possible 'unless there was some League for preservation of Peace to which the United States amongst others were a party'.

On the possibility of negotiations Grey sent an even franker message to be given orally to the President.[95] The messenger was Chandler Anderson, a close friend of Lansing's in the State Department and one of those who followed the high road to posthumous fame for the minor official by keeping a diary; he was returning to Washington after a spell of duty as legal adviser to Page. The message conveyed Grey's view that discussion was premature and said that he wanted the President to know that the Allies would insist, if they could get them, upon the return of Alsace-Lorraine, the payment of an indemnity to France, and Russian acquisition of Constantinople and the Dardanelles.

It was a bleak prospect. The only firm offer was from Britain to discuss the two-point programme. There was an unconfirmed offer from Germany to the same effect. If Bernstorff's assurance was genuine, House could hope that the pacific tips of each side, Grey for the Entente and the Kaiser and Chancellor for the Central Powers, might profitably talk together. But the Kaiser's supposed peaceful inclinations were hardly more than imaginings and Grey had made it as plain as a pikestaff that his inclinations would be held in check by the Allies' demands. These demands, if advanced seriously, put out the faint hope of a peace between equals. Constantinople could be surrendered at the expense of Turkey but Germany could not possibly see a restoration of Alsace-Lorraine in any other terms than as an admission of defeat.

So when House decided to go to Europe, it was not with any real hope of bringing about an agreement but with the object of finding out at first hand whether the prospect was quite as gloomy as it looked. He proposed to put it to the President that they had done all they could do through ambassadors and that the only thing now was for him to take the matter up directly with London and afterwards with Berlin. He wanted to see the President anyway about another project, an ambitious plan for a pact with the South and Central American Republics, so on 12 January he took the midday train from New York. McAdoo and Grayson met him at the station and after he had dressed for dinner he went into the President's study. 'We had exactly twelve minutes' conversation before dinner, and during those twelve minutes it was decided that I should go to Europe on January 30.'[96] After dinner to House's surprise the President, instead of discussing all the matters of importance that House had on foot, read from A. G. Gardiner's 'sketches of prominent men'* until it was time to go to bed, interrupting himself only for a visit from Senator La Follette. House interpreted this to mean that the President had confidence in his doing the work without his help.

The following morning House managed to get in a few more minutes after breakfast when the President and he strolled from the elevator to the President's study. It was decided that House should see Spring Rice and also Bryan and break to the latter the news of his impending visit. House met Spring Rice at 10.45 a.m. and found him in what he described as 'rather a sulky mood';[97] the Allies would not receive the good offices of the President cordially, he said. House told him that the President would have nothing to do with terms of peace but wanted to see what was possible about a guarantee for the future. Asked whether the United States would be a guarantor, he gave the same answer as before. Spring Rice demanded that House tell the French and Russian ambassadors what he was doing so that they might not take offence. House was against this but was persuaded and so they all met at 4 p.m. House had asked Spring Rice to get them into a receptive frame of mind, but he had not done so and was, House noted, 'not particularly nice in helping me out'. It was an awkward interview, both ambassadors denouncing the Germans violently and telling House that his mission would be entirely fruitless, but they agreed that there was no harm in his finding that out for himself.

House then went on to break the news to Bryan who 'was distinctly disappointed when he heard I was to go to Europe as the peace emissary. He said he had planned to do this himself.' House replied that the President thought it would be unwise for anyone to go officially (he in fact told House that he would let Bryan resign rather than let him go on such a mission); and Bryan said generously that if it was unofficial, House was the man best fitted for the job. Then House went back to report to Wilson and they discussed a letter of instructions and a code to be used.

On 14 January Spring Rice telegraphed to Grey that House intended to come. The announcement arrived in the midst of the perturbation caused by the voyage of the *Dacia*. Grey's cable of 18 January† was expressed as being sent to warn House of the state of British public opinion. However, in the edited version which the Colonel received, Grey said that it would give him great pleasure to see House.

Of course, he understands that all that can be promised here is that if Germany

---

* A. G. Gardiner was at this time the editor of the London *Daily News*, a leading Liberal newspaper in which his 'sketches' were a prominent feature. Many were reprinted in book form; a volume entitled *Pillars of Society* was published in 1913.   † See p. 187 above.

seriously and sincerely desires peace, I will consult our friends as to what terms of peace are acceptable.[98]

On 24 January House went to Washington again for a last word. Wilson told him to tell Grey everything, to explain the bypassing of Bryan, and to say that the President was acting directly through House and eliminating all intermediaries. Then in his diary House quotes Wilson direct: 'There is not much for us to talk over, for the reason that we are both of the same mind and it is not necessary to go into details with you.'

Wilson prepared and typed out himself, so that not even his confidential stenographer would see it, a letter addressed to House and to be used as his credentials. He was supplying through House, the President wrote, 'a channel of confidential communication' through which the nations at war might have a preliminary interchange of views about peace. He had no thought of suggesting terms unless asked to do so.

If we can be instrumental in ascertaining for each side in the contest what is the real disposition, the real wish, the real purpose of the other with regard to a settlement, your mission and my whole desire in this matter will have been accomplished.[99]

Then House took his leave and the President insisted on driving to the station with him and walking with him to the train.

The President's eyes were moist when he said his last words of farewell. He said: 'Your unselfish and intelligent friendship has meant much to me,' and he expressed his gratitude again and again, calling me his 'most trusted friend'. He declared I was the only one in all the world to whom he could open his entire mind. . . .

I asked if he remembered the first day we met, some three and a half years ago. He replied, 'Yes, but we have known one another always, and merely came in touch then, for our purposes and thoughts were as one.' I told him how much he had been to me; how I had tried all my life to find someone with whom I could work out the things I had so deeply at heart, and I had begun to despair, believing my life would be more or less a failure when he came into it, giving me the opportunity for which I had been longing.[100]

On 30 January House sailed from New York in the *Lusitania* on one of her last voyages. He had to turn a blind eye on the American flag she hoisted when she entered the war zone. In London he took up his quarters in the Washington Hotel in Curzon Street.

IX

HOUSE IN EUROPE

THE moment that House parted from Wilson on the station platform at Washington was the peak of their friendship. Not that there was any sharp decline or that when House returned four months later there was any outward change, but House's unique position was inevitably eroded by Wilson's marriage to a very possessive woman.

When the President's engagement to Mrs. Norman Galt, formerly Edith Bolling, was announced on 6 October 1915, he composed and typed out the following statement for the press:

Mrs. Norman Galt is the widow of a well known business man of Washington who died some eight years ago. She has lived in Washington since her marriage in 1896. She was Miss Edith Bolling and was born in Wytheville, Virginia, where her girlhood was spent and where her father, the Hon. William H. Bolling, a man of remarkable character and charm, won distinction as one of the ablest, most interesting and most individual lawyers of a State famous for its lawyers. In the circle of cultivated and interesting people who have had the privilege of knowing her Mrs. Galt has enjoyed an enviable distinction, not only because of her unusual beauty and natural charm, but also because of her very unusual character and gifts. She has always been sought out as a delightful friend, and her thoughtfulness and quick capacity for anything she chose to undertake have made her friendship invaluable to those who were fortunate enough to win it.

It was Miss Margaret Wilson and her cousin Miss Bones who drew Mrs. Galt into the White House circle. They met her first in the early part of the present year, and were so much attracted by her that they sought her out more and more frequently and the friendship among them quickly ripened into an affectionate intimacy. It was through this association with his daughter and cousin that the President had the opportunity to meet Mrs. Galt, who spent a month at Cornish this summer as Miss Wilson's guest. It is, indeed, the most interesting circumstance connected with the engagement just announced that the President's daughters should have picked Mrs. Galt out for their special admiration and friendship before their father did.[1]

In this hand-out the second paragraph, as will be seen, diplomatically enlarges the parts played by the minor characters in the drama, particularly Miss Margaret Wilson's, and hardly does justice to the *élan* of the leading man.

The age of the leading lady was naturally not displayed. Mrs. Galt was in fact forty-two, sixteen years younger than her betrothed. Certainly she was beautiful—a dark, luscious beauty with a full figure. She was attractive too, with vivacity rather than intelligence and sparkle rather than wit. She had been brought up in gentility and poverty in a large Virginian family that had owned its plantation before the Civil War; she was devoted to all its members and their ways. Not much is known about Mr. Galt. In her substantial volume of memoirs written in 1939, he is mentioned when they married and when he died. The memoirs consist chiefly of social adventures with a special appeal to those interested in the doings of quasi-royalty. There are few men and almost no women who can write an account of their own lives without making themselves look rather silly in places and the second Mrs. Wilson was not in the minority. She shows herself as a woman of warm romantic temperament and a sweet manner stiffened with a little extra glucose for people she disapproved of; and even for those who merited worse, her censure is sorrow-sugared rather than anger-spiced.

Edith's first husband was nine years her senior, but, she says, seemed much older. She was fond of him but clearly not in love and the wooing was lengthy; 'after four years his patience and persistence overcame me'.[2] She was then twenty-four. They had no children; one miscarried. Mr. Galt had a jewellery business in Washington and when he died after twelve years of marriage he left her the business, and it produced a more than adequate income for her; but not, since it left her 'in trade', a social position. Dr. Grayson was in love with Altrude Gordon, a young girl, the daughter of an old friend of Mrs. Galt's who spent much time in her company. Thus the doctor came to see quite a lot of Mrs. Galt. One day he asked if he could bring Helen Bones to call; she needed company and outdoor exercise, he said. Mrs. Galt replied, to use her own words:

My dear Doctor, as you know, I am not a society person. I have never had any contacts with official Washington, and don't desire any. I am therefore the last person in the world able to help you.[3]

However, Helen Bones did come and the two women got into the habit of taking long walks together in Rock Creek Park and returning for tea to Mrs. Galt's house at 1328 Twentieth Street. One afternoon in the middle of March 1915, when the walk was over, Helen Bones suggested that they should go to tea at the White House. Mrs. Galt protested that she was very muddy, but, on being assured that Cousin Woodrow was out golfing, she agreed to go. Coming out of the elevator on the second floor they ran straight into the President and Dr. Grayson who had just got back from the golf course. Although muddy, Mrs. Galt was wearing, as she recalled, a smart black tailored suit which Worth had made for her in Paris and a tricot hat which she thought completed a very good-looking ensemble. They all had tea in the Oval room and an hour of delightful talk. The President was obviously attracted. He asked her to stay to dinner, but she declined. A fortnight or so later on 7 April Helen suggested a drive. When Mrs. Galt reached the White House she was amazed to find that the President was coming too. This time she stayed to dinner and he talked to her intimately of his childhood. Thus began a series of rides. Statesmen who fall under the spell of younger women are tempted to substitute for the homage of youth the flattery of confidences. As Asquith was doing at this very time and as Disraeli had done before him, Wilson on these rides around Washington scattered secrets of state plentifully before his lady. Then on 28 April there was his first note accompanying a book for her to read and on 30 April a more formal dinner party at which Mrs. Galt wore a princess black *charmeuse* which Worth had created for her. Then on 4 May there came the evening after dinner at which Wilson declared his love. He had told the others what he was going to do, so that the two were left alone on the south portico. It was just over six weeks since they had first met.

Mrs. Galt had not, so far as her memoirs disclose, been speculating about the nature of these marked attentions. Being an extremely conventional person, it is unlikely that she thought of a proposal of marriage after so short an acquaintance and so soon after Mrs. Wilson's death. If she had, being also a kind person, she would not, as she did, have blurted that out. Yes, Wilson answered, but time was not measured by weeks or months or years, but by deep human experience; and since his wife's death he had lived a lifetime of loneliness and heartache.

There is no call to doubt his sincerity. He had, as he had written to Ellen sixteen years before, 'an insatiable desire to be loved—an infinite passion of love in me, longing to be spent'.[4] So long as she lived, it was spent on her alone. If ever there was a monogamist, it was Wilson: it was not merely that only one woman could be his wife but also that he always had to have one. At this moment he was like a man who, having heard the first theme in the adagio of Beethoven's last symphony and at once thought it impossible that any lovelier melody could ever entrance his emotions, has been assailed by the second theme and has known, again at once, that, while the first will come back perpetually, to the second he must succumb.

The conversation was continued in decorous terms. He would be less than a gentleman, Wilson said, if he continued to make opportunities to see her without telling her that he wanted her to be his wife. Mrs. Galt held back. She had no ambition to marry the President of the United States. She would marry him only if she was in love with him and that she had yet to find out. So the courtship continued with Wilson seeing her whenever and wherever the conventions allowed, writing her long letters every day and sometimes twice a day, breathing ardour upon her hesitations. This was how things were when House re-entered the scene.

In the five or six weeks that passed between the time that Grey first agreed to discuss peacemaking on the basis of the two-point programme and the time that House and he began actually to talk, the diplomatic situation had changed considerably. It changed further while House was in England and long before the end of his stay it was on 26 April 1915 completely altered by the Treaty of London. The change was due to the developing ambitions of the Allies. Their precipitation into the Great War had been too sudden and their absorption in averting defeat too intense to allow time for counting up the prizes which they would expect to have awarded to them in the event of victory. The prizes anyway would be incidental to their paramount object which was to beat down Germany. Russia's proposal in August 1914 to create an autonomous kingdom of Poland was more of a military manœuvre to improve conditions on and around her main battleground than the initiation of a new settlement. Its appearance was bland for it meant undoing the partition of 1772 and a sacrifice of territory by Russia as well as by Germany.

On 5 September 1914 the Entente powers signed an agreement not to make peace except in common but the treaty contained no definition of aims. Britain was the first to proclaim in general terms what she was fighting for. At first the Prime Minister spoke oratorically about German militarism and the invasion of Belgium, though he did on 2 October 1914 say that the British Empire had no desire to expand. Then on 9 November at the Lord Mayor's Banquet at Guildhall he used slightly more precise, though still rhetorical words:

We shall never sheathe the sword which we have not lightly drawn until Belgium recovers in full measure all and more than all that she has sacrificed, until France is adequately secured against the menace of aggression, until the rights of the smaller nationalities of Europe are placed upon an unassailable foundation, and until the military domination of Prussia is wholly and finally destroyed.[5]

It was not made clear—it was doubtless not easy to be particular—whether these general objectives could be attained for France, Belgium, and the smaller nationalities without any change of territory. France soon made it plain that for her they could not; the President of the Chamber said on 22 December 1914 that France would lay down her arms only 'when the provinces torn from her had been restored to her for ever'.[6] These provinces were of course Alsace and Lorraine. The fact that they lay between France and Germany and had a mixed population was bound to make them a bone of contention. But in 1871, when after the Franco-Prussian War Germany demanded and obtained their cession, they had been held by France for upwards of two centuries and the sentiment of the majority was passionately French. Gladstone felt all the wrong of this though he had no sympathy with the French talk about the inviolability of their soil. He failed to persuade his Cabinet, as he recorded with regret, to make an effort to speak with the other neutral powers against the transfer of Alsace and Lorraine without reference to their populations. Since Bismarck then insisted on the cession without a plebiscite, France now demanded that they should be similarly restored.

So matters stood at the end of 1914 and the Entente powers made no further public statement of their intentions if victorious until two years later.

The first of the secret treaties was made to satisfy Russia. The possession of Constantinople had long been a Russian ambition. She wanted it mainly so as to control the Straits. Her only warm-water ports were in the Black Sea and more than half her trade passed through the Straits, so that their control was genuinely vital since they could be used to strangle her. When in April 1912 Turkey closed them for a fortnight against a possible Italian attack, there had been an economic crisis in Russia.

Turkey, although at first apparently neutral, had in fact on 2 August 1914 signed a treaty of alliance with Germany against Russia. The sentiment in her army was strongly pro-German. She believed that the Entente powers if victorious would partition her empire. There was good reason for this belief; the Ottoman Empire had been for so long on its death-bed that the inheritance had been closely discussed, particularly by Russia and Britain. In August 1914 Russia offered a high price for Turkish neutrality but it was rejected. On 26 September Turkey closed the Straits to commercial traffic and on 28 October allowed two German cruisers into the Black Sea to bombard Odessa. Accordingly on 1 November the Entente declared war. This was soon followed by the proposal of a British naval attack on the Dardanelles. The move was welcomed, if not invited, by the Russians, but they were nevertheless fearful that it might lead to the British occupation of Constantinople. On 4 March 1915 the Russian Foreign Minister demanded that the Straits, i.e. the Bosphorus and the Dardanelles and the territory adjoining them including Constantinople, should become Russian; he offered to extend to his allies 'the same sympathy for realization of desiderata which they may form in other regions of Ottoman Empire and elsewhere'.[7]

The invitation to formulate desiderata set the British Government for the first time to contemplating the fruits of victory. Constantinople could not be obtained except by the complete defeat of Turkey which would place what Asquith called 'the carcase of the Turk'[8] on the table ready for the carving knife. On 10 March he summoned a War Council to which the Conservative leaders were bidden.[9] There was general agreement to accept the Russian demand and the discussion was about what should be the price required for what was, as Asquith had termed it, 'a complete reversal of our old traditional policy'.[10] The situation was not unforeseen. In November 1914 Grey had as good as told Russia that she could have what she wanted. About the same time Herbert Samuel, a Jewish member of the Cabinet, had begun to compose what Asquith called a 'dithyrambic memorandum'[11] advocating the annexation of Palestine to the British Empire and its colonization by Jews. There was also the hope that Russia, gratified by Constantinople, might concede to Britain a larger sphere of influence in Persia. What about Mesopotamia? Alexandretta at the north-eastern tip of the Mediterranean would, the soldiers and sailors at the War Council thought, make a good naval base. From this the talk at the Council broadened to the elimination of the German Navy and the emasculation of Kiel.

Not all of this partitioning would conform to the ideas of France who speedily laid claim to Syria and Cilicia as well as Palestine. France and Britain decided to sign an immediate agreement with Russia, which they did on 25 March, postponing the adjustment of their own affairs. On 8 April Asquith set up a committee to consider the nature of British desiderata in Turkey-in-Asia.

The second secret treaty was the Treaty of London made on 26 April 1915 and it embodied the inducements offered to Italy to desert the Triple Alliance. In October 1914 her Premier brought out the magnificent phrase *sacro egoismo* as expressing the principle which would guide her conduct. Thereafter she considered carefully the offers she got from both sides; but as the territory she chiefly wanted was what only a defeated Austria could be expected to yield, the Allies were able to make the more attractive bid. In November 1914 Baron Sonnino became Italy's Foreign Minister and held the post for the rest of the war and throughout the Peace Conference. It was he who conducted the bargaining in 1915. He was not a typical Italian. His father was a rich Italian Jew, his mother Welsh, and he was born and remained a Protestant. These hybrid origins made him all the more passionately patriotic. *Sacro egoismo* meant that Italy, so newly born as a nation, owed a sacred duty to herself and to the world to be one of the great powers of Europe. In 1914 she was not quite that. She was, as it were, asked to most of the big parties but she was not quite one of the set. The feeling that her position was not taken for granted exasperated her susceptibilities and animated her resolve to use the war to gain such additional territory abroad as would put her status beyond doubt. That was the ambition of most politically minded Italians and with Sidney Sonnino nothing else counted at all. He was no wheedling negotiator but a tough man with a hawk nose who drove his bargains with an angry persistence.

Italy had one legitimate aspiration, Italia Irredenta. The Trentino with its mainly Italian population subject to Austria was to Italy what Alsace-Lorraine was to France. But so that she might have a strategic frontier on her north-east, she wanted to go beyond the Trentino and annex South Tyrol up to the Brenner. This meant that a quarter of a million unwilling Austrians would be transferred to her rule. Her second great wish was to make the Adriatic an Italian lake by securing that all the surrounding land from Venice in the north down to where Albania comes out to meet the Italian heel should either belong to her or at least be removed from any hostile influence. So she stipulated for Trieste, for Istria and Dalmatia with their mainly Slav population, for numerous islands, rocks, and islets, for full sovereignty over Valona, Albania's capital, and the right to make Albania a satellite state: all the rest of the opposing Adriatic coast was to be neutralized. Thirdly, she wanted to increase her power in the Mediterranean and so the partitioning of Turkey was an opportunity not to be lost. She stipulated for her 'just share', which was to be the province of Adalia where Asia Minor makes the north coast of the Eastern Mediterranean; she was also to be given formal sovereignty over the Dodecanese, twelve Greek islands which she already occupied as a result of her war with Turkey in 1912. At the conclusion of the bargain all these demands were met; and for good measure she received as well an assurance of 'compensation' if France and Britain increased their African possessions at the expense of Germany, a loan of £50,000,000 and a promise of 'a share of the war indemnity', this being the first time that an indemnity was mentioned between the Allies. Although the details were kept secret, no one who cared to know was in doubt that a deal was being done. Page reported it to the State Department on 8 May 1915, saying that Italy would get 'very large parts of Austrian territory' against the wishes of Serbia.[12]

It was plain enough that Grey did not care for this sort of thing. He acknowledged the necessity: better to make certain of victory at the cost of some principles than to risk losing all of them by defeat. But he had no stomach for the haggling. In and out of the Cabinet he was being constantly prodded by Lloyd George and Churchill. 'War plays havoc with the refinements of conscience', Lloyd George later observed,[13] and complained that Grey, mistaking correctitude for rectitude, was coldly critical of the Italian advances. By design or by fortune Grey went on holiday before the negotiations closed and Asquith took them over and did the deed. He approached them in the manner of the nineteenth-century English gentleman abroad who knows that it is necessary to distribute *baksheesh*. Characteristically, he found a line in the *Inferno* which, he said, 'gives an air of respectability to their claims'.[14]

Then there were the Balkans, that is chiefly, Serbia, Roumania, Bulgaria, and Greece, nineteenth-century nations created out of the slow ruination of the Ottoman Empire. Every Balkan nation reckoned to make something out of a war. There they were in 1914 with their armies ready to be hired as mercenaries to the highest bidder. But the bidding was far from simple. It was conducted not in cash but in territory and the most attractive bids had to be made up of the choice pieces which each nation wanted. Since delivery could not be made until after victory, the receiving nation had to give credit, which meant that it must study carefully creditworthiness as it fluctuated from time to time with the fortunes of war. Likewise the bidder must study carefully the state of the market and the hopes and fears of prospective suppliers. The state of the market resulted largely from the two Balkan wars of 1912–13. In the first war Bulgaria, Serbia, and Greece in alliance attacked Turkey. While Bulgaria bore the bulk of the serious fighting, Greece and Serbia overran the weakly held territories of Thrace and Macedonia, the latter with a large Bulgarian population. They refused to give Bulgaria her share of the conquered territory; and when in the second Balkan war she turned on them, not only was she defeated, but in her weakness she was attacked from the other side by Roumania and lost to her the Black Sea Province of the Dobrudja.

On the outbreak of the war the Entente was of course aligned with Serbia; and Greece almost at once on 19 August 1914 offered an Alliance. This put Bulgaria naturally into the other camp. Notwithstanding this, on a broad and imaginative view of the situation the Entente would appear to have been fortunately placed. The Balkan countries were compressed between Austria-Hungary on the north and Turkey on the south. Thus the natural suppliers of territory for the hungry Balkans were the enemies of the Entente. A Cabinet which contained at one and the same time two out of the three greatest war ministers whom Britain has ever had could not be blind to the chances thus offered in the grand strategy of war. Churchill was the first to see the point and was soon followed by Lloyd George. In the second half of the nineteenth century the idea of a Balkan Federation had been talked about: and Churchill's plan was to induce the Balkans into a unified force which would expand north and south making its gains at the expense of their common foes instead of at the expense of each other. As early as 23 September 1914, a month before Turkey was in the war but when her hostility was no longer in doubt, Churchill was urging Grey to adopt this policy of securing common action. By 28 November Asquith was writing: 'Desperate efforts are being made to find some territorial formula which will bring Bulgaria and Roumania into the fighting lines alongside Serbia and Greece.'[15] As late as February 1915 and in the teeth of Grey's opposition Lloyd George was proposing himself as a special plenipotentiary to deal with the situation over the heads of the ambassadors: 'Germany has not depended upon her Bax-Ironsides',* he wrote.[16]

Doubtless the plan looked more promising from a distance than close to. Unity would be extremely difficult to achieve and without it general promises of expansion would cut no ice. There would have to be internal concessions and juggling with territories. Bulgaria wanted especially Macedonia to which she had natural claims and which she would have had after the Balkan wars if she had not been cheated out of it by Serbia. Serbia insisted upon sticking to it and withstood every effort to induce her to exchange it for Bosnia and Herzegovina to be taken from Austria. No step could be taken without all the Allies, Russia always suspicious, being brought into line. The plan might have failed, but historians agree that it was only half-heartedly attempted.

This sort of thing was not Grey's métier. He had rejected the Greek offer of alliance for fear of offending a supposedly neutral Turkey and arousing Russian anxiety about Constantinople. It turned out to be an error which he tried in vain to repair. Even Asquith became a little pressing, writing on 2 January 1915 that he had urged Grey to put the strongest possible pressure upon Roumania and Greece to form with Allied military help a real Balkan bloc.[17] In the end the Entente lost Bulgaria but gained Roumania.

So diplomacy in the early part of 1915 was made up of bribes for the Balkans, the seduction of Italy, the satisfaction of Russia, and the recognition of Britain and France as Ottoman legatees. Churchill in particular was keen on 'some equivalent share of the spoils', Asquith wrote[18] on 25 March, the day the Russian treaty was signed. Winston is recorded about this time as having 'sketched an Entente map for fighters, showing what those who fought for us would get': 'for every one there was a definite prize'.[19] Lord Bryce too joined in with a gusto that would have startled Wilson. He wrote:

Greece must be promised Smyrna and all the islands that Italy can be persuaded not to press for. We might even think of dangling Cyprus before her.... Roumania, of course, will have Transylvania, a great prize for her.[20]

* Sir Henry Bax-Ironside, 1859-1937, Minister Plenipotentiary to Bulgaria 1910-15.

Lord Crewe, whose judgement Asquith rated 'highest of any of my colleagues',[21] thought that Britain should have Mesopotamia as an outlet
for Indian emigration. Asquith wrote on 25 March that he believed Grey
and himself to be the only two who thought that 'in the real interests of
our own future the best thing would be if at the end of the War we could say
that we had taken and gained nothing'.[22] But this presumably was on the
supposition that nobody else took and gained anything either. At the War
Council on 19 March he said with imperial unctuousness:

> If, for one reason or another, because we did'nt want more territory or because
> we did'nt feel equal to the responsibility, we were to leave the other nations to
> scramble for Turkey without taking anything ourselves, we should not be doing
> our duty.[23]

Outside Europe there was one keen nation with her way to make in the
world. This was Japan. Her immediate ambitions on the mainland centred
on the Chinese province of Shantung. The Yellow Sea that opens in the
south into the China Seas is on its other sides surrounded by lands that were
once all part of the Chinese Empire: on the east Korea dropping down
towards Japan, on the north Manchuria with Russia pressing from above,
and on the west the Chinese mainland with the province of Shantung about
the 36th parallel. When in the second half of the nineteenth century Japan
emerged from her seclusion, she naturally vied with the European powers
in their efforts to prise territories, leases, and concessions out of China's
slackening grip. Her methods were more thorough than theirs and in 1894
she began the career of aggression which fifty years later was shattered by
the atom bomb. A victorious war brought her in 1895 Formosa and China's
recognition of the independence of Korea. China agreed also to cede Port
Arthur at the top of the Yellow Sea, but Russia, France, and Germany combined to oppose the cession and Japan had to give way. Japan knew that she
would have to struggle with Russia for the mastery of Korea, so in 1902 she
made a treaty with Britain whereunder each party was to aid the other if
attacked by more than one power. This meant that Japan could not again
be overborne by a combination of powers as she was in 1895 and left her free
to settle the issue with Russia alone. When she defeated Russia in 1905
her paramountcy in Korea was recognized (in 1910 she annexed it) and she
got also the rights she wanted in and around Port Arthur; so that in 1914
she was naturally interested in the German position in Shantung.

This had been obtained in 1897 by methods that were not unusual.
Two German missionaries were murdered in Shantung and Germany made
this an excuse to seize the port of Tsingtao and other territory around
Kiaochow Bay and to exact railway and mining concessions over the rest

of the province. In 1914 Japan saw the outbreak of the European war as a good opportunity to acquire these desirable rights. There was also a number of German islands to be picked up in the Pacific, for Germany could not hope to defend any of her Asian property. Although the Anglo-Japanese alliance did not call for her intervention and although Britain did nothing to encourage it, Japan on 15 August 1914, using the alliance as a pretext, sent an ultimatum to Germany demanding the cession of her Shantung property 'with a view to the eventual restoration of the same to China'.[24] On 23 August, over the protest of China, she sent an expedition into Shantung and by November had defeated the German troops there at a cost of 1,800 casualties to herself. Meanwhile in October she captured and occupied all the German islands north of the equator. Britain's initial reluctance to sponsor these activities had been because of the alarm that they might cause to Australia and New Zealand who had been busily capturing the German islands south of the equator. By the end of 1914 Britain had come to realize that Japanese naval co-operation in the Pacific would prove a valuable asset and was seeking to allay Anzac fears. On 6 December Harcourt, the Colonial Secretary, warned the Governor-General of Australia that he

ought in the most gradual and diplomatic way to begin to prepare the mind of your Ministers for the possibility that at the end of the War Japan may be left in possession of the Northern Islands and we with everything south of the Equator.

The Governor-General replied reassuringly that he had not found much antipathy to this suggestion though it was felt that 'our fractious U.S.A. Coz' would not like it.

Grey himself accepted that Japan must have compensation after the war 'proportionate to her efforts'. But on 17 December 1914 he laid it down that

with regard to all territory conquered and newly occupied during the war the only acceptable basis is that it should be without prejudice to final arrangements to be made in time of peace.

He applied this principle of 'conquest without prejudice' to all colonial territory as it was brought into the bag. But he realized from the first that he was on thin ice, for he had minuted as early as 19 August 1914 that it was not to be expected that Japan would spend blood and treasure in Shantung and get nothing for it.

In addition to Britain's allies, present and prospective, there had also to be considered her dominions. By 1915 Germany had lost not only all her Pacific possessions but also a great deal of territory in Africa. In a memorandum which Harcourt presented to the Cabinet on 25 March 1915 and which he suitably entitled 'The Spoils', arrangements were outlined for the consumption of these and other fruits of victory.

It is out of the question to part with any of the territories now in the occupation of Australia and New Zealand . . . If German South West Africa is occupied by the Union Government, it must obviously be retained as part of the British Empire . . . German East Africa forms the missing link in the chain of British possessions from the Cape to Cairo. It would make an admirable colony for Indian emigration of the class which wants to trade and not to cultivate, assuming that the latter will be provided for in Mesopotamia.[25]

Harcourt had not hitherto been classed as a Liberal Imperialist. If these were his sentiments, the enthusiasm among the Cape-to-Cairo dreamers of the Boer War period can well be imagined. Their chief anxiety was that Britain and her empire should keep well ahead in the scramble in which France, Belgium, and Portugal would also be front runners. The opportunity for a general exchange and mart, in which old acquisitions should be traded as well as new, should not be lost. In a plan of redistribution publicly presented to the Royal Geographical Society in February 1915 the author justified his admitted generosity to the British flag by his conviction that 'our rule was more beneficial than that of any other Power to the Africans'.[26]

Grey did not underestimate the difficulties. Sir Horace Plunkett was an Irishman, a son of the 16th Lord Dunsany, who had spent five years of his youth on a ranch in Wyoming and had friends among the great in both countries; he made himself a contact-man between House, Grey, and Balfour. Talking to him on 6 February, the day before House came, Grey replied to his suggestion that England should ask for no territory so that the sincerity of her desire for peace should be proved, by saying that there was one insuperable objection and that was that the self-governing colonies would not give up what they had taken. Grey noted this also at the War Council on 10 March* where he recorded his own opposition to annexation.

There was nothing to embarrass Grey personally in his dealings with House. He had not invited the discussion. He had placed it firmly on the basis that his views were not necessarily those of his colleagues, still less of the Allies. He had let it be known what France and Russia were demanding. He had told the French and Russian Governments formally what he was doing, though of course their ambassadors in Washington knew it already. He had told Plunkett, and was later to say the same thing directly to House, about British colonial demands. The specific promises to be made to Russia

* See p. 257 above.

and Italy and to be held out in the Balkans had not yet solidified. But Grey intended to talk frankly about the Allied attempts to bring Italy, Roumania, and Greece into the war and to neutralize Bulgaria; anyway, no one could possibly have thought that any of these nations would go to war because she had suddenly become convinced that the Central Powers were morally wrong.

Each man, Grey and House, held a brief in which he did not quite believe. Both men believed that the Allies were in the right, that Germany must be shown that war did not pay and made to consent to a permanent settlement. They differed slightly in that House thought, while Grey did not, that this object could be achieved by a drawn peace. But fundamentally they were of the same mind. Nevertheless, House was the emissary of a neutral power and his brief was to press for peace on any terms that could be found. Grey was the foreign minister of a power at war; and his brief was, while keeping America persuaded of Britain's peaceful and honourable intentions, to resist peace at a price which might appear reasonable to neutrals but not to belligerents. How much should he disclose of arrangements which might streak the candid garments in which Britain had vested her nobler aims?

Both men took pains over the preliminaries to their meeting. House wanted to meet Grey directly and immediately without having to go through Page. Through Spring Rice he asked Grey to send word to the ship on arrival as to how and where they were to meet 'for a few minutes conversation with you alone immediately upon arrival in strictest secrecy'.[27] He was due to arrive in Southampton in the afternoon of Saturday, 6 February. Spring Rice asked him if he wanted Grey to remain in London over the weekend and he replied that Monday lunch would do.

But Grey spent the weekend in London. Saturday was the only day on which he could see Plunkett (who had just got back from the States) and he wanted perhaps to get the feel of the situation. He arranged to see House at eleven on Sunday morning at 33 Eccleston Square. They talked for two hours. Then House stayed to lunch and they talked on until 2.30. They seem to have come together just as if they were friends meeting to discuss in a practical way how to further a cause in which they both believed. They never looked at their briefs at all. The two-point programme was not mentioned. Grey simply assumed that what House would want to know was what was being done about winning the war. 'We discussed the situation as frankly as you and I would have done in Washington,' House reported to Wilson, 'he telling me frankly the position the Allies were in, their difficulties, their resources, and their expectations.'[28] They talked about the prospects of bringing in Italy and Roumania ('not as encouraging as I had hoped', House reported) and the difficulty of getting Bulgaria and Serbia together; of Russia's inadequate transport system which prevented her from maintaining more than two million men at the front; of Russian and French territorial demands and the nature of the final settlement. At the end Grey smiled and said: 'Here I am helping to direct the affairs of a nation at war, and yet I have been talking for $3\frac{1}{2}$ hours like a neutral.' If he had, House had certainly been listening as an ally. He was enchanted by this approach and complimented beyond measure, he told Wilson, that Grey had such confidence in his discretion and integrity. Possibly it did not take much to bring out the true community of interest between the two men, but whatever it took, this conversation did it. House usually had his negotiating tricks and a place up his sleeve for cards, but he was incapable of responding to this overture with anything less than equal frankness. He made no pretence of impartiality. What he was now clear about was that, whatever peace was made, it must be the sort of reasonable peace that Britain, or at least Grey, wanted. Peacemaking became thereafter for House a collaboration between himself and Grey in which he saw them both as working as much against the rapacity of the Allies as against Germany. After this conversation he wrote:

If every belligerent nation had a Sir Edward Grey at the head of its affairs, there would be no war; and if there were war, it would soon be ended upon lines broad enough to satisfy any excepting the prejudiced and selfish.[29]

In the days that followed Grey and House met frequently, sometimes at lunch and with others, but generally around seven o'clock in the evening at Grey's house. It was Grey's habit to leave the office early enough to spend an hour at home before dinner. Hankey, reading the House diaries when they were published in 1926, was horrified at the freedom with which Grey spoke.[30] As he said, Grey had treated House exactly as if he were a Cabinet colleague and he found things in the diaries that were so secret that he (Hankey) was recording them in manuscript in the War Council's minutes. The two men continued to talk about the progress of the war and House offered his comments and criticisms: 'I again urged upon him better co-ordination between the eastern and western fronts.'[31] But the two main subjects were House's proposed visit to Germany and the matter which Grey thought so important, the nature of the post-war settlement.

The former subject was broached at luncheon with Page at the American embassy on 10 February, Tyrrell, Grey's private secretary, also being present.[32] House maintained that Germany was in earnest and that the Kaiser was ready for peace while Grey maintained that Germany was fencing so as to embarrass the Allies in their negotiations with Bulgaria. But Grey repeated, as Page reported to Wilson that day,[33] that England at least would welcome any sincere proposal which included the restoration of Belgium and security for the future—the two-point programme. House said that he had no intention of pushing the question of peace. He wrote in his diary the next day:

In my opinion, it could not be brought about, in any event, before the middle of May or the 1st of June. I could see the necessity for the Allies to try out their new armies in the Spring, and I could also see the necessity for Germany not to be in such an advantageous position as now, for the reason she would be less likely to make terms that would ensure permanent peace.

After this conversation he cabled Wilson that the Allies had not achieved sufficient military success to ensure the acceptance of their demand for permanent peace. On the same day he wrote more fully:

I think the Allies will not consent to final peace terms until they have had a try at Germany during the coming Spring. I explained to Grey, however, that it was not too early to get the machinery in order and that if it developed that Germany would give now terms that would be acceptable, it would be foolish to sacrifice so many useful lives.

There is an inconsistency here about what House was saying to Grey and what he was reporting to Wilson. Since Grey had repeated at this interview that he was willing to discuss a sincere offer on the terms he had always stated as minimal, House, when he said he would not push for peace, must have meant that he was accepting the argument that Germany would not agree to such terms, particularly those relating to permanent peace, until after she had sustained some reverse. But he reported to Wilson only the argument, not that he had accepted it. It may be that he was not yet ready to tell Wilson how much of a collaborator he had become. The non-disclosure had no consequences, for the very next day House received the long-promised 'confirmation' from Zimmermann which showed that Grey's argument was right. Zimmermann's letter, dated 4 February, welcomed an interview with House, but on the crucial point he wrote: 'There are certain limits which we are unable to overstep. What you suggest concerning the paying of an indemnity to Belgium seems hardly feasible to me.'[35]

The next day, 13 February, House took this letter round to Grey and after lunch at 33 Eccleston Square they 'sat by the fire in his library, facing one another discussing every phase of the situation with a single mind and purpose'. They discussed the letter long and carefully. Two factors must have been plain enough. The first was that Bernstorff's assurance that there would be 'no obstacles' to the evacuation and indemnity of Belgium were false. The basis of the proposed deal had collapsed. Grey doubtless was too generous to say 'I told you so'.

The second factor was that the indemnity was a minimum term, not only in the sense that Grey would agree to nothing less (and if he would not, no one would), but also in the sense that no peacemaker with the moral feeling of Wilson or House could press him further. Wherever the blame lay for beginning the war, it did not lie on Belgium. It would make nonsense of international morality and law if she were not to be compensated or if the compensation were to be paid not by the offender but by those who had opposed the offence. It would make an absurdity of any post-war treaty for permanent peace if it was to begin by condoning Germany's breach of the Belgian treaty. House agreed, as he told Grey in rhetorical language, that it was better to go on fighting if the right settlement could be brought about in no other way. But he did not want to give up trying; and he thought that as America's relations with Germany were getting worse, if he did not go soon he would not be welcome. Grey thought that negotiations would be useless unless the military situation changed. He had information that Germany was starting an enveloping movement upon the Russian front with a view to impressing the Balkan states. He did not believe that the civilians in the German Government could do anything until after the campaign was over. House was to lunch with the Prime Minister on 17 February, and a decision was deferred until after that. If House thought that he made any impression at the luncheon table he does not record it. Asquith's attitude to peacemongers was firm and unvarying; they had excellent intentions and were the victims of grievous self-delusion. A fortnight later he used the occasion of his speech at the commencement of the British blockade* to say just that, and added: 'It is like the twittering of sparrows amid the storms and tumult of a tempest which is shaking the foundations of the world.'[36] He finished by quoting from his 'never sheathe the sword' speech at the Guildhall in the previous November.

Grey's information about Germany's strategic plan was correct. At the end of 1914 Germany feared that Allied diplomacy might succeed in bringing Italy and the Balkans into the war on their side, thus threatening the collapse of Austria-Hungary and Turkey. In January 1915 she decided to stand on the defensive on the west and to attack in the east, where a resounding victory over the Russians would strengthen Austria and Turkey and allure the Balkans. In this strategy she was brilliantly right and the war in 1915 went in her favour. While the British and French wore themselves out with futile offensives in the west, Germany drove Russia out of Poland and Galicia with a loss of 750,000 men, gained Bulgaria as an ally, invaded and annihilated Serbia, and opened up the road to Constantinople. Indeed, when Grey spoke, the battle to the north of Warsaw that was to be called the Winter Battle in Masuria had begun and resulted after nine days in the encirclement and near destruction of the Russian Tenth Army.

* See p. 203 above.

Meanwhile, Grey was being careful to inform France and Russia of House's visit. He spoke to the French Foreign Minister in London and on 12 February sent a telegram to Petrograd :[37] this on 16 February he showed to House who agreed with it. It said that House believed and that he, Grey, doubted that Germany desired peace, that if she expressed such a desire the Allies would formulate their conditions in common, and that he had impressed on the Colonel the danger of saying anything that Germany could represent as separate negotiation.

House took several days to compose his reply to Zimmermann's letter of 4 February. He had received the letter on 12 February and he dispatched his answer on 17 February.

All of our conversations with the Ambassadors in Washington, representing the belligerent nations were based upon the supposition that Germany would consent to evacuate and indemnify Belgium and would be willing to make a settlement looking towards permanent peace. I can readily understand the difficulty that your Government would encounter with regard to an indemnity; therefore, if that question might for the moment be waived, may we assume that your Government, would let the other two points make the beginning of conversations?

If we could be placed in so fortunate a position, I feel confident that parleys could at least be commenced.[38]

This letter was written after House had talked to Asquith and Grey and they had agreed, so House said, that he should write along these lines. If this means that House thought that the Englishmen might drop their demand for an indemnity for Belgium it is hard to believe that he understood them correctly. The contrary is plainly indicated in a memorandum by Grey on 24 February in which he gives a composite summary of his conversations with House.[39] It is true that later in the year Grey authorized Eric Drummond, who in May succeeded Tyrrell as his private secretary, to say unofficially that, if the indemnity were the only obstacle to peace, the question might be settled by arbitration. But the context makes it plain that he conceived of the indemnity as having to be paid unless Belgium had been guilty of 'trafficking her neutrality', which he knew she had not, and that he

would really rather like the German people to know the truth after the war was over, by having every document that had passed between Belgium and us produced to some Tribunal that could pronounce upon them.[40]

Meanwhile, Gerard was flying a German kite. The fourteen days between 4 February and 18 February made up the period that elapsed between the German Declaration of submarine war and the date when it was due to come into effect. The neutral reaction to the Declaration alarmed the civilians, Bethmann and Jagow going so far as to propose that it should be revoked. This began another round in the intense German conflict over the submarine war. In this atmosphere someone got to work on the excitable Gerard. The ambassador believed that Germany was winning the war. She would get a separate peace from Russia, he thought, then overwhelm France, and then completely blockade England. With these prospects Germany would not herself propose peace, but if a reasonable offer was made

very many men of influence would be inclined to use their efforts to induce Germany to accept the proposition . . . It is my belief that if you seize the present opportunity you will be the instrument of bringing about the greatest peace which has ever been signed, but it will be fatal to hesitate or wait a moment; success is dependent on immediate action.[41]

This is what Gerard cabled to Wilson on 11 February. Wilson replied by referring him to House; and he also cabled to House, saying that Gerard's method was not the right one, but asking if House had had any intimation from Berlin. Gerard on 15 February wrote direct to House that the Allies should send the peace proposal or an offer to talk peace to him verbally and secretly.[42] If it was sent within a matter of days, even hours, he was, he said, sure of its acceptance. What exactly it should consist of, he did not state, beyond saying that Germany would pay no indemnity to Belgium or anyone else. From a later cable[43] it appears that what was being thought about in Germany (or what Gerard thought was being thought about) was the evacuation of Belgium without indemnity and the evacuation of the north of France in exchange for colonial territory or cash. It may be that the 'very many men of influence' (Gerard, it is plain, knew of them only at second-hand) included Falkenhayn who felt that the best that Germany could now hope for was a compromise peace in her favour.

House took Gerard's letter to Grey on 18 February and Grey said that such terms would be entertained when Gerard's predictions of utter defeat had been fulfilled and not before. House replied tactfully to Gerard on 19 February that Grey found it 'utterly impossible to make any such hasty proposal as you thought the situation required';[44] and later he soothed the ambassador's feelings by pointing out that the British were a slow-moving people.[45]

Wilson in Washington had naturally fallen behind the pace of House's development from intermediary to collaborator. House had now been nearly a fortnight in his task of ascertaining 'the real disposition, the real wish, the real purpose'* of the Allies, and, so far as Wilson knew, his only reason for not ascertaining the mind of Germany (where, if Gerard was to be believed, there was some disposition to receive a proposal) was that the Allies wanted first to better themselves militarily. On 20 February he sent

*See p. 251 above.

a cable which shows that, while he deferred much to House's judgement, he retained the superintendence of the enterprise.

It will of course occur to you that you cannot go too far in allowing the English government to determine when it is best to go to Germany because they naturally desire to await some time when they have the advantage because of events in the field or elsewhere. If the impression were to be created in Berlin that you were to come only when the British government thought it the opportune time for you to come, you might be regarded when you reached there as their spokesman rather than as mine. Do you think we can frankly state this dilemma to Grey?[46]

But House stood his ground. In a cable of 22 February he gave his reasons and elaborated them in a long letter the next day.[47] There was no reason he wrote, to believe that Germany was ready to make such terms as the Allies were ready to accept. She refused to indemnify Belgium and refused to make any proposition herself. She might or might not be willing to evacuate Belgium and consider proposals looking to permanent peace, but even if she conceded these two cardinal points, neither Russia nor France was willing to make peace on such terms. Grey was anxious for England to take the highest possible grounds and not ask for anything except the evacuation and indemnifying of Belgium and the permanent peace settlement. But he was coming into conflict with colonial opinion—South Africa and Australia would not give up what they had taken—and though he was trying assiduously to work up an opinion on broader lines, he might not be successful. If, he said, he went to Berlin when Germany was not ready to discuss terms the Allies would accept, he would lose the sympathetic interest of England and she would probably cease to consider Wilson as a medium.

Although House put it more widely, the crux of the matter was the indemnity for Belgium. If House wanted to persuade Germany to concede this point on which she was apparently adamant, the time to do it was not in the moment of her Russian triumph. If, on the other hand, he was going to try to make peace without providing for the indemnity, he was no doubt right in thinking he would forfeit the confidence of Grey. Wilson's failure to denounce as immoral the invasion of Belgium could be accepted though not applauded; but if he pressed for a peace which condoned it, that would be too much. House wrote in this letter:

The one sane big figure here is Sir Edward Grey; and the chances are all in favour of his being the dominant personality when the final settlement comes, and I believe it is the path of wisdom to continue to keep in as close and sympathetic touch with him as now.[48]

Grey's memorandum to Asquith of 24 February suggests that House may have exaggerated the British concern with his visit. In it Grey reported that

October 1915. David Lloyd George, Minister of Munitions, and Winston Churchill, formerly First Lord of the Admiralty, in Whitehall

Lord Kitchener of Khartoum, Secretary of State for War, with Sir Edward Grey, British Foreign Secretary, in Paris

Colonel Maurice Hankey,
Secretary of the Committee
of Imperial Defence

Sir Eyre Crowe, Head of the
Contraband Department at the
Foreign Office

he had told House that the refusal of the indemnity for Belgium provided no
'terrain' on which Britain could negotiate; and that with her success against
Russia, and so long as she believed that she could win on land, Germany was
not likely to listen to any terms that Britain or the Allies could accept. But,
he said, he would be very glad if House went to Berlin, if only to satisfy his,
Grey's, curiosity as to what the German mind really was.

Meanwhile, Wilson was becoming alive to the fact that the basis for the
talks had broken down. On 22 February he cabled House:

Do you get it direct from Zimmermann or through Gerard that the terms you
suggested as a basis for parleys in your letter to Zimmermann would not be considered? I understand the situation but want to be sure of each element in it.[49]

Then on 25 February he wired:

Your cables enable me to understand the situation in all its phases. I greatly
appreciate them. I am of course content to be guided by your judgment as to
each step.[50]

A letter from Zimmermann written on 2 March finally disposed of the
'two-point' programme. He would not take as a starting-point even the
modified basis which House had proposed, that is, the evacuation of Belgium
without indemnity. He wrote:

You are taking as a basis a more or less defeated Germany . . . Although I can
assure you that Germany has the welfare of Belgium very much at heart, still
she is not able to forget what a terrific cost was paid for the resistance our men
encountered there.[51]

If England would give up her claim to a monopoly of the seas, he thought it
might be a good beginning. As a little extra encouragement Jagow sent
a message through Gerard hoping that the Colonel would come to Berlin
soon.[52] But when on 13 March 1915 the Colonel left for France *en route* for
Germany, he no longer had any hope of initiating discussions. He went
simply to meet people whose minds he wanted to probe himself. When later
he summed up the situation for Bryan, he wrote:

Germany is not willing to evacuate Belgium at all, nor even France, without
an indemnity, and Count von Bernstorff's suggestion that this could be arranged
was wide afield. The Allies, of course, will not consent to anything less; and there
the situation rests.[53]

Or, as Grey put it, Bernstorff's peace talk in Washington was 'fudge'.[54]

When he got to Germany, however, House found a topic which he hoped
might keep both sides talking and also provide a basis for the post-war

settlement. This was his plan for the Freedom of the Seas. It was a topic which enabled House to employ a device in whose use he felt himself to be skilled. The device was to take a proposal which would be of international benefit, present it to each side as if it benefited that side alone and then, leading each party towards what it took to be its own self-interest, bring both out of the narrow defiles along which they had been walking into the wide space of the common good. To understand how the plan began to form in House's mind it is necessary to go back to the beginning of his visit and describe the talks he had on Grey's ideas for the post-war settlement.

While he was on board the *Lusitania*, House had given thought to the post-war settlement but he had not modified his opposition to Grey's idea that America should be a party to a league to enforce peace. What he was thinking about was an agreement by which all nations should cease to manufacture arms for a period of ten years, at the end of which everything would automatically be obsolete and the world put on a peace footing. But Grey intended to use House's visit to push his plan; and he told Plunkett when he saw him on 6 February that he looked to America to 'play the big part' and to come into a league of peace which would submit its quarrels to arbitration and 'put pressure' on anyone who refused.[55] Grey raised this at his first talk with House on 8 February. 'There was one thing Grey was fairly insistent upon,' House reported to the President, 'and that was that we should come into some general guarantee for world wide peace.'[56] House was willing that America and other neutrals should take part in a separate post-treaty convention codifying the Hague rules; but Grey, House told the President, 'did not accept this as our full duty'.

At the luncheon at the American embassy on 10 February Grey brought up his ideas again and this time House told him directly that it would not do; 'it was not only the unwritten law of our country but also our fixed policy not to become involved in European affairs'.[57] Much to House's surprise, Page disagreed with him and so did Tyrrell, who was also at the lunch. An argument followed in which House stuck to his point that the most that could be done was American participation in a convention to agree upon rules of warfare that would take away much of the horror of war. When House reported to Wilson on 15 February he mentioned only a convention called for this limited purpose at which Wilson would preside.[58] If peace was not in sight by August, he wrote, it could perhaps be called then and used as a medium of bringing about peace. But Page passed on to Wilson the full expansion of Grey's idea. He wrote on 10 February:

If it were definitely known by England that in the discussion that must follow the laying down of arms, all the moral power of the world—our power in particular—would be actively and strenuously exerted for the making of a programme of forcible security for the future—in that event England might consent to end the war as a drawn contest.[59]

To return to the lunch-table conversation, House pursuing his own thoughts went on to elaborate on some of the new rules which would take away much of the horror of war. Among other things he spoke of safety lanes at sea where shipping, both belligerent and neutral, would not be subject to attack. Grey said that he thought that Britain would be willing to agree that all merchant shipping should be immune. House was pleased to learn that Britain would go so far. At lunch the next day with Tyrrell there was further talk about the 'second convention'.[60] Tyrrell thought that if there were such a convention, Britain would consent to the absolute freedom of merchantmen of all nations to sail the seas in time of war unmolested. The submarine, he said, had changed the status of maritime warfare and Britain would be better protected by such a policy than by an overwhelming navy. This was an echo of the British policy which had led to the Declaration of London. It was from this talk that House took his plan for Freedom of the Seas. But it would be, he obviously felt, a wicked diplomatic waste to allow it to be put forward by Britain. Since it meant the end of British naval domination in time of war, it should be welcomed by Germany. The thing to do was for House to present it to the Germans as something which American mediation might secure in return for some concession on Germany's part. House outlined this plan to Wilson in his letter of 23 February. He said that Grey was now occasionally speaking of 'that second convention which the President may call'; and continued:

I have reason to believe that this government will be ready to make great concessions in that convention in regard to the future of shipping, commerce, etc., during periods of war. It is my purpose to keep this 'up my sleeve', and, when I go to Germany, use it to bring favourable opinion to you by intimating that I believe that when the end comes, you will insist upon this being done; in other words, that with your initiative and with Germany's co-operation Great Britain can be induced to make these terms.[61]

Zimmermann in his letter of 2 March hinted that negotiations might be started if Britain gave up her claim to maritime supremacy; the hint offered House an opportunity to introduce his plan. Gerard, although he now saw no prospect of peace, pressed House to come so that he could at least acquaint himself with the situation. House would not stir without Grey's approval, for he saw in Grey the only hope of the sort of peace he wanted; as he later recorded, if this was brought about it would be 'through the sanity and justice of Sir Edward Grey and British opinion'.[62] Grey offered no objection. Indeed, from House's diary it would look as if all his movements were decided jointly by himself and Grey, but it is difficult to believe that Grey felt himself so deeply concerned. Anyway, on 7 March it was decided that House should go first to France and then to Germany. Wilson bestowed his usual plenary blessing, saying that he had a feeling that there was at last some real hope—a statement which indicates that his belief in House was so complete that he was not really trying to understand what was going on.[63]

A few days before he left, House met another British statesman whom he found almost as congenial as Grey. This was A. J. Balfour, who two years later succeeded Grey as Foreign Secretary and as such was the second British delegate at the Paris conference. Arthur James Balfour was then sixty-seven, eight years older than Wilson, in experience already a veteran yet still with so much to do. Like Grey he came from the leisured class. His father, who was born of Scottish gentry and inherited a fortune made in India, married the daughter of the second Marquess of Salisbury, so that Balfour's mother was a Cecil. Balfour himself never married. He had a place in Scotland, a big house in London, 4 Carlton Gardens, and all the money he wanted; he probably never thought about money as mattering one way or the other.

The Cecil family was founded by the two great Elizabethans, William who was Lord Burghley and his son Robert whom James I made Earl of Salisbury. After that, Lord Salisbury's daughter and biographer writes, 'the general mediocrity of intelligence which the family displayed was only varied by instances of quite exceptional stupidity'.[64] The seventh earl owed his step in the peerage to his wife. Then there began a second blossoming; and another Robert, ninth earl and third marquess, became the last of Victoria's Prime Ministers. It is not wrong to think of Balfour also as a Cecil. His father died when he was eight and the two great influences in his life were his mother and after her his uncle. He was Salisbury's pupil, colleague, deputy, and successor; and he had with him at the Foreign Office and at Paris in 1919 another Cecil, sixteen years his junior, his cousin Robert, Salisbury's third son.

As befitted the Cecils of that and succeeding generations Balfour's family life was built gaily upon a foundation of earnestness and among the things of the intellect. Drawn by his uncle into politics he moved along the easy line apparently without ambition. He got into Parliament in 1874 but it was more than two years before he made his maiden speech. His real interest then was in the study of metaphysics. In 1878 he published his first book *The Defence of Philosophic Doubt*. It got him a reputation that clung; the reader may remember Wilson's reference to him in 1902 as 'a philosophical dreamer'.* When he stood for Parliament for the second time in 1880 he was resolved, if defeated, as he thought he might be for the land slid away from the Tories, to quit politics for philosophy. But he was elected; and when in 1885 Salisbury formed his first government, he included Balfour who soon disproved any suspicion of nepotism. Thereafter the Conservatives remained in power for an almost unbroken period of twenty years and Balfour's success in office was such that in 1902, the year in which Wilson became president of Princeton, he followed almost inevitably his uncle as Prime Minister. But he had not the talent of democratic leadership. Neither in the Boer War (to which his attitude was not very different from that of the Liberal Imperialists)† nor in any other matter did he lead either his Cabinet or his party; his time was occupied in trying to keep them whole on the divisive issue of tariff reform.

The long Tory ascendancy was ended by crashing defeat at the 1906 election. Balfour never became Prime Minister again: yet only half his great career was over. In 1911 he gave up the leadership of his party and assumed the role of elder statesman. When Prime Minister he had founded the Committee of Imperial Defence. At Asquith's request he continued to sit on it and so was naturally brought into consultation when the war broke out. 'Dining tonight with Winston and Fisher to talk naval shop' he noted on 10 November 1914;[65] in February 1915 he was helping with the diplomatic difficulties with the United States. When Asquith in May 1915 formed the first coalition Balfour succeeded Churchill at the Admiralty.

Yet throughout his long life he seemed to hold himself aloof from the affairs in which he played so great a part. This was perhaps because he never lost his love of metaphysics. 'Though very exceptionally hardworked in the region of public affairs', he wrote from 10 Downing Street, he had had time 'to look more or less perfunctorily, through Dewey's book, some of Schiller's Essays, and the articles in this quarter's *Mind*'.[66] Politics was never more than a part of his life. He never thought about them in bed, he said. The detachment was emphasized by an air of languor left over from his youth and then diagnosed in the vague medical language of the day as 'low vitality'. The air matured into an easy and unflappable pose—the tall figure, over six feet, almost lanky, slightly stooping, the large luminous eyes, the downturned moustache, the hand resting on the lapel of the frock-coat. House felt his charm.

I took a liking to him at once, and have a sincere desire that it should be reciprocated. I like the quality of his mind. It is not possible to allow one's wits to lag when one is in active discussion with him. In that respect, he reminds me somewhat of the President. I am inclined to rank him along with the President and Mr. Asquith in intellectuality, and this, to my mind, places him at the summit.[67]

* See p. 10 above.　　　　† See pp. 114–15 above.

It is true that Balfour had been 'very complimentary in regard to the suggestions I have made, and said they were unique and practicable as far as he could see at the moment'.[68] But the fact that Balfour was the sort of man who would find an early opportunity of paying a compliment gracefully does not mean that his appreciation was not genuine enough. In September 1915, talking about House to Plunkett, he said that

he liked House immensely, and Wilson because he appreciated House. We agreed that House was not intellectually brilliant, but, what was far better, intellectually honest.[69]

House saw a lot of Balfour and his first impression was confirmed. In May 1915 he wrote:

I talk to Balfour with more freedom than any man in Great Britain with the exception of Grey, for I trust him implicitly. Grey and Balfour are two great gentlemen, and I feel sure of their discretion.[70]

Later, when writing to Wilson, he referred to Grey and Balfour and himself as 'the only three who speak your language'.[71]

House was in Paris from 11 to 17 March. He had a formal interview with the French Foreign Minister at which compliments were exchanged and Wilson's 'keen interest and noble desire to bring about peace' duly noted.[72] But there was no Grey to treat his motives seriously and it was generally thought that the President was getting anxious about the German vote at the 1916 election and was trying to find an opportunity of playing the peacemaker. 'There is nothing that even looks like peace within sight', House reported to the President; and he delivered one of his sweeping judgements: 'I find that the ruling class in France do not desire peace, but that a large part of the people and the men in the trenches would welcome it.'

House was in Germany from 20 to 30 March. There was a dinner party at the embassy for him on the day he arrived; it was one of the rare occasions when Mrs. House slips out of the shadows, Grew describing her as 'very pretty and charming'.[73] Dr. Rathenau, who was to play a great part in the post-war Germany, was there; he urged House not to cease in his efforts to bring about peace but he admitted that he stood alone.

Soon House was in conference with Zimmermann whom he had always liked and now found exceedingly cordial and delightful. But the Colonel had to report that 'there is nothing that even looks like peace within sight'.[74] He made no attempt to pursue the two-point programme. He not only accepted Zimmermann's assurance 'that if peace parleys were begun now upon any terms that would have any chance of acceptance, it would mean the overthrow of this Government and the Kaiser',[75] but adapted his tone to it, saying that the time for peace had not yet come and that in France they were totally wild, in England somewhat less. He was sadly disappointed, he wrote to the President towards the end of his visit, 'that we were misled into believing that peace parleys might be begun upon a basis of evacuation of France and Belgium'.

But House never gave in and always consoled himself with what he had accomplished for what he had failed to do. He had established cordial relations in all three capitals, taken the measure of all the men with whom he hoped later to deal, and prepared them for the President's entry as mediator when the scene shifted. He had found a way which he thought might keep conversations alive, at least on paper. This was his ingenious plan for Freedom of the Seas. He first brought it forward at his meeting with Bethmann on 27 March. It was his first meeting with the Chancellor, whom he found courteous and kind: 'one of the best types of German I have met'.[76] House was at his most devious in presenting his plan. 'I shivered in Berlin', he said later, 'when I proposed it to the Chancellor and the Foreign Office, for fear they would see that it was more to England's advantage than their own.'[77]

The Chancellor, according to House, was very enthusiastic, 'the first thread to be thrown across the chasm which would finally have to be bridged' he said. This was a matter, House told him, in which America had a common interest with Germany and in the 'second convention' she would stand fully behind Germany to bring about the desired result. His thoughts, House said, went far beyond the Declarations of Paris and London; he had in mind the absolute freedom of commerce in future warfare and that navies should be used almost wholly for protection against invasion. The way House handled his theme was to use it as a re-entry into the two-point programme. If England would consent to Freedom of the Seas, he told the Chancellor, the German Government could say to its people that Belgium was no longer needed as a base for German naval activity, since England was being brought to terms.

What House's ingenuity overlooked was that a government cannot hold private communications with its people. In the honeycomb of Wall Street it is no doubt possible for a buyer secluded in one cell to persuade his backers that he is picking up something at a bargain price while the seller in another persuades another set of backers that he is unloading a liability. But if both propositions are to be shouted from the housetops their incompatibility demands attention. The British would not be attracted by the idea that the abandonment of 'Britannia Rules the Waves' was to be the inducement to Germany to restore what she had unlawfully seized. Whatever the

Germans thought of the idea as a road to peace, they found it irresistible as propaganda. So used, Britain's naval supremacy could be made to provide a plausible argument for the acquisition and retention of Belgium. The moment that Germany announced, as she did through her propaganda machine in America, that if England granted the freedom of the seas, she would retire from Belgium, and if England refused, she would use it as a fortified base on the Channel, not only did the idea become completely unsaleable (which it probably would have been anyway to the British people at large) but the label Freedom of the Seas began to stink as 'made in Germany'. This was what was to happen in the not very remote future. But there were a few weeks left in which House canvassed for it energetically and in which Wilson was able to describe it as 'very promising'.[78] After that the term degenerated into a handy expression of the thought that Prussian militarism was not the only threat to freedom, there was also British 'navalism'[79]—a word coined by German propaganda in America towards the end of 1914 and widely adopted by the critics of the British blockade. Eventually Freedom of the Seas became one of the Fourteen Points on which Wilson proposed peace, but it could not survive the discovery that it was inconsistent with the new order embodied in the League of Nations. The idea was born in House's mind at a time when he was rejecting the League of Nations and he thought of it as part of the new international law which would civilize warfare. When the sights were lifted from the civilizing to the abolishing of war freedom of the seas became irrelevant. As Grey was almost immediately to point out, though without taking the point right to its logical conclusion, 'the sea is free in times of peace anyhow'; there would be no sense in protecting the maritime trade of the aggressor or the outlaw when he was being punished or restrained by the navies of the League.

House left Germany on 30 March for meetings at Nice and Biarritz with the American ambassadors to Italy and Spain. The former gave him the latest news on the Allied offers to bring Italy into the war; the ambassador did not think they were large enough. Then House went back to Paris where he spent nearly three weeks. While there he wrote to Grey that he had made some progress with Freedom of the Seas, but he did not say that it was to be a *quid pro quo* for the evacuation of Belgium. Grey on 24 April replied in effect that Freedom of the Seas was one side of the coin. 'If Germany means that her commerce is to go free upon the sea in times of war, while she remains free to make war upon other nations at will, it is not a fair proposition'.[80] But if she would join a post-war League of Nations expenditure on armament might be reduced and new rules to secure Freedom of the Seas made. Subsequently in conversation he told House that public opinion, particularly Conservative opinion, would have to be educated in the matter;

and he advised House to discuss it with Bonar Law, the Conservative leader, and others in his party.

If House did so, he does not record their reactions. He discussed it with Loreburn, a former Lord Chancellor,* and also with Haldane just after he had been so unfairly thrown out of the Government; he reported their enthusiastic approval. But they were perforce armchair supporters. Grey was evidently himself convinced; it was after all the logical result of the pre-war policy that led to the Declaration of London. He returned to the question as the result of the conversation he had with House on 14 May† which led to the renewal of the proposal for a *modus vivendi*. On 7 June a telegram was drafted for him to send to Spring Rice[81] as a summary of the personal views which he had expressed to House and which the ambassador was told that there could be no objection to his making use of 'as a personal expression of your own opinions'. The telegram was substantially a repetition of Grey's letter to House of 24 April but was rather more precise about the 'new rules', intimating that Britain 'might give up the right to interfere with merchant shipping'. Grey, who was about to leave for Fallodon for the second time that year to rest his eyes, scrawled on it an almost illegible endorsement, adding the point that the future development of the submarine and Britain's excessive dependence on overseas commerce made it to her interest that the seas should be free in time of war. Drummond, now Grey's private secretary, submitted the draft to the Prime Minister and to Balfour, the new First Lord of the Admiralty. From the latter the reply came on 8 June that he would prefer to have no responsibility; he had no particular objection, he said, but it was not the kind of telegram he would have sent himself.[82] The Prime Minister replied on 10 June that he thought it advisable to let the matter drop.[83] Drummond, who was later to become the first Secretary-General of the League of Nations, was certainly in sympathy with his chief's view. He encased the draft in a memorandum which he prepared on 11 June on the theme of disarmament.[84] The burden of armaments, already before the war becoming intolerable, must, he said, be removed; and this could not be done 'unless the governments of the civilized world make an effort to ensure that any nation undertaking an aggressive war in the future will be an outlaw'. He hinted that there must be naval as well as military disarmament; there was a very real danger to Anglo-American relations if what was known as 'navalism' was not moderated. Hankey on the same day issued a counter-blast expressing his disbelief in the value of international agreements; he agreed that 'American opinion must not be outraged by the offer of a blank negative' and advised stalling.[85] The point got no further.

* See p. 558 below.   † See p. 292 below.

Nor did the counterpoint get any further in Germany where they were all for disarmament on sea but not on land. On 16 June Gerard wrote to House:

I am sorry to report that while authorities here think the idea of the seas good, they think the idea of freedom of land too vague . . . Germany will never agree directly or indirectly to any freedom of land or disarmament proposal.[86]

House had got back to London on 28 April. He had been there for over a week, spent mainly in discussing the Freedom of the Seas and his hope of starting a correspondence between London and Berlin which would ultimately lead to a peace conference, when the sinking of the *Lusitania* jolted everyone out of peace talk. House was among those who thought it meant war and his counsel to the President reflects this feeling. When Wilson had asked him what to do about the *Gulflight* House had cabled on 5 May that a sharp note demanding full reparation would be sufficient. Now, after the *Lusitania*, by cable of 9 May followed by a letter House advised an immediate demand that Germany cease her policy of making war upon noncombatants. It would come to that sooner or later, House said, and Wilson would lose prestige by postponing the issue. If war followed, it would not be a new war, but an endeavour to end more speedily an old one. He concluded his cable:

America has come to the parting of the ways, when she must determine whether she stands for civilized or uncivilized warfare. We can no longer remain neutral spectators. Her action in this crisis will determine the part we will play when peace is made, and how far we may influence a settlement for the lasting good of humanity. We are being weighed in the balance, and our position amongst nations is being assessed by mankind.[87]

House showed this cable to Balfour who complimented him warmly. He also had a long talk with Lord Kitchener, the Secretary of State for War.[88] Britain would not urge America to come in, Kitchener told him, but if she did come in, the war would be enormously shortened. This was doubtless one of the 'very guarded' responses which Lord Crewe in a private letter to Spring Rice on 18 June referred to as customary.[89] Actually, Crewe wrote, the majority of the Cabinet thought that it would be 'very greatly to our advantage if the United States decided on hostilities'. The four reasons he gave did not include military or naval help; one was the moral effect on other neutrals and another the strengthening to the point of impregnability of the financial and economic position.

House spent the rest of the month in an attempt, which will be described in the next chapter, to re-open the *modus vivendi*, the deal whereby the unrestricted submarine war was to be traded against the food blockade. The attempt failed; and House, concluding that war was inevitable, decided to return home, intending, so he told Plunkett, to persuade the President not to conduct a milk-and-water war. On 3 June he had a farewell lunch with Crewe (now regularly in charge of the Foreign Office in Grey's absences) and on 4 June with Balfour (who had been primed that morning by Hankey for a discussion on 'navalism'),[90] and impressed on them America's difficulties over the British blockade. If the submarine controversy with Germany was settled by war, there would be no need for an answer to the Note of 30 March; but if it was settled peacefully, House declared, an immediate answer must be forthcoming.

The Colonel had now been from house to house in London ('my comings and goings as unchronicled as if I were a crossing sweeper';[91] he never went to government offices if he could avoid it), meeting, except for one person, everyone who mattered in Britain, whether in or out of power. Power in England then resided in the War Council, a small body which emerged in November 1914 composed of the leading members of the Cabinet and the heads of the armed forces; later it became the Dardanelles Committee and then the War Committee. House, as befitted his known status, entered the halls of power through the front door. Had he been the House of the pre-Wilson era, he would before entering have surveyed the premises and noted the man on duty at the back door. He did not do that and consequently he never talked to Hankey. The omission was piquant, for in many ways Hankey was to the rulers of Britain what House was to President Wilson. He had not of course a vote in the War Council, but then it was not a body that settled things by vote. To all intents and purposes his voice was as strong as any. The memoranda which he constantly prepared and submitted were as well considered as those by any minister. He had the ear of each one individually. 'I have just been having a talk with Hankey', Asquith noted on 13 February 1915, 'whose views are always worth hearing.'[92] As Churchill has summarized it: 'He knew everything, he could put his hand on anything; he said nothing, he gained the confidence of all.' The two men, House and Hankey, were similar in that they both worked behind the scenes (though Hankey kept much further behind than House) and they both wrote up diaries, recording their successes in somewhat similar language. 'He avoided the pitfalls I had feared he might slip into', Hankey would write;[93] and 'he gave as his reason that I was the only person who had any influence over the P.M.';[94] and 'I lunched alone with the P.M. as I always do before his big speeches . . . I was very glad that I got him to insert some passages'.[95] But in outlook they were entirely different. House's mind travelled over wide fields and his ambitions were boundless. Hankey's mind operated within narrow limits. Both concerned themselves with organization but while with House this was a means to an end, with Hankey proficiency in organization was an end in itself. He asked no questions of the existing order. He believed in Britain and in sea power and in the efficacy of the blockade. House and Hankey met only once during America's neutrality and that was in January 1916 at a dinner party given by Strachey, the editor of the *Spectator*, when House noted that a 'Colonel Hankey of the National Defence Board' was among the guests. But House had the Archbishop of Canterbury on his right and the King's private secretary on his left and he records no conversation with Hankey. Hankey's diary also has a note of meeting House at what he calls a depressing dinner. 'Like most of the naval and military world I was frankly suspicious of him . . . I disagreed with almost everything he said.'[96] After America had come into the war, the two men met frequently and got to know and like each other well. If before that House had known of Hankey as anything more than a subordinate official, he might have cultivated him as assiduously as he did other men of power. He might have made some impression on him, but it is doubtful. Hankey with his insignificant appearance and his almost ridiculously insignificant English name was the nineteenth-century Briton who would admit the twentieth century only on the terms that it recognized that Britain was still supreme.

When House left on 5 June he had been in Europe for four months and had spent more than half his time in England. Mr. Baker depicts him as ensnared by British diplomacy, 'the sheer persuasiveness and charm of the British statesman at his best',[97] talking House's heart away with 'nature, solitude, Wordsworth' (these were topics which House confessed to conversing about with Grey one day at luncheon when he felt he ought to leave business until after the meal), while House, ears closed to the voice of Gerard crying peace and eyes shut to the arms of Zimmermann outstretched across the water, was adroitly diverted by Asquith and Grey from his duty to his master. There is no reason to think that House's visit to Germany would have been any less productive if it had been made a month earlier. But every day's delay, Mr. Baker feels, was precious to the British, a day gained towards their objective of staving off peace and drawing America into the war. The vision of England as the land of the lotus may be exaggerated, but there can be no doubt that House found it a very satisfactory place.

X

AFTER THE *LUSITANIA*

Methods of submarine warfare; cruiser rules and unrestricted war — the stages in the German-American dispute — 'Too proud to fight' — the first *Lusitania* Note: 13 May 1915 — the starvation policy and another *modus vivendi* — the second *Lusitania* Note: 9 June 1915 — Bryan's resignation — the return of Colonel House — the new Secretary of State; Lansing's character — did Wilson take advice? — Bethmann's first victory — the third *Lusitania* Note: 21 July 1915 — improvement in German-American relations

WE must consider now the two methods of submarine warfare against merchantmen. Neither was unobjectionable. In the less objectionable the submarine followed the practice of the intercepting cruiser as far as her nature allowed. She used her power of submergence only to conceal her approach. Then she surfaced and warned. But her vulnerability on the surface denied her the time to search the ship and she had not the men to put a prize crew on board. So she could not capture. She could only, after allowing the crew to abandon ship, sink the vessel. The law permitted destruction of an enemy merchantman only if in exceptional circumstances capture was impracticable, and of a neutral ship never at all. So this method was usually illegal; and something worse than illegal in that it exposed the crew, and maybe passengers as well, to the perils of an open boat in mid ocean. But it was not deemed to be grossly inhumane and even came to be called euphemistically warfare in accordance with cruiser rules. As such it was contrasted with the death–dealing method of the unheralded torpedo for which the euphemistic term was unrestricted warfare.

The sinking of the *Lusitania* was the supreme act of unrestricted warfare. Twenty-three months passed between that act and the American declaration of war. Rather more than half this time was taken up by Wilson's efforts to get Germany to abandon or moderate submarine warfare against the non-combatant ship. In the beginning he hoped that Germany would be as stunned as the rest of the world by the magnitude of the disaster and that she would see that a weapon which could lead to results which he felt she could never really have contemplated would have to be abandoned. For in the age of 1915 the sinking of the *Lusitania* was a barbarity. The destruction of the ship herself could be accepted as an act of war, illegitimate but not detestable. As causing the death of the crew, it was indefensible but not utterly outrageous. But the death of women and children was beyond the pale. Brutal death was the point at which the line had always been drawn. Women and children had died of starvation as a regrettable consequence of a prolonged siege, but the world which accepted that sort of death had exclaimed at the barbarousness of a soldiery which put them to the sword. The line was conventional but not logical: a civilization which is not yet secure and is still throwing up its defences against savagery where and how it can has to defend conventional lines.

Here then was an act, as unlawful and as shocking as the rape of Belgium, which affected America, as the invasion of Belgium did not, in that it took American lives. Americans like Theodore Roosevelt could deplore the invasion of Belgium but they could not resent it without infringing the golden rule of nineteenth-century international behaviour, which hitherto only Gladstone had questioned, that nations must mind their own business. American citizens lawfully on the high seas *were* America's business. So the sinking of the *Lusitania* was a *casus belli* in the sense that no moralist—at least if the sin was unconfessed and without promise of amendment—could deny America's right to go to war. There was a large number of Americans who thought that, unless satisfaction was given, she ought to go to war, some because they had always thought so and were now dispensed from observance of the golden rule, some because they now saw a challenge which it would be cowardly not to meet head on, and some like Colonel House because they thought America would have to meet it sooner or later and that delay would be purchased by loss of honour without hope of peace. There was also a large number of Americans, for whom Bryan was the protagonist, who could not see that there was anything to resent, any more than there would have been if a party of American women had wandered into no man's land between the trenches. In between there was the majority of Americans who felt shock and resentment which they wished to express as loudly as possible so long as it did not lead to war.

Wilson's attitude was that of the majority, though for him it was based on something more than the desire for action without its consequences. His thinking put him in the company of those who knew that the challenge could not be evaded, but his feeling and his whole nature put him against the resort to war. Reconciliation between thought and feeling was achieved by his belief, or at least his strong hope, that an appeal to conscience would prove as powerful a weapon as the threat of force. Thus once again Wilson's convictions led him towards the policy which was politically expedient, a policy which sacrificed neither peace nor irretrievably prestige and gained time for a country which was mentally and physically unprepared to fight. But it was a policy which might lead to war. If the appeal to conscience failed, America would, unless she could find some honourable way of escape, be confronted with a choice between a loss of prestige immeasurably greater than if she had adopted forthwith the Bryanist policy of non-involvement, a loss so great as to be tantamount to humiliation, and the threat of intervention which might have to be made good.

The appeal to conscience failed completely. It is fairer to attribute the failure to the inherent weakness of the appeal than to defects in the German conscience. Although in form an appeal to conscience, it was in substance an appeal to law. The conscience of humanity still recognizes that even in war there are things that ought not to be done, but what such things should be is a matter about which men can conscientiously differ. In 1915 virtually no German believed that the sinking of the *Lusitania* was morally wrong. He drew no moral distinction between drowning non-combatants and starving them. He spoke rather wildly about starvation at a time when as yet no one in Germany was going short of food, but starvation was undoubtedly the object of the British blockade. The only possible answer to the German argument was that international law permitted starvation but not drowning. This answer was certainly not incontestable. Food for civilians was not contraband and so (except in the siege and the close blockade) they could not legally be starved. After March 1915 the British tried to get round this by pleading retaliation. But if it is permissible to retaliate by starving, why not also by drowning? The only response to that is that starvation sounds more respectable because more gradual and comes closer to precedent because of its acceptance in siege warfare. In short, the complaint against Germany in so far as it was logical relied not on morality but on convention; and for its appeal relied on the emotional distress caused by an unprecedented advance in the horrors of war. It could not really, as it tried to do, strike the conscience by invoking the eternal verities.

Since the complaint was not strong enough to touch the hearts and minds of the German people, it is not surprising that it made no impact whatever on their high command. Bernstorff went no further than to express his regrets to the State Department that 'the events of the war' had led to the loss of American lives.[1] Jagow in Berlin said that responsibility rested with the British plan to prevent imports of food, adding, when Gerard queried that, imports of raw materials.[2] Thereafter the German Government, while willing to evade or placate, would yield nothing in principle nor would it admit any wrongdoing over the *Lusitania*. Germany did not succeed in driving Wilson off the diplomacy of continuous expostulation but she did force him to fight for his gains on the more usual ground of diplomatic negotiation and to take them in the form of piecemeal concessions granted in response to threats. Tirpitz and the Navy were unwilling to make any concessions at all and they had the support of public opinion; they doubted whether Wilson would proceed from words to deeds and they reckoned, such was their belief in the submarine, that if he did Britain could be defeated before he could do anything effective. Bethmann and the civilians believed that American intervention would mean the defeat of Germany and that unrestricted submarine warfare would inevitably bring America in. To avoid this they were willing, if necessary, to abandon submarine warfare altogether, but their object was to get as much out of the submarine as they could without antagonizing America to the point of war. It was not until 1916 that the military command aligned itself firmly with the naval on this issue. By adroit manœuvring Bethmann managed at first to hold his position with the Kaiser even against their combined strength. Thus for this period the German Government followed Bethmann's policy of retreat when America threatened and, when she was acquiescent, of advance by way of concession to the navy and public opinion.

In the first post-*Lusitania* stage, although Wilson had uttered no threat, the fear that another incident like it would precipitate American intervention caused orders to be given to the submarine fleet not to attack neutral ships or any large liners, whether neutral or enemy. This was done early in June. The order about neutral ships was made public; that about liners was kept secret. On 19 August 1915, while the *Lusitania* controversy was still unresolved, a submarine sank without warning the *Arabic*, a large British liner; there were forty-four casualties, including two American citizens. Without putting any threats on paper Wilson let it be known that, if Germany did not give satisfaction, he was contemplating breaking off relations. By this means he obtained what was called the *Arabic* pledge. This was in effect the publication of the instructions regarding liners which had hitherto been kept secret, and their enlargement by the omission of any qualification of the liner's size. The terms of the declaration were: 'Liners will not be sunk by our submarines without warning.' There followed a period of uneasiness during which 'mistakes' occurred. They culminated on 24 March 1916 in the torpedoing without warning of the *Sussex*, a British channel steamer on her regular voyage from Folkestone to Dieppe; there were about eighty casualties of whom four were American. This produced from Wilson what was tantamount to an ultimatum, a statement that unless the German Government abandoned 'its present practices of submarine warfare' America would sever diplomatic relations altogether. This secured on 5 May 1916 the *Sussex* 'pledge', whereby Germany suspended unrestricted submarine warfare. But she made the suspension conditional upon American efforts to compel the British to abandon their blockade and reserved her rights if those efforts should fail. It was Bethmann's last victory, secured almost on the anniversary of the *Lusitania*, and it kept the peace for eight months. After that the new army command, the Hindenburg–Ludendorff combination, came down decisively against him. On 31 January 1917 Germany withdrew her undertaking. For two months Wilson searched in vain for a way out of the impasse and then there was war.

This chapter and the next take the narrative up to the end of the *Arabic* crisis. The dates on which the action hinges are:

1915

7 May	sinking of the *Lusitania*
13 May	first *Lusitania* Note
28 May	German reply
9 June	second *Lusitania* Note
8 July	German reply
21 July	third *Lusitania* Note
19 August	sinking of the *Arabic*
7 September	Germany's first *Arabic* Note
6 October	Germany's second *Arabic* Note: the settlement
30 October	Germany's third *Arabic* Note

The sinking of the *Lusitania* was an infuriating shock to Americans. It was as if one of two pugilists had suddenly lashed out at a ringside spectator. There was astonishment as well as anger. Popular indignation was such, Bernstorff wrote, that 'even the German-Americans were terror-stricken by its violence'.[3] There were no ears for excuses or explanations. Bernstorff himself prudently went into seclusion until the storm blew over. 'Our propaganda', he reported to the Chancellor, 'has completely collapsed . . .[4] Another event like the present one would certainly mean war with the United States.'

The shock drove Wilson in accordance with his nature into himself and not outwards to seek relief in talk with others. It was after lunch and he was leaving for his round of golf when he received the bare news of the sinking. He waited indoors and when in the evening the report came that the loss of life would be heavy, he went out and walked alone in the streets of Washington. The next day was Saturday and he kept to his usual weekend routine, golf with Grayson on the Saturday morning, then a three hours' motor drive in the afternoon, church on Sunday and another country drive.

When the Monday came, he still saw no one—none of the reporters who besieged Tumulty, not even the Chairman of the Senate Foreign Relations Committee who came to call. He did not send for his Secretary of State. He had issued a statement saying that he was 'considering very earnestly, but very calmly, the right course of action to pursue',[5] and this was all the world knew of his mind until the Monday evening, 10 May. He then fulfilled an engagement in Philadelphia to address four thousand newly naturalized citizens and he spoke to them about American ideals.

The example of America must be a special example. The example of America must be the example not merely of peace because it will not fight, but of peace because peace is the healing and elevating influence of the world and strife is not. There is such a thing as a man being too proud to fight. There is such a thing as a nation being so right that it does not need to convince others by force that it is right.[6]

The world had waited three days to hear from the President what America's retort was going to be. For many outside America, to whom he figured only as the American President, this was the first revelation of his individuality. What did it mean, 'too proud to fight'? For some it was a coward's plea, for others a fragment of Christianity tossed out into a wicked world. Taken in the smaller context of the speech itself, the phrase epitomized a noble thought, that might is not right and that the mighty should scorn to prove their point by force. As Tumulty wrote in his memoirs: 'Self mastery is sometimes more heroic than fighting, or as the bible states it, "he that ruleth his own spirit is greater than he that taketh a city".'[7] But in the larger context of Wilson's wartime utterances the phrase sparkles with his conceit that America was not as other vulgar and quarrelsome nations. It expressed his pride in her aloofness, keeping her head when all about her were losing theirs. It poised her somewhere between heaven and earth, to be appealed to and maybe to extend a well-washed hand in blessing. There is in Chapter 16 of the Book of Proverbs, from which Tumulty quoted, another and better-known proverb: 'Pride goeth before destruction and an haughty spirit before a fall.' When in 1917 the haughty tumbled into the puddle of war, she got her hands as dirty as those of any of her friends and was liked the better for it. But meanwhile the phrase had made Wilson's image in a million minds and fixed it for the years to come.

Incredible though it may seem, it had not occurred to Wilson that what he had said at Philadelphia might be taken to relate to the sinking of the *Lusitania*. He was only repeating as an abstraction his deeply felt sentiment that to fight was not the grandest answer to provocation. Only three weeks before he had spoken of neutrality as requiring 'absolute self-control and self-mastery';[8] and at the beginning of the Mexican troubles he had spoken of the 'self-restraint of a really great nation'.[9]

Questioned by the press after his Philadelphia speech, he said that he was expressing a personal attitude, nothing more. But there can be little doubt that he was not going to strike the blow that House and the militants expected. Tumulty says that when he tried to call his attention to some of the tragic details of the *Lusitania*, Wilson told him that it was much wiser not to dwell too much upon such matters. Tumulty's record of what he then said is not to be taken word for word but may be a fairly reliable compound of what Wilson was saying then and later. He was keenly aware that the feeling of the country was now at fever heat. But would the present emotionalism last long enough to sustain action?

The vastness of this country; its variegated elements; the conflicting cross-currents of national feelings bid us wait and withhold ourselves from hasty or precipitate action. When we move against Germany we must be certain that the whole country not only moves with us but is willing to go forward to the end with enthusiasm. I know that we shall be condemned for waiting, but in the last analysis I am the trustee of this nation, and the cost of it all must be considered in the reckoning before we go forward.[10]

On the Monday advice began to come in. There was House's cable already recorded. There was a predictable one from Page reporting unofficial feeling in Britain that failure to act definitely would shut the United States out of all European respect for a generation.[11] There was an equally predictable reaction from Bryan who fastened on the fact that the *Lusitania* was carrying contraband, including 4,200 cases of cartridges. 'England has been using our citizens to protect her ammunition', he said to his wife;[12] and he put it to Wilson once again that Americans should not be allowed to travel on such ships. 'Like putting women and children in front of an army', he wrote: the American people would be thankful 'that a believer in peace is in the White House at this time'. Almost alone among his fellow citizens he seemed indifferent to what they regarded as the enormity of the crime; on the Sunday he had seen the German ambassador and offered him much consolation, saying according to Bernstorff that the indignation was ridiculous.[13] There was a different reaction from Lansing whose pen was already outstretched towards the draft of a Note. But Wilson wanted no draft and no advice. He had taken three days of solitary thought because he needed to go back to first principles and think out again from them what his attitude should be to the menace of the submarine.

In the result he brought himself back to the point from which Bryan had begun to dislodge him and confirmed himself in his first choice of the radical solution. Not only did he come down decisively in favour of the claim that Americans must be allowed to travel as they wished; he also struck at the root of what put non-combatants in jeopardy, which was any use whatsoever against them of the submarine. It was impossible for the submarine to visit and search or to capture. She could only sink and leave all on board to the mercy of the sea in small boats. This meant an 'inevitable violation of many sacred principles of justice and humanity'.[14] The Note, first drafted on his typewriter, was a call to Germany to abandon altogether the submarine campaign which she had just initiated. This was not put in a form as high as a demand because it was couched in the Wilsonian terminology of assumption that the German Government, which had always stood for justice and humanity, would, as soon as its attention was called to its unfortunate lapse, put things right. But it came to the same thing since what was 'confidently expected' was a 'disavowal' (the word became crucial) of the acts of all the submarine commanders in every incident from the *Falaba* onwards, reparation, and steps to prevent recurrence. The consequences, if expectation went unfulfilled, were veiled. But the phrase 'strict accountability' was used again. As it read in the final version the German Government was not

to expect the Government of the United States to omit any word or any act necessary to the performance of its sacred duty of maintaining the rights of the United States and its citizens and of safeguarding their free exercise and enjoyment.

The draft was ready for the Cabinet meeting on Tuesday 11 May. The President prepared the meeting for strong action by reading House's cable* which the neglected Bryan had not even seen. No one questioned the tenor of the draft but there was much talk about consequences and incidentals. Wilson refused to contemplate war but he did not rule out a diplomatic break. Some members talked of a warning to Americans as a matter of wisdom not to travel on belligerent ships; others suggested holding the balance even by a note of complaint to Britain; and there was some talk of postponing settlement, which would mean reservation of rights instead of the demand for disavowal. It may be surmised that Bryan's was the leading voice, for these were the three emollients which thereafter he pressed upon the President, advocating now one and now another as occasion offered. Burleson and Daniels were ready to give him some support but not to the point of opposition to the President; the great majority of the Cabinet was for firm action.

The Cabinet meeting brought to Bryan the first knowledge he had of the President's mind. Thinking it over after the meeting and after the draft had

* See p. 280 above.

been sent to Lansing to put into diplomatic style, Bryan's worries increased. He would join in the document, he wrote to the President on the next day, 12 May, but 'with a heavy heart'.[15] He followed this on the same day with another letter suggesting that there should be issued at the same time as the Note a government statement to the effect that 'strict accountability' did not mean immediate settlement, which could await the restoration of peace. With this he won a temporary success. Wilson said that he would sleep on the idea and the next day he replied with a draft of a press notice, beginning about there being 'a good deal of confidence in Administration circles that Germany will respond to this note in a spirit of accommodation'.[16] The rest of it was vaguer than Bryan had proposed but enough to carry the impression that Germany could talk her way out of trouble. It contained a strong hint that the United States would be willing to arbitrate. Bryan was overjoyed. The Note was due to go to Berlin that afternoon and Bryan intended to send the press notice as well and tell Gerard to deliver it at the same time. In his simplicity and delight he told Lansing and Tumulty what was afoot. They were horrified and mobilized Garrison, the Secretary of War, and Burleson. Just as Wilson listened to Lansing on matters of law (Lansing was 'Mr. Wilson's legal conscience', Bernstorff said)[17] so he listened to Burleson and Tumulty when they spoke as his political conscience. There would be a 'terrible howl', Tumulty said; the President would be accused of 'double-dealing'.[18] Bryan, Wilson replied, was a wise politician. Nevertheless, he agreed to hold the statement for the time being. Tumulty—'white as a ghost' he said he was—reported this to Garrison. There was nothing more that they could do.

Wilson changed his mind. The reason he gave to Bryan was that he had heard that Bernstorff was saying that the United States 'were not in earnest, would speak only in a Pickwickian sense';[19] and he, Wilson, dared not lend colour to any indication that the Note 'was merely the first word in a prolonged debate'. So the Note of 13 May was dispatched without the gloss.

Disappointed on this ground, Bryan shifted to another. He was now seriously frightened that Wilson's tactics would lead to war and desperately anxious to use any expedient that would keep the peace. He was lying awake at night, jotting down his thoughts, losing three or four hours sleep. He tried yet again for a warning against travel, but on this Wilson's mind was quite made up. Even if it would have been the right thing in the first place, he had told Bryan on 11 May, after the outrage it was too late.

Bryan made greater headway with the idea of holding the balance even by sending a Note to Britain protesting against her irregularities. Here he had the support of Lansing, who always felt strongly about any sort of illegality, and a draft was put in hand. Certainly Wilson wanted to make a protest sooner or later and, as has been seen,* was at this time telling House to put pressure on Grey. But after he had given it some thought, Wilson on 20 May came down in favour of postponement. He feared that Germany would regard such action as showing 'uneasiness and hedging'.[20] He may also have had the feeling, which he afterwards revealed, that it was unwise to fight on two fronts at once. Finally, there had been a development in London which made a protest at that moment inopportune.

The phrase, mangled out of context and shouted on posters—'We are too proud to fight: Woodrow Wilson'—had been received with ribaldry by Englishmen and with shame by Americans in London. The worst impression was effaced, in government circles at any rate, by the terms of the Note of 13 May. By condemning the whole submarine campaign as illegal and inhumane, Wilson seemed at last to be striking the high tone of morality which he had left unsounded at the rape of Belgium. 'Nothing less than the conscience of humanity', the London *Times* proclaimed, 'makes itself audible in his measured and incisive sentences . . . The moral interests of the United States and the Allies are henceforward indissolubly linked.'[21] On the practical side Germany appeared to be faced with a choice between the hostility of the United States and the total abandonment of her submarine campaign. Either would be a substantial gain for Britain. From all sides congratulations poured into the American embassy which Page forwarded to the State Department together with his own. Bryan passed them on to Wilson with the wry comment: 'I am glad to note that it will not take a generation to regain the respect with the loss of which we were threatened.'[22]

On 14 May House and Grey were lunching together and the principal topic of conversation was naturally the Note and its consequences. Grey asked House what he thought Germany's reply would be. House said that if he were writing it, he would say that if England would lift the embargo on food Germany would discontinue her submarine policy. Grey said that if Germany would discontinue also the use of poison gas and the ruthless killing of non-combatants England would lift the embargo. Germany had released poison gas for the first time a few weeks before. This was more than a clear breach of what had been decided at the First Hague Conference in 1899; it dirtied the idea, still vigorously alive, that war could be waged as a clean fight. House immediately reported Grey's observation to the President who replied that he was deeply interested and told House to find out how far the British Cabinet would go. Page was discouraging. It

* See p. 215 above.

was only, he pointed out, the old *modus vivendi* which both sides had already rejected.

On Wilson's insistence House had of course to pursue the matter but it soon became apparent that Wilson and Grey were at cross purposes. What Wilson wanted and immediately urged was in effect an abandonment of both blockades and a return on Britain's part to the *status quo* before reprisals began. The test of that was whether Britain would allow the import not only of food for civilians but also of all other non-contraband materials. On the face of things such a request was reasonable. The object of reprisals is achieved when the illegality complained of ceases; and if the object of Britain's blockade was to force Germany to desist from her submarine blockade, then on the cessation of the latter the whole of the former should go and not merely a part of it. But in truth Britain's blockade was not a genuine reprisal at all; it was an independent measure of war. So for that matter was Germany's submarine blockade. They were both weapons of war; and so long as each side remained confident that its weapon would in the end prove the stronger, there was no prospect of a deal.

Of course if Britain had ever conceded that the only justification for her blockade was as a reprisal, she could, when she offered only a limited withdrawal, have been put dialectically on the spot. But she was too clever to do that. She always left herself room to plead that as a blockade it was within at least the penumbra of international law. Although in a court of law the point was unarguable, in the less restricted arena of diplomatic correspondence the idea of adapting the classical blockade to modern conditions could be made to sound very persuasive. Inevitably it provoked the counterattack that changed conditions justified also the submarine war. The answer to that was that changed conditions could never justify inhumanity. This led to the rejoinder that to starve civilians was just as inhumane as to drown them. So the argument came full circle back to food.

This was what Grey's prescience perceived. What he had in mind (he never suggested anything more) was not a mutual cessation of reprisals but a mutual cessation, as it were, of barbarities—on the one side the drowning of non-combatants and the use of poison gas, on the other starvation. Perhaps he would not have thought of the British blockade as barbarous. But it was represented by Germany to be so and Grey foresaw that the force of the representation, as yet still weakened by the fact that there was no food shortage in Germany, would increase correspondingly with the success of the blockade. In the future there might be a real advantage to be gained from a mutual abandonment of inhumanities, and meanwhile a propaganda advantage from making the offer.

So in spite of Page's forebodings, House when he went to see Grey again found him still receptive. A memorandum was prepared (though, House noted, it was not necessary 'for he remembers well what he says and never recedes from his word'),[23] embodying the arrangements. Staple foodstuffs were to be allowed to go to neutral ports in exchange for the abandonment of submarine and gas warfare. As between Britain and the United States all foodstuffs then detained were to be brought before the Prize Court as quickly as possible. This was on 19 May. Two days later Grey was able to tell House that he had consulted the Cabinet and that, if Germany made the proposal, it would be considered.

Although he was twice urged by Wilson to press Grey for the wider arrangement covering all non-contraband, House does not appear to have said anything at all about it. It would certainly have been rejected by Grey who would probably also have been disappointed in House if he had tried to press on him something that went so far beyond the scope of what Grey had originally volunteered. House—and Page also, as has been seen— regarded their relationship with Grey as something very special and his confidence in them as an asset personal to themselves and not to be put in jeopardy on instruction from above. Wilson at any rate made no complaint when he got the terms of the memorandum. He passed it on to the German Foreign Office through Gerard where it met with the predictable answer, which, as Jagow said, he had given before, that an arrangement could be considered only if raw materials such as cotton, copper, and rubber were included.[24] Germany, Jagow told Gerard, was in no need of food. The Allies, House said when Gerard reported back, would never allow raw materials; and that, probably to House's relief, finished the matter. Wilson accepted the conclusion with disappointment and said that the German demand for raw material for munitions was 'manifestly impossible': 'it looks as if we were again in a blind alley'.[25]

But for Grey it had been a successful piece of diplomacy. He had stifled the German wailing about starvation. As House pointed out to Wilson, 'this does away with their contention that the starving of Germany justifies the submarine'.[26] And as Grey said to House when they lunched together on 26 May it made the point that England was not trying to push America into war. At the very moment when Wilson had apparently put Germany into the position of either having to abandon her submarine campaign or face the possibility of war with the United States, Grey offered her a way of abandoning the campaign without loss of face and with a *quid pro quo*.

But diplomacy apart Grey was worried about the future of the starvation policy. He told House at the lunch on 26 May that some members of the Government had said that if Germany was actually running short of food, it would not be well to relax. He, Grey, did not agree with this. It is significant too that when the week before Grey told House that he would put the proposal to the Cabinet, he had added that if in ordinary times the Cabinet did not accept his view he would resign, but that he could not do that in wartime. At Fallodon in June he continued to worry about this and about the kindred point on Freedom of the Seas. The argument on both was the same. In the long run would it not be better for Britain to obtain security for her maritime trade: in the short run could she not gain a diplomatic advantage with the United States? Grey put the double point in a letter to Crewe from Fallodon dated 14 June which he asked should be shown to Asquith. Crewe did not try to resurrect Freedom of the Seas which, as we have seen,* Asquith had just killed. But he prepared a memorandum for the Cabinet in which he reported on the abortive negotiations for the *modus vivendi*. 'It seems worth consideration', he wrote, 'whether some formal offer ought not to be made to the United States in order to put ourselves right with public opinion there.'[27] The approach was half-hearted and came to nothing except that it produced from Hankey a paper which he himself called 'a crushing reply . . . much appreciated by P.M. and Mr. Balfour'[28] and which contained an interesting assessment of the rival blockades. The results of the submarine blockade to date did not make, he thought, its abandonment worth any concession; on the other hand, the Allies could not hope to starve Germany out this year. There was in fact here too little of an underemphasis. The starvation policy had not as yet made any impact at all. Indeed at this very time, on 27 May, Lansing had a long conversation with Spring Rice in which he tried, as he thought successfully, to persuade the ambassador of its futility. They were incurring all the odium of it with nothing to gain: 'the legality of the attempt was neither here nor there', Lansing said, 'since the very idea was repugnant to the humane elements of modern society'.[29] Spring Rice promised to urge the point on Grey; but he passed it on only as a suggestion that might be made by the State Department.[30] But Hankey, doggedness and prescience combined, was looking forward to 1916 when, he said, the possibility of starvation could not be dismissed. Even if Germany could not be starved into surrender, the effect of serious military reverses would depend on morale and here the combination of economic and food pressure would help. Hankey concluded:

Finally, when the war reaches its inevitable end, and terms of peace are discussed, one of the greatest assets remaining in our hands is the fact that we cut off the enemy from access by sea to the outer world. Unless our enemies are willing to buy back from us the right of free communication, and to give the price we ask, we can refuse to come to terms.[31]

* See p. 279 above.

One other effect the abortive *modus vivendi* had. It set the British Cabinet thinking about what they should do in the unfortunate event of Germany being driven by the United States to abandon submarine warfare. How then could retaliation be maintained? By things like the Scarborough bombardment (now seven months old) and poison gas perhaps: but maybe it would be better just to declare everything contraband. Grey in a note for the Cabinet on 17 July 1915 suggested as an additional argument for continuing retaliation that the British blockade 'has barely commenced as yet to be seriously inconvenient to Germany' while the submarine had destroyed 300,000 tons of shipping, not to mention lives and cargoes; Britain could not be expected to discontinue her retaliation before its effect was felt unless Germany paid compensation.

   The German Government's reply dated 28 May 1915 to the first *Lusitania* Note reached Wilson on 31 May.[32] In it Germany accepted responsibility for any attack on neutral vessels which, she said, was contrary to explicit instructions. This met much of the complaint about the earlier incidents. But on the *Lusitania*, which overshadowed all, the reply was, and was intended to be, temporizing. The Government had not yet decided how far it would go to avoid American hostility and until the controversy on this point between the civilian and naval wings was settled, there was nothing for it but to temporize. The Note, Jagow explained at a press interview, was an attempt to establish a common basis of fact to serve as the groundwork for further conversation.[33] Germany had already, the Note said, expressed her regret for the loss of neutral lives. But there should be agreement about the facts and certain important ones had escaped the attention of the American Government. The *Lusitania* had been constructed as an auxiliary cruiser. She left New York with guns 'mounted under decks and masked'. She had been advised to use neutral flags and ram submarines. She had previously carried Canadian troops. She was carrying a cargo of ammunition 'destined for the destruction of brave German soldiers' and her rapid sinking was due to the explosion of this cargo. The German Government recommended these facts* 'to a careful examination by the American Government' and

---

* Although the American Government in its reply was tart about these allegations ('It was its duty to see to it that the Lusitania was not armed for offensive action, that she was not serving as a transport, that she did not carry a cargo prohibited by the statutes of the United States . . . it performed that duty'; FRUS. 437), some of the facts are still in dispute. There was nothing in the auxiliary cruiser point; many liners, German as well as British, were constructed so that in time of war they *could* be used as cruisers. Admittedly the *Lusitania* was carrying cartridges but petty explosions could not have contributed to the disaster. It has been asserted that she was secretly carrying high explosive. This has never been proved, but, on the other hand, no convincing explanation has been given of the rapidity of the sinking. It would have been illegal under American law to load high explosives in a ship that was

concluded with the reflection that the *modus vivendi* had been rejected by Britain.

Wilson was flummoxed. His first Note had been applauded because it satisfied so nicely the twin desiderata of no yielding and no threats. It had sounded the highest possible moral tone and given the lowest possible indication of what might happen if there was an inharmonious response. The German reply did not controvert Wilson's principles: it ignored them. It reduced the matter to the level of an ordinary case in which, once the facts were settled, a bargain could presumably be struck. Since the facts said to be in doubt could not affect the question whether submarine war was ever permissible, the Note was by implication a complete rejection of Wilson's appeal. There was no meeting on the high ground he had chosen. What then should be the next step? In the interval sentiment in the country had moved further away from involvement so that the natural response of stepping up the threats, even if acceptable to Wilson, might prove politically unsound. As Spring Rice summed it up in mid June 1915:

> The American people are ready to accept any reasonable excuse from Germany. I doubt if on the present record the United States will go to war, that is, unless some new and striking incident occurs.[34]

The degree of Wilson's perplexity is shown by the fact that, instead of following his usual course of preparing a draft and inviting approval, he threw the matter over to the Cabinet. This produced only confused talk and Wilson then asked the State Department for an outline of a second Note. Neither Bryan nor Lansing ventured on that and on 3 June the President himself composed the second *Lusitania* Note.[35] It was a weak document, no more than a repetition of the first, without any additional statement of unpleasant consequences. It ended prayerfully: 'The Government of the United States, therefore, very earnestly and very solemnly renews the representations of its note' of 13 May; and this doxology was preceded by the familiar invocations of humanity and expressions of confidence in the intentions of the Great Imperial German Government. It was saved from the appearance of inanity by the fact that it caused the resignation of Bryan and so led the world to believe that it must have meant much more than it said.

Bryan's resignation was in fact due to his stress of mind and to his realization that he would never get his views to prevail. At the Cabinet meeting on 1 June, the day after he received the German Note, Wilson brought it up and invited full and free discussion. The intrepid Garrison led off with the

---

also carrying passengers, but in international law high explosive is not distinguishable from other contraband. The whole subject is covered in *Lusitania* by Colin Simpson (London, 1972).

suggestion that Germany should be made to say whether or not she accepted the principle of the first *Lusitania* Note; if she did not, there was nothing to discuss. Then someone reverted to the idea of a strong protest to London. Bryan, who, so Spring Rice put it, regarded 'the torpedo and the Prize Court with equal abhorrence',[36] said excitedly that this was what he had always wanted. He seemed to his colleagues to be under great strain. He ended his harangue by saying: 'You people are not neutral. You are taking sides.'[37] Wilson rebuked him sharply in a tone of voice which, it was later reported to House, had not been heard in Cabinet since the occasion when some member unnamed 'had transgressed in some way the proprieties'.[38]

Another unusual step which Wilson took was to receive personally the German ambassador. This he did on 2 June 1915. It was, Bernstorff reported, a cordial exchange of views in which the President urged a complete cessation of submarine warfare and pressed the point that Germany and the United States had both always been in favour of Freedom of the Seas. This resulted in Bernstorff urging his government to lift in their next Note the discussion to the level of the humanitarian standpoint. At this interview Wilson gave privately the indication which he would not give openly that if submarine war ended he would press for the raising of the English hunger blockade. He kept them distinct in his own mind by calling one an insistence on America's rights and the other a service which she would be in a position to render once her rights were secured. Bernstorff would not have been so nice about removing the taint of a bargain.

This day and the next Bryan bombarded Wilson with letters, long and diffuse and all on the old rejected themes, and Wilson dealt with them as firmly and kindly as he could. At the Cabinet meeting on 4 June when Wilson read his conciliatory draft there was no opposition, only what Houston called 'a confused and tiresome discussion'.[39] It was plain that Bryan was beaten. He could not find any fault with the language of this Note as compared with the first. It was simply that he felt he could not sign another Note like the first, regarding both of them, as he did, as one-sided and a flirtation with war. There were added to this the accumulating miseries of his position, now only that of a figurehead (as his wife, who perhaps felt it more keenly than he, said to McAdoo).[40] The President was used to consulting with House and Lansing; the Secretary was not even a station on the route to House and on that to Lansing he was often bypassed. He felt too, so Tumulty thought, that he was under suspicion. An unfortunate matter had come to light shortly before. When Gerard had gone to see Zimmermann about the proposed foodstuffs deal and had talked perhaps a little too grandiosely about American determination, Zimmermann had been provoked into showing him a report from Dumba, the Austrian ambassador in Washington, in which the ambassador said that Bryan had assured him 'that American notes, however strongly worded, meant no harm, but had to be written in order to pacify the excited public opinion of Americans'.[41] Gerard duly reported this to Washington and the story soon got out. Bryan hotly denied the words attributed to him. It is improbable that he said anything quite like that, but it is very probable that, as when talking with Bernstorff, he failed to conceal his lack of sympathy with the President's policy and that the knowledge of his attitude accounted to some extent for Germany's cavalier treatment of the Note.

The next day was a Saturday, 5 June. At lunchtime Bryan called on McAdoo and asked him to find out from his father-in-law how he could resign so as to cause the least embarrassment.[42] McAdoo persuaded the Bryans to go away for the weekend to think things over. Bryan seems to have spent much of it in marshalling his thoughts for a final appeal to the President which he put on paper and followed up with an interview on the Monday morning in which he passionately pleaded for 'Christian forbearance'[43] and the President endeavoured to dissuade him from resignation. But that was now inevitable. At the end he said to Wilson: 'Colonel House has been your Secretary of State, not I, and I have never had your full confidence.'[44] So he made his personal complaint for the first and the last time. Then full of grace he went out into the political wilderness, whence he never returned, to face unarmed the malice of his foes, the taunts that he had deserted his post, and the public silence of his colleagues. There was an affecting scene at the University Club on 8 June where he entertained them to a farewell luncheon. All of them were sad to see him go. There was another moment of emotion on 9 June, the day his resignation was announced, when he took formal leave of Wilson at the White House, each invoking the blessing of God upon the other. Then he walked to the State Department for the last time together with Tumulty, their arms around each other.

The incident upset Wilson. He was curt and obviously irritated when questioned by the press and he suffered from a series of blinding headaches. But though he had sincerely tried to dissuade Bryan from resigning, fearing that it would be taken as a sign of government disunity, he was relieved when he went and much happier after he had gone. Wilson was then left as the only man of stature in the Democratic party. The Cabinet diminished in importance when it lost the man who had been for twenty years the Democratic leader. Foreign policy was not discussed there again until the crisis of 1917. It is noteworthy that Houston, who described in his memoirs in detail the Cabinet discussions in early June, wrote of the next six months, a period in which tension with Germany increased to near breaking-point and hostility with Britain also mounted, as follows:

The period from June 1915 to the middle of December was one of great and growing activity and strain; but, in the field of foreign relations, there was no departure in policy which caused or demanded much discussion or consideration at the hands of the Cabinet.[45]

The second *Lusitania* Note was dated 9 June 1915. In the unusually argumentative atmosphere that engendered it two ideas emerged, one still-born and one that came later to fruition. Both ideas centred on the point that it was too much to ask of Germany that she should abandon altogether the use of the submarine against merchantmen. McAdoo discussed with Lansing, who was rather doubtful about it, an addition to the Note to say that, provided submarine operations did not jeopardize human life or cause indiscriminate destruction of neutral property, the United States would be willing to consider proposals modifying the existing rules of international law. This was on 7 June but McAdoo did not raise the point in the Cabinet the next day. Perhaps he allowed it to be submerged in Houston's variation. Houston did not favour any formal modification of the law but he did not see why Germany should not be allowed to use the submarine in accordance with cruiser rules. The German blockade would not then be paralysed. He wanted Wilson to emphasize American rights. If the people were to be made ready for war, he said, they must understand it as an American issue. He put this point to Wilson on 5 June when Wilson rather unexpectedly called him on the telephone to ask if he had got any clear notion of the Cabinet's views the day before. He developed it further at the Cabinet meeting on 8 June when Wilson made notes and indicated agreement. Wilson did not alter the Note which was then ready to be dispatched but, as will be seen, it became the point of departure for the third *Lusitania* Note.

Bryan also left an important idea behind him. In the whole course of the debate over the two Notes he had won only one meaningful verbal concession. Wilson's draft of the first *Lusitania* Note claimed protection for American travel on unarmed merchantmen. Lansing, commissioned to put the Note into diplomatic style, altered the word 'unarmed' to 'unresisting'. What he had in mind was doubtless the rule of international law that permitted a merchantman to be armed for defensive purposes. Bryan objected to the change, saying with unlawyerlike sense: 'It is presumed that an armed vessel will resist—that is what the arms are for.'[46] Wilson restored the original word. This technical issue was the hinge on which the next great debate turned.

In the lull which followed all these excitements Colonel House returned.

On 13 June his boat arrived in New York and he was taken off in a revenue cutter. While at sea he had heard of Bryan's resignation; the thoughtful Plunkett had sent him a wireless. He dismissed all the gossip that he would be the new Secretary of State. He heard without comment the gossip about Mrs. Galt. It was unthinkable of course that his health would permit him to go to Washington in the summer heat. Anyway, Wilson was coming to New York on 24 June on his way through to Cornish for his summer holiday, and he sent McAdoo to discuss with House as soon as he returned the only question of urgency, which was the appointment of the new Secretary of State. House gave his views on that in a letter to Wilson written on 16 June which was also his formal report on the conclusion of his mission. There was not much to say about the latter that Wilson did not know. The sinking of the *Lusitania*, the use of poisonous gas, and other breaches of international law had put an end, House wrote, to his discussions in England on the Freedom of the Seas and on a peace covenant. Otherwise, he said, by midsummer the belligerents would have been discussing peace terms through Wilson. House was humbugging himself as well as Wilson when he wrote this, but like many over-confident men he hated to admit failure.

His judgement was sounder on the future than on the past. He prophesied that the German Navy would force the continuance of the submarine policy, leaving the Foreign Office to explain 'unfortunate incidents'. He concluded:

> I think we shall find ourselves drifting into war with Germany ... regrettable as this would be, there would be compensations. The war would be more speedily ended, and we would be in a strong position to aid the other great democracies in turning the world into the right paths.[47]

For, as he had said earlier, if the Allies failed to win, it would mean a reversal of the entire American policy.

The two ambassadors, British and German, came to call on House in New York while he was waiting there for Wilson: and then on 24 June the two friends met. There were two great topics for discussion. The first of them was Lansing, whom Wilson had formally appointed that morning as Secretary of State. He was, Wilson said, practically his own Secretary of State and Lansing would not be troublesome by obtruding his views. He suggested that House should see Lansing and tell him of their special relationship, not fully of his work in Europe, but enough to get him to work in harmony. Then Wilson said to House that he had an intimate personal matter to discuss with him. As House recorded it in his diary, Wilson said:

> You are the only person in the world with whom I can discuss everything. There

are some I can tell one thing and others another, but you are the only one to whom I can make an entire clearance of mind.[48]

Then he spoke of his love for Mrs. Galt and his wish to marry. It was indeed a delicate topic. House felt that Wilson would not be healthy and happy unless he married again but he was afraid he would be criticized for the briefness of the interval. So while approving he urged postponement until the following spring. Then each went to his summer residence, House to Manchester on the coast of Massachusetts and Wilson to Cornish where Mrs. Galt and the family awaited him. Early in July Mrs. Galt admitted that she loved him. She said that she would marry him if he was defeated in the 1916 election but that, if he was not, she still felt uncertain of assuming the responsibilities. Each morning, however, they worked together on the official pouch.

On Bryan's resignation Wilson, as the obvious thing to do, had appointed Lansing as Acting Secretary. But he was not then minded to confirm him in the post because, as he told Houston, Lansing was not big enough. He lacked imagination and initiative and, Wilson added because he always liked to think of himself as one who could take hard knocks in discussion, would not sufficiently vigorously combat or question his views. 'Only a clerk in the State Department isn't he?',[49] Mrs. Galt had said when asked her advice by her suitor as they leant over the rail of the *Mayflower*, the Presidential yacht, on a cruise down the Potomac; and she told a story about a play she had once seen, which illustrated the rightness of getting rid of Bryan. Mrs. Galt was now constantly being asked for her advice on matters of State. But it was the asking, not the answering, that mattered, since it is unlikely when she gave it that she ever supported it with any reasons that would need a moment's consideration and there is no instance of Wilson doing anything silly in consequence.

Wilson knew that House would not take the job, so he did not dwell on him. For a fleeting moment he had a wild thought of appointing a Mr. Jones. Thomas D. Jones was one of the Princeton trustees who had warmly supported Wilson in the great fight. Wilson's desire to promote him—not to reward him, Wilson did not think that way, he thought simply that those who believed in him must be the best men—had caused only the year before a tussle which Professor Link has characterized as 'one of the bitterest and most significant episodes of the first Wilson administration';[50] for that reason the story is worth recalling. In June 1914 Wilson had to make appointments, which required confirmation by the Senate, to the newly created Federal Reserve Board. Mr. Jones, who was a wealthy Chicago businessman, did not seek the appointment; but on the face of things he seemed well fitted for it and Wilson persuaded him to allow himself to be nominated so

May 1915. Lord Robert Cecil (*left*), Under-Secretary of State at the Foreign Office

October 1916. The Prime Minister, Mr. H. H. Asquith, leaving the War Office

Berlin, 1916. Theobald von Bethmann Hollweg, the German Chancellor, with the German Foreign Minister Gottlieb von Jagow (*centre*) and Dr. Karl Helfferich, later Vice-Chancellor

that, as Wilson told him, he could have 'men about me whom I know and have seen tested'.[51] Wilson commended him to the Senate as the 'one man of the whole number who was in a peculiar sense my personal choice'.[52] Rightly or wrongly the appointments were regarded as reactionary and were fought in the Senate by Senator Reed of Missouri who thereby qualified himself for the occupation of another page in Wilson's bad books. A drawback to Mr. Jones was that he was a director of the International Harvester Company, the so-called Harvester Trust, which at that very time was under indictment under the anti-trust laws. Wilson explained this to the Senate by saying that Mr. Jones had gone into the board of the Harvester Company for the purposes of assisting to withdraw it from the control which had led to anti-trust purposes and that in this he had been very effective. Unfortunately, when called to testify before the Senate Banking Committee, Mr. Jones said candidly that he had been a director for the past five years, that he had joined the board in order to oblige Cyrus H. McCormick, the company's chief owner and from the anti-trust point of view also the chief villain, and that he had fully approved of all the company's policies during that five years. He added for good measure that he was one of the principal owners of another trust, popularly known as the Zinc Trust. Accordingly the Senate Committee voted to disapprove the nomination. Wilson carried the fight to the floor of the Senate and Bryan, Burleson, and Tumulty all applied their heaviest pressure. But as the number of insurgent senators increased, Wilson had to concede defeat and to get Mr. Jones to ask for his nomination to be withdrawn.

After resting lightly on Jones, Wilson's mind turned to Houston, the man whom in his Cabinet he most admired, but he was altogether lacking in experience of foreign affairs. McAdoo wanted a good party man but there was no one who filled the bill. House's first nominee was Page. If House had converted Wilson to his point of view that the sooner America entered the war the better, Page would have been a very suitable appointment. But as an executive of a policy of neutrality, the appointment of an ambassador from any belligerent capital, let alone Page, would necessarily have been bad. So in the end Wilson had to come back to Lansing; and though he seemed to be reverting to the man he had first discarded, he was in truth proceeding to the conclusion that he must make himself his own Secretary of State. House approved Lansing as an alternative choice. It is hard to believe, but it is a fact, that House, although he had been so closely concerned with foreign affairs, had met Lansing only once and then for a few minutes when, as he told Wilson, 'his mentality did not impress me unduly', but 'the most important thing is to get a man with not too many ideas of his own and one that will be entirely guided by you without unnecessary argument'.[53]

Lansing was conscious that he had been promoted beyond expectation. He was socially well connected; one of his predecessors as Secretary of State was his father-in-law, John Foster.* He looked distinguished: 'scholarly and philosophical', McAdoo thought, 'decidedly conservative'.[54] Like many a man whose ability is at war with his appearance, he was vain. He enjoyed his rank and all that went with it in Washington society. He was a great diner-out.

He had a slow and legalistic mind. He rarely said anything in Cabinet, perhaps because he was basically out of sympathy with Wilson's foreign policy but more probably because he did not think quickly enough to say it. He must have been aware that when talking with men like Wilson, House, and Page he was meeting minds nimbler than his own. He got the reassurance he needed by preparing elaborate memoranda, as he said, 'for his own guidance'[55] (some of them were titled rather like minor poems, such as 'Thoughts suggested by . . .' ('Considerations on . . .', etc.), which would prove that he was right in the long run. They were written rotundly for he was not a man to use one word if there was room for more. It was Lansing's pedantry and fussiness that drove Page mad. (Page tended to dislike anyone in the State Department anyway. He loathed so deeply Bryan and his pacifism that he pursued him even in retirement with venomous epithets: 'the most repulsive demagogue in all history, dirty, greasy, treacherous'.)[56] When Lansing was Acting Secretary, Sargent, the celebrated portrait painter who lived in London, wished to return through diplomatic channels his German decoration. Page, who was only too delighted to perform a service of that sort, telegraphed Lansing for instructions. Lansing wired back saying that the State Department could have no connection with such a matter and instructing Page to obtain from Sargent the reimbursement of $5, the cost of the telegrams.[57] What a man!

Lansing's conception of diplomacy was simple but not ineffective. It was that the Secretary of State resolutely upheld the honour and dignity of the United States. This ensured both that her voice would be heard respectfully in foreign capitals and that the American people (whose resolution he erroneously supposed to be equal to his own) would give him their support.

On the whole Lansing's character is likely to be rated too low than too high. He was so ponderous and the label of a second-class lawyer stuck so plainly on him that those who dealt with him might overlook that he was a good second class, and also that below his legalisms he had in a high degree the lawyer's virtues, a sound and balanced judgement and a deep sense of fairness. They make his dicta on Wilson historically very valuable:

* One of his successors was his nephew, John Foster Dulles, President Eisenhower's Secretary of State.

although he fell out with Wilson in the end, he seemed always able to assess dispassionately his qualities and defects, and on balance he greatly admired him. It was this dispassionate sense of fairness that separated him from Page—this together with his more limited vision. He believed almost as strongly as Page in the rightness of the Allied cause and was as convinced that American interest demanded an Allied victory. Hardly more than a fortnight after his appointment he wrote in one of his private memoranda: 'Germany must not be permitted to win this war or to break even, though to prevent it this country is forced to take an active part.'[58] But he kept his mind firmly on his job, which was to administer a policy of neutrality; so long as America was neutral, both sides were entitled to equal treatment according to the rules and he did his best to see that they got it. He suppressed his personal feelings as successfully as a professional advocate conducting a case he did not believe in. Until the fall of 1916 he walked through the war in blinkers which he took off only to write his memoranda.

But should a minister remain in office to carry out a policy of which he disapproves? In the British system it would be impossible; such a man would be bound in conscience to resign. But Lansing was neither constitutionally nor morally responsible for the policy he administered. If his appointment had been a political one, he might have felt more awkward than he did. But he had no interest in politics; spiritually he was a civil servant; no one thought of him except as Wilson's instrument. He justified himself to himself by the reflection that action had to be deferred until by a process of education and enlightenment the American people had been brought to a full understanding of the matter. It was none of his business to take part in that.

When Wilson appointed Lansing, he told him that he was convinced that they were of the same mind concerning international policies. If that was true at the time of the *Lusitania* crisis, the conformity did not survive many days. But while he would put forward hints and guarded views on specific points, Lansing never disclosed the width of the divergence between his memoranda and his speech with Wilson. It might be doing him an injustice to say that he did not want to risk his job, but at any rate he saw no sense in losing it through banging his head against a brick wall. So he treated Wilson rather as a family solicitor might treat a pigheaded client whom he did not want to lose. He felt that he understood Wilson's temperament and concluded, he says, that 'success in an attempt to change his views seemed to lie in moderation and in partial approval of his purpose rather than in bluntly arguing that it was wholly wrong'.[59] He studied Wilson in smaller matters too: for example, in his use of language. He soon got to recognize the choicer bits of phrasing and saw that any amendments he suggested did not interfere with them. He knew that Wilson liked things presented in writing rather than orally and that suited his own taste for memoranda. Wilson on his side treated Lansing with scrupulous courtesy (they always addressed each other as 'My Dear Mr. President' and 'My Dear Mr. Secretary'), concealing behind a façade of collaboration the fact that Lansing had to do just what he was told. In fact Wilson got a good deal of valuable help from him, and more than help on the one or two occasions when he let him take the initiative.

Lansing in his memoirs, and Tumulty also, insist that it is wrong to say of Wilson that he never asked for advice. Certainly Wilson did not repel discussion while his mind was in process of being made up. He listened patiently, interrupting only occasionally to check repetition; as much as the waste of time, he disliked the implication that he needed to have a thing said to him twice. But he wanted to be concisely informed on all the relevant facts before he came to a decision and to have expert opinions on any matters on which he did not consider himself a competent judge—as, for example, political consequences, where he respected Tumulty's views. He never resented, even if he did not solicit, a reasoned argument on any point on which he had not made up his mind. When it was made up, he would avoid further discussion if he could; if he had to grant an interview, he would listen always with courtesy and apparent attention though the interloper would probably lower himself in Wilson's opinion. If he persisted to the point of trying to argue Wilson out of his decision, he would lower himself very far. Garrison, Tumulty's 'high type of equity judge', was an offender in this respect. Wilson told Baker:

> Garrison is an intensely argumentative man. He wore me out with argument. When he met a fact, instead of accepting it as facts must be accepted, as inevitable, he wanted to argue about it indefinitely.[60]

Bryan also was an argumentative man, he said, to whom facts were not acceptable. In due course Garrison followed Bryan in resigning from the Cabinet; manifestly the 'fact' that was unacceptable was Wilson's own opinion. 'His overpowering self-esteem', Garrison wrote, 'left no place for common counsel of which he talked so much and in which he did not indulge at all.'[61]

Wilson was like a judge sitting in court. He received the evidence on fact, listened to expert witnesses and to the respectful submissions of counsel, reserved judgement, and then gave his decision. After that the court was closed. If a judge can be said to be advised by counsel and witnesses—for this is what the processes described by Lansing and Tumulty amount to—then Wilson took advice. But he never took advice in the sense of preferring somebody else's judgement to his own. He was wearied, though he always tried not to show it, by someone like Page who simply wanted to tell him what his judgement should be. Such a man had no useful contribution to make. All he had done was to put his mind to work on the problem in the same way as Wilson proposed to or had already put his. But Wilson was equipped to do his own thinking. He had no use for someone else's mental machinery; he was quite convinced that his was superior. What was still worse was when his would-be adviser had not put his mind to work at all—or perhaps had not got a mind or at any rate one that worked like Wilson's—and had merely come to tell him, on the strength of some hunch or intuition which he could not clearly expound, what he would do if he were in Wilson's place.

What this means is that, except from House to whom he had given the *entrée*, Wilson did not value advice as such. He was interested only in the grounds for an opinion and not in the fact that it had been formed by a person whose judgement was worthy of respect. He was so little interested in the personality of the self-appointed adviser that he preferred, as Lansing had discovered, to read what he had to say rather than to listen to it. He never even tried discussion with a group (unless receiving the opinions of his Cabinet can be called that) as a means of arriving at a collective decision. House noted on 23 December 1916: 'It is practically impossible to get the President to have a general consultation.'[62]

Wilson, like many men of his sort, really believed that he did take advice. He once told House that he always sought advice. House says that he 'almost laughed at this statement':[63] for he had just been told by McAdoo that when the President got Admiral Mayo's telegram reporting his action in demanding an apology from Huerta, he never even mentioned it to McAdoo who was staying with him at the time. The other members of the Cabinet, House added, all told the same story.

In Berlin, Bethmann in June won the upper hand. Germany, like Britain, was faced with the choice between the unrestricted use of a most powerful weapon and the hostility of the United States. But whereas with Britain the law produced no clear line which she could cross only at her peril, in Germany's case the injection into the controversy of the sacred principles of humanity and the clear demand for the abandonment of the submarine campaign seriously limited her room for manœuvre. Bethmann himself would, if absolutely necessary, have abandoned the campaign. Rightly as it turned out, he assessed the cost of American hostility as too high a price to pay for the submarine blockade. But his power to follow his own choice was conditioned by two factors. First, it was politically impossible to surrender the use of a weapon which the whole of Germany believed to be legitimate and effective. The 'disavowal' for which Wilson asked would be an admission of wrongdoing to be swallowed only in defeat. Formal abandonment of the campaign was virtually out of the question. The second factor upon which Bethmann's power to restrain the use of the submarine depended was a precarious alliance with the military. Falkenhayn, the Chief of the General Staff, had not the same direct fear as Bethmann of American hostility, but he thought that a declaration of war by America would precipitate similar action by European neutrals with armies to put into the field and in 1915 he did not want to run the risk of that. His support for Bethmann therefore depended upon his assessment of the military situation, which was of course variable.

So for the time being Bethmann's hand was strong enough to achieve a limited objective, namely, the conduct of the submarine campaign in such a way as not to create another incident of the same sort—it could hardly be of the same size—as the *Lusitania*. It was not strong enough to win even that much without a fight. The fight with the Navy was still on when the answer to the first *Lusitania* Note was being composed. A few days after its dispatch Bethmann was victorious. On 1 and 6 June 1915 the Kaiser issued two orders to his fleet. The first was that attacks on neutral ships were to cease and commanders were instructed that in case of doubt it was better to let an enemy escape than to sink a neutral. The second and supplementary order said that no large liner, not even an enemy one, was to be sunk. This supplementary order was, as a concession to the Navy, to be kept absolutely secret.

When the second *Lusitania* Note arrived on 11 June Bethmann, concentrating on the practical side of it, planned to meet it by finding some way of giving American transatlantic passengers the sort of accommodation which they evidently desired. Actually there was no difficulty in doing this since it was now settled that large liners were not to be attacked; the question was whether that could be published without loss of prestige. While in the German Foreign Office they were considering various expedients, Gerard volunteered in the manner of Page a helping hand and on 3 and 5 July 1915 he sent to Washington for comment, but without disclosing his own participation, drafts of what was being concocted. It was not that normally he had much sympathy with the German case, but, as he said in his telegram of 5 July:

Anyway, when Americans have reasonable opportunity to cross the ocean why should we enter a great war because some American wants to cross on a ship where he can have a private bathroom or because Americans may be hired to protect by their presence cargoes of ammunition? On land no American sitting on an ammunition wagon could prevent its being fired on on its way to the front and England made land rules applicable to the sea when she set the example of declaring part of the open sea war territory; nor can English passenger ships sailing with orders to ram submarines and often armed be put quite in the category of altogether peaceful merchantmen.[64]

On 8 July 1915 the German Note was delivered.[65] Three-quarters of it was either what Tirpitz rudely called 'ornamental' (references to sacred principles, including 'the lofty idea of freedom of the sea'); or, as Lansing said, 'framed for home consumption',[66] as, for example, this intonation:

> Just as was the case with the Boers, the German people is now to be given the choice of perishing from starvation, with its women and children, or of relinquishing its independence.

The operative part, largely Gerard's contribution, was in the undertaking. German submarines would be instructed to permit the safe passage, if notified in advance, of American liners with special markings, the American Government being confidently expected to see that they carried no contraband. The same protection would be extended to a reasonable number of neutral liners flying the American flag. The Imperial Government could not see why Americans had to travel on enemy liners; but if not enough American and neutral liners were available, it would guarantee safe passage for four enemy liners to be placed under the American flag.

Wilson received the full text of the German reply while he was still at Cornish enjoying a wonderful holiday with his golf and automobile rides in the New Hampshire Hills, and with Mrs. Galt and his family such bliss as a year before he had not expected could ever be his again. 'I have not had such a period of comparative rest and freedom for four years', he wrote to McAdoo.[67] He gave up his afternoon ride to study the text, but he already knew the substance from Gerard's cables. Since House was now back in America he was naturally the first to be consulted and letters went almost daily to and fro between Cornish and Manchester. Wilson decided on two important tactical changes. First he decided to lower his sights from the abandonment of submarine warfare to its conduct in accordance with cruiser rules. Secondly, he decided that he must relax his pressure for verbal admissions. He would state firmly his modified demands and leave Germany to conform by deeds rather than by words. Moreover, he must have decided that he would not scan the seas too closely for signs of non-conformity. Not long after the delivery of the German reply there came news of an attack on 9 July on the *Orduna*. She was a large Cunard liner west-bound from New York with a passenger list of 227 including 21 Americans. The case might have been a minor *Lusitania* but that the torpedo did not find its target. Failure could not affect the principle but it could soften the impact; Wilson allowed the incident to be buried without full diplomatic honours.

Wilson's change of attitude in the third *Lusitania* Note was at least in part a response to the anti-war sentiment in the country. When on 14 July he sent to House as a sample an anti-war letter from a senator,[68] House replied the next day that he had talked with a great many people (who on earth were they?) who without exception expressed a wish for a firmer answer and who, when pressed further, said that the country would be willing to accept the consequences. House could not really have believed this. Only the previous week he had written to Grey:

> The sentiment of the country continues to be clearly against war, and I have serious doubts whether the President would be strongly sustained by Congress in the event he decided upon drastic action, unless, indeed, Germany goes beyond the limit of endurance.[69]

House was here employing one of his favourite tactics, from whose operation not even Wilson was immune, of subjecting two parties in opposition to contrary pressures so as to push them nearer to the spot he had designed as the meeting place: from Wilson he wanted a firmer attitude and from Grey less expectation.

In fact there could be no doubt about anti-war sentiment and as the summer went on House began to appreciate more truly the President's difficulties. Bryan was an active crusader; while he might not get much theoretical support for his pacifism, his practical point about travel was, as Lansing puts it,

> more or less appealing to the average man who is not strongly impressed with the idea that individuals should insist on exercising a legal right when such exercise will cause serious international differences.[70]

This was indeed the hub of the matter. The clothing in the language of high principle of Wilson's demand for the abandonment of submarine warfare obscures somewhat the fact that the demand embodied a sound policy. If it had been conceded, it would have been not only a triumph of principle but also a clean solution, whereas the modified demand for compliance with cruiser rules would be bound to lead to 'incidents'. There seems at first sight a lot of bluff common sense in Houston's line that the President should not try to tell Germany how she should use her submarines so long as she kept to cruiser rules and that America should concentrate on American rights. But if one asked what were the rights to be protected and got the answer, as Gerard put it, 'having a stateroom with a bath', the common sense became less convincing. Yet this was then the attitude of many

Americans. They were unwilling to submit to the indignity of being told how they should travel but very doubtful whether dignity was worth a war. As Wilson wrote to Lansing on 13 July:

> Two things are plain to me, in themselves inconsistent, viz that our people want this thing handled in a way that will bring about a definite settlement without endless correspondence, and that they will expect us not to hasten an issue or so conduct the correspondence as to make an unfriendly issue inevitable.[71]

So Wilson tried to reconcile the inconsistencies by stepping half-way down. House did not disapprove of the change of front. When first asked for advice he had on 10 July hung out some words on the high line ('the soul of humanity cries out against the destruction of the lives of innocent non-combatants, it matters not, etc. . . .':[72] he did not do it nearly as well as Wilson) and in answer to the German denunciation of the hunger blockade had taken the opportunity of rubbing in once more Germany's rejection of the foodstuffs offer. But he also made the practical point:

> Since your first note, the German government has not committed any act against either the letter or the spirit of it; and it may be, even though they protest that they are unable to meet your demands, they may continue to observe them.

It was a shrewd guess at what Germany was then in fact doing and a point that Wilson came to handle cleverly in his draft. House, while not disputing the new policy, had no high hope of its success. He wrote on 13 July:

> The incident will then be closed until Germany commits what we would consider some overt act. I have never changed my opinion as to the inevitable result.[73]

Thus the test of the 'overt act', which played a great part in the last scene of the drama, came into being.

So by the time he got the full text of the German reply on 21 July an outline of his answer was already clear in Wilson's mind and he was able the very next morning to send it to Lansing. The only thing he was doubtful about was the end. What should be the concluding terms of demand, he asked Lansing. Lansing dodged that. Although one might suppose that the language of a diplomatic note should suit its demands rather than vice versa, the reverse process offered Lansing an avenue of escape. His reply deserves embalmment as a specimen of platitudinous non-commitment in full panoply:

> Frankly I am not prepared yet to answer that question. I would prefer to wait until the note is drafted in a tentative form and see what demands would be consistent and appropriate. Of course the demands we make will be the most

difficult part of the note. Is it possible to be firm and at the same time to compromise?

I think that in formulating the demands the possible consequences must be considered with the greatest care. In case of a flat refusal what will happen? In case of counter proposals what then? Should the demands be so worded as to admit of only 'Yes' or 'No' as an answer, or should a loophole be given for counter proposals? Can we take a course which will permit further correspondence? These are the questions which are running through my mind and I have not as yet been able to answer them, I wish more time to consider them.[74]

But he did enclose thirteen memoranda of 'undigested notes' and eight and a half pages of closely reasoned analysis. And he did eventually produce a final paragraph which said that the United States would 'adopt the steps necessary to ensure' respect for American rights.[75] This was an uninspired repetition of the conclusion to the pre-*Lusitania* 'strict accountability' Note. For some reason Wilson thought it had the tone of an ultimatum. Yet he substituted for it the strongest words he had yet used, a reference to deliberate unfriendliness. He took the phrase from the thought he had expressed to House on 14 July: 'They must be made to feel that they must continue in their new way unless they deliberately wish to prove to us that they are unfriendly and wish war.'[76]

The President went to Washington to see the Note settled and sent off and it was dispatched on 21 July.[77] In its final form it was a most adroit shift of position. On 30 June a submarine had stopped a British ship, the *Armenian*, off the coast of Cornwall and after warning had sunk her. Under the principles hitherto expounded this would have called for condemnation. Now Wilson by an oblique reference to it put it forward as an example of the way things could and should be done. The kernel of the third *Lusitania* Note was the statement that it had now been clearly demonstrated that it was possible to conduct the submarine campaign in substantial accord with cruiser rules. So it was manifestly possible to 'lift the whole practice of submarine attack above the criticism which it had aroused and remove the chief causes of offence'.

Gerard's proposals, although they got some backing in the State Department, were firmly turned down: any such agreement would by implication subject other vessels to illegal attack and would be a curtailment of principles 'which in times of calmer counsels every nation would concede as of course'. Concerned with the future more than with the past, Wilson might have glided over the case of the *Lusitania* itself if Lansing had not kept him down to it. Wilson, handling it deftly, used it as a vehicle for his ideas on retaliation. The German Note, while not expressly raising retaliation as a defence, had put forward as the only justification for submarine warfare that it had been obliged to adopt it 'to meet the declared intentions of our enemies and the method of warfare adopted by them in contravention of international law'.[78] In answer to this Wilson stated decisively, and as if it were one of those principles which in times of calmer counsel would be conceded as of course, the American doctrine that the right of retaliation could not be exercised so as to affect neutrals.

Illegal and inhuman acts, however justifiable they may be thought to be against an enemy who is believed to have acted in contravention of law and humanity, are manifestly indefensible when they deprive neutrals of their acknowledged rights, particularly when they violate the right to life itself. If a belligerent cannot retaliate against an enemy without injuring the lives of neutrals, as well as their property, humanity, as well as justice and a due regard for the dignity of neutral powers, should dictate that the practice be discontinued. If persisted in, it would in such circumstances constitute an unpardonable offense against the sovereignty of the neutral nation affected.[79]

So, as Wilson put it,

a belligerent act of retaliation is *per se* an act beyond the law, and the defense of an act as retaliatory is an admission that it is illegal.

And so in view of this admission,

the Government of the United States cannot believe that the Imperial Government will longer refrain from disavowing the wanton act of its naval commander in sinking the *Lusitania*.

After that Wilson went as near as he could in public to offer action against Britain: he invited Germany's co-operation in contending for the freedom of the seas and said that the United States would insist on it 'by whomsoever violated or ignored'. Finally, he limited and concentrated his threat, such as it was, to breaches of cruiser rules involving American lives.

Repetition by the commanders of German naval vessels of acts in contravention of those rights must be regarded by the Government of the United States, when they affect American citizens, as deliberately unfriendly.

The Note was well received in Britain, the general opinion being that it made war inevitable. In Germany it caused great indignation. Gerard had handled the thing clumsily. He had badly misjudged Washington's reaction to his solution. When he cabled the draft of the German Note to Lansing, he said that it was sent 'with the knowledge of friends in the Foreign Office'[80] and that the Note would not be dispatched until he had heard that the plan was acceptable. Nevertheless, in spite of a rebuff from Lansing, he allowed his friends in the Foreign Office to deliver it. They, having naturally supposed that by adopting Gerard's suggestion they were doing just what was wanted, were very upset. So skilfully had Wilson managed his descent from the high horse that the great reduction in his demands was not at first appreciated. The Kaiser, who had a childish habit of scrawling epithets in the margin, emphasized the reaction. 'In tone and bearing this is about the most impudent note which I have ever read since the Japanese note of August last! It ends with a direct threat!'[81]

Part of the new practical diplomacy was to impress upon Bernstorff that America meant business and both House and Lansing were commissioned to talk to him while the Note was still *en route*. Lansing told him on 22 July that America would not continue writing Notes and must receive explicit assurances.[82] Moreover, Lansing had got his teeth into the demand for a *Lusitania* 'disavowal' and was unwilling to leave it alone. Bernstorff in his report home said the demands of the United States were for the *Lusitania* 'a full apology in some form or another' and for the future an undertaking that no passenger ships should be sunk without warning.

After his interview with Bernstorff, Lansing and his wife went off to spend a weekend with the Houses at Manchester. Naturally House would not allow too much time to pass before improving on his brief acquaintance with the new Secretary. House spoke a little of his visit to Europe and the President's hopes of mediation. He himself had now given up any idea of negotiating a peace with Germany on the basis of freedom of the seas or anything else. He thought that Germany's good will was now irrevocably lost and the important thing was not to lose that of the Allies, especially England's, as well. America would have much at stake in the final settlement in which England would, House thought, if the Allies won, be the dominant factor; and it would be unwise to press present differences too hard. He successfully indoctrinated Lansing with a good deal of this. Subsequent events suggest that Lansing's legal conscience may have had some misgivings about not pressing England but on this occasion he did agree with the Colonel that friendly relations must not be seriously endangered. On 22 July House had written in the same vein but more cautiously to Wilson himself. If America pressed hard enough, he said, over the shipping troubles, England would probably yield but her resentment would be felt at the peace conference.[83]

By the end of the month there had been an unexpectedly rapid improvement in German-American relations. Bernstorff writing to House referred ruefully to 'such strong language'[84] in the American Note, but at the same time he was pointing out to his superiors that 'the President has definitely come close to our position, for he now considers the submarine war as legitimate, while he earlier thought that it could not be executed at all according to international law'.

German hope was fed on talk of American action against England. On 24 July Gerard (not without some chagrined comment about his being of no account in Washington) advised that the American Note need not be answered; and in Washington Lansing was letting Bernstorff understand the same thing. Great pleasure was given in Washington when on 30 July in settlement of an ancient dispute over an American merchantman the German Government not only admitted in full their obligation under the ordinary law, but in accordance with the terms of two Prussian-American treaties of the eighteenth century offered to pay compensation for the destruction of an American merchantman even when she was carrying contraband. This sweetened an informal suggestion by Bethmann to Gerard that the question of an indemnity for the *Lusitania* should be referred to arbitration in The Hague. The President, when he heard this, wrote to Lansing on 9 August that he did not think public opinion would allow arbitration 'at present', but he was willing to allow the case to rest.[85] It seemed as if the bright flash of principle had ignited nothing and that the traumatic effect of the *Lusitania* was exhausted.

XI

THE *ARABIC* SETTLEMENT

IN the early days of August the President's mind was occupied with troubles in Mexico and Haiti and these took him to Washington. House in Manchester went on placidly with his unofficial chores. Frank L. Polk—New York lawyer, anti-Tammany Democrat, and close friend to McAdoo—was selected to fill Lansing's former office and presented himself at Manchester as the man 'we had chosen' so as to have 'outlined something of his duties as I imagined Lansing would want them to be'.[1] At the same time House commended him to Lansing as loyal to the core, with a political instinct, and a cultivated gentleman.

House set himself also the task of justifying to his British friends the President's new attitude and lowering the expectations with which he had left them at the end of May. To Lord Bryce he wrote that he wished the British

understood the difficulties under which the President has laboured. I wish they knew with what courage he has resisted all efforts to force him to change our policy in regard to the shipment of munitions of war, and in regard to his treatment of the question of neutral shipping.[2]

Page received a good talking to. He had written to House on 21 July enclosing a pamphlet called *A Merry Ballad of Woodrow Wilson*, and adding his own exegesis.

This thing alone is, of course, of no consequence. But it is symptomatic. There is much feeling about the slowness with which he acts. One hundred and twenty people (Americans) were drowned on the Lusitania and we are still writing notes about it—to the damnedest pirates that ever blew up a ship . . . We are bound to get into the war. For the Germans will blow up more American travellers without notice. And by dallying with them we do not change the ultimate result, but we take away from ourselves the spunk and credit of getting in instead of being kicked and cursed in.[3]

Sapped of its vigour this would not go so very far beyond what House himself thought. But Page must be made to understand the other side of the case.

Sir Edward and you cannot know the true situation here. I did not know it myself until I returned and began to plumb it. 90% of our people do not want the President to involve us in war. They desire him to be firm in his treatment of Germany, but they do not wish him to go to such lengths that war will follow. He went to the very limit in his last note to Germany . . . He sees the situation just as you see it and as I do, but he must necessarily heed the rocks.[4]

Wilson and he, House went on, taking some liberties with facts and probabilities, had heeded the Allies' wishes and but for that could have started peace parleys in November which would have forced the evacuation of France and Belgium and finally forced a peace eliminating militarism both on land and sea. He was sorry, House said, that there was anyone in England who thought so ill of the President as to write the *Merry Ballad*. The Allies had received munitions in unrestricted volume and the President had demanded of Germany a cessation of her submarine policy to the extent of the threat of war. What other neutral nation had done so much? Americans could take care of themselves; it was sympathy that made them help France and England and not the fear of what might follow from their defeat.

The same day, 4 August 1915, House wrote to Wilson suggesting that Page should have thirty or forty days in America. 'The war has gotten on his nerves and he has no idea what the sentiment of the people in this country is in regard to it.'[5] Wilson replied mildly that no doubt Page needed 'a bath in American opinion', but 'is it not after all, rather useful to have him give us the English view so straight'?[6] And Wilson meant this because on 10 September he himself wrote one of his rare letters to Page:

Your letters are of real service to me. They give me what it would not be possible for me to get in any other way, and if it is not too great a tax upon you to write them as often as you do, I hope you will not leave out a single line or item which is interesting your own thought. It is only in this way that I can get the atmosphere, which, after all, is quite as important as the event because it is out of the atmosphere that the event arises.[7]

Wilson was taking more from Page than he would have taken from most of his other servants. This was due in part perhaps to friendship and respect. But after the *Lusitania* he was taking it not as advice intended to influence his judgement but as evidence of what was being thought and said in England; and indeed this is the form in which Page disguised his own views when writing to the President, though not to House. In his letter Wilson inquired after Page's health and suggested a vacation, but he put it too delicately and Page replied that he was very well, that he could not enjoy a vacation, and that House must be forgiven 'his kindly mistaken solicitude'.[8] Thus he escaped for a while the bath in American opinion.

In the first part of August 1915 there was in German-American affairs a stillness such as preceded the sinking of the *Lusitania*. Not tempests but shoals in calm waters seemed to lie ahead and they should be navigable. It was then that the gods that fought against Germany intervened for a second time, choosing as their instruments Geheimrat Dr. Heinrich Albert and Commander Schneider. Of the two the latter was by far the more important for he was the perpetrator of the 'deliberately unfriendly' act. But the impact of that would not have been so formidable if some affliction—Pallas Athene according to Homer often used the weapon of temporary amnesia—had not some weeks before caused the Geheimrat, who was commercial attaché in the German embassy, to leave his brief-case in a Sixth Avenue elevated train when he got off at 50th Street. It had been suspected for some time past that members of the German embassy staff had been engaged in unneutral activities. German reservists had been helped, even to the extent of providing false passports, to return home and supplies had been arranged for German cruisers at sea. The American Government had for the sake of peace taken action only when it had to and had refrained from pressing any charges as far as the embassy itself. But during 1915 evidence had been accumulating that German agents were actively interfering with the delivery of munitions, even to the point of sabotage by the destruction of property, and to stirring up trouble with Mexico in the hope of diverting the supply of munitions from the Allies; and suspicion had been growing that the embassy was not unconcerned.

So it happened that in the same streetcar as Dr. Albert there was a secret service operator who immediately picked up the briefcase and left the car. The Geheimrat, seeing what had happened, rushed in pursuit, but the operator, as was to be expected, was more agile. The documents contained no evidence of sabotage but much evidence of undercover activity, principally by way of subsidizing newspapers and journalists. The documents were sent at once to McAdoo, the secret service being a branch of the Treasury, and about the end of July he took them to Wilson

at Cornish. Wilson told him to consult Lansing and House. After a talk
with House at Manchester on 10 August, it was decided to give the documents to Frank Cobb, the editor of the *New York World*, to use as he
thought fit without disclosing his source. It might lead to war, House
wrote to Wilson, but it would deaden the effect of German propaganda
and weaken such 'agitators' as Bryan. Cobb published the documents
in the *World* in instalments from 15 to 23 August. They aroused great
indignation and were important that summer in giving Wilson a backing
for firm action if he wanted to take it. But the longer-lasting effect of the
incident was to leave the American Government with a settled distrust
of Bernstorff and the suspicion that he was involved in the graver offences.
McAdoo wanted to send him packing. Wilson would not do that; but he
wrote to House on 29 July, about 'the acute difficulty of our own public
opinion, which is being deliberately framed against us. I do not feel that
Bernstorff is dealing frankly with us somehow';[9] and again on 4 August
saying that he was sure that the country was honeycombed with German
intrigue and infested with German spies.

On 19 August 1915 in the usual hunting ground off the south coast of
Ireland Commander Schneider in the U24 sighted a steamer which he took
to be a cargo ship of about 5,000 tons. She was in fact the British White
Star Liner *Arabic* of nearly 16,000 tons westward bound from Liverpool.
The U24 had just sunk a small British freighter by gunfire after her crew
had abandoned ship. The commander, so he wrote in his log, had four
days before been fired on by a large ship. So when he saw the *Arabic* he
decided to submerge and attack her. An hour or so later he torpedoed her
without warning and sank her. There were forty-four casualties, including
two American citizens.

When the news reached Washington Wilson was at the White House
still engaged on Mexican affairs. He sent at once for Lansing. He did not
now need to isolate himself and settle principles. These all cut and
dried. Unless appearances were false this was the deliberate unfriendliness
which everyone, Germany included, had supposed would result in a diplomatic break. Nor had he to fear lack of political support. He felt, rightly
the evidence suggests, that the mood of the country, while always hesitant,
was to leave it to him. Perhaps the thought of his personal power over the
issue of peace and war slightly unnerved him. At any rate he seemed to
recoil from the thought of decision. For public consumption he gave it
out sensibly enough that he would take no action until he had a full report
from the American consul. But although there could be little doubt about

what the report would be, he did not want to discuss the consequences or prepare even provisionally for action. On 21 August he negatived Lansing's suggestion of a Cabinet meeting; all the facts should first be known, he said: haste would give a wrong impression.[10] On the same day he wrote to House a letter which seemed to presage a return to the Bryanist policy of sending strong notes to both sides.

I greatly need your advice what to *do* in view of the sinking of the Arabic, if it turns out to be the simple case it seems . . . Two things are plain to me: one, the people of this country count on me to keep them out of the war; two, it would be a calamity to the world at large if we should be drawn actively into the conflict and so deprived of all disinterested influence over the settlement. We must write to England, and in very definite terms. Do you think that there is any chance of our getting them to rescind the Order-in-Council? . . .[11]

By 22 August he seemed to have become sufficiently clear about what he ought to do to inspire a news report, a course of action by which he did not burn his boats. If the facts were against Germany, there would most likely be a break, the report said; and ended:

It was stated on the highest authority today that the President will act quickly and firmly if the testimony shows that the German Government wantonly disregarded his solemn warning in the last note on the Lusitania tragedy.[12]

House when he got Wilson's letter was rather shocked by the shilly-shallying. He wrote in his diary: 'I am surprised at the attitude he takes. He evidently will go to great lengths to avoid war. He should have determined his policy when he wrote his notes of February, May, June and July.'[13] Not even Wilson's great need of advice could induce House into risking his health in Washington in August; or perhaps he felt that what he had to say might be put more effectively by letter. He wrote on 22 August:

Our people do not want war, but even less do they want to recede from the position you have taken. Neither do they want to shirk the responsibility which should be ours. Your first note to Germany after the sinking of the Lusitania made you not only the first citizen of America, but the first citizen of the world. If by any word or act you should hurt our pride of nationality, you would lose your commanding position overnight.

Further notes would disappoint our own people and would cause something of derision abroad. In view of what has been said and in view of what has been done it is clearly up to this Government to act. The question is when and how?[14]

House then went on to consider the alternatives of breaking off relations, which 'would be the first act of war' or of calling Congress to assume responsibility. All this was clear enough and no one but Wilson could grasp the nettle. But he noted plaintively for Mrs. Galt: 'You see he does not advise: he puts it up to me!'[15]

Into the vacuum created by Wilson's withdrawal from decision thoughts were entering from other quarters as well as from House. Chandler Anderson felt that the third *Lusitania* Note had put the United States on the wrong foot in law. He considered that by abandoning the objection to the submarine campaign as a whole Wilson had as a matter of law implicitly accepted that the campaign was a legitimate reprisal; how then could the United States object if her citizens got hurt in the course of a legitimate reprisal?

This is an odd interpretation of a Note which had insisted expressly and clearly that a reprisal which injured the lives or property of neutrals would be 'an unpardonable offense'.* Nevertheless, on 22 August Anderson seems to have persuaded Lansing that Wilson must be rescued from his 'unfortunate' position;[16] and that the way to do it was to go back to the idea of complete abandonment and seek to achieve it, no longer by simple demand and exhortation which had failed, but by persuading Bernstorff that Germany's best course was to become completely sheep-like and so to leave Britain as the only goat for America to argue with. Lansing told Anderson to put this to Bernstorff, which he did at the Ritz-Carlton at New York on the following day. Bernstorff liked the idea and said he would draft a message to Berlin for Lansing to approve before it went.

Plainly what attracted Bernstorff to the idea was not so much the amenities of the sheepfold as the prospect of the other goat being herded into it. The draft he prepared and sent to Lansing on 24 August made no mention of Germany giving up submarine warfare; on the contrary it said that that was not the idea. The suggestion, as Bernstorff was prepared to pass it on, was that

we should refrain from attacking passenger ships without warning pending negotiations, which would put the burden on England to refrain from unlawful blockade pending negotiations.[17]

What was unsaid but clearly implied was that it would be America's business as the go-between in the negotiation to see that Britain's burden was not left unshouldered.

On 25 and 26 August messages from Berlin arrived which made it clear that if the reports on the *Arabic* case were true the submarine's action would be disavowed. Moreover, in his talk with Gerard Jagow let the cat out of the bag.[18] He said that if the torpedoing was as reported, it was

* See p. 313 above.

contrary to instructions. What instructions, Gerard asked; and thus the secret order that large liners were not to be torpedoed without warning came out.

This relieved the tension and also strengthened Lansing's hand. When he saw Bernstorff on 26 August he did not object to the way Bernstorff had turned Anderson's offer;[19] he could hardly have done so since it was the logical development of Wilson's offer to co-operate in the third *Lusitania* Note. But he said that negotiations would not begin until the *Arabic* incident was settled satisfactorily and that he would not wait long for an explanation. Bernstorff agreed to add this to his message which he sent off on 27 August. At some stage Wilson was of course told of the talks with Bernstorff though presumably not that they were originally designed as a rescue operation. Apart from that he would undoubtedly have approved, partly because he approved of talks anyway and partly because they were tending to a solution based on a protest to Britain which his letter to House shows that he himself had in mind. He certainly approved Lansing's written report of the interview of 26 August, penning on it for Mrs. Galt the delighted comment: 'Don't you think Lansing does these things well?'[20]

As it turned out Anderson's intervention was unnecessary and probably its only effect was to raise Germany's hopes about the prospect of a deal. The Foreign Office in Berlin was almost as outraged by the sinking as the State Department. It appeared to be a clear sign of the Navy's insubordination to the orders which Bethmann had wrested from the Kaiser in June. In both cases, that is, the *Orduna* (not yet buried) and the *Arabic*, the liners were westbound so that there could be no question of traffic in contraband or even of blockade. 'Unhappily, it depends upon the attitude of a single submarine commander whether America will or will not declare war', Bethmann wrote to the Chief of the Naval Cabinet on 25 August.[21]

The Chancellor had now acquired a useful ally outside the Foreign Office. He was Karl Helfferich, at this time at the Treasury and later to be made Vice-Chancellor, an academic economist with a first-rate mind that worked on practical affairs and made him a shade too pleased with himself (after all he had not a 'von') to make many friends in government circles. He was not against the submarine as a commerce destroyer—no German was—but he thought that it must not be used in a way that would bring the United States into the war. Once there, he said, she would finance the Allies for ever and in a war of exhaustion they would win. The right way to use the submarine, he considered, was to trade it with the United States in exchange for her intervention against the British blockade. He had written a powerful memorandum to this effect on 5 August. Bethmann now proceeded on these lines. He demanded a quick report on the facts of the *Arabic* incident, saying that the only solution was complete acceptance of cruiser rules, the order to that effect to be communicated to Washington with an admission of liability for the *Lusitania* as well as the *Arabic*, and with a request that in return America should start negotiations with England to put the war at sea on the basis of the Declaration of London. He himself took action by sending to Washington the soothing messages of 25 and 26 August.

The Navy fought these proposals as they had fought the last and again they were defeated, this time with slaughter. Tirpitz was snubbed by a temporary withdrawal of the special rights given to him on the outbreak of war:* Admiral Bachmann, who had succeeded von Pohl as Chief of the Naval Staff, was dismissed: the Kaiser found his outspokenness displeasing.

Falkenhayn's influence was decisive. He was then planning an offensive against Serbia based on an alliance with Bulgaria and Bethmann's negotiations with the Bulgarians were at a delicate stage. This was the immediate worry. But it was only a facet of the whole military situation and Falkenhayn's assessment of that was prescient and gloomy. He was not seduced by Germany's enormous successes in the east—Warsaw had fallen on 9 August and with the conquest of Poland Germany had got as far as she wanted—from his belief that fundamentally the war was one of exhaustion. He wrote:

There can be no more doubt that our enemies, after realizing that they cannot defeat Germany with weapons, will now try to reach their goal by a war of exhaustion. It will be up to us to prevent this with military measures. It is doubtful if we can succeed, but I most firmly hope that we can. At any rate, our situation is so serious that it would be irresponsible to make it worse. An open allying of the United States on the side of our enemies would mean just such a worsening, and a very serious worsening, indeed. Aside from all the immediate effects on public opinion in Germany and on our economic life during the war and afterward, it would bring a chilling of our relations with all the states that have so far been neutral—Holland, Sweden, Denmark, Switzerland, Bulgaria, Greece, and Roumania. In order to break this war of exhaustion, we need the help of the neutrals.

If, therefore, the responsible leader of German policy makes demands regarding the conduct of submarine war in order to maintain peace with the United States, then according to my conviction there is no other choice but to oblige him, unless one could prove that the assumption that the United States would go to war was wrong.[22]

Bethmann's offer to Washington did not go as far as the course with

---

* See p. 190 above.

which he had threatened the Navy. He put the offer under three heads in his instructions to Bernstorff. First, an offer of arbitration for the *Lusitania* and 'perhaps' the *Arabic*; the award was not to cover the legality of the submarine campaign. Secondly, passenger liners would be sunk only after warning; Bernstorff was authorized to widen the term 'liner' to 'passenger ship' but not to include enemy freighters. Further he was to say that if England abused the concession, for example, by protecting her freighters with single American passengers, there would have to be further talks. Thirdly, efforts were expected from America to re-establish the freedom of the seas and Germany would co-operate. If these were successful she would conduct the submarine war only in accord with the Declaration of London; otherwise, she reserved the right of decision.

These instructions were sent on 28 August. They fitted in quite well with the proposals made in the dispatch which Bernstorff had telegraphed on the same day, except that they said nothing about the settlement of the *Arabic* itself, which Lansing had made a condition precedent to all further discussion. In this connection Lansing had also demanded to be told officially—what he already knew unofficially through Gerard—what instructions the commander of the *Arabic* had. On 30 August Bernstorff sent a telegram in hopeful terms but emphasizing this crucial point:

It is not so much a matter of making apologies or giving explanations, but rather of making a full statement to this Government as to the instructions given to our submarine commanders. If we can prove by this means that after the *Lusitania* incident, orders had been given to attack no passenger ships while negotiations with the United States were going on, or to do so only under certain conditions, all outstanding questions could be solved without difficulty.[23]

Bethmann replied at once that he could not deal with the facts of the *Arabic* because the submarine concerned had not yet returned to port, but he authorized Bernstorff to tell Lansing confidentially that for several months submarine commanders had had orders not to attack large liners without warning, that the orders had now been modified to include all passenger ships and would remain in force for the duration of the negotiations. At this delicate stage of the affair Gerard refused to transmit Bethmann's message. This was a bit of privateering on his part in a reprisal for the failure of the Kaiser to grant him an audience; he was being treated worse than American newspaper correspondents, he said. So the dispatch had to be sent via Stockholm and did not arrive until 1 September. Bernstorff took it immediately to Lansing. But the Secretary said firmly that it would not do: the statement must be public, not confidential. Bernstorff took the plunge. He gave Lansing for publication the letter which contained the '*Arabic* pledge'.

Liners will not be sunk by our submarines without warning and without safety of the lives of non–combatants, provided that the liners do not try to escape or offer resistance.[24]

For this clear breach of his instructions Bernstorff later received a mild reprimand. As he says, there was no sense in imposing confidence; the nature of the orders to submarines was already known unofficially and would have been all over Washington in a matter of days. Perhaps more significant was the fact that Bernstorff omitted the qualification that the 'pledge' was 'pending negotiations'. Without this qualification it could be said to be a complete climb down and was hailed as that in America. But Germany was not entirely without consolation; on 7 September her alliance with Bulgaria was satisfactorily concluded.

Almost at once it began to look as if rejoicings were premature. The bells had been rung, both in the press and in official circles, on the assumption that within days, as soon as Germany had her own report of the *Arabic* incident, a disavowal would be forthcoming. On 3 September Bernstorff wrote to Lansing to say that the only submarine which could have sunk the *Arabic* had not yet returned to port.[25] The laconic communication left room for the suspicion that perhaps she was very conveniently not going to return at all. As early as 25 August Wilson, as he told House, had begun to suspect that Bernstorff's request that judgement be suspended until the German side of the case was forthcoming was merely sparring for time until their plans in the Balkans matured. Did House think this too far-fetched a suspicion?[26]

Then on 4 September a violent explosion shattered the British liner *Hesperian* and eight persons were killed; there was one American on board, a member of the crew, who was unhurt. The ship's officers were sure that steel fragments on the deck came from a torpedo and not a mine. Suspicion was heavy until 23 September when the German Foreign Office declared that they could say with certainty that no submarine was operating in the area.[27] Even then the State Department was not entirely satisfied; and rightly not. It was not revealed until after the war, but in fact it had been a bid to re-enter history by Commander Schweiger of the U20, he who sank the *Lusitania*; he said that he thought the *Hesperian*, which was armed with a 6-in. gun astern, was an auxiliary cruiser.

Worst of all there were on 6 September shocking revelations about

Baron Dumba, the Austrian ambassador, which implicated the German embassy as well. When a Dutch liner called at Falmouth on 30 August the British arrested an American journalist called Archibald who was on his way to Berlin and Vienna and whom they knew from messages they had intercepted to be in German pay. Among the documents in his possession there was a memorandum addressed to Dumba with a plan for stimulating by bribery and otherwise strikes in American munition factories. There was attached to it an enthusiastic letter from Dumba to the Austrian Foreign Minister: there were good prospects, he said, of disorganizing production in Bethlehem and the Middle West, if not of entirely preventing it, and the German military attaché thought this to be of great importance. The attaché was von Papen, he who twenty years later became Chancellor of the Reich and then served under Hitler. There were other unfortunate letters, one from Dumba describing the President as 'self-willed' and another from Papen to his wife which talked of 'imbecile yankees'.[28] Papen's connection with the affair was, as Bernstorff says in his memoirs, 'very compromising for us'. Moreover, Bernstorff was himself known to be well acquainted with Archibald. On 19 August, a day doubly unfortunate for Germany for it was also the day the *Arabic* was torpedoed, Bernstorff and Dumba had both been dining quite openly with Archibald on the roof terrace of the Ritz-Carlton. This was the very occasion on which Dumba gave him the documents to take back to Vienna. Bernstorff, as he says in effect, was too spry to entrust Archibald with any papers from him. The British gave to Ambassador Page the documents they had seized and sent a copy of Dumba's letter to the press. The President, acting at once, demanded Dumba's recall on 9 September. He would have liked to have had Bernstorff, whom he felt sure was implicated, recalled as well. But the evidence against him was thin and, as Wilson wrote to House, it would be hard to ask for his recall without giving the impression of a diplomatic breach.

At last on 9 September 1915 the German Note on the *Arabic*, looked forward to as a simple disavowal, arrived. It was very unsatisfactory.[29] The U24 had in fact got home on 26 August. It was not until six days later that Commander Schneider put in his report. According to the Note the commander was just about to sink by gunfire the abandoned freighter when he observed the *Arabic*. Altering course, she made directly for him, thus leading him to suppose that she was about to attack and ram. So he dived and fired the torpedo which struck her.

No one who had called for the log of the submarine could believe this. The story in it* was quite different; and in particular said not a word

* See p. 319 above.

about the attempted ramming. The commander knew that he was forbidden to torpedo without warning except in case of flight or resistance. If he had really thought there had been an attempt to ram, it is inconceivable that he would not have recorded it in his log. No doubt when he learnt that his original story would not give satisfaction, he allowed his imagination to amplify it. Evidently the German Foreign Office preferred to believe the second version. It was perhaps politically impossible for them to challenge, even interdepartmentally, the word of a naval officer, let alone to repudiate it in public. Possibly also they were misled by the last sentence of Bernstorff's Note of 30 August* into thinking that what America primarily wanted was the pledge for the future. Whatever the reason, their Note of 9 September was, to say the least, offhand. After saying that the action of the *Arabic* undoubtedly gave the commander good grounds for supposing that an attack on him was intended, it rejected liability even on the hypothesis that he was mistaken. If the American Government disagreed, the dispute could be referred to The Hague Tribunal, subject to the reservation that the award was not to touch upon the legality or otherwise of German submarine warfare.

Even without the advantage of seeing the log, Wilson and Lansing disbelieved the German story. It was contrary to all the evidence from the *Arabic*. Then on 10 September they were disturbed by a dispatch from Gerard giving the opinion of the American naval attaché (which in fact was quite erroneous) that the German Note was the result of a new situation in which the Navy had subdued the Foreign Office. They felt that Bernstorff had led them up the garden path and that, as Lansing wrote to Wilson on 11 September, 'the Bernstorff statement of principle is valueless'.[30] Lansing advised an open demand for the disavowal and punishment of the commander, failure to comply to be treated as 'deliberate unfriendliness' and to result in a diplomatic breach: 'continued discussion of this subject would, I believe, be contrary to the dignity of the United States'.

Wilson decided that Germany should be given a last chance in private before the public threat. Meanwhile Bernstorff, startled out of his summer residence in Long Island by the angry press comment, sought an interview with Lansing. The Secretary received him on 13 September and found him extremely docile, with none of the aggressiveness he sometimes showed, but doubtful of what he could accomplish.[31] The result was that Bernstorff sent home an alarming cable. Lansing gave him permission to cable in cipher direct through the State Department without the message being overlooked. The German Note, Bernstorff told his chief, had been taken

* See p. 324 above.

as a manifestation of bad faith, a sign that Germany, though she gave way in principle, would in practice evade her obligations. He reported Lansing as convinced that the submarine commander was not acting in self-defence; the evidence had been forwarded to Gerard. If, Bernstorff advised, Germany maintained that the commander was only obeying orders, there was no hope of agreement; and if no agreement, there would be a severance of relations.

Both Wilson and Lansing gave 'off the record' interviews to the press briefing them for a probable crisis; Wilson was not going to hedge, the papers said, even if it meant war. While he waited for the answer Wilson found the anxiety very wearing. He had no confidence, he wrote to a friend, that Germany would yield sufficiently. The heat in Washington was intense and his nerves were frayed. His marginal notes for Mrs. Galt were becoming almost as petulant as the Kaiser's. 'I wish they would hand this idiot his passports', he wrote of Gerard;[32] and in another he noted that he was an ass.

The Foreign Office in Berlin was quite astounded by the reaction in the American press and by Bernstorff's report which arrived on 16 September. Bethmann and Jagow were willing to go very far indeed to keep the peace but not to the point of publicly expressing their disbelief of the commander's tale. Bernstorff was instructed to say that, while the good faith of the commander could not be doubted, if it was proved that he had exceeded his instructions, Germany would pay an indemnity out of friendliness. On 18 September Jagow called the Berlin correspondent of the Associated Press to his office so as to publicize his hopes of and belief in a settlement. Surely, he said, there could be an honest difference of opinion about the facts? How could the Foreign Office go behind the report of the commander or do more than agree to arbitrate? He was confident that there would be no further incidents, Jagow said; mistakes could not be eliminated entirely in war but every precaution had been taken. This last was no more than the truth. Bernstorff had concluded his report with the grim sentence that there was no doubt that a second *Arabic* case would mean war; and a top secret order had on 18 September 1915 been given to the fleet that all submarine activity in the Western Approaches, i.e. the approaches to the Channel and the Irish Sea, was to cease. By the end of September the first submarine campaign had, except in the Mediterranean, come to an end.

Bernstorff, anxiously awaiting his further instructions, went on 16 September to see House who had now got as far south as Long Island.[33] His main trouble, he told House, was in getting his people to believe that Wilson was in earnest. He thought he might get Berlin to say that they believed the submarine commander was mistaken. House told him to get Berlin to go as far as he could and then he, House, would find out un-officially whether it was acceptable. House impressed on him also that while the people as a whole were averse to war, they trusted the President's judgement and he was sure that they would sustain him, however far he went.

House duly reported to Wilson who wrote back on 20 September express-ing his continuing distrust. He feared that when Germany had gained the time she needed, in the Balkans, for example, she would resume her old ways and they would be back where they started. Without an explicit disavowal of the *Arabic* offence, any general avowal of a better purpose was untrustworthy.[34]

Lansing went away on a short vacation, a fact which gave Bernstorff, across whose mind optimism and pessimism were always chasing each other, great relief. The heat in Washington had subsided enough for House to venture there. He found the President firm and even belligerent. He wrote in his diary on 22 September:

much to my surprise, he said he had never been sure that we ought not to take part in the conflict and, if it seemed evident that Germany and her militaristic ideas were to win, the obligation upon us was greater than ever.[35]

On 26 September Bernstorff called on House in New York to give him the gist of the instructions which had been dispatched to him on 17 Sep-tember.[36] This was the offer of arbitration and the friendly indemnity: it was not the disavowal that had been demanded. He asked House if this was satisfactory: if not, should he consult Berlin at once or wait until Lansing got back to Washington? House passed this on to the President who replied that he, Wilson, would wait until 2 October when Bernstorff could see Lansing in New York and that Bernstorff had better take it for granted that disavowal would be insisted on. Passing this on to Lansing, Wilson wrote: 'You will know better than I can as yet just what line to take with the Ambassador when you see him.'[37]

While Bernstorff was waiting to see Lansing his final instructions were being formulated in Berlin. They were sent on 27 September and he got them on 28 September. The Foreign Office had completed its investiga-tion, the dispatch said, and had no doubt that the commander believed the *Arabic* intended to ram and had every reason for such belief. Affidavits in support were being sent at once. However, the German Government would not disbelieve the evidence of the *Arabic* and so would agree that in reality no such intention existed. The attack of the submarine was thus unfortunately not in accordance with instructions and a communication to that effect would be made to the commander. The offer of a friendly indemnity was repeated.

This would surely be enough for anyone with any willingness to compromise, but it was not in terms a disavowal. It represented, the dispatch said, the limit of possible concessions. Bernstorff used it as the basis of a formal Note which he gave to Lansing at the Hotel Biltmore in New York on 2 October. The meeting was brief, Lansing, as was to be expected, reserving judgement. He took the Note to Washington and Wilson and he discussed it in the evening of 3 October. The American Government, Wilson agreed, 'could not accept a note of that sort'.[38]

Wilson was now getting himself into an extremely dangerous, if not almost impossible, position. He had got a clear agreement about how Germany was to behave in future. Was he going to go to war because Germany had not behaved in the past as she had promised to do in the future? This for a man of peace would be surprising, even if it were established that Germany had in fact so behaved. But there was a dispute about the facts, apparently a genuine dispute, in which Germany had submitted her evidence and offered arbitration. Did Wilson think the dispute irrelevant: would he, if the award had found that the commander did honestly although erroneously believe that he was about to be rammed, still have thought the incident an occasion for war? Or believing the dispute to be relevant, did he prefer to solve it by war rather than by arbitration? Would he go to war because the indemnity he claimed was offered *ex gratia* instead of with an admission of liability? A possible course perhaps when the denial of liability suggests a likelihood of repetition but hardly when it is accompanied by an undertaking to the contrary. What had happened to change the hesitancy and indecision at the beginning of the crisis into the firm and almost foolhardy stance at the end?

There are many men about whom such a question would not need to be asked. There are negotiators who know intuitively when they have got their adversary on the run and when they can be bold, even to the point of bluffing, without being rash. For such men the temptation to seize the favourable moment and settle once and for all and triumphantly an issue that would otherwise float around in the doldrums of arbitration might be irresistible. But Wilson with his patience and caution and anxiety to keep out of war was not at all of that type. He was quite unused to bluffing and would have found the art repugnant. There is nothing to indicate that in this case he was bluffing. So far as the evidence goes (it rests on Lansing's report to House of the meeting on 3 October) Wilson said simply that the Note would not do at all, not that it was good enough but that they might as well try for something better.

There are two things to be considered before speculating further. One is that an offer of arbitration would not appeal to Wilson unless he was himself uncertain about what he wanted to do. At first sight it is astonishing that the man who so frequently insisted that he must know all the facts before he could safely reach a decision should not have welcomed their ascertainment by impartial inquiry at The Hague; and that he who proclaimed justice and not national gain as the object of American policy should treat at all lightly the processes by which justice is commonly made manifest. But Wilson, though he had learnt the trade of law and even practised it for a year, had not absorbed so much as a modicum of an idea of what the processes of justice had to do with justice itself. The dictum that justice must not only be done but must be seen to be done would, if he ever heard of it, have meant little to him. The process of trial and argument whereby the truth is beaten out of the evidence in an arena where all can see it and which thus fashioned bears a mark that makes it also what is known and believed to be the truth, all this was outside his experience. Justice was for him a cloistered virtue to be practised in the study, if not completely in solitude then certainly not as part of a public brawl. He did not think it necessary, as he was sadly to prove at Versailles, to hear and examine what the other side *wanted* to say. Given the material which he required, he himself was the artificer of justice. Even when party to the cause he did not doubt that he could be impartial. So when he had seen what he wanted to see, he made up his mind; and when he had made up his mind, what was the use of arbitration? He was then so sure that he was right (as indeed in this instance he was) that he could not conceive of his decision being sincerely questioned.

But what makes the great difference in his treatment of the two parts of the *Arabic* crisis (and this is the second factor to be considered) is that between them he had come to the conclusion that Germany, and Bernstorff in particular, were not to be trusted. He saw the Note of 7 September as a dishonest attempt to wriggle out of the settlement made on 1 September. This is shown clearly enough in the letters and comments already quoted. He had an emotional repugnance to dealing with people he did not trust. In part no doubt this was due to a praiseworthy dislike of trickery and bad faith, but it may also have been due to a less praiseworthy animosity against people who could suppose that he was a man to be outwitted. Bernstorff and the Germans he represented were now being given a touch of the brush with which Wilson had tarred Huerta the Mexican and the Princeton troublemakers. He had written of Huerta that he was slippery and like quicksilver. On 15 September he wrote to a friend that the Germans 'do not know how to keep faith with anybody and we are walking on quicksand'.[39] The suspicion of German treachery lit a flame which was not extinguished with the passing of the crisis. The remark made on 22 September which so surprised House did not spring from momentary exasperation. It was a change of mood which under the stimulus of House became a change of policy.

The foregoing may help to explain why Wilson was not in early October the patient and long-suffering statesman he had been for the preceding five months; but it is not a sufficient explanation of how it came that he was ready to run such a considerable risk of either a political or a diplomatic débâcle. House and Lansing both believed that war was desirable as well as inevitable sooner or later. House believed that the American people would now follow where Wilson led. Lansing, although not a professional politician, seemed now to think that he owed it to the political character of his office to dabble a little in thoughts about what the people would do; but he could not be expected to feel the weight of any responsibility in the matter. On 24 August at the beginning of the crisis he had written to Wilson a significant letter. In view of the probability that relations would be severed, he had been considering, he wrote, the effect of war upon the part America would play in a peace settlement. She had hoped to occupy the position of a mutual friend, acting as an intermediary to open negotiations and as a restraint upon both parties. But as the war progressed he had become more and more convinced that America was losing the friendship of both. He thought that she had lost irretrievably any influence over Germany and that her attitude was misunderstood in Great Britain. If there was war with Germany there would be a complete restoration of friendship and confidence with the Allies and she would be in a position to influence them towards leniency in their demands. Thus her usefulness in the restoration of peace—the letter was written by Lansing with his eye on Wilson's ambition to be a peacemaker—would not be lessened by war and might even be increased. He did not know what effect war would have upon the American people but was convinced it would not arouse very much enthusiasm. 'Beyond this', he concluded weightily, 'I do not wish at the present time to express an opinion.'[40]

But Wilson, unlike his advisers, had not yet come to think that war on the side of the Entente was desirable; and even if he had thought it was desirable and inevitable as well, he was much more attentive than they to the need for carrying the people with him. How could he do that unless there was some piece of intolerable behaviour which roused the nation as well as himself? He could not lead the nation into war simply because he himself had come to distrust Germany. She had not as yet openly broken faith; he could not say that an offer to arbitrate instead of the submission he wanted was a breach of faith.

But it is unlikely that Wilson felt that he had to estimate the political risk involved because it seems so improbable, especially when one considers his hesitations in February and March 1917, that in October 1915 he seriously intended to push matters to a breach. But then was he not running a grave diplomatic risk if he appeared to reject what Germany said was her last word and it was in fact her last word and then he had to accept it? Even though it was all done in secret, he would lose his strongest diplomatic weapon against Germany, which was Bernstorff's belief that he meant what he said. Perhaps the answer is that Lansing from the first had wanted to be tough and Wilson was now in the mood to give Lansing his head. Historians can only ask the questions which (as will be seen) Count von Bernstorff, by exceeding his instructions, has for ever prevented them from answering.

What is certain is that whether it was bluff or not, Lansing put on a most determined front. The press was briefed to say that the Note of 2 October was unacceptable and that a final refusal by Germany might bring about a breach; and Lansing telegraphed to Bernstorff, who had gone back to Long Island, to come at once. The interview took place at the State Department on 5 October at 10.30 a.m.[41] Lansing said that the President and he were agreed that the Note offered was unsatisfactory. First, the acceptable statement that the commander acted contrary to his instructions was apparently contradicted by the statement that he had good reasons for doing so. Secondly, although a disavowal might be implied, it was not frankly stated; the word 'regret' was used. Thirdly, the American Government would not accept an indemnity as an act of grace. Lansing then gave him the Note with the necessary changes pencilled in. Bernstorff said he would return to his embassy to examine his instructions to see if they were broad enough to permit the changes and would send back a new Note within the hour. Of course they were not broad enough. But Bernstorff was completely convinced, the more so perhaps because Lansing had left the threat to be inferred from his manner instead of putting it into words, that if Germany did not comply it would mean war. By 12.15 p.m. he had sent back the amended Note which read:

The orders issued by His Majesty the Emperor to the commanders of the German submarines—of which I notified you on a previous occasion—have been made so stringent that the recurrence of incidents similar to the *Arabic* case is considered out of the question.

According to the report of Commander Schneider of the submarine that sank the *Arabic* and his affidavit as well as those of his men, Commander Schneider was convinced that the *Arabic* intended to ram the submarine. On the other hand, the Imperial Government does not doubt the good faith of the affidavits of the British officers of the *Arabic*, according to which the *Arabic* did not intend to ram the submarine. The attack of the submarine, therefore, was undertaken against the instructions issued to the commander. The Imperial Government regrets and disavows this act and has notified Commander Schneider accordingly.

Under these circumstances my Government is prepared to pay an indemnity for the American lives which, to its deep regret, have been lost on the *Arabic*. I am authorized to negotiate with you about the amount of this indemnity.[42]

This time Bernstorff did not get off so lightly. Through an oversight in the State Department his telegram to Berlin reporting the settlement was not sent off and Bethmann read the terms in the London press. In giving the pledge Bernstorff had not made it conditional (as he had been told to do) on British behaviour; and now he had committed the forbidden act of disavowal. As to the first, Bernstorff protested that he had always reserved freedom of action for Germany if England did not come half-way; as to the second, he could only persist in saying that any other course 'would infallibly have led us into a new war'.[43] For the Foreign Office the second was the more serious because of its repercussions on the Navy, aggravated by Bernstorff's carelessness in mentioning Schneider's name. But the Foreign Office was in a jam. It could and did severely reprimand Bernstorff in private but his recall or any published censure would have been taken as a repudiation of the settlement. Jagow sought a way out by sending on 30 October a formal Note to Lansing expressly approving the settlement and impliedly disapproving its terms.[44] The new Note did this by following its expression of approval with a recitation from the old Note before it was amended. 'I may therefore', Jagow said blandly, 'repeat Count Bernstorff's statement that the attack of the submarine, to our regret, was not in accordance with the instructions issued, and that the commander has been *notified** accordingly.' The indemnity would be paid out of friendly consideration.

A month earlier this would have been received in Washington, and with justification, as new and overwhelming proof of German untrustworthiness. Perhaps it did have its influence on Wilson's growing anti-German sentiment. But by then the triumph had been celebrated and all the heat had gone out of the crisis. The Note remained unanswered.

For the American public the *Arabic* settlement was the culminating act in the successful repulse of the first assault upon their country's neutrality.

* Italics inserted.

She could now return to her seat at the ringside, perhaps not quite as neutral in thought as she had been in August 1914 but still as determined as ever to maintain neutrality in action. Yet there were now, beneath the surface, a number of important men who thought otherwise. Within the Administration they included, as we have seen, House and Lansing and several of the Cabinet. On the Republican side the two most influential in foreign affairs were Senators Root and Lodge. Senator Root, though cautious, non-committal, and for long neutral in action, had never been neutral in thought. His hopes, he wrote to Bryce on 23 September 1914, were 'pinned upon the success of your arms'.[45] Had he still been Secretary of State, he told another friend, he would have protested over Belgium. When after the *Lusitania* Lansing sent Anderson on 15 May to find out what the elder statesman thought, he returned an oracular answer that seemed to favour vigorous action.[46] Senator Lodge was by nature pro-British, anti-German, and anti-Wilson. He said in August 1914, and no doubt sincerely believed that he favoured an 'honest neutrality',[47] but what was pro-British was much more likely to appeal to his sense of honesty than what was pro-German. He was seeing Spring Rice constantly. Like Root he felt that there ought to have been a protest over Belgium and he was contemptuous of Wilson's inaction from the *Gulflight* onwards. He believed, he wrote in his memoirs, that if Wilson had gone to war over the *Lusitania* he would have had more support than in 1917. He was friendly with Dean Andrew West of Princeton and had no respect for Wilson. He wrote about him in October 1912:

A man can change one or two of his opinions for his own advantage and change them perfectly honestly, but when a man changes all the well considered opinions of a lifetime and changes them all at once for his own popular advantage it seems to me that he must lack in loyalty of conviction.[48]

But neither Root nor Lodge spoke out against the President. They had come out against him on the Ship Purchase Bill and defeated him. But on what was pure foreign policy there was an unwillingness to create a discordance. Lodge especially

held very strongly the opinion that in a matter of foreign relations it is our duty always to stand by the President of the United States just so far as it is possible to do so without violating one's convictions.[49]

Former President Taft was more sympathetic to the President.[50] He gave for use in the mid-term elections on 3 November 1914 a commendation of the stand Wilson had taken on neutrality. He wrote to Wilson on 10 May doubting whether war was the necessary answer to the *Lusitania* outrage. He publicly approved the first *Lusitania* Note and said privately that

Roosevelt was making an ass of himself. The *Arabic* settlement gave him another chance for a dig at his rival. He wrote to a friend on 3 September that Teddy was 'deeply grieved over the fact that Wilson seems to have won a substantial victory in his stand with Germany'.[51]

Roosevelt was the only man of the first rank to hurl himself against the President. His initial neutrality in August 1914 was genuine enough but well before the sinking of the *Lusitania* he had come to regret it. He was neither anti-British nor anti-German; he had found much to admire in both nations and had friends in both. He was especially fond of Grey, 'one of the finest fellows I have ever met'[52] (perhaps their common love of wild life had something to do with that), but thoroughly disapproved of Asquith, 'fundamentally the Wilson type'. He was not entirely repelled by the invasion of Belgium. The act divided his emotions. He was attracted by the spectacle of ruthless might and by the sentiment that the prize should go to the strong and the determined, that there was a penalty to be paid for weakness and that necessity knows no law. Perhaps if the thing had been done chivalrously, as a strong man might set aside a woman who blocked his path, and amends made thereafter, he would have accepted it. But when it presented itself to him as the act of a bully it aroused his loathing. It was not in his nature to protest in words and not in deeds; a man who was not ready to hit ought to hold his tongue. After some months he began to persuade himself that if he had been President, he would have made a protest and backed it with force. Although he warned his British friends against pressing America too hard with their blockade, he would not protest about it because it was 'ignoble to protest against the seizure of copper and not against the violation of Belgium'.[53] There are two passages taken from letters he wrote in December 1914 which show how his ideas were taking shape. The first was to Dr. Dernburg who sought his sympathy for Germany's intention to absorb Belgium economically and with territorial guarantees.

Now, my dear Dr. Dernburg, this is simply a frank avowal that there is no such thing as international morality . . . I understand entirely the great difficulties of Germany's position with France on one side and Russia on the other. But I do not and cannot accept and I never shall accept the German theory of international morality.[54]

He expressed the essence of his creed when he wrote that a nation

should fearlessly and where possible effectively take action against wrongdoing; that it should prepare itself so as to make it unsafe for any other nation to do wrong to it; and that in its turn it should scrupulously do justice to every nation that acts rightly.[55]

And by February he was beginning to think that there could be no neutrality between right and wrong. At the end of a long dictated letter to Strachey, the editor of the *Spectator*, he added a postscript in his own hand:

> More and more I come to the view that in a really tremendous world struggle, with a great moral issue involved, neutrality does not serve righteousness; for to be neutral between right and wrong is to serve wrong.[56]

So when the wrongdoer turned to provoke America, there should be no faltering. He had not to wait for the shock of the *Lusitania*. Over the *Gulflight* he thought that Wilson and Bryan had behaved with 'abject cowardice'.[57] When he got the news of the sinking of the *Lusitania*, he did not himself hesitate though it came for him at an awkward moment. It was in the middle of a libel action at Syracuse in which he was the defendant.[58] He was having his 'bad moments' because the judge, although 'a thoroughly upright man', was 'excessively legalistic' and had ruled out all his most important evidence. There were two German-Americans on the jury. A cautious man would have kept his thoughts on Germany to himself until after the verdict. Roosevelt spoke out at once: 'Piracy on a vaster scale of murder than old time pirates ever practised . . . Warfare against innocent men, women and children.' 'Too proud to fight' he called 'the nadir of cowardly infamy.'[59]

In this spirit he entered upon his last great fight which finished only with his death two months after the end of the war. His energy was stupendous. In articles, speeches, and pages of letters he poured out his convictions, setting for his countrymen, as his biographer has written, 'an unparalleled example of intolerance and hatred, of duty and devotion, and of high resolute courage'.[60]

But Roosevelt was out of tune. In the American press the extravagance of praise that had greeted the first *Arabic* victory was renewed upon the second. 'A divinely appointed leader.'[61] 'Laurelled with victory.' 'A tremendous moral victory.' On 6 October 1915 House wrote to Page that it was 'the greatest diplomatic triumph of this generation'.[62] But Page was not impressed.

Some of Wilson's admirers looked only at the beginning and at the end. The dialogue had begun with the demand for the recognition by Germany of the sacred principles of humanity and had ended with her almost humiliating capitulation. So they saw it as a great moral victory. It was not really that at all. It was not a conquest of the high ground by Wilsonian principles but a remarkable win on the low ground in a diplomatic dogfight. What had made Germany yield was the threat of war. She had given in to pressure skilfully applied not without bluff. Her capitulation was not by a long chalk total victory. Wilson began by aiming at the abandonment of the submarine as a commerce destroyer. A cynic who was unimpressed by the principles of humanity would have told him that he was asking for too much and that he should never have aimed at more than the imposition of cruiser rules, to which in his third Note he reduced his demand. Yet he did not get as much as that. What he got was founded on a distinction, made in Germany in order to limit a concession rather than on any basis of logic, between liners and freighters. Bernstorff reported on 15 October:

Only a few of the most rabid of the pro-English papers venture openly to reproach President Wilson with having achieved nothing but the security of passenger ships, but all Americans are prepared to admit in confidence that the Government has completely departed from its original position.[63]

In the beginning of the final squeeze at their interview on 13 September —the one at which Bernstorff had been 'extremely docile'*—Lansing had suggested that the undertaking should apply to all merchant shipping and Bernstorff had passed this on as something that 'everyone here would be much gratified' about.[64] There had been no response to that and the suggestion was not further pressed. Without this extension, the undertaking was untidy both in theory and practice. In theory it could be criticized as putting one value on an American life in a liner and another when it was in a freighter. In practice, what would happen if an American on a freighter was killed? Undoubtedly the main danger was loss of life on liners but the lesser danger to Americans as crew or supercargo was left as a potential worry. A greater worry than that, so long as the distinction persisted, lay in the opportunities it offered to submarine commanders to mistake liners for freighters.

Nevertheless the gain, while not all that had been hoped for, was very considerable. Wilson played his hand just right. If he had overplayed by threatening war too openly or too soon, dissenting voices in Congress might have encouraged Bernstorff to think that he could disregard the threat. If he had underplayed, he would not have pushed Bernstorff over the brink into disobedience. The success owed much to Lansing's tactics but Wilson was the commander in the field. If told that he had done an excellent job of ordinary diplomatic work, he might not have been so pleased, but served up as a moral victory it was very sweet.

Was it in truth, when related to the larger objects of statesmanship, a gain of real significance? If Wilson's object as a statesman had been to secure for Americans a safe crossing of the Atlantic on such liners as they chose to patronize, his diplomacy would have been entirely successful. But his

---

* See p. 327 above.

object was greater than that. It was to keep out of the war and to do it in such a manner as, first, would not dishonour America and, secondly, would enable her to play the part of impartial peacemaker if opportunity offered. Safety of transatlantic travel in a vessel of the passenger's own choosing was relevant only if the loss of it would amount to a loss of national honour and dignity. Wilson considered that it would and that he must take his stand on the law and tolerate no abridgement of it. It was, however, a very small abridgement on a doubtful point of law. Wilson's object being to keep out of war unless honour forced him into it, it would have been statesmanlike to accept any compromise that was not a shameful evasion.

But then Wilson, it is clear, was never in any doubt about the law. Neither apparently was Lansing. Lansing was probably ready to admit that the submarine decree of 4 February 1915 was as a reprisal 'justified', the word he used to mean that it was a valid reprisal against the enemy, provided that Germany accepted responsibility for any consequence suffered by the neutral.[65] America, who was herself denouncing British illegalities, could not argue convincingly that there was no case at all for the submarine decree as a 'justifiable' reprisal. Thus Lansing's first reaction to the decree, before he realized that it might menace the United States, was favourable.*

Moreover, the action threatened was hardly a grave annoyance to America. If Lansing saw this last point, he did not get it over to Wilson. The American argument in the third *Lusitania* Note drew a superficially attractive distinction between injury to property and injury to life. Under the belligerent doctrine the limit of a reprisal is that it must not cause the neutral to suffer a disproportionate degree of inconvenience; injury to life and limb, it can be strongly argued, is not a matter of convenience at all nor one that can be condoned by a willingness to compensate; and so can never form part of a reprisal.

But unless the measure of reprisal inevitably puts the neutral in peril, this argument cannot apply. If there is an alternative open to him, which he can take with safety, the test must be whether taking the alternative puts him to unreasonable inconvenience. The British war zone decree of November 1914, for example, admittedly put neutral ships in the North Sea in peril if they did not keep to the safety lanes. It could not, however, be argued that as a reprisal it was excessive simply because if the neutral insisted on his full rights he might get hurt; the true question would be whether it was excessively inconvenient to expect him to keep to safety lanes. So on the belligerent doctrine the question for America was whether it was excessively inconvenient for her citizens when they crossed the

* See p. 200 above.

Atlantic to take passage only in a neutral vessel. Even if it could be plausibly argued that it was, the argument would have to meet the offer in the second German reply of safety for some belligerent liners. This was surely enough to remove any cause for complaint. Thus if the belligerent view— that is, the British and German view—of the nature of the doctrine of reprisals was correct, America had as against Germany at this stage a very weak case indeed. Even if there was no more than room for argument, Wilson's diplomacy would, in relation to his object of keeping the peace, be seriously at fault. There is no loss of dignity or honour about a compromise on a doubtful point. A man spoiling for a fight may insist on his own view of his rights; a man anxious for peace must take into account his opponent's view and be willing at least to discuss it.

But Wilson did not see it as a doubtful point. He seems to have considered the belligerents' view as unarguable. They themselves were partly to blame for that. America could not be expected to put their case for them. Lansing's failure to test the strength of America's legal case may have been due in part to the feebleness with which the opposite case was presented. Although it was the Allies' best point and Germany's only one both sides fought shy of it. Whatever its legal strength, the point was lacking in appeal and both belligerents were more concerned to retain America's goodwill than to worst her in legal argument. After the submarine decree of 4 February and before the March Order-in-Council that was the answer to it, Britain in a memorandum to the State Department of 19 February 1915 announced her expectation that reprisals would not be challenged.[66] But the expectation was not well received and Spring Rice in June advised strongly against using the argument.[67] Another reason for not using it may have been the fear that it might be too successful. If it resulted in the withdrawal of the submarine decree, Britain would have been left with nothing to retaliate against which would not have suited her at all. Consequently in her Note of 24 July 1915 she talked of self-defence rather than retaliation. In a letter of 20 August 1915 Spring Rice pressed his objection in language likely to appeal to Grey. Britain was fighting to uphold the law, he wrote; she should not, by breaking it because Germany did, play the German game. 'You will not I hope think me impertinent if I remind you what your signature means to the world at large and that I hope and pray that meaning may never be impaired.'[68]

Germany also began firmly enough in February 1915 with the point that the object of the submarine decree was to induce neutrals to compel Britain to observe the law. But she had to tread delicately after the loss of life in the *Lusitania*. In 1916 both sides put the argument briefly and cogently, Germany in a Note on 16 February[69] and the Allies, at French insistence, in their Note of 24 April.[70] But by then it was too late. The President, as we have seen,* had made up his mind and stated it, a double process which secured him against change.

Yet between June 1915 and February 1917 the only issue between the United States and Germany concerned the American right to travel (after March 1916, the right to travel on an armed ship), a right surely of trifling value. Even if he was correct in law, as a leader who considered that statesmanship meant keeping out of war, Wilson can surely be criticized for failing to perceive—or if he perceived, for failing to explain to his countrymen—that America no more than any other neutral was immune from the inconveniences of war; and that this was an inconvenience which could be accepted without any loss of honour and dignity. Now it may well be that, whatever Wilson perceived or missed in the logic of the situation, it was for one reason or another just in this direction that the current of his thought was flowing when it was stemmed by the sinking of the *Lusitania*. This was an event bound to knock any statesman off his course. Americans were not given time to digest the possible consequences to them of Germany's method of reprisal before 120 of them were slaughtered by a stroke of uncivilized warfare. A democratic leader was bound to respond to the nation's mood and to alter course while it lasted. But ought Wilson to have let it deflect him permanently? Correctly he diagnosed the emotion as indignation rather than pugnacity and acting on that he withheld the threat of war. Yet he took up a stand which meant that unless Germany was subservient the threat would sooner or later have to be made. Ought he not to have left himself a way of escape from the conclusion that the loss of any American life in the future would be a cause for war? If so, what was wanted was not clarity but obfuscation and ambiguity. Unfortunately Wilson was not a master of these.

If the first *Lusitania* Note had not been written the world would have been spiritually a poorer place. But diplomatically the Note was a mistake and the sort of mistake that is made by a man who is so sure of what he wants to say that he does not take counsel. If Wilson had put policy to his Cabinet and not just a draft for polishing, he might have been made to see that he was uttering demands from which he would almost certainly have to recede. If he had substituted for some of his solitary meditation a few hours of uninhibited discussion, he might have been brought to realize the dangers of his new course. The *Arabic* settlement put the United States in an unnecessarily exposed position. If Germany withdrew her undertaking, the United States had either to confess the bluff or go to war so as to keep Cunard liners safe for the occasional American to travel in.

* See p. 313 above.

She escaped from this predicament only because before the end Germany made less trivial demands upon her honour.

Another criticism of Wilson's diplomacy is that it did not improve the way towards one of his secondary objectives, that is, the holding aloof in such a manner as would retain his influence for peacemaking. Germany did not want his mediation and would never have accepted him as impartial whatever he did. Wilson did not appreciate that and so it must be counted against his diplomacy that he gave her grounds for suspecting his impartiality. By requesting at the beginning absolutely as much as, if not more than, the law gave him, a request so far-reaching that to comply with it Germany would have to drop the only naval weapon she had, by threatening war over a point of doubtful law and negligible substance, and by pushing it almost brutally to the point of forcing Germany to submit to his version of a disputed story, he had done more than show hostility, he had given her cause for fearing that the object of his diplomacy was to scarify rather than to heal.

Britain had no real cause for complaint about Wilson's impartiality. However, she was not looking for signs of impartiality but for signs of support. In answer to House's reproachful letter to Page—'what neutral nation has done so much?'—Page wrote on 23 August:

> The question is not what we have done for the Allies, not what any other neutral country has done or has failed to do—such comparisons, I think, are far from the point. The question is when the right moment arrives for us to save our self-respect, our honour, and the esteem and fear (or the contempt) in which the world will hold us.[71]

Most Britons would have answered in the same way. They could not see impartiality as a virtue in the struggle between good and evil. Wilson's acceptability by them as a mediator would depend upon his satisfying them that, however things might look, he could not in the end be indifferent to a moral issue such as was raised by the invasion of Belgium. It must therefore be counted against his diplomacy that by raising and dashing British hopes in this respect he left them lower than before. By his first protest over the sinking of the *Lusitania* he obtained as much respect as he would have got if he had protested in like terms over the invasion of Belgium. They were both outrages against the laws of civilized warfare, but, the fair Briton must admit, America was not materially concerned with the first: would Britain have gone to war if she had had no material interest in the balance of European power? As soon as a moral issue arose in which also American rights were infringed, Wilson had spoken out in splendid language. That was the beginning. Then the morality had tailed off into an argument about liners and opened a prospect of two buddies getting together over the freedom of the seas. Would it be unfair to say that Wilson began with a high-principled denunciation of German inhumanity and ended with an offer to co-operate so long as American lives were not endangered? That is how the British saw it and what Page meant by a loss of respect. On 26 August Grey wrote to House from his Hampshire cottage:

I have said nothing about the sinking of the *Arabic* because it is to us only one amongst several incidents every week of sinking merchant and passenger vessels without regard to civilian lives. But people here are of course watching with intense interest what you are going to do about it. There is I think disappointment that the feeling in America is not more combative. The ruthless invasion of Belgium by Germany, the revelations of the crimes committed there,* the sinking of the *Lusitania* and now the *Arabic* each in turn produces emotion and indignation in America which seems to evaporate; and people here become less hopeful of the United States in taking a hand and more critical of the President.

On the latter point I tell people what an American said to me the other day: viz. that if the President said he must take action against Germany he would have the whole country behind him, but solely because he had convinced the country that he had done his best to keep out of war; they must accept it, though they desired to avoid it.

If I could feel that your people were sure to say, sooner or later, 'though we have no concern with territorial changes between the belligerents themselves, who must settle things of that kind by themselves, there can be no peace till the cause of Belgium is fairly settled in the interest of public morals and future peace,' I should be content.[72]

---

* This was a reference to the report of the Committee on Alleged German Outrages published on 12 May 1915. The committee was presided over by Lord Bryce and consequently its account of the atrocities committed by the Germans in Belgium carried great weight in the United States. It was as fair a document as could be expected from a partisan source issuing at a time when feeling was still hot; subsequent investigation has confirmed broadly its findings of terrorization. Cf. Link 3: 41.

XII

THE END OF 1915

THE year 1915 was a bad year for the Entente and a good year for the Central Powers, but not good enough. On the western front all the Entente offensives had been costly failures. In December after the last British autumn offensive at Loos, Sir John French, the commander-in-chief, was replaced by Sir Douglas Haig. The failures meant deadlock but not defeat. The following year would see thrown into battle the new British armies—Kitchener's armies, they were called, since they consisted of civilians who had responded to his call and who in 1915 were being made into soldiers. Germany had hoped by then to have only one front on which to concentrate all her troops. But while her conquests in the east had been enormous and she had 'liberated' Poland, Courland, and Lithuania, she had not, as she had hoped, driven Russia to sue for peace. Bethmann, always anxious to negotiate from a position of military strength, was continually putting out feelers, but the Tsar Nicholas II rejected them all. This pathetic little man, who struggled weakly and incompetently to manage his enormous empire as if it were his family property, kept his grip on one idea, that he would not let his allies down. He wrote on 8 July 1915 to his royal cousin George V: 'It will soon be a year that this terrible war has been raging and goodness knows how long it may still last but *we shall fight* to the end!'[1] The Baltic provinces which he had lost were only on the fringe of his vast territories and he still had huge reserves of manpower. Russia could be driven back but never defeated until her will to fight was cracked.

Yet for the Entente it was sadly disappointing. There had been much talk in 1914 of the 'Russian steamroller', slow to start, it was said, but irresistible when on the move. Now it had been decisively checked and one way out of the deadlock on the western front had been blocked. There was no other way showing any better prospect. The British 'side-shows' in the Dardanelles and at Gallipoli had collapsed with a consequent loss of prestige in the Balkans; the main evacuation was completed in December. Serbia, who in 1914 had successfully repulsed an Austrian invasion, was now threatened by a Bulgarian army supported by German troops. In a belated and rather futile attempt to come to Serbia's aid the Entente landed a force in Salonika which never did any good at all. Italy, after her declaration of war on Austria on 22 May, launched two offensives with negligible results. So at the end of the year the position was that the Central Powers had made substantial gains but were not yet within sight of victory.

Except when covering military operations, which still in northern latitudes had to defer to the onset of winter, history does not usually accommodate itself with exactitude to the revolution of the globe. Yet as it happens most of the narratives which intertwine in this story reached a cardinal point at or about the end of the year.

Wilson's romance bloomed into marriage on 18 December 1915; he returned from his honeymoon to begin life again on 3 January.

The American legal offensive against Britain, arrested by the *Lusitania* crisis, now surged forward. It was discharged into an atmosphere which was even less receptive than in 1914 to protests against the blockade and at a time when the British Government, reconstituted in the political crisis of May 1915, was under mounting pressure to get on more ruthlessly with the war. Grey's influence was declining and at the end of the year, when on 30 December he and several other ministers were persuaded to withdraw their resignations, the Government narrowly survived a second internal crisis.

There was a general realization that the United States was not adequately armed to meet a diplomatic crisis such as the *Lusitania*. The inevitable euphemism selected to label the new movement was the clumsy word 'preparedness'. Wilson in the summer of 1915 took command of the preparedness movement and, running into difficulties with Congress, decided upon an appeal to the country. This decision he took on 18 January 1916.

The *Arabic* settlement turned out to be only a truce in the diplomatic struggle over the submarine which was resumed in the winter of 1915 and continued into the following spring. Two liners, the *Ancona* on 7 November 1915 and the *Persia* on 30 December, were sunk with loss of life. The latter is a convenient day for a pause in this narrative, for coincidentally it was also on that day in Berlin that Falkenhayn withdrew support from Bethmann.

During the autumn of 1915 House was preparing a plan for intervention, the boldest he had yet conceived. On 28 December he left the United States to put it into execution.

All these stories hang together and this chapter takes each of them so far on its way.

At the beginning of 1915 the Liberal party had been in power for nine years, a long stretch in British political life. It was first returned with an enormous majority in 1906. Balked in its radical measures by the Opposition in the House of Lords, it engaged on what was then seen as a momentous constitutional battle in which with the passing of the Parliament Act 1911 the Upper House acknowledged defeat. The battle involved two general elections in 1910, from which the two great parties in the Commons emerged about equal in numbers, but the general support afforded by the small Labour party and the Irish Nationalists gave the last Liberal Government a decisive majority. The Parliament Act limited the life of a parliament to five years. It would be unprecedented for any political party to win four consecutive elections, so that to all appearances when the war broke out the Liberal party was at the fag end of its long prosperity.

As a collection of personalities the Liberal Cabinets from 1906 to 1915 were scintillating. H. H. Asquith (it was still an age of surnames and initials) must be counted among the greatest of peacetime Prime Ministers; and in Lloyd George and Churchill the Cabinet in 1915 contained two future Prime Ministers who were to prove themselves great war ministers. Asquith has been called the last of the Romans and also the last of the Whigs. Both names are appropriate, suggestive alike of the imposing features and cast of mind. Above all things he possessed *gravitas*. The structure of his mind was classical, monumental and yet mobile. Mentally he moved with the weighty speed of a Rolls-Royce. Although he came from the middle classes of Yorkshire, he had a patrician disdain for popular clamour and a confidence in his own ascendancy. In his retention of the first place for so long his loyalty to his colleagues proved as serviceable a quality as his incapacity for intrigue. Even at the end Lloyd George was the only Liberal in the Cabinet who questioned his right to remain.

Lloyd George since 1908 had been Chancellor of the Exchequer, then regarded as the second office in the Cabinet. Like Asquith he was a self-made politician but made in a very different factory and out of very different material. The raw material of Asquith's personality was the solidity of the Yorkshireman and of Lloyd George's the volatility of the Welsh. While Asquith's mind and culture had been developed in the classical atmosphere of Balliol College, where he won the most distinguished prizes, Lloyd George's had been fed on what he picked up at the village school and in home teaching. Neither man had inherited wealth so that both had to enter politics through a profession. Both chose the law, Asquith coming by way of the Bar and Lloyd George as a solicitor, then considered to be the lower branch of the legal profession. While Asquith moved easily and inevitably into the upper classes, enjoying their food and drink, their society, and especially their intellectual pleasures, Lloyd George remained always a man of the people. Although Roosevelt's characterization of Asquith as 'fundamentally the Wilson type' was far too shallow, their minds were of the same metal, while Lloyd George's mind was the 'quicksilver' which Wilson could not trust. None of the three was an unemotional man, though Wilson and Asquith appeared to be so. Both these two needed the sustenance of women. Asquith, more of a rover than Wilson, mortgaged his heart in platonic friendships with younger women. Lloyd George, as potent and attractive in body as in mind, demanded from them physical satisfaction and obtained it with a boldness which in the first and second decades of the century was almost incredibly foolhardy. House put him in a quite different category from Asquith, Grey, or Balfour. He wrote of him in May 1915:

> He reminds me more of the virile aggressive type of American politician than any member of the Cabinet. He lacks the learning, the culture and the trustworthiness of his government associates. He has something dynamic within him which his colleagues have not and which is badly needed in this great hour.[2]

Given the political situation in 1914 a coalition sooner or later was inevitable. A general election in wartime was undesirable, yet the statutory limit imposed by the Parliament Act could hardly be suspended without all-party consent. The Conservative party was under the leadership of Bonar Law, who had been the compromise candidate in 1912. He was an able and uninteresting businessman, who, if he had not become Prime Minister for a brief period in 1922 after Lloyd George was ousted, would hardly have rated a biography. His talents did not enable him to talk with Asquith on a footing of equality and he was overshadowed by Balfour whom he had replaced; by Austen Chamberlain and even by Long, the rivals between whom he had risen; and by the imperious Curzon, whom House described as the 'worst jingo I have ever met'[3] and whose desire it was, so he told House, that peace should be made only in Berlin. But Law was after all tenaciously ensconced at the top; to underrate him was a mistake which Asquith made and which Lloyd George did not.

The Conservatives after the outbreak of war gave patriotic support to the Government while reserving the right to criticize. By May 1915 criticism had reached the point at which it was best answered by absorption and Asquith formed what was later called the first Coalition Government. Winston Churchill, his reputation shrivelled on a pyre of the public's misjudgements of him which his hubris had kindled, ended the first phase of his heroic career with a tumble into minor office which he soon left. Haldane's fondness for German philosophy was twisted into a charge of pro-Germanism which drove him into private life. In forcing these expulsions, as well as in their demand for a more strenuous prosecution of the war, the Tories sang in tune with the Northcliffe press. Alfred Harmsworth, the creator of popular journalism in Britain, was in 1905 at the age of thirty-nine raised to the peerage as Baron Northcliffe. In 1896 he founded the *Daily Mail* which in 1915 had the largest circulation of any newspaper, just over a million. In 1908 he bought *The Times* and by dropping its price to a penny in 1914 trebled its circulation to 145,000. Thus he bestrode the division between the 'popular' and the 'quality' press. He had a bubble of genius which ultimately burst into megalomania. He used his newspapers to spread hatred of Germany. He was an instigator of the first coalition (as witness his conversation with House)* and later of the second. He was vehement against Asquith whom he believed would lose the war and sought to drive from office. As an end this was justifiable: the means he used were those of the yellow press and of his transatlantic contemporary, William Randolph Hearst, whom it is not undeservedly offensive to him to say that he resembled. Asquith ignored Northcliffe but Lloyd George did not.

The formation of the first coalition started the decline of Asquith. The movement was slow, spread over eighteen months, and even at the end he might have kept his place and much of his power if he had been less self-confident and more astute. What kept him so long in an office for which in wartime he was not well fitted was his immense prestige on the one hand and on the other the lack of any clear alternative, because of the insignificance of Law who as leader of the other party had the strongest political claim, and the distrust of Lloyd George whose quality was increasingly being recognized as what was needed. Asquith remained in war as he was in peace the ideal chairman of a body the size of the Cabinet. In peacetime matters were rarely so urgent that where decision was difficult it was not better to adjourn or compromise rather than to force the issue and risk a split. Asquith had a constitutional reverence for what he called the *plenum* of the Cabinet that hindered him from making an effective instrument out of the War Council and the other Cabinet committees which were from time to time created. His imperturbability came close to lethargy. He con-

* See p. 215 above.

tinued his immense correspondence with his women friends, principally Venetia Stanley to whom he wrote almost every day. Often written in Cabinet while his slower colleagues were catching up, these letters may have been an anodyne to impatience which would have been better on a freer rein. Always quite a heavy drinker, there was a degree of instability after dinner which disquieted some of his colleagues. By 1916 he was in the sixty-fifth year of his age and the ninth of his service as Prime Minister, the longest continuous service for a century.

Lloyd George, ten years younger, was in every way a contrast: vital, alert, and agile, pressing here, there, and everywhere, leaping from point to point, and making short work of the distance between extremes. He had been reluctant to come into the war but once there he was in it heart and soul. By May 1915 the manufacture and supply of munitions had got beyond the War Office and in the new Government Lloyd George, keeping a hold on the reversion of the second place in the Cabinet and retaining as security for it the Chancellor's residence at 11 Downing Street, stepped down to start the new Ministry of Munitions.

Edwin Montagu was one of the lesser casualties of the new coalition. He was a young man of thirty-six who had been in the Cabinet for only four months in a minor office which now had to be used to accommodate Churchill. He was a Jew and very conscious of it, 'a nervous and sensitive person' as he described himself.[4] He was almost unique in the Liberal hierarchy in being an admirer of Lloyd George and devoted to Asquith. It was he who by the irony of fate and after three years of persistent wooing had drawn into wedlock and out of Asquith's orbit the young Venetia Stanley. He remained in the Government in junior office but it was the close continuing friendship with Asquith that made him of some importance.

In the new Cabinet there was, to use the terminology of half a century later, a strengthening of the 'hawks' over the 'doves'. This caused a hardening of the British Government's attitude to America. It was also the chief cause of the decline in Grey's influence. He had been the most dove-like in the old Cabinet, especially towards America, but now he was no longer working only among his party colleagues who with few exceptions had always regarded with reverence his conduct of foreign affairs. One of the exceptions was Lloyd George who was irritated by what he called his 'correctitude'; and Lloyd George was now the rising star. When in the autumn Bulgaria joined the Central Powers, with disastrous results for Serbia, Grey was blamed, though maybe the defeats in the Dardanelles and Gallipoli had as much to do with Bulgaria's choice as defective diplomacy. Grey was now in his tenth year as Foreign Secretary. Although only fifty-three the wear and tear of office had been increased by his weakening eyesight which kept him from his desk in April and again in June 1915. He was saddened by the shocking ingratitude with which his old friend Haldane had been treated; in peacetime, he said, he would have left the Cabinet with him.

The reader who wants to refresh his memory about the state of Anglo-American relations will have to go back to Chapter VII and the American Note of 30 March 1915.* Thereafter German-American relations occupied the limelight, beginning with the *Falaba* which was sunk just before the Note was sent and passing through the crises of the *Lusitania* and the *Arabic* with the fear of war swelling and receding. During this period, however, Anglo-American relations had not been amicably quiescent but had been infected by increasing irritation on both sides. By the Note of 30 March, it may be remembered, the President had put Britain on probation; she would be given time to see whether she lived up to her assurances of good behaviour. But within only six weeks Wilson was ready to summon her for a breach of her recognizances. Already in May he had authorized the preparation of a draft Note and in June had instructed House, then in London, to put pressure on Grey.† He had decided that he must finish with Germany first, but in July Secretary Lansing was saying privately that British violations of the law were 'indefensible and beyond belief'.[5]

The administration of the March Order-in-Council creating the economic blockade had many teething troubles. American shippers, who had been told that intercepted cargoes would be paid for and who expected prompt cash settlements, were grievously disappointed. The Chicago meatpackers, for example, a well-organized body with many food cargoes consigned to Scandinavian ports (and with, Lord Robert Cecil suspected, a justifiable grievance)[6] found themselves faced with a lot of questions to answer. Who exactly was the consignee? For if he was suspected of being an enemy agent, the transaction would fall under the earlier Order-in-Council of 29 October 1914, the food be seized as contraband, and no payment made. If there was a doubt about this, the case must go to court. In the Prize Court cases did not seem to come on and there was the usual wrangle about which side was to blame for the delay; for the Crown the Solicitor-General said in court on 14 June 1915 that it was all the fault of the claimants themselves.[7] Sometimes there was a question about who was to get the cash, claims being made by both shipper and consignee. Frequently there was a dispute about amount; the British said that the meatpackers were making exorbitant demands. Another grievance was that there was no arrangement for pay-

---

* See pp. 205–6 above.   † See pp. 291–2 above.

ment of demurrage. Mr. Skinner, the American consul-general in London, a fair man but far from as Anglophil as the ambassador, reporting to the Secretary of State on 28 June, wrote:

If our British friends would only put their administrative machinery in order, and deal with neutral cargoes and ships in a spirit of fairness, and also with some efficiency, they probably would carry out their program, while at the same time reducing complaints to a very low figure indeed. Their whole attitude is one of negation, and they seem to be incapable of undertaking anything helpful or constructive.[8]

Mr. Skinner was not being uncharitable; the British Cabinet had, as we have seen,* already decided that the new Order-in-Council should be used as a scourge on the backs of the unrighteous. In this atmosphere many nasty charges were made on both sides. The British said that the meatpackers were deliberately shipping unmarketable stuff and trying to get compensation for its seizure. On the other side it was being said that British trade with neutral countries was increasing in the very commodities which, coming from America, were being intercepted. There was good ground for this: Cecil minuted on 17 July:

Our continued permission of the export of articles to Holland and Scandinavia from this country which we were stopping when coming from America seems impossible to defend.[9]

Page himself investigated and dismissed an active rumour that the cotton commandeered was being resold at a profit. But while there was no bad faith, there was great laxity, as was manifest from the statistics with which Skinner was bombarding the State Department. The reason was that Britain's domestic machinery controlling trade with neutrals was as yet working far less efficiently than her organization of the blockade: angry Americans found a more sinister explanation in the suspicion that she was using the war to edge America out of her markets. A cable from Lansing to Page on 16 July talked of things 'reaching a crisis' and asked him, if he could do so without offence, to intimate to Grey that the matter should be treated as a Cabinet question:[10] he did so and Grey assured him that every important question was.[11] On 22 July the Cabinet decided to make the not very relevant concession that American ships outward bound from German ports, and which might therefore be carrying enemy goods for export, should not be searched.

Cotton was the subject which brought bad feeling on both sides to the boil. Rather ridiculously, since it was an essential ingredient in high explosive, it had been put on the free list of the Declaration of London.

---

* See p. 184 above.

Partly because of this but chiefly because of the importance of the trade to the Southern States of America, Grey had persuaded the Cabinet in 1914 against the wishes of the French not to put it on the list of contraband.* In the early summer of 1915 a press campaign, led by the *Daily Mail*, was started against what the *Mail* called the 'Cotton Crime'. The *Mail* printed a daily announcement that cotton was not yet contraband and laced it from time to time with remarks about every bale of cotton in Germany making an Allied cripple or corpse. The agitation alarmed the cotton planters, politically a strong and voluble group. Four million people were directly employed in the production of cotton and the prosperity of the South depended on it. The 1914 crop, which would begin to move about 1 August, was the largest ever and the planters were excessively nervous about their markets. They could see only the loss of the German market, and did not, as Skinner pointed out, set against it the enormously increased purchases by the Allies.[12] To the vulgar on each side the issue was extremely simple. One side wanted to know how long the Americans were to be allowed to go on supplying high explosive to the Hun; and the other side how long the British were to be allowed to impoverish countless American homes.

A like issue, but with contentions reversed, had been joined half a century before; and the Allies, if their memories had served them better, could have answered America with American words. During the Civil War the blockade by which the North sought to strangle the South by cutting off her exports of raw cotton strangled also the cloth factories of Europe. To the reproaches made Secretary Seward answered for President Lincoln, that 'the President had considered well and carefully the subject of the distress in Europe',[13] but was determined that the United States should not be 'diverted from its course by any foreign persuasions, intimidation or constraint'. The European mind was occupied with a fresh supply of cotton while the vital question which engaged America concerned 'all human interests, all human rights, all moral principles, and all political systems throughout the world, with all their influences upon civilization'. 'Our cause is now', Mr. Seward said, 'as it was at the time of our great revolution, the cause of human nature.'

In June 1915 the agitation to put cotton on the contraband list was taken up in Parliament. In fact after the March Order-in-Council it ceased to matter what was on the list and what was not, except that what was on the list could be seized without being paid for. The difficulty of stopping imports into Germany was simply that of ascertaining what consignments to neutral ports had an ultimate enemy destination and this difficulty would not be removed by calling cotton contraband. Lord Robert Cecil pointed

* See p. 185 above.

this out when the matter was raised in Parliament on 22 June 1915.[14] The only advantage of putting cotton on the list was that there would be a more orthodox answer to American protests if cotton was detained under the ordinary law as contraband than if under the contested provisions of the Order-in-Council. The French were anxious about this, but it was not a point which troubled the British agitators who always asserted that America would not or could not oppose action. Indeed, the hawks in the Cabinet now believed that the right thing to do was to go all out, defy the United States, and throttle her trade with the Northern neutrals.

On 5 July 1915 Lord Crewe in Grey's absence raised in the Cabinet the question of the new cotton crop and, with the aid of the now familiar allegation that the German Government was monopolizing the commodity, suggested that it should be made absolute contraband.[15] When Grey got back he found awaiting him a thoughtful minute written by Cecil.[16] British international lawyers, of whom Cecil was one, were not all happy about the 'blockade' aspect of the March Order-in-Council. Indeed, one of the most distinguished, Lord Justice Phillimore, who was later to play a considerable part in the development of the League of Nations idea, wrote to Grey on 27 March 1915 to protest: 'we are champions of the law quoad Belgium and yet breakers of law quoad the Neutrals of the World.'[17]* Cecil was more cautious: he said that Americans seriously doubted whether the blockade was justifiable in international law and added: 'I am not sure that they are wrong.' Would it not be better, he asked, to get back to the old law and justify the seizure of cotton—and of food also, though for this the case was not argumentatively so strong—as contraband? We should still want to restrict German exports, but this was 'far less burdensome to neutrals' and could be justified as a reprisal.

Grey on 22 July circulated the Cabinet on these lines although, it is interesting to note, he shied away from the use of the reprisals argument.[18] But the change of course would have meant the repeal or drastic modification of the March Order-in-Council and it seems unlikely that Grey would have persuaded the Cabinet to do that. Politics were involved as well as economics and it would have been reckoned an admission of defeat. It was at this juncture that Sir Richard Crawford, the British commercial attaché in Washington, devised a bold and ingenious solution of the cotton crisis. It was that cotton should be declared absolute contraband and that at the same time the British Government should support the market up to 10 cents a pound. This was substantially below the price of the 1913 crop which averaged $13\frac{1}{2}$ cents but a good margin over the existing market price of 8 cents. The boldness of the plan was in the double forecast: first, that if the

---

* See also Bryce's letter, p. 506 below.

greatly feared declaration of cotton as contraband was seen to affect the market only for the better, the agitation in America would quickly subside; secondly, that the crisis was temporary and that in the long term the demand for cotton would ensure that an obligation to buy up to 10 cents would not be unreasonably onerous. Behind the double forecast was the hope that if on both sides of the Atlantic the cotton agitation was quieted, the volume of discontent on each side about other commodities, on the one side because they were thought to be ruinously detained and on the other because they were said to be flowing unhindered into the factories of Germany, would fall back to the normal and not unmanageable size. All these forecasts and hopes were brilliantly made good; in particular by mid October 1915 the price of cotton per pound had risen to 12 cents.

Of course the ingenuity of the idea was not enough for its success. That needed also thorough and skilful execution. Finance had to be arranged and the passive acquiescence (official approval was naturally out of the question) of the President and Secretary ensured. House was in on all this and there were at Manchester, Mass., in early August closetings with the British ambassador. House gave the scheme his blessing and reported accordingly to the President.[19]

Then Bernstorff got wind of it. He wrote to Lansing on 6 August 1915 that he had heard that Britain had offered to buy $2\frac{1}{2}$ million bales of cotton at 10 cents a pound in order to pave the way for making cotton contraband.[20] He assumed that the offer would be rejected, but if it was being considered, the German Government would offer to buy 3 million bales at the normal price, provided the cotton 'could be transported to Germany through neutral countries according to the rules of international law'. Later he intimated that he was willing to go up to 30 cents a pound. It was, as Wilson said, 'a palpable bribe', and a very tiny one. If Germany lost 20 cents on every bale of the 3 million, the price for the embroilment of Britain and the United States over the burning issue of the day would be $600,000. Lansing, whose short-sightedness, whether due to nature or to blinkers, was sometimes almost beyond belief, passed the offer on to Wilson on 7 August with the observation that it might be of great value in clearing up the troubles of the cotton states. This from the man who the week before had agreed with House that friendly relations with the Entente must never be seriously endangered and who a fortnight later was to write to Wilson himself in that vein![21]* Wilson of course turned Bernstorff down at once, more in sorrow for the mind that thought to offer a bribe to the United States than in surprise at its inadequacy. 'How little they understand us.'[22]

On 11 August Grey presented the final plan to the British Cabinet, where

---

* See pp. 314 and 332 above.

it was approved.[23] Spring Rice was authorized to choose the best moment for the announcement that cotton was henceforward absolute contraband. The news of the sinking of the *Arabic* came most conveniently and on 20 August the proclamation was made. Bernstorff in his memoirs paid a tribute to British skill in handling their differences with America.[24] The comparatively unimportant incident, as he called it, of the *Arabic* stole the headlines while the extremely important economic measure was hardly noticed.

The *Arabic* affair on the one hand and on the other the amicable solution of the cotton crisis combined to produce an atmosphere favourable for Britain at a time when she needed it. In the summer of 1915 she found herself in the first stages of the financial predicament which was later to become so grave. She had not so far suffered from the Bryan ban on loans* to foreign governments because it had not been extended to private credit. But this situation began to change as a result of the action of the Federal Reserve Board on 2 April 1915. The Board was the creation of the Federal Reserve Act, one of Wilson's great domestic achievements, which came into force on 23 December 1913. Instead of having a central bank publicly controlled, an idea which in the America of that time would have been politically impossible, the Act provided for a Federal Reserve Board with supervisory powers and with a membership nominated by the President. Paul M. Warburg was, as we have seen, one of those members and by reason of his ability an influential one. He was strongly pro-German and felt keenly that the United States was acting one-sidedly in supplying the Allies with munitions. The Board, largely due to his persuasion and in the absence of McAdoo, issued on 2 April 1915 Regulation J which prohibited the regional banks from rediscounting bills arising out of the sale of munitions. The justification claimed for this was that the regional banks were public institutions so that their financing of war trade would be a violation of neutrality. Private banks shied away from discounting bills which the regional bank would not rediscount. In May, Britain, who handled the finances of the Allies in the United States, was running a trade deficit of between 50 and 75 million dollars a month. By August she was having difficulty in holding the pound at the official exchange rate of $4·86; on 18 August the pound dropped to $4·65. On that day in London McKenna, the Chancellor of the Exchequer, raised the matter in the Cabinet. A week later he advised that the Allies must face the necessity of raising cash from the American public by an issue of bonds and the Cabinet approved

* See p. 176 above.

of a reconnaissance being made through J. P. Morgan & Co., the United States agents of the British Government.

Meanwhile, McAdoo had entered the fray. A dominating man himself, he did not approve of the exertion on the Board of influences other than his own. On the question of financing Allied purchases his attitude was untainted by sympathy for either side. He saw it simply as a matter of American prosperity: this depended on the maintenance of war trade, which was lawful commerce and should therefore be financed in the same way as any other lawful commerce. The Board took counsel's opinion and were told on 20 July 1915 that banks were not public institutions and that Regulation J was unlawful. At the Board meeting on 10 August there was deadlock: Warburg and his supporters, though driven off the legal point, continued to maintain that the financing was unneutral.

J. P. Morgan & Co. were now sounding out Lansing as well as McAdoo about a public flotation. This was a matter for a presidential decision and Wilson gave it on 26 August. He would not, as both his ministers wanted, formally revoke the Bryan ban; but he said that it could be orally conveyed—nothing to be put in writing—that if a loan was floated the Government would take no action either for or against it. This was good enough for the Allies and a commission under Lord Reading to negotiate the terms of the loan arrived on 10 September. Both Bryan and Stone came out against the loan. Terms were agreed on 28 September for $5,000,000 at 6 per cent, a rate of interest which was considered exorbitant by the British Cabinet but grumblingly approved. But even at this rate the loan, though it produced the cash for the Allies, made no appeal to the American public. Nearly 40 per cent of the issue was left with underwriters and another 20 per cent was taken up by six large war contractors; only 6 or 7 per cent came from non-institutional investors. Perhaps the greatest gain was that on 7 September 1915 Regulation J was repealed.

The great American indictment, postponed until after the *Arabic* settlement, was dispatched to Page on 21 October 1915 in an ambience of sadness rather than wrath, and delivered to the Foreign Office on 5 November. It made not much impact but thickened the gloom in which the Entente's unhappy year was drawing to an end. Page, who on 26 September had taken immediate advantage of the President's encouragement and written him a voluminous letter, described the atmosphere as it then was.

There is great confusion, great fear, very great depression—far greater, I think, than England has felt, certainly since the Napoleonic scare and probably since the threat of the Armada. Nobody, I think, supposes that England herself will be conquered; confidence in the navy is supreme. But the fear of a practical defeat of the Allies on the continent is become general.[25]

Page told the President also of 'increasing feeling that the Prime Minister does not lead the nation'; of the possibility that Lloyd George might resign and then be asked to form a new Government, 'since he is, as the public sees it, the most active and efficient man in political life'; of Grey's depression, greater than Page had ever known, and of the rumours that 'if all the Balkan states fail the Allies, Sir Edward Grey will be reckoned a failure and must resign; and you even now hear talk of Mr. Balfour's succeeding him'. Then he played his signature tune:

In the meantime our prestige (if that be the right word), in British judgement, is gone. As they regard it . . . the peace-at-any-price sentiment so dominates American opinion and the American Government that we will submit to any indignity or insult—that we will learn the German's real character when it is too late to save our honour or dignity. There is no doubt of the definiteness or depth of this opinion.

On 27 September House had Spring Rice to lunch to prepare him for the blow. 'He understands, or pretends to understand, the great difficulties under which the President is working', House reported.[26] 'You may expect a pretty strong communication', Sir Cecil telegraphed home. But when on 14 October he saw the draft, he was quite unsteadied. 'I suppose you know', he said to House, 'that the record will forever stand that when the laws of God and Man were violated, there came no protest from America.'[27] And when House said something about Bernstorff, Spring Rice burst out:

I would be glad if you would not mention Bernstorff's name in my presence again; I do not want to talk to anyone who has just come from talking to him or to Germans. At this moment I do not know how many of my relatives have been killed in England by the raid of the German zeppelins last night.

House said this was insulting and he would not permit it. There followed an amplitude of apologies and they parted amicably. House recorded in his diary on the same day that Washington was no place for a nervous and delicate ambassador. 'He is a cultivated, highminded and scholarly gentleman and, when normal, is of the very best type of British Diplomat.'[28] After that for a while the overwrought ambassador went out of his way at the State Department to emphasize his sympathy for them in their shipping troubles.

The Note to Britain was drafted during October 1915 by Anderson, topped up by Lansing, and decorated by him with some more severities.[29] It was 7,000 words long with several appendices. No doubt it was, as Wilson commented, 'an unanswerable paper'.[30] It was in form an answer to the

British Note of 23 July (itself an answer to the American Note of 30 March) and it elaborated all the legal points which Lansing had not been allowed to put into the latter Note. The British in reply could and did parry some peripheral thrusts but on the main counts they could only shift from one legal leg to another, hoping that neither would have to carry too much weight for too long. While the writing of it must have given satisfaction to the legal authors, and the reading have pleased the pro-Germans and the strict neutralists and cast down the interventionists, it did not convey the impression that anything much was going to be done. Wilson, now nearing the peak of his private unneutrality, was uncharacteristically uninterested. 'I merely touched up its phraseology here and there.'[31] Lansing, having regard to his secret resolve not to do anything seriously unfriendly, presumably considered that hard words would break no bones. On 11 November Grey wrote to House a rather weary letter saying that it was 'before our Legal Advisers'. He went on:

We must either continue the difference of opinion with your Government, or give up definitely and openly any attempt to stop goods going to and from Germany through neutral ports . . . It looks as if the United States might now strike the weapon of sea power out of our hands, and thereby ensure a German victory.[32]

Page, who had of course been against sending the Note, was no less depressed at Christmas than at Michaelmas. He had, he wrote to his family, spent the evening with a Cabinet Minister and the military news was so bad that 'to-night I almost share this man's opinion that the war will last until 1918. That isn't impossible.'[33]

In 1914 the United States had a considerable navy, ranking next after those of Britain and Germany, but still, judged by European standards and in relation to the world importance of the United States, disproportionately low. She had no army to speak of. Military and naval spokesmen naturally seized the occasion of a great European war to point out America's shortsomings. The thought that America should be 'prepared' appealed to the Republican right. Roosevelt took up the cry in the *Outlook* which was his journalistic organ and now one of the chief ways by which he made his influence felt. Senator Lodge tried to get going a congressional investigation into the state of the nation's defences. House also was in favour of a 'war machine commensurate with our standing among nations'[34] so that America might be in a position to enforce peace; and he claimed to have pressed this on the President from the beginning. It may be doubted that he did so with any ardour until after the *Lusitania* when there was no need for more than an occasional prod. There is certainly no contemporary record of his saying anything to Wilson before then and it would have been uncharacteristic of him to have pressed on Wilson a policy to which Wilson was at first implacably opposed. Wilson tried with the nippers of scorn to kill the movement in the bud. In his second Annual Message to Congress on 8 December 1914 he said that America would do in the future as she had done in the past and rely for her defence 'upon a citizenry trained and accustomed to arms'.[35] She would not alter her attitude 'because some amongst us are nervous and excited'. This was the Address in which he first spoke of the war ('whose causes cannot touch us') as having nothing to do with America except that it afforded 'opportunities of friendship and disinterested service which should make us ashamed of any thought of hostility or fearful preparation for trouble'.

It was House's practice, he told his biographer, to drop any subject on which the President and he disagreed until the time came when he had a new argument to present.[36] But in this case either he underwent a temporary conversion or he felt that silence would be too unattractive. After the speech he wrote to Wilson:

> You go far enough to satisfy any reasonable man and your reasons for not going further are, I think, conclusive. It must be patent to all that our protection lies in the navy and must always largely be so.[37]

In December 1914 Wilson's attitude was generally applauded. But the *Lusitania* crisis caused both President and public to realize that America's contact with the European war might not be limited to opportunities for disinterested service. Wilson had to reverse himself sharply and he did. He had no thought of turning America into a great military power and he realized that the creation of any army that Europe would respect as a force behind her diplomacy would take far too long. But he noted it as doubtful whether the Army was even strong enough to quell a pro-German rising in the United States if war with Germany broke out. On 21 July 1915 he instructed the Secretaries for War and the Navy to plan for 'adequate national defense'[38] and it was not long before he made these instructions public. By that time popular support for increased armaments had grown considerably. Lodge wrote that Wilson was 'seeing votes' in the change of policy.[39] But the need for the change was obvious and naturally occurred to others besides Wilson.

On 15 October the President approved the Navy's plan for spending $500,000,000 over five years to build 10 battleships, 6 battle cruisers, 10 cruisers, 50 destroyers, and 100 submarines. On 6 November Garrison's plan for the Army was published. It provided for an increase in the Regular

Army of about 40 per cent to 140,000 men and the creation of a reserve force, called the Continental Army, of 400,000 men, each man to be on active duty for two months a year for three years and thereafter to be on reserve. Wilson laid these plans before Congress on 7 December 1915 in his third Annual Message, which struck a very different note from the Message of the year before.[40] He wound up with an attack on disloyalty. This was provoked chiefly by revelations in November about the activities of von Papen and another attaché at the German embassy in Washington which had resulted in their expulsion on 1 December and come uncomfortably close to Bernstorff himself.

But Wilson added words which Bernstorff thought were intended to strike at bad behaviour in London and Paris[41] and which certainly came uncomfortably close to Page.

There are some men among us, and many resident abroad who, though born and bred in the United States and calling themselves Americans, have so forgotten themselves and their honor as citizens as to put their passionate sympathy with one or the other side in the great European conflict above their regard for the peace and dignity of the United States. They also preach and practise disloyalty. No laws, I suppose, can reach corruptions of the mind and heart; but, . . . etc.

He had not, Wilson said in the course of this address, any thought of any immediate or particular danger; there was reason to hope that no question in controversy with other governments would lead to any serious breach of amicable relations. Why then, the critics asked, was there any need for such a great change in military policy as the creation of a continental army and of so huge an increase in naval strength? Acquiescence was not to be expected from those who thought of America as a country far above the troubles of the world and dedicated to peaceable ways. This was the group to which, until May 1915, Wilson had himself belonged and whose aspirations about America's role in the world he had constantly voiced. While Lodge and his followers felt the indignation towards latecomers of those who had already worked long hours in the vineyard, many of Wilson's supporters, hitherto the staunchest, felt the greater indignation of the betrayed. They were given soothing assurances that the arms were wanted only for defence. But defence against whom? Who was threatening? Where was the invader? Wilson had no convincing answer to such questions. The only threat against American lives and property that had so far taken any tangible form was limited to when they were on British liners and Wilson had just received the plaudits of the nation for removing that. In truth he wanted an army and navy not just for manning the battlements but so that he could if necessary deliver the sort of counterstroke that may have to be made by a nation which in a wicked world insists on holding every inch of what she owns. How to distinguish this from aggression?

'This nation does not need burglars' tools unless it intends to make burglary its business', cried Bryan.[42] Of course he had flung himself into the fray. He spoke through his journal, *The Commoner*, which rivalled Roosevelt's *Outlook*, and on innumerable platforms throughout the country. He called the new programme 'a challenge to the spirit of Christianity'. He caught the echo of Wilson's first war speeches when he urged 'the influence of others by example rather than by exciting fear'. If the country was really in danger, he said '100,000 patriots would spring to arms between sunrise and sunset';[43] pitchforks, scythes, and some shotguns would doubtless be available but Bryan did not suggest any other arms they were to spring to.

It was clear that Wilson was going to have trouble with his own party in Congress. The new majority leader in the House of Representatives, successor to Underwood, Wilson's rival for the nomination in 1912, was Claud H. Kitchin, a farmer lawyer from North Carolina. He was fervently opposed to the programme and a formidable opponent, for he was a powerful debater and also much liked. Wilson said of him that he 'never knew a man who could state his position more lucidly or yours more fairly'.[44] The President had to woo Champ Clark again and to invite Republican support. Besides the pacifist opponents of the programme there were those who were distressed by the prospect of increased taxation and those who disliked Garrison's plan for a continental army, preferring the strengthening of the National Guard which consisted of state militias and had more of the flavour of a yeomanry. There were many congressmen still uncommitted and who like local retailers were reluctant to stock a new article unless it was nationally advertised. Tumulty wrote to the President on 17 January 1916: 'I cannot impress upon you too forcibly the importance of an appeal to the country at this time on the question of preparedness.'[45] The next day Wilson announced his decision to go to the country in a 'swing around the circle'.

In a man whom religious education has secured from licentious indulgences, the passion of love, when once it has seized him, is exceedingly strong; being unimpaired by dissipation, and totally concentrated in one object.[46]

So Boswell wrote about Johnson and so a biographer may write about Wilson at this time. No man of sixty can be unstirred by the thought that a desirable woman, much younger than himself, has fallen in love with him. The revelation intensified passion in Wilson and brought him to a pitch of joy that pushed out of his mind all care for what he was doing. Politically he was behaving with some recklessness. It was not as if the White House circle, even when it was not in mourning, had often been refreshed by new and handsome entrants. Now Mrs. Galt was constantly dining there and joining the President in his automobile rides. She had been for a cruise with him in the presidential yacht and by the end of July 1915 had spent six weeks at the Cornish holiday home, ostensibly as the guest of Miss Margaret Wilson. All this was now generally known. The outcome must be supposed to be marriage, but this supposition could not in the circumstances have its customary effect of stifling ill-natured criticism. In every age an interval has been thought necessary to prevent the funeral meats from coldly furnishing forth the marriage table. In the convention of the nineteenth century which still prevailed in 1915 a year was the bare minimum between the funeral and marriage announcements. Anything less, if it was not positive evidence of lack of affection, showed at least a lack of respect for the dead and indeed for the institution of monogamy.

The three daughters were all pleased, for they knew their father's need and that its satisfaction did not touch their mother's memory. But they were no longer part of the White House entourage and there feeling was mixed. Helen Bones rejoiced but the others were a little disconcerted by the sudden change from despondency to ardour in almost less than the time that it took spring to turn into summer. Tumulty was seriously upset. By disposition he was one of those who frowned on second marriages, and but for the fact that for him Wilson, though he might err, could not sin, he would have been shocked by the rapid replacement of the woman whom he had looked on almost as a second mother. Grayson hovered enigmatically between approval of the end and some discouragement of the means. The gentle stream of companionship he had thought to provide for Helen Bones had burst its banks and was rushing into another outlet in a torrent compared to which his own leisurely courtship was still meandering. The President, he told House, was infatuated and, claiming House's approval, was wholly absorbed in the affair and neglecting everything else. But he agreed with House that if Wilson did not marry he would go into a decline. House himself, who was not in Washington during the critical period, continued to tread carefully and wrote in his diary on 31 July: 'I am sorry the President has fallen in love at this time, for he will be criticised for not waiting longer after Mrs. Wilson's death.'[47] Mrs. Galt spent August visiting friends and receiving Wilson's daily or twice-daily letters. Wilson went back to Washington on 12 August and on 1 September, the evening of Mrs. Galt's return, they dined together in the White House. Her absence had made Wilson quite desperate and he pressed for a conclusion. Perhaps unconscious of it, he resorted to the tactics he had used with Ellen.* Had he any right, he pro-

* See p. 17 above.

fessed to doubt, to ask her to share a load that was breaking his back?[48] Put that way, there was by then only one answer, and on 3 September they were formally but still secretly engaged. Mrs. Galt still wanted the announcement delayed until after the election.

So for different reasons did many others. Tumulty thought the announcement would be fatal to Wilson's chances. The party managers, when they met in early September to consider the affair, agreed with him. The verdict was unanimous but no one was willing to be foreman.

Rumours spread and inevitably they featured Mrs. Peck whose name had already emerged in the 1912 election. She had divorced her husband not long before and so was a free woman—free in the eyes of the law. Did she dare to imagine that if Wilson contemplated remarriage she would be his first choice? Perhaps others imagined it for her. Whether she was disappointed or merely indiscreet, she must have been talkative enough to let it be widely known that she was the possessor of a packet of letters; that said, the contents could be assumed. Rumour declared them to be compromising and declared also that Mrs. Peck was threatening to come out with them. Gossip could compose many variations on the theme. The divorce must have been prearranged, it was suggested, and now Mrs. Peck, poised for the leap into the White House, was being rudely pushed over by another aspiring First Lady. She was threatening a suit for breach of promise, so it was said, and the rich Mrs. Galt was trying to buy her off.

In fact, Mrs. Peck, whose only fault probably was that she did not conceal the extent of her acquaintance with the famous, was proceeding in a much more pedestrian manner. She was now in Southern California where her son was struggling to raise fruit and she to raise money. She owned some mortgages that she could not succeed in selling. This she wrote to Wilson in June 1915. Wilson interpreted it, as was perhaps intended, as a cry for help and on 14 September he sent her a banker's draft for $7,500. He told Grayson what he was doing and Grayson told McAdoo. Then or thereafter in progress from mouth to ear the sum rose to $15,000. McAdoo was very disturbed; and indeed nothing could have been more unfortunate than a payment of such a sum at such a time. He dared not tackle the President directly about it and, apparently in the hope of getting Wilson to open up, he invented an anonymous letter which he told Wilson had been sent to him from Los Angeles saying that Mrs. Peck was showing the correspondence and doing Wilson much harm.

Wilson reacted with immediate courage. He acknowledged to himself, as later he did to House, that his letters to Mrs. Peck had been warmer than was prudent. But the friendship had been platonic and he would not let himself be blackmailed, no matter how deeply he might be humiliated in

spirit by publication. He went straight to Mrs. Galt, told her the whole
story, and begged her to stand by him. This was the evening of Saturday
18 September. Mrs. Galt was startled and at first unsure. Not that she did
not accept the story just as Wilson told it, but to a woman as protected as she
had always been it must have come as quite a shock to realize that she was
engaged to a man who had in the phraseology of the time 'got himself
talked about'. Perhaps too she was a little hurt to discover that there had
been in Wilson's life, albeit imported only platonically, a woman whom she
had not known about. She sent him away without complete reassurance.
But when by the early hours of the Sunday morning she had thought it out,
she wrote him a letter in which her strong love is firmly delineated beneath
the draperies of her style—'the hideous dark of the hour before the dawn
has been lost in the gracious gift of light' and so forth.[49] What she effectively said was that she was sorry she had been unreasonable, that she was
not afraid of gossip or threat, and that she would stand by him: this she
pledged.

Wilson was overjoyed. Though it cost him something to do so, he told
the whole story once again to House on the evening of 22 September. He
could not understand about Mrs. Peck, he said, and 'thought that she must
have fallen under some evil influence'.[50] House, who had arrived in Washington the day before, had already heard from McAdoo the story of his manœuvre
and felt that he could not give him away. But he was able to reassure Wilson
by scouting the possibility of blackmail. He recorded in his diary:

> His loneliness is pathetic. With the weight of the burdens upon him, it seems
> but a small concession which public opinion might make in behalf of this man not
> to criticise him too much for doing what one in a humbler station of life would be
> able to do without comment.[51]

The only result of McAdoo's *démarche* was that Wilson's determination
to announce the engagement was strengthened and Mrs. Galt the more
easily persuaded. The announcement was made on 6 October and the loyal
Tumulty released on the same day as an antidote a statement that the
President intended to vote for women's suffrage in New Jersey. Above the
surface there was curiosity and enthusiasm provoked by the beauty of Mrs.
Galt and below there was much unpleasantness. 'A certain lack of propriety', was a mild comment. 'A vulgar marriage', was Senator Lodge's.[52]
There were tales of supposed neglect by Wilson of his first wife and a Hearst
reporter found that he had not yet put up a tombstone on her grave. It was
a good opportunity to give an airing to the hardy type of smoking-room
story that was always in need of a new peg: 'she was so surprised when the
President proposed that she fell out of bed.' Much of this sort of thing,

ludicrously false to the decorum of the courtship, hung about Wilson's reputation for a long time thereafter.

The publication of the engagement enabled Wilson to spend as much time as he wanted with his fiancée. House recorded complaints from Washington that he was neglecting business. No doubt he was distracted but there is no substantial evidence of neglect. The fact is that Wilson never kept long hours; he did his work in a concentrated fashion. The engagement was not prolonged and on 18 December the wedding took place quietly at Mrs. Galt's home. The new Mrs. Wilson was, in the old parlance, a helpmate. She enjoyed more than her husband did the splendours of establishment and pride of place. But in all essentials she fitted completely into his life, which outwardly continued as before but which inwardly she transformed. She had no greater liking than he for social life; that she was untouched by 'the small spirit of the society folk of the place'[53] was one of the many commendations which Wilson bestowed on her when announcing the engagement to his friends and relatives. The family gathering was for her as for him the ideal of entertainment. She enjoyed too all his well-tried pleasures, the game of golf, the automobile ride, and the twice-weekly vaudeville at Keith's Theatre—respectable performances they must have been, since she shared also his abhorrence of the *risqué*. She loved working with him, doing the secret chores like decoding, or just sitting in the study while he worked or talked with House and others. She rarely offered political advice and when she did it was not more weighty than her light dismissal of Bryan over the rail of the *Mayflower*.* Gerard has reported that at one of these secret conferences she showed a deep knowledge of foreign affairs and 'at times asked pertinent questions',[54] but Gerard was not much of a judge either of foreign affairs or of pertinence. It would not have mattered anyway what advice she gave. What mattered was the reassurance and the echoing sympathy. She looked after him and enjoyed his pretence of looking after her. She could make him relax; 'the kind of woman to make him forget his many cares', House wrote to Page.[55]

She engulfed his capacity for friendship. The once smart and dashing Mrs. Peck makes only one more appearance. She came to lunch at Los Angeles four years later when Wilson was sweeping the country on his last great appeal to the people. 'She came—a faded, sweet-looking woman who was absorbed in an only son. She told many stories of her struggle to maintain herself and help him to get his start.' She stayed too long, 'poor woman, weighed down with her own problems, of course she did not understand'.[56]

Mrs. Wilson was very sorry for her.

There were of course no more letters to Mrs. Peck or to the other

* See p. 302 above.

'cultivated and conversable' women. The second Mrs. Wilson wanted to reign alone over her husband's heart even if it meant, as for a time it came to do, reigning over the United States as well. Within a few years, out of all her husband's familiars only the shadowy Grayson remained. She thought of the others as defectors, not as the ousted. For eight years out of the eighty-nine of her life she lived on the peak with her hero and her beloved and when it was over the facts dissolved into melodrama. Twenty years after the event she wrote in her memoirs an entirely fictitious account of what was for her the crisis of 18 September.[57] It was not, as she remembered it then, Woodrow Wilson himself who came to her but Grayson. It was his duty, Wilson had told Grayson, to protect Mrs. Galt from backstairs gossip.

So he had set himself to write and tell me but, to quote Dr. Grayson: 'He went white at the lips, and his hand shook as I sat watching him try to write; his jaw set, determined no matter what it cost him, to spare you; but after a long time he put the pen down and said: "I cannot bring myself to write this; you go, Grayson, and tell her everything and say my only alternative is to release her from any promise".' The little Doctor choked as he repeated this.

Mrs. Galt's answer was that she would write. And so she did. But Wilson felt sure that the letter meant his rejection; he could not bring himself to face the written word; he put the letter in his pocket unopened. Two days went by and Edith felt hurt and humiliated. About noon of the third day Dr. Grayson came again.

Grave anxiety marked his chiselled features . . . The President is very ill and you are the only person who can help. I can do nothing . . . Broken on the wheel. He does not speak or sleep or eat.

Could it be, Edith asked herself, that her letter had fallen into alien hands? She decided to go to the President although unchaperoned save by the little doctor.

He went quickly to a door which he opened and beckoned me to follow. The curtains were drawn and the room dark; on the pillow I saw a white, drawn face with burning eyes dark with hidden pain. Brooks, the coloured valet, was by the bed. No word was spoken, only an eager hand held out in welcome, which I took to find icy cold, and when I unclasped it we were alone.

Thus there was fortunately averted what might have been a grand tragedy in the nineteenth-century mode of Silence Misunderstood.

When on 2 October 1915 Bernstorff tendered to Lansing at the Hotel Biltmore the draft which formed the basis of the *Arabic* settlement, he tendered also a draft on the *Lusitania*. But Lansing then put the latter aside in order to obtain a quick and definite settlement of the former. Bernstorff thought that he would hear no more about the *Lusitania*. Reporting to Berlin on 15 October, he said that the American Government was well satisfied with the *Arabic* settlement and that the *Lusitania* might well be left to drag on and referred to The Hague after the war.[58] On 20 October he reported that House had said 'let it drift'.[59] There is no doubt that House did give this advice, for he recorded it in his diary; for his new plan, which involved a show of mediation, a renewal of the *Lusitania* controversy might be an embarrassment.

But Germany did not want the *Lusitania* to drift out of sight without leaving behind her what she regarded as her *quid pro quo* for the *Arabic* settlement; so on 30 October 1915 Bernstorff called on House to inquire whether he did not think the time propitious for doing something 'to maintain the doctrine of the freedom of the seas'.[60] The Colonel in reply used a classic formula of discouragement (not doing anything to 'make it more difficult of accomplishment when the right moment comes') and reported accordingly to Lansing. But he did not report that he had told Bernstorff to let the *Lusitania* drift. Probably Lansing would not have let it drift anyway, for he was not the sort of man to be happy with an unclosed file. At any rate, if when the ambassador called at the State Department on 2 November he had planned to take the offensive, he had to submit to it being wrested from him by the Secretary. The draft of 2 October, with its justification of the sinking as a reprisal and its offer to submit the question of an indemnity to The Hague, would not do, the Secretary said; Germany must admit liability. Bernstorff said that his Government would never do that. Lansing, who knew that the ambassador had been rapped for going too far in the *Arabic* negotiations, did not press him harder. He offered to take the draft for further study, doing this perhaps so as to give Bernstorff an opportunity of procuring something better.

Just possibly if there had been no further incident the affair would have stopped there. Lansing might have been unappeased, but it seems unlikely that Wilson, who had after all been virtually prepared to accept this solution at the end of July, would allow a *casus belli* to develop out of a case now six months old. But on 7 November the Italian liner *Ancona*, 8,000 tons, bound from Naples to New York, was sunk by shellfire and eventually by torpedo in the Mediterranean with great loss of life, including nine out of the twelve Americans on board. According to the survivors the submarine commander behaved brutally, opening fire without warning and giving passengers and crew no time to escape. The American press headlined it as 'Another Lusitania Incident'. In London *Punch* had a Bernard Partridge cartoon of President Wilson pen in hand. 'This calls for a note—Mr.

Secretary, just bring me in a copy of our usual No. 1 note to Germany—humanity series.'[61] On the President's desk the cartoonist showed a pile of volumes—*The Polite Letter Writer*, *Fences and How to Sit on Them*, and such like.

Such sneers were typical of those which so upset Page. Had they been designed simply to taunt America into the war the motivation would have destroyed the power to hurt. What hurt was that the average Briton was genuinely indifferent about whether America came in or not. Britain was then at the height of her imperial pride and did not consider that she needed America, other than in the capacity of a supplier to help her win the war. This sort of cartoon expressed the sentiment of the age, that to get into a fight was an admirable thing to do and to keep out of it rather despicable. If America's role was to stay out and make money out of munitions, the nice British were sympathetic and the nasty sneered. Times change, and nice and nasty alike who lived another twenty years lived long enough to see Britain, a country divided in sympathy between the rival ideologies in the Spanish Civil War and petrified at the thought of another conflagration, play a humiliating part in the farce of non-intervention.

In all countries the responsibility for the *Ancona* sinking was generally believed to be German. This was no doubt a rash assumption since the submarine was undoubtedly flying the Austrian ensign and Austria accepted responsibility. But it was in fact true: the submarine was the German U38. This was not known until after the war and in 1915 the State Department had to deal with Austria. But nobody really believed Germany was entirely guiltless. This and the fact that November was the month of the revelations about unneutrality and worse which led to the expulsion of von Papen and his colleague may account in part for Wilson's assent to the renewed pressure on Germany over the *Lusitania*.

Lansing, following his successful method in the *Arabic* case when he had practically dictated the terms of Germany's Note, drafted another Note for her to send which went all the way in admitting liability without actually using the disputed word 'disavowal'. He submitted his draft to the President on 11 November 1915. Wilson replied on 17 November:

> I believe that neither you nor I are satisfied with this formula, but I think that it is probably the best that can be drawn, and I hope that you will press it upon the German Imperial Government. I have kept it in the hope that I could suggest something more satisfactory, but I have not been able to formulate anything that pleased me at all.[62]

Promptly that afternoon Lansing sent for Bernstorff and presented him with the draft. The ambassador said that he would submit it to his Government and Lansing urged a speedy settlement, the time, he said, being 'especially opportune on account of our recent note to Great Britain'.[63] He said also that the *Ancona* sinking had aroused deep feeling and added (perhaps with his tongue a little way in his cheek) that 'the peculiar thing was that in spite of the Austrian admission the blame was falling upon Germany as being the dominant power in the Central Alliance'. It was even possible, he said, that Congress when it met in December might declare war. Lansing himself was certainly prepared for extremes. Reporting on this conversation to Wilson, he said that they were coming to an impasse and that if Germany refused to give satisfaction, the Administration must either break relations or lay the entire matter before Congress to decide for war or peace. 'From the selfish standpoint of politics I think that the people generally are very much dissatisfied with the continuance of negotiations.' The Administration, he wrote, had irrevocably lost the pro-German vote and unless it was rigid it would lose the anti-German vote as well.

The election was now under twelve months away and Lansing, just because he was not a politician, felt perhaps that it was necessary for him to face up to the facts of political life by accepting the need for votes. It is unlikely that his counsel made any impression on Wilson. Already for months past observers, so many that it would be tedious to chronicle all that they wrote and said, had been attributing this or that action on Wilson's part to his desire to get this or that sectional vote. But there is not a trace in any of his private letters or in his most secret and confidential talks that he was concerned to frame his policy with even half an eye on re-election. There were other things besides fighting that Woodrow Wilson was too proud to do.

Lansing's demand for a speedy settlement was made on 17 November and a week passed without result. In the interval he received from the President all the authority he needed. Wilson was back on square one and defined his position there in a letter to the Secretary on 21 November:

> The matter of the Lusitania is just as important and just as acute now as it was the day the news of her sinking arrived, and a failure to secure a satisfactory settlement will disclose the same questions of future action that then lay in the background. . . . I think the Ambassador cannot be too explicit with his government in this matter.[64]

So on 24 November Lansing dispatched a curt reminder. But the ambassador did not take it very seriously. Lansing had not, as he had in the *Arabic* ultimatum, spoken in the name of the President. Bernstorff, believing that House who had said that the *Lusitania* would drift knew the President's mind and that Lansing did not, had decided that Lansing was out on a foray of his own and that on his own he was no danger. So he had sent home an untroubled report of the meeting on 17 November. Now in reply to Lansing's reminder he said that he had reported to Berlin by ordinary mail ('as you know, I have no other means for confidential communications'),[65] that he would not get an answer for several weeks, and that when he did he thought it would be unfavourable. After his talk with the President* in which 'the President showed me a common ground on which we could meet, viz. his policy of "the freedom of the seas"', he had, he said, recommended to his Government the policy which they had adopted. 'The President left no doubt in my mind, that if we gave binding assurances for the future, the past would cause no more friction.' Germany, he wrote, was unlikely to make any further concessions until the American Note to Britain had had some effect. Pressure to do so might result in her concluding that the policy of concessions to obtain 'the great and common object of the freedom of the sea' was wrong and returning to a policy of severe reprisals.

Bernstorff stopped dawdling after Lansing sent for him on 1 December to tell him that two of his attachés, von Papen and another, were *personae non gratae*. The ambassador was very relieved to find that he was not himself accused and when House saw him the next day he found him 'visibly shaken'.[66] So the telegram to Berlin on 2 December (House had evidently suggested a telegram) while not alarmist, was certainly more urgent than before. In it Bernstorff said that the United States Government had lost its nerve over the von Papen affair, the *Ancona*, and the impending Congress. 'Colonel House who is a good reader of the barometer here, sees no danger.'[67] But Germany must 'be prepared to do *something* with regard to the Lusitania question'. The American press was now full of revelations about plotting and intrigues by German agents and on 7 December Bernstorff sent another telegram. He feared he said, that Congress might take radical action and they must look for a formula on the *Lusitania* that skimmed over the points of contention.

Meanwhile, on 13 December, Lansing submitted to the President a draft of a very peremptory note to Austria on the *Ancona*.[68] The essential facts, he claimed, were not in dispute.

With full knowledge on the part of the Austro-Hungarian Government of the views of the Government of the United States as expressed in no uncertain terms to the ally of Austria-Hungary, the commander of the submarine which attacked the Ancona failed to put in a place of safety the crew and passengers of the vessel which they purposed to destroy.

The language was much stronger than in anything that had been sent to Germany. The meat in the humble pie prepared for Austrian consumption

* The interview on 2 June 1915; see p. 298 above.

was a demand for a prompt disavowal, along with punishment of the commander responsible and payment of an appropriate indemnity. The trimmings included the adjectives 'inhumane' and 'barbarous' and there were references to 'this outrage' and 'wanton slaughter'. Wilson approved this on 5 December and it was sent to Vienna the next day.

Wilson was giving Lansing his head again; or perhaps he had his mind on matrimony. Later, as will be seen, he got cold feet over the *Ancona*; and clearly he was a bit out of touch with the *Lusitania* situation. The note he typed to Lansing on 21 November shows that he was then under the impression that the instructions to submarines in force at the time of the *Arabic* had also been given to the submarine that sank the *Lusitania*.[69] On this hypothesis it might be taken as a sign of bad faith if the German Government refused to apply the *Arabic* formula to the *Lusitania*—'little less than a repudiation of the assurances then given to us', as Wilson said. But since this was not so, what the United States was doing was to insist on adding to the promise of amendment she had got for the future a confession to cover the past. It would be rash of Wilson to allow Lansing to go on in this way for a negligible gain unless he shared Lansing's determination (which in fact he did not) to break off relations if Germany was not brought to heel.

Lansing continued to go full steam ahead. On 15 December when a fortnight had passed since his last interview with Bernstorff, the Secretary wrote to him: 'I feel that continued delay in reaching an agreement in this matter may precipitate a situation which both of us would seriously regret.'[70] This finally pushed Bernstorff off his could-not-care-less attitude. He went to New York the following morning to see House. It looked as if the United States was deliberately going for a break with both Germany and Austria, he said; given time he was sure he could do something. House had nothing to say that would help and Bernstorff sent off Lansing's letter by wireless to Berlin where it caught up with his earlier 'not to worry' messages. Bethmann now realized that something had to be done and began to prepare careful instructions which would not this time leave Bernstorff with any scope for the initiative.

Meanwhile, on 17 December, the State Department received the Austrian reply.[71] It was far from deferential. Before using such sharp language, the Note said in effect, would it not have been better if Mr. Lansing had presented the facts more precisely, giving the names of witnesses and stating why he regarded them as more credible than a commander in the Imperial and Royal Navy. There was a rebuke for the failure to give 'any information whatsoever as to the number, names and more precise fate of the American citizens who were on board'. Would the United States Government 'formulate the particular points of law' and not merely refer 'to an exchange of correspondence which it has conducted with another government in other cases'?

Lansing emerged from under this cold douche as angry as a man can be expected to be when he is faced with a caricature of his own methods. 'Special pleading consisting of technicalities and quibbles', he wrote to the President.[72] He was still angry when he composed his memoirs: 'vapid and colorless', he called the Note, 'an insult to one's intelligence'.[73] He prepared on the same day, 17 December, a strong reply which, as he wrote to the President when he sent him the draft, was practically an ultimatum. But, he asked, what other course was open if the United States Government was to maintain its self-respect? 'The principles of law and humanity cannot be debated. I feel that it would be contrary to our dignity to continue a discussion of this sort.'[74]

On 18 December Baron Zwiedinek, the Austrian chargé during the interregnum after Dumba's abrupt departure, called to reveal the chief of 'the particular points of law' which his Government had in mind—whether a merchantman lost her immunity if she attempted to escape.[75] Lansing refused to discuss the point. The *Ancona*, he said, had practically surrendered and the murderous attack on her was like the indefensible slaughtering of prisoners. The Austrian Note, he said, was 'more or less frivolous' and had made a very bad impression. The Baron retired showing, Lansing reported, 'very much emotion'.

This day was Wilson's wedding day. The ceremony took place in the evening and he spent the morning with, metaphorically speaking, the cartoonist's *Polite Letter Writer* in front of him, toning down Lansing's draft and adding some pieces of courtesy. The Note went to Vienna the next day.[76]

On 21 December the Secretary gave two interviews. One was to the Baron who returned to say that it was very difficult for the Austrian Government to punish the submarine commander, especially if he was following instructions (and even more difficult, he might have added, if he was a German commander following German instructions; but possibly the chargé had no suspicion of that). Very well, Lansing said, if the submarine commander was not guilty, the Austrian Government was: the Government could, if it wished, exonerate the commander, assume the guilt itself, and apologize. Three days later Lansing received a telegram from the American ambassador in Vienna saying that the Government still thought the American demands 'based on inaccurate and insufficient evidence'[77] and that they would probably propose arbitration. Lansing was displeased by this. His attitude to arbitration was that of the diplomat rather than the lawyer: if you wanted to be conciliatory, you agreed to it, and if you did not you said that it was contrary to the dignity of the American people. Lansing did not want to be conciliatory. Moreover, if granted for the *Ancona*, Germany would demand it for the *Lusitania*; and while the American people might be complacent about an arbitration with Austria, they would not, Lansing believed, stand for so much as discussing an arbitration with Germany. So Zwiedinek got short shrift when on that day, 24 December, he called to say that because of the Christmas holiday the Austrian answer could not be expected before the end of the following week.[78] Lansing told him that a delay of several days would be very unfortunate: the issue was too distinct to require long consideration. The chargé telegraphed Vienna accordingly.

The other interview on 21 December 1915 was with Senator Stone.[79] Lansing was entirely wrong in supposing that his own bellicosity was lagging behind sentiment in Congress. He was in fact far ahead and the wing of the Democratic party for which Stone and Kitchin, both in controlling positions, were spokesmen, was alarmed by the severity of the Note to Austria. The senator suggested to Lansing that he was bearing down too hard on the Central Powers and not hard enough on Britain. Lansing argued the familiar distinction between life and property but Stone said that German babies were dying because Britain would not allow the United States to send condensed milk.*

The senator's lack of fervour did not cause Lansing to let up at all on his needling of Bernstorff who was now getting quite desperate at the dilatoriness in Berlin which he had at first condoned. On 20 December he passed on to Lansing a message he had that day received saying that instructions were on their way by mail. Replying the same day, Lansing regretted that the instructions had not been telegraphed; the time taken by mail might seriously affect the negotiations and a delay of two weeks would make a satisfactory adjustment well-nigh impossible. A day or two earlier Lansing had a message from Bethmann through Gerard pointing out the difficulty he was in caused by his inability to communicate with Bernstorff by cipher cablegram. So in his letter Lansing said that he would allow secret and coded messages to be sent via the American embassy in Berlin and the Tuckerton radio station; and he suggested that the mailed instructions should be repeated immediately by this route. Bernstorff on 21 December telegraphed

---

* This was something widely believed in America at this time. Shortage of milk for babies was one of the many grievances mentioned by von Papen in a rather tearful farewell conversation on 6 December 1915. On the instructions of the State Department Gerard had a report prepared by Dr. Taylor, a member of his staff, who found in April 1916 no evidence of any reduction in the milk supplied to nursing mothers and infants and no evidence that any children were suffering from lack of milk. The report was published in the United States in July 1916 without objection by the German Government and its conclusions were not challenged by them. See FRUS., pp. 960–5 and LP. p. 92.

Lansing's letter to Berlin and asked that this be done. Getting no reply he sent another telegram on 24 December and another on Christmas Day: 'hysteria grows daily': 'break with Austria-Hungary seems almost unavoidable'.[80] He had advised the Austrian chargé to tell his Government that if American demands were not conceded, there would be a breach; but at the same time he thought it 'not conceivable that the Austrian Government could swallow this bitter pill'.

After Christmas Lansing, realizing that the crunch on the *Ancona* was coming, wrote to obtain Wilson's final word. He had already reported on the interview with Senator Stone which had left Lansing himself undisturbed. He did not think that the Senator would oppose the Administration's policy, but it was, as he said, awkward having as chief of the Foreign Relations Committee a man who did not support the policy wholeheartedly, especially with Senator Lodge heading the minority on the committee, 'radically pro-Ally' and looking for possibilities of political advantage. As to policy, Lansing was in no doubt that if Austria did not submit, the United States ought to break off relations. Since this would inevitably mean war, ought Congress as the war-making power to be consulted first? This was the only question he posed.

Lansing wrote this on 28 December and Wilson, still on his brief honeymoon at Hot Springs, read it the next day with apprehension.[81] Up till then he had not discouraged Lansing at all. He had had a report of the Secretary's interview on 21 December with the Austrian chargé and had written on 24 December saying that it was very wise to make him see the position of the United States 'without any penumbra about the edges of the statement'.[82] (Penumbra—or rather the absence of penumbra—was one of Wilson's choice expressions.) But he could hardly be expected to view Senator Stone's lack of enthusiasm with all of Lansing's unconcern. Anyway Lansing's use of ultimatums was so alien to Wilson's ordinary policy—the *Arabic* was surely an exception—that he was bound to have misgivings when brought to the brink. Probably he would not have allowed things to go so far if he had been following them with his usual concentration, but he is hardly to be blamed if during this time his thoughts were a little distracted. Now, however, after Christmas he applied the brake very firmly. He had seen the ambassador's message from Vienna about arbitration and he dealt with this first on 27 December. His reaction must have taken Lansing by surprise. If arbitration could not be considered for the *Arabic*, why for the *Ancona*? Wilson, however, now thought that to refuse arbitration would be contrary to America's traditions and place her in a position which it would be difficult to justify in the opinion of the world: did not Lansing think so too?[83]

Then on 29 December he replied to Lansing's letter of 28 December. He did not think it would be wise to lay the matter before Congress since that would be treated as an announcement that war was expected. But they might seek useful guidance in private from 'wise and experienced men on the Senate Committee on Foreign Relations'. This was the only allusion, rather disconcerting for Lansing, to Senator Stone's views. Anyway, if the Austrian Government thought America bound in fairness to consider further representations, 'how can we refuse to discuss the matter with them until all the world is convinced that rock bottom has been reached?'[84]

How Lansing would have adjusted his diplomacy to this new directive can only be conjectured. On the same day that it arrived there arrived also a telegram from the Vienna embassy saying that the Austrian reply was being translated and enciphered and was a practical compliance with American demands.[85] When it arrived in Washington it proved to be, in contrast with the harsh tones of its predecessor, a mellifluously gentle retreat into unconditional surrender, overlooking on the way ('in consideration of the humanely deeply deplorable incident') some gaps in the evidence and the lack of reply to some of the justified questions put earlier, offering obeisance to 'the sacred demands of humanity', agreeing substantially with 'the principle expressed in the very esteemed note' of the United States Government, concluding that the commander was to blame and announcing that he had been punished, and finally accepting liability to indemnify.

Here was another triumph for the Lansing method which was succeeding all along the line with Bernstorff as well. The ambassador's jauntiness had been put to flight by the Secretary's aggressive tactics (there was another sharp reminder on 29 December)[86] and the moment he got his instructions from Berlin, he took them to Lansing. Nor was he deterred either by their rigidity or by his previous experience from embroidering them with pacificatory remarks.

Bethmann's decision to send the instructions by the ordinary mail had been deliberate. He wanted them to arrive about the same time as the *Ancona* submission which he relied on to produce a good atmosphere for their reception. He had indeed brought some pressure to bear in Vienna to secure a humble submission which he would never had made himself; doubtless he thought the Austrian gullet better able than the German to swallow the bitter pill. The instructions consisted of three alternative proposals set out in order, the second and third each going slightly further than the one before.[87] The first was the old formula of denial of liability coupled with an offer of arbitration. The second maintained the denial, but offered instead of arbitration a friendly indemnity. The third skirted liability and offered simply the friendly indemnity. Only stylistic changes could be made, Bernstorff was told.

Bernstorff saw Lansing on 31 December and as instructed put forward the first proposal first but hardly waited for its rejection before saying that he expected further instructions.[88] He asked, as he had been told to do, why the United States Government rejected arbitration; and then volunteered his belief that, if a good case could be made out against arbitration, his Government might adopt the course taken by Austria in the *Ancona*. On this hopeful note the interview terminated, to be followed the next day by the news of the sinking in the Mediterranean of the British liner *Persia*, 8,000 tons, with loss of life, including two Americans. This created a commotion which brought Wilson back to Washington. The commotion subsided when further facts emerged, but the case gave a new turn to the *Lusitania* negotiations.

In February 1916 the United States and Great Britain entered into a secret pact. It provided for a peace conference to be called by the President at which he was to propound 'reasonable' terms and thereafter to make war upon the side which refused to accept them—indeed a novel conception of a *casus belli*. Any risk of Britain being upon the wrong side was to be avoided by the reasonable terms being settled in advance as acceptable to her and by leaving it to her to say when the moment for action had arrived.

The architects of this pact, embodied in the House–Grey Memorandum of 22 February 1916, were House, Wilson, and Grey. They must be put in that order because House was the head designer. But Wilson was involved not merely as House's principal. He personally approved the design and finally settled the draft. For House the pact was the logical consequence of his firm opinion that America's entry into the war was inevitable; on this premise the pact achieved the two desirable objectives of hastening the inevitable and thus shortening the war and of curbing the Allies' greed for conquest. How far Wilson really came to share this view, and, if and in so far as he did not, what he made of the pact in his own mind are questions to be explored in succeeding chapters. Initially two things can be said.

The first is that undoubtedly, for reasons which have been indicated or surmised in the narrative up to this point, Wilson's attitude towards involvement had changed. In April 1915 he had reached the conclusion that both sides were almost equally unreasonable—the 'almost' covering a slight reservation in favour of the Allies—and that there was nothing to be done with either of them. This was his summation of the position, the fruit no doubt of House's reports from the capitals of Europe, which he bade Bryan give to the Japanese ambassador in answer to an inquiry about rumours of peace:

I am sorry to say that there is only one thing we can truthfully say to the Japanese Ambassador in reply to his inquiry—and perhaps it will be useful to say it—namely, that there are no terms of peace spoken of (at any rate in Germany) which are not so selfish and impossible that the other side are ready to resist them to their last man and dollar. Reasonableness has not yet been burned into them, and what they are thinking of is, not the peace and prosperity of Europe, but their own aggrandisement, an impossible modern basis (it might be well for Japan to reflect) for peace.[89]

But then a number of things happened. In May there was the shock of the *Lusitania*. Bryan's influence was withdrawn. On 31 July Wilson had read and noted 'as amazing in its detailed revelation of the whole German state of mind'[90] a report from Gerard which said among other things that the German people were united in full approval of her war methods, including the sinking of the *Lusitania*, and that, except for the majority socialists, they were determined to keep Belgium. They were confident of ultimate victory and 'dangerously mad', Gerard said.[91] Next month Wilson read Lansing's anti-German letter of 24 August* and sent him two days later a note of appreciation, saying 'it runs along very much the same lines as my own thought'.[92] Germany's dealings had been guileful, so Wilson thought, and in September 1915 he believed that she was trying to wriggle out of the *Arabic* pledge. He had come too near to war over the submarine to leave him as confident as he had been that America's destiny was to remain aloof. The change in Wilson's mind bubbled to the surface in his remark to House when they talked in his study on 22 September†—the occasion also on which he talked to House so intimately of his private life—that he had never been sure that America ought not to take part in the conflict. This remark was the mainspring of House's plan.

The second thing to be noticed initially is the likelihood, to be assessed in what follows, that House and Wilson did not look at the project from the same angle, House seeing it as the channel of entry into the war on the terms he wanted and Wilson seeing it as primarily an exercise in peacemaking with war as the last resort.

On the British side Grey was the only architect, the other British ministers being largely indifferent, which they could afford to be, since Britain was only taking an option. For Grey the pact stood at the crossways between his statesmanship and his political consciousness. As a world statesman he realized more acutely than any other Briton then in office that the future of Europe, and indeed of the world, depended upon the creation of a new

* See p. 332 above.   † See p. 329 above.

international instrument for the avoidance of war and that such an instrument could not be effective without the co-operation of the United States. As a politician he appreciated the hostility of most of his countrymen to any idea of being put on terms by the United States. He was not good at putting his political craftsmanship, of which he had not much, to work for the ends he believed in as a statesman. Thus he will be found making a statesmanlike advance to House and then throwing up against the response a barrage of political difficulties; House must understand that he was speaking only for himself, that he would have to consult his colleagues and ask the Allies, and so on. Against the indifference of his colleagues he lacked the skill to prevail. Perhaps also he lacked the high power of conviction that would have been necessary. In particular he never really made up his mind about how thoroughly he wanted Germany to be beaten. He did not want to trample on her but he wanted her to realize that she was saved from being trampled on not by her own might but by the magnanimity of her conquerors. Only in this way could she be made to see that aggression did not pay. This was the ideal, but was it worth the sacrifice if an adequate peace could be bought more cheaply? On this question Grey often vacillated, as he did too less frequently on his assessment of the ideal. He was not always as sure as his colleagues were that a drawn peace would be a misfortune to be contemplated only when the hope of total victory had been abandoned. This was the crucial point on which House and Grey differed and on which Grey, hampered perhaps in part by his own uncertainty and in part by his sense of his responsibility for keeping America's support, never made the difference clear. House, at any rate until America came into the war and proximity shortened the view so that it stopped at the wall of the arena, did not want in any circumstances the utter defeat of the Central Powers.

Yet Grey's statesmanship was not unavailing. It is better to proceed at half speed in the right direction than to go full ahead in the wrong one. Grey went far enough on the right road to secure his fame unless mankind itself destroys the way to a complete civilization. If it does not, there will come a time when a civilization based on a world order will lie like a great city built at the mouth of a river. What course the river will take in its lower reaches we cannot now foresee, nor all the gorges and valleys through which it will earlier have run, nor its tributaries and the confluences. But surely we can perceive its source in the trickle that flowed out of 33 Eccleston Square? This house that was once Winston Churchill's and was Grey's residence during the last part of his Secretaryship still stands (a commemorating tablet bears the name of Churchill only) tall and narrow, a typical small London house of its time. It was in his study there, that Grey first tried to persuade House and through him Wilson of the need for a world authority in which America must join. In the beginning he was unsuccessful but he persevered and the commitment came first secretly as the basis of the pact of 22 February, then publicly in Wilson's epoch-making speech of 27 May 1916* and thereafter in the Covenant that Wilson secured in Paris and embodied in the League of Nations. For years past visionaries had foreseen the new order and already in 1915 many men of learning and intelligence were at work on post-war schemes. These are the underground waters of change and they are always plentiful. What counts is the force that drives them up to the surface where governments take action and the skill that channels the rivulet so that it is not dammed or diverted or wasted in a bog. Of the men who accomplished this Grey was the first in time.†

We have seen how consistently he had pressed House throughout his stay in England in the early part of the year to concede the need for American participation in a new world order. When he went to Fallodon a few days before House left England, he wrote to him again from there.

The more I consider this war the more I feel that your Government must take a hand in the larger aspects of the peace, if human ideals are to get and keep the ascendancy over material militarism and political ambition. Germany is the peril to-day, but the peril will recur every century in Europe if Europe is left to itself.[93]

Again on 10 August he wrote to House on the same topic.

My own mind revolves more and more about the point that the refusal of a Conference was the fatal step that decided peace or war last year, and about the moral to be drawn from it: which is that the pearl of great price, if it can be found, would be some League of Nations that could be relied on to insist that disputes between any two nations must be settled by the arbitration, mediation or conference of others. International Law has hitherto had no sanction. The lesson of this war is that the Powers must bind themselves to give it a sanction. If that can be secured, freedom of the seas and many other things will become easy.[94]

On 26 August he wrote more pointedly about mediation by the United States. Several neutrals, he said, had pressed him about a conference to undertake mediation. He had replied that no conference would be much use

---

* See p. 489 below.

† In the first half of 1915 a League of Nations Society was formed in England and a League to Enforce Peace in America. Lowes Dickinson is generally credited with the invention of the name 'League of Nations'. See H. G. Wells, *Experiment in Autobiography*, Gollancz, 1934, vol. 2, p. 694: A. J. P. Taylor, *Politics in Wartime*, Hamish Hamilton, 1964, p. 96: E. M. Forster, *Goldsworthy Lowes Dickinson*, Arnold, 1938, pp. 163-73. Shortly after the outbreak of war Dickinson formed a group to discuss a scheme for a League. It was chaired by Bryce and called the Bryce group. See Edmund Ions, *James Bryce and American Democracy*, Macmillan, 1968, pp. 266-72. Grey was in touch with the Bryce group and could have got the name 'League of Nations' from it. Leonard Woolf was also a member of the Bryce group. He wrote a book on *International Government* which was used by the British delegation at the Peace Conference. See Leonard Woolf, *Beginning Again*, Hogarth Press, 1964, pp. 183-92.

unless the United States was in it. While the Allies of course were concentrating on victory, it was in his mind continually that the awful sufferings of the war would have been in vain unless at the end of it nations were
determined that future generations should not fall into such a catastrophe
again. He looked to America under the guidance of the President to help 'in
those larger conditions of peace' which should interest neutrals as much as
belligerents.[95] At a dinner party in London on 1 September where, Tyrrell,
who had been Grey's private secretary, met Van Dyke, Wilson's former
Princeton colleague, now ambassador at The Hague, the two men had an
hour's conversation. Tyrrell pressed Grey's ideas, especially about a league
of nations, with the obvious intent that his thoughts should be passed on.[96]

As always House responded quickly to the slightest hint of mediation.
Impetuously he replied to Grey on 3 September:

> Do you think the President could make peace proposals to the belligerents at
> this time upon the broad basis of the elimination of militarism and navalism and
> a return, as nearly as possible, to the status quo? Will you not advise me?[97]

A little later the Colonel began to wonder whether it was really worth a try.
He recurred to the thought which he had expressed to Lansing in July*
that the opportunity of getting Germany to make peace had passed. On
14 September he wrote to Grey begging him not to take the suggestion too
seriously: 'from all that I can hear from Germany, it is utterly hopeless to
think in that direction now.'[98]

But then came Wilson's remark on 22 September about taking part in
the conflict.† It opened up unexpected possibilities. On 8 October the
President and Mrs. Galt came to New York and the Houses gave a dinner
to celebrate their engagement, just announced. They all went to the theatre
to see one of the successes of the period, Cyril Maude in *Grumpy*. But
House managed to get twenty minutes with the President and this is his
account of what he said.

> I thought we had lost our opportunity to break with Germany, and it looked as
> if she had a better chance than ever of winning, and if she did win our turn would
> come next; and we were not only unprepared, but there would be no one to help
> us stand the first shock. Therefore, we should do something decisive now—some-
> thing that would either end the war in a way to abolish militarism or that would
> bring us in with the Allies to help them do it. My suggestion is to ask the Allies,
> unofficially, to let me know whether or not it would be agreeable to them to have
> us demand that hostilities cease. We should put it upon the high ground that the
> neutral world was suffering along with the belligerents and that we had rights as
> well as they, and that peace parleys should begin upon the broad basis of both

       * See p. 314 above.   † See p. 377 above.

military and naval disarmament . . . If the Allies understood our purpose, we could be as severe in our language concerning them as we were with the Central Powers. The Allies, after some hesitation, could accept our offer or demand and, if the Central Powers accepted, we would then have accomplished a master-stroke of diplomacy. If the Central Powers refused to acquiesce, we could then push our insistence to a point where diplomatic relations would first be broken off, and later the whole force of our Government—and perhaps the force of every neutral— might be brought against them.

The President was startled by this plan. He seemed to acquiesce by silence.[99] Three days later House had Polk to lunch and unfolded the plan to him. Polk, he recorded, 'thought the idea was good from every stand-point'.[100] Two days after that House put the plan to Lansing who, he said, agreed with him absolutely.

Just as he took silence for acquiescence, so House was apt to take acquiescence for warm approval. Lansing's reaction is perhaps better gauged by the letter he wrote six weeks later when House had put the plan on paper and Wilson sent it to him for his comments.

In regard to the discussion relative to peace, I think that there is a possibility that it might work out along the lines suggested but there are so many problems connected with it—such as boundaries, colonial possessions and indemnities, that I hardly like to express an opinion until it takes a more definite form.[101]

This marks not only the extent of the Secretary's enthusiasm but also the beginning and end of his curiosity. At this time he was juggling with the *Lusitania*, the *Ancona*, and *personae non gratae* at the German and Austrian embassies; and the passage quoted was sandwiched between others relating to these tastier topics. He had not, as Bryan had, any envy of the Colonel's role, nor had he Bryan's apostolic zeal for peace. He preferred to stay at home and keep house. The President made the great new commitment three months later without any further consultation with his Secretary of State.

Meanwhile Grey, ignorant of course of the startling development, had been composing a response to House in the same minor key in which the overture had been played. Grey's letter was sent on 22 September and the British ambassador handed it to House in Washington on 13 October. All that Grey really wanted—and in this he was the world statesman rather than the British Foreign Secretary—was to get America committed to the idea of the League of Nations. What House appeared to want was the acceptance by Britain of peace based on the return to the *status quo*, and so far he had given no indication that he had changed his mind about the possibilities of an American commitment. Grey put the point bluntly.[102] Would the President, he wrote, propose that there should be a League of Nations binding themselves to side against any Power which broke a treaty, which broke the rules of warfare on sea or land, or which refused in case of dispute to adopt some other method of settlement than that of war? Only in some such system was there any hope for disarmament and only the American Government could propose it. As to the possibilities of peace on the basis of the *status quo*, Grey could not answer without consulting his Cabinet and the Allies. If the President was really prepared to make the proposal, he would consult them. Personally he thought that neither side was ready to discuss peace.

England is bound to fight on with her Allies as long as they will fight, to secure victory, and I do long to see the bullied provinces of Alsace-Lorraine restored to the freer government of France, and Russia ought to get her outlet to the sea. But the minimum to avoid disaster is the restoration of Belgium and the preservation of France in the terms of peace.

At the same time Grey cabled a rather warmer message to be delivered through Spring Rice. Spring Rice was to tell House that Grey had entire confidence in him and was always prepared to listen to anything he had to say. If he had reason to believe that Germany really wanted peace on terms 'fair to us and our friends' it would be worth his while to come over.[103] There was added the usual warning that Grey's opinion did not count until the Cabinet and the other parties had been consulted; and also a suggestion that communications should not be made through Spring Rice unless the French ambassador was associated with him.

On 14 October the Colonel took Grey's letter to the White House. Wilson had now had six days in which to consider the suggestion of intervention and House was pleased to find him cordially acquiescing. House took three days over the preparation of the answer to Grey, 'one of the most important letters I ever wrote' he called it. There follows the draft which he sent to Wilson on 17 October.

It has occurred to me that the time may soon come when this Government should intervene between the belligerents and demand that peace parleys begin upon the broad basis of the elimination of militarism and navalism . . .

In my opinion, it would be a world-wide calamity if the war should continue to a point where the Allies could not, with the aid of the United States, bring about a peace along the lines you and I have so often discussed. What I want you to know is that, whenever you consider the time is propitious for this intervention, I will propose it to the President. He may then desire me to go to Europe in order that a more intimate understanding as to procedure may be had.

It is in my mind that, after conferring with your Government, I should proceed to Berlin and tell them that it was the President's purpose to intervene and stop this destructive war, provided the weight of our United States thrown on the side that accepted our proposal could do it.

I would not let Berlin know, of course, of any understanding had with the Allies, but would rather lead them to think our proposal would be rejected by the Allies. This might induce Berlin to accept the proposal, but, if they did not do so, it would nevertheless be the purpose to intervene. If the Central Powers were still obdurate, it would* be necessary for us to join the Allies and force the issue.

I want to call your attention to the danger of postponing action too long. If the Allies should be unsuccessful and become unable to do their full share, it would be increasingly difficult, if not impossible, for us to intervene. I would have made this proposal to the President last Autumn, but you will remember that it was not agreeable to the Allies.[104]

The plan was to be put forward as House's own idea and as not yet considered by the President. Indeed, House put into the letter the diplomatic untruth that he would not suggest it to the President until he knew that it would meet with the approval of the Allies. He said also that he would tell Sir Cecil that at present it was merely a discussion 'between friend and friend'.

Wilson returned the draft on 18 October with two alterations, one purely textual and the other one which House noted in his diary as 'quite important'.[105] Where House had written 'it would be necessary for us to join the Allies and force the issue', Wilson added 'probably'. Wilson himself attached no importance to the qualification. He wrote to House:

I have made one or two unimportant verbal changes in this, but they do not alter the sense of it. I do not want to make it inevitable quite that we should take part to force terms on Germany, because the exact circumstances of such a crisis are impossible to determine. The letter is altogether right. I pray God it may bring results.[106]

On 19 October the letter still dated 17 October, was sent to Grey split into two parts mailed from separate post offices and with a separate letter of instruction to Grey as to how to put them together again. Unfortunately one of the essential parts went on a British ship that was not sailing directly to England but via Canadian ports to pick up troops. Grey did not receive the whole confection until about 8 November.

It certainly did not make the impact upon him that House had hoped for. House thought of it as an offer which was 'practically to ensure a victory to the Allies'.[107] Perhaps if Grey had known, as House did, that it actually had the approval of the President who had written of it as something that made it only just short of inevitable that America should take part in bringing

---

* At this point Wilson inserted 'probably'.

Germany to terms, he might have displayed more eagerness. Without these accompaniments the letter, even after making all allowance for the use of euphemisms appropriate to any discussion of war-making, reads ambiguously. Certainly it was a proposal leading to American intervention in some form, but in what? What was meant by throwing in weight? Joining the Allies and forcing the issue sounded definite but left behind it the nagging afterthought that if it meant getting into the war, why did it not say so plainly? The penultimate paragraph of the letter managed to say almost as much as that in its second sentence and then to take most of it back in its third. 'If the Allies should . . . become unable to do their full share' surely must mean that America was going to share something with the Allies; and what could they share except the fighting? But then the reader learnt that this proposal would have been made a year ago if it had then been agreeable to the Allies; and whatever House had proposed or thought of proposing the year before it was not America's entry into the war.

But anyway Grey was handicapped. Even if there were no ambiguities in the message and no 'probably' and even if he had felt sure that it would be the friendliness of House that would control the President's mind and not the hostility of the State Department manifested in the Note of 5 November which he had received only a few days before, Grey knew that 'a peace along the lines you and I have so often discussed' would not be enough for the majority of his colleagues or for any of the Allies. He could let House come and talk about it if he wished on the chance that it might lead to something but he could not decently offer any encouragement.

So the point which evidently struck him most forcibly was that House still avoided any commitment to American involvement in the League of Nations. This was his immediate reaction to the message and he cabled to House on 9 November asking exactly what was meant by the 'elimination of militarism and navalism'.[108] Did it mean that the President would propose a League of Nations as suggested in his (Grey's) letter of 22 September?

This question made it imperative for House to come off the fence. There is nothing specific to show what finally caused him to change his mind about American involvement; perhaps it was simply that acceptance of it was now plainly required for the fulfilment of his plan. He composed for Wilson's approval a brief answer which said yes; the proposal contemplated was 'broadly speaking' along the lines of Grey's letter of 22 September. It is this tailpiece rather than the momentous letter of 17 October that history will emphasize; the latter led only to an abortive pact but the former was the beginning of the end of American isolation. It meant, as House wrote later in his diary, 'the reversal of the foreign policy of this government',[109] and, he might have added of every American Government that had ever been.

It was for this that he had to get Wilson's approval and the letter that accompanied the draft was one of the sort he reserved for the occasions when Wilson had to be brought to the highest pitch. He ended it:

> This is the part I think you are destined to play in this world tragedy, and it is the noblest part that has ever come to a son of man. This country will follow you along such a path, no matter what the cost may be.[110]

He need not have exerted himself. Although Wilson had never discussed as a matter of practical politics the abandonment of Washington's celebrated advice against European entanglement, he was not on this issue anything of a traditionalist. For him the annexation of the Philippines had meant the end of isolationism. 'We stepped into the arena of the world since the Spanish war', he said in a lecture at the end of 1900, 'and entered a new century.' The annexation, unless it was to be justified as conquest, thereby sinking the new world to the level of the old, had to mean that America was concerning herself with the welfare of other nations. In his *Atlantic Monthly* article in 1901* Wilson far outstripped contemporary thinking.[111] 'The whole world has already become a single vicinage', he there wrote; and he wrote of American isolationism as a thing of the past and 'quite without parallel in modern history'. But, he said, had it not been for the Philippines America might not have seen where her duty lay.

On 6 August 1914 President Eliot of Harvard, horrified by the outrageous behaviour of Germany, suggested in a letter to the President a combination of nations to enforce a blockade against her.[112] Would not the people of the United States, Eliot asked, now approve of the abandonment of Washington's advice? The plan did not appeal at all to Wilson and Eliot himself reconsidered it. But the letter may have put thoughts into Wilson's mind. Stockton Axson, his brother-in-law, recalled many years later a conversation with Wilson in August 1914 in which he had spoken of a post-war association of nations bound together to protect the peace.[113] On 4 January 1915 he wrote to a friend that he was very much interested in creating a world federation although he had to stand aloof at present.[114] So he immediately approved House's draft, his only comment on it being the favourable one that 'broadly speaking' might be omitted.[115] The cable was dispatched on 11 November. At last Grey had won his point.

A thought struck Wilson. If America came to the conference as sponsoring a League of Nations, could she not remain on high at that altruistic level and leave all territorial squabbling to be done by the belligerents themselves? He wrote to House the next day that he thought that the paragraph in Grey's letter contained the *necessary* programme. This began the edging

* See p. 113 above.

out of territorial questions from the agenda. On 19 November House told Bernstorff of the project. As he put it to him it was a suggestion that if Germany would consent to general disarmament America would throw in her weight and demand that the war cease; America, House said, was not concerned regarding territorial questions or indemnity. It was of course no part of House's plan to discuss such questions with Germany anyway. But it looked as if at some time after this House decided to drop the point altogether or at least to push it well into the background. It is difficult to say exactly when or why. Its omission emasculated House's plan; how could he enforce moderation in the Allies' terms without discussing them? But it was not only the President who was disinclined to discuss them; Grey also was plainly reluctant.

After his cable asking for elucidation there was no word from Grey until 25 November. Then there arrived a long letter which he had written on 11 November. Most of it was taken up with his lamentations over the tenor of the State Department's Note of 5 November. The part of it which dealt with House's offer was depressingly cool. He must have a definite proposal, Grey wrote, to put to the Cabinet and to the Allies and that was why he had cabled to ask exactly what House meant.

> I do not see how they could commit themselves in advance to any proposition without knowing exactly what it was and knowing that the United States was prepared to intervene and make good if they accepted it.[116]

It would be nice to talk things over with House, Grey said, but he could not urge him to come since his presence would not have any practical effect at the moment; the Allies had made up their minds to a winter campaign.

House was grieved. Grey surely could not have appreciated the magnitude of the offer. 'The British are in many ways dull', he wrote in his diary.[117] During the last weekend in November the President and the Secretary were both in New York, the former with his fiancée and the latter with his wife, to see the Army–Navy football game on the Saturday. On the Sunday the Lansings lunched with the Houses. The Colonel's conversation with the Secretary was about the need for 'a complete and satisfactory understanding' with the British;[118] some way must be found of 'making it clear to the Allies that we considered their cause our cause'. At five o'clock the same day House had an hour and a half with the President and took the same line.[119] Wilson appeared to agree but asked how they could make the point; the ambassadors were hopeless; the only thing was for House to go to London. House did not much like that. He was willing to go of course, he wrote to Wilson on 1 December, but he doubted the necessity for precipitate action.[120] 'We are now in the most delicate situation that has yet arisen', he wrote in his diary.[121] What Grey had asked for in his letter of 11 November was a precise formulation of what was meant by 'intervention' and of how America proposed to make it good. This, if America meant business, could conveniently have been given in writing and that was what House had contemplated. For he had written to Grey on 11 November (their letters crossed on the high seas):

> I think we should go as far as possible by correspondence, for it would not be wise for me to go to England until we had a thorough understanding as to what we should do and whether to act. It may be that the time will not be propitious until Spring or Summer, but you will know best about that and I must necessarily be guided by your advice.[122]

But Wilson evidently felt that he would rather have their thoughts and intentions by word of mouth than in writing. Wilson's enthusiasm for a detailed commitment was cooling. As will be seen, it sank to its lowest level just before House left for Europe and did not rise again until House brought back the pact for approval.

Washington now began to concentrate on the problem which the inactivity of Grey had brought into the limelight. The situation made very apparent the disadvantage of having an ambassador who had no diplomatic training in doing what he disliked. Page would have disliked very much—up to the point of non-intervention—a manœuvre designed to let America sneak into the war by a postern gate instead of marching in with flags flying over a lowered drawbridge. Moreover, he would not try to make Grey under-stand that the American proposal was tied up with their differences over the blockade. While House was disturbed by Grey's reproach in his letter of 11 November that America was striking the weapon of sea power out of British hands and thus ensuring a German victory, and wanted to make it plain that on the contrary they had a common cause, Wilson wanted to make it plain that America, however friendly *au fond*, was not going to go on indefinitely being pushed around by illegalities and consequently that when she made peace proposals as a way out of the legal impasse she must be listened to. Wilson was not content with the plop made by the Note of 5 November; American grievances were justified, he told House in December, and must be actively supported.[123]

But Page had got almost to the point where the only grievances he could support were the British against America. He was now taking very literally Wilson's request not to 'leave out a single line or item which is interesting your own thought'.* At first he spared Wilson 'the insulting remarks that go about London'.[124] But by January 1916 he was considering it his

---

* See p. 317 above.

duty to tell the President things which probably no one else did and which, he said, House in particular declined to take seriously. The list of things to be told included the information that a common nickname for Americans was 'too prouds' and that Wilson's picture on the screen had caused such hissing and booing that it was hastily removed. The racy letters in Page's fine hand which Wilson had so enjoyed were now making sickly reading for him. Sometimes they were cloyed with pathos that could be acceptable only to a fellow devotee; they were almost insulting in their assumption that the reader could hardly believe in the neutrality he preached. Wilson began to pass them over to House in unopened packets.

But the chief target for Washington's dissatisfaction was the British ambassador. Everybody was now finding him impossible to talk to. On 15 November in conversation with Polk as House described it in a heady brew of mixed metaphors, Spring Rice blew off the lid and threw down the gauntlet.[125] Lansing thought that he should be replaced by Bryce. Wilson was for by-passing the obstacle rather than removing it and suggested that House should tell Grey that they could not deal with a 'highly excitable invalid'.[126]

House's tactics on intervention were now those of postponement, smothering Grey with reassurance without pressure, while at the same time he tried to solve the ambassadorial difficulty without a visit. To these ends he made use of Plunkett with whom he had several talks in early December. The chief trouble in the Anglo-American situation, House told him, was the temperament of Sir Cecil. What about having Plunkett in his place? 'A delightfully American idea', Plunkett thought, 'I know no foreign languages, have no wife or plate':[127] the plate was then, as are still the wife and the foreign languages, an important part of an ambassador's equipment. But his health, like House's, would not stand the climate of Washington. On intervention House's view was that it was best to refrain from decisive action until the wearing-down process had continued some months longer. But Wilson and he were determined to see the Allies through, he told Plunkett, and America would make the terms of peace even if she did not participate in the war.

On 7 December he sent Grey a message through Plunkett saying that his mind was no longer running towards peace even on the broad lines spoken of before. What was needful, he said, was a better working understanding: 'the machinery we are using is not altogether satisfactory. Just why I cannot explain here and it may be necessary for me to see you in person.'[128] Then on 10 December he wrote direct to Grey suggesting that he should send his private secretary, Eric Drummond, over to talk. He referred mysteriously to most important decisions in the making and to 'the policy which we have determined upon and of which you have only the vaguest idea'.[129]

There was now more than a possibility that House's plan would be over-taken by events. The peremptory note on the *Ancona* was sent on 6 December and Lansing was still determined to press Bernstorff hard on the *Lusitania*. On 12 December House wrote to Page: 'We are much nearer a break with the Central Powers than at any time before. It would be as well for you to call to the attention of our friends in England the fact that the lower their fortunes seem the more ready we are to help.'[130] But he did not foresee for himself any great role in the immediate future and indeed was thinking of going to Texas for a few weeks.

Three days later House was disconcerted, and doubtless a little embar-rassed also after all he had been saying to 'our friends in England', by a change of presidential wind. Except perhaps for the disinclination he had shown to putting anything further in writing, Wilson had given House no hint that his distaste for embroilment was returning. The two men had a long talk at the White House on 15 December which House recorded for his diary as follows:

I found the President not quite as belligerent as he was the last time we were together. He seemed to think we would be able to keep out of the war. His general idea is that if the Allies were not able to defeat Germany alone, they could scarcely do so with the help of the United States because it would take too long for us to get in a state of preparedness. It would therefore be a useless sacrifice on our part to go in. I called his attention to the necessity of our having the Allies on our side for the reason we would have to undertake the task alone when Germany was ready to deal with us. He admits this, and yet I cannot quite get him up to the point where he is willing to take action. By action, I mean not to declare war, but to let the Allies know we are definitely on their side and that it is not our intention to permit Germany to win if the strength of this country can prevent it. The last time we talked he was quite ready to take this stand, but he has visibly weakened.[131]

Nevertheless, Wilson was insistent that House should go to London, overruling the objections of Lansing who thought it might be better to wait and see whether or not the pressure he was using over the *Lusitania* and *Ancona* negotiations resulted in a breach. It was absolutely urgent, Wilson said, to explain to the British Cabinet direct the American point of view. House of course accepted the decision. He gave out to everyone, including Page, that he had no peace plans. The public was told that the object of the visit to London, Paris, Berlin, and perhaps Rome was to brief ambassadors who could not conveniently be brought home. Spring Rice was told this by House when they met on 17 December and passed the information on to Grey coupled with the assurance that there was no 'mission'. House and the ambassador were together for an hour and a half and Sir Cecil nearly undid all the bad work he had been doing. House wrote: 'I have never seen

him more entertaining, affectionate and reasonable. He was all we know
he can be on occasions . . . How can I go to London and demand his head?
I am trying to think of some way to save him.'[132] House saw Bernstorff also
on 16 December and again on the 22nd when he conveyed an invitation
to House to go to Berlin to discuss peace upon the general terms of military
and naval disarmament. House reported to Wilson—now on his honeymoon:

> In the conversation which Bernstorff repeated to his Government, I said I
> believed if they would consent to a plan which embraced general disarmament you
> would be willing to throw the weight of this Government into the scales and
> demand that the war cease. That we were not concerned regarding territorial
> questions or indemnity, but we were concerned regarding the larger questions,
> which involved not only the belligerents but the neutrals also.
>
> The Allies will take care of the territorial and indemnity questions, and we need
> not go into that at this time. If we start with such discussions, it would involve us
> in controversies that might be endless and footless.[133]

In this letter House also asked for instructions and for suitable messages
to be handed to the men he was to meet. 'It is hard to estimate the effect of
flattery and politeness upon Europeans, and this may be said of the British
and Germans as well as of the Latin races.'

Wilson replied at some length from Hot Springs on Christmas Eve.
He had written on the same day to Lansing in reply to his 'disturbing'
account of Senator Stone's charge that the Administration was too kind
to Britain,* saying that it made 'House's errand all the more pressing and
opportune'.[134] His letter to House began by passing the diplomats under
unfavourable review. Everything Bernstorff said had to be corroborated
from Berlin. Spring Rice was 'puzzling and incalculable . . . some less
childish man should take his place'. This was 'the errand upon which you
are primarily bound' and 'the demand in the Senate for further, immediate
and imperative pressure on England and her allies makes the necessity for
it the more pressing'. 'About the possibilities in the direction of peace',
Wilson wrote as follows:

> You ask for instructions as to what attitude and tone you are to take at the
> several capitals. I feel that you do not need any. Your own letters (for example,
> this one in which you report your conversation with Bernstorff) exactly echo my
> own views and purposes. I agree with you that we have nothing to do with local
> settlements,—territorial questions, indemnities, and the like,—but are concerned
> only in the future peace of the world and the guarantees to be given for that. The
> only possible guarantees, that is, the only guarantees that any rational man could
> accept are (a) military and naval disarmament and (b) a league of nations, to secure

---

* See pp. 373-4 above.

each nation against aggression and maintain the absolute freedom of the seas. If either party to the present war will let us say to the other that they are willing to discuss peace on such terms, it will clearly be our duty to use our utmost moral force to oblige the other to parley, and I do not see how they could stand in the opinion of the world if they refused.[135]

House replied on 26 December: 'I think we agree entirely.'[136] Notwithstanding these mutual professions of comprehension an outsider may be left in doubt about just what House was supposed to do. He had to talk to Grey and what Grey would have in front of him would be the proposal of 17 October. Was House to tell him that this was now scrapped? Did America's lack of interest in territorial questions extend to cover the restoration of Belgium, Grey's 'minimum to avoid disaster'? If it did, what hope was there of interesting the Allies? If it did not, what, if anything, was America prepared to do if Germany refused to evacuate Belgium at the sound of morality's trumpet? It is hard to believe that House thought he could make any impression in England or anywhere on the Continent with a proposal to arraign before the bar of public opinion any belligerent who refused to discuss disarmament in a territorial vacuum. But perhaps he felt that it did not much matter. House was not now looking for quick results. It is evident that he did not think that his plan would work until the Allies had suffered some reverse; it was when their fortunes were low that America could come in on her own terms.

Whatever was in his mind House and his wife and secretary left New York on a Dutch liner on 28 December 1915 with Wilson's gratitude 'for the incomparable and inestimable services you are rendering the country and me your friend' and with the assurance that his counsel on domestic matters would be greatly missed.[137]

XIII

HOUSE TRIES HIS HAND

Peace sentiment in America and Britain – House in London: 5–20 January 1916 – Wilson's preparedness speeches: 27 January to 4 February 1916 – Germany's change of submarine policy: January 1916 – *Lusitania* negotiations: 7 January to 8 February 1916 – armed ships and another *modus vivendi* – House in Berlin and Paris: January and February 1916 – collapse of the *modus vivendi*: 15 February 1916

IN 1915 quite an appreciable number of Americans besides Bryan were becoming convinced that the war ought to be stopped somehow. They were animated partly perhaps by the nervous fear that if it was not stopped America would sooner or later get embroiled, but just as much by the feeling that the war was becoming an insensate performance that debased humanity. Within three weeks of its outbreak the Niagara Section of the New York Peace Society was preparing to raise a million dollars to set up a commission to investigate the cause of the war and produce a plan for settling it; 'looks to me very dangerous', Wilson noted.[1] Thereafter delegations descended upon the White House and the State Department and, thinned down to individuals, visited House to promote the idea of a Peace Conference in some neutral capital. The Colonel was disposed to treat all such people as cranks: their intentions were good but they had no idea how to set about them: they were like children entering for a chess tournament before they had learnt the moves. Yet since in the end House was no more successful than they, it is worth, in order to set it beside House's more sophisticated methods, just noticing the effort of one who was not an ineffective man, Henry Ford, the millionaire motor manufacturer and founder of the great organization which bears his name.

Stimulated by pacifist bodies, mainly female, he went to see House on 22 November 1915 and the President on the following day. He told Wilson that he would give his entire fortune ('I guess I know how to make some more') to end the war in Europe and put down militarism wherever it existed. The following day he announced his project—the voyage of a 'peace ship' to sail for Europe with a cargo of evangelists to spread the word.[2] The object was to have the men out of the trenches by Christmas. House declined the invitation to become a passenger. Bryan found it more important to stay at home to fight preparedness and other leading pacifists made similar excuses. The ship sailed on 14 December 1915 in a gust of ridicule and the project evaporated after a nine days wonder. Ford returned disillusioned. It had not taken him long to grasp the point. The people responsible, he said, were not, as he had supposed, the bankers, militarists, and munition manufacturers, but the men who were getting slaughtered. This was a discovery that Wilson and House might with advantage have noted.

In Britain there was nothing in the shape of a mass movement against the war. There had been from the first a small minority, chiefly among the intellectuals, who regarded the war as wicked or at least unnecessary. A sample of the high intellectual response may be obtained from a look at the society of the élite at Cambridge University that was called the Apostles. Its membership in 1914 had in it many names that have outlived their time. Rupert Brooke, the war poet, was among them: 'now God be praised who has matched us with His hour.' But the majority thought differently. Bertrand Russell, the philosopher who lived long enough to condemn the war in Vietnam half a century later, was the most energetic, as he was intellectually the most distinguished, of those who were anti-war. He was an emotional pacifist, shocked by the horrors and futility of war, whatever its cause. Some went further. There was a man called Sanger, one of those who, as in every society of this sort, is regarded with exceptional affection and esteem by his friends but who leaves no mark on the world beyond: he became a barrister and if he had not found a place in the biographies of his successful contemporaries he would have enjoyed only the restricted fame of an editor of *Jarman on Wills*. He wrote to Russell on 7 August 1915:

As you know I have always regarded Grey as one of the most wicked and dangerous criminals that has ever disgraced civilisation, but it is awful that a Liberal Cabinet should have been party to engineering a war to destroy Teutonic civilisation in favour of Servians and the Russian autocracy.[3]

Lytton Strachey, later to be more celebrated than his cousin St. Loe, the editor of the *Spectator*, and holding very different views from him, was active with Russell in support of conscientious objectors in 1916 after conscription had come into force. Maynard Keynes, another Apostle, soon absorbed in government service, shifted uneasily in his seat in the Treasury: Russell and Strachey felt that he had let them down. But Russell was surprised to find that many of his friends were of a different way of thinking about the war. On the evening of 4 August he quarrelled with G. M. Trevelyan, the historian, 'along the whole length of the Strand'. Gilbert Murray, who had been pro-Boer, 'went out of his way to write about the wickedness of the Germans'. A. N. Whitehead, joint author with Russell of *Principia Mathematica*, the work with which he made his name at the beginning of the century, was 'savagely war-like'. In October 1914 Russell met T. S. Eliot, the poet, in New Oxford Street and asked him what he thought of the war; Eliot replied that he was not a pacifist. 'That is to say', Russell commented, 'he considered any excuse good enough for homicide.'[4]

Sanger's view of the cause of the conflict was extreme. Most opponents of the war, including Russell himself, thought that Germany was chiefly to blame but that the Allies were not guiltless. Two other Cambridge Apostles, Lowes Dickinson and Leonard Woolf, who were active in promoting schemes for a League of Nations, thought the same. This was probably also the view of Morley ('You and I are in accord on this breakdown of right and political wisdom', he wrote to Russell),[5] who resigned from the Cabinet on this issue in August 1914. The stronghold of these men and the place where they met with those active politicians who thought likewise (Morley retired into privacy and silence) was in the Union of Democratic Control, a body formed on the outbreak of war, the name signifying the creed that aristocracies and oligarchies were the cause of war. Its secretary and mainspring was a man called E. D. Morel, one of those men to whom conformity of any sort is abhorrent. As essential equipment for his difficult duties, he was well provided with the inability to see any point of view except his own: those who disagreed with him were 'dishonest' or possibly 'a personal force for evil'. His championship of Germany was so extreme that the German Socialists had to ask him to pipe down lest he spoilt their case against their own Government. Trailing behind him, many of them at a considerable distance, were the few Liberal and Labour members of Parliament who on this issue had detached themselves from their party. The Labour party had not given much thought to foreign policy. In its manifesto for the General Election of 1906 it devoted to foreign affairs, as Mr. Taylor points out,[6] only one half of a sentence, the whole being: 'Wars are fought to make the rich richer and school-children are still neglected.' When in 1914 patriotism proved more powerful than the undesirability of making the rich richer, Ramsay Macdonald, the Leader of the Parliamentary Party, who was to be Prime Minister in the first Labour Government in 1923, resigned his post. Charles Trevelyan, the elder brother of G. M., resigned at the same time from a junior position in the Liberal Government. Arthur Ponsonby and Noel Buxton were two other Liberal M.P.s who shared his view. These three subsequently became Socialists.

Until conscription was threatened all that a pacifist could do was to discourage individuals from volunteering for the army or for war work and to press for a negotiated peace. As the war dragged on inconclusively through 1915, the latter objective began to attract men not in sympathy with the former. Liberals who had acted initially in revulsion to German arrogance and brutality began to ask themselves whether the issue was as black and white as they had supposed. Nothing short of stark opposition between good and evil could justify prolonging the miseries of war to the bitter end; if one side was even partly to blame, the issue should be negotiable. Conscription acted as a catalyst for these ideas. There was talk of this measure almost as soon as the first coalition was formed. In June 1915 Lloyd George took it up publicly. Throughout the rest of the year Asquith, who himself disliked it but was chiefly concerned to avoid a party split, fought a delaying action; eventually the Military Service Bill became law in May 1916. It seems now astounding that there was so much opposition in principle to the idea of sharing fairly the burdens of military service. But Britain was not quite yet a nation at war; fighting was still an individual rather than a national obligation and still dependent upon patriotism. Liberals, who had supported the war because it was a war for freedom, asked what would become of freedom if men were forced to fight. Conscription meant, the *Manchester Guardian* said, 'the moral defeat of the British system and the victory of German methods'.[7] It was hard to accept the logic of a war for freedom—that men must pay in coinage for the safety of the treasure. In this atmosphere a few more men began to question whether the war had not gone on long enough.

Differences over conscription on the Liberal side of the Government led indirectly to a short and sharp crisis while House was crossing the ocean and nearly resulted in Grey not being at the Foreign Office to meet him at the other end. Only one minister resigned on the issue of principle but two others threatened resignation because of the effect of conscription on industrial production. Grey supported them, but his letter of resignation to the Prime Minister on 29 December 1915 suggests that what really moved him was his increasing weariness.[8] The strain of war was telling on him more than on most. 'I hated it beforehand and I hate it now', he wrote to Churchill on 13 November.[9] Five months later Mrs. Churchill described him to her husband as 'terribly aged and worn-looking'.[10] So now he wrote to Asquith that he had always felt that he ought to have left the Cabinet when Haldane went in May. Asquith replied the same day that he was filled with despair at the thought of being deserted by all his oldest and best friends. Grey was much touched and stayed; and McKenna and Runciman compromised. Only Sir John Simon resigned, an act which he later thought mistaken.[11]

Mr. House is here again and I hope that you can dine with me tomorrow, Fri, 8.15.[12]

Here again. Would it be wrong to imagine a hint of surfeit between the lines of Page's invitation to Grey sent on 5 January 1916? House's sea voyage ended at Falmouth that afternoon. Less favoured passengers, he noted, were not allowed off the ship for twenty-four hours 'because of examinations incident to the war'.[13] But there was nothing contraband about House; naval officers escorted him and his party to the railway station and put him on a sleeper for Paddington. Either Grey could not dine or House could not wait or (more probably) wanted to talk first without Page. In the afternoon of 6 January the two men were in conference. The 'primary purpose' of the Colonel's mission had a short life.

I touched lightly upon the British Ambassador and his temperamental unfitness for the position he occupies. I did not push this further but will perhaps pick it up later.[14]

So House noted his first conversation with Grey: and so he reported to Wilson, but without the qualifying 'perhaps'. He later suggested to Grey that Bryce might go to Washington under cover of some employment,[15] but he did not push hard against the natural obstacles to such a proposal including 'the wounding of ambassadorial dignity'. Bryce advised strongly against any application for Sir Cecil's removal and on 13 January House wrote to Wilson that the matter was better left in abeyance lest it interfered with their other plans.

Undoubtedly the application would have failed. Grey was intensely loyal to his subordinates and had, moreover, a great affection and admiration for Spring Rice and especially for his ardent patriotism. 'We are all patriotic', Grey wrote more than fifteen years later, 'but the welfare of his country was a matter of daily concern to him.'[16] Grey took an early opportunity of letting the proposed victim know that he ridiculed the idea of a special mission. On 24 March he wrote personally to 'My dear Springy' to tell him of the most gratifying letters he had received from America, praising him exceedingly and contrasting him most favourably with Bernstorff.[17] The encomium seems to have been taken from a letter from Senator Lodge about 'one of the oldest and best friends I have in the world'.[18] To conclude the affair the Foreign Secretary recommended Spring Rice for the G.C.M.G.

As for Page, he had just sent off on 4 January a 'purposely restrained' telegram[19] to the State Department to which, being unable, as he said, to do any real service by mincing matters, he had reported that the only way in which America could preserve English respect and elevate herself above the level of a third or fourth class power was by the immediate dismissal of every German and Austrian official in Washington. However, House found him 'exceedingly cordial and pleasant'[20] and reported to the President that the ambassador had done what he could. After this the Colonel seems to have forgotten all about the two ambassadors and the primary purpose of his visit; and so apparently did Wilson. Already by 10 January House was referring in his diary to his peace plan as 'the real purpose of my visit'.[21]

The plan that was unfolded to Grey on 6 January contained a more grandiose idea than the simple thought in Wilson's parting letter that America should come down against whichever side refused disarmament. It envisaged a union of democracies based upon freedom of the seas and the curtailment of militarism. The plan seems to have assumed, no doubt rightly, that the curtailment of militarism was a purely democratic object which Germany would oppose; and consequently what House had to do to make it work was to get Britain to agree to freedom of the seas. This would enable the United States to intervene. Grey appears to have listened with gratifying attention to the familiar argument about the advantages which freedom of the seas would bring Britain and to have asked no awkward questions about any more precise terms of peace or about what was meant by intervention, not even when House said that intervention was preferable to the United States drifting into the war through a diplomatic breach. He confessed to Grey that he had advised Wilson against a breach because he hoped for this sort of agreement about intervention. This could hardly have left Grey with the impression that the intervention might be confined to moral force. But Grey, it seems clear, was not seeking any immediate action. What he wanted was to clinch America's participation in the post-war settlement. As yet he had nothing direct from the President himself. On the plea that his colleagues would like it, he got House to cable Wilson for 'some assurance of your willingness to co-operate in a policy seeking to bring about and maintain permanent peace'.[22]

House saw Balfour the same evening but it was at a dinner party at Brooks's and there was no detailed conversation.[23] It was arranged that the three, House, Grey, and Balfour, should lunch together on 10 January so that House could elaborate the plan to Balfour. They would then consider what other members of the Cabinet should be brought in.

House had allowed himself a fortnight in England before he went to

Germany and within a day of his arrival his engagement book was full, including what turned out to be 'a pleasant hour with the King'.[24] He had Page to lunch on 7 January but all they discussed was the unpopularity of the President in Great Britain. Page asked whether he thought the President would be offended with what he had written and House thought it quite likely. House had Drummond to lunch next day and emphasized to him, as he had to Grey and did to other ministers, the difficulties in the way of an understanding caused by Britain's high-handed and irritating policy upon the seas.[25] He may even have made a slight impression. At any rate on 9 February Grey sent out a circular about annoyance to neutrals; and asked for instructions to be given that courtesy, consideration, and civility should be shown.[26]

On 9 January Wilson duly cabled the required assurance but stuck firmly to generalities.

Willing and glad when the opportunity comes to co-operate in a policy seeking to bring about and maintain permanent peace among civilized nations.[27]

With this fortification House met Grey and Balfour on 10 January 1916. Balfour and House did most of the talking beginning with Freedom of the Seas. When House mooted the subject in June 1915 Balfour, as we have seen,* had been non-committal. House

found him not very constructive, but analytical and argumentative. Time and again he would start with the wrong premises. I would gently touch him on the shoulder and ask for a word and would bring back the discussion to the contention we had laid down and not what he was imagining it to be.[28]

House in his diary paints an improbable picture of Grey and Balfour as 'full of suppressed excitement'.[29] Apart from the fact that neither was an excitable man, there was nothing from their point of view to get excited about. That Grey was dubious emerges from everything he wrote and said; and that Balfour was 'argumentative' is what House himself says. Even if themselves persuaded of the practicability of House's plan, they knew how slender was the chance of getting it past their colleagues and the Allies. Of course they must want to see America in the war. But House was assuming a great deal when he took it for granted that they would not only want to see her in the war but also want as ardently as he did to see her controlling the peace. He was asking a good deal of human nature if he expected them to be favourably excited when he told them, as he had already told Grey, that he was largely responsible for the fact that America had not already broken off relations with Germany when 'we would be merely in the ruck of the war along with the balance of them'.[30]

* See p. 279 above.

Anyway nothing was settled. House arranged for another meeting on 15 January and decided meanwhile to get Bryce's advice before taking up the discussion again. The next evening Page had various ministers to dinner and a symposium.[31] He had been asked, Page said, to start things off with the question, what did the United States wish Britain to do? 'The United States', House replied, 'would like Great Britain to do those things which would enable the United States to help Great Britain win the war.' He followed this with a discourse on the burden that the blockade was placing on the President. Lloyd George was one of the guests and so was Lord Reading, the Lord Chief Justice. At the end of dinner Reading took House aside and suggested confidential talks with Lloyd George, a proposal which House accepted and which led him into the temptation, which hitherto he had resisted, of a discussion on territorial terms.

Rufus Isaacs, created Lord Reading when he became Chief Justice in 1913, had been a brilliantly successful barrister. He was an ambitious man with an ambition for the glitter rather than the gold. The Chief Justiceship was a prize which he took but with which he was not contented. His abilities were such that he could not fail in the office; but even if it had not been for the war and the natural feeling it brought that his talents could be better employed, he would soon have found the work tedious. Before he became Chief Justice he had been Attorney-General with a seat in the Cabinet. His charm gave him an easy friendship with all his colleagues but he was especially close to Lloyd George. When at the Bar he had appeared for him in one of the two libel actions in which Lloyd George repelled suggestions of adultery; and when in office the two men had passed together through the ordeal of what was called the Marconi Scandal, an affair in which they were charged with trafficking in the shares of a company then negotiating for a valuable government contract. They were acquitted of dishonesty but not of a grave error of judgement; and from an error of judgement in a matter of this sort a politician is lucky to escape with his public life.

It was to Lloyd George, then Chancellor of the Exchequer, that Reading turned on the outbreak of war. He was given a room in the Treasury where he did great work in helping to sort out the financial problems consequent upon the war. In June 1915 Lloyd George got him a G.C.B., the first of many such honours. In September 1915 he headed a mission to the United States to negotiate the first Anglo-French loan. In New York on 2 October he met House. In fact it was House who arranged to meet him and the two men took to each other at once. House found him, as he wrote later, 'a calm clear-minded statesman with more of the political than the judicial mind'.[32]

On 16 October they breakfasted together on the morning of Reading's departure for England and agreed to keep in touch.

Lloyd George knew nothing about House's plan. But by the end of 1915 his mind was ranging over every possibility that could bring Britain to victory and so inevitably making calculations about American intervention and its consequences. Lloyd George was not the man to leave that sort of thing to the Foreign Office. He got Reading to arrange a quiet meeting on the side; neither Lloyd George nor House, Reading suggested to the latter, would be willing to open his mind fully to the other unless they were alone. The solitude did not exclude Reading himself who had an indirect interest in the conversations since he saw in them opportunities for his own negotiating talents and possibly even then had his eye on the Washington embassy which he later obtained.[33]

So on 14 January the three men dined alone in the Princess Ida Room at the Savoy.[34] When the waiters had withdrawn Lloyd George stated the purpose of the meeting. He believed that the war could go on indefinitely and would do so unless the President intervened. But he thought that intervention, to be effective, should not be offered until around 1 September. By then the big battles of the summer would have been fought; he did not expect them to be conclusive but thought that a forecast could then be made of what the final end might be. As to the peace, he agreed that navalism must go as well as militarism and that the freedom of the seas was at least debatable. He insisted that the Turkish empire should go and that Poland should again become a nation and they discussed at considerable length what House the next day described as Lloyd George's 'division of the world'. What struck House most was his insistence 'that the war could only be brought to an end by the President, and that terms could be dictated by him which the belligerents would never agree upon if left to themselves'.

So when House the next day went to his meeting with Balfour and Grey at the former's residence at 4 Carlton House Gardens, and found the map of South Eastern Europe and Anatolia conveniently placed on a wall, he gave the other two 'in detail the division of the world, as George had outlined it, and the extraordinary part he would have the President play'.[35] He was surprised to learn that they had not discussed the matter with him. They warned him that Lloyd George 'jumps at conclusions quickly, but as quickly forms another'.[36]

Then they reverted to House's proposal. Again Balfour did most of the talking and again House found him argumentative. There were many difficulties. Neither Grey nor Balfour thought it prudent to discuss the matter with their colleagues and certainly not with their Allies. Even if they could do both, the people could not be told and without their knowledge of the advantageous position in which Britain would be placed, they would never endorse the plan. Balfour seemed even to be doubtful about the merits of the post-war settlement; Germany, he thought, would never play fair. So the plan advanced only to the stage of bringing a few more people into the discussion, principally the Prime Minister. Lloyd George and Reading had got half-way there already, so they were to be told; and to be told also were the two ambassadors whom House had come to eliminate. Then when House got back from the Continent the British and he would talk again.

But it does not look as if Grey was expecting anything immediate or dramatic to come out of further talk. A secret memorandum which he wrote on 14 January was concerned with the spring offensive which the army command wanted. He was impressed by the arguments against it but impressed still more by the fact that all military opinion was in favour of it and that without it there would be a paralysis of strategy. He wrote: 'I believe that the only chance of victory is to hammer the Germans hard in the first eight months of this year. If this is impossible, we had better make up our minds to an inconclusive peace.'[37] Nor did he suspend until the Colonel's return the 'division of the world' which they had discussed with Lloyd George and Balfour at the Savoy and at Carlton House Gardens. The consideration of British desiderata in Asiatic Turkey,[38] begun in the spring of 1915* and complicated by the prospect of obtaining in exchange for appropriate promises Arab support for the Allies, had resulted in discussions between England and France which produced by the end of the year substantial accord as to how their interests could be satisfied. On 4 February Grey approved the agreement, known as the Sykes–Picot Agreement, for submission to Russia for her endorsement.

In his reports to the President from England House gave a broad summary of his discussions. He had told Grey and Balfour, he said, that 'you believed that in order to justify fully our existence as a great nation, it might be necessary to bring to bear all our power in behalf of peace and the maintenance of it'.[39] He had told them that the President would make no agreement concerning European affairs—only upon broad questions such as the elimination of militarism and navalism. He had endeavoured to shake their confidence in ultimate military success. Wilson on 12 January had sent House a cable 'for your information and guidance' saying that it looked as if the difficulties with Germany would be presently adjusted and then there would be a demand, especially from the Senate, for the United States to force England 'to make at least equal concessions to our

* See p. 257 above.

unanswerable claims of right'.[40] House reported on 13 January that he had taken this up without success with nearly every member of the Cabinet; he said that if the point was pressed Sir Edward was likely to go and that would be a calamity.[41] As for Germany, he wrote on 16 January that there should be no serious breach unless she sank another passenger ship, in which case diplomatic relations should be immediately broken.[42]

These reports do not give the full flavour of House's conversations. 'Bring to bear all our power' was an ambiguity that might fit either physical or moral force; House had not left the British in doubt that he was talking about the former. He did not report to Wilson his phrase about the United States helping Great Britain to win the war nor that he had begun to flirt with the territorial terms of peace. There is no reason to think that these omissions were intended to deceive. When, for example, he used his 'helping the Allies to help themselves' titbit on a later occasion—it became one of his motifs—he did report it.* He was certainly allowing himself a large measure of discretion. He had, for instance, dropped entirely the 'primary purpose' of his mission. He had reported that fact to Wilson without expecting or incurring any rebuke. Other matters had to be more delicately handled, but he did not doubt, rightly as it turned out, his ability to persuade Wilson to honour any bargain he made. When in one of his talks with Grey and Balfour, the latter had wondered whether the President would be able to carry out the proposed agreement, House

told them it would be easier for me to persuade the President to accede to what I would be willing to agree to, than it would be for them to succeed with their colleagues. I had only one man to convince and I knew him sufficiently well to know what he would accept and what refuse.[43]

House was certainly not going beyond the original brief which the President had authorized in the message to Grey of 17 October and he was probably not much put out by Wilson's subsequent modifications. He had to face the fact that the two parties, Wilson and Grey, who had seemed to come quite close to each other in September, had drifted apart. He had not sufficiently attracted Grey with the offer of American help in exchange for a decisive voice in moderating the terms; and Wilson by the end of December had lost interest both in giving the help and in framing the terms. But House would not have been the broker he was if he had abandoned hope of bringing the parties together again. If he could induce the British to be more forthcoming, might he not also induce the President to revert to his earlier enthusiasm for the original plan which at the time Wilson had thought altogether right and had prayed God might bring

* See p. 424 below.

results? When House left England he was less hopeful about the British than he was about Wilson. The day before his departure he recorded in his diary his fear that British conservatism would make improbable any real accomplishment and his wish that Lloyd George was Prime Minister with Grey as Foreign Minister: boldness was what was needed at this time.

House left London on 20 January 1916, took a few days off in Paris (he intended to talk to the French on his way back), and then proceeded via Geneva to Berlin where he arrived on 26 January. Wilson was then just opening the preparedness campaign with three speeches in New York on 27 January. He left for his 'swing around' on 28 January. Preparation for war does not of itself imply recourse to war: this was the line that Wilson took with emphasis upon his own specific achievements and intentions. The tour was a great success. It was as well that no one in his audiences had had a glimpse of the message to Grey of 17 October 1915, which Wilson had never countermanded, or an inkling of what House had been talking about in London. The country was to be prepared, Wilson told the citizens of Pittsburgh, 'not for war, not for anything that smacks in the least of aggression, but for adequate national defense'.[44] He was filled with a strange feeling, he said, when it seemed to be implied that he was not the friend of peace. 'If these gentlemen could have sat with me reading the dispatches and handling the questions which arise every hour of the twenty-four, they would have known how infinitely difficult it had been to maintain peace.' It had needed watchfulness and unremitting patience to avoid the entanglements which beset him on every side: but he had done so. At Des Moines he said:

There are actually men in America who are preaching war, who are preaching the duty of the United States to do what it would never do before—seek the entanglement in the controversies which have arisen on the other side of the water—abandon its habitual and traditional policy and deliberately engage in the conflict which is now engulfing the rest of the world. I do not know what the standards of citizenship of these gentlemen may be. I know only that I for one cannot subscribe to those standards. I believe that I more truly speak the spirit of America when I say that that is a spirit of peace. Why, no voice has ever come to any public man more audibly, more unmistakably, than the voice of this great people has come to me, bearing this impressive lesson, 'We are counting upon you to keep this country out of war'. And I call you to witness, my fellow countrymen, that I have spent every thought and energy that has been vouchsafed me in order to keep this country out of war. It cannot be disclosed now, perhaps it can never be disclosed, how anxious and difficult that task has been, but my heart has been in it.[45]

He was equally emphatic about his intentions. 'You may count upon my heart and resolution to keep you out of the war, but you must be ready if it is necessary that I should maintain your honour.'[46] But he must be able to protect the nation against things he could not control. 'There is constant danger, every day of the week, that her spiritual interests may suffer serious affront.'[47] He reminded his audience at Milwaukee that he had kept the nation out of war. 'So far I have done so, and I pledge you my word that, God helping me, I will if it is possible.'

By the time House reached Berlin nearly a month had passed since he had left Washington and within that month much had happened in the German-American struggle over the submarine. Lansing had pressed to such extremes his efforts to obtain an admission of illegality in the eight-month-old *Lusitania* case that at the end of January there were rumours in Washington of war within days. At the same time he had put the cat among the London pigeons with a proposal for yet another *modus vivendi*. In Berlin there had been a significant shift in the forces that were for and against unrestricted submarine warfare.

Of these three movements the one that proved in the end to be the most important was the last. But by the end of January it had not taken effect and its progress until then can be chronicled briefly. It has been recorded* that when Bethmann won the battle of the *Arabic*, Bachmann, the Chief of the Naval Staff, was dismissed. His successor, Admiral Henning von Holtzendorff, a distant relative of Admiral Muller, chief of the Kaiser's Naval Cabinet, was selected by the latter as a man who would smooth the ways between the Navy and the political branch. As a smoother of ways he was doubtless well chosen, for he was not a strong man and he shuttle-cocked between the promptings of the Navy and the blandishments of Bethmann. In practice this meant that he usually began with a statement of the Navy's case and then succumbed to a greater or less degree to Beth-mann's influence. In the autumn of 1915, however, he was under the influence of Tirpitz and accordingly in favour, though less passionately than his mentor, of unrestricted U-boat war. He believed, as he wrote in a memorandum of 7 January 1916, that if Germany could not win a favourable decision by the autumn of 1916, the chance of concluding a satisfactory peace would disappear; and that even the defeat of the French might not bring about a decisive result.[48]

But the crucial factor at the end of the year was not the adherence of Holtzendorff but the conversion of Falkenhayn. When on 30 December

---

* See p. 323 above.

1915 the general and the two admirals met in the War Ministry in Berlin Falkenhayn withdrew his objections to unrestricted warfare. He no longer had any fears, he said, that a break with America would precipitate a crisis in the Balkans; Bulgaria had joined the Central Powers, Serbia was knocked out, and the route to Constantinople secure.

Thus the general removed the veto he had imposed on military grounds. But he did not come down decisively on the larger question of policy. Unrestricted warfare, Bethmann declared, was Germany's last card. If it failed, it was *finis Germaniae*, for it would bring America into the war and that in the long term meant defeat. Would it, Falkenhayn asked, bring victory before the end of 1916? The naval chiefs assured him that it would. They had now fifty-eight submarines in service, nearly three times the force with which they began the first campaign in February 1915. Falkenhayn said it was up to the Kaiser to decide. The Kaiser on 15 January decided on a middle course. Bethmann was to prepare the way diplomatically for a submarine campaign to begin on 1 March, while the Navy was to investigate the possibility of sparing neutral shipping. The provisional order, which on 18 January the Kaiser approved, did not directly sanction destruction of neutral shipping but went nearly as far: neutral ships were to be treated as enemy vessels unless they could be positively identified as neutral.

On the last day of the old year Bernstorff had made a promising beginning in the attempt to find a formula on the *Lusitania* that would satisfy Lansing.* It looked at first as if the sinking of the *Persia* might damage his prospects. But Wilson, brought back from his honeymoon to cope with the situation, refused to be hustled. Tumulty talked with him on 4 January 1916 and reported this interview:

> My attitude toward this matter was for action, and action all along the line. This did not seem to meet with a very hearty response from the President. He informed us that it would not be the thing for us to take action against any government without our government being in full possession of all the facts.[49]

The facts turned out to be inconclusive. Nobody had seen a submarine or a torpedo or its track. But Bernstorff had been a little alarmed by the commotion and when on 7 January he resumed the *Lusitania* negotiations he proceeded at once to the third and broadest of the proposals which he had been authorized to make. This was the friendly indemnity without mention of liability. Lansing passed on the offer to Wilson.[50] If in any way, he wrote, the agreement to pay the indemnity could be construed into a recognition

* See p. 376 above.

of liability, it would seem as if a final settlement of the case was very near. Wilson replied on 10 January that he had tried hard to find something in it out of which a satisfactory answer could be made and had failed: it was a concession of grace and not at all of right.

Lansing needed no further encouragement. On 24 January he wrote to Wilson that he proposed to tell Bernstorff that further conversations were useless and to demand formally an admission of illegality under pain of diplomatic breach.[51] Wilson in reply agreed in principle. But he reminded Lansing of House's cable in which he had asked that no step should be taken against Germany until his letter (it was written on 16 January* and had not yet arrived) had been received. So Wilson suggested that Lansing should feel his way for a few days.

On 25 January Lansing told Bernstorff that the draft he had submitted was unsatisfactory: there was no admission that the sinking of the *Lusitania*, being an act of reprisal, was an illegal act. What, Bernstorff asked, did Lansing wish him to do? Lansing said that he could see no good reason for continuing the informal conversations unless Germany frankly admitted the illegality. Bernstorff said that he was convinced that his Government would not do that. This seemed to show, Lansing replied, that they had both reached the same conclusion, namely, that further informal negotiations would be useless. Lansing's note of the interview continues.

The Ambassador seemed greatly perturbed and sat for several moments considering the situation. He finally said: 'and what would be your course in case my Government will not accede to these terms, which seem harsh?' I replied: 'I see no other course, Mr Ambassador, except to break off diplomatic relations'. The Ambassador said: 'I do not see how the matter could stop with the breaking off of diplomatic relations. It would go further than that.' I replied: 'Doubtless you are correct in this view'.[52]

The German ambassador made a final effort. He came back to the State Department the following morning with a revised memorandum. The Secretary told him that it was not satisfactory. Bernstorff then invited Lansing to say what changes he wanted, Lansing obliged, and the ambassador there and then dictated a new memorandum which he said he would submit to Berlin. The crucial passage, the one that followed on the statement that the sinking of the *Lusitania* had caused the death of American citizens, ran as follows:

Thereby the German retaliation affected neutrals, which was not the intention as retaliation becomes an illegal act if applied to other than enemy subjects.

The Imperial Government, having, subsequent to the event, issued to its

---

* See p. 402 above.

naval officers the new instructions which are now prevailing, expresses profound regret that citizens of the United States suffered by the sinking of the Lusitania and, recognizing the illegality of causing their death, and admitting liability therefor, offers to make reparation for the lives of the citizens of the United States who were lost by the payment of a suitable indemnity.

Lansing then prepared for the worst. On 26 January 1916 he sent a long telegram to Gerard and House in Berlin explaining the position. He drafted a Note to follow the breakdown of informal negotiations. The effect of it was that unless the German Government made a declaration in the terms demanded, diplomatic relations would be severed. The draft stated expressly that the subject was not open to further discussion. On 28 January Lansing advised the press that the *Lusitania* negotiations were going badly and that the President was determined to end them soon if the German Government did not make a satisfactory disavowal. The situation, he said, was now graver than it had been for some time.

When on 29 January Bernstorff's dispatch with America's final word arrived in Berlin, House had been there for three days. On 27 January he was given a hint of the impending change in the balance of forces that controlled the use of the submarine. Solf, the Colonial Secretary, came to a meal at the American embassy which he regarded as breakfast and House as lunch and said in the strictest confidence that Falkenhayn was inclining towards the naval view.[53] For the moment, Solf said, the Chancellor held the ascendancy but the outcome was uncertain. Then on 29 January Zimmermann, just after seeing Bernstorff's dispatch, lunched with Gerard and House and told them firmly that the German Government would not yield. He wrote a strong letter to House for transmission to Wilson;[54] and Gerard cabled Lansing the same day that both he and House agreed that something less than an explicit admission of wrongdoing should suffice.

Lansing was not at all pleased with the action of interlopers who did not, as he thought, understand the point.[55] On 24 January he had told Gerard in reply to a tart telegram from the ambassador ('It may have escaped your notice but I am utterly without information as to your negotiations on Lusitania case') that there was nothing he wanted him to do. This in turn displeased Gerard who by cable of 29 January advised Lansing exactly what to say so as to close the incident. Lansing riposted on 31 January with a warning to 'offer no encouragement'; and he wrote to Wilson, who had reached Kansas City on his preparedness tour, suggesting that he should reply to Gerard 'explaining the point at issue'. Wilson wired back instructing him to do so.

This was at 7.07 p.m. on 2 February. At some time between then and

4.22 p.m. the next day, when he sent another telegram to Lansing telling him to hold his hand, Wilson changed course. Perhaps he reflected that he had been telling his audiences for some days now that there was no specific crisis in foreign relations and that he did not foresee one. Certainly it would have been difficult to represent a difference of opinion on a point of international law, a difference that was made academic by Germany's willingness to pay an indemnity anyway, as amounting to the spiritual affront which on the day before he had told the citizens of Des Moines might drive America to war.* Lansing, impelled by his conviction that, as he had told Bernstorff, the dignity and honour of the United States was at stake, would have gone to war over the wording of a Note as enthusiastically as if the tragedy it was embalming had occurred the day before. It is inconceivable that Wilson would have allowed that to happen. But if he had gone any further, he could have avoided war only by submitting to a diplomatic rebuff. Bernstorff was right in thinking that there was no hope of Germany accepting the Lansing formula. Probably she would not have considered it anyway, but at the very moment when she was contemplating the resumption of submarine warfare, an admission of its illegality was out of the question. Jagow told Gerard at dinner in the evening of 31 January[56] that there could be no admission.

Bethmann was ready to thrash out the issue in public. On 2 February he released the news of the crisis and on following days he and Zimmermann gave out statements to the American press describing the American demand as an impossible humiliation,[57] statements which got a sympathetic response from Stone and Flood, the two congressional chairmen of the committees on foreign affairs, and from the anti-war party in Congress. So far from there having been, as Lansing had supposed there would be, dissatisfaction expressed in Congress when it met in January over the delay in settlement of the *Lusitania* affair, the feeling turned out to be all the other way. In Washington anti-German and anti-British sentiment came and went in waves and as one receded its opposite flowed in to claim the vacant space. The great anti-German wave of the autumn, started by the sinking of the *Arabic* and impelled by the Bryce report on Belgian atrocities, the shooting of Nurse Cavell for helping British and Belgian prisoners to escape, and the sabotage revelations, culminated in the sinking of the *Persia*; and when doubt was thrown on German responsibility for that, it ebbed away.

The spirit of Congress was described by Spring Rice in a letter to Grey of 13 January as

somewhat menacing. Congress was opened in stormy meetings in which violent

* See p. 403 above.

attacks were made upon our commercial policy. Senator Lodge's intervention in the Senate in which he said that his heart was more moved by the thought of a drowned baby than an unsold bale of cotton, was very effective and changed for a time the tone of the debate. But the general tone of the debate was not favourable to us. The same could be said of the House of Representatives. Violent language was used against the measures in restriction of trade. Lodge's son-in-law, Mr. Gardner, of Massachusetts did what was very rare in Congress, that is, made a speech in favour of England . . . It is expected that an arrangement on the Lusitania question will shortly be announced, and then, as they say here, the sheet of Germany will be cleared and the account against England re-opened.[58]

Two telegrams from House which reached Wilson after he had left Kansas City focused the situation for him. They were probably the immediate cause of his change of policy and certainly the justification for it which he gave to Lansing. House had waited until he reached Geneva on his way back to France before on 30 January he cabled Wilson a clear and forceful appreciation of the position in Berlin.

The situation is like this. A great controversy is going on in Germany regarding undersea warfare. The navy backed more or less by the army, believe that Great Britain can be effectively blockaded, provided Germany can use their new and powerful submarines indiscriminately and not be hampered by any laws whatsoever. They also believe failure has resulted from our interference and Germany's endeavour to conform to our demands. They think war with us would not be so disastrous as Great Britain's blockade. The civil Government believe that if the blockade continues, they may be forced to yield to the navy; consequently they are unwilling to admit illegality of their undersea warfare. They will yield anything but this. If you insist upon that point, I believe war will follow. Gerard understands the question and I would suggest letting him try to arrange something satisfactory direct. I hope final action may not be taken until I have had an opportunity of talking with you . . .[59]

House followed this up with a telegram from Paris on 2 February in which he said that he doubted whether a crisis with Germany could long be avoided. She would attempt to break the British blockade by submarine warfare. America would then be compelled to sever relations and it would be much better to do so then than 'over a nine months old issue and largely upon the wording of a suitable apology'.[60]

Wilson got back to Washington on 4 February and he sent House's telegrams to Lansing with an accompanying note: 'Do you not think that we could frame a handsome apology from Germany which we could accept without explicit disavowal?'[61]

That afternoon Bernstorff called at the State Department with some

ingenious amendments which Jagow had devised to the Lansing formula.
As amended it read:

> Thereby the German retaliation affected neutrals which was not the intention
> as retaliation *must not aim** at other than enemy subjects.
> The Imperial Government . . . expresses profound regret that citizens of the
> United States suffered by the sinking of the Lusitania, and *assuming** liability
> therefore, offers to make reparation etc.[62]

By these amendments the references to illegality were removed. Instead
of 'admitting' liability, Germany 'assumed' it, the doubtful point of law
remaining unsolved. It was correct on any view of the law to say that a
reprisal must not be 'aimed' at a neutral, although its application might hurt
them. Lansing was (or felt it prudent to be) favourably impressed by these
semantics. He thought there was a recognition that retaliatory acts though
'justifiable' (i.e. against the enemy) were not 'lawful'; and he found it
possible to consider that the declaration that 'retaliation' must not aim
at 'other than enemy subjects' meant that it was unlawful so far as neutrals
were concerned. He reported to Wilson: 'I believe we could state our
understanding of the language in order to show in our acceptance that we
consider there is a direct admission of wrong.'[63] A 'high authority' in the
State Department announced that German concessions had removed the
danger of a break in relations, even though the situation was grave.[64]

The Secretary and the ambassador met on 8 February 1916 to discuss
some of the finer points of wording; and on 16 February Bernstorff left
a draft which, looked at by itself, the President and the Secretary were prepared to approve. But they felt they had now to consider it in the light of
a declaration which Germany had made on 10 February about her policy
towards armed merchantmen. To understand this it is necessary to go
back to the beginning of the armed ships controversy and trace the course
of a new *modus vivendi*. In doing so we can take leave of the *Lusitania*.
What was left of the dispute disappeared in the armed ships imbroglio and
did not emerge until the post-war settlement. The final formula, reached
after untold labour as Bernstorff reported, was dubbed by Lansing 'acceptable but not satisfactory'.[65] But the ambassador regarded it as a draw in
Germany's favour: Wilson had lost out on the word 'illegal'.

A merchantman who seeks to resist capture commits no breach of
international law but she loses thereby her non-combatant status. The
choice between yielding and fighting is hers and she may not be attacked

* Italics added.

unless she shows fight or tries to escape. It follows that she can be armed for resistance. But there must be a limit to her armament, otherwise she could be made into a warship. And in wartime many merchantmen are converted into auxiliary cruisers. The limit, which it is easier to define than to apply, is that the armament must be defensive and not offensive. This is a distinction which, as the Dutch Minister of Marine sapiently observed at the beginning of the war, *he* could perceive but he was afraid that 'people might not'.[66] The prime object of defensive armament, and doubtless the reason why it was sanctioned by international law, was for use against pirates and privateers. Privateers were private vessels commissioned by a belligerent government to capture enemy merchantmen; since they were armed quite lightly a small gun might keep one at bay. But there were no longer any pirates in the Atlantic and privateering had died out early in the nineteenth century (it was indeed officially abolished by the Declaration of Paris in 1856) and no armament that could possibly be described as defensive would tempt a merchantman to try conclusions with a cruiser or a destroyer. No one before 1914 contemplated the submarine as the merchantman's foe. But there was the possibility that a belligerent might use lightly armed surface interceptors comparable with privateers. On 17 March 1914 Churchill told Parliament 'that Britain proposed to arm 70 merchantmen with two 4·7″ guns apiece so as to make them "thoroughly capable of self-defence against an enemy armed merchantman"':[67] they would not be allowed to fight with any ship of war and they would be directed to surrender if overtaken by one.

Churchill was dealing with a subject which, as he said, 'has proved a stumbling-block to many'. In 1913 a Dr. Schramm, a German international lawyer with a higher respect for logic than for tradition, had subjected the whole muddled concept to a disconcerting analysis. What was its basis, he asked? If it was based on the right of self-defence, that was a right exercisable only against illegal interference; but the belligerent seeking to visit and search was acting legally. It was for this reason that no one suggested that a *neutral* ship could be armed for resistance; she had no right of self-defence; she must submit to visit and search. So the alleged right flowed from belligerent status. How then could it be exercised so as to avoid the normal consequences of belligerency? Neither a nation nor a ship could be semi-belligerent. But his was a lone voice. Not even German Prize Law gave him full support. It prescribed that merchant seamen whose resistance was overcome should be treated as prisoners of war, whereas under the law the life of a non-combatant who resisted was at mercy. International law seemed to have created in the merchant seaman a curious creature, a non-combatant with the option of combating, 'a class of persons', as an American authority* put it, 'that comes rather between combatants and noncombatants'. Not a class, the Germans might say, with a strong claim to immunity from the risks of war accepted by naval ranks.

Dr. Schramm's opinions were denounced in a massive memorandum[68] prepared for the British Cabinet in February 1916 which it is difficult to believe that any of them comfortably digested. Batteries of legal precedents like trains of horse-drawn culverins were wheeled into position and judicial dicta from the Napoleonic wars were hurled like cannon-balls against the doctor's daring propositions. While the chief hope of victory was staked on the mass of tradition flung against him in frontal attack, there was also permitted as a sideshow an effective piece of infiltration into his logic. If a merchantman must be unarmed and unresisting, was she to submit to capture by any enemy ship also unarmed, that got within hailing distance? The flaw was mentioned in the Cabinet paper and passed lightly over, for it seemed fantastic to suppose that with the great German Navy bottled up in the North Sea an unarmed or weakly armed raider could be roaming the Atlantic. But for the lawyer the flaw was disintegrating. International law could not formulate itself on the assumption that a Britannia who ruled the waves would be a party to every war. It must provide for equality of force and for the possibility, which indeed even Britain had contemplated in her pre-war strategy, that lightly armed marauders might be at large. But if the law required a merchantman to surrender at sight, why should the raider bother to be armed at all? To avoid this absurdity, the law, instead of prescribing how light a ship's armament must be so that she could call herself defensive, would have to prescribe how heavy it must be to entitle her to call herself aggressive. The only way of escape from these difficulties was by a movement away from them towards one extreme or the other—the one of allowing every unarmed ship to proceed on her way unmolested, that is, Freedom of the Seas; and the other of treating as a warlike operation all trade with a belligerent in wartime, that is, Total War.

Within a year and with the introduction of the convoy system, events had put the movement on the latter course. But meanwhile, since warships in time of war were subject to disabilities in neutral waters—for example, they could not as a general rule stay longer than twenty-four hours in a neutral port—the distinction between a warship and a defensively armed merchantman had to be formally drawn. The United States did this for her own purposes in a Declaration entitled *The Status of Armed Merchant Vessels* issued on 19 September 1914.[69] When any armament at all was carried, the Declaration put upon the shipowner the onus of showing that it was solely for defence, but it gave as indications of a defensive purpose

* Admiral C. H. Stockton, *Manual of International Law for the Use of Naval Officers*, 1911, p. 179.

such factors as that the calibre of the guns did not exceed 6 in. and that they were not mounted forward. By an inevitable process of construction the Declaration (which was of course drafted before submarine warfare had been experienced) was treated as permission to carry a 6-in. gun aft, a grave deterrent to a submarine on the surface. A single shot which pierced her hull would, by making it impossible for her to dive, leave her an easy prey to an enemy destroyer.

Lansing had the strict legal position in mind when in the draft of the first *Lusitania* Note he altered Wilson's reference to 'unarmed' merchant-men to 'unresisting'.* This made the point that it was the resistance and not the arming that deprived the merchantman of her non-combatant status. Wilson, to please Bryan, restored the original word. It was not until the *Hesperian* was sunk on 4 September 1915† that Wilson realized quite what he had done and he then apologized handsomely to Lansing for his error.[70] The *Hesperian* was certainly unresisting but was carrying a 6-in. gun astern. Germany used the point to justify the hypothetical torpedoing (it was not established satisfactorily at the time) and her contention got some support in the American press. Gerard's opinion, expressed cogently to House when the row was on in February 1916, was that of many Americans.

It seems to me to be an absurd proposition that a submarine must come to the surface, give warning, offer to put passengers and crew in safety, and constitute itself a target for merchant ships, that not only make a practice of firing at submarines at sight, but have undoubtedly received orders to do so.[71]

In August 1915 the helplessness of a submarine against minor armament was dramatically illustrated in the case of the *Baralong*.[72] She was a decoy ship, a tramp with a concealed armament of twelve-pounder guns. On 19 August near the Scilly Isles the U27 stopped a British steamer, the *Nicosian*. The *Baralong* came on the scene after the *Nicosian*'s crew had taken to the boats and when the U27 was beginning to shell her. The *Baralong* was flying the American flag. Approaching so that the *Nicosian* lay between herself and the submarine and so that the latter could not see what she was doing, the *Baralong* ran up the White Ensign, unmasked her guns, and trained them on the spot where the U27 would appear from behind the *Nicosian*'s bows. As soon as she did appear she was shelled at 600 yards and sunk at once. Twelve of the submarine's crew escaped and made for the *Nicosian*. Some were shot and killed in the water and others as they clambered up the *Nicosian*'s side. Then the *Baralong* sent a party of marines to hunt down the remainder with orders to take no prisoners.

* See p. 300 above.   † See p. 325 above.

These details did not appear in the report which the commander of the *Baralong* made to the Admiralty.[73] A search of the *Nicosian*, he wrote, resulted in six of the enemy being found and they all shortly afterwards succumbed to injuries received in the shelling of the submarine. The record does not show whether the Admiralty were struck by the probability of six German sailors *in extremis* swimming to the *Nicosian*, climbing her side, and then expiring in unison. Unfortunately for Britain's good name, there were in the crew of the *Nicosian* five Americans who told the story in spite of being asked by the commander of the *Baralong* to keep quiet about it. Page obtained affidavits from three of them and on 26 and 29 August sent them to the State Department. 'Horrible', Wilson commented: 'one of the most unspeakable performances.'[74]

On 6 December 1915 the German Government sent to Britain through the United States a demand for the court-martialling of the *Baralong*'s commander on a charge of murder.[75] Balfour refused. The matter came several times before the Cabinet so that his evasive tactics might be approved.[76] The Admiralty made no admissions on the facts: neither did they expose the commander's story. But if the Germans had had any doubt about their ability to bring home the charge, which was after all based entirely on neutral evidence, they would hardly have suggested a British court martial; and if the British had had any confidence in their defence, they would not have declined the suggestion. Instead they selected three recent allegations of German atrocities and offered to submit the *Baralong* together with these three to an impartial tribunal. Germany refused the offer. So the neutral world had to be content with the conclusion that neither set of warriors cared to risk its reputation. The United States Government, since no American lives had been lost, behaved with cold correctitude.[77] The only matter to which they were prepared to give official consideration was whether the American flag was still at the mast of the *Baralong* when the firing started. On this point the conflict of evidence was such, Lansing told Bernstorff, that he did not feel warranted in taking up the matter with the British Government.

About the time of the *Baralong* incident a British steamer, the *Waimana*, entered the port of Norfolk in Virginia armed with one 4·7 gun mounted aft. At the beginning of the war on 25 August 1914 the British Government had, 'in view of the fact that a number of British armed merchantmen will now be visiting United States ports',[78] assured the American Government that they would never be used for purposes of attack and would never fire unless first fired upon. But in fact the *Waimana* was only the third armed vessel to call. The Declaration of 19 September 1914, although it gave a number of indications of what was inoffensive—such as the calibre of the gun, not to exceed 6 in., and its position on board, not to be mounted forward—required the authorities to satisfy themselves in each case that the vessel would not be used for offensive operations. After two visits of armed ships in the autumn of 1914 the American Government suggested that the position was embarrassing and the British Government apparently accepted that it was.

Then came the *Waimana* with her gun. On 25 August 1915 Lansing sent Spring Rice a letter which hoped that he might find it possible to instruct the captain to remove the gun. On 10 September the ambassador replied that the British Government, while anxious to oblige, were reluctant to create a precedent: was there any respect in which the vessel contravened the regulations? The next day Lansing replied bluntly that 'it has come to the knowledge of the Department that British merchant vessels which carry arms have used them for offensive purposes in attacks upon submarines'.[79] If he was not satisfied about this in the case of the *Waimana*, the gun must be removed else she would be interned as a ship of war. On 12 September he wrote to Wilson suggesting that changed conditions required a new declaration under which merchantmen with any armament at all would be excluded from American ports. Wilson instructed him the next day to prepare an amended Declaration but not to put it into effect 'until we see what we are going to be able to work out of this Arabic business'.[80]

Meanwhile, there was disquiet in London about what Grey described as a 'volte-face' showing 'great nervousness' on the part of the United States.[81] He sent Balfour the draft of a telegram which the latter (apart from doubting whether 'gruesome' was a good diplomatic expression) approved.[82] But Balfour also submitted to Grey (while being by no means sure that it was worth sending) the draft of a letter to House. In the end it was decided to rely upon this. The British did not want a test case and the *Waimana* was instructed to unship her gun and sail without it. The Collector of Taxes at Norfolk rubbed salt in the wound by assessing her to tonnage tax $300·54 on the ground that she had landed 'valuable dutiable goods'.[83]

In his letter to House, dated 12 September 1915, Balfour said that he was taking advantage of House's permission to write to him privately and 'as between man and man'.[84] He did not deny, he wrote, that merchantmen were in fact aggressive. But, he said, they were dealing with an enemy who knew no law and who repeatedly sank peaceful traders without notice. Jumping the point that if a merchantman got an opportunity for aggression it was precisely because the submarine had surfaced to warn in accordance with the law and was *not* trying to sink without notice, he concluded with an appeal to 'a broad spirit' which would not modify the law 'in the direction favourable to the perpetrator of outrages and hostile to his victims'. The appeal might have been more effective if it had not had to try to keep its head above water in the wake of the *Baralong*. But anyway, Wilson, to whom House sent the letter, was more concerned with the concrete question of whether it was fair to ask a submarine commander to give warning when it inevitably brought him within range. It was a question, he said, which was giving Lansing and himself some perplexed moments. House had a talk with Reading on the subject when he saw him on 2 October and warned him that sooner or later Germany would press the point[85] and he wrote likewise to Balfour reporting the President's views. House himself felt that he could see the English point of view better than Lansing but still did not consider it wholly fair.

To appreciate the reason for the British alarm it has to be understood that at this stage of the war, and indeed until the middle of 1917, the gun was considered the only effective answer to the submarine; and in 1915 merchantmen were being armed as fast as supplies permitted, though not nearly fast enough. Of course the gun was useless against underwater attack. But compliance with international law was by no means the only motive inducing a submarine to operate on the surface. The craft of 1915 were primitive. They could not undertake an ocean voyage (which was why their hunting grounds were limited to the North Sea, the Western Approaches, and the Mediterranean) and 60 miles at a stretch was about the limit of an underwater voyage. The torpedo was a costly weapon which took time to manufacture. A submarine in 1915 could carry from 8 to 20 torpedoes according to size, while she could carry as much ammunition and bombs as she could use. So the commander had to husband his limited supply of torpedoes. Wherever possible he would surface and use his gun to force the merchantman to surrender. Then when the crew had taken to the boats, he could destroy the vessel by gunfire or put a party on board her with time bombs. Three-quarters of the merchantmen sunk by submarine before unrestricted warfare was declared in February 1917 were sunk either by gunfire or by bombs. The British Admiralty were right in supposing that in this form of warfare the merchantman's gun would prove of great value. It did not often bring outright victory; the superior speed of the submarine on the surface enabled it to flee and submerge if defeat threatened. Out of 175 submarines destroyed by the British navy during the whole course of the war only five were destroyed by merchantmen. But what the gun did was to keep the submarine at bay and allow the merchantman to escape. Up to the end of 1915 no merchantman with a gun had been sunk. In the first half of 1916 the number sunk was still fairly small. Thereafter it increased considerably as newer and larger U-boats with bigger guns were coming into service. But over the whole period of thirteen months before the beginning of unrestricted warfare, that is from 1 January 1916 to 31 January 1917, the statistics show conclusively the advantage enjoyed by the armed ship. During this period armed and unarmed ships were attacked in about equal numbers, 310 of the former and 302 of the latter. Of the armed ships 236 escaped and only 67 of the unarmed. Of the armed ships that did not escape 62 were sunk without warning and only 12 after an encounter on the surface.

Germany alleged from the first that British merchantmen had instructions to attack submarines on the surface by gunfire or, if weaponless, by ramming. Whatever the wording of their instructions there is little doubt that that is what they were expected to do if they could not escape. Secret instructions sent out in April and May 1915 contain no trace of the direction to surrender when overtaken as stipulated by Churchill before the war. In one set the master was told that, if escape was impossible, he was to 'turn and steer straight for submarine':[86] likewise as to the use of the gun, nothing was said in accordance with the assurance of 25 August 1914 about not firing unless fired upon. Another set, marked 'not to be allowed to fall into the hands of the enemy', reads:

If a submarine is obviously pursuing a ship by day, and it is evident to the master that she has hostile intentions, the ship pursued should open fire in self-defence, notwithstanding the submarine may not have committed a definite hostile act such as firing a gun or torpedo.[87]

The instructions offer no guidance as to what is to be taken to be evidence of hostile intention nor any elucidation of the phrase itself. A pursuing submarine would not have purely amicable intentions: at the least she would intend to stop the merchantman according to cruiser rules and then sink her: would this be enough to justify attack? The point is simplified— for naval practice, if not for international law—by a recommendation in a later paragraph to open fire anyway if the submarine got to within 800 yards.

In October 1915, possibly as a result of the *Waimana* incident, revised instructions were issued in which the tone was much more subdued. Masters were reminded that the armament was supplied solely for the purpose of resisting attack and that their object should be to avoid action whenever possible. In case of deliberate approach or pursuit, 'fire may be opened in self-defence in order to prevent the hostile craft closing to a range at which resistance to a sudden attack with bomb or torpedo would be impossible'.[88] This is not perhaps remaining strictly on the defensive. It reflects the insoluble difficulty of making rules for non-aggression when neither side trusts the other. With the German record of submarine warfare it would be folly for a merchantman to forget that a torpedo might be released at any moment, while it would be an imprudent submarine which, in order to parley with a merchantman, went within effective range of her gun: and over the area between them there hovered the danger that a 'mistake' might be made by either side. In March 1916 the British, so as to rebut German charges of aggression, published the revised instructions, but unfortunately the Germans had obtained copies of the earlier sets.

This then was the background to the *Waimana* incident. Lansing mentioned it in a telegram to Page on 18 October 1915. He referred also to the *Baralong* and hinted that the American Government might have 'to change its lenient attitude towards the arming of merchant vessels for defensive purposes'.[89] But he did nothing further until after the sinking of the *Persia* on 30 December. Whether or not the *Persia* was torpedoed she was certainly armed. On 2 January 1916 Lansing wrote to the President to inquire whether it might not now be an opportune moment to issue the revised Declaration.[90] But then he had a better idea, another *modus vivendi*, the Central Powers agreeing not to torpedo without warning in consideration of an agreement by the Entente to disarm their merchantmen. He did not see, Lansing wrote to Wilson on 7 January, 'how the Entente powers could reasonably object to such an arrangement'.[91] Wilson thought it 'thoroughly worth trying'[92] and even, as he later told House, 'a capital stroke'[93] for England, ensuring that their merchantmen could no longer be torpedoed at sight.

Certainly it was an admirable solution on paper. Presented in peacetime at a pre-war Hague Convention, it would have seemed a logical development. But in wartime it postulated a confidence in the power of international law which the British as warmakers were unlikely to have. Would not the Germans continue to torpedo just as before, accusing the British of arming their ships? Mistakes in perception could easily be made through a periscope. Moreover, while the new law would, if it were observed, save British lives, it would also by making surface warfare easier for the Germans mean a greater loss of British ships and cargoes. Were the British to acquiesce in an amendment to the laws of war which would help the German blockade? These arguments could, as indeed they were when the proposal was put forward, be combined with and blurred by emotional overtones. Here was the Hun with his barbaric methods of warfare and all America proposed to do about it was to alter the law in his favour so that he could get on with the job!

But since Lansing was operating on paper he went ahead with Wilson's entire approval. He had on reflection some misgivings about the Allied response. As the Central Powers would probably return a speedy acceptance (so he wrote to Wilson on 17 January) and Allied failure to concur would intensify the rising anti-Entente sentiment in the United States, he proposed to deliver the Note to the Entente Governments first.[94] If they rejected it, it could then, if so desired, be kept secret.

The Note was dispatched on 18 January 1916.[95] After setting out the need for a *modus vivendi*—some way must be found of saving non-combatant life without depriving Germany of 'the proper use of submarines in the interruption of enemy commerce'—the Note formulated 'a reasonable and reciprocally just arrangement' as follows. On the one hand submarines must adhere strictly to cruiser rules, stopping belligerent merchant vessels and removing the crews and passengers to 'places of safety', that is, open boats in mid ocean, before sinking them as prizes of war. Merchantmen on the other hand would be prohibited from carrying any armament whatever. His government, Lansing added menacingly, was seriously considering treating armed merchantmen as auxiliary cruisers.

On 22 January Grey received from Spring Rice a cabled paraphrase of the Note. About a fortnight earlier he had had from the ambassador a report of an informal conversation with Lansing on 31 December about the American Note of 5 November* to which the Secretary was awaiting an answer.[96] It would be a good thing, the Secretary had said, if the answer could announce some concessions at least in form: Germany might come to an arrangement about the *Lusitania* (Lansing had in fact had on the same day a hopeful interview with Bernstorff)† and then public opinion would demand some concessions from Britain. Lansing probably had in mind only some concessions to appearances of the sort which Bryce wrote about in the following month.‡ But his words set off some indignant minuting in the Foreign Office: 'The idea that *we* should be made to pay for the Lusitania outrage could only occur to a German—or a hyphenated American.'[97] To which Crowe added: 'It certainly occurs to President Wilson.'

Grey also had taken a serious view of Lansing's advice. On 12 January he had sent for the French ambassador and told him that things had taken a 'serious turn'.[98] The American Government, he said, had settled, or thought that they had settled, the *Lusitania* and Britain's turn was coming. If she refused to give way, he feared an embargo on munitions or some other retaliation, perhaps even an attempt by the American Navy to break the blockade.

---

* See p. 357 above.   † See p. 376 above.   ‡ See p. 506 below.

So when he heard of the *modus vivendi* Grey suspected that it was part of a *Lusitania* settlement. Spring Rice firmly believed that Lansing had told the Italian ambassador so; and the *New York Tribune*, which was currently running a series of articles on presidential policy for the 1916 election, had forecast the attractions of a settlement secured by a promise of vigorous anti-British action. In fact of course Lansing was on quite a different tack. So far from using the *modus* as bait for Germany, he was trying it out first on Britain: the stumbling-block in the way of a settlement was his insistence, which could only be pleasing to the British, upon an admission of illegality.

On 25 January Grey sent for Page, who knew nothing of the *modus*, and asked him for House's address; he wanted to make it clear that at their recent talks he had had no idea that this Note was in the offing. He had to meet in the House of Commons the next day a hostile resolution, which had much support in the press, that all overseas traffic with Germany should be prevented by blockade—in effect, that responsibility for the blockade should be transferred from the Foreign Office to the Admiralty; he would not mention the subject in the House, he told Page, for if he did it would cause a storm that would drive every other subject out of the mind of the House. Page at once transmitted these remarks to Washington together with his own lamentations[99] and Grey on the same day cabled his reply to Spring Rice. It was full of painful surprise and disappointment and dismay which he said he could not adequately express. The wholesale sinking of merchant vessels was to be justified and no chance of defence was to be allowed. The law was to be altered in favour of Germany at the very time when the United States was pressing upon Britain outmoded conceptions. Page followed this up with another cable sent on 28 January after he had made further contacts, strongly advising that the proposal be dropped and offering the sensible comment that 'at this stage of the war it is doubtful if any agreement can be made on any subject between all the belligerents'.[100]

It may be remembered that the change in submarine policy which the Kaiser had decided upon on 15 January* was still provisional. There is no evidence that at this stage Lansing's *démarche* was known in Berlin. But Germany had for some time past been complaining about attacks by merchantmen on submarines and the Navy felt that if they could not obtain a total removal of restrictions, submarines should be allowed at least to operate without warning against armed merchantmen. The idea was put

* See p. 405 above.

to the Kaiser on 24 January. He at once approved of the compromise and instructed the Chancellor to prepare the appropriate declaration based on the treatment of armed merchantmen as auxiliary cruisers. Thus by a not unnatural coincidence, but one which inevitably thickened the suspicion of a plot, the German Foreign Office and the State Department were moving on parallel lines. Lansing's indiscretion allowed the lines to converge.

On 26 January he received Baron Zwiedinek, the Austrian chargé, who had come to protest against an armed Italian liner being allowed into the port of New York.[101] Lansing said that the liner had been cleared because the Italian ambassador had pledged that her guns would not be used offensively against a submarine. Moreover, Lansing said, transgressing his own precept of secrecy, he had already proposed to the Allies that they should stop arming merchantmen altogether. Zwiedinek responded with alacrity. The Central Powers, he said, held that submarines could not warn armed merchantmen and were contemplating issuing a declaration to that effect. He would welcome that, Lansing said; but he advised delay for a month or so before issuing fresh instructions to submarines in order to see if the Allies accepted the *modus vivendi*.

Spring Rice presented Grey's cable to Lansing on 27 January at a heated interview—heated at any rate by Spring Rice.[102] What, he asked, would the Americans do if the Germans continued to sink disarmed ships without warning? That would be an unfriendly act, Lansing said, a *casus belli*. The Americans would do, Spring Rice went on, preferring to answer his own question, what they had done in the past, investigate, procrastinate, and express displeasure. This *modus vivendi*, he said, was obviously part of a larger agreement being negotiated with Germany. Lansing at once repudiated this.

Lansing was upset by Spring Rice's outburst but not deterred. Grey seemed to be disappointed, he reported to Wilson, because America was failing to save British commerce from attack by Germany.[103] The end of it would be that armed merchantmen would have to be treated as auxiliary cruisers. Wilson was just about to leave Washington on the preparedness tour but he gave Lansing three-quarters of an hour on the evening of 28 January. He seems to have backed him up completely and told him to ask House to intervene in Paris and London. Thus emboldened, Lansing talked pretty freely to the press and the *modus vivendi* was in substance made public on 29 January. On 2 February Lansing cabled House in Paris giving a summary of its terms and deploring the Allies' refusal to consider it calmly.[104] Grey was seriously distressed, Lansing reported, but he himself thought it the fair and only humane solution. House replied the next day direct to Wilson begging him not to take action until his return.

We must now go back to 26 January and report House's doings in Berlin and then in Paris. He spent only three or four days in Berlin. He had a long talk with Bethmann after dinner at the American embassy on 28 January.[105] Nothing came of it and it was unlikely that anything would. House tried to draw Bethmann out by giving him an exaggerated idea of British anti-Americanism and willingness to talk peace. Bethmann offered in reply his hope of an understanding between Germany, Britain, and America which even now might be brought about, 'the dream of his life' he said.

In fact the intervening months had not altered the basic German policy contained in the September Programme,* and support for it in the country had not been effectively diminished. It is true that the Social Democrats, who had joined enthusiastically with the parties of the Right and Centre in the entry into the war, were now becoming disturbed by the attitude of their associates. As Mr. Watt puts it:

> Their own pre-war warnings that Europe's capitalist rulers intended to foment an expansionist war in order to stave off the inevitable collapse of their society seemed now to have been borne out in practice.[106]

On 9 December 1915 the Government made its fifth application to the Reichstag for war credits. In the Socialist party caucus that preceded the vote in the Reichstag, the party divided 66 in favour and 44 against; and when the vote was taken, 20 opposed and 22 abstained. This was to result in the spring of 1916 in the secession of eighteen 'Independent Socialists', the remaining bulk being known thereafter as the 'Majority Socialists'. The resolution which the Reichstag passed on 9 December, known as the Declaration of War Aims Majority, was in the following terms:

> In complete unity and quiet determination we await the hour which shall make possible peace negotiations in which Germany's military, economic, financial and political interests must be permanently guaranteed to their full extent and by all means, including the necessary territorial acquisitions.[107]

This was in accord with Bethmann's speech which preceded it.[108] The Chancellor did not refer explicitly to 'territorial acquisitions'; he spoke in a more gingerly way of 'guarantees' and of holding 'gateways' against aggression. The more bitterly the enemy waged war, the bigger the guarantees that would be necessary, he said.

So he told House on this occasion, 28 January 1916, that permanent peace meant no menace from the British side or the Belgian side and that there

---

* See p. 387 above.

must be an indemnity for giving up the north of France. House reported to Wilson that Bethmann was most unreasonable. 'Time and again I brought him back to the point that his expression of a desire for peace meant a victorious peace and one which included indemnity from his antagonists.'[109]

House did not even mention to Bethmann the plan with which he had started out, the conference to be called by Wilson to proclaim disarmament coupled with sanctions of some sort against the side that refused to come in and with the parties settling the peace terms for themselves. It would not have impressed Bethmann if he had. The Chancellor's policy was still, as it had been from the first, to avoid a general conference and to negotiate separately with his opponents; and he was kept busy with this during the next six months. Germany had already set on foot talks with King Albert of the Belgians on the basis of what she called a *rapprochement*, which in January 1916 looked quite promising. But when the *rapprochement* revealed itself as an uncomfortably close hug nothing came of it, though the Entente was sufficiently alarmed to send an emissary to talk to King Albert in February 1916. Conversations begun with the Japanese Minister in Stockholm in April 1916 were on the basis of the secession by Germany of her interests in the Far East in return for Japan taking herself out of the war and Russia with her, and there was also the possibility of a German-Russian-Japanese understanding such as imperial dreams are made of. Rumours of what was going on disturbed the British Foreign Office but the conversations broke down on 17 May 1916. At the end of May the German Minister at Berne was in touch with 'a prominent member of the French Radical Socialist Party', the suggestion being that France, by making a separate peace and thus breaking up the Allies could earn a substantial rebate in German territorial demands; but the rebate offered was not good enough even for the Radical Socialists.

All that House took away with him from Berlin was a strong conviction, which was derived from his talks with Solf and Zimmermann and which he at once communicated to Wilson,* that there would soon be unrestricted submarine warfare. The effect of this on House's mind was (since he believed that unrestricted warfare would bring America in) to make him feel that if he was to do a deal with the Allies before America came in, it was now or never; and that since the British had given him no encouragement at all, there was nothing to be lost by trying it out on the French. This appears from his final report to Wilson written on 9 February where he said:

Up to the present I have been confidential with the British Government alone, and have left to them the bringing into line of their allies.

However, I was never more impressed by their slowness and lack of initiative

---

* See p. 407 above.

as upon this trip, and I concluded that we had better take the risk and talk plainly to the French. The result was surprisingly satisfactory.[110]

In Paris he had two conversations with Briand, the Premier, and Jules Cambon, formerly French ambassador in Berlin, on 2 and 7 February. After the second he cabled to Wilson that it was the most important conference he had had in Europe. He started off by trying to create a good atmosphere. This led him past his motif that, apropos of shipping troubles, what America wanted most 'was for them to do those things which would help us to help them best',[111] and on to a statement that 'the lower the fortunes of the Allies ebbed, the closer the United States would stand by them'.[112] The former he reported to Wilson in so many words in his first letter of 3 February, and the latter he paraphrased accurately enough in his final report of 9 February.[113] He had to slur over this when he got to London and wanted to urge action without waiting for near defeat.[114]

In his report House gave the kernel of the talks as follows:

It was finally understood that in the event of the Allies had some notable victories in the spring and summer, you would not intervene; and in the event that the tide of war went against them, or remained stationary, you would intervene.

After reporting what he had said to the French about the need for secrecy and keeping in touch, the letter goes on:

Briand and Cambon know and seemed to agree to the advice I gave you concerning the settlement of the Lusitania matter. It is impossible for any unprejudiced person to believe that it would be wise for America to take part in this war unless it comes about by intervention based upon the highest human motives. We are the only nation left on earth with sufficient power to lead them out, and with us once in, the war would have to go to a finish with all its appalling consequences. It is better for the Central Powers and it is better for the Allies, as indeed it is better for us, to act in this way; and I have not hesitated to say this to the British and French Governments, and have intimated it to Germany.

A great opportunity is yours my friend, the greatest, perhaps, that has ever come to any man. The way out seems clear to me and, when I can lay the facts before you, I believe it will be clear to you also.

Fortunately for the historian it is unnecessary for him to try to determine exactly what House was saying that Wilson would do since any understanding he made in Paris was superseded by the House-Grey Memorandum in London. So the letter need be looked at only for the indication it gives of what was in House's mind and for what it may be supposed to have conveyed to Wilson.

The most important paragraph, that which recorded what was 'finally understood', suggests that House had now resigned himself to the fact that the Allies would not welcome intervention if they were likely to be victorious and that consequently nothing could be done until after the summer's campaigning had shown the form. In the cable in which he said that it was the most important conference he had had, House added that it was 'along the line of my conversation with Lloyd George before leaving London, but much more gratifying'. This must be a reference to his talk with Lloyd George on 14 January 1916 in which the latter advised that the offer of intervention should be made about 1 September.

But what sort of intervention and on what terms? Here the reader must levitate into the clouds of 'intervention based upon the highest human motives'. The key to this obscure paragraph may be in the first sentence. House's concern seems to have been to justify to everybody his advice to the President not to get into the war over the *Lusitania* issue. It would be better for everybody, he thought, that the United States should come in voluntarily as peacemakers and not be dragged in as warmakers. He had told this to the British and the French, House said, and intimated it to Germany. What form his intimations to Germany took, and how in any event anything he was planning could possibly make things better for the Central Powers, are questions which are quite unanswerable. Certainly he made his point with the British. How far did he make it with the French?

M. Cambon kept a note of the conversations. The two things which struck him most were, first, House's statement that there would be unrestricted submarine warfare which would bring the United States into the war before the end of the year; and secondly his opinion that American mediation was not possible at the present time. Undoubtedly House meant the first statement seriously because it so surprised M. Cambon that he got House to repeat it. On the second point the impression left with the French was that the mediation was not imminent. If by the autumn things had gone well with the Allies the United States would intervene peacefully; if they went badly, she would intervene militarily. As to terms, House was told that France must have Alsace-Lorraine. House replied that this might be done by giving equivalent compensation to Germany and Russia; Turkey would have to disappear. But France and England must agree on peace terms in a broad and liberal spirit and then the United States would support them and enter the war if Germany did not accept them. Briand and Cambon both said that the time for a peace initiative had not come and that they could discuss peace only in accord with their Allies. House replied that it was England's and France's business to bring the Allies into line. He emphasized the danger of delay and of too much optimism about the prospects of victory.

Nothing was said in Paris about the *modus vivendi*. Grey had told the French what was going on and emphasized the gravity of the matter but the French kept clear of it in their talks with House. House left Paris on 8 February and motored to Boulogne where he spent the night and had a talk with King Albert of the Belgians at his headquarters. They discussed peace terms. House's suggestion that Germany might be allowed to purchase the Belgian Congo as part of a scheme of compensation for Germany in return for her agreement to cede Alsace-Lorraine was not too badly received. The next day House crossed the Channel and took up his quarters at the Ritz where he dined with Page that evening. There was a note waiting from Grey saying that he would be pleased to see House the next morning. Page was most pessimistic and told House he would be able to do nothing with the British Government because of the *modus vivendi* and the impending *Lusitania* settlement, and that Grey had said as much.

During the first part of House's visit the situation did not improve. The Austrian chargé had lost no time in communicating to Vienna and Berlin the glad news of Lansing's attitude. On 9 February 1916, the day that Page was bemoaning the whole affair, Zwiedinek called again upon Lansing to tell him that within a few days the Central Powers were going to publish a declaration 'welcomed by Mr. Lansing' that thereafter armed ships would be treated as auxiliary cruisers.[115] Lansing was disturbed by 'welcomed'. He had not used that word, he said; what he had said was 'the sooner it was done the better'. Lansing was also seeing Bernstorff at this time and they were putting the finishing touches to an acceptable formula for the settlement of the *Lusitania*. The Secretary took occasion to point out that from the first *Lusitania* Note onwards the United States had stipulated for immunity only for unarmed vessels. He would not give Bernstorff a copy of the *modus vivendi*, he said, until he had received an answer from the Allies which he expected would be a refusal.

In accordance with Lansing's wish Zwiedinek telegraphed that the word 'welcomed' must not be misunderstood: it did not imply any initiative on Lansing's part, but he had repeated his opinion that there were certain reasons that might justify the declaration by the Central Powers. This naturally was not interpreted as a discouragement and on 10 February the Central Powers announced their instructions to their navies that on and after 29 February 1916 armed merchantmen were to be treated as warships: they added a caution to submarine commanders to make absolutely certain of the existence of the armament.[116] They did not find it difficult to make out a strong case on the facts. They were able to produce sets of Admiralty instructions[117] (found on the S.S. *Woodfield* whose master seems to have been rather careless) issued between February and May 1915 which were based on an extended notion of self-defence and were hardly in keeping with the assurances given to the American Government in August 1914.* The American press, announcing the declaration, reported that Administration officials were not disturbed by British protests against the new policy and that there was a strong possibility that the American Government would define armed merchantmen as warships.[118]

What House and Grey said to each other about all this can only be conjectured but undoubtedly they came to some understanding which is nowhere recorded. When they met on 10 February† Grey asked why America did not come into the war on the submarine issue instead of by demanding a conference; he cannot have been reassured by House's answer that it would be best for the *Lusitania* incident to be smoothed over. At this very time there was being prepared for Grey a paper to put before the Cabinet in which he voiced his suspicion that the *modus vivendi* and a *Lusitania* settlement formed 'part of a *transaction* between the two Powers' with 'the appearance of producing a grave position of affairs in our relations with America'. The *modus vivendi*, the paper said, was 'an attempt to re-adjust the balance of sea power in favour of our enemies' and was 'if not unfriendly, at least unneutral'.[119]

At the end of their talk on 10 February the two men arranged a programme to bring the Prime Minister and others into the discussions on the House plan. The discussions and the Cabinet paper could hardly run along parallel lines. Grey must have told House that America must drop either the *modus vivendi* or the House plan. Probably he did it in a very gentlemanly way and it looks as if he postponed the ultimatum for as long as he could. It was not until the morning of 14 February, the day set for the decisive discussion, that House cabled the President. 'There are so many other issues involved in the controversy concerning armed merchantmen that I sincerely hope you will leave it in abeyance until I return. I cannot emphasize too strongly the importance of this.'[120]

House would have been able to assure Grey that he knew nothing of the *modus vivendi*. Did he also assure him that he could put a stop to it? The behaviour of both men suggests that he did. When on that same day, 14 February, Chandler Anderson asked House if any critical questions were likely to arise with Britain over the disarming of merchant ships, House said no.[121] On that day too House in his diary referred to Grey as

* See p. 414 above.   † See p. 432 below.

a 'colleague' and said that he found him 'far more sympathetic than Page'.[122]

The Cabinet paper was printed and certainly got as far as the Prime Minister.[123] What happened to it after that no one knows; at the Cabinet meeting on 16 February the subject was not mentioned.[124] Grey cabled Spring Rice on that day but only to report what House had said to the President.[125] On 18 February Grey wrote to Balfour with a lightheartedness contrasting with his earlier anxiety. Lansing would expect a reply, he said, and none of the Allies would draft one. 'So I suspect we must draft one and I fear (I really mean "am glad") that it is for you to say what line the reply should take.'[126] But by 18 February Grey had doubtless heard the substance at any rate of Lansing's circular telegram to embassies[127] sent on 16 February and knew that the *modus vivendi* was scotched.

House's cable to Lansing arrived in the evening of 14 February. On the following morning there was a Cabinet meeting in Washington and before it Lansing was in conference with the President. In the afternoon Lansing summoned the press to the State Department and announced a drastic modification of policy.

What caused the change is again a matter of surmise, whether it was a decision of principle or of expediency and how far it was influenced by House's emphatic advice. Wilson's endorsement of the policy and his overriding of Grey's protest had been made when he saw Lansing in Washington just before he set off on his tour; he may then have followed the Lansing line without giving much thought to it. It may be that in studying Grey's argument later he was more impressed by it; the point that the law could not be changed unilaterally is one that would have appealed to him. He had entertained the proposal originally in the belief that it would be welcome to both sides and, thinking as he did that it was the underwater attack that the British feared, he was amazed that they did not see it as an opportunity to gain a great advantage without losing anything. If he made the switch purely in deference to House, there could be no reason why he should not tell House so. In fact he told House later that he thought the whole *démarche* had been a mistake and that he blamed himself as much as Lansing.[128]

It was not an easy task for Lansing to extricate himself from the position into which he had wedged himself so securely, but it was one of those happy occasions when too many words were preferable to too few. He took cover behind the distinction between offensive and defensive armament. The Administration, he told the press, still regarded the *modus vivendi* as a good thing, but, if rejected, it would accept the position and would not classify defensively armed merchantmen as warships. But then a merchantman's armament was ordinarily superior to that of a submarine; so ordinarily it might be considered to be offensively armed. The Administration would not warn Americans against travelling on merchantmen armed solely for defence. While on the one hand it would be a breach of international law if submarines sank defensively armed vessels without warning, on the other hand the new German order was not necessarily unlawful. Mistakes were bound to occur. And the Administration's attitude, if Americans lost their lives, would depend on all the circumstances.

The *modus vivendi* would have saved civilian lives. But this was not the first object of either of the belligerents. For them the first object was the winning of the war. So regarded, each side thought on the evidence it had that the *modus vivendi* would give it the worst of the bargain. Germany looked forward to more powerful submarines and the all-out underwater campaign and would not give that up. If Britain had not relieved her of the 'odium' she too would undoubtedly have rejected the proposal. The sum which Britain had to do in the crude figuring of war required her to put in one column the saving of lives and in the other the increased loss of ships and cargoes; and to add to the latter the loss of her chief propaganda weapon against Germany. The *modus vivendi*, if it had been agreed and observed, might have kept America out of the war. On a cold calculation this would not be something for Britain to look forward to.

But in truth her attitude was not a matter of calculation. Indeed, she would have done better to have played the whole thing more coolly and put up a show of reasonableness. The British response to the *modus vivendi* was emotional. Even if Grey's judgement had not been warped by his suspicion of a German-American deal, it would have been impossible for him politically to have overcome the inevitable charge that he was leaving defenceless merchantmen to the mercies of the Hun. The debate he had referred to when he spoke to Page* was only one vent for the criticism he was having to meet in the press and Parliament and which resulted in March 1916 in the creation of a separate Ministry of Blockade.

The *modus vivendi*, as proposed in Lansing's Note of 18 January 1916, had still to be officially rejected and this was done formally on 23 March.[129] The rejection was sweetened by an informal assurance that all armament was intended solely for defence.

Lansing compiled (and on 26 April issued as a memorandum dated 25 March) an elaboration of his closing thoughts based upon a new doctrine of 'presumptions' more easily comprehensible by a lawyer than by a naval

* See p. 420 above.

officer who had to act upon them.[130] An enemy ship must presume that a merchantman was armed for protection only and so immune from attack, unless there was 'primary and direct evidence' that she had an aggressive purpose. A neutral government on the other hand might presume that she was armed for aggression and so to be treated in a neutral port as a warship, unless there was 'secondary or collateral evidence' that she had no aggressive purpose. The requirement of secondary or collateral evidence, whatever this might mean, was enough to make the British very careful about allowing any armed merchantman to call at an American port; and this no doubt was the object that Lansing desired.

The incident was inevitably the seed of ill-will. What fostered antagonism to Britain in official circles in Washington in 1916 was partly the thought that she would do nothing to ease America's difficulties as a neutral and partly resentment because she treated the spirit of the law as a weapon to be used when it suited her and not as a commandment to be honoured. The case for the armed merchantman needed in order to succeed nothing more or less than insistence on the letter of the obsolete law. Balfour should have had his tongue in his cheek when he wrote in his letter to House of 12 September 1915:* 'I am, as you know, the last person to suggest that in the presence of the ever-varying conditions of war, old rules can remain unmodified.' The British needed unmodification to sustain their attitude to the submarine and the armed ship; and modification to justify their own blockade.

* See p. 415 above.

XIV
THE HOUSE-GREY MEMORANDUM

House makes the Pact: 22 February 1916 — rebellion in Congress: 21 February — Bethmann wins another victory: 3 March — so does Wilson: 7 March — Lansing's fanciful tale — Wilson ratifies the Pact: 7 March — Grey freezes the Pact: 21 March — did the Allies make 'a monumental blunder'? — was Grey less than frank? — was House fooled? — was Wilson a doubledealer? — his capacity for deceit — the conditions in which he worked — was he betrayed by his fondness for House?

WHILE House was on the Continent Page had heard something of his plan and thought it 'purely academical nonsensical stuff'.[1] Page himself on 22 January had cabled to Washington his 'profound conviction' that America must now make up her mind whether she wanted the war to end as a draw or in the decisive defeat of Germany.[2] If the former, she might obtain it by obstructing the British blockade: but then, Page warned, the war would end with Britain unable to oppose the depredations which he had been told Japan intended to make in the Pacific. Lansing wondered whether this was written after consultation with House, but Wilson thought it unsafe to assume that it had 'any admixture or colour of House's views in it'.[3] Nevertheless, he said that it deserved to be thought over. It may have been the seed of an idea about the Yellow Peril that Wilson came out with a year later. But if it was, it sprouted as an argument against intervention instead of for it.

Page's opinion of House's plan did not alter as the Colonel expounded it over the dinner table at Page's home at 6 Grosvenor Square on the day of his arrival in London, 9 February 1916. It was a very disagreeable evening for both men as they immediately made clear in their respective diaries. Page's record has the merit of setting out more clearly than it appears from House's letters what was in House's mind—in effect, a reversion to the original scheme of 17 October 1915.*

First, his plan was that he and I and a group of the British Cabinet (Grey, Asquith, Lloyd George, Reading etc.,) should at once work out a minimum

* See p. 382 above.

programme of peace—the least that the Allies would accept, which, he assumed, would be unacceptable to the Germans: and that the President would take this programme and present it to both sides; the side that declined would be responsible for continuing the war. Then, to end the war, the President would help the other side, that is, the Allies. House had talked more or less with some members of the French Government, who, he said, were enthusiastic about it. I wonder if they understood what he said, or whether he understood what they said? Then, too, the King of the Belgians approved it. Of course, the fatal moral weakness of the foregoing scheme is that we should plunge into the war, not on the merits of the cause, but by a carefully sprung trick. When I said that the way to get into the war was for a proper cause—then House objected that we must do it the President's own way. Of course such a morally weak indirect scheme is doomed to failure—is wrong, in fact.[4]

House wrote in his diary:

He frets me to such an extent that I fear I talked to him rather roughly. Everything the President was doing was wrong, the contempt of the British and Europe generally for us was growing stronger every day, and the United States was in bad odor everywhere. In reply I literally flayed him, and I was surprised afterward that he took it so kindly. The man hinders me my work because he tries to discourage me, and would totally do so if I were of a different temperament.[5]

Early the next morning, 10 February, Reading—'the inevitable Rufus' as Montagu called him[6]—was at the Ritz after breakfast. House, who was just off to 33 Eccleston Square, could see him only for a few minutes but that was long enough for him to arrange a quiet dinner the next day so that Lloyd George and House could resume where they had left off in January. Reading was able also to offer a dinner party at his house in Curzon Street as the venue for the main conference.

House began his talk with Grey by reporting on the situation in Berlin. Would it not be better, Grey asked—he had heard something of the Paris talks from the French ambassador—for America to come into the war on the submarine issue? She could at any time declare that she was ready to make a separate peace on her own terms. House replied that this was impracticable; once she was in she would have to stay in until the point of exhaustion or decisive defeat. The best plan for the good of all was to smooth over the *Lusitania* incident and intervene by demanding a conference. House convinced Grey, he says, of the wisdom of this: at any rate he convinced Grey that it was no use arguing. They decided on their programme of further discussions—a lunch at No. 33 on the next day, Friday, to which the Prime Minister and Balfour would come; and then the dinner at Reading's on Monday the 14th, when he and Lloyd George and Page would be brought in.

That evening House sat down to write to Wilson a euphoric account of his first day's work. He seemed still buoyed up by his conviction that he had made a great breakthrough in Paris. As for London, Grey, he reported, had put the point about the *Lusitania*, 'but in ten minutes I had brought him round'. In the same spirit he went on:

After going over the situation with great care and taking up every detail of foreign affairs, we finally agreed that it would be best for you to demand that the belligerents permit you to call a conference for the discussion of peace terms. We concluded this would be better than intervention (on the submarine issue) and it was understood, though not definitely agreed upon, that you might do this within a very short time—perhaps soon after I returned.

The Allies will agree to the conference, and, if Germany does not, I have promised for you that we will throw in all our weight in order to bring her to terms.

You will see that we have progressed pretty far since I left Paris—further than I had any idea that it was possible to do.

I cannot say with certitude what attitude Asquith and Balfour will take to-morrow, but I doubt whether Grey would have been as positive if he had not been reasonably certain of their co-operation.

I am very happy to be able to write you this, and I hope to-morrow I may be able to confirm it by cable. If you can hold the situation at Washington clear of all complications, sending no notes, protests etc., etc., to any of the belligerents, it looks as if something momentous may soon happen.[7]

From Paris House had written on 3 February (though indeed with little or no justification): 'I am as sure as I ever am of anything that by the end of the summer you can intervene.'[8] Now a week later, he was saying that 'we have progressed pretty far since I left Paris' and was encouraging Wilson to expect the intervention soon after his return. There is nothing to show that Grey said anything which would justify this. If he did, it was certainly not echoed in the wider conversations that now began.

The luncheon on Friday, 11 February, marked the formal introduction of the Prime Minister to the House plan. By this time the reaction of the others was manifest, Grey sympathetic to the idea but doubtful of its practicability, Lloyd George and Balfour both curious, neither of them hidebound, the one always ready to explore and the other to analyse. Asquith became and remained, it is safe to say (if one discounts a report by Reading[9] who as a go-between had to manufacture lubricant out of stray remarks), only very mildly interested. It is surprising that House, who had just said to Grey that if America came into the war over the submarine issue it would mean a fight to the finish, did not readily see that many Englishmen would feel the same way about England.

At lunch Balfour, House records, was 'less argumentative':[10] he did not realize that that was a bad sign. All three Englishmen expressed the view that Britain, who so far had been the least hurt by the war, could do nothing until her allies were ready to discuss peace. If, Grey thought, one of them proposed peace discussions, then he could say that America was ready to intervene. What assurance, Balfour asked, did House wish to take back to the President? A definite understanding, House replied, that it would be agreeable to the British Government, when the time was propitious, to have the United States propose cessation of war and a conference to discuss peace terms. He warned them that if they waited until Germany had a decisive victory, or nearly so, they need not expect action from America. Then, with House and Grey arranging to meet again on the Monday morning, all the conspirators left separately. Grey said later that if it were known that they had been discussing peace, 'every window in my house would be smashed',[11] while Page told House only half humorously that he would be lucky if he was not thrown into the Thames.[12]

Situated conveniently near to the Thames was Lord Milner's house at 17 Great College Street and there in these same months of January and February 1916 another set of conspirators, including the editor of *The Times*, was secretly meeting to plot the overthrow of Asquith and work for the more vigorous prosecution of the war.[13] Unmolested, however, the Colonel moved on to tea at the American embassy where he did not find Page at all changed in his opinion. The ambassador said that he was not coming to the dinner on Monday:[14] it would be ridiculous for him to talk about closer relations with Britain when America was doing everything she could to irritate her. A day or two later he noted in his diary that he must try to undo the harm that House was doing and that if House came again he would quit. He added:

All the vain and silly talk about 'intervention' i.e. about submitting proposals to the belligerents and about standing in waiting for a peace proposal from one belligerent to the other—this is all mere aloof moonshine.[15]

The busy day ended with the quiet dinner at Reading's house at 32 Curzon Street to meet Lloyd George. Nothing new was said. Again House had to talk 'George and Reading out of the belief that it was best for us to enter the war at this time on the *Lusitania* issue'.[16]

On Monday, 14 February 1916, the meeting, to which all the others had been preliminary, took place. Dinner at 8.30 at 32 Curzon Street. House must have felt it to be a historic occasion for he noted precisely in his diary the order of arrival and the seating at table. The Prime Minister, fresh from a weekend at Walmer Castle and a game of golf with Mrs. Churchill, was on the host's right, House on his left, Grey on House's left; Balfour and

Lloyd George made up the sextet.[17] It was not until the butler withdrew, as House records, that the talk moved out of conversational channels into a discussion on the war. House usually encouraged some war talk since it gave him an opportunity to rub into the British that their prospects were not so rosy as they thought. He forecast that Germany would attack in the west without waiting for the spring, perhaps at Verdun. This was a good forecast (or perhaps House had picked it up in Berlin where the talk was not always tight), being made a week before the Battle of Verdun began. It was 10.30 before they got down to House's plan. Lloyd George set the pace and outlined what he thought a peace conference might do. They discussed the remaking of Europe, 'we all cheerfully divided up Turkey, both in Asia and Europe. The discussion hung for a long while around the fate of Constantinople.'[18]

It was getting late when House got them to the real point of the meeting: when should the United States demand that the war should cease and a conference be held? House felt that he got Lloyd George thoroughly committed to the intervention except that he was chary of fixing a time. Grey alone seemed to be thinking of an immediate venture. In answer to Asquith, House said that if the Allies could make an impression on the German lines of sufficient importance to discourage Germany, that would be the psychological moment. The others tentatively agreed though Lloyd George and Balfour inclined to further postponement.

It was now 12 o'clock and the Prime Minister made a move to go. While the conference was not conclusive, there was at least a common agreement reached in regard to the essential feature; that is, the President should at some time, to be later agreed upon, call a halt and demand a conference. I did not expect to go beyond that, and I was quite content.[19]

It was Asquith who in the course of the evening had asked the most significant question and got the answer that was perhaps—if the discussion had swayed him at all—determinative for him.

Asquith again asked what the President would do in the event he presided at a peace conference, and the Allies proposed a settlement which he considered unjust. I replied that he would probably withdraw from the conference and leave them to their own devices. On the other hand, he wished to know what the President would do in the event of Germany proposing something totally unfair, and against the interests of civilisation and humanity. In these circumstances, I thought the President would throw the weight of the United States on the side of the Allies. In other words, he would throw the weight of the United States on the side of those wanting a just settlement—a settlement which would make another such war impossible, and which would look to the advancement of civilisation and the comity of nations.[20]

In other words, it was to be a Wilsonian peace. Granted that Wilson and Asquith would both in a general way want the same sort of peace, was Britain ready to submit its terms to the arbitrament of Wilson? House's answer made it plain that the President would keep the ace in his own hand; a threat by the president and convenor of the conference to withdraw if Britain did not toe the line would be a potent weapon and one which Asquith was not the man to place in the hands of any foreign power, however friendly.

Was Lloyd George the man to do it? House's impression that he had got him committed was confirmed the next day by Grey who congratulated House on his achievement. But neither of them knew Lloyd George as well as the woman who was then his secretary and his mistress and became his lifelong companion and his second wife. It took time for her to learn—and she said that many men never learnt it—that until Lloyd George actually said 'yes' to a proposal there was every prospect that he would say 'no'. She has written:

I have known him talk around a project, even a most ridiculous one, with every appearance of favouring it but without the slightest intention of accepting it. I have seen him go right up to the threshold of acceptance when he knew that he would not enter, though many would have sworn that the matter was settled.[21]

She was not writing apropos of this particular affair, for she knew very little about it. She knew that Lloyd George was going to the dinner—rather unwillingly, but they had told him he must be there—'to discuss points of policy between England and U.S.A.';[22] he promised to tell her what happened but did not have time to do so.

When House called upon Grey the morning after for a brief talk before he went on to the palace, he found him quite moved at the thought that what they had done might shorten the war and save the lives of millions of men. He thought that there was no need for any more general discussion and that he could write a memorandum of the understanding reached. In fact Grey and House drew up the Memorandum together at 33 Eccleston Square on 17 February. Grey had by then obtained a detailed account from the French ambassador of House's conversations in Paris and the Memorandum was intended to cover the understanding reached in both capitals. On the morning of 23 February Grey gave House his copy of the Memorandum and on 25 February House sailed from Falmouth, declining Grey's offer of a special train since, as he noted prosaically, the train service was very convenient.[23]

The House-Grey Memorandum, dated 22 February, was expressed as written by Grey, and ran as follows:

Colonel House told me that President Wilson was ready, on hearing from

France and England that the moment was opportune, to propose that a Conference should be summoned to put an end to the war. Should the Allies accept this proposal, and should Germany refuse it, the United States would probably enter the war against Germany.

Colonel House expressed the opinion that, if such a Conference met, it would secure peace on terms not unfavourable to the Allies; and, if it failed to secure peace, the United States would* leave the Conference as a belligerent on the side of the Allies, if Germany was unreasonable. Colonel House expressed an opinion decidedly favourable to the restoration of Belgium, the transfer of Alsace and Lorraine to France, and the acquisition by Russia of an outlet to the sea, though he thought that the loss of territory incurred by Germany in one place would have to be compensated to her by concessions to her in other places outside Europe. If the Allies delayed accepting the offer of President Wilson, and if, later on, the course of the war was so unfavourable to them that the intervention of the United States would not be effective, the United States would probably disinterest themselves in Europe and look to their own protection in their own way.

I said that I felt the statement, coming from the President of the United States to be a matter of such importance that I must inform the Prime Minister and my colleagues; but that I could say nothing until it had received their consideration. The British Government could, under no circumstances, accept or make any proposal except in consultation and agreement with the Allies. I thought that the Cabinet would probably feel that the present situation would not justify them in approaching their Allies on this subject at the present moment; but, as Colonel House had had an intimate conversation with M. Briand and M. Jules Cambon in Paris, I should think it right to tell M. Briand privately, through the French Ambassador in London, what Colonel House had said to us; and I should, of course, whenever there was an opportunity, be ready to talk the matter over with M. Briand, if he desired it.[24]

A week earlier Page had by implication given a forthright opinion on the scheme, which he had been told was the President's own, in a cable addressed to the President himself. Balfour, who through Plunkett was shown a copy of it, said that he had never seen such a communication from an ambassador to his master.[25] Page prefaced his advice by saying: 'My loyalty to you would not be absolute if I shrank from respectfully sending my solemn conviction of our duty and opportunity.'[26] Return to your original *Lusitania* Notes, Page all but commanded, and refuse to yield a jot or a tittle of them: at once sever diplomatic relations. There would be no need for more. 'I do not believe we should have to fire a gun or risk a man.' Economic measures, moral weight, and the threat of war would bring an early peace and immortal credit would be the reward. 'Longer delay *or any other plan*,† will bring us

---

* A second 'probably' was here inserted by Wilson.

† Italics added. Page repeated the same argument in a cable of 26 March marked 'for the President only', LP. 706.

only a thankless, opulent and dangerous isolation. The Lusitania is the turning point and the time for action is come.' Lansing was relieved (or said he was) to be assured by the President that this was not, as he had at first thought, the fruit of House's labours in London.

This was a singular instance of Page allowing his enthusiasm for the cause to expel his natural candour. He did not in fact believe that peace could be obtained by threats; he noted in his diary on 14 February that economic war would lead to actual war.[27]

The day on which the House–Grey Memorandum was signed in London was also the day on which Wilson in Washington faced the fiercest challenge to his leadership that he had yet experienced.

Lansing had not succeeded in the difficult task of burying the *modus vivendi* without further prayers for its soul. His disquisition on 15 February on offensive and defensive armaments had not only come as a sudden reversal of policy but had not much enlightened the ordinary Congressman on the vital questions he was now asking himself. Was the Administration or was it not asserting the right of Americans to travel in safety on armed ships; and what would it do about it if they did and were killed? On 17 February Representative McLemore, a Democrat, introduced into the House a resolution requesting the President to warn all American citizens to refrain from travelling on armed merchant vessels. There were already in the Senate bills introduced by Senator Gore designed to prohibit the issue of passports to Americans travelling on belligerent ships or on neutral ships carrying contraband. Positively to forbid Americans was one thing; to discourage them another. There seemed to be nothing objectionable about the McLemore resolution; indeed, in the light of what Lansing had said, it seemed hardly more than a sensible precaution. The Administration had declined to say that the German order was unlawful or to say in advance what it would do if a submarine sank an armed ship with Americans on board. It was true that Lansing had said that the Administration would not warn Americans against travelling on merchantmen armed solely for defence. But the only armament in question was a gun; and prospective passengers might be pardoned for feeling some uncertainty about whether it would go off aggressively or defensively and for feeling insufficiently reassured by Lansing's statement that mistakes would be bound to occur. A warning of the sort contemplated would not interfere with British commerce; it was certainly not an unneutral act and could hardly be represented as an unfriendly one.

In this bewildering state of affairs, Senator Stone called on the President on 21 February 1916 to find out what the Administration had in mind. He himself, he said, was in the dark. Wilson for his part was puzzled by the signs of Congressional interference with his conduct of foreign affairs. He suggested that the senator should return for a full discussion bringing the Senate majority leader and Representative Flood, Chairman of the House Committee on Foreign Affairs.

The meeting took place that same afternoon. Wilson was never at his best in round-table discussions of this sort. The suspicion that he was being thwarted was liable to make him, as it had done at Princeton, say something foolish, particularly if he had not clearly formulated in advance what his line would be. On this occasion he does not seem to have worked out anything beyond Lansing's statement or to have considered adequately the difficulties which it involved. He began by repeating what Lansing had said about the *modus vivendi*. Perhaps he stressed the importance of pending diplomatic negotiations and of their possible embarrassment by Congressional action; his hearers would have understood this as a reference to the *Lusitania* negotiations that were known to have reached a difficult stage. Then perhaps something that was said nettled him. At any rate he went further than it was necessary or prudent to go. The American Government, he said, would go to almost any lengths to defend the right of Americans to travel on defensively armed merchant ships. He would consider it his duty to hold Germany to strict account if a German war vessel should torpedo without warning an armed merchant vessel carrying American passengers. Indeed, he would sever diplomatic relations if this occurred. Moreover, he would regard adoption of a resolution warning Americans against travelling on armed ships as a rank discourtesy. Thus he dispelled Lansing's careful obfuscations.

Stone banged the table. The American people, he said, did not want to go to war to vindicate the right of a few people to travel or work on armed vessels. They should be warned to stay off. Otherwise it might mean war and in such a matter he must follow his conscience.

The conversation was carried back no doubt with embellishments. The account of it merged with the rumour that the German Foreign Minister had just said that submarines would attack without warning all armed merchant ships, whether carrying passengers or not. If both he and Wilson were heading for war, was not war inevitable? There was a sense of sudden crisis, almost of panic, a feeling that unless something was done there would be an immediate break. Flood called a meeting of the Democratic members of his committee and told them that the President would not yield and was prepared to go to war to vindicate the right of Americans to travel on armed ships. Every member present signified that he favoured the McLemore resolution and the meeting insisted on what amounted to an ultimatum to the President that unless he changed his policy within forty-eight hours the House would adopt the resolution. The loyal efforts of leading Democrats in Congress, including Stone and Flood, notwithstanding that all of them sympathized with the resolution, aided no doubt by Burleson and Tumulty employing the usual methods, succeeded in keeping the subject off the floor of the House on the 23rd and 24th. At 3.30 on the 24th Speaker Clark called Tumulty and told him that he and Flood and Kitchin, the majority leader in the House, would like to see the President as soon as possible. Wilson kept them kicking their heels until 6.15 and then did not send for them.

The issue was no longer whether or not Americans should be warned. It was whether or not Wilson was to submit. In a crisis of this sort Wilson always preferred pen and paper to spoken words, that is, when the words could be answered back. And he had been given the chance of entrenching himself behind a written statement of his position, for he had just received a long letter from Senator Stone.[28] The letter was only an expression of the senator's anguish, his feeling that it would be indefensible to plunge the nation into the vortex because 'of our own people recklessly risking their lives on armed belligerent ships' and his anxiety to stand by Wilson and not to embarrass his diplomatic negotiations. Wilson was employed all that afternoon in drafting his reply. Speaking, he said, in deep solemnity and without heat, he wrote as follows.

You are right in assuming that I shall do everything in my power to keep the United States out of war . . . So far I have succeeded. I do not doubt that I shall continue to succeed . . . But in any event our duty is clear. No nation, no group of nations, has the right while war is in progress to alter or disregard the principles which all nations have agreed upon in mitigation of the horrors and sufferings of war; and if the clear rights of American citizens should ever unhappily be abridged or denied by any such action we should, it seems to me, have in honor no choice as to what our own course should be.

For my own part, I cannot consent to any abridgment of the rights of American citizens in any respect. The honor and self-respect of the nation is involved. We covet peace, and shall preserve it at any cost but the loss of honor. To forbid our people to exercise their rights for fear we might be called upon to vindicate them would be a deep humiliation indeed. It would be an implicit, all but an explicit, acquiescence in the violation of the rights of mankind everywhere, and of whatever nation or allegiance. It would be a deliberate abdication of our hitherto proud position as a spokesman, even amidst the turmoil of war, for the law and the right. It would make everything this government has attempted, and everything that it has achieved during this terrible struggle of nations meaningless and futile.

It is important to reflect that if in this instance we allowed expediency to take

the place of principle, the door would inevitably be opened to still further concessions. Once accept a single abatement of right, and many other humiliations
would certainly follow, and the whole fine fabric of international law might
crumble under our hands piece by piece.[29]

When Wilson had finished typing this he gave both it and Senator Stone's
letter to the press and told Tumulty to tell the Speaker that the President
would receive a delegation from the House of Representatives at 9 o'clock
the following morning, 26 February.

Champ Clark was the spokesman for the delegation.[30] He had come not
to argue, he said, but simply to inform the President that the warning
resolution would be carried by at least two to one. Wilson was calm. He
intended to see this thing through, he said, and he could not help it if
Congress would not support him. Any yielding to Germany now, particularly by the adoption of the warning resolution, would encourage further
transgression of American rights by both sides and the whole fabric of
international law would fall to pieces. What would happen, he was asked,
if a German submarine sank an armed merchantman with Americans
aboard? 'I believe we should sever diplomatic relations', he replied. What
would happen then? 'Count von Bernstorff told Secretary Lansing', Wilson
replied, 'that a break in diplomatic relations would be followed by a declaration of war by Germany.' The effect of American participation, he added,
might be to bring the war to an end much sooner than appeared possible.
Clark said that Wilson would have his support only so long as his policy
did not lead to war; he reserved the right to leave the Chair and oppose the
President if his policy seemed to foreshadow hostilities. Wilson remained
unmoved. He displayed some emotion only when he was told that people
were saying that he wanted war with Germany. 'In God's name', he cried,
'could anyone have done more than I to show a desire for peace?' The
delegation departed. It was very clear to all, Clark reported, that the President stood on his letter to Senator Stone.

But they found that the mood of Congress was changing. Everyone had
read Wilson's letter in the morning newspapers. This and what Clark told
them made it clear to every supporter of the resolution that he could get
his way only by open defiance of the President. Burleson must have been
satisfied that Wilson would win, for at a Cabinet meeting later in the morning he urged him to press for outright defeat of the McLemore resolution.
But Wilson did not at that stage want a showdown. He told Lansing to make
it clear that his letter applied to armed ships only if they were armed for
defence, and that he was willing to discuss the proper definition of defensive
armament with the Berlin authorities. This offered a way out and McLemore
announced that he would not press for a vote on his resolution, at least until

the President had had time to conduct negotiations with Germany. The crisis dissolved as rapidly as it had crystallized. A canvass at the end of that day found that two-thirds of the Democrats and five-sixths of the Republicans in the House would stand by the President. It was as triumphant an assertion of personal authority as has ever happened in a democracy.

Three days later Wilson decided that the situation had changed and that he must move into the attack. The change sprang from the German reaction to the collapse of the *modus vivendi*. Germany, it will be remembered,* had on 11 February 1916 published her declaration that after 29 February enemy merchantmen carrying guns would be regarded as warships and she had done so with the Secretary's blessing. The encouragement was vivid enough whether it was displayed, as Lansing disputed, by the word 'welcome' or, as he claimed, by the phrase 'the sooner the better'. The day on which Lansing back-pedalled was 15 February.† The next day, when the German ambassador called at the State Department with the final draft of the *Lusitania* settlement all ready for signing and delivering, he was told coolly by the Secretary that he could express no opinion on it. The *Arabic* assurances, Lansing wrote to Wilson on 17 February, had been given with the full knowledge that Britain armed her merchantmen and the declaration of 10 February was contradictory of the assurances and nullified them. Wilson replied the same day. But for the declaration, he said, the German draft should clearly be accepted, but the declaration threw doubt on the whole future. He suggested 'a frank conversation' with the ambassador, telling him how difficult it was to interpret the *Arabic* assurances 'in the light of the new and dangerous policy' and indeed to understand the new policy at all.[31] Lansing was equal to the occasion. After all, his legal position was as impregnable as his diplomatic was vulnerable. What he had proposed was a new agreement requiring the assent of both belligerents and it now appeared that Allied assent would not be forthcoming. Germany had acted without waiting for the agreement. Even if it was a prod from Lansing himself that had made her jump the gun, nevertheless she had acted on her own responsibility. Bernstorff was too old a hand to levy reproaches. It was a fair point too that the declaration made no exception for passenger liners and Lansing rubbed in the danger of the mistaken sinking of an unarmed liner. Bernstorff put Lansing's change of front into the correct perspective. He treated it as a withdrawal of the 'welcome' to the declaration of 10 February, but not as a renewal of the pressure for a *Lusitania* settlement. Indeed, when on 18 February he reported the conversation to Berlin, he expressed his belief that no more would be heard of the *Lusitania* affair. But he added his customary warning 'that, if a catastrophe similar to the Lusitania case

* See p. 426 above.   † See p. 428 above.

occurs again, war with the United States cannot be prevented by any art known to diplomacy'.[32]

The warning came as some reinforcement to the German Chancellor, who was being hard pressed by the war chiefs now all aligned against him. The declaration of 10 February, so far from satisfying them, had led them to hope that Bethmann was on the run and that by following the chase they could get all they wanted. Falkenhayn was by now fully converted. He expressed his conclusion in a memorandum to Bethmann on 13 February. He stuck to his military last, basing his opinion on his requirement that Belgium should be a place of assembly for the troops required for the protection of Germany's industrial regions. There must, he said, be 'unconditional military dominion' over Belgium; otherwise 'Germany's war in the west is lost'.[33] But this, he agreed, would mean for England that she would have lost and thus could be achieved only by her defeat: so 'those who are conducting this war have not the right to refuse to make use of U-boat warfare'. On the same day, 13 February, Tirpitz weighed in with his contribution. On 19 February Holtzendorff completed an elaborate memorandum, the prototype for those that were to follow throughout the next eleven months, accompanied by graphs and statistics to prove that unrestricted warfare would force England to her knees within six months. Surprisingly he was persuaded by Bethmann to amend on 24 February the declaration of 10 February by exempting from it all liners whether armed or not. Perhaps he felt that this sharpened the coming encounter in which he hoped for total victory; the more diplomacy clogged the drive of the submarines, the stronger the case for the clean warlike decision.

The publication on 25 February of Wilson's intransigent letter to Senator Stone convinced Bethmann and Jagow that America had a secret understanding with England. As they saw it, the question to be decided was simply whether the submarine could end the war in the short term before the long-term consequences became effective. The Chancellor on 29 February prepared a paper for the Kaiser which, like Holtzendorff's which it was designed to counter, set the pattern of his argument in the months to come.[34] He questioned the calculation on which the Navy's forecast of triumph was based. He elaborated on the consequences of America's certain entry into the war; on this issue he was aided by the fears of Austria and Turkey as expressed by their foreign ministers. He foresaw—wrongly as the event proved—that American entry into the war would bring with it that of Holland and Denmark. Finally, he went as far as he could to meet naval demands. If the unrestricted U-boat war exempted neutral shipping and unarmed enemy liners, he believed that war with America could be avoided; at any rate, he was prepared to run that risk.

Three days were scheduled for the great debate at Charleville. On the evening of 2 March the Chancellor handed his paper to the Kaiser. On the morning of the next day he had an interview with His Majesty who said he would not permit the 'folly' of provoking America into the war and would arrange everything with Falkenhayn and Holtzendorff. Bethmann succeeded in inflaming the Kaiser against Tirpitz to the extent of procuring an order transferring the press bureau from the Grand Admiral's Department to Holtzendorff's. On this last point the Kaiser adhered to his resolve, but in the matter of the settlement of Falkenhayn and Holtzendorff he did not. After a talk with the former on the next day the Kaiser veered right round. Bethmann had to play all his cards, including the last trump of resignation (tactfully presented as an unwillingness to assume responsibility) in order to ensure that what emerged from the Kaiser at the end of the three days was no worse than continued indecision. Holtzendorff indeed thought that he had won and that the Kaiser had accepted his argument that the war must be ended in 1916, that six to eight months must be allowed to the U-boats to do it, and that consequently Bethmann could have only until 1 April to make the best diplomatic preparations he could. But Bethmann was in the strong position of being the draftsman and the Imperial commands, as they came out in writing, were:

1. The immediate anouncement of an unlimited submarine campaign is rejected.

2. During the month of March the ground with America and the European neutrals will be explored with the aim of making possible the beginning of an unlimited submarine campaign on April 1, thus avoiding a break with America.

3. His Majesty reserves to himself the decision whether and actually when all-out submarine warfare is to begin.[35]

Bethmann sent a blow-by-blow account of the whole affair in a long letter to Jagow dated 5 March which he ended with apologies for his poor penmanship: 'my nerves are somewhat uneasy'.[36] Tirpitz's resignation, as a result of the implicit rebuke, was the outward sign of the Chancellor's new lease of life. The broad result of the Charleville 'Grand Council of War', that is, that 'Von Tirpitz lost', soon came to the ears of Gerard; and Washington got the news from him on 7 March.[37]

Meanwhile in Washington Bernstorff had been seeking to give some comfort to the Congressional rebels who had been worsted on 26 February. On 27 February he received a dispatch sent on 18 February containing a long justification of the declaration of 11 February which Berlin then believed to accord with the American position. He was told nothing of the amending order of 24 February exempting liners. He did the best he could with an announcement that Germany was willing to discuss the definition of offensive and defensive armament; but he said also that the German Government urged that Americans be warned not to travel on armed ships. Zwiedinek and he had decided that it would be unwise to embarrass Lansing by publishing the 'welcome' conversation and Zwiedinek had so reported to his superiors on 20 February. Jagow on 28 February suggested to Bernstorff that he should tell Lansing that the Central Powers had instituted their action against armed ships in response to the Secretary's own statements and that they would feel obliged to publish these statements if war occurred. But the ambassador knew enough of Wilson to know that a touch of blackmail would not be the way to handle him.

But Bernstorff with his talk of a warning against travel had said enough for Wilson to suspect that he was trying to reopen the controversy. The President decided to move in for the kill. The McLemore resolution must be brought up for execution. 'The report', Wilson declared on 29 February 'that there are divided counsels in Congress in regard to the foreign policy of the government is being made industrious use of in foreign capitals.'[38] He asked that an early vote should be taken upon the resolutions. On 1 March Stone, Clark, Flood, and Kitchin all went to the White House again to plead for delay. But Wilson was adamant. He could not conduct foreign policy, he said, so long as the German Government believed that Congress had repudiated his policies. There was another fight in which all the power of patronage was used. In the Senate on 2 March Senator Gore said that he had it on good authority that the President told Congressional leaders that he expected war and that American participation might end the struggle by midsummer and be a blessing to civilization. Wilson described the report that he 'was trying in some way to bring on war' as 'grotesquely false'.[39] Bryan hurried to Washington to help the insurgents. On 3 March in the Senate Wilson got his way by 68 votes to 14. Senator Stone reported on 'another very frank talk' with Wilson. 'So far from the President desiring to involve this country in this disastrous European war', Stone said, 'his supreme wish is to avoid that calamity.'[40] On 7 March Wilson triumphed in the House by 275 votes to 135.

While pro-Allied feeling in the United States was naturally jubilant, as was Wilson himself, at his smashing victory, pro-German and pacifist feeling was not ill-pleased. McLemore claimed that 90 per cent of the House would have voted for his resolution if they had not been brought under threat. Bryan also in his paper *The Commoner* contended with much force that the vote was irrelevant.

The real object had been accomplished by the discussion. The people of the

United States are not willing to go to war to vindicate the right of Americans to take these risks; neither is Congress. The President knows it and we can now return to our work and await the results, confident that the Jingoes cannot drive us into war.[41]

Both ambassadors were gratified. Spring Rice, reporting on the first stage of the struggle, wrote:

Every sort of pressure was put upon him and he appeared for the moment to be in a minority in both Houses . . . grew hourly stronger, and at the present moment it is generally believed that he will be able to carry the day. He is said to have shown great heat in the discussion. He produced a letter which is extremely firm in its language and shows no symptoms of yielding.[42]

Bernstorff, when it was all over, said it was a Pyrrhic victory. He reported:

We have gained the following remarkable advantage as the result of the past weeks, that the American people have expressed themselves through their chosen representatives against a war with Germany. Your Excellency is well aware that I have always prophesied that this would be the feeling of Congress, although Mr. Lansing, in his talks with me in the course of the negotiations concerning the Lusitania, always asserted the contrary.[43]

What emerged at the end of it all as the most significant factor was Wilson's letter to Senator Stone. It contained a new definition of his last ditch. Since he had taken his first stand on the proposition that Americans must be free to travel and to trade without danger to life a number of complicating refinements had appeared. Americans might be passengers on liners or on cargo ships; they might be members of the crew; the ships might be American, Allied, or neutral, armed or unarmed; the armament might be offensive or defensive. Wilson had now made it clear that Americans —he had not distinguished specifically between passengers and crew or between liners and cargo ships—were not to be endangered on ships defensively armed.

But the letter went further than that in its statement of general principle. It shut the door on change in the law. It clearly implied that if in breach of the law American lives were endangered, America would if necessary go to war. The letter was composed under stress and time pressure and without real consultation. There was a talk with Tumulty who had prepared a draft which was made use of. The letter was discussed with Lansing on the telephone but he was given no time to consider it. Perhaps Wilson might on reflection have been more cautious but, granted his methods of meeting opposition, it is doubtful. It was a crisis of obedience and opposition must be quelled. What he had to oppose was the apparently innocuous idea that Americans should be warned of the risks they ran and what he needed for his opposition was a convincing statement of principle. It would be difficult to formulate any narrower principle that would have served the purpose. At any rate, this was what he had written and it was now for ever in the books.

Lansing emerged from the incident without the bad mark which his indiscretion deserved. In his memoirs he has left behind a tale of exculpation[44] which as an illustration of an autobiographer's flight of fancy rivals Mrs. Wilson's dramatization of her love affair. But while Edith gave way to her romantic sense, the Secretary of State yielded to vanity; he did not like to look indiscreet and inconsistent even if only in the mirror in his own chamber. The heart of the affair according to his account was an attempt by Bernstorff to drive him out of office. The German seized on what Lansing calls the Austrian Zwiedinek's 'unintentional mistake' in reporting the Secretary as having said on 26 January that he would welcome the proposed German declaration classing armed merchantmen as warships. What an indiscretion, Bernstorff must have thought (as indeed it was—to welcome the declaration before it was issued and thus make it appear that the United States had initiated the action): Lansing could now be smitten hip and thigh. But Bernstorff, as the story goes, chortled over his impending triumph with a lady friend and the conversation was reported to Lansing. The prospective victim acted promptly. He sent for the copy of Zwiedinek's telegram in the State Department files and found that it did indeed use the word 'welcome'. He immediately summoned the Austrian chargé and told him that he had misunderstood the conversation. Zwiedinek wanted, Lansing says, to amend his report but Bernstorff threatened to have him recalled if he did so. Lansing, however, telegraphed to Berlin and Vienna explaining how Zwiedinek had misunderstood his words and the explanation was accepted. 'I can imagine', Lansing reminisced, 'the chagrin of Bernstorff upon learning how I had slipped through his fingers.'

But why was not the phrase that Lansing admittedly used, 'the sooner the better', just as good as 'welcome' for the purposes of Bernstorff's plot? Lansing explains why the two were quite different. According to this explanation, when on 26 January Lansing heard of the proposed declaration, so far from welcoming it as in step with the *modus vivendi*, he at once perceived that it might wreck the *Lusitania* negotiations. This is to say that the reason Lansing gave for stalling the negotiations and which, so far as there is any contemporary record, was first expressed by him on 16 February, the day after the abandonment of the *modus vivendi*, was in fact in his mind three weeks earlier. Lansing thought, so he says, that it would be most embarrassing if a *Lusitania* settlement was at once followed by the declaration since the United States would have to denounce the declaration immediately it was made. Better, Lansing thought, that the declaration should be issued as soon as possible, so that he could demand its withdrawal as a term of the *Lusitania* settlement. So, according to his memoir:

> Perceiving the strategic advantage to be gained if the Central Powers were induced to act promptly, I told Zwiedinek that I deplored such proposed action since it would reopen the submarine controversy, but that, if his Government persisted in its intention to issue such a declaration, 'the sooner it was done the better'.

Lansing's idea of 'a strategic advantage' was odd. What was to be gained by leading the Central Powers into making a declaration so that the United States could immediately demand its withdrawal? The simple course was to say at once that if such a declaration was made it would put an end to the *Lusitania* negotiations. Indeed, if the declaration was thought to affect in any way the *Lusitania* settlement, it was urgent that Bernstorff should be told so at once. It was on that very day, 26 January, that Lansing had given Bernstorff his final terms for transmission to Berlin.

The truth is that Lansing never began to disapprove of the proposed declaration until after he had been driven off the *modus vivendi*. Not only is there no record of his earlier disapproval, but the record so far as it goes, is against it. On 9 February Bernstorff reported to Berlin that Lansing had reminded him of the fact that from the beginning of the controversy the American Government had always spoken of unarmed merchant vessels.[45] This would imply that Lansing saw no inconsistency between the proposed declaration and the American position in the *Lusitania* controversy. Lansing's answer to this—first put on record a month later—is that Bernstorff's report is false and that in fact he had always told Bernstorff exactly the contrary.[46] Now, all these reports to Berlin went over the State Department's wire and were scrutinized to see that they did not involve the United States in any unneutrality. Lansing himself saw this particular message at the time. He made no comment, he says, because messages were not being scrutinized for accuracy and a correction on one occasion might lead to the assumption that an uncorrected version was an agreed version. He did, however, make a note to correct 'if the opportunity offered'.

Lansing can hardly have supposed that a correction made when opportunity offers is either more potent or less objectionable than one made promptly. What prevented him from immediately telling Bernstorff that while he did not normally vet his telegrams for accuracy, he had on this occasion perceived signs of a misunderstanding which could seriously mislead Berlin? The German embassy was of course well aware that its messages were scrutinized, but Lansing seems to have regarded this activity as being in the same class as the performance of the natural functions, that is, as one which is universally known to take place but which ought not to be remarked upon. In fact no opportunity offered, he said, because the subject was not drawn to his attention officially. Presumably he wanted Bernstorff to raise the subject in an official call which would give him the opportunity of correcting the false impression without a specific reference to the inaccurate report; meanwhile the perpetuation of the false impression in Berlin was to be preferred to the indelicacy of an allusion to the process of scrutiny. If it were anyone other than Lansing who was offering this explanation, it could be treated derisively; but in his case and considering his natural pedantry it is one that ought at least to be taken seriously.

The Secretary had, however, the misfortune to be misinterpreted by Zwiedinek as well as by Bernstorff. The Austrian chargé, immediately after the interview with Lansing on 26 January in which he mentioned that the declaration was contemplated,* telegraphed to his government on the State Department wire the news that the Secretary would welcome it. Lansing saw the message that day, observed the word 'welcome' and made a note to correct it, but again only 'if opportunity offers'.[47] On this occasion opportunity was kinder and the Central Powers were left under a misapprehension for no more than a fortnight. On 9 February, two days before the declaration was made, Zwiedinek called to announce its forthcoming publication and brought with him a telegram from his government in which it was referred to as the declaration 'welcomed by Mr. Lansing'. This permitted the Secretary to go into action without a reference to the message of 26 January. It was Zwiedinek who had the indecency to refer to the latter and to inquire why the point was not taken then. Lansing replied with an explanation of his inhibitions. Nevertheless, it is clear from Lansing's contemporary memorandum of the interview[48] that the Baron stood his ground: the language used, he said, warranted the report he had made. To this Lansing replied that his language was unfortunate but that he had not intended the meaning conveyed and hoped that Zwiedinek would so advise his government. Zwiedinek—the telegram has already been summarized†—advised his government exactly to this effect. He did not amend 'welcome'— he had not been asked to do so—and he added that the Secretary still thought the declaration to some extent justifiable.

But all this is playing with words. The fault in the Austrian's report, if Lansing is right, lay not in the paraphrasing by 'welcome' of 'the sooner the better' but in the total omission from it of Lansing's statement that he deplored the declaration and that it was only if the Central Powers insisted

* See p. 421 above.   † See p. 426 above.

on making it that he wanted it accelerated. This omission distorted the whole sense of the conversation and one is forced to wonder whether even Lansing could suppose that its rectification could be left to a convenient opportunity. When the opportunity did occur Lansing made no complaint except of the inaccurate paraphrase of his own unfortunate language.

Four days elapsed between 16 February when Bernstorff learnt from Lansing that the declaration was now unwelcome* and 20 February when he and Zwiedinek decided that it would be unwise to embarrass Lansing by publicizing his change of front.† Maybe that was just enough time for Bernstorff to contrive and abandon the plot which Lansing attributed to him and divulge it to the lady friend on a tapped telephone whence it got easy access to the mind of Lansing. Whether or not the plot existed it adds no credibility to Lansing's attempt to explain away his own blundering. There can be no doubt on the contemporary documents that he did, before he was forced to change his attitude to the *modus vivendi*, welcome the declaration, that he led the Central Powers to believe that he did, and that he lacked the strength needed for a simple admission that he had gone too fast and too far. He did not of course know of Bernstorff's decision not to embarrass him and remained fearful that sooner or later it would be brought up against him that he had instigated the declaration. In early March he sent long telegrams on the subject to the American ambassadors in Berlin and Vienna.[49] He prepared also a memorandum for the Cabinet which, he felt,

ought to know something of the difficulties which we have had to face and particularly the adroit efforts made by the German Ambassador, for I consider Zwiedinek acting more or less under his direction, to cause embarrassment and place this Government in a false light.[50]

The President, who read the memorandum to the Cabinet on 7 March, was very sympathetic and suggested an amendment to the telegram so that Lansing 'might not even seem to admit any excuse for Zwiedinek's misrepresentation'.[51]

The episode, as Lansing justly observes in his memoirs, 'is interesting as showing what was going on behind the scenes'.

House reached New York on 5 March when Wilson's victory in the Congress was virtually assured. By the time their first meeting took place, Wilson had proved that if what the House–Grey Memorandum needed for its implementing was power and determination put behind it, he had both. He had also repeatedly and clearly given pledges totally inconsistent with it.

* See p. 442 above.　　　† See p. 445 above.

A fair summary of his public position is that he had pledged himself not to go to war unless there was a breach of international law affecting America's honour or her interests. With that pledge he had solicited votes to give him the means to go to war if necessary and with its aid he had defeated his opponents in Congress, learning thereby that the feeling in Congress was such that without the pledge he would have lost the day.

If Germany refused to attend the conference summoned by the President or if, having attended it, she refused to accept terms 'not unfavourable to the Allies', she would commit no breach of international law, she would not thereby dishonour America and, unless it was to be said (contrary to the whole idea of the neutrality which Wilson had constantly proclaimed) that America's interests required that the Allies should win the war, she would do nothing affecting America's interests. Her refusal to fall in with American ideas of peacemaking could hardly be described as the spiritual affront which Wilson had spoken of at Des Moines.* Yet it was in these circumstances that the Memorandum required America 'probably' to go to war on the side of the Allies. If Wilson assented to the Memorandum, either he made ready to dishonour his pledge, or, keeping it, he cheated the Allies. Whether House had grasped the inconsistency must be a matter of conjecture. Probably he had not received reports of the speeches in the Middle West. We do not know if he had seen the assurances given to Senator Stone and compared them with his own statement, made to a friend just before he left England, that in thirty days the United States would be in the thick of it;[52] or what he thought of Wilson's description as 'grotesquely false' of the charge that he was trying to bring on war.† Wilson, one must at least begin by supposing, understood the inconsistency well enough. He knew what was in the Memorandum and he knew what he had told the country; and indeed after endorsing the Memorandum he stuck to his theme. The day on which he was settling the reply to Grey, 7 March, was also the day of the 'frank talk' with Senator Stone in which he said that it was his supreme wish to avoid involving the country 'in this disastrous European war'.† On 13 March he assured a visiting delegation of Scandinavians: 'Nothing is nearer my heart than keeping this country out of war and doing anything that the United States can do to show its preference for peace.'[53]

The Colonel was careful in the way he presented the Memorandum to Wilson and there was good reason why he should be. First, he had gone outside his brief and even beyond the terms of his original message to Grey of 17 October‡ in discussing territorial arrangements and in specifying in the Memorandum those which he considered to be reasonable. Secondly, there was the question whether Wilson really intended the use of physical force.

* See p. 404 above. † See p. 445 above. ‡ See p. 382 above.

Had Wilson's final letter of 24 December* superseded on this point the original message? If so, all that House had done foundered on a misapprehension. In his intermediate messages, House had used ambiguous phraseology, referring to intervention or forcing the issue or 'throwing in all our weight'. The Memorandum he now had to present was unambiguously based on the original message and unmistakably clear in its language—'enter the war', 'leave the Conference as a belligerent'.

House travelled down to Washington on the day he arrived in New York. The following day, 6 March, he lunched at the White House and then he and the President and the new Mrs. Wilson took an automobile ride of something over two hours during which, he says, he outlined every important detail of his mission. He was dropped at the State Department on the way back and spent an hour with Lansing. Then he went back to the White House and showed Wilson the Memorandum. Wilson seems to have been delighted with it and with everything that House had reported. 'It would be impossible', he told House warmly, 'to imagine a more difficult task than the one placed in your hands, but you have accomplished it in a way beyond my expectations.'[54] They were to meet the next day to settle the terms of the reply to Grey.

The following morning, 7 March, House saw Spring Rice and told him that the United States would finish by taking part in the war. The moment for intervention had not yet come, but it would come, and the President's ideas on the subject were in process of formation. He added for good measure that Britain would do well to tighten her blockade of Germany since it was one of the most effective weapons that the Allies possessed. The ambassador does not record whether gratification, astonishment, or disbelief was uppermost in his mind as he listened to these remarks. At any rate he did not pause to reason why. At 11.30 a.m. he telegraphed to the Foreign Office that he had a message directly from the President that they could delay their reply to the great American indictment of 5 November 1915.[55] As for the arming of merchant ships, a short Note, he thought, would do, stating that the Allies preferred to maintain the existing practice and renewing their assurances that guns would be used defensively.

Then the Colonel returned to the White House where Wilson first wrote out in shorthand and then transcribed on his typewriter the reply to Grey. It was to be sent in House's name and read as follows:

I reported to the President the general conclusions of our Conference of February 14 and in the light of those conclusions he authorises me to say that, so far as he can speak for the future action of the United States, he agrees to the memorandum with which you furnished me with only this correction that the

* See p. 390 above.

word 'probably' be added after the word 'would' and before the word 'leave' in line number 9.[56]

With this insertion Wilson tidied up a loose end in the Memorandum, bringing it into line with the original message. The original message, since it did not deal with the terms of peace, had contemplated only one contingency in which America would join the Allies, namely, the refusal of Germany to agree to a conference. The Memorandum contemplated another, namely, the refusal of Germany at the Conference to agree to reasonable terms. Just as Wilson had qualified the first statement, in order not to make it quite inevitable, as he had written at the time, that America should take part in forcing terms on Germany since the exact circumstances of the crisis could not be foreseen, so he qualified the second. Presumably it remained in his view 'an unimportant verbal change' which did not alter the sense of the Memorandum. 'The fact that he has approved in writing all that I have done gives me great satisfaction', House recorded in his diary that day.[57]

On 8 March House cabled the ratification to Grey and two days later he followed this up with a letter. The President, he said, had completely approved of what he had done, his recent victory in Congress was complete, and the matter now entirely in the President's hands: 'it is now squarely up to you to make the next move and a cable from you at any time will be sufficient.'[58] On 12 March he wrote to Wilson: 'I believe our plan will work out before midsummer and perhaps much sooner.'[59] He was reporting on a conversation with Bernstorff whom he had told that the President might intervene after the battles in the West were over, perhaps in several months. The report goes on: 'He thought Germany would welcome the intervention and asked if I thought the Allies would accept it. My opinion was that I thought the English would resent our interference. This is true, but of course, it was given to him for a purpose.'

It is difficult to see why Wilson and House were so exhilarated and the latter so convinced of success. A survey from a distance of what the Colonel had brought back shows his mission as a failure. He had achieved neither of the objectives primarily given to him in the President's Christmas Eve letter.* One he had quietly dropped;† as to the other—trying to make the British Cabinet realize American feeling about the blockade—he had confessed to getting nowhere.‡ As to what the President had then called 'possibilities in the direction of peace', he had gone to Europe to persuade the Allies to agree to Wilson's calling a conference which would result in the President presiding over the peace. He had been instructed to keep off any

---

* See p. 390 above.   † See p. 396 above.   ‡ See p. 402 above.

discussion of the actual terms of peace, sticking to the high line of the elimination of militarism and navalism as the objective of the conference. The Allies had first induced him to come off it and talk terms, thus obtaining some useful information about American ideas on the settlement; and then they had given him the same answer as he had got three months earlier before he went to Europe. Then Grey had told him that his visit could have no practical result. Now in the Memorandum Grey told him that Britain would do nothing without the agreement of her allies and that 'the Cabinet would probably feel that the present situation would not justify them in approaching their allies on this subject at the present moment'. If House did not read that to mean that things would have to get worse before the Allies would allow Wilson to interfere, he could not understand diplomatic English.

But clearly House was bubbling over with enthusiasm which he must have communicated to Wilson during the two hours of conversation before he produced the Memorandum. Possibly the Allied statesmen had been more forthcoming in talk than they had been in writing or possibly House thought that they had been. Lord Reading, whom House planned to have in Washington as the go-between and who may therefore have been grooming himself for the assignment, told House on 22 February that Asquith had spoken privately 'much more strongly in favour of the agreement' than he had at the dinner party.[60] There is an occasional reference in the diary to remarks by Grey which show him as more eager than his colleagues, but there is not recorded any concrete statement by anybody at variance with the terms of the Memorandum. Nor was anybody other than studiously vague about the date of its translation into action. Possibly Wilson and House, who would believe that the terms endorsed by House corresponded more nearly to the Allies' desiderata than in fact they did and who would view more realistically than the Allies themselves their chances of obtaining them without American aid, felt that, although the Allies might maintain a bold front on paper and in conversation, it would be impossible for them when they took counsel among themselves to reject so attractive an offer.

The prospect of these attractions was not causing any excitement in London. On the day the Memorandum was dated, 22 February, there was a routine meeting of the War Committee with a long agenda.[61] Sandwiched between the Cameroons (which the committee 'provisionally' divided up with France) and the supply of acid to Russia and Italy, there was a paper by General Robertson on the diplomatic policy of the Allies; he wanted Britain to exert greater control. There was quite a long discussion on this, ending up with the consideration of what could be done with the neutrals: could Holland, for example, be brought in? With regard to the United States, Grey said, there was nothing to be done (except to be careful not to cause friction with the blockade) unless the Allies gave up 'all idea of being able to finish the war'. Lloyd George said that it would be better to leave the United States alone; perhaps they might like to come in later. Asquith said (Grey disagreeing) that they were determined not to come in, but that there was no harm in trying. Balfour said nothing. Colonel House was mentioned only as having recently been in London.

The Colonel was in fact still in London—he left on the following day—and the reason why the Memorandum was not mentioned was doubtless that Grey and he were not yet agreed on the extent to which it should be circulated. But enough was said at the War Committee to show that, except for Reading who did not count, none of the Curzon Street diners was likely to give it a rapturous reception. Grey gave a copy to the French ambassador who remarked that neither French nor British public opinion would tolerate such a proposal.[62] Hankey already knew from conversations with McKenna and Balfour ('curious how they all confide in me!') a good deal of what was afoot.[63] Moreover, at the Stracheys' dinner party on 18 January at which House and Hankey first met,* one of the guests was Captain Hall, the Director of Naval Intelligence. He had not found the 'do-it-yourself' cipher which Wilson and House had contrived very difficult to crack and for some time past had been intercepting House's cables to Wilson including the recent ones sent from Berlin. He was miserly in the way he dispensed from his store of secret information. But Hankey and he were old friends and both at the time shared a suspicion of House. Hankey learned from him about House's 'peace stunt' and was shown copies of the telegrams. His chief reaction was one of horror at finding that House, apparently with Grey's connivance, was trading Freedom of the Seas against German militarism. But there was also in House's telegrams the 'priceless information' of Germany's submarine plans which might force America into the war.

On 7 March House talked with Montagu, the Prime Minister's confidant, and the upshot was that Montagu urged on Asquith that General Robertson, the Chief of Staff should be told of the proposal. Montagu, unlike most of his fellow Liberals, believed in smashing Germany. He said so at a dinner party on 11 March at the McKennas' ('short dinner, but 3 menservants', Arnold Bennett, the author, noted).[64] Earlier that day, at lunch at the Carlton, Hankey and Montagu had agreed that Robertson should be told; he should be asked whether in his opinion the Germans

* See p. 282 above.

could be defeated in the summer and warned that after that economic pressure would probably compel a reduction in the Allies' maximum effort. If Robertson was not sanguine of success, Hankey thought that House's suggestion ought to be tested 'in order either (1) to discuss peace before we passed our zenith, or (2) to get the United States of America behind us, in which case we could go on forever'.[65] On the 14th Hankey warned Robertson that the House question was coming up and that the decision would largely depend upon what he and the First Sea Lord thought about the prospects of the war.

On 15 March Grey, having by then received the Presidential confirmation, circulated the Memorandum to the War Committee:

> We ought to come to some decision as to whether President Wilson's suggestion should be discarded, or regarded as premature, or encouraged. This decision depends, I imagine, upon the opinion of military and naval authorities on the prospects of the war.[66]

On the following morning Hankey went to see the Prime Minister who, being in bed with a nasty attack of bronchitis, decided to postpone the War Committee meeting from the 17th to the 21st. They talked of House and the Prime Minister asked Hankey to see Grey and get him to talk to Robertson informally. 'The Prime Minister himself', Hankey recorded in his diary, 'affects to regard the whole thing as humbug and a mere manœuvre of American politics.'[67] Although Hankey uses the word 'affects', it seems clear from what he says elsewhere that it was a view he shared. It was the view universally held by the French. What seemed to experienced politicians to be the extreme *naïveté* of the plan led to the suspicion that it was not intended to be taken seriously: its object, they thought, was so that the President could say in the coming elections that he had gestured towards peace. Hankey's diary continues:

> In the afternoon I had a talk with Grey about House, and he told me the whole story. He spoke of the heavy responsibility which this laid on him. If he took no notice of it, and the war went wrong, he would have missed a great opportunity either to get a decent peace or to bring in America. If, however, we were likely to be completely victorious it would be better to ignore it. A middle course was to postpone action, but this would probably be to miss our opportunity.

Edwin Montagu recorded in August 1916 his sweeping belief in the contemptibility and untrustworthiness of the American politician of all parties when it came to international politics.[68] This is reflected in the reasons for discarding the Memorandum which on 18 March 1916 he put down on paper for Asquith to see.[69] First, the proposal was not honest or fair to Germany: possibly House had made a similar proposal to the Germans. Second, there was no guarantee that Wilson would stand by the terms.

Third, the terms could only be justified on the assumption that the Allies could not win the war; indeed, they were such that Prussian militarists could claim that they had won the war.

At the meeting of the War Committee on 21 March there was again a long agenda with the Memorandum coming last.[70] Grey posed the question as being whether he ought or ought not to take it up with the French on his forthcoming visit to Paris, his information being, he added later, that they would not wish to avail themselves of the offer. If, however, there was a prospect of deadlock at the end of six months through our inability to continue financing our Allies or any prospect of the defeat of an ally, e.g. Russia, the French ought to be consulted. So saying, Grey, as he was now making it his habit to do, laid the matter before the military oracle. General Robertson was inevitably oracular in his reply but confessed that all his own instincts were opposed to Colonel House's suggestion.

If one could imagine anything so improbable as Colonel House in a toga, the subsequent scene could have resembled Caesar's assassination in the Senate. Surely the Colonel would have been as startled as the great Julius when one by one his friends displayed, like daggers from beneath their cloaks, their unvarnished opinions of his plan. He would not of course have expected much good from Bonar Law who anyway had been outside the circle. Law spoke first and said the negotiations would be based on the *status quo ante* which would be equivalent to defeat; public opinion would not have it. Law was not to be the only man who referred to the proposals in the Memorandum as the *status quo ante*, as if the surrender of Alsace Lorraine and Constantinople would leave the map of Europe unaltered. Even if (though for Germany alone) the would was to be salved by concessions elsewhere, it seems improbable that the humiliation of the surrender would give, as Montagu thought, the Prussian militarists cause for rejoicing.

Then Asquith, whose strong approval had been bespoken by Reading, delivered his blow; the proposal should be put aside for the present and he doubted anyway whether Wilson could carry it through. Then what a rent Mr. Balfour made! The proposal, he said, was not worth five minutes' thought; its object was to get the President out of political difficulties. Lloyd George was quite non-committal, speaking only to the peripheral point of the vulnerability of Russia. Before he spoke at all, the issue had virtually been settled: so that for him there was nothing left to be gained by commitment and non-commitment might pay dividends. He drew these twenty years later for use in his vendetta against Grey.*

Why was this conference never summoned? Who was responsible? . . . The world would have been saved a whole year of ruin, havoc and devastation . . .

* See p. 239 above.

The world was once more sacrificed to the timidity of statesmanship. This great and at one time promising plan thus fell through. The bloody campaigns of 1916 . . . etc.[71]

His memoirs thunder on. The terms of the Memorandum, he says, were acceptable to all the Curzon Street diners (Asquith and Balfour included), but Grey took refuge in the 'probably' (there is no record of Grey mentioning the word), his real reason being that he was frightened of the Allies.

McKenna, the Chancellor of the Exchequer, was the last contributor. From the scraps of his conversation that have survived, he would seem to have been the least disinclined of all the senior ministers to a compromise peace. But on this occasion he stuck to his last and spoke only on finance; he said that the American exchange situation was safe until July. This led to a brief wrangle with Law about credit and to the Prime Minister saying that 'the discussion was now passing rather beyond the scope of Sir Edward Grey's point'. No decision was recorded. Grey had not asked for one, saying at the beginning that he had felt he must share his responsibility—presumably for what he did or did not say to the French—with the War Committee. He intervened to disagree with Asquith's view that Wilson could not carry the Memorandum through. But he displayed no advocacy. His attitude, to which he always subsequently adhered, was that he had an option worth preserving in case the market fell: no more than that. For House, if he had been there, the lukewarmness of Brutus Grey, though it was neither more nor less than the Memorandum itself said, might have been the unkindest cut of all. While there was no formal decision, no one doubted the result as Hankey recorded it in his diary: 'At the outset discussed House's proposals . . . decided not to adopt them at present.'[72]

Grey did not convey the decision to House in this blunt form. On 24 March he wrote to House that he could not put the matter before any of the other Allies unless in concert with the French Government.[73] Asquith and he were going to Paris on 30 March and if the French Premier had any views to express on the subject he would no doubt state them then. On 7 April Grey wrote again to House to say that the French had not mentioned the Memorandum at Paris and he therefore had not brought it up.

In a general talk with the French Foreign Minister on 12 April Grey observed that not one of the Allies had as yet hinted to the others that the time for discussing peace had come and the Minister entirely agreed that none could feel that the time had come when satisfactory terms could be secured.[74]

Asquith had gone on from Paris to Rome where on 1 April he called on the Pope. His Holiness made some suggestion about the desirability of an early peace but, Hankey records, 'the Prime Minister pursed up his mouth and said words to the effect that we should continue to the end'.[75] Bertie, the British ambassador in Paris, who was a strong opponent of a negotiated peace, was reassured by talks he had in mid April with Balfour and Lloyd George: 'no idea of a lame peace', he recorded in his diary.[76]

Although by the end of March 1916 the House–Grey Memorandum was frozen stiff, it lives on in history to unsettle the graves of the statesmen who were parties to it. Were the Allies right in treating so lightly the chance of ending the slaughter? 'History will lay a grave charge', House reports Grey as saying on 17 February, 'against those of us who refuse to accept your proffered services at this time.'[77] Certainly, when Grey was writing his memoirs, he thought that the world had perhaps had to pay with two more years of war for the peace it got at Versailles:[78] was not the price too high?

There are other questions which historians have asked themselves and tried to answer. Did Grey deal honestly with House? House on reflection had doubts. It was almost diplomatic dishonesty not to tell him of the secret treaties; 'the English are close traders, don't fool yourself', he said to his biographer.[79] Does the whole affair make a fool of House? And does it show up Wilson, the high-minded preacher, as a diplomatic double-dealer?

Let us begin with the general question. Was the Memorandum worthy of something better than stillbirth? The rejection of the idea of a drawn peace was not, as the narrative will show Wilson and House coming to believe, the reaction of stupidity or vengeance or greed for territorial aggrandisement. When more than a year later in August 1917 Pope Benedict XV addressed to all belligerents a Note suggesting a settlement based on restoration of occupied territory, disarmament, and international arbitration, and House thought it might be an occasion for a 'notable utterance'[80] by Wilson, Wilson was at first inclined not to take any notice of it at all. It was hardly fair, he thought, to ask the Allies to discuss terms with a military autocracy whose acts throughout the war made it impossible for other governments to accept its assurances.[81] On 17 August Wilson discussed the Note with a group of senators. The Pope, Wilson said, 'does not touch the objects for which we are fighting'. One senator thought that the Bishop of Rome should be told that it was none of his business. Everyone was agreed, Senator Lodge recorded, that there could be no real peace until America and the Allies were able to dictate it,[82] but Wilson thought that that could not be said at this time. When he did reply, it was briefly to the effect that the Allies were fighting German militarism and would not negotiate with it. The reply filled Grey with satisfaction and was much admired by Lord Robert Cecil.

But then of course America was at war. In 1916 her mission was peace-making; and stubbornness, a virtue that Wilson much admired in a fighter, appears to a peacemaker as bloody obstinacy that makes his task impossible. Neither Wilson nor even House appreciated at this time the depth of feeling against Germany that made her utter defeat the only worthwhile object. In supposing that this was mainly an 'official' view they were in error. Page put the British feeling more bluntly than Grey dared. On 9 February 1916 in the middle of House's talks in London he had written that no member of the Government could afford to discuss the subject; and on 23 May he wrote to House:

This German military caste caused all the trouble and there can be no security in Europe as long as it lives in authority. That's the English view. It raped nuns in Belgium, it took food from the people, it even now levies indemnities on all towns, it planned the destruction of the Lusitania, and it now coos like a sucking dove in the United States. It'll do anything. Now, since it has become evident that it is going to be beaten, it wants peace—on terms which will give it a continued lease of life.[83]

And again on 30 May:

All the peace talk that comes from the United States causes surprise and is taken to confirm the old opinion that the people in the United States do not yet know anything about the war . . . There is not any early peace in sight here, and any discussion of the subject at all puts the British and the French on edge.[84]

When in 1917 war weariness was much greater and the movement for a negotiated peace came out into the open, it got support from only a small minority.

In one of the weeklies in April 1916 there was a perceptive article in which the writer, who was clearly sympathetic to the peace movement—probably he was Maynard Keynes—analysed its weakness.[85] It had, he said, to demonstrate two propositions, the first that the war was in deadlock and the second that a stalemate peace would be durable. If there was any reasonable chance of dictating terms, public opinion would take it: if a drawn peace would not endure, it was better to fight on in the hope that the deadlock would be broken. There were many, the author thought, who would accept one or other proposition but not many who would accept both, not enough to kindle a conscious demand: 'for men do not reason quickly or clearly on a subject on which they are told it is unpatriotic to reason at all.'

Subsequent events did not bring all the benefits that were in 1916 expected from the humiliation of Germany. In the middle twenties of the century many Britons surveying the wreck of the peace made at Versailles, and asking themselves whether the price was not too high, would have felt as

Grey did about the answer. Looking back in 1933 House said that the rejection of his offer was 'one of the monumental blunders of the war'.[86] But the responsibility for the waste of what was bought by so many lives and so much suffering rests, as Grey hinted in his memoirs,[87] not only on those who made the peace but also on those who used the peace they made.

Even if the statesmen of 1916 had seen that a drawn peace was to be preferred to victory or at least that it was not worth an extra year of bloodshed, it does not follow that the rejection of the House plan was a monumental blunder. There were other powerful objections to it. Page rightly called it academic stuff. It is certain that if the Allies had acted on the House plan, Germany would have rejected the terms which Wilson had approved; but what Wilson would have done when it came to the point must be conjectural. A declaration of war by the United States simply on the ground that she thought the fighting ought to stop would have been to formulate a *casus belli* of staggering novelty. From time immemorial great nations had settled their differences in their own way and made peace on their own terms and neutrals had minded their own business and kept clear. Was the world as it entered the twentieth century ready for this revolutionary concept? It meant that the United States would discharge single-handed the duties of a League to Enforce the Peace while that idea was still in embryo. Certainly it offered to Wilson, as House put it, a noble part and a great opportunity. But if Wilson took it, would America follow? Spring Rice had persistently and correctly told his government that the American people did not want to get into the war. Even if the Allies were sure of Wilson's firmness of purpose, would he not in the end have to resort to his 'probablies' to extricate himself from a position too far advanced?

Thinking back nine years later, House decided that the Allies had come to the conclusion that the amount of military help they would get from America would not compensate them for her interference with the terms of peace.[88] This is one way of putting it, but does not necessarily mean that the Allies were afraid of interference with rapacity. Even if they had accepted generally Wilson's views on what was reasonable as set out in the Memorandum, many points of important detail would be sure to arise. While they were not asked to bind themselves in advance to his arbitrament, he could deal them a serious blow by withdrawing from the conference if they disagreed with him. An abortive peace venture might be disastrous for morale. House makes too little of the difficulties of democratic peacemaking. When the nerves of a whole people are strung up for war, they cannot be relaxed and easily made taut again. The leaders whose task it is to keep them to the pitch dare not allow any talk of peace until the end is clear in sight.

All in all the statesmen of 1916 cannot be blamed for taking an earthbound view of the proposal. It offered a possible way out but with so many twists and turns in it that it would have been unwise to take it unless the straight road ahead became decisively blocked.

Ought they, and Grey in particular, to have been more open with House than they were? The two men had established a relationship of mutual frankness rising above diplomatic fencing. But there is no reason to think that Grey and his colleagues, although never impressed by House's plan, were not genuine in exploring it, evaluating it for what they thought it to be worth, and dealing with it accordingly. It would have been foolish of them to treat it tactlessly; short of that, Grey, as is plain from the record, was discouraging about it from start to finish and House's high hopes at the end were of his own manufacture. His complaint that he was not told about the secret treaties is an irrelevant afterthought. If Grey would have been justified in talking to House about them at all, it could not have been till the point was reached when they became a serious obstacle to the plan; and it never was. In fact House knew a good deal about what was going on at the time and would then probably have resented the suggestion that he was so naïve as to suppose that Italy and the Balkan countries were entering the war for love.

What then of House himself? He was excessively optimistic; but what pessimist has turned the current of events? Undoubtedly the episode makes him look a little foolish, the more so since he was so obviously revelling in every minute of all that happened 'When the Butler Withdrew'. Here he was, discussing epochal events with the men in charge of them. London, Berlin, Paris, and London again, he slipped through the barriers set by war, moving mysteriously behind a cloud of speculation, not the decorated ambassador but the spirit of the new diplomacy, the small man in the soft hat. Was he in fact only a donkey trotting after an English carrot? That would be far too scathing. His mind was not quite in the first class and his sudden transfiguration into a person of world importance left him just a little too pleased with himself. He was not as modest and unassuming as he appeared to be. In his diary and among a few friends he liked to magnify his triumphs. Plunkett records: 'House told us that he had put the British case to the French in a way which made Balfour exclaim: "That's the best speech I have ever heard!".'[89] He believed himself immune from the defects which he enjoyed pointing out in others—the susceptibility to subtle flattery and the erroneous supposition that a man who agrees outwardly has been inwardly convinced.

But the notion that he was a gullible fool cannot be reconciled with the judgement of his contemporaries. The British statesmen who dealt with him treated him with a respect which was due as much to his own personality as to the credentials he carried. In the tributes they paid to him at the time and in retrospect there is not to be detected any trace of mockery. They cannot all have been speaking tongue in cheek, men like Asquith and Grey in particular. Lloyd George was not the sort of man who in his memoirs would have resisted a taunt at someone he thought he had made a fool of; he said of House that he was 'adroit and wise in all things appertaining to the management of men and affairs . . . a well-balanced but not a powerful mind'.[90] Balfour, who liked him immensely, thought him 'not intellectually brilliant';[91] but then Balfour's intellectual standards were high.

It is, however, possible to assess House as a shrewd and intelligent man and at the same time to accept that in common with most Americans of his time he thought that there was nothing to learn about diplomacy. Elihu Root once said: 'In this country international law was regarded as a rather antiquated branch of useless learning, diplomacy as a foolish mystery and the foreign service as a superfluous expense.'[92] Indeed, in 1897 Champ Clark had proposed the abolition of the diplomatic corps! There is something of the too clever amateur about House's devices, something of the raw smartness of the litigant in person when he feels that his natural ingenuity has alighted upon a good technical point. Lloyd George in his memoirs wrote of him:

When I recognise that he was honourable in all his dealings, it is not inconsistent with this characteristic to say that he possessed craft. It is perhaps to his credit that he was not nearly as cunning as he thought he was.[93]

It cannot be often that a proposal of an alliance from the most powerful neutral, and a nation, moreover, whose ill-will, as Grey wrote, meant certain defeat,[94] produces no more satisfactory answer than that she will be notified when her services are required. 'Balfour made the remark', House recorded on one of their early talks, 'that he would see what concessions his colleagues would be willing to make to American opinion. I asked him to please not put it in that way, since we did not consider they were making any concessions whatever to us, but it was quite the other way round.'[95] All the same House never threw off in London the habit of the petitioner or ejected from the discussion the underlying British assumption that because they were fighting, so they thought, against tyranny and for honour among nations, they were fighting America's battles too and serving her and themselves and the world. It may be that House's talents were imprisoned in a like assumption and that he was an unsuccessful emissary, even as Page was a bad ambassador, because he felt about it more deeply than a diplomat ought to feel.

Grey and House are small fry in history compared to Wilson. Their failings and follies, such as they had, can be buried with them. But Wilson in the twentieth century represents idealism in action. If this episode shows that the evangelist who crossed the Atlantic three years later was just a politician using promises to serve his own ends, it will leave its mark on him and on history. It has not in this aspect of it received from Wilson's apologists all the attention it deserves. Some of them seek to dismiss the whole enterprise as one of House's pranks while others half ignore it on the ground that Wilson's 'probably' destroyed the pith of the Memorandum.

As to the first, it is of course possible to argue that in negotiating the Memorandum House exceeded his instructions. To judge of this one must ask what his instructions were. Was he to negotiate something on the lines of the message of 17 October 1915? Or were the implications of that entirely superseded by the letter of 24 December 1915 which was intended to restrict any pledge to the use of moral force? Or were both merely guidelines which House was to follow to the extent he thought best in accordance with Wilson's usual practice of giving him *carte blanche*? How to answer these questions is arguable but is also academic. Once Wilson had seen and approved the Memorandum, it ceased to matter whether or not it reflected accurately his state of mind in the previous October or the previous December. The President of the United States is not an infant or a mental defective to be protected from the undue influence of his attorney. If House exceeded his instructions, why did not Wilson say so? If the President himself did not rebuke his agent, why do his biographers?

Where House was at fault was in the way he inflated the chances of the pact being put into effect. This, however, tells, if anything, the other way. If Wilson had been led to believe that all the pact did was to confer an option unlikely to be exercised, it might have been easier for him to feel that he was not making an effective commitment to war. Or again if House had encouraged Wilson to think that Germany would accept the 'reasonable terms', he might have been misled into treating the pact as offering a real chance of peacemaking to which the risk of war could be subordinated. Whether Wilson did in fact think this is a point to be explored later. But if he did, the fault does not lie with House. There is no record that when the two men discussed the Memorandum the probable German reaction to the reasonable terms was touched upon at all. If Wilson was under any illusion that it might conceivably be favourable, he could not have read

House's report from Berlin.* There is no evidence that House ever obscured the meaning of the Memorandum; and its meaning plainly was that when the Allies pressed the button, as they were expected soon to do, they inevitably started a process designed to bring America into the war.

What about 'probably'? 'A potent word', Mr. Baker, Wilson's first apologist called it:[96] 'a momentous change' is how he described what his hero called an unimportant verbal alteration. There is not much in this. The issue is not whether Wilson was saying that, come what may, he would go to war or whether he was saying that he would probably go to war. Clearly he was saying the latter. The alteration was unimportant because it was implicit anyway in the sort of undertaking that Wilson was giving; he could not be expected to pledge himself absolutely and in all circumstances. Everyone knew that the power to declare war resided in the Congress. The least meaning that the Memorandum carries is that Wilson sincerely intended to bring the United States into the war on the side of the Allies if the Central Powers refused to discuss reasonable terms. This was the secret promise. The only meaning that the public promise can bear is that Wilson sincerely intended to keep the United States out of the war.

'Probably' detracts from the value of a promise to its recipient because it shows the promisor to be aware of possibilities that might frustrate his purpose, but it is not a word to be used by a man who wishes it thereby to be understood that he is reserving his liberty of action. 'Probably' diminished the strength of the promise but did not change its character; the language of the Memorandum was not thereby sublimated into the 'moral force' of the Christmas Eve letter. Moral force is hardly more than metaphorical force. 'Poor, silly Bryan' took that point. When, after the German declaration of submarine war in February 1915, Van Dyke from The Hague inquired whether if a Dutch ship was sunk, the Netherlands could count on 'the moral support of the United States',[97] Bryan replied that they could count on a 'sympathetic attitude . . . I do not understand what moral support means'.

When the distractions of the 'probablies' are put aside the charge of deceit emerges as one that Wilson's admirers have to face squarely; and when facing it they would be wise at the outset to concede two points. The first is that the idea that Wilson was a liar and a humbug is not one that would have seemed at all strange to his political opponents. The second is that even his friends accepted his capacity for a high-minded form of deceit.

When Wilson's name came up casually in conversation in October 1915 Taft said that Wilson was in his judgement, having known a good many Presidents, the most unblushing and ruthless opportunist that he had ever

* See p. 423 above.

met. In the following year, as the election campaign aroused animosities, Taft's feelings became even stronger. 'No one', he wrote to a friend, 'in the campaign has as much contempt for Wilson as I have. My contempt is based on the fact that I regard him as a ruthless hypocrite, and as an opportunist who has no convictions that he would not barter at once for votes.'[98] 'A far more dangerous and mischievous demigod than poor, silly, emotionally sincere Bryan', Theodore Roosevelt wrote to Sir Horace Plunkett about the same time.[99] Root told Chandler Anderson: 'We have had weak presidents and wrong-headed presidents, but never until Wilson have we had an unscrupulous and dishonest President.'[100] None of these was an impartial judge, but they were all big men, generally accounted men of probity, speaking their thoughts in private conversations and not for the record. None of them would have been startled if he had had a sight of the House–Grey Memorandum at that time. He would have said that it was just another thing revealing the true Wilson that lay behind the public pieties.

Let us then consider a hostile hypothesis. Wilson was uninterested in European affairs and in the great issues to which later his tongue gave such rich adornments, until his eyes were opened to the stage upon which he could play 'the noblest part that has ever come to a son of man'.[101] He saw himself, as indeed for a little time he became, the greatest man in the world, the peacemaker, the lawgiver, the one to whom the dumb millions brought their woes that he might speak out with the voice which God had not granted to them. He would take the teaching of the American fathers and enlighten not a fraction of a new and empty continent but all mankind. It was egoism and not nobility that led him beyond the boundaries of America, the sort of insatiable egoism that led Alexander and Napoleon into their wars of conquest; but Woodrow Wilson was to be a new world conqueror who fought not with the sword but with the book. If this projected spiritual conquest meant that the American people must probably go to war, then Wilson could be as ruthless about that as any material conqueror might be. He knew of course that to play his part he must remain President and so must be re-elected in 1916, and he was a shrewd enough politician to guess that it was keeping the country out of war that would win the votes, as in fact it did. So he spoke peace from the rostrum and war in the chancelleries until after his re-election, when he went to war within four months.

This hypothesis pictures Wilson as a megalomaniac. There is an alternative hypothesis that presents him as a man whose struggles to do his best took him into deep water. If he had wanted to lead the country into war, he could have done so at any time after the *Lusitania* crisis; thereafter it was his influence that kept her out: by leadership in war he could have obtained more easily than in any other way paramountcy at home and abroad. The truth is in this view simple and undramatic; he found himself in the position of being unable to square his acts and his words, an absence of parallelism that leaves many politicians undisturbed. Not that a plausible biographer would put it as meanly as that. Few public men have passed their lives in telling the truth, the whole truth, and nothing but the truth. As Carlyle says, the ordinary man can hold off interrogation and it is the misfortune of the hero or superior man that he is subjected to impertinent inquiries which he cannot always refuse to answer. There is a task for an anthologist in the collection of all the different ingenuities of apology to which the deceitfulness of great men has stimulated the writers of their lives. Carlyle admits that Cromwell was a liar, but he puts the word in inverted commas. 'Each party understood him to be meaning *this*, heard him even say so, and behold he turns out to have been meaning *that*!'[102] The superior man, Carlyle says, must have reticences in him; if he were to explain to lower men the deeper insight he had, they would shudder aghast at it. Wilson himself, speaking of Jefferson and perhaps with Carlyle in mind, wrote of 'the sort of insincerity which subtle natures yield to without loss of essential integrity'.[103] He several times told House that he felt entirely justified in lying to reporters when they asked questions about public policy.[104] All the same he disliked the bluntness of the outright lie; he preferred, as House put it, to 'graze the truth'.[105] When he did, it seems to have amused him to make a sort of parlour game of it; he would indulge his love of exactitude in words, and perhaps also his contempt for the 'lower men', by using words which, if they were as clever as he, would tell them nothing; and if obtuse, mislead them.

A code of private morals cannot be applied without qualification to the different conditions of public life and some measure of duplicity, using the word in its literal rather than in its offensive sense, is a necessary part of the political art. It was Wilson's 'too-clever-by-half' tactics that irritated his fellow politicians and earned him among his enemies his reputation for dishonesty. But it cannot be said—and he would not himself have argued for it—that in his speeches to the people he was playing with impertinent questioners. His words were being spoken then on an issue of peace and war that touched the flesh and blood of any whom he duped.

When the facts disclose a prima facie case of deceit, the commonest form of defence is to plead misunderstanding. 'Find my client guilty', the advocate will cry, 'of folly and muddleheadedness, if you will, but not of fraud.' When the question is put in these broad terms, it becomes vital to appraise a man's character as a whole. While it raises an issue on which a reader of this book or of the many other biographies of Wilson must in the end be left to form his own judgement, it is permissible for an author to express his. I think that Woodrow Wilson, while fundamentally an honourable man in all his public as well as his private undertakings, was capable of deceit under three conditions. The first is, as he admits, when the questioning was impertinent; and there are many who will deny that in such a case there is moral fault. The second is when he let himself become emotional, usually when he felt thwarted; and then to an extent he, as it were, lost control of the truth. The third is when he was deceiving himself as well as others. None of these conditions was present in the matter we are now considering.

But then, it must be asked, is it any more in accord with Wilson's character that he should be guilty of muddleheadedness and confusion? Had he not on the contrary an exceptional capacity for clear and thorough thinking? This indeed creates a dilemma from which it is tempting to escape by concluding that Wilson must have been misled and by featuring House as the culprit. If this temptation is resisted, as I think it should be, there is nothing for it but to accept that in this instance Wilson did not fully understand what he was doing. There are three factors which make this conclusion less improbable than it might otherwise seem. The first lies in the conditions under which Wilson chose to work; the second in the functioning of what he called his 'single track mind'; and the third in the extraordinary relationship between himself and House.

As to the conditions, Wilson preferred study to conference. He placed little or no value on general discussion. In discussion a subject is turned over with a thoroughness that the mind working by itself can rarely achieve. If discussion throws only a diffuse light as compared with the beam of a penetrating mind, it ensures that no corner is left in darkness. Without discussion even the finest intelligence can sometimes altogether miss the point. In foreign affairs Wilson made no real use of the State Department. Presidents and Prime Ministers have before and since assumed personal direction of foreign affairs, but never without the help of a group of able assistants. Lloyd George built a garden annexe to 10 Downing Street to accommodate his secretariat. Franklin Roosevelt always had at least half a dozen first-class brains around him. President Kennedy threw all his subjects for decision into a group to be thrashed out. By then of course the White House had a large executive staff. Towards the end of the Second World War it numbered nearly seven hundred. President Wilson had in the White House, apart from a small clerical staff, Mrs. Wilson and Tumulty. Mrs. Wilson coded and decoded and blotted signatures. Tumulty was invaluable in party matters but not equipped to serve in any other sphere. The President might almost have been running a parish with the help of his wife and a curate and a portable typewriter.

Many observers speak of the President's aloofness. The British and the German ambassadors were in agreement on this point. Spring Rice wrote:

It is difficult to explain exactly the way in which business is conducted here. The President rarely sees anybody. He practically never sees ambassadors, and when he does, exchanges no ideas with them. Mr. Lansing is treated as a clerk who receives orders which he has to obey at once and without question. His communications to the press have been several times contradicted from the White House. He practically never expresses an opinion to a foreign representative.[106]

Bernstorff in his memoirs wrote:

Audiences with the President, when they were obtainable at all, proceeded on the lines that the visitor put forward his suggestions, upon which Wilson delivered a more or less detailed exposition of his own views. Then the audience was at an end, unless the visitor was very persistent in which case he did not fail to forfeit the President's favour, who would in the end hand him over to House.[107]

The most vivid picture has been left by Page, who eventually in the summer of 1916 came over for the long-deferred bath of American opinion. He was invited twice to luncheon at the White House where, apart from the American ambassador to France on the second occasion who was in the same plight as himself, he met only Miss Bones, the Misses Smiths of New Orleans, and Tom Bolling, the President's brother-in-law. The President, he was told, had at his table family connections only and, except for the regular notables at the set dinners, no distinguished men and women.

What an unspeakably lamentable loss of opportunity! This is the more remarkable and lamentable because the President is a charming personality, an uncommonly good talker, a man who could easily make personal friends of all the world. He does his own thinking, untouched by other men's ideas. He receives nothing from the outside.[108]

Later he wrote to the First Secretary of his embassy in London:

The President dominates the whole show in a most extraordinary way. The men about him (and he sees them only on 'business') are very nearly all very very small fry, or worse, the narrowest twopenny lot I have ever come across. He has no real companions. Nobody talks to him freely and frankly. I have never known quite such a condition in American life.

Thus Wilson worked alone. There was no body of men to prepare the issues for his decision or, as he took his mind continuously from problem to problem, to see that in a moment of weariness or in a time of tautness (such as the crisis with Congress not quite over by 6 March) he did not miss the point. But when all allowance is made for this, there is left only the supposition that Wilson had no ears for what he did not want to hear. He had no aptitude for European politics and no more wish to learn about them than he had to learn about Tammany's methods of obtaining votes; both subjects were at best 'painfully interesting'. He wanted passionately to bring the war to an end and for that, as he saw it, he needed a platform from which to address the world. He thought that House had succeeded in constructing one and that was enough for him; he was not interested in what it was made of but only in what he said when he got on to it. While House was mindful of Constantinople and colonies and the division of Turkey, Wilson may have seen all that as detail which could settle itself once the great task was put in hand. As House talked of this and that, Wilson, it may be, was chiselling at the phrases that would persuade the German people of the wrong they had done to France in taking from her Alsace-Lorraine half a century before and of their sin against Belgium, and bring them to repentance. Perhaps Wilson was sure in his own mind that the Germans would succumb to moral force.

When in April 1917 America went to war, Page put down on paper the President's two fundamental errors as he saw them. His first was of course his policy of neutrality of thought and his failure to understand the moral quality in the British case as Page so often put it to him. Then Page went on:

> The second error he made was in thinking he could play a great part as a peacemaker—come and give a blessing to these erring children. This was strong in his hopes and ambitions. There was a condescension in this attitude that was offensive.
>
> He shut himself up with these two ideas and engaged in what he called 'thought'. The air currents of the world never ventilated his mind.[109]

It may be then that Wilson simply did not understand what it was that his emissary was getting at. Wilson would not think of peacemaking as a work of patching and adjusting differences and bargaining over territory, but as a proclamation of universal truths in such a manner as to command assent. 'I have an invincible confidence in the prevalence of the right if it is fearlessly set forth', he wrote to a friend[110] after his call to the world for 'peace without victory' later in the year. The practical consequences of the transfer of territory and the proper compensation to be tendered for it were minor matters compared with the correct formulation of the appropriate principles. For Wilson's mind processed a principle with the efficiency of a machine designed for that purpose and no other; and with the same efficiency mechanically rejected the material upon which it was not designed to operate.

Yet is even this enough to account for his endorsement of the Memorandum? What made him apparently oblivious to the element in it that

Page called a 'carefully sprung trick'* and that struck Montagu as dishonest and unfair to Germany?† Had Wilson forgotten the Christmas Eve letter about moral force?‡ Why did he never tackle House about this or about the 'terms not unfavorable to the Allies' which House had made entirely on his own, or think twice about the acquisition by Russia of Constantinople?

These are questions for psychology rather than for history. Wilson's intense sensitivity 'to the feeling others may have for me'§ may have meant not only that he was himself easily wounded but also that where he loved he could not bear to wound. He had a fondness for House of the sort that where there is no suggestion of homosexuality usually goes with family ties. If House had been a favourite son or a beloved younger brother, an explanation would easily be found for a reluctance to doubt, an inhibition on questioning, and an unwillingness to spoil a triumph. The attachment of the one man to the other, especially strong on Wilson's side, the lavishness of his approvals and the absence of criticism, the fervid growth in the beginning and (what was yet to come) the unexplained suddenness of the end, point to a peculiar relationship whose effects cannot be left out of account in any analysis of Wilson's actions.||

* See p. 432 above.   † See p. 456 above.   ‡ See p. 390 above.   § See p. 14 above.
|| Wilson's character has been made the subject of psychological study and indeed he has been post-humously pyschoanalysed by the great Freud himself upon the basis of facts or assertions supplied by William C. Bullitt, a Wilson disciple who abjured. (Sigmund Freud and William C. Bullitt, *Thomas Woodrow Wilson: A Psychological Study*, Weidenfeld & Nicholson, London, 1967.) Wilson's feeling for his father is said to be the dominant fact in his life. A succession of 'younger brothers' began with the real younger brother, Joseph, ten years Woodrow's junior (he who was denied the postmastership) and continued with Hibben, Tumulty, and House. 'Normally the elder brother in his unconscious becomes father to the younger brother and also identifies himself with the younger brother, so that in the relationship he plays father to himself'. Thus House became 'my second personality . . . my independent self' and thus Wilson re-established his infantile relationship to his father (p. 126).

XV
THE NEW ORDER PROCLAIMED

Mexico — the *Sussex* crisis — the League to Enforce Peace and the Address of 27 May 1916 — the end of the House plan — Mexico again — Wilson's and House's suspicions of Britain

LESS than three weeks passed between Wilson's ratification of the House plan on 7 March 1916 and the torpedoing of the *Sussex* on 24 March which put the plan and the Colonel's hopes for it into suspense. They were not restful weeks for Wilson. Few weeks were. These were occupied with another of the recurrent crises in Mexican affairs. Even before the villain Huerta had been driven from Mexico, Carranza's leadership was being challenged by his principal lieutenant Villa. A period of internal warfare followed until September 1915 when Villa was defeated in the field. Wilson then rather reluctantly ('I think I have never known of a man more impossible to deal with on human principles than this man Carranza', he had written on 2 July 1915)[1] gave *de facto* recognition to Carranza's Government. Villa remained an unsubdued rebel in the north of Mexico, his remaining assets being a company of loyal, if undisciplined, followers, a talent for guerrilla warfare, and the power to operate on the border of New Mexico so as to facilitate embroilment with the United States. On 10 January 1916 a group of his banditry had pulled seventeen Americans out of a train in north-west Mexico and robbed and murdered them. There was indignation in America comparable to that which followed on the sinking of the *Lusitania* and an outcry for armed intervention. Carranza at Wilson's demand promised immediate action. But he could not catch Villa.

This was the situation when on 9 March 1916 Villa attacked Columbus, an American border town. There was a pitched battle with over seventy Mexican casualties and about twenty American. Wilson, to forestall Congressional action, resolved upon a punitive expedition. Carranza on 11 March stated that he would regard the dispatch of an expedition without his permission as an act of war. Wilson was as determined to avoid war with Mexico, if he could, as he was war with Germany. He told Tumulty so when Tumulty threatened that if he did not send the expedition at once, he would not win a single electoral vote in the November election. He did not care, he said, if he was called a coward and a quitter.

The gentlemen who criticise me speak as if America were afraid to fight Mexico. Poor Mexico, with its pitiful men, women, and children, fighting to gain a foothold in their own land. They speak of the valour of America. What is true valour?[2]

Then he repeated (or Tumulty inserted in his memoirs) what he had said about valour in a speech about a fortnight before.

I would be just as much ashamed to be rash as I would be to be a coward. Valour is self-respecting. Valour is circumspect. Valour strikes only when it is right to strike. Valour withholds itself from all small implications and entanglements and waits for the great opportunity when the sword will flash as if it carried the light of heaven upon its blade.

The Punitive Expedition, nearly 7,000 strong, set out on 15 March, Carranza acquiescing under protest and Wilson declaring that it was not an invasion of Mexico or an infringement of her sovereignty. Wilson and Lansing were still endeavouring to regularize the affair and reach agreement with Carranza when they had to turn their attention to the graver issue in Europe. It had begun to look as if Germany no longer cared whether or not she brought America into the war.

As yet the Kaiser had not made up his mind about the submarine war, nor had it made up for him. He had postponed the decision until 1 April 1916 instructing Bethmann in the meanwhile to prepare the ground diplomatically for a declaration of all-out warfare. These instructions might be thought to favour the probability of the declaration. Certainly the German naval command thought so and therefore was the less inclined to discourage the zeal of its submarine captains. The incidence of 'mistakes', deliberate or careless, largely depended on what sort of reception the commander thought he was likely to get when he came home. The series of incidents which led to the next crisis in German-American relations was the consequence of general laxity rather than of a throwing down of the gauntlet.

On 16 and 18 March 1916 two Dutch ships, one a liner, were torpedoed. There were no Americans on board but of course there might have been. On 24 March the *Sussex*, a channel steamer, was torpedoed. She had twenty-five Americans on board. There were eighty casualties including four Americans injured. Before the end of March four more British ships were sunk, two of them with Americans in the crew. None of these vessels was armed and all according to first reports were sunk without warning. It was naturally the *Sussex* that got the headlines. But it was the fact that she was only one of a number that made Washington feel that the long controversy was at the crux. The *Arabic* settlement was at stake. The German Government was, it seemed, either deliberately disregarding it or quite unable to secure its observance.

The fact that the *Sussex* had been torpedoed was reported in Washington on the very day it happened, Friday, 24 March, and more details came in over the weekend. Wilson as usual gave no sign of his reaction. When by the Monday Lansing had heard nothing, he wrote to the President a very vigorous letter.[3] All the information, he said, indicated that the *Sussex* had been torpedoed. Moreover, German policy and the submarine attacks of the past ten days raised the presumption that she had been. Accordingly, unless Germany established conclusively her innocence, which he anticipated she would fail to do, diplomatic relations should be broken off, either immediately or under an ultimatum requiring within a time-limit an unequivocal admission of the illegality of submarine warfare. Audaciously he said that the time for writing Notes discussing the subject had passed. If the dignity of the United States permitted delay, he would favour it; but the dignity did not. On the same day and reflecting the opposite point of view, the President had a telephone call from Senator Stone asking him not to take action before they had discussed the position. Wilson replied that he would not do anything drastic without the sanction of Congress.

When he heard the news of the *Sussex*, House felt hardly well enough to go to Washington but could not leave Wilson without advice: 'I am afraid he will delay and write further notes when action is what we need.'[4] He was, he felt, the only man who could strengthen the President's backbone.

The *Sussex* incident did not suit the House plan. It meant another Note; and if the Germans were obdurate, Wilson would either have to climb down or to act. If he climbed down, he would lose entirely the Allies' confidence; and if he acted, the Allies would get the benefit of American participation without having to pay for it by an agreement on moderate terms of peace. Nevertheless, faced with the choice between undesirables, House had no doubt that the supersession of the plan was the lesser. So he went to the White House and was there from 28 to 30 March. The first meeting was disappointing. House recorded:

He evidently does not wish to back up his former notes to Germany upon this subject. He does not seem to realise that one of the main points of criticism against him is that he talks boldly, but acts weakly.[5]

House saw Lansing on 29 March and approved the letter he had written to the President. They both agreed that Wilson would be reluctant to back up his own threats. Then on 30 March he had a long talk with the President. Break off relations, he urged. But who then, Wilson asked, would lead the way out? A distaste for fighting was as always coupled in Wilson's mind with reluctance to abandon the role of the angel of peace hovering above the scuffle and ready to descend and lead the nations out of war. This was the role he would forfeit if he plunged abruptly into the arena as a common belligerent or breaker-off of diplomatic relations. Since this was the part with which House had tempted Wilson to enter the play, he may have felt the argument to be a little embarrassing. But times had changed and House could now point out, as he did, that in the new situation, Wilson would lose all influence with the Allies if he hesitated to act. House also tried adroitly to adopt the House plan to the new situation.

I suggested that, when he sent Von Bernstorff home, he should make a dispassionate statement of the cause of the war and what the Allies were fighting for. I suggested that he should say nothing unkind of the German people, but should strike at the system which had caused this world tragedy, and contend that when that was righted, the trouble with Germany as far as we were concerned, would be ended. Then I thought at the right time—which would perhaps be by midsummer—I could go to Holland and, after a Conference with the Allies and with their consent, I could open negotiations directly with Berlin, telling them upon what terms we were ready to end the war.

I thought the same arrangement could then be carried out; that is, he should preside over the Conference and we should take part. This would make our participation more effective than as a neutral, and we could do greater and better work in this way than we could in the way we planned.[6]

But in the end, the Colonel's only concrete achievement was a commission to see Bernstorff and impress him with the danger: the United States would surely enter the war, he was to say, unless there was a decisive change in Germany's submarine policy. On 30 March, the day House left Washington, Wilson sent a cool letter to Lansing saying that there was no satisfactory proof that the disaster was caused by a torpedo and that if it was, 'there are many particulars to be considered about the course we should pursue as well as the principle of it'.[7] He added that they must have a personal conference 'very soon', but he went off on a weekend cruise.

One might have thought that by this time the principle at least had been settled but the letter to Lansing made it clear that in Wilson's mind nothing was cut and dried. Official Washington was near despair. Phillips, House's protégé in the State Department, went to New York on the Sunday to summon House to return to the assault. Even Grayson was worried;[8] but he did not want to talk to Wilson himself for, as he told House, if anyone tried to make him do what he did not want to do, the President would cease to have any liking for him.

By the time House got back to Washington, the President had taken a tentative step. He had told Lansing to prepare a Note. This followed on the convincing evidence which Wilson found on his return from his week-end cruise that the *Sussex* had been torpedoed without warning and that she was not armed or carrying troops. Lansing at once settled down to the congenial task of drafting the sort of note that had worked so well in the *Ancona* case—wanton and indiscriminate slaughter of helpless men, women, and children; breach of faith in the renewal of an inhuman and illegal practice; reversion to barbarism.[9] In the first *Lusitania* Note, the draft said, the American Government had expressed the opinion that it was impossible legally and humanely to employ submarines as commerce destroyers. This opinion had now become a settled conviction. The German Government must now announce its purpose to discontinue, and must actually discontinue, the employment of submarines against commercial vessels of belligerent as well as of neutral nationality. Having thus demanded the total cessation of submarine activity, whether or not cruiser rules were observed, the Secretary in his draft offered Wilson the choice between the alternatives proposed in his letter of 30 March, the immediate severance or the ultimatum.

Colonel House and the draft arrived at the White House about the same time in the evening of 5 April. The Colonel did not tackle the President that night but he intercepted him in the following morning on the way to his office and they fell into a long talk. As an alternative to what House said was an inevitable break, they discussed the possibilities of the House-Grey Memorandum. Should they try to make sure of it by pressing Grey to act on it at once? Eventually Wilson himself drafted a cable to Grey ('in his own handwriting, as we call his little typewriter'):

Since it seems probable that this country must break with Germany on the submarine question unless the unexpected happens, and since, if this country should once become a belligerent, the war would undoubtedly be prolonged, I beg to suggest that if you had any thought of acting at an early date on the plan we agreed upon, you might wish now to consult with your allies with a view to acting immediately.[10]

Looking back nine years later House realized that this was diplomatically a mistake. He was in effect asking Grey to hurry up and buy American action and at the same time telling him that, if he waited, he might get it nothing. But the mistake was so glaring that House could not have been blind to it at the time unless he had wildly overestimated Grey's enthusiasm for a peace of moderation as well as his power of bringing into line colleagues who at best could be hooked to American mediation only with the bait of belligerency. Back in New York on 7 April, House followed up the cable with a letter in which he added as an additional reason that the American people would respond to the higher and nobler issue of stopping the war more surely than they would to the submarine issue. This might have overstrained Grey's belief in the nobility of the American people, but anyway he had answered the cable before he got the letter, telegraphing on 6 April that the time was not yet ripe.

Meanwhile, Bernstorff was as usual taking things lightly until on 8 April House jolted him with the statement that if submarines were really sinking liners without warning, the President would break relations. 'House paints the feeling resulting from the Sussex case in very dark colours', Bernstorff at once telegraphed to Berlin, and asked for instructions which would enable him to reassure the American Government 'which now once more is entertaining doubts of our good faith'.[11] Berlin was puzzled. Jagow had already told Gerard that if indeed a submarine had attacked the *Sussex* Germany would 'immediately render the necessary redress';[12] but he wanted more information. In fact the commander of the U29 who had done the deed genuinely believed that the vessel he had torpedoed was a minelayer, not without some justification, as the *Sussex* had recently been altered in a way that gave her quite a warlike appearance. The German Admiralty had compared the commander's description with an old photograph of the *Sussex* and they did not tally at all.

Friday, 7 April was the beginning of the second weekend after the incident and Wilson had still done nothing. He went off on the *Mayflower* again taking Lansing's draft with him. It proved far too strong for him. He decided to start anew on his own and came back to the White House on the Saturday afternoon. He worked alone on his draft in his study all the rest of the day, all Sunday, and all Monday (cancelling his appointments), except for a long drive in the afternoon. He finished it late that night. It emerged simply as a diluted version of Lansing's draft but without even the milder of his endings. Wilson must have spent most of his time in trying to decide how far he would go. He began by describing the attack on the *Sussex* and pointing out that it was not isolated. How much better it would have been, he said in effect, if the American Government had insisted on its original position.

It has become painfully evident to it that the position which it took at the very outset is inevitable, namely that the use of submarines for the destruction of an enemy's commerce is of necessity, because of the very character of the vessels employed and the very methods of attack which their employment of course involves, utterly incompatible with the principles of humanity, the long established and incontrovertible rights of neutrals, and the sacred immunities of non-combatants . . .

The Government of the United States is at last forced to the conclusion that there is but one course it can pursue. Unless the Imperial Government should now declare its intention to abandon . . .[13]

Abandon what? Surely the use of the submarine against commerce. But no,

abandon its present practices of submarine warfare and return to a scrupulous observance of the practices clearly prescribed by the law of nations, the Government of the United States can have no choice but to sever diplomatic relations with the German Empire altogether. It will await an early announcement of the future policy of the Imperial Government in the earnest hope that this unwelcome course will not be forced upon it.

'Its present practices' could only mean its failure to follow cruiser rules. So the draft ended simply with yet another demand that Germany should conform to the rules and obey the law.

House came to Washington by the midnight train and breakfasted with the Wilsons at the White House on the morning of Tuesday, 11 April.[14] The three of them went to the President's study at 9 a.m. and the President read his draft. House thought the conclusion weak and Mrs. Wilson agreed with him. Be consistent and demand complete abandonment, House advised; otherwise there will only be prolonged argument about 'present practices'. Wilson said, as was indeed true, that that would be tantamount to a declaration of war. He listened patiently to argument but in the end all he would do was to tighten the conclusion a little so as to demand an immediate answer. At 11 a.m. he had to leave for a Cabinet meeting. He was doubtful about reading the draft to the Cabinet. He did not care for their opinion, he said, and was afraid to trust them with a draft. He decided to read the text, not as a Note but as an argument he had in mind.

Wilson then passed his draft over to Lansing. The Secretary interpreted with exceptional boldness his mandate to go over it for form,* style, and accuracy. He accepted the rejection of his demand for the abandonment of the submarine as an anti-commerce weapon and also the watering down of the language used, saying in accordance with his usual policy that he was 'very heartily in accord'. But the conclusion, with its prospect of waiting for 'an early announcement', stuck in his gizzard. Perhaps he was stimulated by the press reception of the German Note which arrived on

---

* his meant diplomatic style—points like 'having the honour to inform' instead of merely inform-
was not Lansing's duty to improve the English.

12 April;[15] the doubts expressed in the Note about whether a German submarine had really torpedoed the *Sussex* were greeted with anger and the offer of a Hague inquiry with derision. Anyway Lansing turned the conclusion of the draft into a statement that relations were severed and would not be resumed until Germany abandoned 'present practices'. In an accompanying letter of extraordinary frankness he said that Wilson's ending weakened the communication very much, and would be construed as indefinite as to time and as giving an opening for discussion.

The impression I get is this, that we say we will wait and see if you sink another vessel with Americans on board. If you do we will recall our Ambassador. Why should we postpone to the happening of another outrage action which I feel will do much to prevent such outrage? . . .
I feel strongly in favour of the action I have proposed.[16]

On 15 April Lansing passed on to the President a tale produced by Jusserand, the French ambassador, that the *Sussex* had been sunk by the U18, whose commander had subsequently been decorated. There was nothing in the tale but it did not matter anyway, since Wilson could never be inflamed into action. He replied with a polite implication of doubt and the comment that 'circumstances of this sort are of course very disturbing'.[17] Lansing's second letter on the same day was more to the point. In it he put forward another suggestion for strengthening the draft. In order to avoid discussion about what 'present practices' were, he proposed the substitution of 'present method of submarine warfare against passenger and freight-carrying vessels'.[18]

Wilson had these letters and the affidavits from the *Sussex* passengers in front of him on Saturday, 15 April when he spent the day working on the final form of the Note. He turned down Lansing's suggestion of a breach of diplomatic relations pending resumption of good behaviour. But he accepted the clarification of 'present practices'. Lansing's words pin-pointed the difference between the *Arabic* 'pledge' and the *Sussex* 'pledge' that was to come and solidified the new gain which the difference contained. The *Arabic* formula covered only liners, but now the distinction between passenger and cargo vessels would be abolished and all shipping would be secured against attack without warning. The final draft (with a slightly strengthened conclusion; instead of 'awaiting an early announcement' the Note demanded an 'immediate declaration') was ready on 17 April.[19]

Wilson was oppressed by the undertaking he had given to Senator Stone. He was determined not to have a round-table discussion with congressional leaders in which they would doubtless try to maul his draft. He decided that the dispatch of the Note should come first and the consultation second.

So the Note went out in the evening of 18 April, Congress was summoned for 1 p.m. on 19 April, and in between at 10 a.m. on 19 April Wilson saw Stone and Flood and their compeers and gave them a summary of the Note. Stone was not pleased. Wilson in his address to Congress, which he read from his own typescript, went a little further towards the exclusion of a *via media* between submission and war.

We owe it to the due regard for our own rights as a nation, to our sense of duty as a representative of the rights of neutrals the world over, and to a just conception of the rights of mankind to take this stand now with the utmost solemnity and firmness. I have taken it, and taken it in the confidence that it will meet with your approval and support.[20]

All the world took this as practically an ultimatum which would probably bring America into the war. Clemenceau, later as French Premier to preside over victory, apostrophized in his journal: 'Hail to you, American citizens, who march back into the history of Europe under a great arch, on the front of which Washington, Jefferson, and so many others have carved the noblest claims of humanity.'[21]

In Germany the immediate reaction to the Note was that it made war inevitable. The nation could not yield. The best that could be done, Bethmann thought at first, was a gentle answer that would encourage anti-war sentiment in Congress. But as the stark truth—that America really meant what she said—began to penetrate, German resolution began also to falter. Few leaders in early 1916 wanted to shoulder the responsibility of adding so formidable a power to the enemies of the Reich. Once again it was Wilson's achievement to get it across without immoderate language that might have upset the apple cart that the choice lay only between acceptance and war. In the end this came out unmarred by his earlier hesitancies. A telegram from Bernstorff on 23 April, following a long exploratory interview with the Secretary on 20 April in which the latter was immovable, was an added warning against the gamble that Wilson was bluffing.[22] Germany might negotiate if she wished, the Secretary said, but she must suspend the underwater attack while she did so. On 28 April Lansing cabled Gerard telling him to press for a prompt answer and to make it quite clear that America would not bargain about taking action against Britain.[23] No one can now say whether or not, if Germany had been obdurate, Wilson would have sent another Note. At any rate while he was waiting for an answer, his firmness showed no decrease. After a talk with him and Lansing on 3 May House recorded:

l the President set in his determination to make Germany recede from ition regarding submarines. He spoke with much feeling concerning

Germany's responsibility for this world wide calamity, and thought those guilty should have personal punishment.[24]

Meanwhile, Bethmann was working hard to increase his room for manœuvre. He exchanged cables with Bernstorff; he had talks with Gerard to see what leeway he had there, and with his naval and military colleagues to see how far he could get them to go. Falkenhayn emerged as his most determined opponent. The General had come to the conclusion that the submarine campaign offered the only hope of subduing England and therefore, since he had given up the prospect of outright victory on land, the only alternative to a war of exhaustion. He backed up his arguments with the threat to abandon the Verdun offensive. But the offensive anyway was not coming up to expectation and Falkenhayn's influence, now on the decline, was soon to be extinguished. Thus the attitude of the Navy was crucial and it was not as firm as Tirpitz (who from his retirement delivered another blast 'in this dark hour') hoped. Some said that submarines could be made just as effective under cruiser rules. The wavering Holtzendorf as Chief of the Naval General Staff was the key figure. He began by saying that Wilson's demand was out of the question, but then expressed a willingness to give up the campaign if England gave up her starvation policy. This was on 22 April. On 30 April he prepared another memorandum in which, following the Helfferich line,* he stressed the economic disadvantages which would result from war with America. The crux of his reasoning was that the best solution for Germany would be the abandonment of the British blockade. He summed up in a passage which was to form the basis for the German Note.

If we are able to maintain peace with America, and if we, by concessions concerning the conduct of the submarine war, prompt America to exert pressure on England so that she will permit legal commerce between belligerents and neutrals, we will have obtained the economic succour which would put us in a position to preserve our advantageous military situation for a long time and consequently to win the war.[25]

Bethmann seized on this memorandum and got it before the Kaiser as representing the Navy's views. At the beginning of May there was a long weekend conference with the Kaiser at Charleville.[26] Gerard was in attendance throughout. The highlight for him was luncheon on the Sunday and a ding-dong conversation with the Kaiser. But the object of having him there was to explore the possibility of an understanding on the lines of the Holtzendorf memorandum. Gerard gave the correct diplomatic reply that the President might be expected to go some way towards doing

* See p. 322 above.

what he would never bargain to do. House also had advised the German Government through Bernstorff against trying to do a deal.[27] Working under this handicap Bethmann nevertheless succeeded. He persuaded the Kaiser that the decision was in the last analysis a political one and that the Kaiser should accept his view. Thus he got his way. It was for the last time, as he knew. On 11 May he sent for Gerard, and told him, without intending 'the least trace of a threat', that if in four or six weeks nothing was done by America to enforce international law against England, his position would become untenable.[28] His estimate of time was too pessimistic but otherwise his prophecy was correct.

Germany's reply to America was in two Notes, the first on 4 May 1916 dealing with submarine warfare generally,[29] and the second on 8 May with the incident of the *Sussex*.[30] The first Note, after the appropriate denial of any evil intention, stated that the Navy had been ordered to conduct submarine operations everywhere in accordance with cruiser rules; but that the order was given in the expectation that the United States would compel the British also to observe international law and that, if their efforts failed, Germany reserved complete liberty of decision. The second Note accepted the evidence supplied by the State Department, regretted the 'deplorable incident', and offered an indemnity; the commander had made an honest mistake for which he had been appropriately punished.

In America the German Note of 4 May was not universally regarded as satisfactory. 'A decidedly insolent tone', Lansing wrote to the President; but added that this was only his third impression and his final judgement would require further study. House, whose advice Wilson asked by telegram, was quite satisfied; from his point of view it was a Note which Wilson could accept without loss of face, leaving open the way back to the House plan. House advised no formal reply,[31] but Wilson alone in his study decided on a rejoinder. He would sever the promise from the condition, accept the former and reject the latter. This he did by one of his favourite devices, that is, by declaring his disbelief that his opponent could really mean what he had plainly said. Although there were certain passages in the German Note, he wrote, susceptible of the construction that German policy was contingent upon the result of negotiations between the United States and other countries, he took it for granted that this was not intended. Then came the punch. 'Responsibility in such matters is single, not joint; absolute, not relative.'[32]

The terseness of the reply owed something to Lansing with whom Wilson had discussed his draft. The letters passing between President and Secretary on this point, as well as those already recorded in the earlier stages of the *Sussex* affair, illustrate very well their method of collaboration and show that Wilson did not resent quite blunt criticism so long as he did not suspect an attempt to drive him off his course. The Secretary's comment on 8 May 1916 after reading the draft was:

I found on reading it that the same impression I had when we discussed it last evening remained with me—namely, that it expressed satisfaction and gratification which do not appeal to me. While I think our note should be polite, I feel we should omit any expression of relief on having avoided a break with Germany. I also thought the note was longer than was necessary and that it should be limited as far as possible.[33]

The Secretary enclosed his own draft and expressed the hope that there should be as little delay as possible. The President replied the same day:

My dear Mr. Secretary: You are probably right about cutting out all 'satisfaction', and I am quite content to have the note go as you have amended it. I am returning it so that it may be sent at once.[34]

The Note was sent off to Gerard that evening and was presented on 10 May. The crisis was over.

On 3 May 1916, by which date it seemed likely that the *Sussex* crisis would be resolved, Wilson and House met to consider the next step and to wonder again why Grey was so slow in the uptake. He had followed his brief cable of 6 April in which he stymied House's approach, with a letter written in his own hand. But the letter merely repeated the theme that the French, who had suffered most, must take the initiative; he would not even discuss it with them unless they mentioned it first. He had, he said, sent a message to Briand that he had heard again from House and he had himself since seen Briand in Paris but Briand had not referred to it; Grey hinted that House might like to deal with the French Premier direct.

Wilson, harking back to Grey's early insistence on America's participation in the post-war settlement as a condition of British acceptance of her mediation, told House that he was willing to give publicly a pledge of her readiness to join a post-war international organization; at the same time he would demand the calling of a conference. Both men were agreed that in any event this would be a good thing to do and could be combined with making a second and even more urgent approach to Grey.

An opportunity for the pledge and the summons to a conference presented itself almost immediately. There had been fixed for 27 May 1916 in New York a meeting of the League to Enforce Peace. This body proposed that all international questions not settled by negotiation should be submitted to a judicial tribunal or council of conciliation; and that force should be used, military and economic, against any nation committing acts of hostility without first making such a submission. The League had been inaugurated about a year before and was now holding its First National Assembly. Former President Taft was its chief sponsor and among the most active workers on its behalf. Many other well-known men were in its membership including Senator Lodge; and, as it happened, most of the prominent ones were Republicans. Wilson had never publicly concerned himself with its objects and he had refused an invitation to address the meeting. On 9 May Wilson accepted House's suggestion that he should be sent another invitation and should agree to make the principal speech following one from Senator Lodge.

The President was perhaps anxious to get a little discreet publicity in higher circles for his plans, for on 12 May he sent for Mr. Baker, the journalist and biographer to be. Baker was thrilled by a wonderful talk, two hours long, from eight to ten in the evening.[35] He was shown into the library upstairs in the White House and had a moment to look about. He admired a copy of Watts's *Love and Life* with a poem of the same title on the bookcase beside, and a striking photograph of the new Mrs. Wilson. He noticed Grey's book on *Fly-Fishing* and felt rightly that Wilson had never cast a fly in his life. He observed the desk with a great litter of books and papers, the filing cabinet behind, and the President's own typewriter desk in the corner: 'it is the quiet retreat where he does all his serious work.' The talk covered many subjects. But, Wilson said, he was thinking more than almost anything else just now about what America might be called upon to do toward helping to bring about peace. Should he outline tentatively some of his plans or ideas at the dinner of the League to Enforce Peace? He asked Mr. Baker's advice and Baker advised 'guarded statements'. 'Just as we were parting he said that his talk with me was not an interview but a conversation, the purpose of which was to enable me to found soundly and truly whatever I might write about him and his policies.'[36]

Meanwhile, House was composing a draft of a cable to Grey which he thought would 'fetch a favourable reply'.[37] Wilson approved it, suggesting only that he should emphasize that he, Wilson, was being pressed to take action, now that the *Sussex* was settled, and that he was faced with the danger of a significant alienation of sympathies from Britain. It was indeed true that peace was now in the air and the politically minded could not be insensitive to the thought that successful mediation would make Wilson .... ble in the election six months ahead. Tumulty, who certainly was ....ng the insensitive, wrote on 16 May a businesslike letter to Wilson: ....e is now at hand for you to act in the matter of *peace*.'[38] He enclosed an article by a Mr. Strunsky* and suggested an appeal to the heart and conscience of the world.

House's cable was dispatched on 10 May. In form it was a request for advice, but for advice on a course which the cable made it pretty clear the President had made up his mind to take. The President would now publicly commit the United States on the lines set out by Grey, in his letter of 22 September 1915,† and would announce at the same time that if the war continued much longer he would call a conference to discuss peace: House would like Grey's opinion on the advisability of this. The cable began and ended on a monitory note. It began:

There is an increasingly insistent demand here that the President should take some action towards bringing the war to a close. The impression grows that the Allies are more determined upon the punishment of Germany than upon exacting terms that neutral opinion would consider just. This feeling will increase if Germany discontinues her illegal submarine activities.

It ended: 'If it is not done now, the opportunity may be forever lost.'[39]

Grey was alarmed by this. A conference called by the President in which he was prepared to propound terms was something whose value could be and had been weighed, the value depending on whether in a given situation in the war the terms proposed were attractive enough. But if the President called a conference without putting terms on the table, it would be to Germany's advantage. She would go into it with her European conquests still intact and all that the Allies would have to bargain with would be the conquered German colonies which the Dominions were unwilling to relinquish anyway. The President and his adviser might have their gaze uplifted from these bargaining factors to a new order of things, but this was how the old diplomacies saw it. As Clemenceau said about the proposal after it had been brought forth: 'What is a mediation that envisages right only beyond the clouds?'[40] Grey cabled back on 12 May that a peace appeal without any indication of definite terms would be a move favourable to Germany.[41]

This left House 'distinctly disappointed'.

I am disappointed that he does not rise to the occasion. For two years he has been telling me that the solution of the problem of international well-being depended upon the United States being willing to take her part in world affairs. Now that we indicate willingness to do so, he halts, stammers and questions.[42]

He thought the Allies over-elated by the repulse of the Germans at Verdun

* Mr. Simeon Strunsky was a friend whose fertility of mind seems to have appealed to Tumulty. A later suggestion in February 1918 which Tumulty passed on to Wilson, but fortunately in vain, was that the United States should guarantee the people of Russia against the return of autocracy: see Baker 7: 564. † See p. 381 above.

and expecting a success with their own coming offensive. Success, he commented sardonically, might change their views about the evils of militarism and navalism. He foresaw trouble with them.

The effect on Wilson was enough to cure him completely of the passing disease of unneutrality and to make him think about what he called 'hard pan'. His predecessor Theodore liked to talk of walking softly and carrying a big stick; Wilson gave a schoolmasterly adaptation of the same thought in an address to the National Press Club on 15 May which was understood to refer to troublesome elements both in Mexico and in Europe.[43] He spoke of 'the present quarrel' as carrying 'those engaged in it so far that they cannot be held to ordinary standards of responsibility'. Since the rest of the world was mad, could America simply have nothing to do with it? No, he answered: if she did, she would lose her moral influence. Then he went on in a Kiplingesque vein: 'If you can only retain your moral influence over a man by occasionally knocking him down, then for the sake of his soul you must do it.' Likewise, 'the shortest road to a boy's moral sense is through his cuticle. There is a direct and, if I may be permitted the pun, a fundamental connection between the surface of his skin and his moral consciousness.' So there might come a time when America would have to act in a way in which she would prefer not to.

So Wilson, advancing on Britain the next day cane in hand, instructed House to send Grey a full cable which 'with the most evident spirit of friendliness' would make him understand that matters had reached a crisis which could not be postponed.

> The at least temporary removal of the acute German question has concentrated attention here on the altogether indefensible course Great Britain is pursuing with regard to the trade to and from neutral ports and her quite intolerable interception of mails on the high seas carried by neutral ships. Recently there has been added the great shock opinion in this country has received from the course of the British Government towards some of the Irish rebels.[44]

Either the United States must make a decided move for peace or she must insist on her rights

> as against Great Britain with the same plain speaking and firmness that she has used against Germany. And the choice must be made immediately. Which does Great Britain prefer? She cannot escape both. To do nothing is now, for us, impossible.

Then he formulated the essence of his thinking.

> ...move for peace, it will be along these lines 1) Such a settlement with
> ...their own immediate interests as the belligerents may be able to agree
> ...have nothing material of any kind to ask for ourselves and are quite

aware that we are in no sense parties to the quarrel. Our interest is only in peace and its guarantees; 2) a universal alliance to maintain freedom of the seas and to prevent any war begun either a) contrary to treaty covenants or b) without warning and full inquiry—a virtual guarantee of territorial integrity and political independence.

House answered the next day with the draft of a cable and some mournful reflections on selfishness and ingratitude; it was Wilson's duty, he said, to press for a peace conference, whether the Allies liked it or not.[45] Wilson in his reply on 18 May asked for help with his address to the League.

> I am thinking a great deal about the speech I am to make on the twenty-seventh, because I realize that it may be the most important I shall ever be called upon to make, and I greatly value your suggestion about the navy programme. . . .
>
> Would you do me the favour to formulate what you would say, in my place, if you were seeking to make the proposal as nearly what you deem Grey and his colleagues to have agreed upon in principle as it is possible to make it when it is concretely formulated as a proposal? Your recollection of your conferences is so much more accurate than mine that I would not trust myself to state the proposition without advice from you, though it may be wise to strengthen and heighten the terms a little.[46]

These two letters suggest that Wilson had relaxed any grasp he ever had of the real object of House's plan. In the first letter his proposal to 'move for peace' shows a return to his former notion of expressing no view upon territorial questions: the terms were to be such as 'the belligerents may be able to agree upon'. In the second letter he expresses a wish to follow the House–Grey Memorandum as closely as possible. But the Memorandum specified territorial terms not imprecisely and Grey had just emphasized the need for them in his cable of 12 May. Plainly Wilson had no adequate recollection of the momentous document, still only two months old, and had not troubled to keep a copy in the filing cabinet which Mr. Baker observed.

The first letter, and the speech at the Press Club which it followed, show also that Wilson's mind had already moved towards the conclusion, which later he dwelt upon so insistently, that the belligerents were fighting about nothing in particular. They refer almost contemptuously to 'the quarrel' and the implication is that the parties would find no difficulty in composing their differences if only they would put themselves to the task.

> Tweedledum and Tweedledee
> Agreed to have a battle;
> For Tweedledum said Tweedledee
> Had spoiled his nice new rattle.

> Just then flew down a monstrous crow,
> As black as a tar-barrel;
> Which frightened both the heroes so,
> They quite forgot their quarrel.

There is room for the gibe that Wilson's conception of his role was very close to that of the monstrous crow and that he thought peace could be obtained as easily as in the nursery rhyme, the warriors ceasing to fight as inconsequently as they had begun. Another interpretation of what was going on in his mind may be that he was for his own purposes choosing to take at their face value the protestations of both sides that they were fighting only to repel aggression and was assuming that if they could be promised the security of a universal alliance to prevent future wars, they could adjust their other differences.

The draft cable to Grey was approved by Wilson and sent off on 19 May. It was firm enough, though House had a little diminished the tone of Wilson's letter of 16 May. He began by saying that America had no desire to urge on the Allies 'something for which they are not ready'; and said also that the conference would not be immediately called and they would be given ample time to demonstrate whether or not the deadlock could be broken. None the less he maintained the pressure.

America has reached the crossroads, and if we cannot soon inaugurate some sort of peace discussion there will come a demand from our people, in which all neutrals will probably join, that we assert our undeniable rights against the Allies with the same insistence we have used towards the Central Powers. . . . If England is indeed fighting for the emancipation of Europe, we are ready to join her in order that the nations of the earth, be they large or small, may live their lives as they may order them and be free from the shadow of autocracy and the spectre of war. If we are to link shields in this mighty cause, then England must recognize the conditions under which alone this can become possible and which we are unable to ignore . . . I would suggest that you talk with the three of your colleagues, with whom we discussed these matters, for it is something that will not bear delay.[47]

The President approved the draft without alteration and the cable was dispatched on 19 May. House followed it up with a letter on 23 May.[48] England and France, he wrote, seemed to prefer the advantage of a crushing victory to a just settlement with American co-operation. This would chill American enthusiasm, 'never, I am afraid, to come again, at least in our day'. If the chance of world-wide peace was lost, 'the fault will not lie

e dictated to his diary that day a passage which showed that he had
pe; and showed also his conception of the partnership at work.

ident and I are getting into deep waters and I am not sure we are coming out as we desire. If he will play our hand with all the strength within our power, I believe we can make them do as we wish.[49]

Grey replied to the cable on 19 May with a promise to consult the Prime Minister at once. This was all that Wilson and House had when they met in New York on 24 May. If House had ever had any thoughts of acting on Grey's hint that he should take the matter up with the French direct, he must have been daunted a little by news of a conversation between Polk and Jusserand on 22 May. The French ambassador was so distressed by indications that the President was contemplating a peace move that he went to the State Department to tell Polk that 'anyone trying at this time to bring about peace would be considered a friend of Germany',[50] and asked that the President should be told at once. The Wilsons had come to New York to attend Grayson's wedding, for his courtship had now ended as successfully as Wilson's. They spent the night in the Houses' apartment and the two men had a long talk. The Entente's attitude, House concluded, was due to France's desire to see Germany crushed, for she could never again hope to have so many allies by her side. They decided that it was now hopeless for the President to call for an immediate conference and that the main theme of his speech to the League to Enforce Peace on 27 May should be a general exposition of the new policy. House thought that if Wilson could now 'strike the high note, the right note, and hold to it', history would give him one of the highest places among the statesmen of the world.[51] Using extensively the draft for which he had asked House, Wilson spent the whole of the next day on the preparation of his address.

It was thus that Wilson's epoch-making speech of 27 May 1916 was composed.[52] Grey's original idea did not expire with the House–Grey Memorandum; it became the stuff of Wilson's thought and the stimulus to a great commitment. The war, Wilson said, had come suddenly and out of secret counsels; had there been time for conference, it might have been averted. The lesson was that there must be a new and more wholesome diplomacy and (here he adopted House's phrase and the simple yet fundamental idea that House believed should be the basis of the new diplomacy) the governing of nations by the same high code of honour that is demanded of individuals. America, Wilson said, was now a participant, whether she would or not, in the life of the world, with obligations and interests in all that affected mankind. The thinking of world statesmen had been set ahead a whole age by the war and came to this—that the principle of public right must henceforth prevail and that the nations of the world must in some way band themselves together to see to it. The United States was willing to become a partner in any feasible association of nations formed in order to realize this object. He was willing, he said in conclusion, to initiate a peace movement; and he put forward in almost the same words the scheme set out in his letter of 16 May, the immediate settlement to be left to the belligerents and for the long term a universal association of nations.

Only a minority—in Europe no more than a handful—recognized this pronouncement as one of the great events of the century. For the second time in history (for one must not forget the rhapsody of the Tsar Alexander I just a hundred years before) a powerful ruler proclaimed as a practical policy the idea of a world order. The wary might mark the immense significance of that and still feel that the promised land was for the enjoyment of their descendants rather than for them. But no wariness could cushion the impact of the declaration by America of a new foreign policy. The venerable admonition of Washington against permanent alliances and the age-old fear of entanglement had at last withered away. The President of the United States had so declared, not only for his own administration but speaking, as he said, 'the mind and will of the people of America', in the presence and with the approval of his Republican predecessor and of Senator Lodge, the mouthpiece of his party in foreign affairs. This was a matter that affected the life, liberty, and happiness of everyone in the civilized world.

But in Europe peace was a hope and war an actuality and neither side could think of anything but victory. Each thought that without victory there could be no tolerable peace and that with victory peace could be made in the image that the victor conceived. Furthermore, in his opening sentences the President had used words which upset those in Britain and France who might otherwise have been the most attracted by the purport of his speech. In emphasizing that America, while profoundly affected by the war, was in no sense a party to what he called 'the present quarrel', he said: 'With its causes and objects we are not concerned. The obscure fountains from which its stupendous flood has burst forth we are not interested to search for or explore.'

These words pained even men like Grey who did not judge Wilson merely by his pronouncements. Up till then they had believed that Wilson, while for good political reasons clinging to neutrality, shared their detestation of German militarism and acknowledged the strength of the ideals that sustained them in battle. To them, as also to the majority of those Americans who were not indifferent to the issues, it seemed plain that the dominating cause of the war was Prussian aggressiveness, that the objects of Ger[many] were her own glorification and aggrandisement, and the objects [were] the very objects that Wilson was by this speech publishing, [mainten]ance of right and respect for the territorial integrity of small [states. Di]d Wilson not see that, while he was talking about territorial integrity, England was fighting for the integrity of Belgium? On this Spring Rice was sarcastic: 'The Good Samaritan did not pass by on the other side and then propose to the authorities at Jericho a bill for the better security of the highroads.'[53] The cold reference to causes and objects implied that there was nothing to choose between the belligerents and that they were a set of quarrelsome folk fighting among themselves for objects not worth bothering about. Moreover, Wilson presented the idea of the League in the form that was the least palatable to Britain. Perhaps with the idea of attracting interest in Germany he put the freedom of the seas as its first object and the prevention of war second. But no one in power in Germany was interested anyway, and British sympathizers were given the impression that America desired the association to be directed primarily against British naval power.

Brand Whitlock, the American ambassador in occupied Brussels, wrote to House: 'It is the most important announcement concerning our foreign policy since the announcement of the Monroe doctrine, although it will take many years before this fact is brought into relief and fully understood.'[54] House wrote to Wilson and recorded in his diary: '. . . a landmark in history. It marks the beginning of the new and the decline of the old order of statesmanship.'[55] But he added, keeping it of course for the diary: 'There was one unfortunate phrase. . . . The Allies will overlook all the good in it and accentuate this.'

House was right about the Allies. There were some who, construing the phrase charitably as they thought, concluded that Wilson had in mind material objects and not principles and that he was stressing America's indifference to the former. Bryce thought that all that it meant was that Mr. Wilson did not propose at that moment to discuss the causes and objects. But generally the speech was received with indignation rather than applause. This bred counter-indignation in Americans usually sympathetic. Both House and Page were annoyed with the Allies for picking on one phrase and ignoring all the rest.

Although in the speech Wilson had refrained from announcing any plan for a conference, he had indicated clearly that he needed only an invitation from one side or the other to take action. This had been as much an object of his speech as the declaration of policy; and in thanking House for his letter of congratulation he wrote: 'I was handling a critical matter and was trying to put it in a way that it would be hard for the Allies to reject, as well as for Germany.'[56] In fact neither found rejection at all difficult. There was no official response to the speech and expressions of public sentiment were hostile. The Allies rejected him because they treated him as disqualified by his deflation of their war aims, while in the eyes of the

Central Powers he had never qualified at all. Thus all he had done was to prove the soundness of the advice which House and Lansing had both given him in the previous summer and which they were to press on him as strongly as tact permitted during the rest of the year, that Germany would never listen to him and that, if he wanted the Allies to listen, he must be careful not to say things which were bound to upset them.

Speakers in the Reichstag and writers in the German press, except in a few socialist newspapers, firmly rejected Wilson as a mediator. But Jagow told Gerard on 14 June that this was not to be taken as official.[57] It had of course been from the first, and still was, the policy of the German Government to humour the President and place the odium of rejection of any peace proposal on the other side; and by mid June, the Allied reactions to the address of 27 May made it safe for Germany to be privately encouraging. At the same time, and independently of the address, the German Government's attitude towards an American initiative was changing. The process of the change was obscured by some ambiguity in the use of the word 'mediation' and perhaps also by some failure in contact between Bethmann and Jagow. The development will be considered in the next chapter.

Grey, it will be remembered, had promised to take counsel with the Prime Minister on House's cable of 19 May 1916 pressing for a decision. The promise was kept with greater amplitude than promptitude. The matter was brought before the War Committee, but not until 24 May. This was the day when Wilson and House were meeting in New York, and, having almost given up hope of the answer, were preparing the address of 27 May. The regurgitation of the House plan in London created what Hankey called 'a frightful row'.[58] The Army Council—that is, the governing body of the War Office, meaning principally General Robertson and the military men—threatened to resign if there was any further inquiry into 'the peace question'. When the War Committee met, the Cabinet Ministers present, turning everyone else out of the room, for nearly an hour went into a huddle. All that is known about what they said comes from the report that McKenna made to Hankey on the way to lunch. Asquith, Grey, Balfour, and himself, McKenna said, were for acceptance, 'owing to the black financial outlook', Law and Lloyd George against. A decision had not been reached but McKenna expected it to be favourable; a draft reply ubmitted by Grey but another was being prepared by Balfour. a was, as we shall see, as Chancellor of the Exchequer much with 'the black financial outlook' and that may have coloured out the likely decision. A better guide to the sense of the meeting is probably to be found in Balfour's draft written the same day. This was a rejection of the proposal as premature, but so carefully phrased as not to sound the last word and upholstered with an elaborate argument to suggest that it 'might be dangerous to the cause we have at heart', that is, a post-war organization to maintain peace. 'The great scheme', Balfour argued, was dependent on a satisfactory peace at the end of the war: a satisfactory peace meant the restoration of Belgium, Alsace and Lorraine, an independent Poland, 'the status of Turkey profoundly modified—*not* in the interests of the Central Powers—and some other changes made in the map of Europe in accordance with the principle of nationality': a premature announcement of intervention would be interpreted as an appeal for peace on the basis of the *status quo ante* and such a peace could not lead to an international organization of the kind the President contemplated.

On a first reading Balfour's draft seems weak almost to the point of futility.[59] Was not the sort of peace it was postulating almost identical with what the House–Grey Memorandum, as yet without response, had offered? But anyone provoked to make that retort would find that there emerged from a second reading questions, hinted at rather than stated, but which he could not very well leave unanswered. Was this a peace which the United States was 'prepared actively to promote by war or the threat of war'? Did she appreciate the extent to which the proposed peace machinery would depend for its effectiveness on sea-power which by diplomatic pressure she might have whittled down? What were the prospects of the organization if it was proposed 'in connection with an inconclusive or disastrous peace accompanied, perhaps promoted, by diplomatic friction between the Allies and the United States over maritime affairs'?

Thus did Balfour parry the probe. The United States in effect was trying to discover whether the Allies were really serious about a reasonable peace; in reply Britain would like to know whether the United States was really serious about war and whether she understood the need to win the war before making the peace and the value of the blockade to winning the war. But this subtle composition was not dispatched. Perhaps it was thought to be too dangerous. The terms of the 'satisfactory peace' outlined by Balfour by no means embraced all the Allies' recent commitments: what if America replied that she accepted the terms and on the faith of them was ready to go to war? Or perhaps Grey thought that the references to the blockade would only irritate. At any rate he sent on 29 May an uninspired reply which concluded with the repetition of his advice to try the French.

Then came the report of the President's Address of 27 May 1916. Grey was seriously upset by it. We knew that the President could not express himself strongly on the side of the Allies, he said to Page when the ambassador called on 27 July to take leave of him before sailing to New York, 'but we did not believe that anyone could play a great part in securing future peace who was really indifferent to the causes and objects of the war'.[60] Grey wanted the ambassador to make various things clear to the President and Page's efforts to do so will be recounted later. The most important was about France. Let Wilson address his Notes jointly. He, Grey, though he knew the President only through Page and House, did not believe those who said that his only motive was vote-catching. A joint Note would make it clear that his motive was not anti-British, for there was no political capital to be made in America by being anti-French. Let him also, if he wanted to put out peace feelers, approach France direct and not rely on ascertaining her views through Britain: he ought to realize that it was impossible for Britain to be the first to suggest that the time had come to make peace.

Grey's correspondence with House dragged reproachingly on until Grey ended it rather acrimoniously in a letter of 28 August 1916.[61] As it happened, it ended also the association between these two good men, for with the collapse of his plan House was on the sidelines in foreign affairs until after America came into the war and by that time Grey was in retirement. It is sad that it ended in some disillusionment on both sides. By 28 August Grey, who had after all only accepted an option, was perhaps getting rather tired of being dunned as a defaulting debtor for failing to take it up. More importantly, he had, as he said in his letter, begun to doubt whether American membership of a League of Nations would mean anything. Had the President—this is not what he said but what he might have asked himself—who publicly professed ignorance and indifference as to what the war was about, ever intended, even privately, to fight on the side of the Allies? If he had, would the American people have followed him; and would they follow the path he had set for them in his League address? He expressed in the letter his doubt about that; and he expressed it also at greater length in a private letter sent on the same day to the League to Enforce Peace which had asked him for a pronouncement in its favour.[62] Since the address, Spring Rice had been drumming into him his distrust of any scheme which committed the American people to active intervention as a guardian of peace. On 14 July Spring Rice wrote:

> It is quite evident that the country does not desire war, even when United States territory had been actually invaded and Americans killed in their own h̲o̲u̲s̲e̲s̲. W̲e̲ ̲m̲ay draw the conclusion that this country is by no means ready to ̲ ̲ ̲ ̲ ̲ ̲tions for the future of Europe in connection with the Peace Treaty, ̲ ̲ ̲able be the objects.[63]

̲ ̲ ̲ce here to United States territory being actually invaded was an allusion to events on the Mexican border: and for the sake of the illustration it is worth picking up the Mexican tale where it was left off at the beginning of this chapter* with the dispatch of the Punitive Expedition.

A state of affairs in which an American army probed more and more deeply into Mexico and never contacted Villa could not go on for long without trouble. Notes were continually being exchanged and incidents as continually occurring. There was one at Parral on 12 April 1916 when there were American casualties and many more Mexican. A tentative agreement for the gradual withdrawal of the expedition, 'inspired by the belief' that the Mexican Government would omit no effort to prevent further invasion of American territory, was upset by an incursion into Texas which caused its Governor to demand the occupation of Mexico. But these were minor affairs compared with the outrage of an American defeat. This occurred on 17 June at Carrizal, deep in Mexico, where the battle was brought on by the provocation of an American officer, acting in disobedience to general orders, in the belief that the Mexicans, if attacked, would notwithstanding their superior numbers run away. Instead they routed the Americans and, though they suffered the greater number of casualties, they took twenty-five prisoners. It was this, the thought that there were American prisoners in Mexican hands, that stirred the country. Tumulty was quite beside himself. He wrote to Lansing:

If I were President this moment or acting as Secretary of State, my message to Carranza would be the following: 'Release those American soldiers or take the consequences'. This would ring around the world. In the name of God, why do we hesitate longer?[64]

The President on 25 June demanded their release in language that was calmer but very firm. He did not expect that Carranza would submit and he prepared for war, to put an end, as he said, to an intolerable situation. The *de facto* Government could not or would not protect Texas, New Mexico, and Arizona against incursion or allow the United States to protect them: Northern Mexico must be cleared of armed forces. On 27 June he prepared an address to Congress on these lines. The next day the prisoners were released. The news started a flood of telegrams to the White House. They were ten to one against any form of war. This reaction touched Wilson deeply. He must have realized how near he had come to a war which he did not want out of a mistaken belief that national sentiment as well as national policy demanded it. He used the occasion of an address on

* See p. 473 above.

30 June to pour out all his thoughts about the futility of war. How easy it is to strike, he cried, but,

> Do you think the glory of America would be enhanced by a war of conquest in Mexico? Do you think that any act of violence by a powerful nation like this against a weak and distracted neighbor would reflect distinction upon the annals of the United States?[65]

The consequence of this was another flood of letters and telegrams and House wrote to tell Wilson how truly he had sensed the feeling of the country. 'The people do not want war with Mexico. They do not want war with anybody, but least of all a country like that.'[66]

All this must have had its effect upon Wilson's attitude to the war in Europe.

The demise of the House plan left the President stern and the Colonel disheartened. Grey's letter of 29 May was clumsily worded. He had, as has been suggested, some reason for not setting out the territorial terms as specified in Balfour's draft; the detailing of them would inevitably provoke the retort that they were the same as those in the House–Grey Memorandum. But it would have been better to provoke the retort than to arouse suspicion. Grey's paraphrase—that the terms of peace must be sufficiently favourable to the Allies to make the German people feel that aggressive militarism had failed—let in the implication that the terms which had been discussed in London were no longer considered good enough and that this was the true reason for the rejection of the American overture. To some extent it was the true reason; and its appearance, when eventually it emerged three months after the Memorandum, was not improved by the smoking out. There seemed to be a lack of frankness.

It is difficult to blame Grey. The easiest thing for him to do so as to preserve the intimacy with House which he valued—and perhaps the best way also of preserving American goodwill for Britain—would be for him to say that the House plan would not, alas, satisfy all the demands of the Allies to whom Britain was committed. To Grey's mind that would have been disloyal to the Allies, to those whose aid the Entente had bought as well as to those whose cause Britain had made her own. Moreover, though it would have contained a part of the truth, it would not have contained the ... act was that the idea of a negotiated peace was unacceptable ... rey's colleagues. If he had said as much as that, he would have ... ing American goodwill for himself at the expense of goodwill ... ry and it was his duty as Foreign Secretary to keep the possibility of American mediation alive for use by his country when, if ever, it would serve her interests. The result was that Grey could not be frank. There is doubtless much to be said for and against frankness and personal friendliness as diplomatic virtues; the danger of frankness is that, when once given, its withdrawal under pressure of circumstances can be very disconcerting. The inevitable consequence of Grey's letter was that Wilson and House suspected that Britain as well as her allies had undisclosed ambitions and that they must be very large if the chance of achieving them seemed to the Allies worth more than American aid. The suspicion was correct. The division of the 'spoils' was now proceeding beyond the point at which it could be excused as bribery to bring in new allies. On the very day of the House–Grey Memorandum the War Committee was, as we have seen,* meeting to settle the fate of the Cameroons. On 23 March the War Committee approved the Sykes–Picot agreement as altered to obtain Russian consent and on 16 May the division of the Ottoman spoils was formulated in letters from Grey to the French and Russian ambassadors.

Suspicion was more deadly in Wilson than in House. House's annoyance was directed against the 'stupidity' of the French and English for prolonging the war when they could get a peace which would mean the end of militarism, though he added: 'It would also mean an end of navalism, and that perhaps is where the shoe pinches.'[67] He wrote to Page in June 1916: 'I have come to feel that if the Allies cannot see more clearly in the future than they have in the past, it is hardly worth while for us to bother as much as we have.'[68] And in almost Wilsonian tones he lamented the lack of response from 'official Great Britain or France'. 'It is not the people who speak, but their masters, and some day, I pray, the voice of the people may have direct expression in international affairs as they are beginning to have it in national affairs.'

House reached the peak of his neutrality with the observation already noted† about the tiresomeness of hearing the English declare that they were fighting for Belgium when their primary reason for being in the war was because they would not tolerate Germany having a dominant navy as well as a dominant army. On another occasion he talked of British 'cant and hypocrisy'.[69] If America entered the war, he said, Britain would make unlimited demands on her and then, when they were all met, accuse her of trying to force her to give better terms to Germany than were warranted. But it may be observed that on neither occasion was the ebullition calculated to do Britain any harm. The first was on 29 June 1916 in talk with a visiting British radical M.P. whose sentiments were much the same; and the second was on 22 September to Page whose anglophilism was impregnable.

* See p. 454 above.   † See p. 140 above.

Wilson's reaction went much deeper. It was expressed in a letter to House on 22 June 1916:

The letters and the glimpses of opinion (official opinion) from the other side of the water are not encouraging, to say the least, and indicate a constantly narrowing instead of a broad and comprehending view of the situation. They are in danger of forgetting the rest of the world, and of waking up some surprising morning to discover that it has a positive right to be heard about the peace of the world. I conclude that it will be up to us to judge for ourselves when the time has arrived for us to make an imperative suggestion. I mean a suggestion which they will have no choice but to heed, because the opinion of the non-official world and the desire of all peoples will be behind it.[70]

But the Presidential term was now moving towards its close and, until he knew whether he was to serve again, Wilson could not embark upon any more international projects. Meanwhile, natural disappointment was added to the unease genuinely caused by the British attitude. The failure of the plan left the United States without any escape from the multiplying troubles of neutrality. Partly for the sake of the plan Wilson had risked a revolt in his party and found now that he had gained nothing by it. It had been House's own pudding, well-mixed with a pound of high purpose to an ounce of American advantage, and the cook would not have been human if he had not been riled to find that it had hardly been tasted by those invited to the feast. Since the Allies had turned down the plan, America had to solve the problems of neutrality as best she could; and the Allies could hardly complain if the solutions were not favourable to them.

With House any feeling of resentment was short-lived. He continued to grumble and he rebuked Jusserand whenever he saw him. As late as 10 October he recorded an interview with the French ambassador in which he

insisted that the Allies made a mistake in not carrying out the tentative agreement we made in Paris and London last February, which would have brought the war to a close in all probability and would have given France a favorable peace. If not, it would have involved us in the struggle.[71]

But there was no disturbance of his fundamental belief that America could o win. In November 1916 when he was talking to Polk the President's tendency to offend the Allies, he said: ar, let it be with Germany by all means. She has for- consideration, and the situation demands, for our we hold with the Allies as long as we can possibly do it he added in his diary: 'I will confess that the Allies beyond endurance.'

So House brought himself to a businesslike acceptance of the fact that if the Allies would not have victory on his terms, then they must have it on their own, for an Allied victory was what America wanted. America's entry into the war he believed to be inevitable; and since he had failed in his attempt to make terms for it in advance, he must rely on the President being able at the peace conference to restrain excesses.

Wilson was more deeply affected. The innate American distrust of British statesmanship had not, as it had with House, been softened by personal acquaintance; he had already, he thought, been given good reason in 1913 to dislike British policy in Mexico; the British still needed to learn a lot more of the elementary doctrine that he had then exhorted Page to pound into them.* He drew a much sharper line than House did between the British ruling class and the people. The people certainly wanted peace but the privileged classes were blocking it because of antiquated ideas which were inconsistent with the new order; and the people in Europe could not make their voice heard because there was not anywhere true democracy in the American sense. In this respect Wilson's thinking was closer than House's to the mean of American thought. It is worth glancing at the reflections on this subject of Houston, a Cabinet Minister as well as a thoughtful intellectual and a strong believer in the Allied cause. Of European countries England and France had come furthest, he thought, with England in the lead. But both were in need of fundamental changes and 'have a long road to travel before they reach the point at which America now stands in the march to individual well-being and social and industrial democracy. Among other things, class distinction and privileges under law or custom must go.[73] Most of southern and eastern Europe, he said, was still medieval, and Russia in a hundred years might possibly get in sight of where America started. Men like Wilson and Houston were full of English sentiment. Wilson's favourite literature was English and much of his political thought and many of his heroes. Oxford was an ideal; and after Princeton the English Lake District mirrored the country nearest his heart. A Briton of the time had no difficulty in understanding that a man might almost worship Bach and Beethoven, admire Goethe, be ruled by Kant, and as fond as he wished of the Bavarian peasantry; and yet abhor the German ruling class. That an American might like Britain and dislike her government seemed a stranger idea. But in fact Americans did not share the British belief that Britain was in reality, if not in form, just as democratic as America; most of them were quite clear that Britain was governed by a ruling class whose habit of thought was aristocratically far behind the times. Anti-war British radicals like Bertrand Russell w

* See p. 120 above.

at this time saying the same thing. Professorially speaking Wilson in 1894 had allowed that Britain and Switzerland as well as the United States were democracies. But in September 1918 in an unguarded moment he referred to 'old Governments like that of Great Britain which did not profess to be democratic'.[74] He had under House's guidance, though perhaps he hardly realized it, himself come to a secret understanding with a professedly undemocratic government. He had been swayed perhaps by the hope that House could make men like Grey and Balfour take what he called in his letter of 22 June the 'broad and comprehending view'. But that had failed, and the failure restored his belief in the open and direct method, the recourse to public opinion, the appeal, as he put it in the letter, to 'the opinion of the non-official world and the desire of all peoples'. When after the election he turned his attention again to foreign affairs, he sailed grandly out of the inland waters of secret negotiation into the high seas of rhetorical diplomacy.

XVI

ANGLO-AMERICAN RELATIONS 1916
THE ELECTION

The U53 – the Irish Rising – increasing effectiveness of the British blockade; the end of the Declaration of London – interference with the mails – the Black List – tobacco and forcible rationing – the threat to retaliate – Page's bath in opinion – Lansing hardly a Secretary of State – election problems – the Democratic Convention – 'Keeping the Country out of War' – Wilson and Roosevelt – the returns – peace, progressivism, and the League of Nations

FOR about nine months, that is from the time of the solution of the *Sussex* crisis in May 1916 until the resumption in February 1917 of the submarine war, Germany and the United States went their separate ways with little or nothing to say to each other. Bernstorff wrote to House in June that he was doing everything to be forgotten.[1] Below the surface there was tension due to the knowledge on each side that the issue was sleeping but not moribund; and above it there were occasional alarums. Tranquillity was shaken by the arrival on the American side of the Atlantic of the new German long-range submarine. It appeared first in July 1916 in the guise of a merchantman, the *Deutschland*, with a cargo of dyestuffs which she unloaded at Baltimore. America was startled by the possibilities and Britain seriously disturbed. Ought such a vessel, Grey asked, to be treated as an ordinary merchantman? Britain, who had not felt any difficulty in applying to submarines the law of visit and search, now queried whether international law ought 'to transfer without modification to submarines, rules and regulations which work fairly well as regards surface vessels'.[2] Lansing would have none of this.

Then in October the armed version appeared. The U53 popped up in Newport harbour, delivered a letter for Bernstorff, and then, just outsi⟨de⟩ territorial waters, sank nine vessels, all without violating the *Sussex* p⟨ledge⟩. This was in the middle of the election campaign and created a gre⟨at hulla⟩baloo. It coincided with two sensational interviews given by Ger⟨ard⟩ just arrived in New York on leave and thought it within th⟨e⟩

ambassadorial duties to warn America of the perils confronting her, which he did by declaring his conviction that there would be a submarine war in the immediate future. Shares tumbled on the New York stock exchange and marine insurance rates rose by 500 per cent. It was rumoured that the commander of the U53 had been given information at Newport about where British merchantmen were to be found (they were in fact stationed in the Channel in full sight of shore) and that at his request an American destroyer had moved to allow a torpedo to be put into an empty ship. Grey told Page of his efforts to 'hold back the almost fierce public feeling'.[3] 'How difficult it is', Wilson sighed, 'to be friends with Great Britain without doing whatever she wants us to do.'[4] 'You people', Franklin D. Roosevelt said to *The Times* Washington correspondent, 'are losing your sense of proportion.'[5]

One constant factor in Wilson's foreign policy was his determination not to be engaged on two fronts at the same time. Another constant was his assessment of German misbehaviour as worse in kind than British because it affected lives and not just property. 'It is interesting and significant', he had written to Bryan in June 1915, 'how often the German Foreign Office goes over the same ground in different words, and always misses the essential point involved, that England's violation of neutral rights is different from Germany's violation of the rights of humanity'.[6] He made the same point in public in the speech in September 1916 in which he accepted the nomination for his second term.[7]

The aggravation caused by British activities was incessant. Being less intense than that caused by German activities, it gave place to the latter while it lasted; but the latter had no sooner begun to dwindle than, as we have seen from his letter to House of 16 May 1916,* Wilson was on the warpath against Britain. He wrote in this letter of Britain's indefensible and intolerable behaviour in the course of the blockade; and then added a new count to the indictment with a reference to 'the great shock opinion in this country has received from the course of the British Government towards some of the Irish rebels'. This was the Sinn Fein rising in Dublin at Easter [...] quelled but was the first step towards the grant [...]d in 1921. The nervousness caused by rebel- [...] war caused the Government in London to [...] everity, disturbing American sentiment far [...] powerful Irish element. Many of the rebels [...] he leader, Sir Roger Casement, was reserved [...] for a torrent of appeals for clemency.[8] Percy, [...] es had renewed his contacts in Washington [...] nercy; Spring Rice repeatedly implored it;

See p. 488 above.

Senator Lodge, not a soft man, sent his earnest hopes that 'some means will be found to avoid execution'. On 29 July 1916 the Senate passed a resolution in favour of clemency and stipulated that it should be presented. Wilson caused it to be presented *à titre d'information*[9] and without instructions which Spring Rice said was 'under the circumstances an act of great courage'.[10] Casement was hanged on 3 August. On 11 August Spring Rice wrote: 'There is no longer a moderate Irish wing. They are all pressing for action against Great Britain.'[11] And Bernstorff rejoiced that 'the Irish have come over into our camp like one man'.[12]

To the minds of men like Asquith and Grey Casement was trebly traitorous—traitorous as a rebel, as a man who had been knighted in the King's service, and as one who had trafficked with the mortal enemy Germany, soliciting aid from her and endeavouring to seduce from their allegiance Irish prisoners of war. Each side invoked the case of Belgium and failed altogether to understand the other's attitude. Grey wrote to House: 'We are not favourably impressed by the action of the Senate in having passed a resolution about the Irish prisoners, though they have taken no notice of outrages in Belgium and massacres of Armenians.'[13] Americans, on the other hand, questioned the sincerity of the English belief that she was fighting to free Belgium from German oppression when she herself was holding down a small nation on her doorstep by methods as ruthless as those which she condemned in others.

On points of this sort waves of anti-British sentiment came and went. The irritation caused by the blockade was perennial and waxed as its effectiveness increased. But there was now in Britain as much irritation with America and just as much hostility against her as there was in America against Britain. When on 15 September 1916 Spring Rice wrote warning the British Government to take heed where they were going, he put his finger on the spring of anti-American feeling. 'The trouble is that we counted on too much, and because we counted on too much we are angry at being disappointed.'[14] The America who thought both sides to blame and stood inflexibly on her trading rights was not at all the America whom Britain had pictured in 1914. Since the end of 1915 there had been a growing feeling that the Foreign Office was being too kind to a neutral interested only in making a good thing out of the war. All the top British admirals thought that the Foreign Office was letting America get away with it.[15] Admiral Jellicoe, in command of the Grand Fleet, wrote to his second-in-command on 22 December 1915: 'They imagine every neutral is anxious to go to war with us and can do us harm.' The rumblings of the admirals reached the First Lord who with Cecil's consent asked Jellicoe to deliver his in writing. The resulting production made Crowe very indignant, not perhaps so much because he disagreed with it as because it was an encroachment on Foreign Office preserves. He wrote on 24 January an angry minute about over-worked departments and press attacks organized by naval officers,[16] which called forth a soothing reply from Cecil.

Whether organized or not the British press as a whole was blaming the Foreign Office for timidity and the Admiralty for subservience to the Foreign Office. An article in the *Morning Post* of 18 January 1916 from its Washington correspondent headed 'The Blockade Farce' gave figures showing the enormous increase in American exports to neutrals of food and other materials such as boots and cotton since the war broke out. The news-paper's conclusion was: 'Had the Navy not been hampered by the Foreign Office it is probable that Germany before this would have been forced to sue for some terms or to surrender, having been starved into submission.'[17] On 25 January the Prime Minister himself attended a confidential meeting of national editors where with Cecil's aid he fended off much hostile questioning.[18] The American consul-general on 17 January reported British opinion as being in 'an angry frame of mind'[19] and this was the atmosphere in Parliament as Grey described it to Page on 25 January.*

All this took place amid the tension already described,† created by the fear that after settling with Germany over the *Lusitania* America would train her guns on Britain. In the letter of 12 January in which he wrote of things taking a 'serious turn' Grey had spoken of the danger of American retaliation, such as an embargo on munitions, and of the desirability of a joint Allied Note to support the blockade. The Foreign Office was working on this.[20] An embargo could be answered by an Allied prohibition (Russia on 19 January promised to help) on the export of raw materials, such as nickel and rubber, which the United States needed and which were under Allied control. The opinion which Crawford sounded in America was unanimous that she could not face the results of such measures. The Board of Trade was asked to report on the prospects of a trade war. A joint Allied Declaration got as far as a draft which would, had it been issued, have been the first proclamation of economic warfare that escaped lip-service to the restraints of the law. Economic pressure, the draft said bluntly, was a valuable weapon; and the Allies declared that they 'will co-operate together and support one another to the utmost of our power in cutting off from Germany, Austria, Turkey and Bulgaria all commercial intercourse with other nations'.

The outward manifestation of the internal stir was the creation in Febru-ary 1916 of a Minister of Blockade with a seat in the Cabinet. This was done on Cecil's recommendation supported by Grey. Grey must have felt con-

* See p. 420 above. † See p. 419 above.

siderable relief in handing over duties which he was now finding repugnant. This came out in a letter to Asquith on 15 February 1915:

> We are now threatened with the complete alienation of Denmark and Norway who are both undoubtedly friendly by nature and I believe we are depriving both countries of things really necessary for their own use.[21]

The new minister was Lord Robert Cecil himself. As a barrister who had practised in international law he was well suited to the post.

Lord Robert was a tall and ungainly man, careless in dress, awkward in manner, and yet commanding. Page describes him as 'ugly, gentle, courteous in the extreme, . . . the ablest of the sons of old Lord Salisbury . . . the only Tory to the *n*th degree that I have ever had a decided liking for'.[22] Cecil believed passionately in a League of Nations and was to become its best-known supporter in Britain. But with equal passion he believed (as did, though with less ardour, his cousin Balfour) that the defeat of Germany was the requisite for a successful League; and on this, the first objective, he was determined and uncompromising. He was a new personality, a hawk in the feathers of an untidy dove, one whose high Toryism made him influential within his party. He continued to be Under-Secretary at the Foreign Office; and when in July 1916 Grey to lighten his burden took a peerage, Cecil became the spokesman on foreign affairs in the Commons. This duty together with his seat in the Cabinet put him in a position of power, the greater because he was not a man who would stay in a place where he could not get his way: he had the 'resigning mind' rather than the 'resigned', Balfour said;[23] and he had also a high-handed touch. In 1918 someone in the State Department rebuked Eustace Percy with the comment that he represented the 'Robert Cecil school of arrogant diplomacy'.[24]

The new ministry unified a motley collection of committees sprawling over various government departments. It substituted central control for the co-ordination attempted by the War Trade Advisory Committee under Lord Crewe, a body which Cecil described in his recommendation as 'too numerous and too oratorical to be of much executive value'.[25] Its creation served notice on the world that the British regarded the blockade no longer as an auxiliary but as a main weapon of war; and Cecil got quickly to work upon making the notice effective with a new Order-in-Council. He thought it unwise and unnecessary to make food, as some critics wanted, absolute contraband: unwise because all the weight of previous British pronouncements could be thrown against it and unnecessary because, as he wrote to Crewe on 29 February, since 'all conditional contraband goods going into Germany are in fact now for the use of the Government', absolute and unconditional contraband could now be treated in 'precisely the same way'. 'For the convenience of the trading community', he said, they would in future be included in one list without distinguishing between them.[26]

True, Article 19 of the Declaration of London forbade the application of the doctrine of continuous voyage to conditional contraband. The new Order, issued on 30 March, made short work of that. It also legalized the seizure of goods consigned to a neutral port if it could be shown that the consignee had ever at any time forwarded imported contraband goods to enemy territory, unless he could prove that in the particular case the destination was innocent. About six weeks before the Order was issued and while doubtless it was in preparation, Bryce had written to Drummond:

> Our international lawyers here, so far as I know their views, agree with American lawyers, in thinking that we are making ducks and drakes of international law, though they maintain a judicious silence on the subject. I can quite understand that H.M. Government think they must stop all trade with Germany by any means, legal or extra-legal, taking their chance of the future, whether in the anger of neutrals or in heavy post-bellum damages. But it is a different question whether something might not be done to make British naval policy deviate less openly from the settled international rules. I believe that Wilson and Lansing would feel relieved if we could make any change which would have at least the appearance of a concession, and would make the divergence of our action from the existing rules less palpable.[27]

But the British evidently did not mind about appearances and under the Order the ducks and drakes played more licentiously than ever before.

The Order was ironically entitled 'The Declaration of London Order-in-Council 1916'.[28] It was the fourth Order in this form, all of them maintaining the pretence that British Prize Law consisted of the Declaration of London with modifications. The Declaration was now in tatters and Lord Robert, who had never personally been involved in it, thought it would be frank to say so. The French made some difficulties about this.[29] The Declaration represented a triumph of continental ideas over maritime and the French might not always be allies. But the French gave way and an Order-in-Council made on 7 July 1916 repealed all previous Orders and thereby freed British Prize Law from dependence on the Declaration.[30] The Order stated Britain's intention 'to act in strict accordance with the law of nations' and, in case any doubts arose about what the law of nations was, went on to enunciate all the latest British ideas on the subject. An accompanying memorandum said that the Declaration 'could not stand the strain imposed by the test of rapidly changing conditions and tendencies which could not have been foreseen'.

The demotion of the Declaration was of no practical importance. The breaking loose from it was just another notice served on the world that Britain had no intention of responding to neutral protests by mending her ways and that she would not in wartime accept the balance between belligerency and neutrality which in peacetime her Government (but fortunately for her not the House of Lords) had thought reasonable and fair.

In Washington Secretary Lansing was waiting for an answer to his Note of 5 November 1915. On 5 January he formally asked the British ambassador to inquire when he might expect to get it.[31] In fact a draft reply was in print by 3 January. But Grey was determined that it should be a joint document from Britain and France. Friendly Americans like Root had for long past been reminding the British that Lafayette was a more popular character in America than George III; and now the fear of a showdown leading to an embargo and perhaps worse made Grey especially anxious for French support. The French were very willing to give it but they had their own ideas about what the Allied Note should say.[32] They rightly regarded the argument of reprisal as the strongest line of defence and said that they would not join in the Note unless it was used; Grey on 4 January 1916 advised against it, saying that it would cause 'irritation and resentment' and stimulate rather than disarm the agitation for an embargo. But he said that it must be settled by the Cabinet in discussion with the French. The draft came before a Cabinet committee on 17 January and discussion went on for three months, the French causing a diversion with a fanciful scheme for scrapping all the Orders-in-Council and declaring an old-fashioned blockade of all German ports including the inaccessible Baltic ports. But they won on the issue of reprisals and two brief but cogent paragraphs in the final Note set out the belligerent argument.

Lansing became impatient. On 21 February he sent a strong message through Page; 'no attention is apparently being paid to our representations and the unwarranted measures to which we are objecting are being continued with unabated vigour'.[33] Grey sent back apologies and promises. But nothing was said in advance to soften the impact of the Order-in-Council of 30 March. This caused Lansing to send a scorcher for Page to deliver. The issuance of the Order, he said, before the Note had been answered could not be regarded 'otherwise than as an act which appears to be intentionally discourteous'.[34] Page does not appear to have passed this on. He had been told to make a formal demand for an answer but he explained that he had not done so because he had been told privately that the Note was ready. The Note was in fact presented on 24 April, stonily received, and never in terms answered.[35] On the particular points with which it dealt, except for reprisals, argument was exhausted; and on reprisals serious argument was never begun.

Interest was now absorbed by two new measures, both attracting indignation, attendant on the blockade, the interception of mails and the publication of a 'Black List' of neutral concerns with whom Britons were forbidden to trade. These two measures infuriated Americans not only because they were oppressive and irritating in themselves but also because they raised issues laden with emotion: who was Britain to censor the letters of free Americans or to tell them with whom they might or might not trade?

The first to make its appearance in order of time was the interception of the mails. The use of the British mail by correspondents of whatever nationality was, of course, subject to British law. The British mails were His Majesty's mails and it was within the prerogative of the Crown to open and inspect any mail at any time. The power was exercised by means of a warrant authorizing examination, very sparingly in peacetime but in wartime whenever it was thought necessary for the prosecution of the war. If a neutral sent his correspondence through Britain—if, for example, American mail to Scandinavia was routed through Britain as it naturally would be—this transit mail was after April 1915 treated as liable to inspection. No legal complaint could be made about that. So the correspondence of neutrals, between themselves or with the enemies of Britain, must, if British censorship was to be avoided, be sent direct to its destination. 'Mails from or to neutral countries', it was said in a Cabinet paper prepared by the Foreign Office and dated 17 November 1915, 'which in peacetime passed through British ports are now being carried by direct neutral steamers'; and, the memorandum added in a tone which seemed to condemn the device as a rather despicable evasion of a natural law, 'there is at least one instance of a new steamship line being started apparently for the express purpose of enabling mails between certain points to escape the Allies' censorship'.[36]

But what about mail on the high seas found on neutral ships that were searched by a belligerent in accordance with international law? Its protection—a subject on which there was little or no international law before 1907—was guaranteed by the Eleventh Hague Convention of that year. The postal correspondence of neutrals or belligerents found on the high seas was thereby made inviolable unless it was destined for or proceeding from a blockaded port. The Convention gave no protection to parcel mail. Parcels could be examined for contraband in the same way as any other cargo. As contraband lists were extended, difficulties arose. Some contraband, such as rubber, could be sent in small quantities by letter mail. This made a case for opening letters. But there was a clear distinction in theory, and one which could be observed to a large extent in practice, between goods and information. The former might be contraband; the latter was free.

Of course the information might be very valuable to Britain. But it was not until the blockade was being tightened in late 1915 that neutrals began to appreciate the perils of using the British mail. In a circular sent out on 23 September 1915 which dealt with the prevention of the transmission of contraband by parcel post, the British Foreign Office stated firmly that the privileges of mails that were protected by the Hague Convention would continue to be carefully observed. But in the autumn of 1915 pressures for a tougher attitude were building up. Possibly the War Office saw the circular and was alarmed at the proclamation of immunity. At any rate, the Foreign Office memorandum already referred to was prepared for the Cabinet. It suggested a reconsideration of the matter, a course strongly supported by the War Office. The Convention obviously created a difficulty, especially since the ink was hardly dry on its affirmation by Britain. But there were two ways round it, the memorandum suggested. There was the familiar bypass along the line that this Convention, like so many other Hague Conventions, was not technically binding since not ratified by all the belligerents; in a war that was now sucking in most of Europe there were certain to be a belligerent or two who had not ratified. The other way was to make use of the exception in the Convention itself, that is, the provision that allowed interception of mail going to a blockaded port. As a result of the March Order-in-Council was not every port now a blockaded port? Might not indeed the British Government weaken its case, consistency being the essence of blockade, if it was *not* to intercept mail? This argument, better calculated perhaps to promote opposition to the March Order-in-Council than to win adherents to the practice of intercepting mail, was not further pursued.

The object of the censorship and the benefits conferred by it were fully set out in a Cabinet Paper prepared by the War Office in May 1916 in the form of a letter addressed to the Foreign Office.[37] It may be inferred from the letter that a good deal more censorship had been going on than Grey was aware of. The value of censorship, both as a means of preventing information from reaching the enemy and of obtaining information useful to the Allies, could, the letter said, scarcely be exaggerated: largely through its means, two enemy plots hatched in the United States and endangering the safety of the British Empire had been discovered and frustrated. Censorship was also indispensable to the blockade.

The value of the censorship as an instrument for suppressing enemy trade and enforcing the blockade is second only to that of the Navy. . . . The Postal Censorship supplies the Prize Court with a volume of clear and reliable evidence which is essential to the equitable and effective conduct of the blockade. . . . Its existence acts as a deterrent upon the loading of enemy goods. . . . effectively exercised, it may paralyse enemy business . . . the information derived from the censorship of letter mails taken from neutral ships is the most valuable acquired from any source during the war.

'Effective exercise', in the estimation of the War Office, required the opening of all letters and the detention of most. All letters in code, for example. They might embody schemes for evading the blockade; if they could not be decoded, they should be detained as indecipherable, and if they could be decoded, they should still be detained because to forward them might give away the fact that they had been deciphered. Letters containing plans for buying up materials that the Allies wanted constituted another objectionable category. So also did letters containing 'commercial propaganda'.

The Foreign Office did not await a Cabinet decision on their 17 November memorandum. As a preliminary step, the memorandum said, British representatives in neutral countries had been told to sound out opinion. Pursuant to these instructions the British Minister at The Hague 'foreshadowed the possibility of' a change.[38] In some excitement the Dutch Foreign Minister telegraphed to the Dutch Minister in Washington that Britain intended 'to no longer respect the inviolability of mails on the open seas', and that he proposed to protest. The Dutch Minister told Lansing, Lansing telegraphed Page on 1 December 1915, and Page saw Grey, who said that no decision had yet been reached but that there was a possibility of the British Government being driven (by unspecified German action in the North Sea and adjacent waters) to change the present practice.

Doubtless it was correct that no decision had been taken. But the British Navy, like the German when it sensed a shift in the wind and a feeling that action would go unrebuked, during December 1915 took the mail off three or four Dutch ships travelling between Holland and America. On 28 December the American Minister in Holland, the former Professor Van Dyke, telegraphed to the State Department recommending 'a prompt peremptory protest . . . to protect the dignity of the United States'.[39] Lansing, ever sensitive to such an appeal and himself indignant at the delay in answering the American Note of 5 November 1915, gladly obliged. On 4 January 1916 he telegraphed instructions to Page to make 'a formal and vigorous protest' and to 'impress upon Sir Edward Grey the necessity for prompt action'.[40]

Thereafter matters proceeded at the tempo the British preferred. On 25 January Page was told that important questions of principle were raised on which the British must consult the French. On 3 April, after a reminder on 19 February, the British and French Governments delivered a Joint

Note.[41] In his protest on 4 January Lansing had made the mistake, to which he was so prone, of overloading. Instead of confining it to the new and hitherto unexplained action of the British in seizing letter mailbags, he devoted nearly half of the telegram to the parcel mail. Since the State Department was, as he said, 'inclined to regard' parcels as being in the same category as any other cargo, this boiled down to a familiar complaint about the blockade generally. Its inclusion enabled the Allies to devote most of their reply to parcel mail and to skirt the subject of letter mail. They did not take the technical point on the Convention, preferring, in accordance with their wont, to use it for the purpose of pointing out how much holier they were than the Germans. The Germans, they said correctly, although they had now desisted from the practice, had in August 1915 taken the mail-bags from three neutral ships and subsequently justified their action by saying that the Hague Convention was inapplicable. Moreover, they did worse than seize mails; during 1915 they had torpedoed thirteen mailships 'without any more concern about the inviolability of the dispatches and correspondence they carried than about the lives of the inoffensive persons aboard the ship'. As to what the Allies themselves intended to do about letter mails, the Joint Note contained only one rather ambiguous paragraph.

True to their engagements and respectful of genuine 'correspondence', the Allied Governments will continue, for the present, to refrain on the high seas from seizing and confiscating such correspondence, letters, or dispatches, and will ensure their speediest possible transmission as soon as the sincerity of their character shall have been ascertained.

The Joint Note did not deal with the cases in which the Navy had undoubtedly seized letters and correspondence and presumably confiscated those whose character was blemished by commercial propaganda and other such insincerities. The paragraph was disingenuous. It was true that the Navy had not seized mail when it was physically 'on the high seas'. What the British did, and intended to continue doing, was to take the mail from neutral ships calling at British ports either because they were ordered to do so by the Navy or because they thought it wise to submit to British arrangements. It might have been better to denounce the Convention altogether than to use this compliance to dodge the observance of it.

These evasions provoked Lansing into strong language. In a Note delivered on 24 May 1916 he described the Joint Note as 'entirely unresponsive' to the American protest.[42] The Allied Governments

compel neutral ships without just cause to enter their own ports or they induce shipping lines, through some form of duress, to send their mail ships via British ports, or they detain all vessels merely calling at British ports, thus acquiring by force or unjustifiable means an illegal jurisdiction. Acting upon this enforced jurisdiction, the authorities remove all mails, genuine correspondence as well as post parcels, take them to London where every piece, even though of neutral origin and destination, is opened and critically examined to determine the 'sincerity of their character', in accordance with the interpretation given that undefined phrase by the British and French censors. Finally the expurgated remainder is forwarded, frequently after irreparable delay, to its destination.

The American Government would not submit to a lawless practice of this character and only a radical change of policy would satisfy it.

The Foreign Office was assailed with equal vigour from its own side. The War Office had not been consulted about the Joint Note and clearly regarded it as lamentably weak.

In the joint Allied note, the discussion was permitted to stray beyond an exposition of the justice and necessity of the military measures being taken and was, to some extent, confused by the intrusion into the argument of political considerations advanced in a spirit of compromise.[43]

The War Office did not think it too late to restore the discussion to the lines from which it should never have been allowed to diverge, that is, an unequivocal declaration that the action of the Allied Governments was no violation of the Hague Convention (because it was not applicable) or of any previous international law. The whole thing was in their view nothing more than 'a mischievous agitation of German origin' which must be 'prevented from assuming dangerous proportions'. Without such firmness they seemed to think that there was no sort of dirty trick that the Hun might not get up to in an attempt to stop his letters being read.

In this predicament the Foreign Office managed to postpone for four months any formal answer to the American Note. They filled in the interval to some extent with informal statements about their methods of censorship designed to show how little delay was in fact caused and by dealing with specific cases of complaint. When eventually they answered on 12 October 1916 they did not, as the War Office recommended, brush the Convention aside. 'In regard to mails found on vessels at sea the Allied Governments have not for the present refused to observe the terms of the convention reasonably interpreted.'[44] They admitted that 'vessels summoned on the high seas and compelled to make for an Allied port' were to be treated as being on the high seas and were protected by the Convention. But they continued to maintain that ships calling 'voluntarily' were not protected. By this time the system was in full swing. There were about 250 censors at Strand House, London, dealing with about 20,000 letters a day. At the price of angering Washington by their artful and dilatory methods the British prevented the issue from being brought to a head.

The operation of a Black List has already been described.* It was a natural belligerent device to stop supplies to the enemy; Germany operated one to the extent that her inferior resources permitted. Britain's measures began with a list of neutral concerns whom she suspected of trading with the enemy. The list was compiled for the use of the contraband committees in their task of deciding whether or not to allow cargoes to proceed to their ostensibly neutral destinations. Trading with the enemy, that is with concerns operating in enemy territory, was forbidden to British subjects from the beginning of the war, but until the end of 1915 the Government relied upon its persuasive powers to stop trade between British subjects and neutrals whom it suspected of favouring the enemy. Then the Government decided to regularize the position, at any rate as regards the worst neutral offenders. On 23 December 1915 the trading with the enemy legislation was amended to give the Government power to publish a list of persons with whom by reason of enemy association British traders were by law forbidden to deal. This list was known as the 'statutory list' to distinguish it from the unpublished list, sometimes called List B, which was still kept in use. The publication of the statutory list brought the British practice out into the open. Lansing regarded the legislation 'as pregnant with possibilities of undue interference with American trade' and on 25 January 1916 protested accordingly.[45] The first list was issued on 29 February 1916 and contained no American names.[46] On 18 July 1916 another list was published in which eighty-five American firms were proscribed.[47]

There was at once a tremendous uproar. Spring Rice and Jusserand, summoned to the State Department, could only wring their hands. On 26 July the Department sent a strong protest, composed chiefly by Wilson himself since Lansing was on vacation.[48] Polk when he dispatched it to Page explained that, 'on account of intense feeling aroused here' they must give it immediate publicity.[49] 'Sheer stupidity', the normally devout Page called it, and 'a bad blunder'.[50]

Certainly it was Whitehall at its least imaginative. The narrow lines on which Lord Robert Cecil drew up his defence were indeed impregnable. 'All we have done', he said in Parliament, 'is to declare that British shipping, British goods, and British credit should not be used for the support and enrichment of those who are actively assisting our enemies.'[51] In fact all he had done was to stir up quite unnecessarily a hornets' nest. The

* See p. 181 above.

unpublicized list, as everyone agreed, was working satisfactorily. A British subject in wartime would not dream of disregarding governmental advice not to trade with someone who was suspected of aiding the enemy; and indeed it was in July 1916 that the Foreign Office made their haughty comment about their inability to suppose otherwise.* Such small advantages as might be gained by putting the matter on a legal basis and in the form of a public list were far outweighed by the American anger, whether reasonable or not, of which the British Government had been forewarned. Those who were on the list objected to being pilloried, as they put it; and those who were not objected to the idea that they traded by permission of the British Government. Such was the power of the British Government in those days over world trade that anyone proclaimed as being in its bad books became virtually untouchable. In one of the many cases which exemplified the protests an American firm of impeccable neutrality bought some cocoa from an Ecuadorian firm to be shipped to America in an American ship and there to be made into American candies for American consumption.[52] When the shipowner heard that the Ecuadorian seller was on the British Black List, he refused to accept the shipment; very probably the ship was on the British White List† and wanted to stay there. The American buyers, who had paid for the cocoa, instructed the sellers to sell it locally, but the British consul in Ecuador threatened to blacklist any buyer. Americans saw this sort of thing as a British attempt to ruin any trader who did not behave exactly as the British wanted.

There was inevitably speculation about the make-up of the list. Why was X on and not Y who seemed to have much closer associations with Germany? Because, it would be suggested, X was being punished for non-co-operation and the omission of Y was due to his having contributed to the Anglo-French loan. More far-reaching suggestions were connected with the Allied Economic Conference that had met in Paris on 14 June 1916. The conference discussed methods of tightening the blockade and this may have stimulated the publication of the enlarged Black List on 18 July. But it discussed also post-war measures to be taken against German commerce and this might mean, as Lansing thought, that neutrals as well as the Central Powers would have to face after the war a powerful trading combination. The suspicion that Britain was using the weapons of belligerence to improve her commercial position in the world was never far away.

Page on his return from America in October 1916 tried to impress upon Grey the resentment felt even among the well-disposed and their feeling that, because it was otherwise pointless, the measure could only be due to

* See p. 181 above.　　　† See p. 181 above.

ill-will.[53] Meanwhile, Lord Robert listened courteously to all remonstrances but remained uncomprehending. Writing more than twenty years later, he said that, while doubting that the Black List was of a real use, he had never been able to understand why it caused such indignation in America.[54]

Blacklisting and mails interference were the major Anglo-American troublemakers in 1916 but there were also in constant supply minor sources of irritation arising out of the blockade. Tobacco, for example. The Americans could not see that its consumption would add to the military effectiveness of the Central Powers and wondered indeed why the Allies should want to discourage their enemies from dissipating their foreign currency in purchases of this sort of commodity; the Allies considered that smoking promoted endurance on the battlefield. But tobacco could not by any stretch of the imagination be called contraband. The Allied case for stopping it had to be based solely on the March Order-in-Council, whose validity the United States did not recognize, so that the State Department, when arguing about tobacco, had always to make the reservation that it ought not to be stopped anyway.

As has been said,* the Allied method of stopping commodities of this sort from eventually reaching Germany was to have an arrangement with the neutral country concerned—in this case Holland—preventing re-export. These arrangements had to be made diplomatically and with some 'give and take'. Part of the 'give' was that tobacco from the Dutch East Indies was allowed in unconditionally, which meant that it could, almost certainly would, be resold to Germany. This angered American tobacco planters who before the war had supplied much of the German and Austrian markets. They said that this was trade discrimination. On 25 November 1915 the British Government yielded the point and specifically agreed that 'for the present' American exporters might sell tobacco to German consumers through merchants in Holland.[55] Then came the tightening of the blockade. On 29 June 1916 the British Government announced that it would revert to its former policy.[56] This enraged the American planters who claimed that, trusting the assurance of 25 November 1915, they had planted large acreages of tobacco suitable for the German and Austrian markets and for which they could not now find purchasers. The controversy was still in full swing at the end of 1916.

The imposition of quotas on the Northern Neutrals inevitably led to diplomatic bickering. The controls fingered their way deep down into even such unwarlike trades as that in oranges and apples, where the British had

* See p. 182 above.

a difficult task in trying to preserve universal goodwill. What about the apples that Denmark re-exported to Russia: was Britain going to include an ally's consumption in the quota? Then as to Holland, there was a Dutch liner which carried fruit from Spain and Portugal; since the rationing scheme was so dependent on Dutch goodwill, it seemed rather scurvy not to allow them a little preferential easement. This led to a thunderous denunciation from Washington; American fruit was being discriminated against. Then there was Britain's ally Italy and her oranges. The American consul-general in London reported in September 1916:

> I am also informed, privately, that the subject of importations of fresh apples from the United States is undoubtedly associated with the difficulty respecting the shipment of oranges from Italy. I deem it quite possible that, but for the necessity of assisting the Italians and disposing of their oranges, the British authorities would take strong grounds against the shipment of apples from the United States, not as a temporary but as a definite measure. The Italians are understood to be very insistent in respect of their desire to forward oranges without restraint into Holland and other northern countries, and it is recognized that if this sort of revenue were cut off, Italian fruit growers would be placed in a very precarious position. On the other hand, it would be difficult to grant free transit to oranges without doing as much for apples.[57]

Official correspondence does not reveal what in the end happened about American apples. They were only one of many sources of friction. Underlying it all was the suspicion that Britain always had her own long-term trading interests in view. This was what the President himself believed as is manifest from his letter of 23 July about to be quoted; and in October he said that she was fighting a commercial war. Certainly Britain was now directing by force the maritime trade of the world, deciding what could be bought and sold and where it could be sent; and using for that purpose, so it seemed, the familiar weapons of the tyrant, intimidation and detention and the scrutiny of private correspondence.

Anti-British feeling in Washington came to a head in July 1916, a month in which each of the many sources of friction had something to contribute. On 29 June Americans were pointedly reminded of the irritations of the blockade by the prohibition on tobacco. On 9 July the *Deutschland* appeared and started off a nervously acrid correspondence on the duties of neutrals. On 18 July the Black List was issued. The chilly reply which the Allies made to the American complaint about the mails was received in Washington on 22 July; the State Department allowed it to be reported in the *New York World* that the reply was considered 'both insolent and imprudent'.[58]

The Senate resolution on 29 July interceding for Casement was the climax to many a memorial meeting honouring the 'Easter martyrs'. Grey circulated to the Cabinet a telegram of 24 July from Spring Rice saying that the President was personally irritated and that 'an unpleasant time is coming'.[59]

It was the Black List which particularly infuriated Wilson and silenced the pro-Allied voices. Wilson wrote to House on 23 July:

> I am, I must admit, about at the end of my patience with Great Britain and the Allies. This blacklist business is the last straw. I have told Spring Rice, and he sees the reasons very clearly. Both he and Jusserand think it a stupid blunder. I am seriously considering asking Congress to authorise me to prohibit loans and restrict exportations to the Allies. It is becoming clear to me that there lies latent in this policy the wish to prevent our merchants getting a foothold in markets which Great Britain has hitherto controlled and all but dominated. Polk and I are compounding a very sharp note. I may feel obliged to make it as sharp and final as the one to Germany on the submarines. What is your own judgment? Can we any longer endure their intolerable course?[60]

The threat of retaliatory legislation which the President spoke of was conveyed more diplomatically to the British ambassador by Polk; it might be necessary, he said, for the Government to take some decided steps to protect its interests.[61] 'It was evident to Polk', Wilson wrote again to House on 27 July, 'that the British Government was not a little disturbed (and surprised, poor boobs!).'[62] The boobs were certainly not surprised and apparently not perturbed. They made a minor concession over tobacco, offering to give free passage to consignments bought and paid for before 4 August.[63] They offered to review the names on the Black List, choosing not to realize that what outraged America was that there should be a Black List at all. On this Cecil was uncompromising. He said to American correspondents on 11 August: 'I cannot see any way by which we can forego our undoubted right to prevent our subjects from providing resources of trade to our enemies. There is not likely to be any change in the policy of the Allies as a result of neutral protests.'[64] This was the type of indirect rejoinder that annoyed Wilson. The protest of 26 July which had come hot from his pen only a week after the announcement of the Black List was not officially answered until 10 October. The formal answer was a more elaborate but equally firm assertion of legal right.[65]

Public opinion in Britain hardened as the year went on. Wilson was debited with all his anti-British activities but given no credit for his anti-German. The second submarine campaign, which was brought to an end with the sinking of the *Sussex*, had lasted only a month but showed every sign of being a striking success. The loss of Allied and neutral shipping was at twice the rate in the first campaign and the seven U-boats that were lost in the second campaign were only a fifth of new construction. Instead of thanking Wilson for having secured this respite, the British despised him for not having acted more forcefully. The hawks reckoned that if he was as flabby with the British as with the Germans they had nothing to fear. It was indeed true that in 1916 America was more prosperous than she had ever been before and that her prosperity depended on Allied trade. Talk of retaliatory legislation, the hawks felt, need not be taken seriously. On 15 June 1916, with the nomination of Wilson as the Democratic candidate, the warning gong had struck and some twisting of the British lion's tail was to be expected before the bout was over.

Lansing had been away for most of July 1916 on vacation and recuperating from a brief illness, which was why Polk had been acting as Secretary of State. The President discussed with him and with Senator Stone and others the nature and terms of the retaliatory legislation. This fell into three categories. The first was a counter-attack on the blockade and on forcible rationing in particular. A country which prevented or restricted the importation into any other country of American products 'contrary to the law and practice of nations' would have its imports into America prohibited or restricted. The second was a counter-attack on the Black List and the White List. Specifically a vessel which discriminated in the acceptance of cargo could be denied clearance from an American port; and generally when 'facilities of commerce' were by the laws or practices of any belligerent denied to American citizens, the citizens of the belligerent could be treated likewise. These provisions were in fact enacted in the beginning of September. They were not mandatory though some in Congress wished to make them so; action depended on the President's discretion. A third category denying the use of American communications to citizens of countries that interfered with American mail was talked of but not enacted. But on 8 September Congress voted a naval appropriation large enough to make the American Navy second only to the British and a close second at that. When on 24 September House suggested that this might account for some of the British irritation, Wilson replied: 'Let us build a navy bigger than hers and do what we please.'[66]

But Wilson had taken the matter as far as he intended at that stage; and deeper consideration brought both British and Americans to a cooler assessment of the consequences of a trade war. Wilson as a historian had written of the sad effects of the retaliatory embargo that preceded the war of 1812; and as President he would have seen a full report from the Secretary of Commerce dated 23 October 1916 which concluded 'that immediate reprisals as authorised by recent laws afford no assurance of success, and threaten even the present basis of neutral commerce'.[67] This report considered, also without much enthusiasm, a proposal for a Congress of Neutrals which in June Lansing (though, as he said, he had previously opposed concerted action) was now ready to consider as a counter-measure to the Allied Economic Conference.[68] The Northern Neutrals, Sweden in particular, had tried very hard during 1916 to entice the United States into joint action over the mails, the Black List, and British malpractices generally, but without success.[69] This must have been a relief to the British. As Cecil told the Cabinet in December, 'very little encouragement from America would make the Governments of Sweden and Holland impossible to deal with'.[70] Whatever reason Wilson had—perhaps a sense of national as well as of personal pride that disliked having to combine—the lack of encouragement turned out fortunately for the United States. For it is sad, but not surprising, to have to report that when the United States entered the war she made no effort at all to influence her associates towards better belligerent behaviour. On the contrary, she profited greatly by British experience and found the idea of a Black List specially appealing. On 6 December 1917 she issued one which contained the names of some 1,600 concerns in Latin America.[71]

Spring Rice was constantly warning that trouble with England was a good electioneering card for both sides, but especially for the party in power. On 17 September 1916 he wrote to the Canadian Prime Minister: 'The situation here is that the President is losing ground and may very probably be beaten. His advisers may tell him that the only thing which can save him is an appeal to American patriotism against the British.'[72] The British ambassador may have been right in thinking that trouble with Britain would be good politics for Wilson. Where he and so many other observers fell into error was in supposing that this was an area in which Wilson played politics. In May Cecil had tipped mediation as the President's election winner. But there had come no offer of mediation and there was to be no provocation of Britain; and the reason was the simple and straightforward one that Wilson was not willing to take any far-reaching steps in foreign affairs until the nation had decided who was to govern it for the next four years. His plan, if re-elected, was to launch with all the authority that re-election would give, a great and, as he hoped, irresistible peace appeal; and probably he had no intention of using his retaliatory powers until after that had failed.

Lansing was another person who concerned himself with Wilson's political prospects. There were two matters, he wrote to the President on 21 September, which were being used against him in the campaign and which ought to be corrected.[73] The first was the Administration's failure to protest against the German invasion of Belgium. This was a hoary subject with Lansing. He had in January 1915 drafted a long statement for the press[74] wherein he drew an interesting distinction between a neutral and a neutralized state which the President had dismissed as 'entirely sound and conclusive from the lawyer's point of view'.[75] The second point, he said, on which the President was being criticized was over the delay in the settlement of the *Lusitania*: ought he to take the matter up with Bernstorff in order to remove the charge that the Administration was letting matters drift? Wilson in a reply negativing the first proposal and discouraging the second, expressed the hope 'that the Department will confine itself as much as possible to routine matters. We should ourselves, no doubt, be unconsciously influenced by political considerations, and that would be most unfair to the country.'[76]

Before Lansing got this reply he had thought of another useful idea which he put to Wilson in a letter of 22 September 1916.[77] As an alternative to a formal protest to Britain about her misbehaviour, should he send a telegram to the chargé in London (Page was then in the United States) expressing his own deep concern? The chargé could then take it upon himself to show the telegram confidentially to Lord Grey. The Secretary enclosed a draft of the proposed telegram in which American grievances were given a reviving spray of verbiage. The gist of it was that if the British Government expected from America an attitude of 'benevolent neutrality', they were much mistaken; that they were straining relations with the United States and that he anticipated that in the near future retaliatory legislation would be put into effect. On the same day as he answered Lansing's earlier letter, 29 September, Wilson answered this one also.

I think it would be quite unjustifiable to do anything for the sake of public opinion which might change the whole face of our foreign relations. Therefore I think it would be most unwise to send a message like this.

I had a talk with Walter Page of the most explicit kind, and am sure that he will be able to convey to the powers that be in London a very clear impression of the lamentable and dangerous mistakes they are making. I covered the whole subject matter here dealt with in a way which I am sure left nothing to be desired in the way of explicitness or firmness of tone; and I think that our letters had better stop at that for the time being. Let us forget the campaign so far as matters of this sort are concerned.[78]

Page arrived in the United States on 11 August 1916 for the visit in which Wilson and House hoped that he might be cleansed in the waters of American opinion, while he hoped that he might make official Washington understand, as he felt that he understood, what it was that the British were about. Neither result was achieved. Page got no sympathy from anyone in the State Department: 'I cannot persuade myself that the fault is entirely ours, or even half ours', Polk wrote to him after he had returned to England.[79]

During the second half of August the President's attention was largely absorbed by a threatened railway strike. Nevertheless, he at once asked his old friend to lunch but gave him no opportunity to talk. At last Page forced a discussion for which he spent the night of 22 September at Shadow Lawn.[80] This was the house, in Long Branch on the New Jersey coast, which Wilson had taken for the summer and from which he intended to fight the election. It was a painful occasion; the two men, who had thought alike on so many things and for so long admired each other, found themselves in the last confrontation far apart. Page could not understand why Wilson had not taken a grip of the great moral issues of the war and instead was clutching at technicalities; Wilson could not understand how Page had allowed himself to be persuaded that England was always right and America always wrong. When the war began, he told Page, he and all the men he met were in hearty sympathy with the Allies, but now he saw no one who was not vexed and irritated by the arbitrary English course. What especially irritated Wilson was the evasiveness of the British, their delay in answering his Notes, their unwillingness to let matters come to a clear issue: as he put it, they would not 'lock horns'. Page told him of the rumour he had heard that Germany wanted an armistice and tried to get him to say that he would not propose one. But Wilson replied that if it was an armistice looking towards peace, he would be glad if Germany proposed it. He said that he would not do anything retaliatory until after the election lest it might seem that he was playing politics; but if after that there were continued provocations, he hinted that he would. The President gave Page the whole morning and was his usual calm and courteous self. The two men parted affectionately and never met again.

Meanwhile, the Secretary of State continued to plod along the path of legal rectitude while bemoaning that it could only lead to disaster. He recorded his deep misgivings in a memorandum which was prepared, he says, before he talked with Page. Nevertheless, his criticism of the President was much the same as the ambassador's.

He does not seem to grasp the full significance of this war or the principles at issue. I have talked it over with him, but the violations of American rights by both sides seem to interest him more than the vital interests as I see them. That German imperialistic ambitions threaten free institutions everywhere apparently has not sunk very deeply into his mind. For six months I have talked about the struggle between Autocracy and Democracy, but I do not see that I have made any great impression. However, I shall keep on talking.[81]

The conclusions to which his meditations brought the Secretary were:

1. There must be no compromise peace with the Germans; the President must not offer mediation which would depress the Allies and encourage Germany.
2. No drastic measures must be taken against Britain.
3. 'Join the Allies as soon as possible and crush down the German autocrats'; this was the true policy which he hoped the President would adopt.

With our knowledge that these were the sentiments irrigating the Secretary's mind, it would have been easy for us to imagine, if no record had been left, the course of the conversations between him and the visiting ambassador. They both had to serve a master whom they thought to be worrying unduly about American rights instead of concentrating on the real principles at issue. They would have expatiated, Page volubly, Lansing far more discreetly, on the difficulties of their position, and upon ways and means of influencing Wilson. They would have considered carefully how far—Page of course willing to go much further than Lansing—America ought to go in making allowances for Britain; obviously as little as possible must be done to blunt the British blockade, since it was one of the strongest weapons in the war between Democracy and Autocracy and must be kept sharp for the day when America would join in.

Alas for the powers of imagination. Both men have left their records which agree in showing that their discussions covered only a catalogue of individual American complaints.[82] The Secretary, Page wrote, 'betrayed not the slightest curiosity about our relations with Great Britain'; all his talk was about 'cases'. To Lansing, Page appeared to be interested only in the feelings of the British public and not at all in 'the pecuniary losses to American citizens'. 'As to the legal principles involved, he seemed to be indifferent.' Violations of law he did not consider important. He was 'full of grumbling complaints at our insistence on American rights, at our lack of vision as to the World War'.

If Lansing had recorded that out of loyalty to Wilson, or out of discretion, he did not open his mind to Page, it would have been understandable. But writing ten years afterwards (for the record is taken from his memoirs) he is unaware of any incongruity. It is in the chapter in which he prints his memorandum 'on the policy which it seemed to me ought to be followed in conducting our controversy with the British Government'[83] that he castigates Page for his indifference to the principles of international law and to the pockets of his countrymen.

Lansing was now living in two worlds. There was what was for him the real and active world, that is the legal world, a world in which he pursued with his nose to the ground all offenders against international law. It was the world which he had inhabited as Counselor and which he ought never to have left. But there was also the world of the Secretary of State. That was a world in which he was hardly allowed to move. He says rather pathetically in his memorandum that for six months he has talked about the struggle between Autocracy and Democracy, without making any great impression. Who were his audience? A little of his talking was done to the President but most of it to himself in the memoranda which he wrote to solace his sense of impotence in a world where he did not really belong.

He had a limited mind: put him on the scent and he would follow it like a hound: take him off it and he was bemused. He is hardly to be blamed if his conduct was no worse than erratic. But was it no worse? His nostrum for Anglo-American relations, as he recorded it in the above memorandum, was to keep on exchanging Notes but to bring nothing to a head. Did he mean by this to write Notes and at the same time and unknown to Wilson give assurances that they would not be acted on? That would be one way of pursuing independently the policy he believed to be right: a deceitful one, no doubt, but a sense of impotence is a cloud on the mind most easily dispelled by self-deceit; and self-deceit spreads easily to the deception of others. On 22 September, the very day on which he was putting before the President his plan of impressing the British Government with the seriousness of the situation by warning Lord Grey of the dangers of retaliation, he was piping a different tune into the ears of the British embassy's trade adviser. He left Sir Richard Crawford with the impression that there was no intention to utilize the power of reprisals:[84] definitely he said that the President would never exercise them except in the last resort. Did he think that the President would have authorized him to say that?

Page, after his return to England was, at any rate until America came into the war, an ambassador only in name. He had made it plain to Lansing that he did not care about his 'cases', so the Secretary channelled them through the consul-general instead. The President had no use for his representative. It would have saddened Page to know that the only effect of their last meeting was, as Lansing thought, probably to strengthen Wilson's anti-British attitude by adding to it a feeling of resentment at the seduction of his ambassador. Page himself now felt that there was nothing more he could do. It was customary for an ambassador to offer his resignation upon the forming of a new administration, whether or not there was a new President. After the election, Page made his letter of resignation more than formal. He made it a last attempt to bring the President around. He wrote in the terms in which Lansing believed himself to talk to the President of the war between

Autocracy and Democracy. He played once again the card that a complete severance of German-American relations would by itself put an end to the war. He asked for 'some sort of active and open identification with the Allies'[85] which would put America in effective protest against German frightfulness and 'in a friendly attitude to the German people themselves, as distinguished from their military rulers . . . There can be no historic approval of neutrality for years while the world is bleeding to death.' There was probably too much of it and certainly far more than the President would read. At least he read enough of it to see that it contained a resignation. He wanted to accept it but could not think of any suitable replacement. At length, after a reminder from Page, he caused Lansing to write and ask the ambassador to remain in his place. Later on 28 March 1917, when House suggested a name to him, Wilson said that recently, in a misguided moment, he had told Page he could continue; and so he supposed 'we would be compelled to have a British American representing the United States at the Court of St. James'.[86]

Undoubtedly Wilson regarded ambassadors as persons of the utmost insignificance. It was the same with Gerard. Though he was careful, because he was a courteous man, to see that they were treated properly by the State Department, he did not mind who they were. He did not communicate through their voices to the chancelleries but on paper to the world. In this form he intended to take his next diplomatic steps but to make them effective he had first to get himself elected.

In his first fight for the presidency Wilson had to struggle for the nomination and when that was secured his election followed quite easily. In his second the nomination was his as soon as in February 1916 he gave a sufficient indication that he would accept it, for he had by then made himself the unchallengeable leader of his party; but the election was one of the closest contests in the history of the United States.

For seventy years after the Civil War the Republican President was the rule and the Democratic the exception who was elected only when for some reason or other the normal Republican majority was cut down or ineffective; the fact that no Democratic President since Andrew Jackson had succeeded himself emphasized the rule. The split in the Republican party which in 1912 made Wilson's election so easy would not occur again; Roosevelt was practically back in the party, hoping to get the nomination and at first much favoured for it. So the Democrats were faced with their usual problem: could they pare enough votes off the standing Republican majority to achieve the exceptional? Their difficulties seemed at first sight to be aggravated by the

fact that Wilson's policies, both domestic and foreign, had strongly antagonized the East. But this last factor, if courageously accepted and firmly
tackled, simplified the problem and showed that the solution was to let the
East go, to rally the West, and to hope to detach from Roosevelt those progressives who disliked his return to the Republican fold. Wilson saw this
as clearly as anyone and the session of 1916 was consequently a busy one.
By the fall the Democratic majority in Congress under the leadership of the
President had put through almost every important measure in the Progressive programme of 1912.

They were not Wilson's personal policies. He had not previously shown
serious interest in any of them and some he had criticized or blocked.
Undoubtedly it was expediency that led him to have a new look at them.
When he examined them afresh he probably did not find them as distasteful
as at first sight; and he did not find it as difficult as he had imagined it would
be to take, as so many liberals were doing at the beginning of the twentieth
century, a few more steps away from *laissez-faire* towards compulsion in
social reform. But the prospect of electoral advantage stimulated him into
a nimbleness that naturally caused comment.

The Republicans' problems nearly all revolved around the personality of
Roosevelt. The Old Guard were determined that he should not get the
nomination, but their own candidate, Elihu Root, could not unite the party.
So on 10 June 1916 at their convention at Chicago they accepted as a compromise Mr. Justice Hughes. Before he was appointed to the Supreme Court in
1910 (and so detached from both sides in the quarrel of 1912), Hughes had
been the leader of the New York Republican progressives and Governor of
the State from 1906. He went to the Chicago Convention in 1916 with a
reputation very like Wilson's in 1912; he was known as a man of high intellectual quality, of great integrity, and with a degree of courage which had
enabled him as Governor to defy the bosses and introduce many reforms. At
the same time he had the reputation of being sane and sound; House thought
he could be shown up 'as a thorough conservative who obtained the name of
progressive because of his refusal to let the bosses dictate to him'.[87]

But Hughes had not the political equivalent of the gardener's green
fingers. Returning ten years later to the Supreme Court he became one of
the great chief justices; as a seeker after votes and in trying to please both
wings of his party he was a failure. For the problems created by Roosevelt
were not merely those that arose out of his personality. His adherence to the
party line and the formal disbanding of his followers could not obliterate
the gulf he had made between two schools of thought, and Hughes was
required to be both regular and progressive. Moreover, the party was
divided on foreign policy as well as on domestic. In the Republican East

sympathy was strongly for the Entente and Wilson's idea of neutrality was condemned as timid and degrading; in the Middle West Republican sentiment was all against intervention, as the party leaders had learnt in the debates in March over the resolutions to keep Americans off British ships. In particular, the big German-American vote, traditionally Republican, was against the Entente. Here again Roosevelt personified the difficulty; for while the progressives generally were for peace, he was active for intervention and so scattered confusion among his former followers. During the campaign Bernstorff wrote: 'If Hughes should be defeated, he can thank Roosevelt. The average American is and remains a pacifist.'[88]

The Democratic Convention opened at St. Louis on 14 June 1916. Wilson had himself written the party platform, and the convention was expected to be an unexciting affair in which the platform of the leader was adopted and his virtues enumerated. Martin Glynn, a former Governor of New York, made the opening speech.[89] In case there should be any feeling that Wilson's foreign policy was too timorous, Glynn had dug out of the history books a number of cases in which American Presidents had submitted to humiliation rather than resort to war, and with American thoroughness had accumulated many more precedents than he meant to use. He began with one in which a Spanish commandant had seized an American vessel and shot the captain, crew, and passengers, over fifty in all. The delegates received this with such enthusiasm that Glynn gave them two more. He would pass over the others, he said, but the delegates shouted: 'Go on, go on.' So he went through the whole list. And after a bit, as he paused after each smack of provocation, the crowd chanted: 'What did we do? What did we do?'; and Glynn bellowed back: 'We didn't go to war.' Bryan, who had disappeared from party counsels and had been rejected even as a delegate from Nebraska, was sitting in the press gallery and wept as Glynn commended to the convention a policy which had not satisfied fire-eaters and swashbucklers but had satisfied the mothers of the land at whose hearth and fireside no jingoistic war had placed an empty chair. He safeguarded the position of the fathers of the land by saying that they would fight when Reason primed the rifle, when Honour drew the sword, and when Justice breathed a blessing on the standards they upheld. The next day Senator James of Kentucky, whom the *New York Times* described as having the face of a prize-fighter and the voice of a pipe-organ, took up the theme and orchestrated it in the grand style.

Without orphaning a single American child, without widowing a single American mother, without firing a single gun, without the shedding of a single drop of blood, he wrung from the most militant spirit that ever brooded above a battlefield an acknowledgement of American rights and an agreement to American demands.

This was followed by a demonstration of twenty-one minutes and a further observation by the senator about the undesirability of the President having at the Last Judgement to exchange places with the blood-spattered monarchs of the Old World. In the evening session Bryan was brought down by acclamation from the gallery; and, being received like a soldier who has been given back his sword and the badges that were stripped from him, he orated too. 'I join with the American people in thanking God that we have a President who does not want this nation plunged into this war.' In this spirit the delegates added to the platform Wilson had drafted: 'In particular we commend to the American people the splendid diplomatic victories of our great President, who has preserved the vital interests of our Government and its citizens, and kept us out of war.'

Wilson was a little startled by this development. But it was true that he had kept the country out of war and it was certain that by June 1916 he was once more clear and undistracted in his determination to go on keeping the country out of war if he could. He could hardly be expected in an election campaign to stress the point that his efforts might not be successful. So again a decision, which had already been reached as a matter of principle, turned out to be the one that was right politically. As far back as 10 May Spring Rice had in writing of the coming electoral campaign forecast the decision correctly. 'No one can doubt', he wrote, 'the President's perfect sincerity in his desire to help in the work of peace. The highest moral principles as well as enlightened interests point that way.'[90]

On 5 July House wrote to Wilson: 'The keeping the country out of war and the great measures you have enacted into law, should be our battle-cry.'[91] But Wilson himself was at first hesitant in his use of the theme. In accordance with ritual the campaign was opened by an oratorical notification to the candidate that he had been nominated. The stage was set for this at Shadow Lawn on 2 September 1916. It was a rambling house with huge porches and great lawns which gave room enough for the 15,000 people assembled for the occasion, and after a suitable introduction by a brass band, whose parade was led by the convert Nugent, Senator James opened the formal dialogue in the customary way.[92] Wilson accepted the nomination in a quiet speech in the course of which he reviewed unemotionally his policy of neutrality. In his next campaign speech on 23 September he spoke only on domestic issues. The speech after that on 30 September was again tuned to domestic issues with a strong bid for the progressive vote. But at the end of it he referred, apparently extemporaneously, to foreign policy, saying that if the Republican party was put into power, there would be a radical change. The country would be drawn, in one form or another, into the embroilments of the European war. Some young men, he said (he was talking to the Young Men's Democratic League), ought to be interested in that. Soft though the reference was, it was loud enough for ears that were stretched. House was no doubt interpreting the general effect of it when he referred to it as a declaration that Hughes's election would mean war. The Colonel, whose anxiety to get Wilson re-elected transcended for the time being his interest in getting America into the war, wrote to Wilson that the Republicans were much concerned with his declaration; he suggested that he should emphasize the point again. Wilson did so, though still not quite bluntly. In a speech on 7 October, he said that the reversal of his policy, which the Republican leader was insisting on, could only be a reversal from peace to war. This was the go-ahead for full amplification. It seemed as if campaign managers and orators had only been waiting for the signal that Wilson would not disapprove. Instructions were given to highlight the peace issue. They were hardly needed by Bryan who was back in his old form and stumping the Middle West on the theme. 'I cannot refrain from dropping you at least a line to express my admiration of the admirable campaign you are conducting', Wilson wrote to him. Five million copies of Glynn's speech were distributed in New York alone. No election address seemed to be complete without some reference to the peace issue. A pamphlet on social reform reminded mothers that Wilson had saved their children from mines, mills, and sweat shops just as he had saved their sons and their husbands from unrighteous battlefields. Three days before polling day a four-page advertisement in the newspapers shouted at the electors: 'If you want WAR vote for HUGHES! If you want peace with honour VOTE FOR WILSON!'

Wilson was obviously glad enough to leave these developments to those who were better masters than himself of stridency. He got the benefit of the issue without giving a personal pledge; he did not get nearer to that than to say that he was not expecting the country to get into the war.

Democratic progressivism competed quite strongly with peace with honour as an electoral attraction. On 31 October eleven out of the nineteen members of the committee that wrote the progressive platform of 1912 issued an appeal for Wilson. Some came reluctantly and with suspicion but they came. Herbert Croly wrote of Wilson: 'The old individualist partisan Democrat, with a political philosophy derived from the Virginia Bill of Rights, is developing into a modern Social Democrat, but the transition is incomplete, and Mr. Wilson expresses himself either in the old language or the new, according to the needs of the occasion.'[93] Walter Lippmann, the other editor of *The New Republic*, the chief organ of progressivism, declared: 'I shall vote not for the Wilson who has uttered a few too many noble sentiments, but for the Wilson who is evolving under experience.'[94] For the general public the attraction was the promise of social justice for the small man against the industrial and commercial interests that dominated the Republican party. Statisticians calculated after the election that Wilson's vote included about 20 per cent of the former progressive vote.

Organization was of course not neglected. Colonel House took a big part in it and claimed to be chiefly responsible for the strategy of the campaign. On 20 June he drew up a plan in which he divided the states into three classes according to the degree of effort needed in each and specified the sort of work that should be done in each. Wilson interested himself very keenly in the choice of party chairman. He pressed House to take it himself, but House insisted that his health would not stand the strain of routine. House, with his eye always on the progressive vote, wanted a man of liberal views. Wilson more appreciative than he had been in 1912 of the workings of the machine, was anxious lest the man chosen should be too 'highbrow' and perhaps intolerant of the 'rougher elements'.[95] But Wilson's personal interest in the campaign—not only did he nominate Glynn and vet his convention speech, but he chose also the chairmen of some of the state conventions—did not mean that he had abandoned all loftier conceptions of the democratic process. On 2 November towards the end of the campaign House recorded:

> The President thought organisation amounted to nothing, and that the people determined such matters themselves. . . . To hear him talk, you would think the man in the street understood the theory and philosophy of government as he does and was actuated by the same motives.[96]

But maybe Wilson was provoked into this statement of electoral simplicities. For this was the day of a great New York rally, elaborately timetabled by House even down to the minutes available for cheering, to which Wilson had unwillingly submitted

> after the most acrimonious debate I have had with him for a long while. . . . I hope everything will work out as planned, though there is a danger it will not—for much must depend upon luck, as matters are supposed to happen spontaneously which are really prepared far in advance.[97]

House was gratified to find that everything went off with a high degree of precision. But he did not of course go to the meeting himself. 'I merely looked in to hear the cheering, and to find that everything was going as planned, and then left for home.' The Colonel regarded a Wilson victory as 'practically certain': so he told Commander Gaunt, the British Naval Intelligence man, on 1 November.[98] He had divided the states into 'certains' and 'doubtfuls' and calculated that out of the 175 votes from the doubtfuls Wilson needed only 34 to win.

There was a lot of anti-Wilson muck-raking. President Hibben of Princeton was approached from Republican headquarters in New York in an attempt to obtain authoritative confirmation of former President Cleveland's charges against Wilson in 1910. He was revolted by the suggestion that they should be used in the campaign and said so. The Peck affair had got about and gossip did not stop at ribaldries, such as allusions to Wilson's 'Peckadillos' and sly references to him as 'Peck's Bad Boy'.[99] It was said that he had bought Mrs. Peck off for $75,000. Worse slanders charged him with infidelities to his first wife descending from adultery to neglect of her grave. Colonel House found a way of answering these without further publicizing the lies. He got Stockton Axson to write an article under the title 'Mr. Wilson as seen by One of His Family Circle'. He edited it himself, cutting out what he called the sob stuff, and it was extensively published.

Wilson, though deeply distressed, ignored in public, as was his habit, all attacks upon him and dealt out generalities. The decision to throw over the East enabled him to hit hard at the same targets all the time, while Hughes could never deliver a knock-out blow lest he floored a supporter as well as an opponent. When Wilson was sent an offensive telegram by an anti-British agitator called O'Leary, he shot back: 'I would feel deeply mortified to have you or anybody like you vote for me. Since you have access to many disloyal Americans and I have not, I will ask you to convey this message to them.'[100] Hughes could do nothing like that. He had to keep within the fold of 'a strict and honest neutrality', as prescribed by the Republican platform, the German and Irish voters, and the Roosevelt musketeers.

Theodore Roosevelt went further than most of his party dared to follow. Wilson and he had for each other the mutual hatred of two rival gospellers. Both were idealists proclaiming different creeds; Mr. Osgood has brilliantly compared them to Nietzsche's Warrior and Priest.[101] For Roosevelt manliness was all: the sign as well of the Victorian gentleman as of the medieval knight; chivalrous and just, tender to the weak, and unsparing of the bully; courage the supreme virtue, cowardice a disfiguring vice, and dishonour the worst fate. A man who submitted to insult lost his virtue and was thereby deflowered like a woman raped. Wilson, the college milksop, who turned the other cheek, who argued instead of acting, and who talked of being too proud to fight, would have got Roosevelt's hearty contempt even if he had kept his ideas to himself. But he was using them to demoralize the nation: he was persuading America that oppression and brutality were no concern of hers, that it was better to submit comfortably than to challenge them, that battle was at any cost to be avoided, and even that it was a noble thing to hang over the arena boasting of clean hands and lecturing the combatants. Such talk was like a castration. It seemed to Roosevelt that the nation was in terrible peril of losing its virility, and that without virility a nation, like a man, must perish miserably.

Perhaps Roosevelt's ideals were a bastard Christianity: certainly what lay between the two men was the age-old divide between the Christ who came with the sword and He who spoke upon the mount. In the end Wilson preached a harder gospel and more profound: and in the end 'the American people were neither so heroic as the Warrior nor so exalted as the Priest'.[102] But in 1916 Wilson appeared mainly as a negative force identified as 'the man who kept us out of war'. That was an evasion that Roosevelt strove against with all his might, and to him the election seemed a struggle between good and evil for the nation's soul. He too could perorate as well as the convention orators of St. Louis. At the end of his last speech in the campaign he remembered the name of Shadow Lawn, and he cried out:

There should be shadows enough at Shadow Lawn; the shadows of men, women and children who have risen from the ooze of the ocean bottom and from graves in foreign lands; . . . the shadows of deeds that were never done; the shadows of lofty words that were followed by no action; the shadows of the tortured dead.[103]

Poor Hughes, straddled between two extreme positions, could hardly say anything that was worth attention; and Wilson was not being too contemptuous when he justified his policy of leaving his opponent's speeches unanswered by saying that it was a good rule not to murder a man who was committing suicide.[104] Nevertheless, most impartial observers thought that the normal Republican majority would decide the result, though by a small margin. The betting in Wall Street at the end was 10 to $8\frac{1}{2}$ in favour of Hughes. Wilson was waiting calmly at Shadow Lawn having refused to have a special wire laid on. Most of the early results came from the East and they showed that the Republican majorities were ominously large. Then at 7 p.m. New York, by far the most important of the 'doubtfuls', declared for Hughes by a substantial majority. This was bad enough, for a presidential victory without New York was almost unknown; it was worse when other big 'doubtfuls' followed suit—Connecticut and New Jersey in the East and Indiana and Illinois in the Middle West. Most Democrats lost heart; and even House, though none of his 'certain' states had defaulted (none ever did), began to feel that defeat was imminent.[105] At ten o'clock the *New York Times* delivered an unqualified verdict for Hughes, and then the *World*, the chief Democratic organ, conceded the election. A thousand Republicans, preceded by two bands, marched to Hughes's hotel, but he was too wise to appear. Roosevelt was less cautious and issued a statement expressing his thankfulness for the 'vindication of our national honor' and denying that he intended to have a hand in Hughes's appointments.[106] Grayson conveyed the news to Shadow Lawn, where they were playing Twenty Questions,[107] and proffered words of consolation which seemed not to be needed. Wilson drank a glass of milk, declining sandwiches and ginger ale, and went to bed. The only thing that seemed to disturb him was what he regarded as the almost certain prospect of war. He had decided, following on a suggestion made by House, that if he were defeated he would not remain in office until the last day of his term on 4 March 1917. He considered the international situation to be far too perilous to be left to a 'lame duck'. Under the Constitution, as it then was, the only way in which he could provide for the victor's immediate succession was to appoint him Secretary of State, whereafter he and the Vice-President would resign, the next in succession being the Secretary. He put the plan in a letter to Lansing on 5 November. When he wrote the letter the odds were against him; it was not the action of a man who, as his opponents suggested, habitually put himself above country.

At the White House Tumulty, attacked by newspapermen who demanded to know if he was ready to 'throw up the sponge', had, he said, to steady himself at his desk to conceal his emotion as he dictated the statement 'Wilson Will Win'.[108] Later that night and during the next day, while he sat at his desk sleepless and without food, he was sustained by telephone messages from a mysterious stranger who assured him that all would be well. True enough, on the next day, 8 November, when the results from the far West began to come in, certainty receded. At the midnight between 8 and 9 November Wilson was narrowly in the lead with 251 electoral votes to Hughes's 247 and 33 still doubtful. Then in the morning, New Mexico and North Dakota, two doubtful states, went for Wilson by narrow majorities. In the evening the Republican chairman for California, the biggest remaining 'doubtful', conceded the state to Wilson. By the end of that day, 9 November, it was safe to assume his victory. He had gone to Williamstown to be godfather at the baptism of a new granddaughter, Jessie's child, and Tumulty sent him a telegram: 'The cause you so nobly represented at last triumphed and we greet you.'[109] Hughes, cautious to the end, did not send his telegram of congratulation till 22 November. 'It was', Wilson said to one of his family, 'a little moth-eaten when it got here but quite legible.'[110]

Wilson ended with 277 electoral votes against 254 for Hughes. His popular vote was $6\frac{1}{2}$ per cent higher than Hughes and nearly half as much again as the vote he got in the split election of 1912.

It was a personal rather than a party victory and indeed in Congress it was a defeat. The Democratic majority in the Senate was reduced to eight. In the House the Republicans led the Democrats by four; but there were five members unaligned. Historians may mark the election, as Page did at the time, as the one in which were laid the foundations of the new Democratic party, which was to become under Franklin D. Roosevelt and his successors the party of the majority as for the half-century before the Republicans had been. It began the combination of the South and the West and the diversion into the Democratic party of liberal and progressive sentiments on which its future electoral triumphs were founded.

It was a victory for peace and progressivism and little else was talked of during the campaign. But Wilson put a greater issue squarely before the electorate. He wrote into the Democratic platform his doctrine that it was the duty of the United States to assist the world in securing settled peace and justice. Their duty is, he wrote, 'to join the other nations of the world in any feasible association that will effectively serve those principles, to maintain inviolate the complete security of the highway of the seas for the common and unhindered use of all nations'.[111] He added—but the words were too strong meat and were painlessly excised at an early stage—'and to prevent any war begun either contrary to treaty covenants or without warning and frank submission of the provocation and causes to the opinion of mankind'. But Wilson fed the country with it in his speeches. He said on 5 October:

It is our duty to lend the full force of this nation, moral and physical, to a league of nations which shall see to it that nobody disturbs the peace of the world without submitting his case first to the opinion of mankind.[112]

He said the same thing again at Cincinnati on 26 October, telling his audience that the business of neutrality was over.[113]

XVII

PEACE SENTIMENTS

Bethmann's peace plans – the rise of Hindenburg and Ludendorff – Wilson postpones his peace move – military stalemate: General Robertson – Lloyd George and the knock-out blow – the submarine peril – the financial peril – the Lansdowne Memorandum – the last of Grey – peace sentiment among the belligerents – Wilson prepares his Note – House disagrees

IN October 1916, while Wilson was in the midst of his election fight, there flew into Shadow Lawn a brace of doves seeking an olive branch, first Bernstorff and then Gerard. These overtures might of course have been, as they had before, escapades started by Gerard's gullibility or Bernstorff's guile. In fact on this occasion they were due to the deliberate decision of Bethmann approved by the Supreme Command; and the Kaiser himself had on 9 October drawn up a memorandum for the President to see. How did it come about that the German Government, whose instructions to Bernstorff only four months before had been to warn Wilson off mediation, was now making an approach?

Bethmann's great victory at Charleville on 5 May 1916 which resulted in the *Sussex* settlement had achieved his immediate object of postponing unrestricted U-boat war but it had neither defeated nor dispersed his opponents. On the contrary, it consolidated the forces in favour of all-out war, now not merely the Army and the Navy but all the political right and some of the centre, and brought them to appreciate that, if they were to succeed in their objectives, they must get rid of Bethmann. The political unity in which the war began had been broken in the spring of 1916. There were now a right, a left, and a centre; and the two points on which the right and the left were most acutely divided were the submarine and war aims— whether or not there should be annexations and indemnities. On the first of these points Bethmann and the Socialists were quite at one, and on the second he was closer to the left than to the right; and it had always been a cornerstone of his policy to keep in with the Socialists since he believed that in the long run the war could not be successfully waged without the support of the working class. As seen from the right Bethmann was now a menace to a victorious peace. The best weapon they had for defeating him was the agitation in favour of the submarine war where they could now command the vocal support of the Army and Navy and much of the press. If in the Reichstag they could obtain enough support in the centre to out-vote Bethmann on this issue, sooner or later he would go. He held his office by the confidence of the Kaiser, not of the Reichstag, but, if he lost command of the Reichstag, his usefulness to the Kaiser would be catastrophically diminished. He was, however, a skilful and determined political fighter and in a series of intricate manœuvres throughout the summer he kept his foes in the Reichstag at bay. Meanwhile, pressure was being maintained by the Navy supported by Falkenhayn. The Battle of the Somme had begun on 1 July 1916 and Falkenhayn was demanding that something be done to interfere with the cross-channel flow of supplies. Submarine commanders complained that they had to let steamer after steamer pass for fear that there might be an American on board. They believed that the British planted Americans, but anyway they had no way of telling. The situation was ripe for another confrontation before the Kaiser and it was set for 29 August 1916 at Pless Castle in Silesia, the Kaiser's headquarters in the East. Just before it took place there occurred the event that was to be decisive in the struggle.

For some time past, and especially since the failure at Verdun, Falkenhayn's position had been insecure. Bethmann—not merely because the General was no longer an ally in the U-boat controversy, but also because the Chancellor was among those who were dissatisfied with his conduct of the war—had been pressing on the vacillations of the Kaiser to dismiss him. The alternative Bethmann had in mind, indeed the only possible alternative, was General von Hindenburg who commanded in the East. The metamorphosis in his mid fifties of Woodrow Wilson from professor to President was rapid enough, but it appears as a stream of events in slow motion when put by the side of the one stroke of fortune which catapulted Paul von Hindenburg into fame at the age of sixty-seven with an impetus which was not exhausted until as President of the German Reich he sank into senility twenty years later. In August 1914 he was a lieutenant-general, three years retired, living quietly in Hanover, looking back on a career which 'had carried me much farther than I had ever dared to hope',[1] with no achievement to his credit beyond the rank he had attained, an elderly officer wondering like so many others when the war broke out whether there was going to be a job for him to do. On 22 August the job was found and a week later the old dug-out was the hero of Tannenberg. It was a victory to which he contributed something, chiefly his steady nerve, but not much.

The story is made more rather than less dramatic by eschewing any romantic revelation of military talents buried in routine and raised miraculously from the grave. Hindenburg in this battle and in the others that followed was just what he had always been, sober and steady, the ideal provider of the lax control and the bountiful sustenance needed by the nervous genius of his Chief of Staff, Major-General Erich Ludendorff. When in August 1914 there was a *crise de nerfs* in the headquarters of the Eastern Command, Ludendorff, a young general, barely fifty, just decorated for capturing the citadel of Liège on the Belgian front, was selected to take charge. Hindenburg was the figurehead who in accordance with German army practice was found for him. He had all the qualifications for that; he came of a Prussian military family, not wealthy but impeccably aristocratic whose ancestors had been among the Teutonic Knights. He looked as Germany thought a German general ought to look, a degree of corpulence, a heavy and immovable face, and a moustache of the right size and shape, the extremes pointing upwards toward the helmet. He was indeed the sort of German the Kaiser ought to have been, no fool, and giving the appearance of being wiser than he was, calm and collected always, the nineteenth-century constitutional monarch who acted on the advice of his minister Ludendorff. The Kaiser had of course the mystique of royalty to which Hindenburg himself paid great devotion; but aside from that, by 1916 the legendary Hindenburg had become the man to whom the whole country looked for salvation. Starting as the figurehead of Ludendorff, he became the figurehead of the German nation.

On 27 August 1916 Roumania, stimulated by the successes of General Brusilov in a Russian offensive against Austria in June, at last decided to chance her arm and declare war on the Central Powers. The Kaiser was upset by the event. He had not, he felt, been sufficiently warned by Falkenhayn of its imminence. This misdemeanour shook the Kaiser and at last toppled the Commander-in-Chief. He was dismissed on 29 August and his place taken by Hindenburg with Ludendorff. Bethmann had cultivated good relations with Hindenburg and believed him to be somewhat of his way of thinking; the Chancellor had told House, for example, when he was in Berlin the previous January, that Hindenburg would support moderate war aims.[2] But Bethmann's hopes for aid from this quarter were almost immediately cast down. Hindenburg, who took Falkenhayn's place at the conference table at Pless, declared himself on 31 August as a strong supporter of the U-boat war.[3] He stipulated only that the decision should be postponed for a short time, one week or two, until the shape of the Roumanian campaign could be seen. The Field-Marshal was not mistaken in asking only for a week or two. Luckier and more accommodating than most deposed generals, Falkenhayn was offered and accepted the command in the Roumanian campaign and discharged his task with such ruthless efficiency that by the end of the year Roumania was virtually out of the war.

Bethmann could not vie with Hindenburg as he had with Falkenhayn; the Field-Marshal's position in the country was far too strong; the Kaiser would have risked his crown if he had dismissed him. Nevertheless, the Chancellor did not give up the fight against what he firmly believed would be the downfall of Germany. Resourcefully he changed his strategy. He disengaged himself as far as possible from the U-boat controversy, adopting a judicial attitude, so as to minimize the injury to his political position if the decision went in favour of the U-boat. At the same time he tried to move the action to another field. If President Wilson were to make a call for peace, it might well postpone the U-boat decision, and shift the discussion from the issue in which the military voice was now predominant to questions of war aims where Bethmann could claim more strongly to be heard and where a nation that was beginning to be war-weary would not so easily allow him to be subdued.

Bethmann's attitude towards Wilson was not in fact very different from Britain's. Neither side wanted Wilson to propose terms of peace, Britain because she knew they would not be favourable enough for the Allies and Germany because she rightly suspected that they would give her far less than she wanted. But neither side wished to lose the help of the United States in the last resort: Britain if she was in peril of defeat and needed American help to avert it; and Germany if, having failed to make peace with one or more of her enemies separately, she was driven into general negotiations. What Germany wanted to avoid, whether she treated in general or in particular, was negotiating from weakness. She did not herself wish to ask for terms. If she could not get any of her enemies to sue, the only alternative was to get a neutral to propose talks. The function which Germany was willing to see discharged by the United States was that of getting the belligerents round a table: that and no more. But as 1916 progressed Bethmann became not only willing but anxious for that. Since the beginning of the year he had been apprehensive about the prospects of the Central Powers in a war of exhaustion. Financially and economically, he contemplated failure in the autumn, though he thought it likely that 'if driven to the wall', they could last still longer.[4] His attempts in 1915 to detach Russia or France from the Entente had failed; and though renewed sporadically in 1916, nothing came of them. The drawn battle of Verdun seemed to stalemate military operations.

At Charleville in the evening of 1 May 1916, the Chancellor talked with Gerard about the President and peace. Saying that Germany had won enough to talk peace without suspicion of weakness, he expressed the hope that the President would take it up and that Colonel House might come again. The hint promptly reached House who promptly took it up with Bernstorff who promptly reported to the Wilhelmstrasse House's understanding that 'we were willing to accept peace mediation by the President'.[5] This, Bethmann replied on 6 May, was premature. A visit from House would be 'very welcome at any time',[6] but Wilson must take some open action against England before he could be accepted by the German people as unbiased. Bernstorff, reporting on the address of 27 May, said that what the President was considering was a conference at The Hague in which the neutrals would participate only in the discussion of the freedom of the seas; the United States would take no part in the actual settlement of the peace conditions.[7] Jagow seems not to have taken this in. In a directive which he dispatched on 7 June regarding 'Mr. Wilson's plans for mediation', he repeated the familiar German objections.[8] The President, so partial to England and so naïve, would be concerned to construct peace on the basis of the *status quo ante* which was not acceptable to Germany. If, therefore, his mediation plans threatened to assume 'a more concrete form' the ambassador must prevent him 'from approaching us with a positive proposal of mediation'. Bernstorff was puzzled by this and in a letter written on 13 July asked exactly what it meant.[9] In common with everyone else in America who so much as dabbled in politics, he assumed that Wilson would for election purposes make some sort of a peace initiative. He pointed out that Wilson was not interested in territorial questions; 'he only wants to play the peacemaker':[10] that, if it led to success, was all that was necessary to assure his election. Was he, the ambassador wanted to know, to stand in the way of such proceedings? Bethmann saw this letter, which was sent by ordinary mail, after he had had news of despondency in Austria coupled with the suggestion that the Central Powers should bestir themselves for peace. On 18 August he instructed Bernstorff by cable that he was ready to accept 'mediation by the President with a view to initiate peace negotiations between the belligerents'; and indeed that this should be encouraged.[11] But in any general peace conference, he said, the participation of neutrals would be acceptable only on general questions such as the freedom of the seas and disarmament. From a conversation which he had on 25 August[12] it is clear that Bethmann was still thinking in terms of a victorious peace though with gains substantially smaller than in the September Programme;* he still wanted the Briey territory but thought that some of Alsace-Lorraine might have to be given up in exchange for it. After the Pless Conference on 31 August, when his hopes of Hindenburg had been shattered, he was prepared to go still

* See p. 242 above.

further. The only way to peace, he told Helfferich then, was through Wilson and it must be taken however uncertain the prospects: it would mean the restoration of Belgium, though subject to some special relationship to be decided in direct negotiation with her.[13] On 2 September in another cable to Bernstorff he put the point directly.[14] He hoped to conclude peace before winter, he said. Would Wilson's mediation be possible and successful if the unconditional restoration of Belgium was guaranteed? Otherwise the U-boat war would have to be carried on in dead earnest. He asked for the ambassador's personal opinion.

The Bernstorffs got themselves invited to lunch at the Houses' summer resort in New Hampshire on 3 September and the Count and the Colonel had a long talk.[15] There would be no mediation until after the election, the Colonel said. The Entente would not be interested just after Roumania's entry into the war and anyway would pay no heed to a presidential candidate; if Wilson was re-elected he would take immediate steps. After that the talk passed to Hindenburg's appointment and to the cause of the war and its future course. He had tentacles reaching into each of the belligerent countries House said, and although in Sunapee quietly resting, he was in close touch with affairs. Bernstorff smiled and answered that it was not necessary to tell him that. The only one of the ambassadors, House noted, 'who has retained his equilibrium and has been able to smile upon the present and philosophize as to the future'.[16]

Bernstorff telegraphed to Bethmann the answer he had got about mediation.[17] He added in a second telegram that if America concerned herself at all with territorial questions, the restoration of Belgium would be her principal interest; and that the attainment of peace through the U-boat war seemed hopeless since the United States would inevitably be drawn in, whatever the result of the election.

Bethmann was not content with the prospect of post-election mediation and decided that more vigorous steps must be taken to galvanize Wilson. On 23 September he approached the Kaiser for authority to make an advance and submitted a draft of instructions to Bernstorff. The draft was revised by the Kaiser himself as well as by Ludendorff to remove what they felt was an implication of weakness. The revised instructions,[18] sent to Bernstorff on 25 September, began with the statement that although the Central Powers were doing very well in the war, it was doubtful whether they could win such a success as to end the war within the year unless they resorted to unrestricted U-boat war. The situation would be changed if the President were to make a proposal for peace mediation. If, however, he desired to wait until shortly before or after his election, it would be too late; Germany was not in a position to remain quiet any longer and must take advantage of the freedom of action preserved in her *Sussex* Note. The ambassador was instructed to 'cautiously discuss' the matter with Colonel House. A peace move by the President, the cable said in conclusion, 'which would appear spontaneous to those viewing it from without', would be given the most serious consideration and should be good for Wilson's election campaign. Gerard, the cable said finally, had asked for leave.

This last sentence referred to a matter that had been afoot for a little time previously. Gerard was not liked in Berlin;[19] and undoubtedly he was undiplomatic, tactless, excitable, and more hostile than not. Even Zimmermann, with whom he got on best, wished that he would not lose his temper. The Germans wanted him recalled and Bernstorff had raised the matter with House. House said that that was impossible but prescribed the same treatment as for a different ailment was being given to Page. While Page was to take the waters of American opinion, a sojourn in America for Gerard would, it was hoped according to Bernstorff, give his nerves 'a chance to rest'.[20] House later suspected unjustly that all this was a deep-laid plot to get Gerard to Washington where he could reinforce Bernstorff's efforts to get the President to act. At least there is no doubt that Bethmann wanted to use the opportunity. Jagow had a talk with Gerard on 25 September and as a result the ambassador cabled the State Department[21] that Germany was anxious to make peace and would accept in general terms a tender of good offices; but there must be no hint that the suggestion came from Berlin or that it was not the spontaneous act of the President. Gerard left from Copenhagen on a Danish ship on 28 September and arrived in New York on 11 October.

Bernstorff was told in his instructions to 'act cautiously' and for once in a way he did. The Foreign Office had slipped the words into the final version of the cable, intending them apparently as a warning to the ambassador against talking too loudly about the resumption of U-boat warfare.[22] Bernstorff, understandably enough, failed to catch this point. The Kaiser's and Ludendorff's stiffening amendments allowed no hint of Bethmann's anxiety to seep through. So Bernstorff repeated the question without added emphasis and received the same answer as before, that is, that there was nothing doing until after the election. He cabled home on 5 October that the situation was unchanged.[23]

The Kaiser at this time was not merely unbellicose but quite maudlin on the subject of peace, a mood which lasted until the fortunes of war began to change with the triumph in Roumania. He is said to have burst into tears on one occasion when peace was mentioned:[24] and on 31 October he wrote to Bethmann about an effort for peace being a moral act and 'appropriate for a monarch who had a soul' and 'the will to liberate the world from its sorrows'. He composed in his own English, which was excellent, a memorandum to be given to Gerard, reminding him of their talk at Charleville and wondering when the President intended to act for peace since 'the German Government foresees the time at which it will be forced to regain the freedom of action that it has reserved to itself in the Note of 4 May last'.[25] Bethmann managed it so that the memorandum was not given to Gerard before he left; the Chancellor feared that the President might be put off by the threat of renewal of the U-boat war which Gerard might over-emphasize. So it was sent to Bernstorff on 9 October with a covering telegram saying it was addressed by the Kaiser to Gerard but that Bernstorff was not to deliver it if he thought it too risky and was to say that it was not to be understood as a threat of a U-boat war. Bernstorff thought it far too dangerous to be handled by Gerard who had just given his sensational interview from the ship which brought him to New York.* So he gave the memorandum to House who sent it direct to the President, having first shown it to Gerard. House noted it in his diary on 19 October as 'a threat to resume submarine warfare in the event the President does not immediately intervene'.[26]

On 9 October Bernstorff had an audience at Shadow Lawn arranged some time before in connection with Polish relief.[27] Though the President spoke very seriously about the U53, the Count found him 'unusually pleasant'. He stated that he had but one wish, to remain neutral and help bring the war to an end; neither side could win a decisive victory. He said repeatedly that he was holding himself ready to mediate, giving the ambassador the impression that he would like to be urged directly; the ambassador said that there was no likelihood of such an appeal by the belligerent powers. Bernstorff telegraphed all this to Berlin.

Bethmann's anxiety was increasing. Hindenburg's attitude towards the U-boat war, as expressed at the Pless Conference, was not of course known to the Chancellor's political opponents who still believed, as the Chancellor had done, that the new appointment might mean an accession of strength for him. Even so they continued to gather support from the Centre. On 7 October the Centre party adopted a resolution in the following terms:

> For the political decision concerning the conduct of the war the Chancellor alone is responsible to the Reichstag. The decision of the Chancellor will have to be supported basically by the conclusion of the Supreme Command. If the decision is against the conduct of a ruthless U-boat war, then the Chancellor may be sure of the agreement of the Reichstag.[28]

On 11 October this resolution was adopted by the Reichstag. The implication

---

* See p. 501 above.

was plain that the Reichstag would accept the view of the Supreme Command whichever way it went and Bethmann knew very well which way it was going to go. On 14 October he cabled to Bernstorff that a definite proposal by Germany for peace mediation was impossible. But he requested again that the President be further encouraged to make 'a spontaneous appeal', if not alone, then in conjunction with the Pope, the King of Spain, and any other neutrals, which 'would assure him of re-election and a place in history'.[29] But Bernstorff cabled back on 20 October that it was not to be expected.

On 24 October Gerard went to Shadow Lawn and talked with the President for the better part of a day. Except for the reports from House, it was the first time Wilson had ever talked with anyone familiar with the German scene and he wanted a lot of information. Nothing that was said, however, altered his decision to leave his intervention until after the election. Yet he was plainly excited at the challenge that he would have to meet if he was President for a second term. On 4 November he wrote to a friend: 'The minute the campaign is over I shall be obliged to prepare some of the most important papers I have yet had to prepare.'[30]

The year 1916 went no better for the Allies than for the Central Powers and it had been a particularly disappointing year for Britain. Her navy, the pride of her imperial power, and her new army, the pick of the nation, the volunteers of 1914, had both fought big battles with indecisive results. The Battle of Jutland on 31 May was the last of the great sea battles in the old style that was ever to be fought. It proved to the German Navy that it had not a superiority in skill or equipment sufficient to offset its numerical inferiority to the Grand Fleet. So Britannia without further challenge ruled the waves for the rest of the war. But it had not been the great naval victory which the British public expected. The public too had high hopes of the year in which with Kitchener's army Britain would, for the first time in the war, exert to the full her military might. Kitchener himself at the beginning of the year had thought it possible that a spring offensive would drive Germany in August to ask for terms which she would first reject but by the end of the year might be forced to swallow. The Battle of the Somme did not begin until 1 July and it expired in the winter rains in mid November. As in the Battle of Verdun earlier in the year, the enormous casualties were about equal on both sides and the territorial gains equally negligible. The Prime Minister's eldest son, Raymond, the nonpareil of his generation, was among the killed. The winnings claimed by Haig, the Commander-in-Chief, were incorporeal and based on judgements sustainable by expectation rather than by evidence, 'a sensible depreciation' of enemy morale, disproof of German invincibility, the demonstration of 'the fighting power of the British race', and so forth.[31] The modesty of the achievement ought not to have surprised the Cabinet for they were quite commensurate with the hopes held out by General Robertson, the Chief of Staff, before the battle began. He had told them that there was not the superiority to obtain a decisive result and that the objectives of the offensive were to relieve the pressure on France and Italy and to inflict as heavy losses as possible upon the German armies. What appalled most of the Cabinet, now that the battle was over, was the realization of the terrible price that had been paid; and what depressed them was the realization that the generals were thinking only of some more of the medicine that seemed to be killing the doctor as well as the patient. 'We shall commence next year's campaign', the Commander-in-Chief wrote, 'with increased knowledge, increased prestige, and a definite balance of morale on our side.' How much further increase of knowledge, prestige, and morale was needed for victory; how much more slaughter to leave a balance large enough to obtain the decisive result? Lloyd George had never believed in the offensive anyway and was saying so to his confidants as early as January 1916. Lunching with Hankey on 1 November he called it 'a bloody and disastrous failure'.[32] Hankey could not offer much comfort. He wrote in his diary: 'The General Staff are so intolerably complacent and self-satisfied that they won't listen to any outside view. Meanwhile they are bleeding us to death . . .'[33]

The fountain-head of the complacency and self-satisfaction was General Robertson, who throughout 1916 was the man who mattered most in Britain. The man whom the public believed to be directing the war until his death on 6 July 1916 was of course Kitchener, the Secretary of State for War. But Kitchener, suffering from an inability to communicate or delegate, was by the middle of 1915 a spent force. When Robertson was made Chief of Staff in November 1915 he stipulated successfully for an increase over his predecessor's powers at the expense of the Secretary of State. 'Wully' Robertson was the first trooper in the British Army to produce a marshal's baton from his knapsack. He had great natural ability and force of character as strong as his vision was limited. His work had been in intelligence and administration (before his appointment as Chief of Staff he had been the extremely successful Quartermaster-General with the British Army in France), and neither his tactical nor his strategical abilities had ever before been tested. He was perhaps not therefore a soldier's soldier and he certainly was not a politician's soldier. To the French he was General Non-Non; and if he elaborated at all on the negative, it was not usually to say more than 'I've 'eard different'. The Prime Minister believed that military operations should be left to soldiers and in accordance with his usual practice gave Robertson 'confidence and a free hand'.[34]

But the Asquithian way of winning the war, the free hand for the generals and for the rest the slow decomposition of difficulties and the gentle stirring of stagnations, was falling into increasing disrepute. Hankey wrote in his diary on 10 November:

> These have been really dreadful War Committees . . . hopelessly congested . . . I could not get a meeting for tomorrow because X was going for a day's shooting, Lord Y for a weekend, and Lord Z to address his former constituents . . . Today's meeting had to end soon after 1 p.m. to enable Ministers to attend official luncheons . . . Thus and thus is the British Empire governed at a critical stage of the war. I have done all I can to get meetings to crystallise woolly discussions into clear-cut decisions, and to promote concord—but the task is a Herculean one'.[35]

Hankey wrote also of Asquith 'writing answers to Parliamentary questions all the time, with the result that the discussion was never kept to the point'.[35a] It was not that Asquith's powers were failing but that the methods of government to which alone his mind was attuned were not answering. His position rested precariously on the lack of an acceptable alternative. Bonar Law had not in him the stuff of a war leader and his modesty prevented him from imagining otherwise. And Lloyd George? Lloyd George was in a state of dithering frustration. He scarcely ever attended Cabinet meetings. He felt, and said quite freely, that Britain was losing the war. He talked continually of resigning. When Kitchener died, he was in the public eye the obvious successor as War Secretary. After first tendering his resignation from the Government and then trying but failing to get Robertson's powers reduced, Lloyd George took the place because he could not afford to let anyone else have it. Thereafter he talked again of resigning. He knew that he ought to be at the summit and he could not see that the only thing that prevented him from walking right up to it was his own reputation for untrustworthiness, which his current behaviour was doing nothing to diminish. He could not make up his mind about the best way to get into Number 10 Downing Street, whether by leaving the Government, rousing the country and taking the place by storm from outside, or by dislodging the occupant from within. As Law put it on November 9: 'Lloyd George is at the same time the right hand man to the Prime Minister, and the leader of the Opposition.'[36]

On 28 September Lloyd George took a step of the sort that was so intensely disliked by his colleagues and which he himself described mildly as causing 'a great deal of perturbation and animadversion'.[37] It was a step which, whether designedly or not, placed him in a good position for an advance on Downing Street, whether from within or without the Government. Asquith's resolution to fight to a finish was as strong as Lloyd George's and more likely to endure, for on this issue Asquith saw only the straight road ahead while Lloyd George's roving eye might well alight on a diversion into peacemaking. But in the public mind Asquith was now thought of as irresolute and Lloyd George as the man with 'fire in his belly'. In September 1916, to use again the language of Lloyd George, 'the highest political circles were sibilant with peace whispers'.[38] The sibilations dated from 7 August, when the Foreign Office completed a massive memorandum, called after its authors the Paget–Tyrrell Memorandum, entitled 'Suggested Bases for a Territorial Settlement in Europe', which discussed a settlement dominated by the principle of nationality but tempered by the claims of the Allies, the two to be reconciled in the light of 'circumstances generally and British interests in particular'.[39] On 29 August Montagu in a Cabinet paper dashed off some generalizations about exacting from Germany everything that could be exacted;[40] and on 30 August Asquith asked the members of the War Council to express their views as to the terms on which peace might be concluded.[41] On 31 August General Robertson submitted a paper with the interesting suggestion that Germany should be left reasonably strong on land but weakened at sea.[42] Memoranda flowed in from Balfour and Lansdowne.[43]

About this time too speculations about Wilson making a pre-election offer were crossing the Atlantic. The British Government believed—rightly, since they had excellent information from their intelligence service—that Germany might be seeking to entice the President into opening the ball; and on 27 August the Foreign Office warned the American embassy (Page was then in Washington) that the British Government would snub Wilson if he fell in with the German plan. Spring Rice and Chandler Anderson were talking on this subject in Washington on 15 September and the latter suggested that the best way of forestalling any presidential move would be by a public statement of the British Government's attitude. Spring Rice passed this on to London. Lloyd George had a copy of this telegram; and he had also precise information, based, it may well be, on an interception of Gerard's telegram of 25 September,* that Gerard was going to Washington to support the German proposal. He did not doubt that Wilson would act upon it before the election. 'He has no international conscience', he wrote, 'he thinks of nothing but the ticket.'[44]

The situation was a delicate one. The policy decision resulting from the House–Grey negotiations was that the possibility of American intervention should be kept open as a last resort. In what way should it be made clear to

* See p. 540 above.

the President that that point had not yet been reached? M. Briand had declared on 19 September, in a great oration which so enthused the Chamber of Deputies that by a majority of 421 votes to 26 they ordered it to be placarded throughout the country, that France would not negotiate. Should a British spokesman reinforce this declaration, or would it be better to wait until the offer was actually made and then deal with it as tactfully as possible? For, as what follows will show, the dependence of the Allies on America was becoming manifest and it was now vital to do nothing that might cause unnecessary offence.

In this situation, Lloyd George, whose department was not directly concerned, without consulting the Prime Minister or the Foreign Secretary or any of his colleagues, gave on 28 September a sensational interview to an American correspondent, warning the President not to butt in.

The fight must be to the finish—to a knock-out . . . Neutrals of the highest purposes and humanitarians with the best motives must know that there can be no outside interference at this stage. Britain asked no intervention when she was not prepared to fight. She will tolerate none now . . .[45]

On any view this was a monstrous thing to do: for just such an offence five and a half years later Lloyd George was to dismiss Montagu from his Cabinet. Grey wrote the offender a pained letter.[46] McKenna, who said that he was now borrowing from America £2,000,000 a day, was furious and said that Lloyd George ought to be 'suppressed'.[47] But there was no one who dared to do the suppressing. He had said just what the vast majority of the British public wanted said—why should America, who had not lifted a finger to help, think that she could tell Britain when to stop?—and by saying it he stood out as the man who could and would win the war. This was the trumpet call that preceded the assault upon the citadel of power. There was still much manœuvring to be done before Lloyd George made through the agency of Sir Max Aitken, later to be rewarded, or perhaps consoled, with the barony of Beaverbrook, the treaty with Bonar Law which brought Asquith down. Striking and becoming 'master of the situation' was how Lloyd George in retrospect described the process.[48]

It is easy to write too censoriously about this. This is not the place to estimate the forces that then moved Lloyd George or to ask how real was loyalty or how strong personal ambition or how clear the call within him that the nation needed such a one as he; a fair answer would have to state all the facts, and they make a long and fascinating tale. In the end the judgement might be that of one of his biographers,[49] that he came to power because he alone of Britons at that time was fully possessed by the spirit of Chatham's arrogant conviction: 'I know that I can save this nation and that no one else can.' When nearly thirty years later, and two days after Lloyd George's death and not two months after the end of the second German war which his old chief had lived to see but not to fight, Winston Churchill as Prime Minister pronounced the valedictory in Parliament, he said that Lloyd George had 'seized' the main power in the State; and when some present questioned the word, he said: 'Seized. I think it was Carlyle who said of Oliver Cromwell: he coveted the place; perhaps the place was his.'

One immediate consequence of the 'knock-out blow' interview was to set the Government thinking more intensely than hitherto about the likelihood of the event. Was Britain in fact, as Lloyd George himself thought, losing the war? As well as the bleak outlook on the western front there came up for consideration in October two other subjects even gloomier in portent, the increasing menace of the German submarine and the economic situation.

In September 1916 the German Navy, while awaiting a final decision about unrestricted U-boat warfare, began a campaign under cruiser rules which achieved a remarkable success. The monthly total of tonnage sunk in September approached that in April 1916, hitherto the peak figure in *unrestricted* warfare, and in the remaining three months of the year substantially exceeded it. To add to this there was the invisible figure of time lost by delay and deviation in avoiding submarines. Losses on this scale did not in their result as yet approach the result achieved by the British blockade and they had the incidental result of reminding those neutrals whose ships were being sunk (in December the neutral losses accounted for a third of the total) of the comparative mildness of the latter. If by now the word 'contraband' had ceased to have much meaning under British practice, it had never had any at all for the submarine which, even under cruiser rules, sunk without examination.

But if the rate of loss continued for much longer or maybe was increased— for the rumours were multiplying that unrestricted warfare would not be long delayed—the balance of the rival blockades would be greatly altered. Sinkings at the existing level, if continued throughout 1917, would mean a loss to British shipping in the year of two million tons, a figure nearly four times as great as Britain's new building in 1916, while the Germans were commissioning five times the number of submarines they lost.

Already by the end of October the forecast was causing great alarm. In a memorandum to the Admiralty on 29 October Jellicoe gave it as his view that the effect of the submarine on trade was the gravest of the perils confronting Britain;[50] he feared that by June 1917 the interference with supplies might force her to accept terms which the military situation would not warrant. The Board of Trade agreed with this prognosis, warning the Cabinet on 9 November of a complete breakdown much sooner than in June 1917. The Navy had no remedy to suggest. Balfour had already told the War Committee that it must be 'content with palliation'. The best of the palliatives seemed to be the arming of merchantmen and in mid November the War Committee decided that this should be given top priority; in the last quarter of 1916 twice as many armed ships as unarmed escaped after attack.

The war was now costing Britain £5,000,000 a day of which 40 per cent was being spent in the United States. So in September 1916 40 per cent of the Allied war supplies, Britain being the purchasing agent for her side, were threatened by the retaliatory legislation that was being enacted by Congress. The British were not, however, seriously alarmed by this. They had considered the matter at the beginning of the year* and reached the conclusion that they were far from powerless in a trade war. Moreover, they did not believe that the threat would be carried out. This was an issue on which, as we have seen,† Lansing was facing both ways. The British saw the reassuring face which he showed to Crawford and Spring Rice. In the first half of September the ambassador was sending very hopeful reports of his talks with the Secretary.[51] The Secretary, he said, was using most conciliatory language; the State Department had ensured that the powers given to the President were optional and not mandatory and hoped confidentially that they would not have to be used. Lansing was even more forthcoming in his talk with Crawford. In the Foreign Office happy minutes were exchanged between Percy on 'electioneering cantankerousness' and Crowe on 'Parliamentary gas and bluff'.[52] Percy thought that what was needed was a 'firm warning' to the United States of the effects that the legislation would have on British public opinion. Reminded by Hurst that in January there had been a report by the Board of Trade on the consequences of a trade war, Percy got it out and said that he would ask the Board 'very much at their leisure' to study the question again. Cecil on 20 September was reported to House as confiding to an American newspaperman that if the President used his retaliatory powers Britain would break off diplomatic relations and end all trade with America. 'Bluff', House said.[53] The old joint declaration (which had never been used, nor was it to be) was brought out, dusted over, and given a more resounding ending in which all the Allies were to declare their 'absolute conviction that were they to abandon any one of the lawful measures of war which they now employ, they would be unfaithful to their citizens and recreant to their duty'.[54]

* See p. 504 above.   † See pp. 520 and 523 above.

So House thought that the British were bluffing and Crowe thought the Americans were! In fact there was an element of bluff on both sides. We have seen* that in Washington during October it was being discovered that all was not plain sailing. In the same month the discovery was being made in London that the sailing would be very difficult indeed. Percy's idea of the Board of Trade taking another look at the trading position was amplified into an interdepartmental committee with himself as Secretary, and the leisureliness was diminished—that is to say, it took only three weeks to set up the committee by the stately process of sending round written invitations to the departments concerned to nominate representatives. The process began on 13 September and by 28 September the committee to Cecil's regret had not met. Grey minuted: 'I do not know who set it in motion and must leave that to whoever it is.'[55] But when it did meet on 3 October it worked quickly. It produced by 13 October a collection of departmental memoranda and a brief over-all report. The concluding sentence of the Board of Trade memorandum put the matter in a nutshell: for numerous essential materials America was an absolutely irreplaceable source of supply. It was an eye-opener for Percy who wrote: 'Our dependence was so vital and complete in every possible respect that it was folly even to consider reprisals.'[56] Only Crowe was undaunted. He wrote on 16 October that any interference with British-American trade 'would rouse a storm in America much more serious than the whimperings about the blacklist and the mails'.[57]

In this fashion the British were reminded that, as Spring Rice put it, 'they would be quarrelling with their victuals if they resented the manners of their grocer'.[58] But they could take comfort from the reflection that the grocer also must be careful not to upset his best—indeed his only remaining—customer. The Entente was now America's export market. As the Foreign Office said: 'It appears almost inconceivable that, unless diplomatic relations become strained to breaking point, she would be so foolish as to imperil her hold on this most valuable market for her goods.'

But this community of economic interest would continue only while the customer had money to spend, and the customer was now reaching the stage when he might not want to give full security for his credit. This was the point that was seized on in the over-all resolution of the interdepartmental committee. A trade war was unthinkable: 'The only probable danger to which we are exposed is the development of a feeling in the United States unfavourable to our loans.' The treasury representative on the committee was Keynes. He was also the secretary to a small committee under Reading which the Chancellor of the Exchequer at once set up to report on the

* See p. 518 above.

financial position. At this time expenditure in America was being met as to 60 per cent by the sale of gold and British-owned American securities and 40 per cent by borrowing. This proportion could not be maintained: the dwindling supply of American securities must be used to bolster the non-American securities to be offered, though with a much smaller margin, as collateral for the money to be raised by loan. Henceforward five-sixths of the amount needed must be borrowed, which meant that £1,650,000 a day must be provided by public or private loans. How long could Britain continue to borrow at this rate? The answer the committee gave was—until 31 March 1917. It was not given very confidently.

> Our financial agents tell us in effect that, by the use of every available device, and possibly at the cost of postponing payments by bank overdrafts, we shall still be solvent on 31st. March. They cannot tell us how this result is to be achieved, but they hope and believe it will be possible.[59]

There was at this time in anti-American circles in Britain a comfortable belief that the unwily Yankees in their greed for profits had plunged too deeply and could not now afford to let the Allies lose. This was not so; the credit the sellers had given so far was well secured. The time was now coming when American businessmen would have to decide whether, for the sake of future profits and to avoid the grave dislocation caused by the loss of so great a market, they would trust for repayment to the customer's prospects. As Grey in his contribution to the symposium put it, 'Americans might well estimate that speedy peace would offer better security for the money they have already invested, than a prolonged war conducted on further American loans.'[60] Further borrowing would be difficult and precarious. The war of attrition was bringing no quick victories and the lack of them was discouraging to the American investor. He might too be put off by irritations such as the Black List and the mails. But on these matters the Foreign Office, unaccustomed to toeing the line, recommended only minor ameliorations such as revising 'in the direction of greater civility' standard forms of reply to inquiries about missing cables.

The extent to which the American public would continue to provide money was, however, only one half of the problem. The other half related to the extent to which the President would continue to permit it. A legal prohibition would not be needed. The British Treasury (whose attitude was much less hopeful than that of the Foreign Office) advised that 'a statement from the United States Executive deprecating or disapproving of such loans would render their flotation in sufficient volume a practical impossibility'.[61] So wrote Keynes on 10 October and added that British policy 'should be so directed as not only to avoid any form of reprisal or active irritation, but also to conciliate and to please'. As McKenna on 24 October summed it up: 'If things go on as at present, I venture to say with certainty that by next June or earlier the President of the American Republic will be in a position, if he wishes, to dictate his own terms to us.'[62] France had in October completely exhausted her gold and dollar resources, and in order to finance her American expenditures for the next six months needed at least £40,000,000 from the British Treasury in addition to the sums already promised. The situation filled 'M. Ribot with sentiments of the gravest despondency and alarm'.[63] 'Who in the world', demanded a sprightly French journalist twenty-four years later, 'remembers M. Ribot, notwithstanding that he was Minister of Finance and then Prime Minister and Foreign Secretary in the course of the last war?'[64] At this juncture he was Finance Minister and nearing both his eighties and the premiership in succession to M. Briand.

A military stalemate as the war entered on its third winter was depressing and the prospect of a grave shortage of supplies alarming. There was probably no one in the Government who seriously feared defeat. Was there anyone who thought that the price of outright victory might be becoming too high? To be the first to raise such an issue needed the sort of level-headed courage that Hankey had. In a memorandum which he sent to Asquith on 6 November 1916 and which predicated that the enemy had given up all idea of an unlimited result, he inquired whether the Allies were still justified in continuing warfare with unlimited objects; if military advice was that they could no longer be hoped for, what should the limited objects be?[65] Asquith as he was apt to do with disruptive memoranda, left it uncirculated. Hankey told Lloyd George on 9 November that 'personally I never had the smallest illusions about crushing Germany. The best I had ever hoped for at any time was a draw in our favour, and a favourable peace extorted by economic pressure.'[66]

If any member of the public had been asked to pick the Cabinet Minister least likely to lend his authority to any ideas of this sort, his choice might well have fallen on Henry Charles Keith Petty Fitzmaurice, fifth Marquess of Lansdowne. This nobleman had after a proconsular career been Foreign Secretary in the last Conservative Government. He remained a pillar of Tory rectitude and as such was part of the coalition structure erected in May 1915. He was the last man, so it might have seemed, to slip out of the grooves in which his career had conventionally run and bear away from the flock. Yet this man in his seventies, to the bewilderment of his family and friends, courted sneers and discredit by asking whether it was time to make peace.

This question, which he first asked in the Cabinet on 13 November 1916, he asked in public a year later in a letter which *The Times* rejected (prophesying the next day that it would be read with 'universal regret and reprobation')[67] and the *Daily Telegraph* published. Throughout 1918 he pressed the cause. The action was generally regarded as the fatal blot upon a long and distinguished career: so his son-in-law and biographer wrote, while admitting the possibility that a future generation might think that he was right after all. Lansdowne himself wrote to his daughter: 'I have long wished to be released, but this is not the kind of last act to which I looked forward for my poor play.'[68]

Lord Lansdowne in his memorandum recalled that members of the War Committee had been asked by the Prime Minister to express their views as to the terms upon which peace might be concluded.[69] Ought they not also to consider, he asked, what Britain's prospects were of being able to dictate terms? He reviewed the gloomy reports which the Cabinet had been receiving.

No one for a moment believes that we are going to lose the War; but what is our chance of winning it in such a manner, and within such limits of time, as will enable us to beat our enemy to the ground and impose upon him the kind of terms which we so freely discuss?

He wrote of the enormous sacrifices Britain was making—'we are slowly but surely killing off the best of the male population of these islands' (he himself had lost a son in October 1914)—which it was her duty to bear only if it could be shown that they would have their reward. He thought it inconceivable that during the winter she would not be sounded about her readiness to discuss peace. Was she prepared with her reply? Things had been said which seemed to commit her to regarding as unfriendly any attempt to extricate her from the impasse. The 'knock-out blow' interview had produced an impression which it would not be easy to efface.

Surely it cannot be our intention, no matter how long the War lasts, no matter what the strain on our resources, to maintain this attitude, or to declare, as M. Briand declared about the same time, that for us too 'the word peace is a sacrilege'. Let our naval, military, and economic advisers tell us frankly whether they are satisfied that the knock-out blow can and will be delivered. The Secretary of State's formula holds the field, and will do so until something else is put in its place.

This led inevitably to a request to Robertson for an appraisal. There was of course no strategy for a knock-out blow. The military advisers were planning a win on points; and Lloyd George in the notorious interview had not in fact held out any hope of quick results in the fight to a finish. Earlier in the month he had asked Robertson to give his opinion on the probable duration of the war and the soldier replied very sensibly in a memorandum of 3 November that it was not merely, or even mainly, a military question;[70] there were naval, economic, and diplomatic factors of which he was ignorant: he thought it unwise to expect the end before the summer of 1918 and how long it might go on after that he could not even guess.

General Robertson would have done well to have left it there. But—egged on, he claims, by Lloyd George—he decided to deliver a knock-out blow himself against those 'miserable members of society' whom he described as 'cranks, cowards, and philosophers, some of whom are afraid of their own skins being hurt'.[71] In a long memorandum he began by posing the question as whether 'we shall win' ('the idea had not before entered my mind that any member of His Majesty's Government had a doubt on the matter'). He ended with the oracular sentence: 'We shall win if we deserve to win.' The large space in between was occupied by a defence of the military conduct of the war to date and an exhortation to increase the war effort. It was not for him, he said, to say what terms of peace should be accepted, but

to conclude peace before we have made our greatest possible effort would be to estrange our overseas dominions, to betray our allies, to sacrifice our own interests, and to dishonour the memory of those who have laid down their lives for the Empire.[72]

As to the question which he was supposed to answer, whether the knock-out blow was possible, Lloyd George summarizes the reply in words which would hardly do as a précis but which catch admirably the spirit of the document. 'Ultimate victory was assured the Allies, provided the advice of the War Office was obediently followed in every particular and its demands patriotically fulfilled in every detail.'[73]

Three more memoranda were placed before the Cabinet on 27 November. There was a dignified rejoinder by Lansdowne.[74] There was a disappointing memorandum from Grey.[75] Two-thirds of it was devoted to a single sentence in Robertson's memorandum in which he had said that diplomacy had seriously failed to assist with regard to Bulgaria and Turkey and to a refutation of this complaint on the familiar lines that diplomacy in war could do nothing without military success. On the question in hand, he wrote that if the naval and military authorities believed that Germany could be defeated or even that the position of the Allies was likely to improve, peace was premature; but that if the said authorities thought that the said position was not likely to improve and might deteriorate, the war should be wound up on the best terms obtainable. There was too much of this sort of waffle in the Asquith Cabinet. Despite Robertson's sensible disclaimer Grey—and there were others like him—was trying to make the Cabinet's advisers decide what it should have decided itself.

In war it is dangerous to talk of compromise unless there is one in sight. What prospect was there of the Central Powers conceding the minimum which the Allies would accept? This is what the Foreign Secretary should have been telling the Cabinet. The Paget–Tyrrell Memorandum, to which Grey did not refer and which had never been discussed in the Cabinet, dealt in its concluding section with the possibilities of an inconclusive peace. Its advice was that a tolerable result in Europe, i.e. the evacuation of Belgium and France, would have to be purchased by colonial concessions by Britain. The result of a draw would be

that Germany will not have obtained all she wanted when she began the war, but will have obtained such an instalment of her ambitions as will enable her government to justify themselves to their people for having gone to war in defence of their territory in 1914; in fact, they will have every reason to claim victory and to represent the Allies as having suffered defeat.[76]

This would be what Cecil called in the memorandum that he put in 'a disastrous peace'.[77] Against it there must be set the military advice offering a reasonable prospect of victory and therefore 'we are bound to continue with the War'.

This was undoubtedly the resolution of the Cabinet and indeed had been expressed a month before by Asquith in the last of his great orations as Leader of the House of Commons.

The strain which the war imposes upon ourselves and our Allies, the hardships which we freely admit it involves on some of those who are not directly concerned in the struggle, the upheaval of trade, the devastation of territory, the loss of irreplaceable lives—this long and sombre procession of cruelty and suffering, lighted up as it is by deathless examples of heroism and chivalry, cannot be allowed to end in some patched up, precarious, dishonouring compromise, masquerading under the name of Peace.[78]

The memoranda of 27 November were not apparently discussed at the Cabinet of 30 November though the report of it, the last to be penned by a Prime Minister's own hand 'with his humble duty to Your Majesty', has for its last paragraph an ominous reference to a warning by the Federal Board of Reserve to American banks 'not to give further borrowing facilities to the Allied Governments'.[79] The long Asquith primacy, having chugged almost to a standstill, now began to rush helter-skelter down the steep declension of its days. On 7 December a new government was being formed. None of the old Liberals were included. Nor of course was Lord Lansdowne whose last deed in government was, as Grey called it in his paper, the performance of a faithful and courageous act.[80]

Grey paid this fitting tribute but he was not of Lansdowne's mind. Before Lansdowne sent out his memorandum Grey asked him and Loreburn to call so that he might put before them 'some of the difficulties of the situation'.[81] Perhaps he put the points better to them than he did in his last Cabinet paper. His notion of peacemaking was in fact simple and clear and one that was proper to a gentleman of his generation. The essence of it was loyalty—the 'disgrace of thinking of peace till the Allies are secure'.[82] He set this out in a covering paper composed about this time and attached to the House–Grey Memorandum;[83] and on 9 December sent both documents to Balfour and Cecil, leaving it to Balfour to decide when 'to make the new Cabinet consider the subject'. He himself was clear, he said in the covering paper, that 'nothing but the defeat of Germany can make a satisfactory end to this war and secure future peace'. But, he went on, this was not a war of Anglo-German rivalry. It was for the Allies 'whose population has been, and is being so grossly ill-treated, rather than for us, to say when it is opportune to speak of peace'. They ought to be told, however, that British support in shipping and finance was going to be curtailed. He feared that one or other of them might then demand that the war be wound up on the best terms available. In this contingency, unless Britain decided to continue alone, President Wilson should be invoked. 'His influence would be exercised whole-heartedly on behalf of Belgium, at any rate: a point on which we cannot yield without sacrifice not only of interest but of honour.' When on 12 December he heard of the German peace note he expressed the same idea briefly in a letter to his private secretary.[84]

This was on the day after he had given up the seals of office. Although he comes back again into the story as a silent and helpless witness of Wilson's last struggle, he had done his lifework. He asked Cecil whether he thought it was wrong of him to be glad to go.[85] He does not appear in 1916 as very effective. But men like he, who neither seek the limelight nor step out of it when they have had enough but stay till every drop of service has been squeezed out, are not to be assessed upon the last year's achievement. Grey may or may not have lost Turkey and Bulgaria about which in his Cabinet paper he was worrying so much. He did not lose America. And he laid some of the stones for the founding of a new world order.

Grey lived for seventeen years longer, years that were compounded as most of his life had been of simple happiness and sharp suffering. He enjoyed only four months more of his beloved Fallodon before it was burnt down; and so in 1923 was his cottage by the Itchen with all its memories. His second marriage lasted for only six years and left him again a widower. He could not see much but he could always tell a bird by its song.

He would not denigrate or embarrass the new Government. When in November 1916 the Cabinet was discussing plans for an inter-allied conference to settle policy for 1917 with two delegates from each country, Grey had suggested that Lloyd George should go with the Prime Minister, for he was the man who could represent most clearly the feeling of the country.[86] He continued to give to the supplanter the credit that was his due. He agreed, he wrote in May 1917, that there were

very many unpleasant circumstances in the way the Asquith Govt. was displaced and many of us including myself had shamefully unfair things said about us, but then so far as I was concerned I was at one time very much overpraised and I was really always miserable and out of place in public life. So long as I am left alone in private life now I have a feeling that it is sort of quits.[87]

But his quittance was not complete. When men leave public office and the gates clang to behind them they are but rarely asked to re-enter. As the old walk out, the young step in. Not so with Grey. The months of ineptitude were sloughed off his reputation; the sterling remained and its brightness was always leaping out to allure his successors. Half blind though he was, he was constantly invited to return; as late as January 1929 Mr. Baldwin wrote to ask him whether he would serve again as Foreign Secretary if the Conservatives were returned to power. But two things only could stir him. One was the League of Nations and the other the liberalism in which he believed.

The same hope of the new world order that attracted Grey was now driving Wilson's pen as he composed his message to the world. But idealism was not now the only spur. A negotiated peace had now become something that America needed in her own interests. The offer of her services to secure it could no longer be, as Wilson would have preferred, purely disinterested. Unless peace came soon she was likely to find herself either at war with Germany or at loggerheads with Britain. A message to the world was not the conventional way of stopping a war; but Wilson, if he had thought it at all necessary to defend the unconventionality, could have argued that it was now the only way left and that it offered a reasonable prospect of success. The diplomatic initiatives had proved to be like country paths that leave the road with a convincing appearance of going somewhere but which in fact are making only for tracklessness; and which reveal, when the diversion has lasted long enough, their intentions in a way that seems to mock the walker for having been taken in. Wilson could not now hope for any response from the Allied Governments. He could hope that the Central Powers would prove more amenable but his plan was not dependent on it. For his plan was to talk to peoples and not to governments.

There was now at the end of 1916 a sizeable minority in every belligerent country in favour of a negotiated peace. It was just possible that a popular appeal by the President could rally enough support for the minority to make the governments think again. The minority in each country was to be found, as was to be expected, on the left and it existed as strongly in Germany as in any other country. Indeed, there was not on the left in any other country a man as courageous and single-minded as Karl Liebknecht, who combined his activities as a socialist deputy at the furthest extremity of the left with underground pamphleteering under the name of Spartacus. He was notorious in the Reichstag for his interpellations: how many Belgian civilians had been shot, he would ask; and when would the Government publish the foreign documents on the responsibility for the war. In the middle of 1916 he was sent to prison for four years, having been arrested at a May Day demonstration, for attempted treason and aggressive disobedience. He was the only man in Germany to be accepted as 'non-opportunist' by Lenin. To his right there were the Independent Socialists, who had split in March 1916, and who were now demanding negotiations for a peace without victors or vanquished and that the Government should state its real war aims. They were obtaining more sympathy in the country as a whole where shortage of food was at last beginning to be felt. The harvest of 1916 was poor. Meat rationing began in May 1916. Butter, sugar, and fats were scarce. The imports, still substantial, of meat, butter, and cheese from surrounding neutrals were being consigned straight to the War Department for troops or to industrial districts for munitions workers; without them, Helfferich thought, the food system would probably have collapsed.[88] There was a potato famine and turnips, usually kept for cattle fodder, were being eaten instead, so that the winter of 1916–17 became known as the 'Turnip Winter'.

In France there was a radical minority of whom M. Brizon, the deputy whose interpellation had on 22 September 1916 been drowned in the deluge of M. Briand's oratory, was an example. In Britain the nearest equivalent to Liebknecht was E. D. Morel. In 1916 he encountered the same fate as Liebknecht but suitably moderated to the English temperament. He was charged, not with treason, but with breach of a regulation which forbade the dispatch of printed matter to a neutral country. Actually, he sent one of his U.D.C. pamphlets to France, but unfortunately for him the recipient had gone to Switzerland and this was thought good enough for six months' imprisonment. Behind Morel, some of them quite close behind, there was as we have seen* a group of Parliamentarians who either opposed the war or were highly suspicious of official and popular thought on the subject. In November 1915 these men first raised in Parliament the call for peace by negotiation and debates on the subject took place on three other occasions during 1916, though on none of them did the dissentients feel strong enough to divide the House.

The Union of Democratic Control constituted the core of the opposition to the war. Beyond its range there were several influential men who by 1916 were ready at least to consider a negotiated peace. These were the men whom House called 'the peace party'.[89] In London in 1915 the Colonel had set out to sample Liberal opinion on peace terms. He made rather an unfortunate choice[90] when he began on February 1916 with J. A. Spender, the most influential journalist of his day, whose character has been sharply rendered by his unpolitical nephew Stephen.[91] Spender was an Asquithian Liberal and a Balliol contemporary of Grey. As a journalist he would have earned Wilson's approval as more interested in measures than in men, for he had never heard of the Colonel. He hastened to report to Grey his meeting with 'a certain Col. House, an American' together with his robust answers to the Colonel's inquiries.

House had a more rewarding interview on 4 March with F. W. Hirst, the editor of the *Economist*,[92] whom he found 'an entirely new type of Englishman', antagonistic to the Government and critical of Grey and Asquith. Hirst took him to see Loreburn who as a former member of the Liberal Cabinet was, Morley being inactive, the prize exhibit of the peace party. Loreburn, another Balliol product, was Lord Chancellor from 1906 to 1912. He came into the Cabinet as a Campbell-Bannerman man and never got over his suspicion of the Liberal Imperialist trio—Asquith, Grey, and Haldane—and resented their superiority in the Cabinet. He complained that he was ignored in Cabinet but Lloyd George thought him petulant and unreasonable and 'always rubbing Grey the wrong way'.[93] In August 1914 he accepted that Britain had to fight for Belgium but as early as October in that year he was corresponding with Bryce about ending the war on the basis of the restoration of Belgium with compensation: on 19 October he wrote that only President Wilson could make his voice heard.[94] House and he had even more in common than this, for he was an ardent supporter of the Declaration of London and receptive to all House's ideas about freedom of the seas.[95] In August 1915 he wrote urging Grey to reconsider his blockade policy.[96] On 10 June 1916 he joined in the correspondence the *Economist* was then running about a negotiated peace[97] with an appeal to Lansdowne as a moderate realist to lead the movement and later he wrote again to Grey in

* See p. 394 above.

support of the Lansdowne line.[98] On 3 July he wrote direct to Wilson promising co-operation whenever the President should decide to make a move.

The adherence to it of men like Lansdowne and Loreburn shows the sort of thoughtful politician, not extremist or cranky, whom the peace movement was attracting. Another of the same sort was Lord Parmoor, a former Conservative M.P. who was to end up in the first Labour Government.* But they all had a hard row to hoe. As Parmoor wrote in June 1916: 'Any genuine attempt to bring about a peaceful solution is treated as almost in the nature of a traitorous suggestion.'[99]

Thus Wilson had from the one side encouragement from the German Government and from the other satisfactory evidence that in England an appeal for peace would not be ignored. Indeed, the British 'peace party', having taken from the address of 27 May 1916 the hint of intervention, were like Jacobites seeking help from over the water; and like Jacobites were excessively optimistic about home-grown support for an invasion. One of the radical M.P.s whom House had met in London in the spring of 1916 was Howard Whitehouse;[100] he had told House then that a public offer of mediation by Wilson would be supported by Grey and Balfour and obtain in the House of Commons a majority of 100. In the autumn he was in the States and called on House on 18 November. He now thought that there would be a close vote in the Commons with the pacifists losing; this would result in the resignation of the progressives from the Government and their replacement by reactionaries; there would then be a military dictatorship and within the year the Government would be overthrown unless it succeeded in making a victorious peace.

The British radicals had other channels to Wilson's mind. Authors like Lowes Dickinson whom Wilson had met in his university days† wrote for papers like *The New Republic*, which Wilson read. There was an American called Buckler,[101] an attaché at the London embassy, who had been at Oxford with Charles Trevelyan and saw a great deal of him and his political friends. He sent regular reports and sometimes messages to House, in this way evading the hostile scrutiny alike of the British censor and of Ambassador Page. Wilson not being an original thinker, his political ideas were usually a distillation from, if not an absorption of, reports of others. Whether or not absorbed from them, the themes he was now developing were those most acceptable to the British radicals.

The result of the election had convinced Wilson that the people relied upon him to keep them out of war and he was determined to throw himself into the effort. Only if it failed was he willing to consider any further step

---

* He was the brother-in-law of Beatrice Webb and the father of Sir Stafford Cripps.

† See p. 92 above.

in the current controversies, the Black List and the mails on the one side and the submarine war on the other. The new campaign which Germany had begun in September was inevitably breaking the cruiser rules with which it was supposed to comply. On 28 October the *Marina*, an armed British merchantman, was torpedoed without warning in heavy seas with great loss of life, including six Americans who were among the crew. Lansing, apparently without consultation with the President, told the press on 1 November that the President was particularly concerned about the incident and determined to hold Germany strictly to the *Sussex* pledge.[102] But when on the next day House mentioned it casually to Wilson, saying that a decision could be deferred until after the election, Wilson replied that he did not 'believe the American people would wish to go to war no matter how many Americans were lost at sea'.[103] He said he was sorry that this was true, but nevertheless it was his opinion. He said also that the understanding with Germany applied only to liners, a remark which House decorously challenged and which much alarmed Lansing when House passed it on to him. On 6 November the British liner *Arabia*, also armed, with American passengers on board, was torpedoed without warning in the Mediterranean; fifty-seven lives were lost, none American. Lansing on 18 November instructed the chargé in Berlin to request an immediate investigation, saying that the American Government was 'unable to square this disaster with the German assurance of 4 May 1916'.[104]

The only effect of these incidents on Wilson's mind was to spur him to greater urgency in the framing of his peace appeal. As soon as he conveniently could after his return to office was assured, he began preparing for it. He assembled the material in a bulky folder containing newspaper articles and editorials, flimsies of dispatches, and extracts from speeches as well as his own notes. On 13 November he told Tumulty to postpone every appointment he could on the ground that 'the President is so engrossed just now with business of the most pressing sort'.[105] He sent for House, who arrived the next evening, and told him that he wanted to write a Note to the belligerents demanding that the war cease. Unless this was done now, he said, America would inevitably drift into war on the submarine issue; he hoped to find sufficient peace sentiment in the Allied countries to make them consent. He asked House for his opinion. For the first time in his life with Wilson House explicitly and firmly dissented. He had indeed written to Wilson only the week before: 'At spare moments I have kept in close touch with the European situation, and I find indisputable evidence that Germany is not yet ready to agree to peace terms that this country could recommend to the Allies.'[106] This letter is very typical of the way in which House dressed up as an expert opinion the conclusion that he wanted his correspondent to accept. His own confident belief in it (and very often, as in this case, he was right) would give him an air which would quietly repel as obtrusive or impertinent any request for details of the 'close touch' or the 'indisputable evidence'.

Now on 14 November House said bluntly to Wilson that the Allies would consider an intervention as made in German interests and as an unfriendly act.[107] Wilson suggested that House might go to Europe so as to be there to ease the passage of the proposal when it was announced; House said he would go, but said it probably in a tone sympathetic to the sentiment he recorded in his diary that he would 'prefer Hades'. His advice was to 'sit tight and await further developments'. But for the President, who felt that Germany had already broken the *Sussex* pledge and thus left him no alternative to mediation but a break in relations, there was no time for delay.

House records also in his diary that Wilson wondered about purchasing the consent of the Allies to mediation by a separate understanding in which America agreed 'to throw our weight in their favor': House replied that the Allies would then ask about terms 'and we would soon get into a hopeless tangle . . . it would be like sitting in a peace conference in advance to determine what the best terms should be'.[108] It seems unlikely that this topic played a key part in the discussion or that it can be taken as signifying a return, even a fleeting one, by Wilson to secret bargaining. In effect it would have meant a return to the House–Grey Memorandum (wherein, it may be observed, House had found no difficulty in determining in advance what the best terms should be); and when House suggested on 7 December the revival of the Memorandum on the ground that it might appeal to the new Prime Minister, Lloyd George, Wilson rejected it flatly saying: 'We cannot go back to those old plans. We must shape new ones.'[109]

The two men spent the whole evening arguing the points over and over again. House had arrived at six o'clock and the President had come at once to his room. They had talked before and after dinner and it was eleven before the President proposed going to bed. He was disturbed and worried by the disagreement and was unusually late the next morning so that House breakfasted alone; which meant, House thought, that he had had a bad night. They resumed their talk and House produced some new arguments. Suppose that the proposal was accepted by Germany and refused by the Allies. Germany would then feel that she could begin unrestricted U–boat warfare. This was a good guess by House since in making the approach to Wilson a secondary object in Bethmann's mind was that, even if it produced no direct results, it might make America less inclined to drastic action when U–boat warfare was resumed. House argued also that if Germany did not resume U–boat warfare, her acceptance of the American overtures and the

Allies' rejection of them would cause America to drift into a sympathetic alliance with Germany, and then the Allies might declare war against America. Wilson retorted that they would not dare to do that and that, if they did, they could do no serious harm. House disagreed, saying that Britain might conceivably destroy the American fleet and land troops from Japan. Eventually, the President said that he had made up his mind and that they could go no further until he had written his views in concrete form; then when he had it in writing and made his points clear, they could go over it again and discuss it with more intelligence. He asked House to see Bernstorff and House suggested that he should see also Lansing and Polk.

House had not to any extent altered his view that the President was making a mistake and his plan now, as he put it to Lansing, was to 'drift for a while until we could get our bearings'.[110] So he suggested to Lansing that he should not press the President on the *Marina* and the *Arabia*. The three of them, House, Lansing, and Polk, 'were unanimous in our belief that it would be stupendous folly to wage war against the Allies'. If war had to come, they thought it should be on their side and not against them. After dinner that evening at the White House the President and House talked again. House said that Lansing and Polk saw no crisis in the U-boat controversy and felt that that quieted the President and put him in better spirits.

House, though not in sympathy with Wilson's decision, carried out his instructions correctly. On 18 November, as already recorded,* he saw Whitehouse, the British radical, and relayed his views to Wilson. He followed it up the next day with a memorandum on peace moves written by Noel Buxton, saying that it represented an important body of opinion. Then he saw Bernstorff on 20 November and told him that 'we were on the ragged edge'.[111] The President would move for peace, he said, at the first opportunity. The Count responded *con amore* that 'peace was on the floor waiting to be picked up': how could the Entente refuse to parley when Germany was willing to evacuate both France and Belgium?

Wilson found all this very encouraging and, as he wrote to House on 21 November, 'corroborating in some degree the impression I expressed to you, that this is very nearly the time, if not the time itself, for our move for peace'.[112] He was about to sketch the paper and would make the best haste he could 'consistent with my desire to make it the strongest and most convincing thing I ever penned'. He had spent most of the week in bed suffering from a bad cold and perhaps too from the strain of all these anxieties coming on top of the election campaign. He would not venture on the work till he was well, for it 'needed the clearest thinking I could do';[113] and he had first to finish the draft of his annual message to Congress.

* See p. 559 above.

XVIII

THE PEACE NOTES

General Ludendorff — the Belgian deportations — Wilson's first draft: House disagrees and Lansing qualifies his admiration — the German Note: 12 December 1916 — peace terms of the Central Powers — the American Note: 18 December 1916 — Lansing's 'verge of war' interview: his disloyalty — a warning to Britain on finance and the Allied replies — peace terms of the Entente — the German reply

---

THE pause for a reckoning between 1916 and 1917 resulted on each side in the decision to fight on and to marshal against each other all the resources of the nation at war. The needs that brought Lloyd George to the top and into uneasy relations with the generals made Ludendorff the moving force in German policy in every field and, after the few months which it took him to bring the civilian ministers to heel, dictator of Germany. He began the process by cajoling Bethmann into dismissing Jagow, 'an intelligent man', he said, 'but not one who can bang his fist on the table'.[1] He was succeeded by Zimmermann on 24 November 1916.

Ludendorff himself was a great banger of tables. At fifty-one he was the ablest and most energetic of all the war leaders as well as the nastiest. He was too nasty to have operated successfully except from behind the façade of Hindenburg. Out in the open, what would have counted against him in Germany would have been not so much his truculence, which fellow-Prussians at any rate would not have found so objectionable, as his un-prepossessing appearance—short-legged, double-chinned, thin-haired, and with a straggling moustache, definitely no Siegfried. But his brain was superb and his industry and command of detail unrivalled. His talent for organization was the equal of his talent for strategy. What he lacked, because he could not comprehend the need for it, was any understanding of politics or diplomacy. Except for Hindenburg, whom he managed so successfully, he could not for long have dealings with anybody who did not take orders.

His dogma, which he relied on in the early days when his universal interference might still be questioned, was that in a total war everything became a military responsibility, which meant his responsibility. His complaint against the civilian authority in the autumn of 1916—as it was Robertson's in Britain—was that the full resources of the nation were not being used. But where Robertson could only exhort, he could act. Judged by his own standards of ruthlessness, he was certainly right and he squeezed out of Germany far more than Bethmann would ever have obtained. His immediate anxiety in September 1916 was manpower. He wanted a labour law to conscript for an 'auxiliary service' every male German between seventeen and sixty. For this he had to come to terms with Bethmann.

But he was not under that handicap in Belgium where a military government ruled. The dislocation of industry as a result of the war had caused unemployment ('pernicious idleness'[2] in the German military vocabulary) in Belgium; Ludendorff's way of solving the problem was to deport the unemployed to Germany to work there. Deportation was not within the powers of an occupying force in international law but that did not trouble Ludendorff. Nor, since he was interested in obtaining the physically fit and the highly skilled and not in the relief of unemployment, were the deportees always selected from the unemployed. This policy caused a world outcry which was as loud in the United States as in the Allied countries, for the treatment of Belgium was of all topics in America the one on which anti-German feeling was most easily aroused. The press was indignant and protest meetings were held in the big cities.

The agitation was at its strongest in the second half of November and was not good for peacemaking. Wilson called it in a confidential message to Bethmann a 'very serious unfavourable reaction in the public opinion of this country . . . at a time when that opinion was more nearly approaching a balance of judgements as to the issues of the war than ever before'.[3] The confidential message accompanied a formal protest ('in a friendly spirit but most solemnly')[4] which on 29 November Wilson instructed Grew as chargé d'affaires to deliver in Berlin. At first he had thought it inconsistent to protest over the deportations when he had not protested over the invasion of Belgium. But he changed his mind. On 21 November Lansing sent him a long and rambling letter in which he explained that he had always 'firmly supported the policy of avoiding all protests on account of inhuman methods of warfare by belligerents'[5] and how much he believed that this policy was wise and should be continued; so, as he said twice, he had nothing to propose except careful consideration 'whether some way cannot be found to bring moral pressure upon Germany'. Wilson replied crisply on 26 November that there was sufficient ground for a 'solemn protest' and told Lansing what to say.

The affair did not disturb Wilson's own inner balance of neutrality. On 24 November he told House to

write to Lord Grey in the strongest terms to the effect that he could be sure that the United States would go to any length in promoting and lending her full might to a League for Peace, and that her people were growing more and more impatient with the intolerable conditions of neutrality, their feeling as hot against Great Britain as it was at first against Germany.[6]

Evidently it crossed his mind that Page might not be a good conductor of the heat, for he suggested to House that it might be well to intimate to Grey

that Page no longer represents the feeling or point of view of the United States any more than do the Americans resident in London . . . it might even be well to intimate that we, in common with the other neutral nations, look upon the continuation of the war through another winter with the utmost distaste and misgiving.

A notification of the President's distaste for war was not likely to impress Grey any more favourably than an intimation that he was not represented by the American ambassador. House transmitted a milder version. On 25 November Wilson told the Governor of the Federal Reserve Board, when talking about credit for the Allies,* that 'our relations with England were more strained than with Germany'.[7]

These were the days, 24 and 25 November, on which Wilson was completing the first draft of what he told his wife 'may prove the greatest piece of work of my life'.[8] Then he summoned House, who set out after recording in his diary that he was 'fearful of its effect'.[9] After dinner on 27 November Wilson read the draft which had not yet got beyond his own typewriter.[10] It began with his reasons for speaking—the disturbance to the life of the world and the intolerable position of neutrals: 'the reasons for this upheaval of the world remain obscure', he said. What prospect was there of an end? If decided by exhaustion, the objects of both sides would be defeated. But so they might be by triumph: 'upon a triumph which overwhelms and humiliates cannot be laid the foundations of peace.' The warring nations seemed to be fighting for the same ideals. Let them define their terms: he urged a conference for the purpose. He was not offering mediation.

I am doing a very simple, a very practical, and a very different thing. I am asking, and assuming that I have the right to ask, for a concrete definition of the guarantees which the belligerents on the one side and the other deem it their duty to demand as a practical satisfaction of the objects they are aiming at in this contest of force, in addition to the very great and substantial guarantee

* See p. 586 below.

which will, I feel perfectly confident, be supplied by a league of nations formed to unite their force in active co-operation for the preservation of the world's peace when this war is over.

House thought it

a wonderfully well-written document, yet, strangely enough, he had fallen again into the same error of saying something which would have made the Allies frantic with rage. I have called attention to this time after time, and yet in almost every instance where he speaks of the war he offends in the same way.[11]

This was of course a reference to the reasons for the upheaval being obscure. House talked to him for ten minutes about that and got him, so he thought, to eliminate it.[12] House pressed other points of the same sort. He wanted something put in which would make the Allies believe that Wilson sympathized with their viewpoint. Wilson would not do that, but he agreed to make it plain that he was not demanding a peace conference. House argued again for delay saying that the way must be prepared; Wilson countered by suggesting again that House should go to England, presumably as a lightning conductor for the thunderbolt in reply. Before he returned to New York on 28 November House saw Lansing and impressed upon him the need for delay until the time was propitious. He wrote in his diary: 'It is too important a matter to bungle, and if he is not careful, that is what he will do.'[13] He felt so strongly that he had one more try. Back in New York on 30 November he sent a letter to Wilson repeating his advice not to risk failure. The Note should not be sent until a background had been laid in France and England. 'If you do not act too hastily you can bring about the desired result. If you do it now, there does not seem to me one chance in ten of success and you will probably lose your potential position for doing it later.'[14] This letter had some effect. Wilson, as he told Lansing on 1 December, decided that it was best not to act hastily and that he would work further on the Note. Lansing, who had been prompted by House, suggested that it would be unfair to ask House to go to Europe and Wilson agreed.[15] House was much relieved to hear this. Lansing disgorged his perturbation on his diary. Suppose that Germany listened to the President and the Allies did not, what, he asked himself, would the situation be? 'When we do go into this war, and we might as well make up our minds that we are going in, we *must* go in on the side of the Allies, for we are a democracy.'[16]

But if the President had in mind any prolonged delay, he changed his mind after a conversation with Gerard. He went on 2 December to New York for the ceremony of the illumination of the Statue of Liberty and Gerard was among the company on the *Mayflower*. Gerard gave the President the advice he wanted to hear, namely, that he should act at once. They discussed a plan which Bryan had confided to Gerard, of the former 'going abroad to fix the whole matter up himself'.[17] Wilson in a letter to House on 3 December gave this as a reason for early action. 'The situation is developing very fast and if we are going to do the proposed thing effectively we must do it very soon.'[18] There were, however, various distractions. The visit to New York was one; the Address to Congress delivered on 5 December was another; and the third was a domestic upset concerning Tumulty which will be mentioned later. Then there was the change of government in Britain which House tried to use as another reason for delay. It was not until 9 December that Wilson sent a second draft to Lansing asking for detailed criticism. He referred to it as 'the demand for definitions'.[19] It had now taken shape in his mind as primarily a demand that each side should define its objectives. It is noteworthy that there was included in the material which he had in his folder an editorial from the *New Republic* of 25 November 1916 in which he had underlined passages about the need for the United States to be told 'the precise nature of the political objects' for which the belligerents were fighting so that she could determine to what extent she could 'appease the apparent irreconcilability' by participation either in the war 'on certain express terms' or in the structure of peace.[20]

Lansing had only one substantial alteration to suggest to the draft and this was to remove the implication that 'the common force' would be at the disposal of the League of Nations.[21] Wilson accepted this and in the final draft referred only in general terms to the object of the League as being 'to ensure peace and justice throughout the world'.[22] In an accompanying letter written on 10 December Lansing went as far as doubtless he felt it prudent to go in support of House. He began with the customary shake of the thurible (the Note was 'admirably presented' and 'certainly justified by our own situation, which grows constantly more intolerable') and then suggested that the proposed course of action had 'its uncertainties which I think should be carefully considered before being finally adopted'.

Suppose that the unacceptable answer comes from the belligerents whom we could least afford to see defeated on account of our national interest and on account of future domination of the principles of liberty and democracy in the world—then what? . . . I have told you how strongly I feel that democracy is the only sure guarantee of peace, so you will understand how these questions are worrying me, and why I think that they should be considered with the greatest deliberation and care before we take a step which cannot be withdrawn once it is taken.[23]

What with one thing and another, a month had now gone by since Wilson's election. Bucharest, the capital of Roumania, had fallen on 6 December. In Berlin on 12 December Bethmann delivered to Grew a Note for transmission to the Allies.[24] The operative part was a bare offer to negotiate and specified no terms, but there was a lengthy preamble referring to 'indestructible strength', 'unshakeable lines', and hope of fresh successes'. The next day the Kaiser in a speech to the troops said that he had proposed negotiations 'in the conviction that we are the absolute conquerors' and asked whether the enemy would think that they had had enough.[25]

How had Bethmann's plan gone awry? What he had been working for was a summons to the conference table by the President couched in terms which it was to be hoped the Entente would not dare to ignore, and which anyway they could accept without loss of face. But now instead of issuing out in the dulcet sonorities of President Wilson the summons was blared into the arena almost as a demand to surrender. Even if it had not been immediately followed by the Kaiser's raucous inquiry as to whether the Entente had had enough—and Bethmann was certainly not responsible for that—it would still have lacked any allure. It had of its nature, because it came direct from a fighter and not from an intermediary, to be pitched high lest it be interpreted as coming from weakness. So pitched, an acceptance of it would be taken as a sign of weakness. Bethmann would seem to have impaled himself on the dilemma which since the spring of 1916 he had been contriving to avoid.

The explanation is manifold. There was an injection into the plan of a demand from Austria for direct negotiations. There was what appeared to Germany to be Wilson's dilatoriness; the invitation that had been given to him in September had been answered by a refusal to move before the election; six weeks after the election he still had not moved nor bound himself to a date. There was the German diplomatic ineptness which disabled Bethmann from seeing either that the language of the announcement doomed it to failure or even that it would interfere with the effectiveness of any move by Wilson. The project had been thrown back and forth between so many participants, Bethmann himself, the Kaiser, Baron Burian, the Austrian Foreign Minister, and the ubiquitous Ludendorff. The multiplicity of cooks had not spoiled the broth but had deprived it of any individual taste. Nevertheless, it had been cooking for so long that it was generally felt that it had better be served up: somebody might be tempted to a sip. Let us go back and examine these influences.

The surprising success of the Brusilov offensive started in Austria a disenchantment with the war which thereafter persisted till the end. On 18 October 1916 at Pless Burian disclosed to Bethmann his ideas about a peace offer.[26] It should be made by the four Central Powers, Germany,

Austria, Turkey, and Bulgaria, and addressed to all neutral powers in the form of a request to them to use their good offices. The request would be a public one and there would be a public statement of the terms on which the Central Powers were willing to treat. Burian had got out a rough sketch of these terms. They were expressed in decent language. Acquisitions of territory were referred to as frontier rectifications or modifications. The same sort of delicacy was observed in the Tyrrell–Paget Memorandum, but there the smaller appetite made it less noticeable. In Burian's sketch 'strategic boundary modifications in favour of Germany and against Russia' included, for example, the annexation of Courland and Lithuania. The terms, if obtained, would result in the Central Powers, taken as a whole, doing pretty well out of the war.

Bethmann was receptive to the idea. It gave him, as he put it, two irons in the fire, the President's invitation, which he still preferred, and the direct approach. He did not at all like publicizing the terms and eventually won his point on that. Nor did he much care for having to be specific about terms at all; hitherto he had always evaded any statement of war aims. While Austria and Germany had made promises to Turkey and Bulgaria to secure their entry into the war, they had no arrangement between themselves. Austria had nothing to bargain with, having lost territory to Russia in the east; her objective was to be restored to her pre-war grandeur with a few small gains. Germany had much to bargain with both in the east and in the west, and wanted to improve considerably on her pre-war position. In suggesting the publication of terms Burian was much more concerned with tying Germany than with notifying the world. Bethmann, although he did not want to commit himself, had to accept that if the two countries were to go to the conference table together they must first agree upon what they wanted. Their aims must be, he noted, framed as maximum terms, but must also seem reasonable 'when submitted to the scrutiny of a fair judgement, untouched by the psychology of war'.[27]

Bethmann took the decision to put the second iron in the fire on 25 October. He had on that day a report of a speech made by Grey on 23 October which, while firm in content, made him sound a good deal more conciliatory than Lloyd George. On 26 October the High Command heard what was afoot. Ludendorff was willing to give his consent, which already had become indispensable, on terms. The terms were that the offer should be made in a favourable military situation (with this Bethmann entirely agreed); that it should be declared as proceeding from strength and not from weakness; and that it should be preceded by the proclamation of an independent kingdom of Poland and the enactment by the Reichstag of a compulsory labour law. The proclamation of a Polish kingdom, that is, of the parts of Poland which Germany had conquered from Russia, was in accordance with Bethmann's idea of creating a buffer state in the east; one advantage of doing it unilaterally before any peace conference began would be, as it was put to Burian, to 'show the world in this way that we regard ourselves as conquerors'.[28] But its immediate interest to Ludendorff was because the German Governor of Poland had told him that it would greatly help recruitment for the German Army. Bethmann would have liked the peace offer to come first; especially he hoped that it might make the labour law more palatable to the German workers. But he had to give way on both points. The Polish proclamation was made on 5 November.

Bethmann now had to obtain the approval of the High Command to a set of terms and then to agree them with Austria. He succeeded in negativing a demand by Ludendorff that, in consideration of Germany contenting herself with taking 'guarantees' from Belgium instead of annexing her, Britain should pay an indemnity; such a demand, he said, 'would instantly bring negotiations to a deadlock'.[29] A long conference with Burian on 15 and 16 November resulted in an agreement of which the main territorial features were as indicated below.

1. *Germany in the west.* The *status quo ante* would be restored (which meant also France restoring what she occupied of Alsace-Lorraine) subject to

   (*a*) Guarantees from Belgium to be negotiated direct with King Albert: alternatively, if no agreement was reached, the annexation of Liège 'with corresponding areas'.[30]

   (*b*) Annexation of Luxembourg.

   (*c*) Annexation from France of Longwy-Briey and some other 'strategic boundary adjustments'.[31]

   (*d*) Indemnity and compensation from France.

2. *Germany in the east.* Russia to lose Courland, Lithuania, and her Polish provinces, the last being made into an independent kingdom.

3. *Austria*

   (*a*) Would get back the provinces she had lost in the east to Russia, that is, chiefly Galicia and Bukovina.

   (*b*) Would take part of Serbia, including Belgrade, other parts going to Bulgaria and Albania, the remainder being restored but to be 'closely connected with the Monarchy from the economic point of view'.[32]

   (*c*) Would establish protectorates over Albania and Montenegro.

4. *Colonies.* Restoration of colonies 'equivalent to those formerly in the possession of Germany':[33] she might take part of the Belgian Congo.

These terms represented some reduction, but not much, for Germany in the west of what Bethmann had visualized in the September Programme.* The great difference was that while the September Programme contained the minimum which Germany would impose, the programme in November 1916 was, in Bethmann's view at any rate, the asking price. He wrote to Ludendorff for example that the annexation of Longwy-Briey was not a *sine qua non*;[34] indeed, in the final draft it was not specifically mentioned, being covered by the general demand for 'economic frontier adjustments'.[35] Burian considered that Germany's demands in the west were 'hardly capable of realization'.[36] Bethmann said at the time that the Austrian demands were 'somewhat ambitious'[37] and after the war that they 'went altogether too far'.[38]

The next step was to obtain the endorsement of Turkey and Bulgaria and, while this was being done, to find out how things were moving in Washington. On 16 November Jagow cabled that question to Bernstorff, mentioning that there were 'other possible steps in the same direction'.[39] Bernstorff, as we know,† saw House on 20 November and cabled on the following day that Wilson would take steps toward mediation, probably before the New Year. Interpreting rightly the implications of the 'other possible steps', the Count added that it was a condition of mediation 'that we should conduct the submarine war in strictest conformity to our promises and not allow any fresh controversies to arise'.[40]

On 22 November Jagow sent Bernstorff more definite news telling him of the imminent announcement, subject to the military situation, by the Central Powers of their willingness to enter on peace negotiations. But the Chancellor was still caring very much about his first iron. He took note of the reference in Bernstorff's cable, which was indeed a repetition of previous warnings, to the perils of the submarine war and obtained the assent of the Navy to a conciliatory Note on the *Marina*.[41] It was dispatched on 25 November and explained the incident as due to the fact that the submarine commander considered the *Marina* to be a horse transport ship and so to be treated as an auxiliary warship; if the American Government found this not to be so, his action would be due to a regrettable mistake. On 2 December Bethmann went straight to the Kaiser to get an order instructing submarine commanders, on account of the *Marina* and *Arabia* incidents, to avoid any action that might lead to complications with America. On 4 December Zimmermann sent to Washington a Note on the *Arabia* in the style of the *Marina* Note but with the substitution of troops for horses.[42] Meanwhile on 26 November Zimmermann telegraphed Bernstorff to say that a move by Wilson was to be preferred to the contemplated

* See p. 242 above.   † See p. 562 above.

announcement.[43] It was urgently desired that he should take action by the time Congress opened (that would be 5 December) or soon thereafter. If put off until the new year when preparations were being made for the spring offensive, military opposition would be strengthened. The ambassador was told to urge this point of view to House 'cautiously and without *empressement*' and to keep Berlin continuously informed. Bernstorff did nothing and was unable thereafter to give any convincing explanation of his inactivity. Perhaps he felt that he had already said enough to House.

If Bethmann did not move soon the die would be cast for the unrestricted U-boat war. How much longer could he afford to wait for Wilson? He had taken care to remove as far as he could any impediment that might be caused by the *Marina* and *Arabia* sinkings. He had not reckoned that the Belgian deportations would be another stumbling-block. On 4 December he received from Bernstorff a cable (sent on 1 December) reporting a conversation with Lansing in which the latter had hinted that unless something could be done to meet the protests of the neutral powers peace negotiations would be affected. On the next day Grew called to present the American protest.*[44] The chargé was instructed to mention, which he did, the great embarrassment caused to the President 'in regard to taking steps looking towards peace' and his distress at having 'his hopes frustrated and his occasion destroyed by such unhappy incidents as the sinking of the *Marina* and the *Arabia* and the Belgian deportations'. The President asked for some 'practical co-operation' in creating a favourable opportunity for some affirmative action by him. There was more than a hint here that the President would do nothing until he got his 'practical co-operation'. The Chancellor had done what he could about the *Marina* and the *Arabia*, but there was nothing he could do about the Belgian deportations; Ludendorff wanted the labour and that was that. Then on 7 December there came another cable from Bernstorff, saying that while everything was ready for the peace move 'the Belgian question stands very definitely in the way'.[45]

This must have decided Bethmann to publish the Central Powers' offer without waiting any longer for Wilson. In the evening of 7 December he went to Pless to get the High Command's approval. But Ludendorff, having obtained in advance what he had bargained for, the Polish proclamation and the labour law, was now minded to make further demands. He had been willing to defer the U-boat war only because of the fear that American intervention might bring in Denmark and Holland. Now that he had troops to spare from the Roumanian campaign he no longer cared about that. On 8 December Hindenburg addressed a memorandum

---

* See p. 564 above.

to the Kaiser in which he stated the conditions under which the peace proposal could be made; these included the new condition that unrestricted
U-boat warfare should be commenced by the end of January.[46] The Kaiser
was requested to instruct the High Command and the political branch to
co-operate on this basis. It was not going to be long before the Kaiser
would accept a *diktat* of this sort without a murmur. But in these early
days of the new régime he was not quite so easily cowed. He gave the
memorandum to Bethmann as soon as the latter arrived at Pless and Bethmann drew up a spirited rejoinder.[47] He would have appreciated it, he said,
if the High Command had postponed the memorandum until after a conference with the political branch. The High Command had already agreed
to the proposal on the assumption that it was not such as to appear as an
indication of weakness: now they put forward new conditions. Unrestricted
U-boat warfare could only be commenced after the promises given to
America and the other neutrals had been withdrawn. This could not be
decided immediately. But, Bethmann said, 'if our peace proposal is rejected, our standpoint in the matter of armed merchant ships will be pressed
with the utmost vigour in the United States'.

This alternative was something for which the Navy had been agitating
for some weeks past: if there was not to be unrestricted warfare, then at
least armed merchantmen—and most of the Allied merchantmen were now
being armed—should be treated as auxiliary warships and torpedoed
without warning. The Wilhelmstrasse had foreshadowed this possibility
on 1 December. A cable of that day had instructed Bernstorff to draw
Colonel House's attention to two incidents.[48] One was the discovery on
8 November on a French steamer, which had in fact fired at a German
submarine at sight, of instructions to commence firing as soon as the submarine was within good range. The other was a speech made by Lord
Crewe in the House of Lords on 15 November in which he blurted out
(Grey immediately suggested the remedy of slipping a qualifying word or
two into Hansard) that 'a German submarine is an enemy which it was
permissible and proper to destroy, if you could, at sight'.[49] Bernstorff had
been instructed to say that the Navy was urging a revision of the American
memorandum of 25 March* and that in order to avoid this question being
opened, Wilson's peace move must be initiated very shortly. Since this
had proved as ineffective as the other promptings to push Wilson into action,
Bethmann was now willing to concede the point. A long debate at Pless on
9 December resulted in compromise. The peace proposal would issue forth
on 12 December and in the event of its rejection Germany's position on
armed ships, which she had never formally abandoned, would be restated.

* See p. 429 above.

In a cable marked 'Confidential for your personal information' Bernstorff was told definitely that the proposal would be made.[50] An ingenious twist was given to the President's demand for 'practical co-operation': Bernstorff was to say that this was the co-operation which Germany offered to the President in his search for a favourable opportunity for action to restore peace.

So on 12 December Bethmann handed the Note to Grew with an expression of his sincere hope that this formal and solemn offer would coincide with the President's wishes. In the Reichstag the same day he had to present it as an offer made from strength but did so as unassertively as he could. During the long and severe years of war His Majesty had been imbued, he said, 'solely with the thought how peace could again be prepared by Germany, firmly secured after victorious battle';[51] and was now convinced that the suitable time had come for an official peace action. The Kaiser's arrogant exegesis of this sentiment in his speech to the troops on the following day was an unlooked-for addendum.[52] It should not have been generally released without the approval of the Wilhelmstrasse, but someone in the High Command, probably Ludendorff himself, found it too succulent to be distributed only as military rations. The best that the Wilhelmstrasse could do thereafter was to send a telegram to the German legations in European neutral countries on 18 December in which the envoys were instructed 'for the purpose of overcoming the effect of possible one-sided misrepresentation and exploitations of this speech' to call attention 'to the high-souled and humane determination of the Monarch' (as mentioned by the Chancellor in the Reichstag) in preference to 'language which was suited to the temper of the purely military establishment'.[53]

Bethmann's hopes for his peace proposal were quite high. In his letter to Hindenburg on 27 November he expressed the view that, given the good military situation for Germany, it would, at least for France, be very difficult to reject.[54] Writing to the German ambassador at Vienna on 15 December he said there were certain reasons to believe that the answer would not be an unconditional rejection;[55] if Germany was asked to disclose her peace conditions or to make binding announcements about Belgium and Serbia, the answer must be a blunt refusal. The general opinion in Berlin was pessimistic about the prospects of peace but felt that there must at least be some discussion. The Allied reaction, however, was swift and brusque. In Paris on 13 December M. Briand referred to 'these pretended proposals' and said it was doubtful whether those whose mediation was sought 'could accept such a delicate task, which might disturb many consciences'.[56] On 15 December the Duma turned it down flat: Russia would fight on for a peace of victory, the Foreign Minister said. On the same day Page cabled that the overwhelming feeling in London was against serious consideration unless Germany put forward definite and favourable terms, which nobody believed she would do.[57]

In Washington Wilson was naturally disconcerted by the German Note.[58] But when he received Bethmann's messages through Bernstorff and Grew about 'practical co-operation' and his hope that the German offer would coincide with the wishes of the President, he felt happier. The German Note was of course known in all the belligerent capitals but Wilson nevertheless had to consider in what terms he should comply with the German request to present it formally for their consideration. He had to consider also what he should do about his own Note. By 15 December he had decided that he would transmit the German Note together with some explanatory observations of his own and that he would also, after an interval sufficient to disconnect the two documents, present his own Note. Accordingly in the evening of 16 December the State Department dispatched the German Note to the American ambassadors in the belligerent capitals with instructions that they were to submit it on behalf of the Central Powers and not as the representative of the Government of the United States. Nevertheless, they were to say:

This Government is deeply interested in the result of these unexpected overtures, would deeply appreciate a confidential intimation of the character and purpose of the response that will be made, and will itself presently have certain very earnest representations to make on behalf of the manifest interests of neutral nations and of humanity itself to which it will ask that very serious consideration be given. It does not make these representations now because it does not wish to connect them with the proposed overtures or have them construed in any way as an attempt at mediation, notwithstanding the fact that these overtures afford an admirable occasion for their consideration. The Government of the United States had it in mind to make them entirely on its own initiative and before it had any knowledge of the present attitude or suggestions of the Central Governments. It will make the same representations to the Governments of the Central Powers and wishes to make them almost immediately, *if necessary*,* but not as associated with the overtures of either group of belligerents. The present overtures have created an unexpected opportunity for looking at the world's case as a whole, but the United States would have itself created the occasion had it fallen out otherwise.[59]

The phrase 'if necessary' shows that, as was apparent also from Wilson's instructions to Lansing, he hoped that the German offer would be accepted; indeed, as late as 19 December he told a friend that he was holding his breath for fear that it might meet with a rebuff. But he had already decided

* Italics added.

on 17 December that the danger of a rebuff was sufficiently great to make it highly necessary, as he wrote to Lansing, to send his own Note at once 'before it be too late to inject new elements into the debate'.[60] So the final version of his Note went off in the evening of 18 December. The instructions to the American ambassadors were that it was to be presented with the utmost earnestness of support and that they were to convey clearly the impression 'that it would be very hard for the Government of the United States to understand a negative reply'.[61] Wilson asked Lansing whether any special instructions ought to go out to Page to make him realize what was expected of him and Lansing replied that he did not see what could be added. It was too late to add anything anyway. Discussing the German Note with Cecil, Page had said, 'speaking quite seriously', that it must not be treated with derision, but that he thought that a reply that the British Government would not 'buy a pig in a poke' would be regarded as adequate by his government.[62] When Cecil inquired further whether the ambassador knew what would be contained in the representations his Government intended to make on their own, he replied that he did not; 'but, as he understood that they were to be made to all the belligerents, he did not think that they could be much more than a pious aspiration for peace, since that was the only thing that was equally applicable to the Germans and to us'. When Wilson's Note arrived with the instructions as to how it was to be presented, Page did what he doubtless regarded as the best that he could do in the circumstances. He read out the formula about the utmost earnestness and the incomprehensibility of a negative reply and elaborated on it by saying that the President had the matter very much at heart, that he was an idealist by temperament, and that this move of his, whether wise or not, was certainly dictated by the purest sentiment of humanity.[63] To which Cecil replied that the step was a very unusual one.

House took no part in the final stages of the draft. In New York he was busying himself on the practical detail of how to get the parties together. For this some knowledge of the German terms was obviously essential. There was no longer a Grey for him to talk to direct. Someone in the British embassy suggested that he should get the Foreign Office to hold their hand so as to give him an opportunity of getting Bernstorff to find out confidentially what the terms were. But the Foreign Office did not in this matter want to be confided in or indeed to confide. They did not act on Wilson's request for a 'confidential intimation' of what they were going to say; and they thanked House politely but said that they could not wait. Wilson wrote to House on 19 December:

Things have moved so fast that I did not have time to get you down here to go over it with you. It was . . . written and sent off within a very few hours, for fear the Governments of the Entente might in the meantime so have committed themselves against peace as to make the situation even more hopeless than it had been.[64]

Wilson sent also the original draft of the Note complete with all its eliminations and changes. House noted that he had seldom seen anything the President had written with so many changes.[65]

The President's Note of 18 December 1916 falls to be considered both as a piece of diplomacy and as a political statement.[66] Leaving aside for the moment the latter, let us consider it as a diplomatic move. As a move to bring peace out of the existing situation, it was practically useless and no one except Wilson and Mr. Baker the biographer have ever, either at the time or later, thought otherwise. In spite of a repeated disclaimer at the beginning of having anything to do with the German Note, it was universally regarded as an endorsement. M. Briand politely but firmly told the American ambassador when he presented it that it was embarrassing and 'unfortunately timed'.[67] Although in language it had diverged greatly from the original draft, its essence was unchanged; it was still designed to lead to a definition by each side of the terms on which it would settle. But it was less demanding in detail. In place of a firm request for 'a concrete definition of guarantees', there was an invitation to an 'avowal of each side's views as to the terms on which the war might be ended'.

Never yet have the authoritative spokesmen of either side avowed the precise objects which would, if attained, satisfy them and their people that the war had been fought out. The world has been left to conjecture what definitive results, what actual exchange of guarantees, what political or territorial changes or readjustments, what stage of military success even would bring the war to an end.

The President did not, as in his first draft urge a conference; but hoped that the interchange of views might lead to a conference in which he would be happy to take the initiative. He did not, as before, demand that the United States should be given without delay some guide by which it could 'intelligently determine its future course of action'; but he pointed out that the United States had an 'intimate interest' in the ending of the war.

The phrase which House so much deplored re-appeared in this form:

the objects which the statesmen of the belligerents on both sides have in mind in this war are virtually the same, as stated in general terms to their own people and to the world.

When he saw what had happened, House lamented: 'He seems obsessed with that thought, and he cannot write or talk on the subject of the war without voicing it . . . it is all so unnecessary.'[68] Certainly the theme was frequently on the President's lips. 'Just a fight . . . to see who is strong enough to prevent the other from fighting better', he said on 30 August.[69] 'Obscure European roots which we do not know how to trace', he said at Omaha on 5 October.[70] And in another election speech at Cincinatti on 26 October: 'Have you ever heard what started the present war? If you have, I wish you would publish it, because nobody else has, so far as I can gather. Nothing in particular started it, but everything in general.'[71] Page after his talk at Shadow Lawn noted that the President seemed to think of the war as 'a quarrel to settle economic rivalries between Germany and England'.[72] This thinking now reflected truly what Wilson felt about the war; and House was closing his eyes to what he did not like to see when he treated it as a sort of tactlessness which, as he said, would make the President unpopular in Allied countries.

In its latest form in the Note of 18 December the thought was more carefully guarded and should not have angered a dispassionate reader, at any rate if he did not look beyond the letter of the text. Wilson was not in words passing judgement but calling attention to the fact that the objects of each side *as stated* were the same. That was the whole point of his argument: since judged by their own statements their objects were the same, let the belligerents state also their terms and see how far they differed. But in December 1916 there were not many careful and dispassionate readers among the Allies; and after Wilson's reference to causes and objects in the address of 27 May they were prepared to read into his words a good deal that was not there and out of them the qualifications that were. They resented the fact that the Note put their professions on no higher level than the German and they refused to attribute the levelling to the necessary impartiality of an umpire. Impartiality was of itself a condemnation, for it meant that Wilson did not believe that they were fighting iniquity. Page reported 'surprise and sorrowful consternation';[73] a luncheon guest at the Palace had told him that the King had wept. 'Don't talk to me about it,' Asquith said, 'it is most disheartening.'[74] On 26 December when Page presented to Cecil a further message from Wilson asking for confidential replies to his Note, Cecil revealed the depth of his feeling in words that shook Page.[75] He could not get rid of the impression, he said, that 'recently American policy had had a somewhat pro-German twist'. He detected in the President's message 'a covert threat'. Britain would disregard it and carry the war to a victorious conclusion; he had hoped that the United States had understood what was at stake. One of Wilson's most virulent British critics, the British ambassador in Paris, he who had been so disgusted with Wilson for using mediation as an electioneering device, had his disgust increased by the thought that Wilson had now no longer 'the vile excuse of Presidential electoral necessities'.[76]

The centre-piece of the Note was the assumption that both parties were equally sincere in intention. On this assumption (and if it was false, the argument collapsed), the fact that they had been fighting each other for over two years while professing the same objects proved that they distrusted each other's professions. This distrust was at the root of the war; each side had made it quite clear that it thought that the other was out to dominate and destroy. Thus the real object of each side was to force the other to submit, because it thought that only by administering a beating could it make sure that the offence was not repeated. This was not the object of only a few bloody-minded men at the top. It was the object which would have been expressed, in differing words no doubt and with differing degrees of emphasis, by about 90 per cent of the populace on either side.

Wilson did not understand the problem which on his assumption he was tackling. If he had, he would have realized that he was dealing with a disorder of the emotions which could be cured perhaps by private and patient persuasion but not by publicly calling for an explanation of the apparently irrational behaviour of two people fighting each other for the same objects. Since he did not believe in the complete sincerity of either side, the protestations of each should have meant no more to him than campaign literature. Instead of putting these aside and getting to the heart of the matter— the distrust that each had for the other—he took the words at their face value and used them as a starting-point for discussion. As a matter of dialectics the approach was excellent. If he could succeed in conducting a Socratic dialogue, he would certainly be able sooner or later to expose the fact that one party or the other had either mis-stated its objects or fallen into error about the means necessary to achieve them. But as a method of stopping a fight in which as House reminded Wilson on 20 December (using the language of a new young friend at the British embassy) 'every belligerent nation had worked themselves up to an exalted enthusiasm of patriotic fervour', it was quite futile: 'do not try to argue with them', House advised.[77]

The eulogy in the official biography illustrates the point. Mr. Baker regarded Wilson's original draft before its dilution by timorous advisers

as one of the strongest papers Wilson ever wrote. It expressed in terms of consummate statesmanship a feasible way out of the misery the world was suffering,—but it was unfortunately addressed to reasonable human beings, when reasonable human beings had momentarily disappeared from off the earth. What could have been more sensible than to ask the fighters to stop for a moment, discuss what the war was all about, and define what each wanted as the price of peace?[78]

Mr. Baker's conclusion about the disappearance of reasonable beings may be right; but in that case observations, however statesmanlike, that are addressed to non-existent persons are bound to have an academic flavour. The suggestion that the fighters might stop for a moment and discuss what the war was all about—and presumably start off again if discussion brought no enlightenment—ignores the character of modern warfare; and explains why, if contrary to Mr. Baker's assumption it was being fought by reasonable beings, they resented the implication that until Wilson called attention to it they had not begun to think why they were killing each other. The voice was the voice of reason but the tone was the tone of mental and moral superiority.

The bleak prospects for this diplomatic initiative were not illuminated by a contribution from Lansing. At his morning press conference on 21 December, the day the Note was published, the Secretary found the idea prevailing that the American Note was in aid of the German overture. At the conference he explained that this was not so. But he felt that the denial needed bolstering. The natural point to make, in order to stress America's independent concern, was that American interests were threatened by a continuance of the war. When one says 'the natural' point, it was not of course, and this was perhaps a small part of the trouble, the point that Wilson would himself have stressed; he would have pointed to the interests of humanity and probably have got away with it even before a bunch of New York press correspondents. But Lansing might well have felt that he would not be able to maintain the discussion at that level. Below that level the motive for the Note, and one which certainly had influenced the President himself, was the impact that both belligerents were making on American rights. Lansing referred to this and said that in this respect the situation was becoming increasingly critical. If he had stopped there, all might have been well, but he expounded further: 'I mean that we are drawing nearer the verge of war ourselves, and therefore we are entitled to know exactly what each belligerent seeks, in order that we may regulate our conduct in the future.' And he concluded by saying:

The sending of this note will indicate the possibility of our being forced into the war. That possibility ought to serve as a restraining and sobering force, safeguarding American rights. It may also serve to force an earlier conclusion of the war. Neither the President nor myself regard this Note as a peace Note; it is merely an effort to get the belligerents to define the end for which they are fighting.[79]

The phrase that was headlined was of course 'verge of war'. There was quite a panic on the New York Stock Exchange. Wilson was understandably very angry; he told House that he had almost decided to dismiss Lansing. Certainly the Secretary's conduct was almost beyond belief. Without even consulting the President, he had interpreted and expanded a Note over whose drafting Wilson had spent many laborious hours; and had even said that the President did not regard it as a peace note.

While Lansing was doubtless furbishing up his favourite weapon in such emergencies, the secret memorandum of self-justification (whose gist in this case has been indicated above) and pondering its periods, Wilson was reaching out for his favourite weapon, the typewriter. The note that was sent round contained no formal rebuke. It was a courteous request for a corrective statement in terms that were firmly delineated; it was not at all in his mind, the Secretary was to say, to intimate any change in the policy of neutrality. Lansing went round to the White House. In his memoirs he puts a bold front on his account of the interview, but its content is best judged by the fact that he did exactly as he was told.[80]

A statement denied is not, however, a statement never made. What, everyone asked, was the Secretary getting at? If the United States stepped off 'the verge', in whose camp would she land? Since the public was quite unprepared for war with the Allies, it was generally assumed that Lansing believed war to be imminent with the Central Powers. However that might be, his intervention diminished the effectiveness of the Note. The inducement to compromise that the United States had to offer depended on her continuing neutrality. If she was coming into the war anyway, each side would be well advised to await the event before moderating its terms.

What was it that Lansing was up to? Was it innocent blundering, tinged maybe by his private disagreement with his chief but not double-dyed in treachery? The affirmative is suggested by the apparent futility of the exercise. Lansing knew that Wilson was not the man to be intimidated by a *fait accompli* and would not be tender to any interference with a project he had thought about so deeply. The best that could be hoped for would be a forced retraction and the worst dismissal: in the event it was the best that happened. Still, the forced retraction does not restore the *status quo ante*. Was the effect that was in fact produced the one that Lansing was deliberately aiming to get?

It is true that Lansing was speaking extempore at the press conference and it would not be fair to condemn him only on an inference drawn from what he there said. It is the external evidence assembled by Professor Link that makes it impossible to doubt that Lansing was guilty of sabotage. This evidence is in two pieces. One is a letter written a month later to a friend in which he confesses to a hidden motive. The letter does not fit in at all with the memorandum prepared for the record. In it he says that he cannot tell the whole story. 'For the present, however, I must bear the blame for having made an unpardonable blunder, and I do so with perfect equanimity knowing that my action accomplished what it was intended to accomplish.'[81]

The other piece of evidence is in the conversations he had with the French and British ambassadors, one on the day before the incident and the other on the day after.[82] What is known about them is derived from Jusserand's reports. What Lansing said explicitly was that America favoured the democracies and would do nothing to harm their interests; the object of the Note was to find out what they wanted. He personally thought that they might ask for Alsace-Lorraine, for indemnities, for an autonomous Poland under Russia, for the annexation of the Trentino by Italy, and the expulsion of Turkey from Europe. The impression he conveyed, if he did not express it in so many words, was that if the President himself was not all for the Allies, his entire Administration was and that the country would not follow him if he took any injurious action against them. He added for himself that he had no faith in Wilson's League of Nations and that only the triumph of democracy could guarantee world peace; the Allies might safely make it clear that they would deal only with a democratic Germany.

The 'blunder', linked with these conversations, told the British and the French all they needed to know. As against them the Note had no teeth in it and could safely be answered by a statement of terms on the lines of the House–Grey Memorandum with a few additions.

Lansing's disloyalty was accompanied by deceit. Some deceit is in the grain of disloyalty since disloyalty unconfessed is the acting of a lie. But on 21 December Lansing told a separate and independent lie to Wilson and to the world. The requirement that he should state that there was no change in America's policy of neutrality was not the only one, nor the most significant, in the typewritten note that Wilson sent. Wilson suspected—who could not?—at the least a lack of sympathy for his policy in Lansing and he asked for what was tantamount to an affirmation of allegiance. Lansing would know how to phrase the statement, the President wrote, 'and how to give your unqualified endorsement to the whole tone and purpose of our note'.[83] The phraseology which Lansing chose was:

I think that the whole tone and language of the Note to the belligerents show the purpose without further comment on my part. It is needless to say that I am unreservedly in support of that purpose and hope to see it accepted.

If he had jibbed at that, it can hardly be doubted that he would have been dismissed. Yet the purpose was one which he did not approve, which he believed to imperil the national interest, and which he intended so far as he could to frustrate.

Disloyalty is not dishonour. There can be a conflict of loyalty where the lesser yields to the greater without dishonour. The man himself is the best judge of when the moment comes at which, in order to escape dishonour, he has to quit the battlefield. Some would say that for Lansing that moment came on 21 December and ask why, unless it was for love of office, did he not then resign rather than perjure himself. Undoubtedly he liked his place but undoubtedly also he had his principles, springing from his profound belief that dignity and duty alike demanded that his country join the fight against tyranny. By staying in office he could best serve his principles if not his master. It would not be easy to determine—maybe he would not truly have known himself—whether he liked better his principles or his place. So that it was fortunate that they went together.

But any diagnosis of his mind on this occasion is complicated by the fact that he was a vain man who was being made to feel as of no account. Indeed, the letter to his friend, which no accomplished deceiver would have written, came out of his vanity: he did not want his friends to think that he had blundered unwittingly, that he was a man who did not know what he was about. In the 'verge of war' statement is there not some pathos in the sentence: 'Neither the President nor myself regard ...'? As if anyone thought it mattered how Lansing regarded what! Yet he was Secretary of State and as such he was cruelly exposed to the temptation of asserting himself. Wilson was not without blame. The President cannot appoint a second-rater to the highest office in the State after his own, deny him any say in policy, and wash his hands of the result. There is another way in which Wilson brought this on himself. Lansing had now made it plain enough by tergiversation what Page had made plain with pungency, namely, that he was out of sympathy with the President's policy. It was a flaw in Wilson's character as an executive that he was so averse to bringing himself to the clear sword-cut which severs the disaffected limb.

The German Note and its developments came at a moment inconvenient to the Allies. On 12 December M. Briand had reshuffled his Government. The new British Government was hardly in the saddle, the new War Cabinet held its first meeting on 9 December, and the new Prime Minister caught a bad cold. This, combined perhaps with some nervous exhaustion after the political crisis, was too much even for Lloyd George's tough physique and on 14 December he was driven to bed. Meanwhile, the new Foreign Secretary was convalescing at Brighton.

A severe attack of influenza had disabled Balfour from more than occasional participation in the discussions about who would serve under whom which had been conducted around the death-bed of the Asquith Cabinet. Neither Asquith himself nor any of the Liberal members of his Cabinet would serve under Lloyd George. The support of Bonar Law did not bring with it the adhesion of any of the Conservative members of the old Cabinet and their attitude to Lloyd George was doubtful. The assembling of the new Cabinet was a skilful piece of political construction and Balfour was its keystone. The difficulty that seemed to stand in the way of the new builder, Lloyd George, was that he had for some time past (to the accompaniment of a running commentary in the press) been extremely critical of Balfour's administration of the Admiralty and had made his removal a condition of a compromise plan that had collapsed. The plan was that Lloyd George should be Chairman of the War Committee with Asquith remaining as Prime Minister. In the first stage of the discussion of the plan Asquith accepted it in principle but refused to move Balfour; in the second stage he rejected it *in toto*. This was well known to Balfour. But Balfour was as detached about himself as he was about the rest of creation. When he heard of the plan and the discussion was still, as he thought, in the first stage, he wrote to Asquith offering his resignation: 'we cannot, I think, go on in the old way: L.G. cannot be lost, the experiment with the War Committee was worth trying and it must be tried on L.G.'s terms.'[84] Lloyd George, when he heard of this, was greatly struck by Balfour's patriotism.[85] Certainly Balfour had that virtue and he had also the dispassion which enabled him to put a just value on Lloyd George's worth. Whether these were the only factors then stirring his inward thoughts could be guessed at only after a detailed account of events and a detailed analysis of a complex character. The outward appearances of the move have been perfectly described by Winston Churchill:

Nothing is more instructive than to follow the dispassionate, cool, correct and at the same time ruthless manner in which Balfour threaded the labyrinth without reproach. He passed from one Cabinet to the other, from the Prime Minister who was his champion to the Prime Minister who had been his most severe critic, like a powerful graceful cat walking delicately and unsoiled across a rather muddy street.[86]

It was typical of him that his acceptance of the Foreign Office was subject to the condition that he should be allowed time to recuperate from his influenza. Thus it came about that at this juncture foreign affairs were in the charge of his cousin, Lord Robert Cecil.

Lloyd George was back at work on 18 December when the Cabinet first

considered the German Note. By this time the opinions of the Allies and
the views of the European neutrals had been collected. The consensus was
that the rejection of the offer should not be unqualified, but should be put
on the ground that an offer on terms unknown was useless. The War Cabinet
decided in this sense and further that the Prime Minister should express
this conclusion in the House of Commons the next day and that there should
be one Note in answer on behalf of all the Allies. In his speech the next
day, his first in Parliament as Prime Minister, Lloyd George struck home
with a quotation from Abraham Lincoln in the American Civil War: 'We
accepted this war for an object, and a worthy object, and the war will end
when that object is attained. Under God I hope it will never end until
that time.' He went on:

> To enter on the invitation of Germany, proclaiming herself victorious, with-
> out any knowledge of the proposals she proposes to make, into a conference, is
> to put our heads into a noose with the rope end in the hands of Germany . . .
> The mere word that led Belgium to her destruction will not satisfy Europe any
> more . . . We shall put our trust in an unbroken army rather than a broken faith.[87]

Before the Allies' reply to the German Note had been further prepared
the American Note was delivered. This was not so simple to deal with.
The first point the British Cabinet had to settle was whether the answer
to it was being addressed to an innocent inquirer or to a potential strangler.

The last item discussed in Asquith's last Cabinet meeting on 30 November 1916 was the action of the Federal Board of Reserve.* In October
the Cabinet had been advised that 'by the use of every available device'
the British position in the United States might remain solvent until 31 March
1917.† One of the expedients, admittedly only temporary, was to get
American banks to buy British and French short-term Treasury Notes.
The day would come when they would have to be funded but until it came
they could go on being renewed. It would have been improvident to embark on this course without first getting the reaction of the Board. When
on 18 November Mr. Davison, the partner in Morgans who was handling
the matter, put up the plan the reception was cool. Mr. Davison, who was
not a very tactful operator, had already let it be known that the issue of a
new British loan was contemplated and had said that he felt the time had
come when it should be accepted without collateral. On 19 November the
Governor of the Board, Mr. Harding, sought an interview with Lansing.
The latter, in his role of family lawyer rather than that of the international
statesman who thought that the Allies ought to win, advised that the Board

* See p. 554 above.   † See p. 550 above.

should be slow to approve unliquid securities with no collateral. On 25 November the Governor went to see the President and took with him a draft announcement warning banks against investing too heavily in these Treasury Notes. The President said that he had hoped that the Board would issue some such statement but had not felt like suggesting it himself. He said that important considerations of foreign policy were involved and that relations with England were more strained than with Germany. He promised his comments on the announcement. He sent them the next day in a letter of more than warm approval in which he suggested that the announcement be made stronger and more pointed and be made to carry explicit advice against investment rather than a mere caution. The strengthened announcement was issued on 27 November. In it the Board deemed it its duty 'to caution the member banks that it does not regard it in the interest of the country at this time that they invest in foreign Treasury bills of this character'.[88] The price of Allied bonds tumbled and the House of Morgan had to buy nearly $20,000,000 of sterling to maintain the exchange.

The alarm was sounded in London on the following day. A War Committee meeting on 28 November to discuss the affairs of the Air Board had adjourned until the evening,[89] but when it met again McKenna had a more exciting topic for its immediate attention, 'the possibility of a very serious situation arising owing to the apparent intention of the United States withholding their financial support from the Allies'. Balfour thought it the most serious matter which had come up for consideration before the War Committee, infinitely more serious even than the submarine menace. Grey wondered whether what was at the back of it was Wilson's intent to bring pressure to bear on both sides; if the submarine menace were to increase, the question of terms must be considered. Bonar Law alone was undisturbed. He took the businessman's view that 'people who had money to lend would always be prepared to lend it in order to make a profit', said that 'the United States were producing wheat and munitions which they must dispose of', and concluded with the thought that 'there was still a means by which we could retaliate upon the United States'.

When the Cabinet met on 30 November they were confronted with advice from the British banks to abandon the gold standard and with advice from Morgans to defy the warning and carry on.[90] They took neither course. They decided not to proceed with the issue of the Treasury Notes, but, as Law had suggested, to make it clear that if facilities were restricted purchases must be also. On 1 December Morgans announced that the bills would be withdrawn because of the Allied Governments' desire 'to show every regard for the Federal Reserve Board'.[91]

The British in Washington were upset and angry. Spring Rice distributed the blame between the intrigues of the pro-German Warburg (he could not blame McAdoo because he was away in California), the vengeance of the Administration upon Morgans who had supported Hughes in the election, and the desperate condition of the United States's finances, though when pressed for details by the Foreign Office he withdrew this last as ill-founded. Crawford was very indignant. If a warning was thought necessary, he asked, why was it not given privately instead of by publicly impugning British credit? Mr. Davison became unwell and retired to White Sulphur Springs. Lansing vehemently denied any hostility to Britain. Governor Harding on 1 December stated publicly that the warning was 'intended in no way to slight the financial status of any foreign country'. When told that Crawford was unmollified, the Governor called at his home on a Sunday morning, 3 December, to say that McAdoo had telegraphed and would endeavour to make amends in a speech he was making on 11 December. Harding went on to speak as a friend and in the strictest confidence. What he said boded ill for the British. He wanted Crawford to know, so Crawford reported,

that the paragraph cautioning individual investors to which I had taken the gravest objection, was not in the original draft as prepared by him, but that he had been instructed to insert it by the highest authority. He advised me also carefully to watch the future foreign policy of the President's Administration with relation to Great Britain.

The President was not at all displeased by the hubbub and its effect upon the British. When a suggestion was made that it might be calming to publish the total amount of foreign securities held by American banks since it was in fact less than generally supposed, he replied on 11 December that the statement should be withheld for the present: 'I am not sure what indirect effect the publication might have on some of our foreign relations.'[92]

This was the situation with which the War Cabinet (the comparatively tight new body which replaced the councils and committees and plenums of Asquith's time) had to deal when it met for the first time on 9 December.[93] Bonar Law, the new Chancellor of the Exchequer, advised that the Federal Reserve Board's announcement had destroyed the hope of seeking in January a loan without collateral of $500,000,000. There was nothing for it except to restrict purchases. The Cabinet decided to do that but without making any announcement.

The future, though not immediately catastrophic, was very very gloomy. A cut of the order of 40 per cent of their supplies would rapidly reduce the Allies to the state to which they hoped by means of the blockade to reduce Germany: and this at a stage when their soldiers could show them no way of winning except by outlasting the enemy. If they lost their staying power, where was their hope of victory?

It was the crisis of the war, less dramatic but more deadly than the battles in the spring of 1918. For in them the enemy was shooting his last bolt; if it hit the target it could rob the Allies of some of the fruits of victory but could never with the American might behind them reduce them to defeat. In January 1917 defeat, total or partial, lurked at the end of the road of dwindling resources.

The French and British reacted to the crisis in their different ways. The French were in favour of treating the American Note almost as brusquely as the German and adding to the reply to America a vigorous protest against the assimilation of the two groups of belligerents. But they were not so close to the financial realities; it was the British who were the bankers of the Entente and who by the end of the war had lent to their allies £1,825 million of which more than half was raised in America. And if it came to the crunch, it was not the French who would starve. Moreover, there was no choice for them between victory and defeat. Germany could allow, as she did, for co-existence with Britain but not with France who must be reduced sufficiently to survive subordinate. The French for their part could not feel safe while the menace of another 1870 hung over them. They were resolved that 1870 should be wiped out, the revenge sealed by the return of Alsace-Lorraine, and that it should never be repeated. On the issues so drawn there could be no compromise. Never again, as House was fond of pointing out, in what seemed their unending quarrel with the Teuton, would the French have ranged on their side so many powerful allies: *il faut en finir*. Thus while House could at least talk terms with the British, he never could with the French. On 3 December he had quite a disagreeable interview with Jusserand in which the latter complained of Wilson's pro-Germanism. House tried to get him to talk of mediation but 'he veered away', House reported to Wilson, 'into the highflown foolish declaration that France would fight to the last man'.[94] This was the French attitude that would have to be cracked before they would even think of compromise. For some it may have been highflown; but that for others it was infrangible they and their children were to prove gloriously between 1940 and 1945 in the resistance to Vichy and its German masters.

The British, as the Cabinet deliberations showed, were as firmly resolved. Although their future as a nation was not at stake, it was not in their nature to be the first to cry quits. Having settled on their goal, they were not put off by their inability to see any way of reaching it other than that of going straight ahead till they dropped. At such moments the British have an obtuseness of vision that served them as well in 1916 as it was to do again in 1940. If one may hazard a guess the most splendidly blinkered was Bonar Law. His influence was now great, especially on this issue; he was at the Exchequer, second in command in the Cabinet and the Leader of the party which sustained the new Government. At the War Committee on 28 November, when the pending disaster was first disclosed, it was he and not Lloyd George who had been the stalwart. He talked always in commercial terms. He spoke of facing 'victory or bankruptcy' as if the alternative to victory was no worse than an appearance in Carey Street. In argument he could be driven round the ring or into a corner, but he could never be knocked down. It was he who on 28 November said: 'There cannot be any slackening of the pace: we must go on as long as we can.' The price of determination was for him greater than for others. In 1917, one in April and one in September, two of his sons were killed in battle.

The other members of the Cabinet manifested the 'do or die' spirit in different fashions. Some were for joining the French in defying the fates and in tweaking the American nose. Others disparaged the difficulties. Others waited for something to turn up; and these were the best vindicated in the result since they had only six weeks to wait. A Cabinet composed of these diverse elements did as the optimistic householder does when he finds his expenditure exceeding his income: he carries on, proceeding with economy but without destructive retrenchment. The advice that would be given to any householder as to how he should behave during the anxious and distressing period between full solvency behind him and the bare cupboard ahead, would certainly include being civil to the grocer. This advice had, as we have seen, been pressed on the Cabinet from all sides. What then does the householder do when, as happened to the Allies on 21 December, the grocer leaves a polite little note on the doorstep with a rather impertinent inquiry to which he says he would not understand a negative answer?

When the Cabinet on 21 December first considered the American Note it did so only to give instructions that a paper should be prepared showing the effect of the maximum pressure which America could bring to bear on the Allies and the effect also of pro-Allied reaction to such pressure in America itself.[95] Lloyd George advised the French that it would be wise for them also to give some thought to their dependence on the United States.[96] The Prime Minister commanded that the Cabinet paper be ready that evening. Hankey, who was in the throes of creating a new secretariat, found this 'tiresome and exacting'.[97] The work 'tremendously upset half the departments in the Government and placed an almost intolerable strain on my office'. He had put his best man, G. M. Young the historian, on to the job, but when the Cabinet next met on 23 December they did not even consider the paper. Hankey was not too well pleased by this too abrupt departure from Asquithian methods.

The Cabinet considered a memorandum from Cecil who advised in favour of stating terms.[98] He did not put this solely, or even primarily, on the ground that American reprisals were to be feared. The President would be much disappointed, he thought, and would undoubtedly look about for the means to make the Allies feel his displeasure; but he thought it unlikely that he would proceed to directly hostile measures though he might do so in time. But, so Cecil argued, the Allies had now an opportunity to show that justice and liberty meant for them something definite and was not mere verbiage; if they refused to state their terms, it would be argued that they were immoderate and indefensible and the refusal would have a bad effect on neutral opinion and on pacific opinion in their own camp. The Cabinet took no final decision but instructed Cecil to prepare a draft on the lines he recommended. A three-day Anglo-French conference was scheduled to meet on 26 December and it is a measure of the importance which the Allies attached to the diplomatic situation that its agenda was made to give way and nearly half the time was spent on discussing the reply to the German and American Notes. There was no substantial difference of opinion on the reply to the German Note, but the French still thought it unwise to answer Wilson with any explicitness about terms while Cecil strongly argued for the contrary view. No decision was reached that day and the matter was not taken up again until 28 December.

In the meanwhile the German reply had been published. No one could fail to see the diplomatic advantage which its negative character gave to the Allies. Indeed, in this diplomatic game the Allies had a double advantage. First they knew from the House–Grey Memorandum and the recent extravagations of Lansing what framework of terms would not, to put it at its lowest, shock America; a diplomatic draughtsman would not be worth much if he could not overlay the frame with a sufficiency of generalities to allow for the comfortable accommodation of all shapes and sizes of treaty that were likely to want to sit on it. Secondly, the Allies could talk, as the Central Powers could not, in terms of restoration, restitution, and liberation. Germany's objective was to retain what she had conquered and to add more as necessary to her future security. It was very difficult to make the distinction between security and aggrandizement sound convincing. Where the Allies asked simply for restoration—Belgium and Serbia— Germany sought acquisitions on a huge scale, parts of Belgium and France, the whole of Luxembourg, and whole provinces in Russia. What were territorial gains for the Allies, such as Alsace-Lorraine for France or the Trentino for Italy, could be described either as the restitution of past robberies or as liberation from foreign domination. The latter head could be stretched, if need be, to compass the break-up of the Austrian and Ottoman Empires. To the former there was a number of heirs, such as the Czechs and the Slovaks, whose claims the Allies could decently support and it was unnecessary at this stage to be precise about what was expected for Roumania. If the Ottoman Empire went, something would have to be done to fill the vacuum; it was likewise unnecessary at this stage to detail the secret arrangements between the Allies designed to ensure that one should not seek to fill it at the expense of another. The expulsion from Europe of the barbarous Turk sounded much better than the acquisition of Constantinople by Russia. In short, they were Democrats talking to a Democracy in a language that was still foreign to the Central Powers.

So it is not surprising that Cecil won his point. A drafting committee was appointed on 28 December and a draft agreed that night. Balfour was anxious to make the point, first made in his abortive memorandum of the previous May,* that the future organization of the world was dependent on the sort of peace the Allies wanted; and it was agreed that he should send a separate paper.

The reply to the German Note was dispatched to Washington on 29 December.[99] It was argumentative in recital and terse in conclusion; a suggestion without any conditions for initiating negotiations was not, it said, an offer of peace but a manœuvre of war. The delivery of the Allied reply to the American Note had to be delayed to get everyone's approval and was not made until 10 January 1917.[100] It took M. Briand's draft as the main text but replaced the cloudy and impenetrable negative at the end with the assertion (which any participant in their deliberations would have found hard to believe) that the Allies experienced no difficulty in replying to the President's request for terms. They could not, they said, make known their objects in detail until the hour of negotiations but they could state what was implied. The reader will by now have no difficulty in guessing what the implications were. But since this was the first occasion on which concrete terms were stated by either side and since the Allied terms were put into a form that was the basis of the Treaty of Versailles it is well to enumerate the heads. These were as follows:

1. The restoration of Belgium and Serbia with indemnities.
2. The evacuation of the invaded territories of France, Russia, and Roumania with 'just reparation'.
3. The restitution of territories taken by force in the past.
4. The liberation of Italians, Slavs, Roumanians, and Czechoslovaks from foreign domination.

* See p. 493 above.

5. The enfranchisement of populations subject to the Turks and the expulsion of Turkey from Europe.

6. The independence of Poland in accordance with the Tsar's proclamation recently reaffirmed.

Finally, the Allies declared that their object was the liberation of Europe 'from the brutal covetousness of Prussian militarism' but not the extermination of the German people or their political disappearance.

Such was the Allied reply and at least it complied with Wilson's request for a statement of terms. Compliance was for Bethmann far more difficult. He was not in mid December unduly depressed by the response to the German Note. The formal answer had not yet been given. Sonnino speaking for Italy had been cautious. Lloyd George's rhetoric had left the door just wide enough open to admit a discussion of terms if any came forward: this was a characteristic of his method, not only at this period but throughout his political life and from its very beginning—'pugnacity and audacity, with an ever-open eye to the chances of compromise' as a recent biographer has well described it.[101] Bethmann's difficulty lay of course in stating his terms. It must have been a considerable disappointment to him that Wilson's Note was in the form of a request for terms instead of a suggestion of a conference. But for Bethmann the prospect of negotiations was all that stood between Germany and the disastrous policy of the unrestricted U-boat war; and he must go on out of desperation if not in hope. It was the risk of Wilson's meddling in the settlement that had so far been decisive in his mind against the statement of terms. It is conceivable that now he would have incurred that: but his difficulty was to make a statement which would neither upset Wilson nor be successfully derided by his opposition at home. The terms in Europe which he had formulated were not all. Solf at the Colonial Office, who sent in a memorandum on 26 December,[102] was still thinking in terms of a German Mittelafrika which would mean Germany taking over the Congo and the Portuguese colonies and more to boot from Britain and France while requiring the restoration of all her own. The Navy, who had also prepared memoranda at the Chancellor's request, wanted Atlantic bases, the Azores for certain, and either the Cape Verde Islands or Dakar and its hinterland.

Germany's formal reply to the American Note was settled promptly with her allies and sent off on 26 December.[103] It was what Bernstorff described as a 'friendly negative' and an attempt to put the project back where Germany wanted it. The direct exchange of views, the reply said, was the most suitable way of arriving at the desired result and the German Government therefore proposed a conference on neutral ground.

But while this Note was being settled in Berlin and agreed with Vienna other avenues were being opened. Before the American Note was dispatched Lansing had discussed it with Bernstorff and said that what was wanted was 'frank statements from the belligerent Powers on their peace conditions'.[104] When Bernstorff said that this would be difficult except through a conference, Lansing replied that the statements could be confidential and might gradually lead to a conference. Bernstorff telegraphed this idea to Berlin on 21 December, adding that the general opinion was that Wilson would like to act as a 'clearing house' for the further steps towards peace;[105] the telegram arrived on 25 December. The idea was made official by the State Department sending out a supplementary telegram to the belligerent Powers on 24 December.[106] In this it was requested that the reply should be made not publicly but in strict confidence so that the United States might convey it in like confidence to the other side, in order that it might in this way be ascertained without publicity whether there was any ground for negotiation or conference.

But Bethmann stuck to his position. Bernstorff was told that interference by the President, even in the form of a 'clearing house', was not acceptable. 'The basis for future conclusion of peace we must decide in direct conference with our enemies if we are not to run the risk of being robbed of our gains by neutral pressure.'[107]

Lansing told Bernstorff that he could not understand why Germany would not name her conditions. When the ambassador replied that German demands were so moderate that they would be interpreted as weakness, Lansing said, as he had said also to the Allied ambassadors, that they could ask for anything at all so long as it provided a starting point for negotiations. But when on 27 December Bernstorff called on House at his request in New York, he had an explanation to give that was more convincing than excessive moderation and which produced a more appealing suggestion. He explained that Berlin feared leaks in the State Department; and this was in truth, the fear not being unjustified, one of the reasons in Bethmann's mind. House suggested that the German terms should be divulged to Wilson and himself in absolute confidence and he offered to ask for the President's approval. He wrote to Wilson: 'I feel sure, if we are persistent and ingenious enough a start can be made, and having once started, final negotiations will follow.'[108]

So on 29 December Bernstorff put this proposal to Berlin. Complete discretion, he said, was assured, 'as Wilson and House, unlike most Americans, are both fairly clever at keeping secrets'.[109] He said also that House had made it clear that there would be no conference without previous confidential negotiations. And he commended the idea. 'With the exception of the Belgian question the American Government ought to bring us more advantage than disadvantage, as the Americans have only just come to realise what England's mastery of the seas means.'[110]

Bethmann was very tempted by this and he went so far as to draft a set of terms for communication. But he had to reckon not only with Zimmerman, who was a much stronger character than Jagow, but with those also to whom Zimmerman was much closer than Bethmann and Jagow had ever been, namely the High Command. Whether because of his own second thoughts or because he gave way to Zimmerman, he scrapped his draft. The telegram dispatched on 7 January 1917 instructed Bernstorff to stall.[111] It was delayed and Bernstorff did not see House until 15 January. By that time—indeed, within forty-eight hours of the telegram's dispatch—Germany had sealed her doom.

XIX
PEACE WITHOUT VICTORY
JANUARY 1917

The old and the new diplomacy — Mrs. Wilson and House and Tumulty — the beginning of the Peace without Victory Address — Paderewski and Poland — the delivery of the Address: 22 January — its reception — British-American diplomacy: Sir William Wiseman — German-American diplomacy: the last word on 31 January — Germany's decision to wage unrestricted war — the gamble and what happened to it — the end of Bethmann

THE Note of 18 December 1916 was the second in the great trilogy whose theme is that the peace of the world is the concern of all, that to wage war unnecessarily is an offence against international morality, and that victory can cost immeasurably more than it can possibly be worth. This was a new and challenging doctrine.

When the twentieth century opened nothing had happened to alter the age-old conception of warfare. It was the affair of the nations who fought. It was the recognized and permitted way of settling a dispute. It was for the disputants to keep the battle within the ring and for other nations to look on. This was how America understood the position in 1914: this was the basis of her neutrality. Before the century was half over, the aeroplane had decimated distance, the atom bomb was annihilating cities, and great adversaries in their efforts to achieve the mastery were shaking the pillars of the world.

Neutrality is in a great war no longer an open house which all who do not care to concern themselves with the battle may freely enter; it has become the precarious refuge of the few whom an accident of nature shelters from the storm. Every thinking man now knows that there can hardly be a war anywhere which will leave him untouched. What Wilson said seems therefore half a century later to be flatly truistic. It did not seem so to the Establishment of 1916. 'Frankly a piece of impertinence.'[1] Lord Hardinge of Penshurst had been the Civil Service head of the Foreign Office from 1906 to 1910 and had after the viceroyalty of India returned to the post in June

1916. He was a Knight of the Garter and a Knight Grand Commander of all the British orders of chivalry except the Order of the British Empire which was not created until 1917 and anyway was below his station in life. The dictum quoted above is the comment on Wilson's Note which he makes in his book of memoirs, appropriately called *The Old Diplomacy*; it is a dictum with which the vast majority of the Knights, Knights Commanders, and Knights Grand Commanders then in Britain would have concurred.

The difference between the old and the new diplomacy has been described by Elihu Root in a letter composed in August 1918 which Professor Zimmern has described as 'one of the classics of American political writing'.

The view now assumed and generally applied is that the use of force by one nation toward another is a matter in which only the two nations concerned are primarily interested, and if any other nation claims a right to be heard on the subject it must show some specific interest of its own in the controversy. That burden of proof rests upon any other nation which seeks to take part if it will relieve itself of the charge of impertinent interference and avoid the resentment which always meets impertinent interference in the affairs of an independent sovereign state. This view was illustrated by Germany in July 1914 when she insisted that the invasion of Serbia by Austria-Hungary was a matter which solely concerned two states, and upon substantially that ground refused to agree to the conference proposed by Sir Edward Grey. The requisite change is an abandonment of this view and a universal, formal and irrevocable acceptance of the view that an international breach of the peace is a matter which concerns every member of the Community of Nations—a matter in which every nation has a direct interest and to which every nation has a right to object.

When this principle is accepted, Root went on,

the practical results which will naturally develop will be as different from those which have come from the old view of national responsibility as are the results which flow from the American Declaration of Independence compared with the results which flow from the Divine Right of Kings.[2]

In this letter to Colonel House, which he doubtless knew was for Wilson to read too, Root cleaned the point of every irrelevance and put it tersely and unemotionally; Wilson in the addresses which he drafted as an appeal to the people of the world enveloped it in warmer and hazier language, but the same new thought was in both. The thing had been said before, of course, by voices raised here and there. But this was the first time that the head of a sovereign state had set an international communication firmly upon the thesis that a war between some nations was the concern of all, that the price of victory, whichever side won, had to be paid by all, and that the price might be too high. Wilson pleaded his justification in these words:

The President therefore feels altogether justified in suggesting an immediate opportunity for a comparison of views as to the terms which must precede those ultimate arrangements for the peace of the world, which all desire and in which the neutral nations as well as those at war are ready to play their full responsible part. If the contest was to continue to proceed towards undefined ends by slow attrition until the one group of belligerents or the other is exhausted; if million after million of human lives must continue to be offered up until on the one side or the other there are no more to offer; if resentments must be kindled that can never cool and despairs engendered from which there can be no recovery, hopes of peace and of the willing concert of free peoples will be rendered vain or idle.

The life of the entire world has been profoundly affected. Every part of the great family of mankind has felt the burden and terror of this unprecedented contest of arms. No nation in the civilized world can be said in truth to stand outside its influence or to be safe against its disturbing effects. And yet the concrete objects for which it is being waged have never been definitively stated.[3]

The Colonel's disagreement with the Peace Note was only on method. Unlike Lansing he was willing to treat with the autocracies; if they would accept reasonable terms, such as would lay the foundation of a good peace, House would do business with them. But he thought that Wilson was setting about it in a way which was bound to fail because ill-prepared and which would unnecessarily irritate the Allies and so weaken the President's position: on both these points he was right diplomatically. Nevertheless, when overruled he set about the tasks assigned to him with his usual assiduity.

Wilson did not summon him back to Washington, as he could have done, to see the Note in its final form. The Colonel left the White House on 13 November and Wilson probably did not decide until 15 November that he was going to send it; as he explained to House, this left very little time. But the re-emergence, although in a different form, of the 'sameness of objects' passage could not have been unwitting and probably Wilson did not want any more comment on it from House. What is perhaps more significant, since confidential diplomacy was House's *métier*, is that Wilson apparently did not consult him before sending off the supplementary Note on 24 December inviting confidential replies. But as House was at the same time talking to Bernstorff on the same lines there was no divergence of purpose.

Probably House was a little shaken by the whole experience. Probably too he was alarmed by Wilson's reluctance even to contemplate war with Germany, especially when contrasted with his airy talk about war with

Britain. In the latter Wilson was indulging his fancy and it is a sign that House was rattled that he should have taken it so seriously: he mentioned it both to Daniels, the Navy Secretary, and to Polk. In his dismay he exaggerated in his diary the effect of the Note, saying that 'the President has nearly destroyed all the work I have done in Europe',[4] and almost for the first time allowed his criticisms to escape from it; on 22 December he let Plunkett understand that he was disgusted at many of Wilson's recent utterances.[5]

This was the beginning of the end of their deep friendship. But there was much besides intimacy that was valuable to Wilson in the association. House remained the efficient and sympathetic minister, and Wilson knew how to appreciate that at its full worth. Moreover, events enabled House to regain most, if not all, of any confidence he had lost. If America had not gone to war the two men would have slipped apart much sooner than they did. But since the war put an end to mediation, the two came together again, happily planning the Fourteen Points and the League of Nations; then, repeating the cycle, the friendship fell away over the settlement of the terms. But this time the flow of sympathy was for ever cut off and the companionship ended. That was two years later. In 1917 the relationship remained outwardly unaltered except for a small thing. The 'Dearest Friend', the salutation with which Wilson began all his letters to House, changed about this time to 'My dear House'; but they still ended 'Affectionately' and often included a warm expression of feeling.

There was another reason for an inner change in the relationship. Edith Wilson was not the sort of woman to accept that there was any part of her husband's life that did not concern her. House soon found out that his advice to her to leave political problems to the President, including therein by implication to himself, was not going to be swallowed neat. Her political interest was personal to her husband but wide enough to cover anything appertaining to his health or happiness; and since he was the President, that could mean a good deal. It centred on his immediate entourage, which meant House himself, Tumulty, and Grayson, the only ones besides herself who had access to the President. Throughout 1916 she concerned herself closely with Grayson's efforts to secure promotion. On the principle of making friends with those who might be dangerous enemies, House allied himself with her on this and other matters. On the surface relations between Mrs. Wilson and House were always cordial; she did nothing rash and he was far too tactful to give offence. But it was inevitable that the all-pervading influence of a very possessive woman should gradually extrude lesser intimacies. The ladies in Wilson's life like morning stars at the rising of the sun receded into the firmament and were seen no more. The men gave place more slowly.

Early in January 1917 Wilson suggested to House that he take Page's place at the London embassy and House declined at once. On 5 March, Inauguration Day, the Colonel dined at the White House. After dinner Mr. and Mrs. Wilson drew apart from the family to watch the fireworks from the Oval Room and invited House to join them. The President was holding his wife's hand and leaning with his face against hers when House spoke of his joy that 'we three', rather than the Hughes family, were looking at the fireworks from the White House.[6] Later in the evening Mrs. Wilson suggested that House should take the London embassy and again he declined. It was not an offer that would have been made, let alone repeated, in the old days. It was an important post, but not one for a 'second personality' or even for the third person of a trinity.

In January 1917 Tumulty's position also sustained a shock. This was a matter of domestic politics in which Mrs. Wilson took an interest and in which she and the Colonel were allies. House had for the last three years been dissatisfied with Tumulty and regretting that he had advocated his appointment, while Mrs. Wilson had never cared for him at all. Tumulty's displeasure at the second marriage has been noted* and, feeling 'pretty bad' about it,[7] he talked to Grayson, which was unwise. There is no doubt that he was hardly the right sort of man to be the President's secretary. He lacked, as House said, refinement and discretion and a broad vision.[8] His political friends were mostly among the less elevating personnel of the Democratic party. His ardent Roman Catholicism had proved an embarrassment, especially during the recent election. He had made one or two serious gaffes. As against all this, there had to be put his unqualified loyalty and devotion. Nevertheless it was natural that at the beginning of a new Administration Wilson should review the position. House had for a long time and with a good deal of support from others in the Administration been urging Tumulty's dismissal. When he was at the White House between 10 and 12 November he and Mrs. Wilson finally talked the President into it. On 15 November Wilson offered his secretary another appointment. Tumulty resisted with a flow of sentiment and by refusing the appointment put Wilson in the position of having to dismiss him. David Lawrence, a journalist who had been one of Wilson's Princeton pupils, intervened on the secretary's behalf and talked to Wilson for three-quarters of an hour on 19 November, after which the President relented.

When on Christmas Eve Wilson dispatched to the belligerent capitals his Note suggesting a confidential exchange of terms, he had done all

* See p. 362 above.

that he could to get negotiations going; over the Christmas holiday he awaited developments. At the White House entertainment and instruction were combined. There was a family dinner for twenty-two on Christmas Day followed by amusing charades, all three Wilson girls in Mrs. Wilson's opinion having 'real histrionic talent'.[9] The next day the Graysons came to dinner with their holiday guests and a 'Colonel Harts gave us his lecture on Washington, and its future development, illustrated by lantern slides'. On 27 December in the evening the German Note arrived and its blankness was discouraging; but it was soon followed by House's hopeful letter* about Bernstorff's attitude.

House had an alternative scheme which he found to coincide with the President's ideas when they met in Washington on 3 January 1917. The President was contemplating another address on the familiar theme, a general settlement to provide security against war and to which territorial adjustments should be subordinate. House thought that terms might be stated with sufficient particularity to describe the sort of settlement which America would be prepared to accept as the basis of the new order. While this would be in effect a proposal of terms to which the belligerents might agree, it could not, when done in this way, be construed as 'meddling with the affairs of the belligerents'. It could be done by way of an address to the Senate in answer to an arranged request for information about the terms on which America would be willing to join a League to Enforce Peace. House records:

> We thought that the main principle he should lay down was the right of nations to determine under what government they should continue to live. This, of course, involves a wide range. We thought that, since Germany and Russia had agreed to free Poland, that should be put in. We naturally agreed upon Belgium and Serbia being restored. Alsace and Lorraine we were not quite certain of, but we agreed that Turkey should cease to exist.
>
> I encouraged him in the thought of doing this great and dramatic thing.[10]

House returned to New York to prepare a detailed plan to be brought with him when he came to Washington on 11 January for the Secretary of State's annual dinner to the President.

Before leaving Washington House saw a number of people including McAdoo, who thought that the President was letting things drift, and Lansing who was very disconsolate. The latter had received no response to a suggestion he made in a letter to the President on 24 December of a daily conference so that he might be 'kept fully acquainted with your views and wishes'.[11] He had received no answer to his letter of 8 December about the

---

* See p. 593 above.

Marina and the *Arabia* in which he had advised that the German explanations should be treated as an admission of guilt and answered by breaking
off relations.[12] The President had ignored also a reminder sent on 21 December. It is indeed very likely that Wilson, freewheeling along the overhead in
pursuit of peace by acclamation, was just not interested in the Secretary's
pedestrian solutions of diurnal problems. Wilson would not even think
about war. 'There will be no war', he told House before he left. 'This
country does not intend to become involved in this war. We are the only
one of the great white nations that is free from war today, and it would be
a crime against civilisation for us to go in.'[13]

House, collecting material in New York, was visited on 8 January by
Ignace Jan Paderewski, the world-famous pianist who had subordinated
his career to work for the freedom of Poland. As the astute reader will
already have foreseen, when Wilson got down to the preparation of the
Peace without Victory Address the refinement of his thoughts tended to
leave territorial questions in the lees. Perhaps they played a larger part in
House's diary record than they did in the actual talk, for what Wilson really
had in mind was a message that would go through governments and touch
the hearts of the peoples. In the end the only point specifically mentioned
was the Polish question, as to which Wilson had a debt to pay both political
and personal.

In addition to a Polish population in the United States with a substantial
vote, there had always been some sentimental attachment between Poland
and the United States. Kosciuszko, friend of Washington and Jefferson,
who had fought for the Americans throughout the War of Independence
and received the thanks of Congress at the end of it, started in 1794 the
unsuccessful revolution against Russia which led to the third partition of
Poland in 1795. That event did not shock contemporary Europe; America
alone through the mouth of Jefferson condemned it as a crime.

The spirit of Poland lived on. The outbreak of a great war always gives
a chance to the oppressed. The Polish patriots split into three groups, one
looking to Russia for restitution, one to Germany, and one to Austria.
Russia was the first to bid with a promise in August 1914 of unity and self-
government 'under the sceptre of the Russian Empire'.[14] A Polish National
Committee was formed in response to the Russian proclamation.

Towards the end of 1915 Paderewski came to the United States as the
representative of this committee and to gain support for it. Concerts combined with propaganda was one method he used and another was the employment of his great charm upon personalities who mattered. He had already

charmed Lloyd George.[15] Lansing's initial suspicions yielded to an admiration of which he found it 'difficult not to speak in superlatives'.[16] House at first disliked what he heard of him; he thought him an offensive egoist. But when they met on 12 November 1915 he was at once attracted by him—his *naïveté*, his child-like simplicity, the reverent way in which the great artist looked up to him. He thought of him as 'a highly sensitive child'[17] and of himself as the prudent father; 'a providential man for my country', Paderewski called the Colonel.[18] 'Through him', House said, 'I became deeply interested in the cause of Poland'; and he passed his views on to Wilson. Paderewski was accorded the unusual honour of an invitation to dinner at the White House. Wilson too was moved. Chopin's nocturnes were followed by tales of injustice and oppression; and politics and morals met over the historic crime and the Polish vote at the forthcoming election. On 6 November 1916, the day before Election Day, Paderewski called at Shadow Lawn to discuss Polish relief and the President doubtless took the opportunity of thanking him for his support in the campaign. Mrs. Wilson recorded in her 'line a day book': 'Mr. P. ended with a beautiful tribute to my husband and expressed his utmost faith in him and his sincere desire to help these suffering people.'[19] She would never forget, she said, his face, fine, tragic and earnest, and his hair like a nimbus around his head.

The first draft of what was to be the Address to the Senate was finished by the time House arrived in Washington in the afternoon of 11 January 1917. Wilson read it aloud in his study before they all set out for the Lansing dinner. House thought it 'a noble document':[20] 'Mr. House was wild about it and says it is the greatest thing he has ever done', Mrs. Wilson recorded.[21] The President decided that it should be cabled in full to American ambassadors abroad (though Wilson hesitated a bit about this on account of the cost), whose duty it would be to see that the full text was published in belligerent newspapers and so to make sure that it would reach the people. So far Wilson had discussed the project only with House. He told House that he would show the draft to Lansing although he did not think that Lansing was 'in sympathy with his purpose to keep out of war'.[22] House got Wilson to remove one or two oblique references to the origins of the war: 'as usual,' he recorded in his diary, 'he struck the wrong note in one instance'.[23] But he missed the note that was to jar, the reference to 'peace without victory'. Lansing, when he saw the draft the next day, took up the phrase and pointed out that the Allies in their latest Note had just re-stated their belief that victory was essential.[24] Wilson was unimpressed by this and, knowing his fondness for phrase-making, Lansing says, he felt any attempt at dissuasion to be useless. The same evening, 12 January, Wilson showed the draft to Senator Stone. Neither he nor Lansing, Wilson wrote to House, was 'very *expressive*, but both acquiesced generously'.[25] If Lansing had been more expressive, he might have selected for comment what he afterwards called the 'questionable if not criticizable' practice of appealing 'to the peoples of the Allied Powers over the heads of their governments'.[26]

The Allies' Note to which Lansing referred was their reply to Wilson's request for terms and was received in Washington on 11 January. Obviously Wilson had to make some reference to it in his Address and he was rather taken aback by the Allied terms. He can hardly have been surprised by the defined objectives which were the sort of things that he and House had been discussing on 3 January. But judging from what he later wrote, he regarded the general reference to the liberating of Italians, Slavs, Roumanians, and Czechoslovaks as heralding the dismemberment of the Austro–Hungarian Empire; and neither this nor the final asseveration that the Allies would not make peace with the Kaiser accorded with his theme of peace without victory. But he made no comment in the Address except to contrast the Entente's reply with that of the Central Powers, saying that the former was 'in general terms, indeed, but with sufficient definiteness to imply details'.[27] He may not have intended this as a pat on the back for the Allies but as such it was generally read.

The Address was ready by 12 January, but was not delivered to the Senate until 22 January. The interval was taken up with elaborate preparations. The text was ciphered and cabled to the embassies with instructions that copies were to be made secretly. Page in London was given a list of newspapers which supported the peace group, such as the *Manchester Guardian*, in which he was to ensure publication. He was horrified at the phrase 'peace without victory' which would 'give great offence in England, since it puts each side in the war on the same moral level'.[28] He cabled to Lansing sincerely praising 'the noblest utterance since the war began' but suggesting that the phrase be altered to 'peace without conquest'. This would have carried Wilson's idea without being a contradiction in terms of the Allied thesis, so recently reiterated, that victory was essential to their war purpose. Lansing ventured to tackle Wilson again, but he replied 'I'll consider it' so brusquely as to signify that he would not.[29]

'Can't you come down and be present, staying with us, of course? Do, please,'[30] Wilson wrote when he told House that the Address would be delivered on 22 January. The secrecy was so strict that it was not until noon on 22 January that the Vice-President read to the Senate the President's letter asking permission to appear; and one hour later he began to speak. Thus Wilson came to deliver the greatest of the three peacetime addresses which, taken together, make up the first and last protestation that history has recorded by a sovereign, not against the wickedness of all war (for Wilson was not a pacifist), but against the extravagance of war as a means to even a good end; the first public statement of the thesis that victory is in its nature inimical to a good peace; the first formal enunciation of the conditions essential to lasting and universal order.[31]

You may make peace, he said in effect to the nations at war, as and when you will. But sooner or later you will have to make it. You may then make what terms you will and we in America can claim no voice in determining what they are to be. But we *shall* have a voice in determining whether those terms are to be made lasting or not. For they cannot be made lasting unless we Americans add our authority and our power to the authority and force of other nations to guarantee them: 'it must be a peace made secure by the organized major force of mankind.' We Americans are ready to perform this service to the world by means of our solemn adherence to a universal covenant, but only if the conditions of the peace we guarantee are such as we approve. Therefore our judgement upon what is fundamental should be spoken now, not afterwards when it may be too late. The essence of the judgement is that 'there must be not a balance of power, but a community of power'.

You have told us, each of you, that you are not struggling for a new balance of power and that it is no part of your purpose to crush the other. But, lest there be any misunderstanding about this, let us see what it implies about the nature of the peace. First,

. . . that it must be a peace without victory. . . . Victory would mean peace forced upon the loser, a victor's terms imposed upon the vanquished. It would be accepted in humiliation, under duress, at an intolerable sacrifice, and would leave a sting, a resentment, a bitter memory upon which terms of peace would rest, not permanently, but only as upon quicksand. Only a peace between equals can last.

Then there must be an equality of rights between big nations and small.

Right must be based upon the common strength, not upon the individual strength, of the nations upon whose concert peace will depend. . . . And there is a deeper thing involved than even equality of right among organized nations. No peace can last, or ought to last, which does not recognize and accept the principle that governments derive all their just powers from the consent of the governed, and that no right anywhere exists to hand peoples about from sovereignty to sovereignty as if they were property.

He gave as his example of this 'a united, independent and autonomous Poland'.

Henceforth inviolable security of life, of worship, and of industrial and social development should be guaranteed to all peoples . . . Any peace which does not recognize and accept this principle will inevitably be upset. It will not rest upon the affections or the convictions of mankind. The ferment of spirit of whole populations will fight subtly and constantly against it, and all the world will sympathize.

Security for development, he said, meant that every nation must have access to the great highways of the sea, which must be kept free.

Then there must be limitation of armaments. 'The statesmen of the world must plan for peace . . . as they have planned for war.'

He believed that he had said what the United States would wish him to say. He believed too

that I am speaking for the silent mass of mankind everywhere who have as yet had no place or opportunity to speak their real hearts out concerning the death and ruin they see to have come already upon the persons and homes they hold most dear.

In holding out the expectation that the United States would join in such a peace as he had outlined, he spoke, he said, confidently because in that promise there was no breach of American tradition but a fulfilment of it. For he proposed that the doctrine of President Monroe should be the doctrine of the world and that all nations should henceforth avoid entangling alliances, for there was no entangling alliance in a concert of power.

These are American principles, American policies. We could stand for no others. And they are also the principles and policies of forward-looking men and women everywhere, of every modern nation, of every enlightened community. They are the principles of mankind and must prevail.

Wilson had put his soul into this last great appeal. The yield though not trifling was hardly commensurate. The American press displayed the enthusiasm that lofty sentiments always evoke. Public opinion was favourable, but then peace by oration or peace without effort was what most Americans wanted. There was in the Senate at the end of the Address tremendous applause but that could have been a tribute as much to its superb presentation and delivery as to its content. The forces that were in the end to defeat the President now began to gather. On 25 January Senator Borah of Idaho introduced a resolution reaffirming the wisdom of isolation and on 1 February Senator Lodge took the opportunity to withdraw his support from the League. Wilson contrasted the noble response in the country with the ignobility of Republican senators. He wrote on 25 January:

I must admit that I have been a little low in my mind the last forty-eight hours because of the absolute lack of any power to see what I am driving at which has been exhibited by the men who are looked upon as the leading Republican members of the Senate. After all, it is upon the Senate that I have to depend for the kind of support which will make acts possible.[32]

In Europe the Address was heard as music shredded in a whirlwind and the theme caught only by those waiting for it and ready to strain their ears. Lowes Dickinson called it 'perhaps the most important international document of all history'.[33] The Pope said it was 'the most courageous document which has appeared since the beginning of the war. . . . It contains many truths and revives the principles of Christian civilization.'[34] In all the belligerent countries it was greeted with enthusiasm by the left wing and with critical respect by the liberals. But the press of war had squeezed most of the liberalism out of the Allies and among them it was generally resented. The man who could not or would not understand that victory over Germany was the essential basis of any durable peace was intentionally or unintentionally doing his best to weaken the will to victory; and why did Wilson seek to let Germany go free from punishment for breaking the very rules he wished to lay down for the future? Bonar Law had a phrase for it which cut all the more sharply because he was not a man who used words for the sake of phrase-making. He said simply: 'What Mr. Wilson is longing for, we are fighting for.'[35]

On New Year's Day 1917 an officer in the Coldstream Guards 'very much wanted to know what the men think about this peace talk'. So he asked Private Robinson. 'The answer', he wrote in his diary, 'was what I had hoped for and thought he would say, "I don't think we can have peace now, sir", he said. "If we don't beat them properly we'll have to fight them again in a few year's time." '[36] Moreover, there were still left in Europe after two years of war some of the emotions that had filled the young men who set out so gaily on the warpath—the call of honour, the thirst for glory, the joy of battle: 'and he is dead who will not fight; and who dies fighting has increase.'[37] For such men peace without victory was a squalidity, a draining into sewage of all the blood poured out, a dishonouring of the dead. Was this war, fought by the free against the tyrants, to be ended by a referee blowing on a whistle and the survivors trailing away from the battlefield while Good and Evil shook hands on it before they parted? What Asquith put into sculptured prose*—was the long and sombre procession of cruelty and suffering, lighted up by deathless examples of heroism and chivalry, to end in some patched-up, precarious, dishonouring compromise?—was decorated by Anatole France's winged similes:

Peace without victory, would this satisfy? Peace without victory is bread with-

---

* See p. 554 above.

out yeast, jugged hare without wine, brill without capers, mushrooms without garlic, love without quarrels, a camel without humps, night without moon, roof without smoke, town without brothel, pork without salt, a pearl without a hole, a rose without a scent, a republic without waste, a leg of mutton without the bone, a cat without fur, a tripe sausage without mustard—in brief, an insipid thing.[38]

'The real people I was speaking to was neither the Senate nor foreign governments, as you will realize, but the *people* of the countries now at war.'[39] Thus Wilson wrote to a friend on 29 January. The preacher as he descends from the pulpit may hope that he has sown seed in the hearts of his congregation which in the fullness of time will fructify into virtue. The red-hot eloquence of a sermon may sometimes work instantaneously, but the fervour that sparks a sudden conversion on the spot cannot be conveyed through a pastoral letter. Wilson could fairly hope that his address would enormously strengthen the peace movement in the belligerent countries and that in the long term they would make themselves felt on their governments. But the long term was just what he had not got. What, one would have liked to have asked him as he took off his surplice and resumed the toga, did he intend to do next? He wanted to amplify his audience and press the truth into their hearts. On 29 January he approached the Carnegie Foundation for Peace to ask if they would back up his Address with systematic propaganda. He wrote: 'I feel that the task of the moment is the rousing of a great body of opinion to very definite thought and purpose.'[40] This was the task of the month or even of the year rather than of the moment. The task of the moment was to get the belligerents to talk together. What was Wilson planning to do about that? The Address was not intended as a diplomatic move and so it is no criticism of it to say that diplomatically it had no effect at all on the British and French Governments and that any effect it had on the German was not good.

British-American relations during January 1917 were muted and confusing. The familiar controversies did not produce any excitements. As with Germany there was an armistice tacitly in force at the presidential level while Wilson was peacemaking. On 27 December 1916 he returned to Lansing some papers on interference with the mails which he had had with him at Shadow Lawn, saying: 'I will be glad to discuss this and other kindred matters with you when we have seen just what the several belligerents are willing to do about discussing terms of peace.'[41] As a result of the renewed submarine activity armed ships were in the offing with a freight of awkward questions. Were the Allies to be allowed heavier armament to cope with more powerful submarines? What should America do about the evidence which Germany had published of Allied instructions to merchantmen to take the offensive? How should she react to Germany's move towards unrestricted war against armed merchantmen? Pursuant to the decision at Pless on 9 December 1916* and to the rejection by the Entente on 29 December of the German peace offer, Bernstorff had on 10 January sent to the State Department a memorandum raising the question for discussion, while saying that of course it did not cancel the *Sussex* pledge.[42]

Some of these matters were discussed at an interview between the Secretary and the British ambassador on 18 January at which the ambassador 'livid with rage', 'wild with passion', with twitching face, blazing eyes, and whitened knuckles hissed at the dignified and impassive Secretary of State that he would be responsible for the murder of helpless people; and then, on being asked to recollect himself, collapsed into a trembling and profuse apology.[43] One of Mr. Lansing's more distinguished successors in office has remarked that he has never seen a memorandum of a conversation in which the author came off second best.[44] If he had unearthed one in the State Department it is improbable that it would have borne the initials R. L. Nevertheless, in this case Lansing's memorandum rings more than half true. There is other testimony, much of it friendly, to Sir Cecil's 'wild outbursts', too much of it to permit any doubt that by 1917 his health was no longer equal to the demands of his office.[45] It is startling to find that at this tense moment in the diplomatic history of the United States, of the four crucial ambassadors in the three capitals of London, Berlin, and Washington only one, Count von Bernstorff, was suited to his job.

The most foreboding, if not the most exciting, question in the State Department was about the British White List. This was the first point— doubtless if Germany had held her hand, it would have been the precursor of many—in which Britain was being forced to choose between the short term and the long term in her need for supplies; her peril being that in grasping for what she could get she might so antagonize America as in the end to lose all. She had begun by denying bunkers to neutral ships that traded with the enemy. Now she was requiring a more positive response and, as she put it on 6 December 1916, was 'unable to guarantee' that facilities could be provided to neutral owners who had not 'undertaken to utilise their vessels in such a way that British or Allied interests are benefited'.[46] On 2 February 1917 the Foreign Office expressed the object as being 'to concentrate any neutral tonnage coming into the market on services most needed by the Allies'.[47] The State Department was satisfied that Britain was using bunkering agreements to secure control of all neutral shipping; American owners, the Department said, were being denied bunkers unless they applied the terms of the agreement not only to the ships to be bunkered but also to all the ships they owned.[48] Polk, who was handling the matter in

* See p. 573 above.

the State Department, began to think that they would get nowhere without an ultimatum; and in this he was probably right. The British now knew all the perils confronting them in their relations with the United States and there is no evidence that they had any policy except to go on to breaking point. But were they gambling—with, as the month went on, the odds moving perceptibly in their favour—on America's entry into the war? There is no doubt that through their interception of cables they knew far more of what was going on in Germany than Washington did; and towards the end of January Colonel House received a hint to this effect from Commander Gaunt.*[49]

The possibility that British policy towards the United States was now being shaped in the light of what was to come is one factor that obscures British-American relations in January 1917. The other is the emergence out of the British embassy of a new actor on the stage whose activities in introducing himself may have been responsible for two rather puzzling incidents. The first is the one already recounted† in which the British seemed first to want to know confidentially what the German terms were and then to say that they could not wait for the information; and the other is an even odder development to be told later. Both featured Sir William Wiseman. The title is not evidence of civil service seniority; he was the tenth baronet and, at this time aged thirty-two, was a captain in the army who had been gassed in Flanders and relegated to home service. He was rather a plump man, neither tall nor short, with a pleasant face and a trim moustache. In 1915 he was recruited for Military Intelligence (M.I.6) and sent to Washington in a position loosely attached to the embassy. His chief duty was the detection of attempts to sabotage the supply of munitions to Britain. So he was not even a temporary diplomat. But his success in diplomacy was such that at the age of thirty-four he was a serious candidate for the Washington embassy. His success was founded on his perception, by luck or by wit, that there was a place to be filled in British-American relations. It was doubtless by wit that he perceived that the ambassador had no intimate contacts with administration figures such as he had with the opposition; and by luck that he was on the stage at the time when House had no longer the easy and direct relationship with London which he had enjoyed through Grey. Grey had indeed cabled that Eric Drummond was staying on as private secretary to Balfour and that House could continue to use their private code. As House wrote to Wilson: 'If Grey had to leave, the next best man in the kingdom for us is Balfour'.[50] But he was very much

---

* Gaunt was, to borrow a footnote from the editor of House's journal, the 'British naval attaché, with whom, following his habit, House had established intimate relations' (House 2: 108).

† See p. 576 above.

next best. House hoped that Plunkett would be raised in influence and that Balfour would look to him for guidance. This was not happening and there was now a vacancy for an intermediary.

The ambassador and the Colonel were generally to be found in different cities, Washington and New York, and when the ambassador had anything to communicate to House which did not require a personal interview, he would send the naval attaché Gaunt. On 17 December Gaunt was on leave and Spring Rice sent Wiseman with a message. According to Wiseman the message 'was of no particular importance';[51] and according to House it was a suggestion (this was three or four days after the German Peace Note had been received) that the Colonel should find out unofficially what Germany's terms were.[52] In fact, there is nothing to show that the British Foreign Office were in the least interested in the terms; and it would have been very singular if without instructions Spring Rice had acted on his own initiative. Perhaps Wiseman suggested to Spring Rice that it might be useful to sound out House on the topic; more probably it was one that emerged when the two men got talking after they had disposed of the unimportant message. For there is no doubt that the Colonel took an immediate liking to the young man; a Wykehamist baronet, quiet and unassuming, intelligent and obviously discreet, was just the type that House fell for. A journalist noted in both their faces despite the dissimilarity, the one lean and the other plump, 'the same appraising competent blue eyes', 'the same stamp of unemotional alertness'.[53] Moreover, Wiseman appeared to be liberal in sympathies and to share House's views about the importance of not inflicting on Germany a crushing defeat.

So the audition went off very well. By the end of it Wiseman had been allotted a speaking part in the great drama. House wrote off that day to Wilson a letter that began:

> Dear Governor:
> The British Ambassador has sent Sir William Wiseman of the Embassy to see me.[54]

Behold the blessings of a baronetcy! Could House have written with the same panache of 'Mr. Wiseman of the Embassy'? The title made it superfluous to amplify the description with any reference to a status which would by comparison have been unimpressive.

This was the first of a number of interviews. Three days later, in a paragraph beginning 'Wiseman says . . .' House was reporting to the President the young man's views on the American press.[55] Wiseman had also views which were passed on about the Allies' resentment of 'any suggestion that they have selfish motives and are not fighting solely for a principle'; this was the peg on which House hung the advice to Wilson already quoted* not to try to argue with them. By mid January the two men were deploring together the fact that Spring Rice, Gaunt, and the embassy staff were so matey with the Republicans and House was observing in his diary that Britain would be far better represented by Wiseman than by 'the older and experienced diplomat'.[56]

House now began to think that the Foreign Office must have at last perceived, what was so obvious to him, that something had better be done to remedy the deficiencies of Spring Rice and were trying out Wiseman as a special emissary. The extent of the confidence he now reposed in Wiseman is shown strikingly by their conversation of 20 January.[57] On that day House received from the President a letter telling him the secret 'locked up in the breasts of Stone, Lansing and W. W.' that on 22 January the President would address the Senate. He at once gave the information to Wiseman (not surreptitiously, for he told Wilson that he had done so)[58] and urged him to advise his government to agree to an immediate peace conference.

On 23 January House reported to the President that Wiseman was in Washington 'in order to get the full opinion of the Allied group' on the Address.[59] It seems as if the 'Allied group', whatever it was, did not greatly outnumber the embassy personnel who saw too much of the Republicans, for all that Wiseman brought back was 'a depressing story'. 'The consensus of the Allied view at Washington', as House relayed it to Wilson on 25 January, was remarkably like that already expressed in the London and Paris newspapers.[60] There followed in House's letter two paragraphs of 'Wiseman's individual view'. The doughier part of this was that peace must come before any plan to enforce arbitration; the effervescent was that every belligerent government was in the hands of the reactionaries who, if America was not careful, would turn 'their concentrated hate for democracy' upon her when peace was made. House recorded all this for Wilson's reading with as much respect as if it had been the reflection of a mature statesman. But fearing perhaps that some of Wiseman's views on the Peace Note and the Address to the Senate might not too strongly appeal to the President, House pointed out that the unfriendly attitude of Spring Rice still warped Wiseman's vision.

On the afternoon of 26 January Wiseman at last knotted the string that secured House. House wrote to Wilson that evening:

He told me in the *gravest confidence* a thing which I had already suspected and that is that he is in direct communication with the Foreign Office, and that the Ambassador and other members of the Embassy are not aware of it.[61]

* See p. 579 above.

No tale, however earnestly told, can carry the conviction that comes from confirmation of what one has oneself been clever enough to suspect. House accepted the statement without question and concluded that Wiseman 'reflects the views of his Government'.

House in his letter underlined the *gravest confidence* and it was a prudent condition for Wiseman to attach to a revelation that would have vanished under scrutiny. It was literally, but only literally, true that Wiseman was in direct communication with the Foreign Office. He wrote routine reports on his anti-sabotage activities which circulated in the Foreign Office as well as in other government departments interested. It is just possible that these reports, since Wiseman first met House, were beginning to attract a little more interest in the Foreign Office than formerly, for he was now including in them some of House's views, explaining that he was taking 'a more active interest in politics than he would ordinarily have considered his duty' because of the unfortunate fact that the Administration had come to regard the embassy officials as Republican partisans.[62]

By 26 January the House–Wiseman situation had come to the crux. The Colonel had already asked the young man to advise his government to agree to an immediate peace conference. When Wiseman came to his apartment that afternoon the Colonel must have been full of the talk he had just had with Bernstorff and of his efforts to persuade Germany to come to the conference table and extremely anxious to know whether Britain would come too. Wiseman gave him to understand that she would. It is not utterly inconceivable that he had some authority for making the gesture. It might have been a gesture of conciliation forced from Britain by her increasing awareness of her dependence on Wilson or it might have been a meaningless gesture which she felt that she could make safely in the knowledge, which by now she probably had, that she would be accepting an invitation that Germany would do more than decline. But no evidence has emerged of any instructions from London to Wiseman or the embassy or of any report back. The probability is that Sir William had come to the conclusion that, if a stream of information beneficent to both countries was to flow between him and House, the time had come to prime the pump. What he said might have proved very embarrassing but, fortunately for him, its significance was almost immediately obliterated by events. Its principal effect has been to create a lot of unnecessary work for historians anxious to find out what exactly Britain was up to in January 1917.

Wiseman had to surmount a little trouble with Gaunt when the latter came back from leave and found that his connection with House, such as it was, had been taken over. No difficulty was made by the Foreign Office. House, appreciating perhaps that he had elevated Wiseman above his claims, was not disconcerted when he found that Balfour knew nothing at all about him. All he did was to suggest to Polk that he should inform the Foreign Office of Wiseman's role; and after that, as his biographer says, the only thing for the Foreign Office to do 'was to make of Wiseman the special emissary he had pretended to be'.[63] In this way Wiseman became the honest broker throughout 1917 and 1918 in Anglo-American relations. Did he win that position for himself by his boldness and finesse or was it conferred upon him by House? The working friendship between Wilson and House is one of the major curiosities of history and that between House and Wiseman one of the minor. It is possible that Wiseman was employing from the first the standard tactics of the middleman who has no buyer and no seller and does not possess what he wants to sell; this is a role which usually requires embellishment of fact. But it is possible too that it was House who was doing most of the embellishing. House's diary is, as we have seen, no plodding ploughman's chronicle. He is a creative diarist in the sense that in recording an interview he seizes on what in it is to him significant; and if he is not Thucydidean in his account of speech, yet sometimes, one suspects, people speak as he expected or believed, or even hoped, that they would speak. House does not intend to deceive. He is indeed quite artless about it, which is why his diary and letters are, with the precaution of careful reading in places, quite reliable. The process can be traced in his report to Wilson of his interview with Wiseman. The first thing that Wiseman says (House's observation being that 'his whole tone had changed') is that 'the atmosphere had cleared wonderfully since yesterday'. In the next paragraph Wiseman 'seemed to now think' that a conference could be brought about if Germany returned a favourable reply. Then a little later, 'he went so far as to discuss with me where the conference should be held'. These noddings and winkings are enough to make House say: 'I take it he has heard directly from his government since yesterday for he seemed to speak with authority.'[64] And finally House calls what has been hinted or implied a 'statement'; and the sentence in which he does so must raise a smile:

I know you will appreciate the difference between any statement coming from the English as against one coming from the Germans.

We must now take up the thread of German-American negotiations at the point where we left them at the end of the last chapter.* The telegram from Berlin, which was the occasion of Bernstorff's visit to House on 15 January 1917, was ominous. American intervention in negotiations was, it said, 'positively not desired', and Bernstorff was to be dilatory about

* See p. 594 above.

stating the terms for which House had asked.[65] The only information the telegram gave about them was that they were moderate and reasonable as compared with those of the Entente; they did not include the annexation of Belgium, but the question of Alsace-Lorraine could not be discussed. Apart from this, all that the ambassador was given to work with was an offer to open immediate negotiations on the agenda for the second conference, the 'Peace League arbitration machinery', etc., to be held 'after a conference of the belligerents had brought about a preliminary peace'. As proof of goodwill Germany was ready to at once negotiate a Bryan cooling-off treaty* and requested the President 'to work out the programme for securing the peace of the world'. As Bernstorff already knew, action against armed ships was beginning immediately; and now this telegram referred to 'the urgent necessity of resorting again to unrestricted submarine warfare' and asked the ambassador for immediate proposals as to how it could be conducted without causing a rupture with America.

Bernstorff would have known that this was the beginning of the end. He decided upon a last fling. That unrestricted warfare would mean America's entry into the war he took for granted as by now everyone in Germany did from the Kaiser downwards. But he believed also, as only Bethmann and a few others in Germany did, that if America came into the war Germany's defeat was certain. He believed that if America did not come into the war Germany could not be beaten. And more than this, what he believed and was alone in believing was that by American mediation in January 1917 Germany could get a better peace than she could get in any other way. He must have felt desperate enough to say anything rather than let this last chance slip. For, having only the telegram to go on, what he offered to House was not just an adornment but a superstructure. He began modestly enough by transmuting the offer to negotiate a Bryan treaty into a promise to sign at once. Then he piled on to the non-annexation of Belgium the independence of Poland and Lithuania and the restoration of Serbia. Finally he said that 'he believed if Lloyd George had stated that there should be *mutual* restoration, reparation and indemnity, his Government would have agreed to enter negotiations on those terms'.[66] Thus he arrived at the *status quo ante* which he himself believed was the true basis for negotiations. House read back his note of the conversation and Bernstorff declared it accurate.

Provided with these sorts of ingredients House could cook a dish to make the mouth water. He wrote at once to Wilson: 'This is the most important communication we have had since the war began and gives a real basis for negotiations and for peace.'[67] On the next day he added:

With the German communication of yesterday you stand in a position to bring

* See p. 145 above.

about a peace much more quickly than I thought possible. They consent to almost everything that liberal opinion in democratic countries have demanded. I think it is important that no move be made now without mature consideration. If a false step is not taken, the end seems in sight.[68]

The point that struck Wilson was the one about arbitration and the Bryan treaty. Would Germany, he asked House by letter on 17 January, be willing to submit to arbitration the terms on which the war should be concluded? If she signed a Bryan treaty, would she suspend unrestricted U-boat warfare during the year's investigation required by the treaty? House said he would write to Bernstorff to get direct answers, which he did that evening. He was still very exhilarated. He told Whitehouse on 18 January that the danger in England was the general belief that they could get a military decision by another offensive; this was a fatal mistake; the President could secure for England everything that was fair in their demands. On the same day he wrote again to Wilson. The liberal element was completely in control in Germany, he said, and the German Government willing to take a stand as advanced as any of the democracies. Ought not he to cable Balfour and Lloyd George that

the German Government had proposed an immediate signing of an arbitration treaty with us, and that they had proposed submitting the question of peace to arbitration, or, as an alternative, that you submit proposals for a conference . . .

If Bernstorff has stated his Government's proposals correctly, peace is in sight for you would be justified in forcing the Allies to consider it.[69]

If there was a receptive answer, he would go to England and press it in person.

Wilson was more cautious but still very responsive. In his reply he called it 'a very striking change of attitude' and 'great encouragement'.[70] He thought that the cable to England should wait until the Address he was about to deliver had had time to sink in a little.

House's paraphrase of what the German Government was proposing went far beyond anything that his own record shows Bernstorff as saying. The ambassador's promise to sign a Bryan treaty was quite different from 'submitting the question of peace to arbitration'; and he had never indicated any departure from the German position that terms must be settled by the belligerents themselves before the general conference under the President's leadership could assemble to discuss the new international order. He replied to House's inquiries with the plain statement that there must be a belligerent conference first. House got this letter on 19 January and sent it on to Wilson saying that it was not precisely what he had understood Bernstorff to say. He wrote on the same day to Bernstorff urging him to divulge German terms and asking what Germany would do about submarine warfare if the United States signed a Bryan treaty with the Berlin Government.

Bernstorff's reply on 20 January reads like the letter of a salesman who is unable to fulfil the orders he has taken because of trouble in the factory. 'I am afraid that it will be very difficult to get any more peace terms from Berlin at this time.'[71] The excuse?

> The exorbitant demands of our enemies, and the insolent language of their note to the President seem to have infuriated public opinion in Germany to such an extent, that the result may be anything but favourable to our peace plans.

The expression of his hope that a statement from the President might have been forthcoming right away led to a delicately worded forecast of the alternative.

> In Berlin they seem to believe that the answer of our enemies to the President has finished the peace movement for a whole long time to come, and I am therefore, afraid that my Government may be forced to act accordingly in a very short time. . . . Every question leads us to the same problem, viz. which methods my Government will be obliged by public opinion to use against the English starvation policy.

He made it quite clear that Germany would not suspend unrestricted U-boat war during a Bryan period of investigation.

House was disappointed. The Germans were 'slippery customers',[72] he wrote when he sent a copy of this letter to Wilson, not like the English who might be stubborn and stupid but were very reliable. The Germans, he thought, might be manœuvring for neutral support in case they resorted to unrestricted U-boat war. But he was not daunted: the great thing was to get a conference going somehow.

> If we can tie up Germany in a conference, so that she cannot resume her un-bridled submarine warfare, it will be a great point gained; and if a conference is once started, it can never break up without peace.

There followed a pause for open diplomacy while the President delivered his Address and waited for it to sink in. Then it was he who took the initiative. He wrote to House on 24 January asking him to see Bernstorff again.

> Tell him that this is the time to accomplish something, if they really and truly want peace; that the indications that come to us are of a sort to lead us to believe that with something reasonable to suggest, as from them, I can bring things about; and that otherwise with the preparations they are apparently making with regard to unrestrained attacks on merchantmen on the plea that they are armed for offense, there is a terrible likelihood that relations between the United States and

Germany may come to a breaking point and everything assume a different aspect. Feelings, exasperations are neither here nor there. Do they in fact want me to help? I am entitled to know because I genuinely want to help and have now put myself in a position to help without favour to either side.[73]

Lansing was becoming obstructive about the extensive use Bernstorff was now making of the permission to communicate with Berlin in code through the State Department, and Bernstorff had to appeal to House and House to the President. Wilson overruled Lansing while upholding him to the extent that he told House in this letter that they must be satisfied that Bernstorff was working for peace; and they 'should in each instance receive his assurance that there is nothing in his dispatches which it would be unneutral for us to transmit'.[74] Whether House took the required action we do not know nor whether it would have deterred Bernstorff if he had. By now, as will be seen, the way the privilege was being used by Berlin was involving the United States not only in unneutrality but in assisting the preparation of hostilities against herself.

The ambassador came to see House on 26 January.[75] He was not hopeful: the military, he said, had taken complete control in Germany. House put the President's plea as earnestly as the President had written it. He put it as the President's view that the Allied terms were impossible of acceptance, need not be considered, were bluff, and that the Address was meant to accord with German views. The President would not interfere with territorial conditions but, if Germany would declare her terms, he was convinced that he could bring about the two peace conferences. Bernstorff said he would send an urgent message to Berlin. He was succeeded as a visitor by Wiseman bringing with him the new rush of hope. House told Wiseman of Wilson's message to Bernstorff; and their busy planning of the conference together shows that he was still optimistic.

It is hard, Wilson wrote to a friend on 30 January, 'to see in the present murky air any landmarks by which to steer'.[76] On that day Bernstorff called up House.[77] He was sending over by messenger tomorrow, he said, a very important letter. Was it an answer, House asked. 'A partial one', was the reply.

On the next day, 31 January, at 4 p.m. the murk lifted and the tempest came.[78] The German ambassador called on the Secretary of State and handed him a Note which he said he had been instructed to deliver. Lansing, who hoped that the call might be to discuss confidential terms, settled down to read slowly and carefully. The Note was an acknowledgement of the copy of the Address to the Senate which the Secretary had sent officially to the German Government.[79] That government found it 'highly gratifying' to see how closely the Address corresponded to the desires and principles of

Germany: how glad Germany would be if in recognition of these principles countries like Ireland and India were to obtain their freedom! Germany's aims were compatible with the rights of other nations. As for Belgium, all that Germany desired was that she should not be used again 'for the purpose of instigating continuous hostile intrigues'. However, the attempt of the Central Powers to bring about peace had failed 'owing to the lust of conquest of their enemies'. There was a good deal more in this vein before the final paragraph referred in a single sentence to two memoranda 'regarding the details of the contemplated military measures at sea'.

The first of these, after expressing the German Government's inability to doubt that the Government of the United States would realize that the now openly disclosed intentions of the Entente to destroy and humiliate the Central Powers gave back to Germany the freedom of action she had reserved in her *Sussex* Note, announced Germany's intention of forcibly preventing all navigation, neutral and belligerent, from and to Allied countries; beginning the next day, all ships met within the specified zone would be sunk.[80]

The second memorandum defined the blockade zones and granted some latitude to neutral ships caught in them by the unexpectedness of the announcement; during a limited period the safety of passengers 'on unarmed enemy passenger ships' was guaranteed.[81] One concession was made to the American right to travel on the high seas. An American liner would be allowed to sail weekly to Falmouth, provided she was painted with red and white stripes on the hull, flew a red and white chequered flag, carried no contraband, and followed a designated lane. She must arrive on a Sunday and depart on a Wednesday. 'The last word of a mad warlord',[82] Houston exclaimed when he heard the terms: 'the farthest limit of dictation.'

Lansing's habitual reluctance to comment after only a first reading and before what he called thorough digestion naturally did not desert him on this momentous occasion. He said no more than that to give only eight hours notice was 'an unfriendly and indefensible act'.[83] Bernstorff begged him to believe that it was not so intended. Lansing was cool in his answer to that, but warmer in his reception of Bernstorff's protest that he personally had worked constantly for peace. He had never doubted that, he said; and the two men parted amicably, shaking hands.

The ambassador at any rate had no doubt about the outcome. At 10 a.m. that day he had carried out his final instructions by giving orders that all German ships in American ports were to be made unfit for service.

The final campaign of conferences, arguments, and decisions which resulted in the defeat of Bethmann and the declaration of unrestricted

U-boat war with all its fatal consequences for Germany, lasted for exactly five months beginning on 29 August 1916 and ending on 29 January 1917. The first of these dates was the day of the Pless Conference at which Hindenburg and Ludendorff expressed the voice of the High Command in favour in principle of unrestricted war. Thereafter the campaign was a rearguard action stubbornly fought by Bethmann. The last engagement so far recorded in this book was again at Pless on 9 December 1916 when the decision in favour of unrestricted war against armed ships was postponed until after the issuing of the German Peace Note. All that Bethmann formally conceded was that if the Note was rejected unrestricted war against armed ships would follow. But in reality, as Bethmann knew, the prospect of peace negotiations was the only weapon with which he could hope to avert unrestricted war *in toto*. If the prospect disappeared he would be defeated in his fight for aversion, but could still fight on for his secondary objective of bringing the declaration about in such a way as not inevitably to precipitate a rupture with the United States.

The end of the campaign was in three stages. The first lasted from 20 to 29 December 1916 when Bethmann secured the last indecision. When he learnt on 30 December of the firm rejection of the German Peace Note he gave up his first objective and struggled only for his second. The second stage finished inevitably with the crucial decision of 9 January 1917 to wage unrestricted war; and the date for it was set at 1 February. The third stage consisted of Bethmann's and Bernstorff's efforts to postpone the date, which ended in failure with the dispatch on 29 January of the final instruction to Washington.

The first stage began with a brief note from Ludendorff to the Chancellor on 20 December in which the former, treating Lloyd George's speech of 18 December as a rejection of the German overtures, said that the U-boat war should now be launched with the greatest vigour.[84] There followed an exchange of argument in the course of which Ludendorff received from Holtzendorff a comprehensive memorandum dated 22 December.[85] The Admiral was now firmly ensconced in the position into which he had been thrust by the Navy of demanding unrestricted war. He guaranteed that England would be forced to sue for peace within five months. We shall want later to glance at the foundations for the guarantee as they were exposed in the memorandum. At this point it is enough to note the conditions attached to it. They were that the war must commence on 1 February and must not be announced until immediately before. Since three weeks of preparation would be needed, the decision to commence must be taken not later than 10 January. It was accepted that it would be at the cost of a break with the United States.

On 23 December a telegram from Hindenburg informed Bethmann of his opinion that unrestricted war against armed ships should begin at once and that diplomatic and military preparations should at once be initiated for launching total unrestricted war by the end of January.[86] When Bethmann demurred, Hindenburg insisted. The terms in which he insisted were symptomatic of the change in power. In the old days the divergence of view between the political and military branches would have been submitted to the Kaiser for settlement. Now Hindenburg proposed simply to announce the divergence and couple with it his insistence, in view of his 'complete responsibility for the successful outcome of the war', on those military measures being taken which he considered appropriate.[87]

Bethmann saw that he could get no further by telegram. On the evening of 28 December he set out for Pless with Helfferich and Zimmermann.[88] Their reception at the railway station on the morning of 29 December was contemptuous. A junior officer was sent to meet them and to say that Helfferich's presence was not desired. Bethmann insisted on taking the Vice-Chancellor with him. The morning passed in complaints about these incivilities and countercharges from Ludendorff that Bethmann was permitting intrigues against the High Command. There was a largely inconclusive discussion about U-boat warfare. All that was decided was the form of the memorandum, to be sent to Washington as soon as the Allies' formal rejection of the peace offer had been received, initiating unrestricted war against armed ships. As to unrestricted war *in toto*, discussions were to proceed between the Foreign Office and the Admiralty.

Thus ended the first stage. Ludendorff's tactics, as they had been from the beginning, were to advance, to pause to observe the effect, and then, if need be, to advance again. After 29 December he needed to advance no further, only to hold his ground. Bethmann and Helfferich acknowledged to themselves that if the High Command continued to insist, they must give way. For with the Kaiser no longer the arbiter in the conflict between the military and political branches, they could not risk a fight in the open which would shake the Empire and which they would probably lose. Any faint hope Bethmann may have harboured that the Kaiser's desire for peace might still be strong enough to keep negotiations alive disappeared with the Allied Note of 29 December. There could be no further talk of an understanding, the Kaiser said, and German war aims must be recast.

Bethmann played for time. He did not start discussions with the Admiralty and he let Bernstorff in Washington go on talking. Then on 5 January Holtzendorff, chief of the Naval Staff, probably goaded from below, took the initiative. He handed to Bethmann his memorandum which the political branch had not as yet seen; and on 6 January he told Ludendorff that he would ask for the final decision from the Kaiser. He went to Pless on 8 January and saw the Kaiser first in the morning and then in the afternoon. In between he saw the two generals to confirm the accord and they discussed who would be Chancellor if Bethmann was obstinate. Holtzendorff suggested Hindenburg himself but the Field-Marshal said he could not talk in the Reichstag. In the afternoon Holtzendorff, with the aid of his memorandum and emphasizing that the High Command were not merely acquiescent but demanding, convinced the Kaiser.

In the old days Bethmann would not have let all this happen without his being on the spot. Now he did not stir until he received on 8 January another of Ludendorff's brief telegrams: 'The military situation is such that unrestricted U-boat warfare can begin on 1 February and for that very reason should begin.'[89] Then he went off to Pless, this time alone. Helfferich sat up all night preparing an answer to Holtzendorff's memorandum. The meeting with the Kaiser was for 6 p.m. on 9 January. When Bethmann got to Pless in the morning, he was told that the matter was as good as settled. He conferred during the day with the two generals but he did not show fight. It was, he told them, the last card and a very serious decision. 'But if the military authorities consider the U-boat war essential, I am not in a position to contradict them.'[90] At midday Helfferich's counter-memorandum arrived by telegraph but the Chancellor did not use it.

The Council in the evening was merely ceremonial. The Kaiser and his councillors stood round a large table on which, an eye-witness records, 'the Emperor, pale and excited, leant on his hand'.[91] Holtzendorff summarized his case. Hindenburg spoke briefly in support. The Kaiser listened impatiently to Bethmann delivering his apologia and explaining why he had opposed unrestricted war and why now, on the Navy's assurance of success, he withdrew his opposition. The Kaiser gave his decision and the secret order was issued that day.

No one in the council chamber seemed to bother with what Austria might feel about so grave a decision that must alter the course of the war for Germany's allies as well as for herself. The aged Emperor Franz Josef had died on 21 November 1916 and had been succeeded by his nephew Karl whose brief incumbency concluded the Hapsburg dynasty. Baron Burian at the Foreign Office was replaced by Count Czernin. The new emperor and the new minister shared an aversion to unrestricted war and a disbelief in the likelihood of its success. Czernin sent his chief of department to Berlin to reinforce the efforts there of the Austrian ambassador. They saw Zimmermann who disguised the fact that the decision had already been taken. 'Show me a way to obtain a reasonable peace and I would be the first to reject the idea of the U-boat warfare', he said. 'As matters now stand, both I and several others have almost been converted to it.'⁹² Germany then paid her ally the compliment of sending Zimmermann and Holtzendorff to Vienna on a mission to convert her. At a Council on 20 January each nation deployed her argument without making any impression on the other, except that the Germans convinced the Austrians that 'Germany had definitely made up her mind to start the campaign in any case, and that all our arguments would be of no practical value'.⁹³ Czernin toyed with the idea of dissociating Austria from the decision even at the risk of ending the alliance, but he did no more than toy with it.

Since the die was cast on 9 January, no more need be said about the effect in Germany of the Allied peace terms than that they shook the moderates like Bethmann and confirmed the view of the military and the right wing. What the Allies were demanding meant the end of Austria-Hungary and Turkey and the stripping and humiliation of Germany. Bethmann said after the war that the conditions imposed at Versailles were in the Allied Note 'pictured in great strokes as territorial conditions absolutely essential to the establishment of peace'.⁹⁴

The Peace without Victory Address made things worse. As a piece of diplomacy it was as much a failure as the Peace Note that preceded it. In the latter Wilson's language gave great offence to the Allies; in the former it gave great offence in Germany. Indeed, it seemed impossible not to give offence to one side or the other. The Allies were indignant because the President had in relation to what they were fighting for put them on an equality with Germany; the Germans were furious because the Allied pretensions to moral superiority in their Note of 30 December went unrebuked in the Address. The Allied conditions—'so unheard of', as Helfferich put it, 'as to be bound to be unacceptable to every nation not actually in a state of collapse'⁹⁵—were characterized by Wilson as bringing the parties 'that much nearer to a definite discussion of the peace'.⁹⁶ 'The principle that governments derive all their just powers from the consent of the governed'⁹⁷ was not one that had ever been accepted in the autocracies; and it seemed to them to be inserted as an endorsement of the break-up of Austria which the Allies were demanding. The 'single example' of this principle which the President selected seemed to exemplify better his capacity for looking at words rather than realities. He said: 'Statesmen everywhere are agreed that there should be a united, independent and autonomous Poland.'⁹⁸ So indeed they had proclaimed, but they were not at all agreed on what sort of an entity the independent Poland should be. Germany meant by Poland only the Russian parts of Poland; Russia meant a Poland under her tutelage.

Kaiser Wilhelm II

Field-Marshal Paul
von Hindenburg and
General Erich Ludendorff

Wilson and his Cabinet, 1917
Left to right, *front row*: W. C. Redfield, R. Lansing, D. F. Houston, Wilson,
W. G. McAdoo, A. S. Burleson. *Back row*: J. Daniels, W. B. Wilson, N. D.
Baker, T. W. Gregory, F. K. Lane

Paderewski had made that clear to House (if he had not understood it before) while the Address was being drafted. On 8 January 1917 House records him as saying that

The proposals of a new Poland made by Russia and Germany were absolutely selfish. Germany proposes to take a part of Russian Poland in order to strengthen her eastern frontier, while Russia wants to create a Poland composed of Russian, German and Austrian Poland for the purposes of securing Danzig for a Russian port.[99]

Then there was the passage in which the President said that 'every great people now struggling towards a full development of its resources and of its powers should be assured a direct outlet to the great highways of the sea'. Germany read that as an acceptance of the Polish demand for the German city of Danzig.

All this confirmed the Wilhelmstrasse's view that Wilson would have proved to be a most unsuitable mediator. In truth his mind was not attuned to German ideas of peacemaking. Germany in her own eyes had thrown back the aggressors and now held parts of their territory by right of conquest. To return any of it was a concession and, if it were territory necessary for her future security (for Germany had no more faith in the new order than France was to display at Versailles), unreasonable even to suggest. Thus the restoration of Belgium subject to control was a generous contribution to a compromise. Bethmann would not have been willing to disclose his formulation of the German terms even confidentially to the President if he had thought that, compared with the Allied terms, they would create an unfavourable impression. When, as we shall see, they were disclosed as 'the terms under which we would have been prepared to enter into negotiations'[100] and the Chancellor so reported to a committee of the Reichstag, he was told by the majority members that if negotiations did after all begin he should not consider himself bound by the terms because they were too moderate.[101] Zimmerman described them as 'concessions of a most extraordinary nature'.[102] Helfferich after the war said that they were 'recognized by everyone to have been very moderate, to have been absolutely nothing in comparison with the Entente proposal'.[103]

If Germany considered the continuation of control over Belgium a moderate requirement, Wilson by contrast never questioned the Allied demand that her unconditional restoration was a necessary first step. There is no reason to think that Wilson, earnestly though he desired mediation, would have tried to get it by disguising his attitude on this point. He never had to consider the matter for he wrote the Address in complete ignorance of feeling in Germany. Gerard in Berlin had not Spring Rice's talent as the trained diplomat for knowing what to report and how to report it. Bernstorff made German feeling sound much more pacific than it was; he knew from the first, as he says, that America would insist on the complete restoration of Belgium and would not mediate under any other conditions and he never in Washington allowed any other thought to escape his lips.[104]

The Allied terms were published three days after the decree of 9 January and the Address ten days after that. One may doubt whether Bethmann would have made any further attempts to postpone the submarine decree if he had not been instigated by Bernstorff who tried desperately to avert the calamity. The ambassador did not know what was impending when he had with House the conversation on 15 January* which led to such high hopes. He cabled his report of it to Berlin the next day; the President, he said, intended to force peace and his next step would be a message to Congress. This cable crossed one from Berlin, sent on the 16th and arriving on the 19th, which was the first Bernstorff heard of the decision of 9 January. The ambassador was told to say nothing until 1 February. The Chancellor said that he knew full well the danger of a breach and possibly war and asked advice about any possible way of diminishing it. This was the news whose impact was reflected in Bernstorff's discouraging letter of 20 January to House in which he said that opinion in Germany had changed.†

The ambassador replied at once to Bethmann that war was inevitable if he proceeded as contemplated; a month's notice might lessen the danger.[105] Again on 21 January he cabled that, if a period of grace was allowed, it was entirely possible that Wilson would merely break relations, at the same time redoubling his efforts for peace.[106] Then on 23 January he cabled that the Address of 22 January was 'looked upon as an additional energetic step in the direction of peace'.[107] If Germany were to announce her peace conditions, Wilson would at once propose a conference. 'I should like to leave nothing undone', the ambassador said. Could not Germany before beginning unrestricted war announce her terms as those which she had had in contemplation before the insolent rejection of her offer? What about winning over public opinion by demanding the independence of Ireland? Immediately after he had seen House on 26 January,‡ the ambassador cabled to Berlin that he had had a very important conference and urgently requested postponement till his report was received. Then on 27 January he cabled a full account of what House had said and concluded with his own clear analysis of the situation.

If the U-boat war is commenced forthwith, the President will look upon this as a slap in the face, and war with the United States will be unavoidable. The war

* See p. 613 above.   † See p. 616 above.   ‡ See p. 617 above.

party on this side will gain the upper hand, and we shall not be able, in my opinion, to tell when the war will end, since the resources of the United States are, in spite of all statements to the contrary, very great. On the other hand, if we meet Wilson's proposition, and if, in spite of that fact, these plans are brought to naught by the obstinacy of our opponents, it will be a very difficult thing for the President to undertake a war against us, even if we were then to start the unrestricted U-boat warfare. Thus, at the present, all we need is a brief delay in order to improve our diplomatic position. In any event, my view of the situation is that at this time we can get a better peace by means of conferences than if the United States should join our enemies.[108]

Bethmann was moved by these pleas. But naval instructions had gone out for unrestricted war and a countermand would reach many of the U-boats too late. Anyway Bethmann knew that it was useless to ask for a countermand. All he could do was to get permission to disclose terms confidentially in the hope that Bernstorff might make something of them. Once again he went to Pless on 29 January.[109] He argued only for taking the chance that the disclosure might, without sacrificing the submarine war, delay America's belligerence. The Kaiser and Hindenburg consented so long as it was made clear that Wilson was not to be at the peace conference, either as mediator or participant.

Immediately thereafter there were dispatched to Bernstorff the Note and memoranda which he delivered to Lansing on 31 January. The letter which at the same time he posted to Colonel House contained the terms which Germany would have offered. Publication of these terms, the ambassador said in accordance with his instructions, would, because the enemies of Germany had published terms aiming at her dishonour and destruction, show a weakness which did not exist. The German Government was therefore showing them to the President personally in proof of its confidence in him.

The terms were those already approved by the Kaiser and the Supreme Command and as dressed by Bethmann for neutral inspection. But the clothing could not conceal the essentials and was not itself in the latest fashion. The words 'strategic and economic' appeared as often as 'liberation' did in the Allied manifesto. Strategy and economics would settle the boundaries of the new Poland. They would settle also, in exchange for financial compensation, the boundaries of the parts of France to be returned to her. The restoration of Belgium would be 'under certain guarantees'. There must be a restitution of colonies which would give Germany territories 'adequate to her population and economic interest'.[110] In conclusion the German Government regretted that it was too late to postpone the submarine blockade. It believed that the blockade would lead to peace very quickly;

and in any event it would be terminated as soon as the efforts of the President, which he was begged to continue, led to an acceptable peace.

If Bethmann hoped that the ambassador would press these thoughts personally upon the President or the Colonel he was to be disappointed. Perhaps Bernstorff had no stomach for it. The terms offered were hardly those which he had led House to expect nor those that he himself believed that Germany could get. He did not try to see House again. When eventually on 15 February he quitted America, appearing, it was reported to House by a friend who saw him off, 'inexpressibly sad', he left a message for him: 'Give him my love and tell him he is the best friend I have in America.'[111]

The great question-mark that for six months had hung over Anglo-American relations is now removed as a stage prop that is no longer wanted. The play ends abruptly and a dissatisfied audience gets up and goes out to empty their minds of the unanswered questions. For how long would the Allies have gone on daring Wilson to do his worst? Would Wilson, when it came to the crunch, ever have done his worst? Would House and Lansing have stood with him if he had? To what sort of peace would Wilson have driven the belligerents if neither had defied him? Or would they have fought on until exhaustion drove them to the precarious compromise that Asquith feared, leaving the United States still in its own world? Or would there have been peace with victory? Was Winston Churchill right when later he wrote:

These prodigious stakes would never have been played if any of those who gathered at Pless had known that a few months later Russia would collapse, and that a new prospect of victory on land would open.[112]

Such questioning leads astray. The answers run rapidly into hypotheses wherein they spawn many more questions than begat them. The reader who is not self-indulgent must drop the book with the blank pages on which the moving finger was not allowed to write. Yet it is permissible to inquire, because it is a matter of actuality, into what went wrong with the plan which cuts the story short.

The calculation in the Holtzendorff Memorandum was for starvation in five months and was based on wheat of which Britain annually imported 75–80 per cent of her consumption. While the submarine blockade would disrupt the supply of other foods, such as fats from Denmark and Holland, and of course of commodities generally, wheat was the yardstick. The 1916 harvest in the northern hemisphere had on the whole been poor, thus offering Germany an opportunity that would not recur. Until in August

1917 the home-grown harvest brought a measure of relief, Britain could add to her stock only by the long haul from Australia or the Argentine, thereby employing a much larger quantity of shipping than that needed to bring in the North American harvest.

The temporary shortage and the long haul were essential factors in the plan, giving it a rigidity which left the Navy without indulgence to grant to diplomacy. The campaign could not be postponed. Surrender day was 1 July. If Britain had not been starved into submission by then, the thought of her own harvest in only a month or so would fortify her to carry on. Consequently the campaign must begin without warning on 1 February. There must be no period of notice during which stocks could be increased and preparations made. The 750,000 tons of German shipping in American ports would, if it could be put immediately into commission, give Britain five weeks' extra life; this was why Bernstorff had been instructed to ensure that the ships were put out of action.

The Memorandum was no model of brevity or clarity. A sprinkling of detailed figures give it a spurious exactitude. But there is nowhere to be found, doubtless because it was incalculable, any estimate of the amount by which the consumption of the average Briton would fall below subsistence level. Two disconnected calculations can be dug out of its many pages. Five months, or, say, twenty-two weeks, was the time allowed for bringing Britain to her knees. The first calculation showed that at the existing level of consumption the stock of wheat in Britain on 1 February 1917 would last for twelve and a half weeks. But the existing level could be lowered by 21 per cent and still leave as much per head as the German was then getting. However, in Germany there was a control organization in good working order and in Britain it would have to be improvised. The Memorandum allowed for a reduction in consumption by rationing of 15 per cent. With this allowance Britain could survive for fourteen weeks without replenishment. What replenishment was to be expected?

The second calculation begins with an estimate of the tonnage on which Britain would reckon for food imports and puts it at 10,750,000, of which about 3,000,000 was neutral tonnage. Forty per cent of the latter could be frightened away by the announcement of unrestricted war, so that there would be an initial loss of 1,200,000. The rest would be sunk at the rate of 600,000 tons a month, which would amount to a reduction of 3,000,000 tons within five months. The grand figure of 10,750,000 would thus be reduced by 4,200,000 or 39 per cent.

What is the relation of this 39 per cent to the quantity of wheat expected to get through the blockade? The Memorandum does not say. Was all this supposed to show that the shipments which Britain had presumably arranged to import so as to maintain the existing level of consumption until the new harvest would be curtailed by 39 per cent? This would put Britain on half-rations for four or five months with the certainty of immediate relief in August and the prospect after that of sustenance from the inexhaustible resources of the United States. The history of siege warfare does not support the conclusion that this is the sort of famine that brings a beleaguered garrison to surrender. It seems more likely that the 39 per cent, in spite of the nicety of the figure, was intended only as indicating the weight of the blow that would be inflicted on British shipping. The Memorandum dwells at length on the psychological effects of the blow, the confusion caused by the uncertainty of whether supplies would arrive or not, and so on. 'The education of the people is such that they have not the discipline essential to meet such a pinch.'[113]

Thus the precise calculation dissolves under inspection into an agglomeration of incalculable factors which might, if all went well, produce in the British the feeling that they would be wise to talk terms which the Germans would listen to. This was the 'guarantee of victory' which the Navy offered to the fatherland.

If Holtzendorff had put forward the submarine as the strongest instrument which for that purpose Germany had at her command and if, without promising a time, he had called it also the speediest, he would have made good his word. But then the word, so constricted, would not have been good enough. For there would then have been substituted for the uncertainties of the short term, i.e. doubts about the immediate economic effect on Britain, the uncertainties of the long term, i.e. doubts about the ultimate economic effect of the United States on the war. Holtzendorff preferred to tackle the former with the aid, as the Reichstag postwar committee of investigation* described it, of

a Heidelberg professor who, by no means, could be considered as an authority of particularly high standing with regard to any question of world commerce or politics, together with several unknown co-operators of inconsiderable reputation.[114]

It was upon this that the plan foundered. The Navy performed its part with the expected success. The estimate of sinkings within the first five months was correct to a margin of 2 per cent. The deterrent effect on neutral shipping was severe: in the early months at any rate the 40 per cent estimate was fulfilled. The estimate of stocks was substantially correct and by mid April it was down to nine weeks' supply, and it fell as low as six. In the 'black fortnight', the second half of April, the British alone lost 400,000

* See p. 635 below.

tons through submarine and mine. Every morning Hankey had on his table the figure of sinkings in the previous day: 'for the first and only time in the war', he has written, 'I suffered from sleepless nights.'[115]

The plan collapsed because the time allowed was simply not enough. Towards the end of it, in June, the Shipping Controller, a formidable Scot appointed by Lloyd George in December 1916, was very gloomy; but his gloom was due to the fear that if losses continued at their present rate, tonnage would fall below the level of the irreducible minimum by January or February 1918—seven or eight months too late. But also in June the effective answer to the submarine peril, the convoy system, which six months before both the British and German Admiralties had decried, was coming into operation. Its effect was electric: a 25 per cent pre-convoy loss was reduced to 1 per cent. In February 1918 the rate of new building in Britain exceeded the rate of British sinkings and the whole shipbuilding industry of the United States was turning out ships for supplies of all sorts to the Allies and for the transportation to Europe of American troops. As a final bonus for the British the wheat harvest of 1917 turned out to be the best of the century.

To return to the Memorandum. What must strike the reader most forcibly about the calculation of shipping losses is the comparatively narrow margin between the yield from unrestricted war *in toto* and that from unrestricted war against armed ships. The estimate for the latter is 400,000 tons compared with 600,000. The estimate of 400,000 was never tested but seems reasonable. In January 1917, the last month before all restrictions were lifted, the losses were just under 300,000 tons. A supplement of a third might easily be expected when the increasing German submarine fleet was at the high point of action and an increasing number of armed ships was being torpedoed without warning. It is true that the torpedoing without warning of armed liners would have defied the President's dictum and that Bernstorff had advised that it would lead to a break.[116] But the evidence shows that it would have been a risk worth taking. The heavier armaments being put on merchantmen, and the orders given to them to act aggressively, would have justified Wilson in changing his attitude; and it is pretty clear that to avoid war he would have done so. In spite of Lansing's continuous proddings, he had taken no action on the *Marina* and the *Arabia*, both armed ships. On 12 January Lansing sent the President a copy of the memorandum on armed ships which Bernstorff had left with him for consideration and discussion and asked for the President's views on the line he should take.[117] Wilson did not reply. The Secretary wrote again on 17 January and Wilson ignored that letter too. On 23 January the Secretary wrote a third time after receipt of a telegram from Gerard. In it Gerard quoted from a Note of 22 January wherein the German Government advised the Northern Neutrals that the merchantmen they were arming might be mistaken for enemy armed merchantmen and so subjected to attack. Gerard regarded this as endeavouring to put the United States into a position where she would passively have consented to attacks without warning on armed merchantmen. The President at last replied on 24 January, saying that Gerard was probably right and wondering 'whether the recent practices of the British in regard to the arming of their merchantmen force upon us an alteration of our own position in that matter'.[118]

Lansing, as he said in a letter to the President on 31 January, was 'greatly agitated' by this, 'more anxious than I have been since the *Sussex* affair'.[119] The whole of his doctrine with its presumptions and its primary and secondary evidence* was at stake. He set to work on a long memorandum to justify the course he urged upon the President, that is, the adoption of 'a firm and uncompromising position as to the right of merchant vessels to arm for defence'.[120] He had just penned these very words, put a comma after them, and written the word 'and', when the German ambassador was shown into the room to deliver his historic communication. Although superseded by the declaration of unrestricted war *in toto*, the Secretary included his memorandum in the documents he sent round to the White House. The discussions that evening touched on it briefly and Wilson indicated a doubt about its soundness. He had already written earlier that day that it was becoming pretty clear to him that the British were going beyond the spirit, at any rate, of the principle hitherto settled.

It would not, however, be fair to surmise that all that Germany gained from her break with America was a rise in the figure of monthly sinkings from 400,000 to 600,000 tons. There was in addition to the 600,000 destroyed the scaring of the neutrals on which the Memorandum counted; and, although the Note of 22 January was directed to just this point, Holtzendorff was not prepared to make any allowance for it if unrestricted war was directed only against armed ships. This meant according to his calculation that Britain would be deprived of only 18 per cent of her available tonnage instead of 39 per cent; this would not be enough in his opinion to force her to sue for peace. Most important, there would be a loss 'of the psychological effects of panic and fear. These effects, which can be brought about only as the result of ruthless U-boat warfare, constitute in my opinion an absolutely essential prerequisite of success.'[121]

Yet one marvels at the prodigality of the hand that threw away American neutrality. It was certainly at this time a stronger force in the President, and probably too in the nation at large, than at any other time in the war. In

* See p. 429 above.

a long report which he wrote on 11 December 1916 about opinion in the press Bernstorff included the following quotation from the *New York Tribune*, 'one of the foremost champions of our opponents':[122]

Despite a very widespread sympathy for France and a well-defined affection for Great Britain in a limited circle of Americans, there has been no acceptation of the Allied point of view as to the war, and there is not now the smallest chance that this will be the case . . . The thing that the British have failed to get before the American people is the belief that the war was one in which the question of humanity and of civilisation was uppermost for the British. The Germans have succeeded in making the Americans in very great numbers believe that it is purely and simply a war of trade and commerce between the British and the Germans.

The prints of the Cabinet papers now filed in the Public Record Office tell the tale of what Britain had to fear from American neutrality. There must in December 1916 have been a score or more of these in the houses of Cabinet Ministers in London. If a master spy had purloined a copy and taken it to Ludendorff, he would have seen that the 39 per cent cut in supplies, on which apparently Holtzendorff calculated, might well come without the employment of a single submarine. Would it have made any difference? Probably not. The Germans had not missed the significance of the President's action in terminating unsecured credits: a paragraph in Holtzendorff's memorandum dealt with it. But it would not bring results 'within a determinable period'.[123] This was the German objective at the end of 1916. For there was then a real doubt, which was not removed until the collapse of the eastern front, about how long she could hold out. The efficiency, determination, and heroism which enabled her to carry on for nearly two more years must not be allowed to obscure the fact that in the winter of 1916-17 she was desperately hard pressed.

Indeed, whatever course Germany took was beset with the sort of uncertainties that actually defeated her submarine campaign. The weight that is given to doubt before action depends on whether or not the action satisfies the instinct. If the nations at war had stated their prime object as Wilson asked them to do and stated the truth and the whole truth, they could have done it in a sentence which would have left him no further forward. For each would have used a sentence with the same words and with irreconcilable import: the humbling of the enemy. The German decision to use the submarine ruthlessly was not a dictatorial one but democratic. The mind of the majority, whether seen through the Reichstag or the press or any other medium, went with it. Germany was no more willing than Britain or France to settle for less than victory; and for Germany the temptation to use a powerful weapon not yet fully tested in action was irresistible. Gerard reported on 21 January 1917: 'Many Germans have informed me lately that the public feeling for the resumption of reckless submarine warfare is so great that they do not see how any government can withstand it.'[124] After the war Bethmann said the same thing:

> Broad circles of the German people were honestly convinced that the U-boat war would save us, and was the only means of salvation . . . No censorship can kill off such a conviction without bringing about the most disastrous results.[125]

In such an atmosphere doubts dissolve when pierced by the call to daring action.

The cardinal error in the German calculation was over the attitude of the United States. Not that she would not come into the war (Germany, though not without a flickering hope, expected that) but that once in, she would not wage war seriously. It was an error in psychology. To say that the Germans did not care about psychology would be wrong. It keeps popping up all over the Holtzendorff Memorandum. But unfortunately for them they got their psychology wrong far more often than they got it right.

What they relied on was the psychology of the blitz. The sudden declaration of unrestricted war was necessary not only so 'that no time be left for preparations' but also so 'that great fear will be injected'.[126] This was why any form of restricted warfare would not do; 'the psychological effect would in the main be dissipated'.[127] This calculation may well have been correct in its application to Denmark and Holland who had the example of Roumania immediately before them; certainly neither of them declared war as the Wilhelmstrasse had foretold. But the flickering hope that America might not come in was also dependent on the shattering effect of the sudden announcement.

> Yes, perhaps the unexpected may happen and even the United States will feel some hesitation about entering into this conflict, with regard to the dangers of which she is thoroughly informed. On the other hand, the entrance of the United States would be almost a necessity if time were to elapse between the announcement and the conduct of the U-boat war the effect of which would be to challenge the United States to a definite and responsible announcement of her attitude.[128]

This was the psychology that made the ruthless submarine war so much more attractive than waiting and watching the slowly tightening purse-strings of the United States. It was not enough for Germany to win in the end by proving herself to be the longer lasting; she must beat her enemies into respect and fear. The concluding section of the Memorandum is devoted to this theme. Why, it asked, had the neutrals submitted with such docility to the British blockade? It was because of Britain's dominion of the seas and her refusal to allow herself to be retarded by any protest of any kind.

> If Germany fails when she still has time to shift her helm and to teach the neutral

Powers that she is in no wise behind England in the matter of determination and in the power which she exercises, the result will be a very serious danger, not only for the present, but for the future as well. To avoid it, the unrestricted U-boat war is the only means at our disposal.[129]

Again:

Hatred and bitterness which the war has produced are least of all to be overcome by making concessions or manifesting consideration for others. But respect may help us where a friendly attitude is lacking. The success of the strong man has really always been the element before which the world has bowed its head.[130]

England's might rested on the belief she had created of her unquestioned predominance on the sea.

If we do not shatter this belief during this war, the reconstruction of our world position will fail as a result . . . The unrestricted U-boat war is the only means given into our hands by which we could bring the whole world back to a true realisation of things as they are. If once we succeed in breaking down the dominion, we shall have fought a victorious fight. There is no middle course between this and Germany's ruin . . . Furthermore, it is only victory which will make it possible for us to nullify the results of the tremendous feeling against us, instigated for the purpose of ruining our position in the eyes of nations.[131]

This was the attraction which drew to it all but a small allergic minority so that they could hardly spare the time to glance at the flippancy of the argument which wrote off the United States. It was assumed, as Helfferich pointed out, that she would act with no greater vigour as an ally than she would as a neutral to save Britain from starvation. One might have thought from the Memorandum that psychology was a purely German handmaiden, for the psychological effect on the Entente of America's entry into the war was not mentioned. As for America, it was assumed that after the British defeat at the end of five months she would quietly give up, so anxious would she be to recover her commercial prosperity. The Navy's guarantee of victory, which would not have got through the most adventurous firm of city solicitors vetting a prospectus, was taken so seriously that no thought at all was given to what would happen in the war if the danger point for Britain of 1 August was passed and she survived into the autumn of 1917 and beyond.

But it is idle to bring a rational eye to bear on the arguments for and against the unrestricted war as they should have appeared in December 1916. The choice was predetermined by Germany's nature and her aspirations: when the moment for decision came she could do none other.

The decision taken on 9 January 1917 would be, Bethmann had

prophesied, *finis Germaniae*. So it was: and it was also, and earlier, *finis Bethmannii*. On the very next day Hindenburg went to the Kaiser and demanded Bethmann's dismissal on the grounds that he had shown such indecision that (a favourite phrase of Ludendorff's) 'he could no longer work with him'.[132] The Kaiser refused. But it was only a matter of time. When six months later the demand was repeated and coupled with the threat of a Hindenburg–Ludendorff resignation, the Kaiser gave way and the twain were respectfully invited to nominate a successor. As a result the All-Highest appointed as his chief minister an obscure official he had never heard of, a man who was believed by Hindenburg to be 'decent and God-fearing' and who would do what he was told.[133]

The work that Bethmann did for Germany was considerable but not such as to commend him to posterity. He sought to make her into a world empire at a time when imperialism was outmoded. He used war as a diplomatic weapon at a time when it was beginning to be thought that it ought to be removed from the armoury. He exercised much skill in the political conduct of the war but it went for nothing when the soldiers took command of politics. Certainly he left his mark. But to be historically great it is not enough to leave footprints in the sands of time. The stream of events may alter course as the river did that left unwatered the great Akbar's city of Fatehpur Sikri; and who except the historically curious will trace the prints that lead to nowhere?

That Bethmann was unsuccessful is not fatal to his claims. Just as martyr-dom admits the unbaptized instantly into the Kingdom of Heaven, so a dramatic failure is often an express ticket to the Pantheon of Fame. The place therein of Woodrow Wilson, whose destiny it was to perish gloriously, his crippled body shielding the heart of the Covenant, has never been in doubt. But Bethmann muffed that too. He did not persevere till the end. It was not in his nature to fight with his back to the wall. He did not even canonize his defeat by crowning it with his resignation. Assessing the odds against him as too great, he withdrew to defend his base. He felt that he alone in his base of power, reduced though it was, stood in the way of what he called 'the machine of war passion'.[134] He thought that there might still be opportunities for negotiation. For these reasons, mixed perhaps with some less worthy, he clung to office until he was removed.

So he can make no claim to being the man who sacrificed his political life in a forlorn attempt to stop Ludendorff from ruining Germany. Ludendorff indeed did not encompass the final ruination. For that a more powerful demon was needed and found in the person of the corporal in Ludendorff's army whom he first met six years later in a beerhall in Munich. The breaking in two of Bismarck's great creation was the work of Hitler. In history as in archaeology there are ruins upon ruins and Ludendorff's reputation lies buried in the lower stratum.

But Bethmann, if he was not a great man, was a good German. When the loss of the Battle of the Marne brought peacemaking back to diplomacy he worked hard for what was practicable in the sort of peace which Germany wanted. Throughout he fought stubbornly and skilfully and with little support against the disaster of American belligerence. For all this he deserves better of his countrymen than he has received. On 20 August 1919 the Reichstag appointed a committee to inquire *inter alia* into 'what opportunities existed during the continuance of the war for bringing about peace parleys, and why such opportunities were brought to naught'.[135] The committee in a majority report, delivered on 18 June 1920, concluded that the opportunities were brought to naught by the decision of 9 January 1917. The report placed 'the historical guilt' upon Bethmann and his colleagues for allowing 'that which they were assured was injurious for the country to occur', while Hindenburg, Ludendorff, and Holtzendorff were found guilty only of aiding and abetting.[136] At least it is time that this curious verdict was quashed.

XX

WILSON BROUGHT TO WAR

Bernstorff sent home: 4 February 1917 — Austrian peace talk — waiting for the overt act — Allied reactions — the Zimmermann telegram — armed neutrality and the eleven 'willful men': 26 February 1917 — sick-bed — the decision for war: 20 March 1917 — the finale: 2 April 1917 — why America went to war — why Wilson went to war — the ideal and the contradictions

---

W E left the Secretary of State saying farewell to Count von Bernstorff—whose eyes, he noted, were filled with tears—as they shook hands for the last time in the afternoon of 31 January. The Secretary telephoned the White House and was told that the President was out. In fact Wilson had shut himself up and given orders that he was not to be disturbed. News in Washington travelled faster in the open air than along the official lines and the President in common with the rest of the public had heard about the German announcement before the ambassador had arrived at the State Department. He emerged to read before dinner the papers which Lansing sent across. At 8.45 he received the Secretary and they talked for an hour and three-quarters.

The President was 'deeply incensed' but in no mood for sharp action.[1] Lansing argued that the only possible course was to break off relations; that was what Wilson in the Note that ended the *Sussex* crisis had said he would do if Germany acted as she now had. But he found Wilson's mind greatly occupied with the sort of 'yellow peril' argument which he had first mentioned to House early in January and which, he said, had begun to impress him more and more. White civilization rested, he said, upon America's ability to keep herself intact, since she would have to build up the nations ravaged by war; as this idea had grown upon him, he had come to feel willing to go to any lengths rather than to war. Lansing urged that the break was bound to come sooner or later and that it was better for the nation to live up to her declared purpose than to wait upon humiliation. But Wilson would not commit himself, harking back to Britain's disregard for neutral rights and displaying his irritation with her as much as his indignation over the insolence of the German notice. The furthest he would go was to authorize Lansing to prepare a tentative draft of a Note breaking off diplomatic relations to be used as a basis for further consideration. Lansing left, much depressed by this indecision.

After Bernstorff had left the State Department Polk telephoned House to get him to come to Washington at once. That evening also House received the letter which Bernstorff had called the 'partial' answer.* It consisted of what would have been Germany's terms for ending the war. The Colonel caught the midnight train from New York and was at the White House for breakfast. He ate it alone and Wilson joined him afterwards.

The high hopes had crashed and Wilson was deeply depressed. As he told his Cabinet the next day, the German announcement came to him as an 'astounding surprise'.[2] He felt, he said to his friend that morning, as if the world had suddenly reversed itself; he could not get his balance.[3] The letter to House was not the opiate which Bethmann had faintly hoped it might be. What it offered was far from the sort of peace which Wilson had thought Germany wanted him to help in making.

Yet he seemed unable that morning to bring himself to do what must be done. Then and on the following day he went over every inch of the ground again, searching for what he could not really expect to find. At any rate, if he had to make the break, he would not allow it to lead to war if he could help it. He reiterated the argument that America must remain at peace to save Europe. But he no longer compared British and German derelictions. Germany, he said, was a 'madman that should be curbed'.[4] Did he think it fair to the Allies, House asked, to expect them to do all the curbing; and thought that Wilson winced.

Discussion died and they waited for Lansing to come with his draft. They could find nothing to do. Wilson fiddled with the books on his shelves and walked up and down. Mrs. Wilson came in and suggested golf but House did not think it would look well. So they played pool till noon when Lansing arrived. The three of them went over the same ground. If the break came now, House and Lansing argued, it might bring the Germans to their senses; if nothing was done, they might think their ultimatum was accepted. When Lansing left, he felt that Wilson had almost reached a decision. Perhaps he was near it in his own mind but he would not be hurried. He had promised Senator Stone, he said, that he would not do anything without notifying him and the senator had to be brought from Missouri. House was not pressed to stay longer and went back to New York in the afternoon.

Outside the White House there was endless and excited talk, mostly taking it for granted that a break was inevitable. Lansing spent the rest of

* See p. 617 above; the contents are summarized on p. 625.

the day preparing a letter to Wilson about what should follow.⁵ Which of two courses, he asked. A declaration that Germany was an international outlaw coupled with a warning to Americans to keep off pirate-infested seas? Or the punishment of the guilty nation? Writing, he believed, without emotion, he came down strongly in favour of the latter. He detailed its advantages, winding up with the thought that it would 'remove all charge of weakness of policy and satisfy, I believe, our own people', though—perhaps in memory of past rebukes on this score—he added in brackets that this was 'not of great importance but the benefit of popular support is not to be ignored'. He sent this round to the President the next morning, 2 February, together with some even more stimulating 'thoughts on Germany's broken promise and the crime of submarine warfare'. Wilson presumably read them after he got back from an early game of golf with his wife and then in the afternoon he presided over the regular meeting of the Cabinet. This was the first of a series at which Wilson permitted—a sure sign of his uncertainty—unbridled discussion of the crisis. The future, if not the present, became much indebted to Secretary Lane for his decision, taking effect as and from that day, to treat this series as of sufficient importance to justify a continuous account in letters to his brother George.

In the Cabinet Wilson posed the question as from an open mind: should he break off diplomatic relations?⁶ He startled his eager listeners by talk of the yellow peril. If it was wise to do nothing, he said, he would do nothing and would submit to any imputation of weakness or cowardice. There followed the sort of excited and disjointed talk that is to be expected when a subject of intense interest is suddenly flung open. McAdoo was vociferous for decisive action and Houston urged a declaration of war. Lansing, who never displayed in Cabinet any of his vigour on paper, murmured—one of the points in his letter—about the Allies fighting absolutism. Someone then asked the President which side he wished to see win. But he answered that he did not wish to see either side win; both had been indifferent to the rights of neutrals; probably greater justice would be done by a draw. Daniels was the chief doubter and several others were impressed by the President's 'long look ahead' at the yellow peril. But on the crisis of the day the general opinion was that to break was the only thing to do.

Wilson went straight from the Cabinet to the Capitol where Stone had just arrived. The Senate had adjourned but Stone got together sixteen Democrats including some of the strongest for neutrality, all from southern or western states. Again Wilson posed the question afresh. There were three courses, he said. First, the immediate break. Second, to wait for an 'overt act', proof that Germany really meant what she said. Third, a final warning. No one spoke for the third and only two, Stone one of them, for the second.

Wilson with his mind made up went home to write a Message to Congress which he finished at midnight. At 10 a.m. the next day, 4 February, he told Tumulty to arrange for him to address Congress at 2 p.m. and then he sent for Lansing to tell him his decision to break off relations. The Message was received with immense enthusiasm. Applause led by Senator Lodge and coming from the whole chamber, floor and galleries, broke into the announcement that relations would be severed. Most of the applauders took it as meaning war. Roosevelt had already applied to the War Office for permission to raise an infantry division. Mr. Baker wrote in his diary that 'no one believes we can escape war'.[7]

Stone moved the resolution in the Senate formally approving the President's act and it was carried by 78 to 5. In the country there was deep division expressing itself in all the usual outlets of democracy, not so much about the step taken as about what should be the next. The anti-war party was much the louder. Bryan got in at once with an appeal to the American people not 'to march under the banner of any European monarch or to die on European soil'.[8] On the other side the American Rights Committee, the group for which President Hibben of Princeton was a spokesman, demanded an immediate declaration of war. In between stood the silent majority, still nearer to Bryan than to Roosevelt, still yearning after what Wilson in a letter to Bryan nearly two years before had called their 'double wish'—'to maintain a firm front in respect of what we demand of Germany and yet do nothing that might by any possibility involve us in the war'.[9] They wanted a way out which did not take them through the valley of humiliation. So did Wilson. While he had perforce taken the first of the courses he put to the sixteen senators, he had in the Message to Congress gone as near as he could to the second. He said:

> I refuse to believe that it is the intention of the German authorities to do in fact what they have warned us they will feel at liberty to do. . . . Only actual overt acts on their part can make me believe it even now. . . . We shall not believe that they are hostile to us unless and until we are obliged to believe it; and we purpose nothing more than the reasonable defense of the undoubted rights of our people. . . . God grant we may not be challenged to defend them by acts of wilful injustice on the part of the Government of Germany.[10]

In the first week of March 1917 Wilson told Franklin D. Roosevelt, Assistant Secretary of the Navy, that he would do nothing that would allow the definitive historians to say that the United States had committed an unfriendly act against the Central Powers.[11] In the beginning he refused to think of war as more than a contingency. He allowed unobtrusive preparations to be made but instructed that there were to be no signs of mobilization. No overt act would be done by him. He drafted a document headed 'Bases of Peace'[12] setting out guarantees for the future peace of the world founded on 'general principles of right and comity', a sort of working document for the conference which apparently he still hoped to call, and on 7 February gave it to Lansing for comment. He made it plain that he was not, if he could help it, going to quarrel with Austria. This was a point he had discussed with House and Lansing in the morning of 1 February.

There had been much fuss and bother about the appointment of a successor to the unfortunate Baron Dumba as Austrian ambassador in Washington. At this critical time the new ambassador, Count Tarnowski, while physically present in Washington, was there only as ambassador designate. This may explain why the Austrian Government's Note on the submarine war, while in identical terms to the German, was not presented in Washington but given to the American ambassador in Vienna to transmit.[13] It had not arrived by 3 February when poor Tarnowski, who had no idea whether his government was following suit or not, called on the Secretary. Lansing told him that the President wished to maintain relations with Austria if possible.[14] No sooner had he left the State Department than the Austrian Note arrived there. Tarnowski was 'visibly perplexed'.[15] He sent off two telegrams to Vienna that evening and another the next morning and the upshot was that Vienna acted with a speed and directness impossible in the old emperor's time. Count Czernin on 5 February telegraphed a cordial acknowledgement of the 'kind words' to Tarnowski. 'A technical modification of the submarine war' was, he said, impossible.[16] Austria, however, was ready to negotiate a peace without victory. But she could not do so while the Entente proposed her dismemberment. Would not Wilson use his influence?

This was the first warm response that Wilson had had to his Peace without Victory Address and, although it came from the combatant who had least to gain by victory and most to lose by defeat, Wilson was highly gratified by it when it was received and deciphered on 7 February. He at once set to work on an appeal to London which he typed out the next morning and took round to Lansing himself.[17] If the Allies, he said, could assure Austria that she would retain at least 'the older units of the Empire', he could in a very short time force the acceptance of peace on the lines of his Senate address. On 10 February Page, as instructed, presented the plea to Lloyd George.

The Austrian angling came as no surprise to the Prime Minister. As early as 5 December he had heard that the Emperor Karl, who on his accession had proclaimed his wish to end the war 'as soon as the malignity of my enemies will allow',[18] was seeking contact with his brother-in-law, Prince

Sixte of Bourbon, an officer in the Belgian Army. The Empress's mother, who lived in Vienna, was the intermediary and she met her son in Switzerland on 29 January. There were said also to be Austrian diplomats in Norway and Denmark ready to talk and on 1 February Britain had sent an emissary there to find out what was afoot. Lloyd George apparently had at this stage no wish to open up a third and wider avenue for a sweeping advance under the command of President Wilson. So he put Page off with the pretence that a separate peace with Austria would merely relieve Germany of an increasing military and economic burden. The Allies had no policy of 'sheer dismemberment', he said, but the just demands of Roumanians, Slavs, Serbians, and Italians must be met by the principle of nationality.[19] He followed this up with many warm words about the President's good influence on peacemaking. Wilson took no further action; there was indeed nothing further he could do.

The President did not, however, allow his anxiety for peace to shift him from his stand on unrestricted warfare. When on 10 February the Swiss Minister in Washington[20] (whom even before the break Spring Rice had described as 'practically a German agent')[21] told Polk that the German Government was willing to negotiate provided that the blockade against England was not broken, Wilson replied at once that the proclamation of 31 January must first be withdrawn. In fact the Minister, as he confessed to Lansing eleven days later 'in a nervous and disjointed way',[22] was acting at the instigation of Bernstorff who, though diplomatically off stage, had not yet left America. The effect on Bernstorff was to make his reception on his return home even chillier than it would otherwise have been. Germany had now no thought of compromise or mediation and there was no longer any point in pretending that she had. Bethmann had shot his bolt and was leaving things to the new Foreign Minister. Zimmermann had learnt with disapproval of Count Czernin's telegram to Lansing on 5 February and told him so the next day;[23] there could be no peace without victory for Germany, he said. Such authority as the Swiss Minister had to intervene was given him on the suggestion that America was looking for an accommodation and was made subject to the condition not only that the submarine blockade should go on but also (which the Minister had concealed) to the resumption of diplomatic relations; it was to be limited to negotiation about the transport of American passengers. Zimmermann made all this public on 13 February.

After his first interview with Page, Lloyd George changed his mind[24] and on 20 February told the ambassador that Britain would give earnest consideration to any formal peace proposal by Austria made through the President provided the affair was kept absolutely secret. Lansing at once sent instructions to Penfield, the ambassador in Vienna. The ambassador had several meetings with Count Czernin, but nothing came of them since, as Penfield wrote in his report of their last conversation on 13 March, the Count said a dozen times in the hour that a separate peace was out of the question.

The Count reported none of this to Berlin. But what he did do, perhaps in the hope of averting the catastrophe which was by then looming so large, was to tell Berlin of a suggestion supposedly made by Penfield at their last talk. This was that if Germany would 'overlook' the American ships then *en route* for England, no more would be sent. Holtzendorff called this 'a flippant and rascally game';[25] and the Kaiser minuted: 'Now, once and for all, an *end* to negotiations with America. If Wilson wants war, let him make it, and let him then have it.'

Throughout February 1917 the President's great problem was how to stand still. How could he prevent the waiting for an overt act from degenerating into a drift either to war or to acquiescence? He studied a plan, which received a good deal of publicity, for a league of armed neutrality. It was put forward by a Professor Hayes of Columbia University who was also a prominent member of the American Union Against Militarism.[26] The object was to elevate the leaguers, that is, the neutral maritime nations, above what was supposed to be the commercial quarrel between Britain and Germany. It did not, however, touch the great problem; armed neutrality is no better adapted to keeping the peace than unarmed belligerency would be to winning a war. Moreover, there was not likely to be a flow of applicants for membership of the league. In his Message to Congress Wilson had 'taken it for granted that all neutral governments will take the same course', that is, of protecting their people in 'their peaceful and legitimate errands on the high seas'.[27] He caused approaches in this sense to be made in the capitals of the Northern Neutrals. But he had snubbed them too often in the past for overtures of this sort now to be well received. Sweden, the most snubbed as well as the most friendly to Germany, observed with ill-concealed glee and diplomatic regret that the United States had chosen not to participate in the system of common measures set up by the Scandinavian countries, preferring to adopt a policy of her own.[28]

It at once became plain that American shipowners were understandably nervous about running 'their peaceful and legitimate errands on the high seas'. Forthwith they cancelled all sailings. Then a Mr. Franklin, the president of one of the largest lines, inquired from the State Department what to do.[29] The inquiry constituted the major topic of discussion at the next regular Cabinet (it met on Tuesdays and Fridays) on 6 February. The expedient of convoy was rejected but apparently only on naval advice. The

Navy Department shared the delusion, common to all admiralties at this time, but to be dispelled by the British a few months later, that convoying only doubled the danger by exposing the warship as well as the merchantman to submarine attack. The decision was that shipowners should be told that they might arm (a step sanctioned by Lansing on the authority of 'the same primitive law of self-defense that justifies an individual in arming and defending himself from a highwayman')[30] but that guns and gunners would not be supplied. The President authorized the preparation of a confidential memorandum to be used by government departments as a guide for answering inquiries. The answer was evidently not intended to be lavish. Inquirers were to be told that the Government could not advise but that shipowners could take 'any necessary measures' to prevent or resist unlawful attack.[31] Lansing read out the confidential memorandum on the telephone to Franklin on 7 February and the latter immediately gave it to the press which published it verbatim on 8 February.

On 9 February the Cabinet was confronted with the difficulty that the defence of a ship against warlike operations was not even in those days of individual enterprise an activity suited to what would now be called 'the private sector'; naval guns could not be bought over the counter and gunners were not on hire. The difficulty was discussed without any decision being reached. The provision of arms is somewhere near the point where presidential and congressional powers touch. The protection of American citizens on their lawful occasions is a matter for the President, a declaration of war a matter for Congress. A careful President would not exercise without the approval of Congress his power of protection in circumstances that might lead to war. Wilson was determined to be very careful. In his Message to Congress he had said that he would come again before them to ask for authority if need be. In Cabinet on the 9th and again on the 13th he said that he would do nothing without Congress and that he would not go to Congress while there was any chance of Germany modifying her position or of her construing any American action as designed to force war. A day or two later he saw Herbert Hoover who 'came away convinced that the President earnestly, and even emotionally, intended to avail himself of any device to keep out, short of sacrifice of national honor'.[32]

The situation was graphically described in a report by Spring Rice later in the month.

The situation is much that of a soda water bottle with the wires cut but the cork unexploded. The President appears to be watching. Germany has declared that she will destroy United States ships if found in the war zone. The United States has declared that Germany will do so at her peril. But so far no United States ship has been destroyed. Is this because no United States ship has been sent into the war zone or because no United States ship has been found there? American ships have certainly passed these waters. Others are on their way. But the great majority have remained in port and the German threat appears to be entirely effective. She has not committed murder, but the threat of murder has kept America off the seas. The result is a stoppage of trade, a congestion in the ports, widespread discomfort and even misery on the coast and inland, even bread riots and a coal famine. These seem to be overt acts. They are at any rate overt facts. But they are not it seems of a sufficiently spectacular character. What is required to arouse the American people is the destruction of an American ship with American passengers. Mr Franklin, a very energetic man, who is in control of the American line, wanted to send his ships in the danger zone with passengers on board if he was allowed to arm them. The Secretary of the Navy told him that to provide guns to a private ship would be an unneutral act, although if he could get them from private sources he was welcome to use them. Mr Franklin said that he knew of no store in New York where 6-inch guns were on sale. He then went back and ordered his crews to be disbanded and the ships unloaded. . . .

There seems to be little doubt that, although the pacifist party in Congress is very strong, Congress will follow the initiative of the President and give him any powers he may desire to have. The country generally is convinced that the President will avoid war if it is possible to avoid it and that any steps which he takes will be purely defensive. The spirit of the country is rising. This does not mean that the desire for peace is less, but that the sense that something must be done to unify the nation and to prepare for war is growing. . . .

But on the whole the President will do all he can to maintain peace and it will be extremely unwise to count with any certainty on the United States entering into the war.[33]

The situation was worse than confusing. It was becoming ridiculous. On 10 February the first freighters to leave America set sail unarmed and Mr. Franklin said that he was ordering two of his ships to leave Liverpool for New York on 14 and 16 February. But, he said, they ought to be protected. On 10 February Daniels, speaking for the Navy, told the President that only the Navy could provide adequate armament and enclosed a memorandum from Assistant-Secretary Roosevelt suggesting how it should be done. There were two more inconclusive Cabinets on 16 and 20 February. After the first several Cabinet officers got together and agreed that the President must do something: 'side with the Allies promptly and wholly', Houston said.[34] After the second of them Lane wrote to brother George: 'We are all, with the exception of one or two pro-Germans, feeling humiliated by the situation, but nothing can be done.'[35] Wilson was lodged in his resolve to do nothing without an overt act. It began to seem as if the only rational course was to pray for the overt act that would release the President from his self-imposed predicament.

But in fact after 16 February (a day on which Spring Rice reported that submission was not impossible)[36] there were signs that Wilson was getting ready to change course. Not that he would take Houston's advice if he could help it. On 19 February he gave one of his rare interviews to outsiders. Talking to Bergson, the great French philosopher, he repeated his belief that England was fighting only for commercial supremacy.[37] But he must have realized that he must come down on one side or the other. Either he must restrict commerce with the Allies to what their own ships could carry, which would have a serious effect on the American economy and would be in substance, if not in form, a surrender to Germany. Or he must protect the trade. It was hopeless in the twentieth century to expect American merchantmen to equip themselves for defensive privateering. The reason why he hesitated almost to the point of absurdity can only be that he saw clearly enough how far armed neutrality would take him on the road to war.

He made up his mind at the latest on 21 February. That evening in his study he wrote out a second Message to Congress in which he asked for legislative authority to arm ships defensively. The following afternoon he summoned Lansing, read to him what he had written, and said he would deliver it to Congress on 26 February. But he told no one else, perhaps because of his usual secretiveness or perhaps because, having fixed 26 February as his deadline, he would not ignore the least chance of a reprieve. So the public uncertainty continued. The last session of the old Congress was due to end with the end of Wilson's first administration on 4 March. The new Congress would not in the ordinary way sit until December. In the Senate neither those who feared national humiliation nor those who feared war were willing to leave the President unwatched. On 23 February they resolved to filibuster appropriation bills so as to force Wilson to call the next Congress into special session. Then at the Cabinet on 23 February the cork almost popped out of the soda-water bottle. Lane wrote:

An animated scene occurred arising out of a very innocent question of mine as to whether it was true that the wives of American Consuls on leaving Germany had been stripped naked, given an acid bath to detect writing on their flesh and subjected to other indignities.[38]

Lane spoke also about the food shortages that were being caused by the shipping stagnation and the reports of bread riots. McAdoo demanded prompt action, Congress or no Congress, and Houston supported him. The President was nettled and said he would have nothing to do with dictatorship. Then he turned on the fire-eaters, especially McAdoo, and reproached them bitterly with appealing to the 'Code Duello', as he called it.

'We couldn't get the idea out of his head, 'Lane wrote, 'that we were bent on pushing the country into war.' After the meeting McAdoo and Houston talked of resignation.

The breach with the Central Powers did not of course leave the Allies uninterested. For the British the immediate point of interest was the financing of the war. For the French it was the effect on the terms of peace.

For a month British statesmen could hardly have dared to look the financial problem in the face; they could only hope that a miracle would happen. And it had. On 5 February at the first meeting of the War Cabinet after the news of the break the chief subject of discussion was its effect on finance and supplies;[39] some members seemed to think that Spring Rice ought already to have got to work on it. It was decided that preparations should be made for telling the United States how she could best assist. It was decided also to settle up with Japan. Britain desperately needed the help of her navy in the submarine war; Japan's price was the Pacific islands north of the equator and the German rights in Shantung which she no longer had it in mind to return to China.* The Cabinet authorized an exchange of assurances whereunder Britain would support Japan's claims, 'it being understood that, in the eventual peace settlement, the Japanese Government will treat Great Britain's claims to the German Islands south of the Equator in the same spirit'.[40] Matters of this sort were best disposed of before the United States joined the Allies.

Another sign of great expectations was to be seen in the discussion in the Cabinet of 5 February about a new Order-in-Council to tighten the blockade. The Order contemplated was to declare that any ship, which was on her way to or from a neutral port affording access to enemy territory and which failed to call at an Allied port *en route*, should be deemed to be carrying goods of enemy destination or origin. This novel provision in international law, which said in effect that anyone who failed to call at a police station should be presumed guilty, had been under discussion for some time between Britain and France and had been vigorously opposed by Jusserand as likely to anger Washington. When the Order was promulgated on 21 February and designated as a reprisal, the State Department made no comment.[41]

Lloyd George did not leave the shopping list, whose preparation the Cabinet had ordered, to wind its way through the ordinary channels. The next day he had a talk with Page. The ambassador's account of it shows him back in his old form and enjoying the new situation.

I called on the Prime Minister yesterday. In a private unofficial talk he said

* See p. 262 above.

that it would be an affectation to conceal his pleasure at our diplomatic break with Germany. He began immediately to talk about the probability of war following. I reminded him that the United States is arranging peace and that war is not in my vocabulary. He replied that it was well to look a little ahead in private conversation. He hoped that in no event would our supply of ammunition to the Allies be curtailed, that a much larger supply of steel could be got from the United States which munition factories here badly need, and he asked earnestly about our merchant shipbuilding activities. . . . Then he asked, 'Is there any way we can serve you? I have already directed our Army Chief of Staff (Robertson) and the first Sea Lord (Jellicoe) to give you all possible information out of our experience that you may ask for'.[42]

In this conversation Lloyd George spoke also of how much he desired the President's participation in the peace conference. He dwelt on this again on 10 February when Page brought him the President's message about Austria and then he made a frank and eloquent appeal to Wilson for help in war and peace. America must be in the war, he said, because her participation was necessary for the complete expression of the moral judgement of the world and so that the President might sit in person at the peace conference. The present belligerents had suffered so heavily that their judgement would also have suffered. Even Britain, who wanted nothing for herself, would be prevented from returning German colonies. Nobody could have so commanding a voice as the President.

These were sentiments genuinely felt, notwithstanding—and if Lloyd George himself would not have admitted this, everyone who knew him would—that they might have to be cut later into shapes that fitted political objectives. Very little that Lloyd George said or did was without a political objective and what he said on this occasion was no exception to the rule. The sentiments were valid not merely as sentiments but also as the most captivating argument for belligerency that could be addressed to Wilson. Page reproduced them in fine style.[43]

Lloyd George made it sound almost as if acceptance of America's help in the war was a price worth paying for her help in the peace. The French Government more soberly came to the conclusion, though not without internal debate, that the benefits the United States would confer as a warmaker were on the whole worth the place at the peace conference to which warmaking would entitle her. They decided therefore to work discreetly for her entry into the war and to do their best diplomatically to convince her of the justice of French aims. In public of course the British were as discreet. They discouraged outbursts of enthusiasm in the press. Spring Rice on 5 February communicated only privately the 'admiration' of the Governor-General of Canada and Wilson pronounced this to be in good taste.[44] This was the kindest thing he had said about the British for quite some time but it was not for long to hold the record. When the British Government communicated with him again on 24 February they received in return his thanks for information of inestimable value and 'his very great appreciation of so marked an act of friendliness'.[45] The events which led up to this astounding encomium must now be set forth.

Germany of course had not been unobservant of America's trouble in Mexico. It tied up a large part of the American Army and so as a stimulant to neutrality in European affairs was something to be fostered. Under the remote superintendence of Bernstorff some of the activity of German agents in the United States was directed towards this object, in particular in trying to arrange the return of Huerta to Mexico. At the same time and by more orthodox methods Herr von Eckhardt, the German Minister in Mexico, was wooing Carranza. Success could be very rewarding. If Mexico's neutrality could be dented, there might be bases for the U53 and her like which could cross the Atlantic. Germany might even hope for the cutting off of the oil which the British Navy needed. Another objective of German diplomacy was to disturb the Anglo–Japanese alliance and from time to time she made overtures to which Japan was not wholly inattentive. The two objectives could be combined. A German–Japanese–Mexican alliance offering the prospect of a Japanese army landing on the Mexican Pacific coast and advancing to the Texan border might, it could be hoped, have a scaring effect.[46]

When in November 1916 it was clear to the Wilhemstrasse that unrestricted submarine war and the consequent estrangement of America were more than possibilities, serious talks were begun. The time was propitious, for negotiations between the United States and Mexico for the withdrawal of the Punitive Expedition were bogged down. Eckhardt was instructed to tell Carranza about the imminence of unrestricted submarine war and the consequent need for bases and to ask what he would care to have in return. So long as Germany had any substantial expectation of keeping America neutral it was risky to be more specific about the *quid pro quo*. But when on 9 January 1917 the die was cast at Pless the Wilhemstrasse decided that the risk was worth taking. An offer of alliance contingent upon the United States entering the war was prepared. The *quid pro quo*, besides 'generous financial support', was the reconquest of 'the lost territory in Texas, New Mexico, and Arizona'. Eckhardt was also to suggest to Carranza that he should invite Japan to join the new alliance.

The safest way of conveying this piece of dynamite across the Atlantic was by the submarine merchantman *Deutschland*, due to leave on 15 January, and this was what was planned. But the trip was cancelled. So Zimmermann decided to dispatch it by the Swedish Roundabout and also via Bernstorff on the State Department 'wire' which the Wilhelmstrasse was then being permitted to use in cipher for the purposes of the German peace offer which Washington then supposed to be in preparation. The message was in fact annexed to the telegram to Bernstorff of 16 January* which brought him the news of the Pless decision; and he was instructed to forward it to Eckhardt by a safe route.

Sending the message in this way was running not, as Zimmermann must have thought, a calculated risk; it was heading for disaster. The British Naval Intelligence at this time was incomparably the best in the world and its organization one of the finest achievements in the history of war. In November 1914 Captain Reginald Hall, R.N., then forty-five and in command of a battle cruiser, was told that his health would not stand the strain of active service and appointed Director of the Intelligence Division. He has been mentioned briefly† as the man who cracked the House–Wilson cipher. This was by no means the highest of his achievements. He constructed out of a miscellaneous collection of 'brains' a department which in 1917 was employing seventy or more cryptographers and clerks besides hundreds of radio monitors. 'A genius', Page called him;[47] and in his rhetorical way wrote of him as one who 'can look through you and see the very muscular movements of your immortal soul'. Certainly Hall had an uncanny way of guessing right. In April 1915 he found in the cellars of the India Office in the neglected baggage of a German vice-consul, who in Persia had had to make a hurried departure, a copy of the German diplomatic codebook 13040. It was one of two used for transmissions between Berlin and Washington. It was used of course with variants introduced from time to time but it provided the structure for the cryptographer to work on. By this means for some time before January 1917 a few people in London— never many, for Admiral Hall, as he had then become, was not a man to share secrets if he could help it—were aware of much that was passing between Bernstorff and his chiefs. Thus it was that on 17 January a publisher and a Presbyterian minister were the first persons outside Germany to learn that 1 February was *der tag*. The annexion for Eckhardt gave them more difficulty. There was a large part in the middle which they could not decode, but they got the proposal for an alliance with Mexico and for negotiations with Japan.

This was enough to tell the Admiral that it was a discovery of immense political importance. But his first thought inevitably was for his sources.

* See p. 624 above.   † See p. 455 above.

If it was to be used, its authenticity would have to be proved to the hilt against an expected German denial; else it would be treated as a clumsy attempt by the British to bring America into the war. How could this be done without ruining an invaluable asset by letting Germany know that Britain was tapping her most secret communications? Hall considered that he had at least a fortnight in which to solve that problem. The announcement of unrestricted war, when it was made on 1 February, might thrust the United States forthwith into the war; and then the interception need never be disclosed.

It was Hall himself who went round to the American embassy to give Page the first news that had reached London of the diplomatic break. If he had asked Page whether it meant war (there is no record that he did), it is unlikely that Page would have been very positive. The ambassador's hopes did not begin high and they dropped lower; on 19 February he wrote: 'I am now ready to record my conviction that we shall not get into the war at all.'[48] At any rate the Admiral decided that he must act; and on the following Monday, 5 February, he took his jewel to the Foreign Office and placed it in the hesitating hands of Lord Hardinge, the Permanent Under-Secretary and the doyen of the old diplomacy. How to handle a stolen treaty is a subject more fully covered in improbable thrillers than by diplomatic expertise. Balfour at any rate had no hesitations that are recorded. But there were still a number of things to be done. Balfour thought it wise to probe gently the thoughts of the Japanese ambassador: the cryptographers were still working on the middle section: a solution had still to be found of the problem of disclosure. Hall was working on the solution, his idea being to disclose the telegram as one intercepted between Washington and Mexico City. But he could not take it for granted that it had actually gone to Mexico City nor without sure knowledge could he fix the date of its dispatch from Washington. Nor would he run the risk that differences, however slight, between the original and the relay might lead the Germans to suspect the interception of the former. What he required was a copy of the relay; and this, since he had an agent in the telegraph office in Mexico City, he thought that, given time, he could get. In fact he got it on 10 February; it showed that Bernstorff had dispatched the telegram by Western Union on 19 January. Then on 19 February the decoders obtained the full rendering including— almost too glamorous to be true—the contemplated reconquest of the lost territories. Also by this time Naval Intelligence had intercepted and decoded a follow-up telegram from Zimmermann to Eckhardt on 5 February. Since Bernstorff was by then excommunicate, it was sent only by the Swedish Roundabout and so the British never revealed that they knew of it. The first instruction had told Eckhardt to wait for the outbreak of war before acting;

the second told him to act at once 'provided there is no danger of secret being betrayed to United States'.[49]

Everything was now ready and Page was consulted, as he had been in the Archibald affair,*about the manner of release. He favoured a touch of ceremony, that the Foreign Secretary should officially hand him the document for transmission to the President. So on 23 February the ambassador called at the Foreign Office and was solemnly handed the telegram in what Balfour, not given to hyperbole, later called 'the most dramatic moment of my life'.[50]

Page then carefully composed an accompaniment to the bombshell and, though pessimistic about what would be blown up, dispatched both the next day. The telegram, he wrote, had been bought in Mexico. The British had obtained early in the war a copy of the German code and had been getting also copies of Bernstorff's telegrams to Mexico. The source of the information must be kept profoundly secret but, Page added with a touch of the wry humour he liked, the British 'put no prohibition on the publication of Zimmermann's telegram itself'.[51] He suggested that the State Department should obtain a copy of the coded text from the cable office in Washington.

It was the weekend. Page on the Saturday morning 24 February had prudently alerted the State Department that a message of great importance would follow. Lansing was away at White Sulphur Springs and Polk waited for it all day. At last it arrived at 8.30 p.m. and after it had been deciphered as rapidly as possible Polk took it straight to the White House. Wilson read it, Polk said, with 'much indignation'[52] and this cannot have been an overstatement. The impudence of the move, when it was made public a few days later, was such as to shock his compatriots; and they could not realize, as Wilson did, the evidence it brought with it of German duplicity—that, as it seemed, since at the latest 19 January Bernstorff had been leading him up the garden path towards the hope of a German peace offer when unrestricted war had already been decided upon.

Two things are clear on Polk's evidence. The first is that Wilson never for a moment doubted (though subsequently many Americans did doubt) the authenticity of the Zimmermann telegram. Indeed, he was to run a substantial political risk in vouching for it when he knew that he could not disclose even as much as he himself knew of how it had been obtained. The moment could hardly have been a better one for setting off a British detonation to bring America into the war, but Wilson never supposed that the British were either so guileful as to have invented the telegram or so guileless as to have been hoaxed. The second thing is that although its publication would greatly reduce his dwindling resources for keeping the peace, he never

* See p. 326 above.

contemplated either suppressing it or feigning doubts about it which he did not have. His first thought was to publish at once. Polk persuaded him to hold his hand until Lansing returned and thereafter Lansing counselled delay. In the end the timing of the release was settled by the course of events in Congress.

For when the President went to Congress the next day, Monday, 26 February, he found that armed neutrality was not going to have an uneventful voyage. His Address to Congress was pitched low.[53] As yet, he said, no American ship had been sunk without warning. (Although Wilson did not know it, the German Admiralty had decided to observe until 28 February cruiser rules against neutral shipping.) The injury to American commerce was because 'so many of our ships are timidly keeping to their home ports'. No overt act had been committed. 'War can come only by the wilful acts and aggressions of others.' It was devoutly to be hoped that force would not have to be used. But before Congress ended its session he wanted, though his own powers were ample, its authority for any action he might be compelled to take. So he asked Congress for specific authority to supply American merchantmen with defensive arms and the means of using them and 'to employ any other instrumentalities or methods that may be necessary or adequate to protect our ships and our people in their legitimate and peaceful pursuits on the seas'. These wide words were to cause difficulty.

Even as Wilson was delivering this Address the rumour was spreading among his hearers that the British liner *Laconia* had been torpedoed. The story was in the newspapers the next morning, 27 February. She was sunk in the Western Approaches during the night of 25 February. She was armed and carrying Americans among passengers and crew. Two Americans, mother and daughter, friends of Mrs. Wilson, died from exposure in the open boats before they reached the safety of Bantry Bay.

This same Tuesday morning Lansing got back from a long weekend and heard about the Zimmermann telegram. He heard also some speculation about how Bernstorff had received it. As to that he had his suspicions and before he went to the White House at 11.30 a.m. he verified them. Bernstorff, he told the President with perhaps a touch of self-satisfaction natural enough in one whose precautions had been overruled,* had received an exceptionally long telegram on 18 January, the day before his cable to Mexico City. While Lansing was stating his premises and unfolding his conclusions, Wilson ejaculated 'Good Lord!' two or three times;[54] and at the end expressed his resentment at this detestable abuse of privilege.

The Armed Ship Bill was now being prepared in the appropriate legisla-

* See p. 617 above.

tive committees in accordance with a memorandum which Wilson had tendered. In the Foreign Relations Committee of the Senate there was no Republican opposition; Lodge wanted to make sure that Wilson would not take refuge in lack of authority. But Stone, the Chairman of the committee and as such the Administration's chief 'instrumentality' in the Senate for foreign affairs, had gone along with Wilson as far as he could and now could go no further. He opposed the Bill. So did three others including Hitchcock of Nebraska, the next Democrat in seniority to Stone on the committee. In the Foreign Affairs Committee of the House various amendments were being proposed to omit the wide words and to forbid the arming of vessels carrying contraband. Wilson did not at all like this: 'the original language was most carefully studied', he told Burleson.[55]

It took the Administration forty-eight hours to overcome the repugnance of Western Union to producing a copy of Bernstorff's telegram to Mexico City. This after all was peacetime in a democratic State! The State Department had it by 28 February. There was then no longer any reason for delaying the revelation and Wilson was determined to apply the spur to Congress. He decided not to make an official announcement but to let the Associated Press have the news for the morning papers of 1 March. At his suggestion Lansing saw Hitchcock in the afternoon of 28 February and showed him the telegram. It was, the senator said, a 'dastardly plot' and he agreed to present the Bill on the floor of the Senate.[56]

It would hardly be correct to describe the publication on 1 March as sensational. Its effect was nearer to the reverse. It stunned. Germany's invasion of Belgium and her sinking of the *Lusitania* paled in comparison with the effrontery of a proposal to assist in the abstraction of three of the forty-eight United States through her back door. Opinion was divided between those who swallowed the news with horrible grimaces and those who spat it out as a poisonous invention. In the Senate Stone pressed to know how the discovery was made—did it come from London?—and another of the four who had opposed the Bill in committee asserted that it was 'a forgery and a sham born in the brain of a scoundrel and a tool'.[57] Underwood, Wilson's rival at the 1912 Convention and now one of the senators from Alabama, was one of the few to remain calm: what was wrong anyway, he asked, with what Zimmermann was doing? In the evening Wilson issued a statement that the Government had evidence establishing the authenticity of the telegram and that it was incompatible with the public interest to say more. Even after this Hearst instructed his editors to treat it as 'in all probability a fake and forgery';[58] and in the evening of 2 March and in the sophisticated atmosphere of the Round Table Dining Club the company, which included Elihu Root, was incredulous. The German-American press of course was unanimous in denunciation. The Mexican Government denied all knowledge.

It was a tricky situation. If Wilson himself needed any more convincing it was easy to provide it. On 2 March the embassy cipher clerk in London decoded the telegram himself at the Admiralty and Page cabled the German text to Washington.[59] But how to convince the public without producing the Western Union telegram and revealing that the code had been cracked? There seemed to be nothing to do except stand on the President's statement, which was accepted, whether believed or not, by those like Lodge who wanted war and disbelieved by those who did not.

The deadlock was broken—to Lansing's 'profound amazement and relief'[60]—in the simplest and most unexpected way. At a press conference on 3 March Zimmermann said that he had sent the telegram. This flabbergasted the pro-Germans, causing some of them to abandon the faith altogether, and added considerably to the devastation created by the explosion.

Secretary Zimmermann has been reviled first for sending the telegram and secondly for admitting that he sent it. These ought not, however, to be made as separate charges, not because it is always wrong to deny the truth—if the maxim applies at all in diplomacy, it would not have been accepted by Zimmermann—but because the justification of both is the same: there being nothing wrong in the deed, there could be no reason to deny it. It was after all, as Senator Underwood perceived, quite normal in nineteenth-century diplomacy to make alliances to operate against prospective enemies; and once war had begun 'prize-dangling', as the Allies had practised it in 1915,* was a recognized part of the process. Germany did not consider even America to be above temptation. 'Perhaps', Moltke had suggested hopefully in August 1914, 'the United States may be induced to turn their navy against Britain if Canada is held out to them as the prize of victory.'[61]

But if it be conceded that the Zimmerman telegram was not a crime, the question may still be asked whether it was a blunder. Would it not have been wiser, hindsight may inquire, to have waited until the rupture occurred before making a proposal which, if it came out, would help to bring on the occurrence? 'If it came out': it was Zimmermann's misfortune rather than his fault that it did. But if it had been suggested to him in January 1917 that the proposal was so perilously freighted that he ought not to run the slightest risk of its miscarrying, undoubtedly he would have asked why. It would have taken a statesman far better informed than Zimmermann to foresee the effect it would have on the American mind.

What in fact it did was to supply an essential ingredient for the compound

* See p. 259 above.

1917. Wilson with his second wife at the inauguration parade in Washington

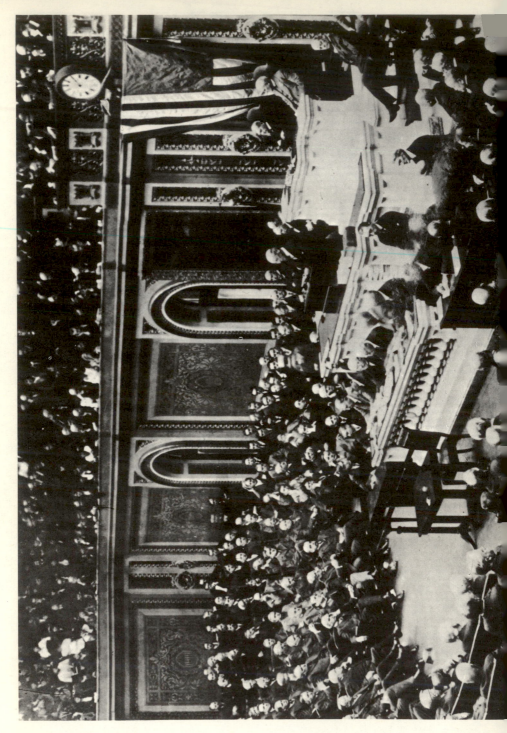

Washington,
April 1917.
Wilson addresses
Congress on the
War Resolution

whose stirring up exhaled American willingness to go to war. Americans were always pleased to hear talk about American dignity and American rights. But when it came to the crunch, no one could think that American travel was worth a war and few that American trade was worth the sort of war that had become a carnage. The impulsion that was needed was the conviction that Germany was a menace to America. Many sophisticated Americans—Roosevelt, Lodge, House, and Lansing—could see that for themselves. For those of them who could not Walter Lippmann in a series of articles in the *New Republic* beginning on 10 February spelt out the argument. A German victory would subvert the sort of civilization in which America lived her life. By substituting might for right it would destroy the fundament of the world system to which all her workings were geared. What had protected America hitherto from the impact of this kind of aggression was Britain's dominion of the seas. If America sat by while Germany wrested that from Britain by the lawless use of the submarine, then sooner or later America would be for it.

But such ideas were too subtle for the simple American. Endangering a world system was not the sort of peril he could visualize. What Zimmermann did was to bring Lippmann's argument to the simple American's doorstep and lay it there in language so crude as to be laughed at by the sophisticated but which the unsophisticated could understand. Moreover, he hit hard at the elements in America hitherto least affected by the war, those in the south for whom Mexico was not so far away and those by the Pacific Ocean where they were always afraid of infiltration by Japanese.

Seen in retrospect the accuracy of aim seems to be so deadly that one wonders how anyone could have hit the target unwittingly. But this would be to ignore the fact that Germany had been forced out of touch with American feeling. Someone who studied Spring Rice's letters would have seen from them that the rock on which anti-war sentiment reposed was in the south and west. But Bernstorff's letters were not of that calibre; and no German could have the inestimable advantage of reading them in the ambience of the talk and crosstalk that flowed out of the constant intercourse between Britons and Americans throughout the war. What would have been an unpardonable blunder for a British diplomat becomes at least excusable for a German.

But one may doubt whether a German diplomat would have seen it that way anyhow. The public exposure is by no means a bad thing, he might have said; it will make Americans understand what it means to go to war with Germany. It would supplement perhaps the fright which Germany hoped to engender in Americans by the suddenness and ferocity of her onslaught on Britain* and help to deter them from interfering. It is not surprising that Zimmermann did not risk a denial which, if it were disproved, would let ignominy rush in where there should be a display of might. The mood of Germany then was shown by what the Kaiser wrote a little later: 'If Wilson wants war, let him make it.'†

It remains only to record that nothing came of the proposed treaty, that there was not much future for Zimmermann, and that he never found out how the secret had escaped. Although Carranza certainly responded to the overture, he told Eckhardt on 14 April that it was stultified by premature publication. By then America had come to terms. The Punitive Expedition was withdrawn on 5 February and Carranza's Government was recognized on 3 March when an American ambassador presented his credentials. Throughout March the Swedish Roundabout buzzed with inquiries from Zimmermann about the leak answered by explanations from Eckhardt about the enormity of his precautions and hints that Bernstorff was to blame. So little did Zimmermann suspect the truth that the interrogation was conducted in the cracked code and the intercepts read with joyful interest by Admiral Hall and his men. Zimmermann's tenure of high office was brief. Although he had striven to accommodate himself to Germany's new masters, they treated him as tarred with Bethmann's brush and both were put out of the Government together.

The first concrete achievement of the Zimmermann telegram was that at the end of the day of its publication the House of Representatives passed the Armed Ship Bill by 403 votes to 13, though an amendment to forbid an armed ship to carry munitions or belligerent nationals was defeated only by 293 to 125. In the Senate, notwithstanding that speakers on both sides agreed that armed neutrality must lead to war, there would have been an even more decisive result had not a group of four pacifists headed by La Follette, the great radical from Wisconsin ('I love these lonely figures', Wilson said of him six years before, 'taunted, laughed at, called back, going steadfastly on . . .'),[62] filibustered to prevent the vote. At noon on Sunday, 4 March the sixty-fourth Congress expired without enacting the Bill.

Wilson got the substance of what he wanted which, since he believed (although in a spasm of annoyance he professed to doubt it) that he had the legal power, was the endorsement by the Senate: seventy-five senators signed a manifesto saying that they would have voted for the Bill if they could. Nevertheless, he was furious and issued a stinging rebuke. Were

---

* See p. 632 above.   † See p. 642 above.

other governments to think that they could act as they pleased without the United States doing anything at all?

The explanation is incredible. The Senate of the United States is the only legislative body in the world which cannot act when its majority is ready for action. A little group of willful men, representing no opinion but their own, have rendered the great Government of the United States helpless and contemptible.[63]

House recorded that he 'showed much excitement and was bitter in his denunciation'.[64] He told Houston that La Follette was vain and Stone slippery;[65] and he said to Tumulty that he would never shake hands with Stone again.[66]

Altogether in this brush with Congress Wilson conducted himself with that emotional mixture of anger and audacity which he so often exhibited when his path was crossed. The terms of his rebuke (though it is fair to say that it was shown to House, McAdoo, and Tumulty among others and approved, even urged, by them) were reckless and unfair. He put in the pillory as the 'willful men' the eleven senators who had opposed the Bill and there they stood to be pelted by an eager press. In fact only four had resolved on the filibuster. The others had committed no crime unless it is criminal to oppose in good conscience a Bill which the whole Senate thought would lead to war. Stone was not one of the four and his punishment was hard. He had travelled a long way with the President since the days when he had fought for Champ Clark in the 1912 Convention. 'One of the strangest things', House noted Wilson as saying in January 1914, 'was that he and Stone had become good friends and that the Senator seemed to have a positive affection for him.'[67] Now Wilson forgot the affection and all the loyal service which Stone had given him and which only his deepest and never-concealed convictions brought to an end.

Stone's fellow senator from Missouri warned him that it would mean his political ruin: 'you are old and you have no property.'[68] But Gum-Shoe Bill could do none other. The time left to him was not enough for poverty to erode. Like all those who opposed the war (Bryan sent a telegram asking the President to enrol him as a private),[69] once the decision was taken Stone flung himself into its prosecution. Travelling to Washington in April 1918 he was struck by a paralysis—brought on, it was said, by his distress over the Allied reverses in France—and almost instantly he died.

Wilson's unfair rebuke had no consequences other than the bad mark which historians have given him for it. Another piece of impetuosity might have had consequences more immediate and graver had not relief come from Germany. As well as his bold endorsement of the Zimmermann telegram, Wilson had in his anxiety to win the battle in Congress thrown into the fight an intimation that he regarded the sinking of the *Laconia* as an overt act. Until then, alike in formal pronouncement and in informal hint, he had been ambiguous, or at least reticent, about whether the characteristic of the overt act would have to be an attack on an American ship or could be an attack on American life in a belligerent ship. He never resiled from the position that American rights included American lives anywhere on the seas, but what he stressed was the safety of American shipping.

This ambiguity was surely wise. It left him free to determine his attitude according to the magnitude of the event. Anything remotely approaching another *Lusitania* he could not overlook, but he would not need to commit himself to extremities because of a single American on an Allied ship. On 7 February the British armed liner *Californian* was torpedoed without warning in the Western Approaches with the loss of forty-one lives, the one American on board being uninjured. Wilson did not regard this as an overt act, for he told Congress on 26 February that none had been committed. Did the loss of two lives from the sinking of the *Laconia*, also armed, put that case so clearly across the borderline? Did Wilson think about this before, almost as soon as he heard the news (how different from his pedantic insistence in times gone by upon waiting for all the facts), he flung the case into the fray? Did the doubt he had expressed to Lansing the month before* about the reasonableness of expecting the submarine to warn the armed ship recur to his mind? Once more he had placed himself on the edge of a war to defend no right more sacred than the right to travel. He could have treated the German declaration of 31 January as by itself a *casus belli* and then he could in justification have pointed to the threat to American shipping. But having said that he would wait for the overt act, expressing his disbelief that it would ever happen, it would be the nature of the act done, and no longer the threat, that would constitute the just cause for war. Suppose that Germany yielded—what was the object of delay if not to give her an opportunity to yield?—to the extent of withdrawing, openly or tacitly, the threat to American ships but not to belligerent liners, how would Wilson stand? But it was not long before Germany spared him the need to answer that question.

On 5 March Wilson was inaugurated into his second term. He delivered his Address outside the Capitol in driving rain and a raw wind with the result that he began the new term with a severe cold. He went to bed on 7 March and remained secluded for over a week. He saw only a few people, Lansing twice, and the regular Cabinet meetings were put off. He went on with

* See p. 630 above.

essential business. For this purpose Mrs. Wilson and not Tumulty was the channel of communication.

A sick-bed gives time for thought, and so we may suppose that on 7 March Wilson began the making of his mind which in all probability he finished in the evening or night of 20 March. We cannot be certain, for there was no concluding record and no one else was privy to the process. He took no counsel, except that at the very end he listened to his Cabinet. Also at the end he unbosomed himself to a friend, Frank Cobb, the editor of the *New York World*, but he was seeking then sympathy and support for the load he had to bear rather than advice. There was probably no one who could have helped him if he had sought help. For all those around him, House, Tumulty, Lansing, Polk, and almost all in his Cabinet, saw no alternative to war. He could have found no one who would comprehend his perplexities. Daniels perhaps would have come nearest to it, but fundamentally the pacifists as well as the warriors were alien to his thought.

He did not summon House to come and watch with him. They were not estranged. House, moving now tangentially, had obtained from Hoover and sent to the President on 13 February a memorandum on the part that the United States should play if she did get into the war.[70] Wilson had sent House a copy of the Zimmermann telegram the day it arrived. House had written to congratulate the President on his Address to Congress ('the last two paragraphs are as fine as anything in the English language') and had stayed at the White House for the Inauguration. But on the great issue the corridor between their minds was closed. House knew it and would say nothing. Anyway, he believed war to be inevitable.

Mrs. Wilson did her best to help her husband. She summoned her family to dinner on the Sunday night, 11 March, and sought to amuse him with an ouija board. She wrote in her diary on 19 March: 'The shadow of war is stretching its dark length over our own dear country.'[71] But that was the limit of her perception. She does not say that he ever talked to her about it. She could not, as Ellen could, sustain him with that lucid conviction of what was right and what was wrong, or give him what he had drawn from Ellen, 'the serene and joyous strength that conquers without effort'.[72]

It rarely, if ever else, has happened that one man, living under democracy, has had with his single voice to give the word for war. It happened to Wilson, not only because he was the supreme executive and in Secretary Lane's words one 'made by nature to tread the winepress alone',[73] but also because behind the tumult and the shouting—the Emergency Peace Federation on the one side with its Twelve Peace Apostles and on the other the American Rights Committee with a meeting of 12,000 in Madison Square Garden and Hibben declaiming 'I am for peace at any price; and the price of peace is now war'[74]—the country was in bulk still as uncertain as Wilson: and those who were certain were about equally divided, so that Wilson was the weight that would bring down either scale. He was not only the President: he was the casting vote of the nation.

Everywhere and always the good man wants peace at any price that is not extortionate but he will not pay for it in that currency which has for its backing honour and true dignity and a just pride and a love of freedom, for these virtues are the metal that makes the walls of the temple of the human spirit. He is right not to pay in coin of that metal, whatever immunities it can purchase, for unless it is treasured the temple cannot be maintained. But often he is no reckoner and the counting up and the balancing is beyond his powers. So the commonalty of the United States made Wilson their steward and put him in charge of their treasure. His doubt and his reluctances and his caution were the qualifications for the trust. They could trust him not to spend their lives and fortunes unless the temple was in danger of being destroyed. If *he* said that they must fight, then they knew that they must fight. They left with him the burden of decision and he knew that he had to take it up: he was their leader. It may be that there has never been another week in history so pregnant as this in mid March 1917. The decision to fight meant another American revolution bringing her into the world of nations. While on one side of the world Wilson was in labour over this, on the other the Russian Revolution had begun; on that Ides of March the Tsar announced his abdication; and thus within a few days of each other there were born into the twentieth century the two giants whose tremendous quarrel burst open doors hitherto kept locked against mankind and brought out weapons whose brandishment has caused the world to quake.

It may be that on such an issue Wilson preferred to be left alone. Six months before, on 4 September 1916, he had delivered at the birthplace of Abraham Lincoln in Kentucky one of the most eloquent of his public addresses.

There is a very holy and terrible isolation for the conscience of every man who seeks to read the destiny in affairs for others as well as for himself, for a nation as well as for individuals. That privacy no man can intrude upon. That lonely search of the spirit for the right perhaps no man can assist.[75]

Wilson could not now stop neutrality, such as he had practised it, slipping out of his grasp. The drastic Order-in-Council of 21 February 1917* went without protest, and clearance was now being given to Allied merchantmen without any questions being asked about the weight of their armament or the use being made of it. When a French ship arrived in New York after

* See p. 646 above.

having sunk a submarine and Jusserand told Polk that details could not be given for security reasons, the latter at once agreed. Some desultory correspondence continued with the French about interference with mails but the heat had evaporated.[76] The dispute over bunkering agreements which Polk in mid January had expected to crystallize into an ultimatum* was heard of no more. The Black List was not mentioned again until Page, apparently on his own initiative, asked for the removal from it of all American names; and the British Cabinet on 4 April readily agreed.[77]

The most significant change was in the field of finance. Not since the Battle of Waterloo had there been for Britain such 'a damned nice thing—the nearest run thing you ever saw in your life'. In October 1916 the Allies' financial advisers had offered them a hesitating prophecy of solvency until 31 March 1917;* and on 22 February Keynes at the Treasury gave them 'four weeks from today'.[78] In early March there were hints from the Federal Reserve Board that an unsecured Anglo-French loan might now be approved. After an urgent dispatch from Page on 5 March warning that Britain might have to go off gold,[79] the Board issued a statement saying that there had been much misunderstanding about its attitude to foreign loans; it regarded them as 'a very important, natural and proper means of settling the balances created in our favor by our large export trade'.[80] This statement was issued on 8 March after Lansing and McAdoo together had visited the invalid, so that he must have approved the change of attitude. In fact there was now less than a month to run before Wilson was asking Congress for the extension to the governments at war with Germany of 'the most liberal financial credits, in order that our resources may so far as possible be added to theirs'.[81]

But that was in April. In the first half of March Wilson was still scouring his mind for anything positive he could do to brake the slide into hostility. He had hoped, he must have hoped, that his firmness on the submarine war would wring out of Germany some further offer on peace terms. He wrote to House on 12 February: 'They must renew and carry out the pledge of last April if they want to talk to us now—or else propose peace on terms they know we can act upon.'[82] What the Zimmermann affair did to him was to destroy the hope of any fruitful discussion. He said on 28 February to a delegate from the Emergency Peace Federation: 'If you knew what I know at this present minute, you would not ask me to attempt further peaceful dealings with the Germans.'[83]

But if Germany remained or was kept at arm's length, what other rational hope was there? Only the hope that armed neutrality would prove a substitute for war. Even if he had been unimpressed by the unanimous feeling

* See p. 550 above.

in the Senate that it would not, Wilson could not, if he permitted himself to reason it out, have failed to see how impracticable armed neutrality was, at least in the form in which America was preparing for it. Defensive armament was only a partial answer to the submarine and by itself could not possibly prevail. It made sense for Britain in 1916 when the use of the torpedo was expensive and impolitic. It could still make sense to the extent that it could prevent Germany from getting cheap results by shellfire. But it could—and in a campaign in which Germany was bound to go to the limit, inevitably would—be answered by submergence. How could a gun fight a torpedo?

The only written records of the business done by Wilson from his sickbed relate to the arming of ships. Lansing started it with a letter on 8 March in which he pressed Wilson to give without delay the order placing armed guards and guns on merchantmen. But the tone of his letter shows that he recommended it only as an alternative to doing nothing. He wrote:

Feeling the present state of affairs is hopeless for ultimate peace and being convinced of the impossibility of founding a policy on the hypothesis that we can remain at peace, it seems to me that we ought to proceed on the theory that we will in a short time be openly at war with Germany.[84]

This was followed by several letters from Daniels about the duties of the armed guard and the use of the gun and on 12 March the President gave the order that Lansing wanted.[85] It was accompanied by detailed regulations. The guard was not to fire at any submarine that lay more than 4,000 yards from the commercial route of the vessel; it was not to pursue or search out submarines or 'engage in any aggressive warfare against them'. Perhaps there was a chance that the submarine would oblige the armed vessel by surfacing within the 4,000 yards. Or perhaps armed guards would see their duty as limited to drowning with the rest of the crew after the unseen submarine fired its torpedo. Thus peace could be preserved. But the likelihood was that the armed ships of neutrals, like those of the belligerents, would become so far as they could hunters of submarines and aggressive. Wilson put the point cogently when he addressed Congress three weeks later.

But armed neutrality, it now appears, is impracticable. Because submarines are in effect outlaws when used as the German submarines have been used against merchant shipping, it is impossible to defend ships against their attacks as the law of nations has assumed that merchantmen would defend themselves against privateers or cruisers, visible craft giving chase upon the open sea. It is common prudence in such circumstances, grim necessity indeed, to endeavour to destroy them before they have shown their own intention. They must be dealt with upon sight, if dealt with at all.[86]

So what else was there? Wilson's meditations on his sick-bed could only take him into a defile and the further he went into it the further out of sight hopes and remote possibilities receded while stark certainties closed in the view. In truth there was, unless he chose to turn and flee, but a single narrow exit. But as yet Wilson refused to see it. Perhaps he hoped for some almost miraculous intervention. We cannot doubt that he prayed much. Perhaps he prayed that there might be given him the power that he had found in Lincoln, 'the power of mind and heart and conscience to which nations yield and history submits its processes'.[87]

Meanwhile he clung to armed neutrality. But rather, one must suppose, as a shield to ward off the final thrust than as a sword which he believed could cut the knot.

The *Algonquin* on 12 March was the first American ship to be sunk by a submarine. She was bound for London, attacked in the Western Approaches without being called on to stop, and shelled while the crew took to the boats; but there was no torpedo and there were no casualties. It was not the most ruthless use of the submarine, but it was indubitably an overt act. Wilson did not say otherwise when the news arrived on 14 March. But he gave it out that it did not change the situation; the Government was already doing everything it could short of war. In the evening of 15 March he received Gerard on his return from Berlin. The President said, Gerard reported, that he had done everything to preserve peace and even yet he hoped that the Germans would abandon the ruthless submarine war.

On 16 March he was well enough, though Dr. Grayson did not like it, to hold a brief Cabinet to deal with a threatened railway strike. He rejoiced in the news from Russia. This was not the Bolshevik Revolution but the Kerensky Revolution that preceded it, the dawn as it seemed then of a great liberal movement. House wrote urging immediate recognition of the new government.[88] Wilson did not need the stimulus; he saw it as the old order giving way to the new.

On Sunday 18 March Washington heard that three American ships had been destroyed. One was sunk by gunfire after warning and with no casualties; another by gunfire without warning and with one sailor wounded. The sinking of the third, the *Vigilancia*, was as ruthless and as overt as could be. She was bound for Le Havre with a general cargo and was torpedoed without warning in the Western Approaches on 16 March. She sank in seven minutes; fifteen of the crew were drowned while launching the boats and the rest landed in the Scilly Isles two days later suffering greatly from exposure.

Wilson followed his usual Sunday routine, a family lunch and a drive in the afternoon, but on Monday morning he sent for Lansing. Yet it was only to say that he did not see what more could be done; the ships now sailing for Europe were carrying four guns and an armed guard of forty. Lansing urged summoning Congress to consider the new sinkings[89] but Wilson said that all he could ask would be for powers to do what he was already doing. Lansing suggested that he should ask Congress to declare war since war, Lansing said, was inevitable. But Wilson was not convinced. He told Daniels of the conversation that afternoon when he discussed with him what more could be done to protect shipping; he still hoped to avert war, he said.

But if he was not convinced, he may have been weakening. The third visitor that day was Frank Cobb and the talk with him was about the consequences of war for the world and for the American way of life and it shows Wilson for the first time as irresolute.[90] It is not after all irresolution to be resolved against war. Wilson's 'inertia', as House and the others called it,[91] proceeded not from indecision but from, they might more forcefully have charged, a refusal to face facts. He said to Cobb that he would take any way out but that he could not see one. And Cobb said there was none.

Lansing that afternoon wrote to House: 'If you agree with me that we should act now, will you not please put your shoulder to the wheel?'[92] Polk also urged House to come. But House did not respond. He had many callers who wanted him to talk to the President or at least find out what Wilson was doing. But House knew well enough that he held at pleasure his shadow office. To displease Wilson seriously—and that meant to do or say anything that could be interpreted as antagonism—would be the equivalent of resignation. Moreover, it was part of his technique that he never pressed himself on Wilson; he liked to wait till sent for. It would not be fair to him to suppose that his main interest was in keeping his position. He knew, none better, that on this issue he could now do no good and might do harm; and he was satisfied, as he had noted on 12 February, that a rapid drift to war had set in.[93]

Lansing, however, did not give up. Instead he climbed to the peak of his humdrum career. For some months now he had been working to bring America into the war, partly in secret and, as we have seen, not altogether creditably, but of late increasingly in the open. He had been pressing his view on Wilson far harder than a year before he would have dared to do. He had none of the finesse which House employed. Yet, beginning perhaps with the part he played in the *Sussex* settlement,* he seems to have found a way of talking quite bluntly to Wilson without arousing his resentment. Maybe he could do it because Wilson was so sure of his subordination; he spoke or wrote always as the confidential clerk, never openly in Cabinet or as the Secretary of State. But he cannot have been unaware of the perils of

* See p. 482 above.

badgering Wilson. House and Grayson,* the two men who knew him most intimately, clearly appreciated it; and indeed, just around this time, House was talking to Gaunt about the danger of losing influence with Wilson.[94]

Lansing had written forthrightly to Wilson in his letter of 8 March. He had spoken again with as much force in the morning of that day, 19 March. Nevertheless, that evening when he got back at 11 p.m. from a dinner at the Japanese embassy, he sat down and wrote another letter to Wilson. It took him two hours. He opened it with a statement of his conviction that armed neutrality was bound to lead to war and that the question was whether it was better to wait or to enter now. He set out what he saw as the five advantages, each in a brief paragraph, of entering now. The fifth was:

I believe that our future influence in world affairs, in which we can no longer refuse to play our part, will be materially increased by prompt, vigorous and definite action in favor of Democracy and against Absolutism. This would be first shown in the peace negotiations and in the general readjustment of international relations. It is my belief that the longer we delay in declaring against the military absolutism which menaces the rule of liberty and justice in the world, so much the less will be our influence in the days when Germany will need a merciful and unselfish foe.[95]

It was a fine letter and it is possible, although it can only be a guess, that it made an impact. For it would have caught Wilson at a time when he was beginning to see that armed neutrality was bound to fail and it pointed to a realignment of policy in language that would please him.

On the next day, 20 March, Wilson presided at the Tuesday Cabinet meeting. On this occasion Lansing as a memorandum-maker eclipsed the efforts of the regular chroniclers, Lane and Houston. The President, he noted,

passed to his place at the head of the table shaking hands with each member and smiling as genially and composedly as if nothing of importance was to be considered. Composure is a marked characteristic of the President. . . . Excitement would seem very much out of place at the Cabinet table with Woodrow Wilson presiding.[96]

The President began with a mention of the railway strike and then said that he desired advice 'on our relations with Germany and the course which should be pursued'. He reviewed the position, referring to the revolution against autocracy in Russia and the prospects of liberalism in Germany. At home he contrasted the indignation and bitterness in the East with the apparent apathy of the Middle West. He gave no hint of an opinion of his own.

* For what Grayson said, see pp. 475–6 above.

McAdoo led the pack with Houston close on his heels, Lansing spoke fifth. His record of his contribution (which, as he said, he would naturally remember more fully than the others) occupies almost as much space in his memorandum as his record of the opinions of the other nine. At one point he spoke with such vehemence that 'the President asked me to lower my voice so that no one in the corridor could hear'.[97] Since, however, the voice did not impinge on the ear of Houston, who recorded bleakly that 'Lansing said little or nothing as usual',[98] it is possible that the Secretary read into the record some of the things that he accidentally omitted to say. Whichever it was, *dictum* or *dicendum*, it expressed what Lansing had for long been saying in private and this is now familiar to the reader. There was, however, one thing in particular he said—Lansing was not sure how it impressed the President—and this was that America should go to war not just because her ships had been sunk and her nationals killed:

the sounder basis was the duty of this and every other democratic nation to suppress an autocratic government like the German because of its atrocious character and because it was a menace to the national safety of this country and of all other countries with liberal systems of government.[99]

The discussion lasted for over two hours. Each man spoke; some at length and some shortly; some gave one reason and some another; but in their conviction they were undivided; even Daniels who that evening wrote in his diary that he 'had hoped and prayed that this cup would pass'.[100]

The President said: 'Well, gentlemen, I think that there is no doubt as to what your advice is. I thank you.'[101] That ended the meeting. The President asked Lansing and Burleson to stay behind and inquired how long it would take to prepare the necessary legislation for submission to Congress. They advised that the earliest date for which Congress could be called was 2 April. Wilson spent that evening alone. On the following morning he summoned Congress to convene on 2 April:

to receive a communication concerning grave matters of national policy which should be taken immediately under consideration.[102]

The summoning of Congress was widely interpreted as signifying a decision for war. House was confident and wrote Page on 21 March that except for the formal declaration the nation was at war.[103] Since we now know what Wilson said to Congress on 2 April and since we can examine in retrospect his secret activities after 21 March, notably his instructions to Daniels on 24 March to establish confidential liaison with the British Admiralty,[104] we can be certain that by the 21st his mind was made up. But, whether out of secretiveness or in the faint hope of a deliverance or just for the sake of postponing commitment, Wilson told no one in so many words. As the silence was eked out in days, anxiety and some doubt set in. At the Cabinets on 23 and 27 March war legislation was discussed but the great question left unanswered. Lansing tried and failed in several ways to get some line on what the President intended to say to Congress. Exclusion brought House and him close together. The Lansings went to New York on 25 March for a dinner party which the Houses gave for them.[105] This gave the two men the opportunity for a good talk, and it may have been as a result of that that on this day the Colonel decided to break with precedent; he wrote inviting himself to the White House.

There was nothing in the least unusual about his reception on 27 March. He arrived in the afternoon, just after the Cabinet meeting was over, and Wilson and he went together into the study. Wilson was not feeling well and complained of a headache. House was the first man to learn from his lips that the decision was taken. He had fought with himself night after night, he said, in the hope of seeing some other way out. 'What else can I do?', he asked. 'Is there anything else I can do?'[106] But he could not have hoped for an answer.

House had seen so much of what he thought of as shilly-shallying that he was afraid that, though Wilson had been forced to a decision, he might prosecute the war so feebly as to lead to discredit and disaster. He was determined to speak out about this as a faithful servant should. Wilson had gambled on mediation and lost and now there must be no more 'peace without victory'. To say this was one of the reasons for his visit. He told Wilson that he was not well fitted to be President in wartime. He served up this assertion with a sauce that made it palatable; Wilson was too refined, too intellectual, too cultivated. It needed a man of coarse fibre and one less of a philosopher to conduct a brutal, vigorous, and successful war. Nevertheless, he must face up to it if his influence was not to be lessened in the great work which would follow the war. He need not worry; it was not really as difficult as many things that he had successfully done. 'He listened with a kindly and sympathetic attention, and, while he argued with me upon many of the points, he did it dispassionately.'[107]

In the evening the two friends went to the theatre together. The next morning, while Wilson was playing his usual game of golf, House had a long talk with the 'pro-German' McAdoo who spoke of quitting the Cabinet and raising a regiment and said that his three sons had enlisted. Then House discussed with the President the terms of the Message to Congress. Wilson produced a memorandum of the points he was going to cover. House approved: 'most of them', he said in his diary, 'were suggestions I have made from time to time'.[108] The main point House stressed in conversation was that there should be a differentiation between the German people and their government. After this talk the Colonel went back to New York, arranging to return on the morning of the day when Congress was to meet. The day after, when Polk telephoned, House told him: 'It's all right.'

But outside the sanctums of the State Department doubts were undispelled. Senator Hitchcock, after an interview with Wilson on 27 March at which he sought to persuade him to rest content with armed neutrality, reported that the President was still keeping an open mind. On the 29th the *New York Times* headlined 'Uncertainty at Washington'. After its meeting on the 30th the Cabinet was still uninformed. Houston refused to speculate upon the possibility that the President would not act; but added that if by any chance he did not, the only decent course for him (Houston) was resignation.[109]

Friday, 30 March was a perfect spring day. Except for an hour's drive in the park and the Cabinet in the afternoon Wilson was at work on the Message. Most of Saturday and Sunday he spent at his typewriter and on the morning of the day itself, Monday, 2 April, he sent what he had written to be printed. House travelled on the midnight train from New York and arrived just as the Wilsons were leaving to play golf. They came back shortly after 11.0 and Lansing came across with a draft of the war resolution for approval. The day drifted on, Wilson apparently calm, but House thought that he could detect signs of nervousness. No one did anything except kill time. A pair of cousins came to lunch. Wilson had expected to address the new Congress at 2.0 but it got bogged down in procedural preliminaries. So in the afternoon Wilson read the Message to House. 'No address he has yet made pleases me more than this one', House noted.[110] But he also wondered in his diary whether Wilson was aware of the contribution which he, House, had made, for he had given no indication of it. This was not the sort of lapse of which House himself was ever guilty. On 5 April he told Lansing that

one of the best parts of the President's address was his statement in regard to democracy being essential to permanent peace and I know you are gratified beyond measure to have your idea brought to the fore so prominently at this time.[111]

No member of the Cabinet knew what Wilson was going to say and House felt that they ought not to have been humiliated to that extent; McAdoo had tried to pump him that morning. House asked Wilson why he had not shown it to the Cabinet and he replied that every man in it would have had some suggestion to make and it would have been picked to pieces if he had heeded their criticism.

Word came that Congress would be ready about 5.0 and Wilson said he would go at 8.30. So they dined at 6.30, half an hour before the Wilsons' usual time. Besides House there were some of the family and they talked, House said, 'of everything excepting the matter in hand'.[112]

Congress had convened at noon and all the afternoon the slow crowds swarmed about the streets of Washington. Many carried little Stars and Stripes. It rained; and as night came on and the sky blackened, the Capitol, floodlit for the first time, stood out in white. The usual police protection was not thought to be enough for the President and, as if it were a symbol of the civil power giving place to the military, a cavalry squadron surrounded the President's automobile and clattered beside it to the Capitol. The corridors of the building were packed. At the door of Senator Lodge's room blows were exchanged. 'You are a damned coward', a pacifist cried.[113] The senator, sixty-seven years old, walked up to him and hit him, saying: 'You are a damned liar.' The pacifist failed to turn the other cheek. The senator was rescued and the pacifist beaten up. 'I am glad that I hit him', the senator said.

The auditorium of the House was crammed. The Cabinet sat to the left of the Speaker, behind them the ambassadors and in front of the Speaker the justices of the Supreme Court. Every representative was in his place. The steps and the doorways were thronged with distinguished visitors. Shortly before half past eight the senators entered and marched solemnly down the centre aisle to their places behind the justices; the Vice-President took his chair beside the Speaker. A minute or two later the Clerk of the House announced: 'The President of the United States.' There was a tremendous ovation and then an intense stillness. The President walked to the rostrum, rested his arm on the high desk and began to read:

Gentlemen of the Congress: I have called the Congress into extraordinary session . . .[114]

Deliberately, quietly, unemotionally, Spring Rice wrote, sentence succeeded sentence.[115] He recited the familiar facts. The challenge, he said, was to all mankind and each nation must make its own choice of the way by which it should be met. He explained why armed neutrality was ineffectual. Then he said:

There is one choice we cannot make—

Chief Justice White had never let his eyes stray from the President's face. He was a veteran of the Civil War; in August 1914 he had said to Houston that if he were thirty years younger he would go to Canada and volunteer.

—we are incapable of making: we will not choose the path of submission—

The sentence was still unfinished when the Chief Justice, as the *New York Times* reported,

dropped the big soft hat he had been holding, raised his hands high in the air, and brought them together with a heartfelt bang; and House, Senate and galleries followed him with a roar like a storm.[116]

The President spoke next of the measures, military, naval, and financial, that would have to be taken. Then he turned to the object of the war. It was the same, he said, as that which in his earlier addresses to Congress he had had in mind.

Our object now, as then, is to vindicate the principles of peace and justice in the life of the world as against selfish and autocratic power and to set up amongst the really free and self-governed peoples of the world such a concert of purpose and of action as will henceforth ensure the observance of those principles.[117]

He introduced House's two ideas, the same standard of morality for governments as for individuals and the innocence of the German people, as well as Lansing's idea upon which House was to congratulate him. He spoke of the 'criminal intrigues' of the 'Prussian autocracy', the spying, the sabotage, and 'the intercepted note', which had all

played their part in serving to convince us at last that that Government entertains no real friendship for us and means to act against our peace and security at its convenience.

The United States would accept this challenge of hostile purpose.

We are glad, now that we see the facts with no veil of false pretence about them, to fight thus for the ultimate peace of the world and for the liberation of its peoples, the German peoples included: for the rights of nations great and small and the privilege of men everywhere to choose their way of life and of obedience. The world must be made safe for democracy. Its peace must be planted upon the tested foundations of political liberty.

They crowded round the President as he left, friends and opponents alike. Senator Lodge shook his hand warmly, saying: 'Mr. President, you have expressed in the loftiest manner possible the sentiments of the American people.'[118] Roosevelt called the next day at the White House to leave his card and his congratulations: 'a great state paper', he said.[119] Ten years afterwards, Lansing, by then the servant whom Wilson had dismissed, wrote of this as Wilson's greatest triumph.

From the moment that he entered the auditorium up to the time that he passed out into the corridors of the Capitol he was master of the situation. His personality was dominant. His vibrant voice, modulated to the solemnity of the occasion and expressive of the grave import of his words, was firm and distinct. He had a great message to deliver and he delivered it greatly. The President's attractiveness of style, the finish of his diction and his persuasive power over his listeners were never better exemplified. His control of language and of his audience was a marvelous exhibition of his genius as an orator. One who heard that impressive address and saw the dignity and sternness of the speaker as he stood on the rostrum, recognized him as a leader of men than whom there was no greater within the boundaries of the United States. . . . Never had I admired President Wilson more or been more proud to be associated with so great a leader, so great an American.[120]

'The world must be made safe for democracy.' The sentence was already on its way round the globe when back in the White House they talked it all over quietly in the Oval Room—Mrs. Wilson, Margaret and Colonel House —'as families are prone to do after some eventful occasion'.[121] Wilson, House records, hardly seemed to have a true conception of the path he was blazing; Webster, Lincoln, and Gladstone had, Wilson thought, all announced the same principles. But for Wilson, if Tumulty is to be believed, the evening did not die away in quiet conversation. After the family had gone to bed, the President, perhaps still far from sleep, wandered off into the Cabinet room and there Tumulty found him. He said: 'My message today was a message of death for our young men. How strange it seems to applaud that!'[122] After that they talked for a long while and it was then that Wilson wept.

Historians are rightly sceptical about this piece of Tumultian melodrama: it is not in Wilson's character and too obviously in Tumulty's. But it should perhaps be disembellished rather than disembowelled. Tumulty, physically near though spiritually afar, cannot have watched without some understanding of his hero's agony of mind. There is at least no doubt that this resolution cost Wilson more than any other that he ever made. It was perhaps the only time in his life when his mind faltered. Problems before had been hard to solve but never torturing. Always before he had gone out boldly towards a decision; this time he was driven. Always before the mind had moved of its own motion to select the right principle and apply it. Sometimes the process was difficult and took time but always it was done without fumbling and without tears. The decision came out of the laboratory of his mind in a neat packet sealed with red wax; all that the apothecary had done was to select with care the right formula and mix his ingredients accordingly. But this time he had had to take a pestle to things in which he passionately believed and grind them up.

Why did Wilson go to war?
One might begin by putting the question impersonally and asking why

America went to war. She gave it out in the formal documents, namely, the Resolution enacted by Congress and the resulting Proclamation by the President, that war had been thrust upon her. It was Wilson's decision to put it that way and, granted his premises, it is quite correct. In these premises Germany was interfering with America's right of passage on the high seas to which by international law she was entitled. This was as much a trespass as if Germany had invaded her territory or seized her physical assets. On her view of the law America had a good cause of action.

But would an impartial international tribunal have upheld her view of the law? The most far-seeing lawyer could not in 1917 have given a confident opinion one way or the other on that. Germany's only defence lay in the doctrine of reprisals and out of this in its application to the German-American dispute three questions arise, none of which is answerable without varying degrees of doubt. The first is whether the doctrine permits any diminution at all of neutral rights: this has already been discussed.* If it does, then the law appears to be tolerably clear that the extent of the diminution must be proportionate to the gravity of the offence that provoked the reprisal. The second question asks whether, as between the retaliator and the neutral, this means the diminution of the other belligerent's rights as well as of the neutral's. The distinction is important since the unrestricted submarine war offered America the choice between sacrificing trading rights and sacrificing lives while as against the Allies it was simply an attack on non-combatant life. Would it be open to counsel for the United States to argue that the reprisal was invalid against the Allies, and so *a fortiori* against all neutrals, since no provocation however great could justify in reprisal the destruction of life? If that point failed, America would have to rely on the interference with her own rights and the answer to the third question would depend upon the tribunal's view of the extent of that interference. Disregarding as negligible such interference as there was with the American right to travel, what was aimed at was the total destruction of American trade with the Allies. In considering the gravity of that the tribunal would have to note that America had not made a *casus belli* of the Allies' destruction of her trade with the Central Powers. A decision, if it had been given, that the destruction of trade was no worse than a supportable inconvenience would presumably have been upheld by posterity, since America in 1939 accepted the total loss of all trade that the belligerents could not fetch and carry for themselves.

But by that time the world had accepted the concept of total war. Obviously much would depend on whether a tribunal in 1917 stuck fast to tradition or let the new concept edge in. Much might depend too on

* See pp. 161–4 above.

whether it stuck to what was legally relevant or let itself be influenced by what seemed to the men of 1917 the exceptional brutality of the German method. Had the Germans the moral right to enforce with the torpedo their view on a doubtful point of law? But a fair answer to that would have to admit that they had in May 1916* given due warning of what they would do if America continued to tolerate the British blockade.

It is not worth while spending more time on these legal perplexities. They do not explain why America went to war. As a matter of law she considered Germany to be hopelessly in the wrong but she did not go to war simply because of that. She considered with almost as much justification that Britain was hopelessly in the wrong too. Nations do not go to war because they have a good cause of action. The ultimatums and diplomatic exchanges reveal only the tip of a complex of calculations and emotions. Theoretically the American Civil War was fought about the doctrine of state sovereignty, but as Wilson wrote in the notes for a lecture he prepared in 1886:

Wars are seldom fought about abstract theories. . . . The North and South fought because their differences and antagonisms had become intolerable and state sovereignty was made the formal basis of the war.[123]

The reasons why America went to war are to be found partly in the contemporary material, notably the Message to Congress and the speeches therein, and partly in what is discernible in retrospect from subsequent events. The historian cannot create the past out of the future, but the future by illuminating the corners of the past can give it its true shape. In one respect it is now agreed that the retrospective process has been carried too far. In the 1930s, in pursuance of the theory then still fashionable that wars are fought to make the rich richer, it came to be thought that America went to war to save her investment in the Allied cause. The careful analysis that American historians have since made disproves this. Indeed, in preceding chapters enough may have been said to show that America was ready to stop trading, painful though it would have been (but then the dislocation of war is bound to bring either poverty or prosperity to neutrals and America had already had plenty of the latter), rather than allow credit.

Another theory that can be disregarded, though for different reasons because it can claim some support from contemporary oratory, is that America went to war to vindicate the law and the rights of neutrals. It is true that she had put herself forward as the custodian of neutral rights and that Wilson had spoken of 'the whole fine fabric of international law' and America's 'proud position as a spokesman, even amidst the turmoil of war, for the law and the right'.† This would be a noble but dry reason for going

* See p. 482 above.   † See p. 440 above.

to war and Wilson had never allowed it to appear cut off from the wells of sacred rights and the redolences of honour and dignity. He himself had no devotion to the law as such. His attitude was the common one that when it is on one's side it ought to be upheld and when it is not it is legalism. When America went to war her disregard of neutral nations was as great as that of the Allies and Wilson made no effort to ameliorate their lot.

Something quite considerable must be allowed for the fact that what was at stake was not just legal principle but America's loud and insistent proclamation of it. National dignity was embroiled. For the fiery in the East this might be enough but for the lukewarm in the West not; and the wisest men in the East could see that outraged dignity, while it makes a good aperitif for war, will not sustain a long struggle. For that there must be some greater unitive force. It could be found in the conviction that an order of things erected on a German victory would not be safe for America or for the world.

For the world or for America. Which first? Wilson would probably have replied to that that it made no difference; and that if in his thoughts and in his Message to Congress he named the world first, it was because it was the greater and the nobler object and because it would be America's pride to think of the new order as a gift from her to others rather than as a blessing for herself. 'We are', he said, 'but one of the champions of the rights of mankind.'[124] But there were others speaking in Congress who thought of America first and America only. No one paid particular attention to what was said by the senator from Ohio because it was not within the compass of the loosest imagination to suppose that he would be the next President of the United States. What Senator Harding said was that he was 'not voting for war in the name of democracy', but only for the 'maintenance of just American rights'.[125] But Wilson after all was the spokesman for the nation and his words were loudly applauded and they touched a chord. The bulk of Americans, if they thought about it at all at this stage, may well have thought it only a matter of emphasis. The idealist emphasis was on the creation of a new order for the benefit of mankind (and thus for America's benefit because she was a part of mankind), for which the defeat of Germany was a prerequisite because of her disregard for law and her bad behaviour. The realist emphasis was on the defeat of Germany because she was an aggressor who, unless curbed, menaced the integrity of the United States: her disregard for law and her bad behaviour were relevant only as showing her to be an aggressor and the creation of a new order relevant only as protection for America against subsequent aggression by Germany or others.

Within this range a man like Lansing, for example, who was not starry-eyed but who thought of the war as a war for democracy, was nearer to the idealist than to the realist position. It would not be possible to say from an analysis of contemporary material which was uppermost in the American mind. This was revealed only when the time of testing came and then the idealists lost. *Victrix causa deis placuit sed victa Catoni.** So the historians rightly see America's entry into the war as her first step towards the realization that she could not for her own security continue to ignore what went on beyond the seas. Essentially there is no difference between this and the British entry two-and-a-half years earlier. Neither nation had an immediate objective. A shocking outrage—in the one case the invasion of Belgium and in the other the sinking of the *Lusitania*, never redeemed but on the contrary exacerbated—led both nations to the conclusion that the devil must be exorcized out of Germany.

So Wilson's was not the *victrix causa*. But the superb effrontery of *sed victa Catoni* was not enough for him. His greater pride did not allow him to believe that he had ever been defeated.

This explanation of the great event of 1917 smoothes the course of history. Self-interest as a motive is easier to handle than self-sacrifice which can lead to awkward historical developments like Christianity. Enlightened self-interest as the source of all progress was still the catchword of the time: its gentle horse-power pulled events quietly along. The explanation that this is what was really at work in America beneath the oratory is strongly confirmed by the great event of 1941 when, the previous exorcism having failed, America had to intervene again, this time without any great flourish of ideals, to help put down Hitler.

A President of the United States who perceived in 1917 that the concerns of Europe were no longer of only remote interest to his country and that Prussian autocracy was an intercontinental menace, one who had the boldness and skill to bring his people out into the world to confront their destiny, would have earned his place in history. It must be tempting to a biographer of Wilson to settle for this. It was in fact his achievement but far short of his intention. To make it the limit of his intention belies his nature and to give him credit for what was not his true intent belies his greatness. Also, while it can be married with the substance (ignoring the language as idealistic garnishment) of the Message of 2 April and subsequent utterances, it would run contrary to more cogent evidence of what was in his mind. What he said both in public and in private before 31 January 1917 makes it certain that he regarded Germany as no worse menace to America than Britain and the war as of no concern to America except in so far as it brought her the opportunity to remake the world according to her likeness. What Germany did on 31 January was what in April 1916 she had warned Wilson she would do if he allowed the British blockade to continue. He preferred to treat a warning

* 'The victorious cause the gods hath pleased, the vanquished hath pleased Cato.' Lucan 1. 128.

of what she would do as a pledge of what she would not do. This would make
it possible, but not very convincing, to argue that the supposed breach of
pledge opened his eyes to her wickedness, were it not that he told the
Cabinet on 2 February that his attitude was unchanged. He did not care, he
said then, which side won and the only menace he talked about was the
yellow peril. It is impossible to suppose that thereafter his attitude was
decisively changed by the crude impact of the Zimmermann affair. Nothing
he said about it suggests a recognition by him of a German peril; and it
would have been so much in tune with Lansing's ideas that the Secretary
would have been bound to pick up the hint of it, if there had been any,
in his conversations in March.

The new order was Wilson's goal and he was not thinking of American
security; he was not clothing in idealistic language a realistic appreciation
of the situation. But the real problem is not to decide which of the two he
was thinking about, but what made him conclude that the defeat of Germany
was a prerequisite to either when only two months before he had been
indifferent about whether she won or lost. Why was she now deemed to be
challenging not America especially but all mankind? What had happened
to thrust her out of the lighted tavern in which she was but one of the
brawlers, albeit the roughest, into the pit of darkness where dwell the enemies
of mankind? What was in Wilson's mind when he decided to go to war?

He said that it was because there was no alternative. This is the only
direct evidence we have of how he came to his decision; all the rest is
inference. But he said it twice, once to Cobb and once to House. So it must
be the starting-point. For though it leads only to another question, to ask
the right question is indispensable to getting the right answer. Why in
Wilson's mind was there no alternative? 'He does not mean to go to war,
but I think he is in the grip of events.'[126] So Lodge wrote to Roosevelt on
2 March 1917. It is true, if it be remembered that the events were of his own
making and that he could unmake them. What had him in their grip were
his own pronouncements. Bryanist non-involvement, if he could get back
to it, was still a perfectly logical and feasible policy. He must on his sick-
bed have gone over in his mind the course he had charted for himself—the
first deceptively simple rejection of the German submarine decree of
4 February 1915, the hesitation over the *Falaba* and the *Gulflight*, the
contemplated withdrawal under the influence of Bryan, the surge forward
in the wake of the *Lusitania*, the hardening of position over the *Arabic*, the
apparent finality of the *Sussex* and, perhaps the most formidable obstacle
of all to retreat, the letter to Senator Stone.*

If the clear rights of American citizens should ever unhappily be abridged or

* See p. 440 above.

denied by any such action we should, it seems to me, have in honor no choice as to what our own course should be.

Could he go back on these words? On the field of battle brave words are often the heralds of retreat. Commanders say that a position must be held to the last, every man dying at his post, and a few days later they surrender. This is not considered to be cowardice. And if it be so, had not Wilson said to his Cabinet on 2 February* that he would submit to any imputation?

He was not caught in any mesh that was not woven of his own words. Politically a retreat into an anti-war position was open. If in March 1917 there had been a referendum on whether the nation should go to war, no one can say what the result would have been. But the confident judgement of Professor Link, whose study of the sources has been wide and deep, is 'that articulate Americans were profoundly divided up to the very end of American neutrality'.[127] The division on the amendment in the House of Representatives on 2 March† showed a minority of 30 per cent striving to avoid involvement and ready at least to look along the path of submission. The fact that this sentiment was geographically concentrated made it much stronger than if it had been dispersed; the 125 in the minority included just under half of the Representatives from the Middle West and just under two-thirds of those from the Far West. And the 125 was an anti-presidential vote as well as anti-war. If the President had put himself at the head of the anti-war party the division might well have been the other way round. Certainly there could be no decision for war which did not contain the moving and unifying force of the Presidency.

Was Wilson qualified to lead a retreat? In such circumstances the expectation of the ordinary politician is not high. He does not when he evacuates an untenable position expect to march out with all the honours of war; he is content if he is able to slither out in a smokescreen of double-talk. Wilson's talent was not for sidestepping, it is true. But he could inject words with a new meaning and forget that the old had ever been in them; and when satisfied in this way of his own integrity and constancy, it came much more easily to him than to most politicians to stand alone. He would not have been so disturbed as they—indeed he might have been stimulated—by the thought that retreat might lose him the support of his Cabinet and of his closest friend. He had always a hankering after the lonely leadership—'leadership of rebuke' he called it in his writings[128]—Bernard, Calvin, Savonarola. 'By methods which would infallibly alienate *individuals* they master multitudes.'

So there *was* an answer to the question. If there had not been, Wilson would not have been so long debating it. But he rejected it. Why? It could

---

* See p. 638 above.   † See p. 656 above.

have been because he would not eat his words and that the man who began by being too proud to fight ended by being too proud to keep the peace. Or it could have been that while he could swallow his own words, he could not tell America to swallow hers; and he had spoken for America and put her dignity in the scales. Though each of these, especially the second, may well have played a part, neither is totally convincing. Wilson was not boasting when he said in this matter, as he had said over Mexico, that he would accept the imputation of cowardice. There is not in the record of his life any time of testing, whether in his public life or in private affairs such as the threat of scandal over the Peck letters, when he is to be found lacking in moral courage. He had unlimited pride, the sort of pride that will not permit a man to be weak and on which therefore courage thrives. It would be a greater humiliation for him to fall in self-esteem than in the esteem of others. There was nothing, he once said, in any decision except choosing between right and wrong;[129] he could not in his own eyes lose dignity by choosing right but would lose it for ever if he chose what he knew to be wrong. As for America, he would not distinguish between her and him. If he kept his dignity, America would keep hers.

There was one reason for rejection which, whether it stood alone or with others, was compelling. This was that, if he and America with him chose the path of submission, his ideal, his hopes, and his dreams of bringing in the new world to regenerate the old would be destroyed. Wilson's critics, contemporary and posthumous, would put that more shortly: they would say that his prospect of cutting a world figure would have vanished. Let us leave that point for consideration later. Whichever way it is put, the reason is compelling. If Wilson turned back now, the ambition which, whether noble and universal or selfish and personal, he had now made a part of himself would perish miserably and he would be left a frustrated man.

Let us assume first that he was under the control of an ideal. It was a noble one. It incorporated and went beyond House's simple notion of honest standards for nations as for individuals. It sought to introduce into international affairs the Christian ideal of peace upon earth for men of goodwill to be brought about through the Christian ethic of service to others. Those who describe as idealistic the simple idea of honest standards for nations cannot mean much more than that it would be hard work to get it accepted. It is not revolutionary to expect a society of nations to regard as appropriate standards which each of its component nations treats within itself as essential to civilized conduct. There is, however, a vast difference between the precept 'Do unto others as you would have done unto you' and the high

Christian virtue of charity. The former is followed by the majority if only on the basis of *quid pro quo* but any appreciable disbursement of the *quid* without the *quo* has never been the practice of more than a few. Only a small minority of individuals in any nation thought of service to others as something that they ought to make of their daily lives. What Wilson was proposing was not just that nations should behave as well as the average of the individuals of which they were composed, but that they should behave much better.

It was almost, but not quite, as if he were trying to bring Christianity into public life. The attempt fell short of that because there were flaws in Wilson's Christianity. The chief of them became significant only in 1919. The one that was already apparent was that his charity, that is, his sense of the duty of service to others which is part of charity and which with Wilson was very real, was marred by condescension. It was Lady Bountiful with her basket of spiritual goodies who was going to cross the Atlantic. Probably the image of Lady Bountiful with its appeal to vanity and self-importance was more saleable than that of St. Francis of Assisi. If Wilson's tone sounds pharisaical, it is to be remembered that the Pharisees came before the Christians and that only a society in which widows are ready to give their mites can afford to despise them. Wilson perceived the need for charity among nations and preached and practised it. The perception, the preaching, and the practice are all necessary to the spreading of a creed and this was the triple task he undertook. It is a creed whose acceptance is now rapidly becoming necessary to the survival of mankind. Wilson failed, of course, as all the world knows. He is and will always be historically great because he was the first to try.

To translate his ideal into action Wilson needed a place, and a dominating one, at the Peace Conference. This was the strategic objective of his foreign policy. There were three tactical approaches to it. The first was by joining the better side and buying a place by a contribution to the war. This was what House wanted; he wanted America to state her terms of entry in the old-fashioned way, as Italy had done and the Balkan countries, but her stipulation would be not for acquisitions for herself but for moderation in the acquisitions of others so that there might be a just and durable peace. Entering the war was the obvious, the traditional, and the only sure way of getting into the Peace Conference. House and also Lansing, beginning with his letter of 24 August 1915,* repeatedly urged it on Wilson. The second approach was made from neutrality and was by angling for an invitation to mediate; this also was traditional. The third approach was a novel compound of the first two. Like the second it was made from neutrality. Like

* See p. 332 above.

the first it was not empty-handed. Gifts would be brought to the peace table in the form of a contribution not to the war effort but to the future peace of the world. As Wilson told the belligerents on 22 January 1917* they could make war without America, they could even make peace without her, but they could not make permanent peace without her.

At the start Wilson adopted the second approach and deviated from it, without fully realizing what he was doing, into the first. The third could not be prepared until he had assembled in his mind the gifts which America could bring: the Freedom of the Seas, the League of Nations, the extension to the world of the Monroe Doctrine, and the guarantees that would ensure these things as well as the rights of small nations and of all peoples to live in democratic freedom. When he had finally grasped, as he had by May 1916, the potentialities of the third approach, its appeal to him was so tremendous that he was moved to make a complete and public commitment.

This was the policy that failed. It had never, as we now know, had any prospect of success. Germany was actively hostile to it and the Entente at the very best indifferent. Wilson was a decade or so in advance of his time in the belief that the peace of the world was too serious a matter to be left to the warmakers. The idea was apprehended by Grey—it was an amplification of his original—and struck sparks from Lloyd George; but the one had not the ardour nor the other the constancy to join in an apostolate.

The destruction of the third approach left Wilson ostensibly with a choice between the other two. But it was not a real choice. The second approach led only to the chair of a conciliator, not of an arbiter. If it was still conceivable that exhaustion might lead the belligerents to accept Wilson as a conciliator, it would give him a place without influence, for he would have nothing of value to offer. What weight could anyone attach to guarantees given by a nation which quaked at the thunder of the guns?

One is reminded of one of the incidents that preceded the cataclysm of August 1914. It occurred in July 1911 and is known as the Agadir Crisis. As well as being the precursor of war it began the metamorphosis of Lloyd George from a Little Englander into a great war minister. Germany had introduced an argument with France over their interests in Morocco by dispatching a gunboat to Agadir and she ignored a communication from Britain on the subject. When after seventeen days Britain was still without an answer, Lloyd George referred to the affair in a speech at the Mansion House in which he used a memorable phrase.

If a situation were to be forced upon us in which peace could only be preserved . . . by allowing Britain to be treated, where her interests were vitally affected, as if she were of no account in the Cabinet of Nations, then I say emphatically

---

* See p. 604 above.

that peace at that price would be a humiliation intolerable to a great country like ours to endure.[130]

It would be idle for Wilson to go to the Peace Conference without a seat in the Cabinet of Nations. The price of the seat was now war. Wilson himself had no doubt of that. As he put it to the Emergency Peace Federation on 28 February, 'If America stayed neutral, the best she could hope for was to "call through a crack in the door".'[131] America must either abandon what Wilson truly believed to be her historic mission on whose accomplishment he had set his heart or else go to war. For Wilson the former could not be.

It took him much searching of mind and conscience to reach this conclusion. But the seven weeks from 1 February to 20 March have not to be accounted for entirely by the struggle to subjugate his hatred of war and conviction of its futility. He had to face up to the fact that while by going to war he made certain of his strategic objective, his abandonment of the selected approach put him into grave tactical difficulties. If his war aims had been materialistic, he would of course have been much better off at the Peace Conference as a belligerent than as a neutral. But for what he wanted to do belligerence was a handicap which he would have to overcome. An America with hands unstained and passions not aroused could have been accepted by both sides as disinterested and impartial. Now he would have to convince beaten foes that the conqueror had no axe to grind. There was a danger not merely that America might appear to lack dispassion but that it might in fact be lacking. This was much on Wilson's mind. Frank Cobb's story of his conversation with Wilson gives it as taking place in the small hours of 2 April, the very day on which the President went to Congress to ask for a declaration of war, and portrays a sleepless Wilson pouring his heart out. Since in fact* Cobb went to the White House less melodramatically at 3.30 p.m. on 19 March, the words he puts into Wilson's mouth may also be touched up. But doubtless he is reliable (there is other evidence to support it) in his account of the chief topic they discussed. This was the havoc of a victorious peace in which America would lose her head with the others and stop weighing right and wrong. The President realized that he could not, whatever he did, escape some sort of surrender. To avoid yielding to Germany he must yield up to the Allies the peace with victory against which he had been fighting. He spoke also of the intolerance, the illiberalism, the brutality, and the ruthlessness that war brought with it. If Cobb has rightly caught his tone, he spoke of these things not as perils to be guarded against but as the forces of evil to which all would inevitably succumb; and he spoke as if seeing through a glass darkly what might be his own fate.

* This is Professor Link's conclusion: L.5.399.

There was another problem. America had unquestionably been the leading neutral; the third approach, if it had succeeded, would have brought Wilson to the presidency of the post-war conference and so without more ado to the dominating position in peacemaking to which he aspired. But where would he stand among the belligerents? There is scriptural warranty for the payment to late-comers to the vineyard of the full wage but there is nothing in the parable about their election as shop stewards. Wilson would have to make a bid for moral leadership of the forces arrayed against Germany with some of his previous pronouncements working formidably against him.

For having decided upon his tactical approach Wilson had pursued it in the single-minded way in which he tackled all his enterprises. He saw clearly the road ahead but he did not look at the terrain he was crossing and took no precautions against the danger of a diversion. Although everyone but himself had expected the blockage, he was astonished by it. There is no reason to think that it was hyperbole when he told House on 1 February that it was as if the world had suddenly reversed itself and was going from west to east. He always found it next to impossible to suppose that people, when told by him what was the right thing to do, might fail to do it. Consequently in the execution of his policy he had not hedged. House, Lansing, and Page had all warned him against saying things that would irritate the Allies and he had ignored their advice. In itself this did not matter too much since American aid would salve the smart. But what he had said about similarity of objects and peace without victory had now come home to roost on a commanding perch. The President could not go to war in Europe as in Mexico by dispatching a professional army on a punitive expedition. He had to summon America to the battlefield and the crowing of the new cock must be made to silence the old. He could not enthuse the nation with the prospect of a draw or inspire it with the thought that, morally speaking, there was nothing to choose between her allies, or associates as he preferred to call them, and the enemy. In the end he could master the difficulty only by a transformation of thought which his words did little to clarify.

It was not difficult to handle convincingly the fact that America was late in joining the quarrel. A quarrel between nations is not so very different from a quarrel between individuals. Though the latter are subject to law and the former not, the legal process has never won its way into the hearts of men as a solvent of disputes. Recourse to law is the last resort in individual affairs as recourse to war is in international. A good and wealthy man may watch with unease his neighbours being bullied by the threat of a lawsuit they have not the means to fight. So long as his own rights are respected he cannot go to law. But if they be infringed, even in small measure, he has to ask himself who, if he submits, will have the courage to resist. In standing up for himself he can sincerely say that he is fighting for justice for all. This was the main theme of the message of 2 April.

The message is not, except at the end when the great ideal blazed out, comparable with the trilogy of peacetime addresses. In preparing it Wilson had to rely on the ideas of others and was handicapped by his own. He put into it—finely expressed, of course—what he had hastily absorbed from House and Lansing. In his main theme, that he was fighting Germany as an enemy of mankind, he could not escape some parochialism; it was natural that he should stress the provocation of America but this was hardly the chief evidence of German hostility to mankind; yet to start before the tail end of her misdeeds might draw too much attention to America's sloth in recognizing the peril. The misdeeds notwithstanding, he succeeded in leaving himself elbow-room for idealism at the Peace Conference by using House's distinction between the German people and their military masters; a hard war for the wicked and a soft peace for the good. He made one attempt to marry the theme of the war message with that of the trilogy. The objects of the war, he said, were those which he had set out in his addresses to Congress, especially that of 22 January 1917. The justification for this in his mind was doubtless that his ideal was unaltered. He aimed now to achieve as a belligerent the sort of peace he had hoped as a neutral to negotiate. This was a façade that a few questions could have knocked down. The usual object of war is victory: was he excluding that? If not, unless he had changed his mind, the sort of peace he was fighting for was one which would not be permanent but would rest 'only as upon quicksand'.*

In the early euphoria after the declaration of war few were disposed to cross-examine or even to scrutinize. But it was not long before Wilson found it necessary to repel inquirers by a display of incomprehension and had to take to preaching with the enthusiasm of a convert doctrine which he had received stonily from the lips of Page. 'It is incomprehensible to me', he wrote on 22 May 1917, 'how any frank or honest person could doubt or question my position with regard to the war and its objects.'[132] The whole conception, he said, had been set forth with the utmost explicitness in his addresses to Congress of 22 January and 2 April. He had exactly the same things in mind on both occasions. When in October 1916 Wilson had asked his audience in Cincinnati† whether any of them had ever heard what started the present war, none had stepped forward with the answer. When Wilson himself discovered the answer, he published it first to the

---

* See p. 604 above.   † See p. 578 above.

Confederate Veterans at Washington on 5 June 1917 and then to the Federation of Labour at Buffalo on 12 November. The war was started by Germany or rather by her military masters: he was willing to let that statement await the verdict of history. Moreover, it was started in pursuance of her plan of world domination—'exact and precise and scientific'—'to throw a broad belt of German military power and control across the very centre of Europe and beyond the Mediterranean into the heart of Asia'.[133] As things stood the plan had largely succeeded, so that it was easy to understand, he said on 14 June,

. . . the eagerness for peace that has been manifested from Berlin ever since the snare was set and sprung. Peace, peace, peace has been the talk of her Foreign Office for now a year and more.[134]

When, as has been recorded,* in August 1917 the Pope suggested a settlement in terms hardly distinguishable from those proclaimed in the Peace without Victory Address, Wilson was able to state the object of the war in language and in sentiment matching the oratory of Asquith.

The object of this war is to deliver the free peoples of the world from the menace and the actual power of a vast military establishment controlled by an irresponsible government which, having secretly planned to dominate the world, proceeded to carry the plan out without regard either to the sacred obligations of treaty or the long established practices and long-cherished principles of international action and honour; which chose its own time for the war; delivered its blow fiercely and suddenly; stopped at no barrier either of law or of mercy; swept a whole continent within the tide of blood—not the blood of soldiers only, but the blood of innocent women and children also and of the helpless poor; and now stands balked but not defeated, the enemy of four-fifths of the world.[135]

The Allies were thrilled. Wilson replied to a congratulatory correspondent:

There seemed to me to be no other answer and, therefore, this one was comparatively easy to write.[136]

Any of Page's letters to Wilson could now have been disinterred and safely published as a presidential address. It is conceivable that some of them might actually have been pillaged. Page himself was left happily mystified. He wrote on his copy of the Address of 22 January:

Compare this Senate speech with his speech in April calling for war: Just when and how did the President come to see the true nature of the German? What made him change from Peace-Maker to War-Maker?[137]

Roosevelt, who soon rebounded from his enthusiasm for 'the great state paper' of 2 April, wrote less kindly:

But what is perfectly impossible, what represents really nauseous hypocrisy, is

* See p. 459 above.

to say that we have gone to war to make the world safe for democracy in April, when sixty days previously we had been announcing that we wished a peace without victory and had no concern with the 'causes or objects' of the war.[138]

The inconsistency is sharp enough to furnish a formidable weapon for those who regard Wilson as at worst an ambitious opportunist and at best a victim of his own mental dishonesty. Wilson, they argue, was determined to become a dominating world figure and was prepared to play whatever part kept him in the centre of the stage. The role of the great arbiter between the warring nations had at first seemed the most promising. That necessitated the United States keeping out of the war (which was politically the most convenient course) and resulted in a series of impartial pronouncements by Wilson condemning both sides as equally sinful and inviting them to come to him for absolution. When this invitation was firmly declined it looked as if Wilson might have to leave the stage for the time being and that he might not even be allotted a speaking part at the Peace Conference. So that he was not at all displeased when Germany's change of policy gave him a chance to emerge suddenly in a new character—that of the leader of a world crusade against the enemy of all mankind. His sentiments, obsequious to his ambition, changed overnight from tender to tough. The strong snub administered to the Pope, who was so impertinent as to try to steal the show in the role that Wilson had discarded, emphasized the change.

It cannot be denied that this is legitimate inference from Wilson's public acts. If it were all the evidence available, the conclusion that he was merely an opportunist, widely held by contemporaries who saw only the public image, could be neither proved nor refuted. This is why what he said and did in private has to be studied in such detail. It is significant not so much for its positive as for its negative effect. There are many men whose ambition is only for self-glorification but who do not parade it in public, but not many who conceal all traces of it from those in close contact. In Wilson's case there is no private witness of insincerity. His daily life disproves decisively any suggestion that he was in love with the vulgarities of glory—place and precedence and their trappings, obeisances and pomp. This on the one hand. On the other, destiny did not call him to unchronicled deeds and, if it had, it is unlikely that he would have answered the call. Refinements of glory, the honour paid by the reverence or respect of right-thinking men and the incense of gratitude from the humble at heart, he would not have been indifferent to, though there is nothing to show that he thirsted after them. Anyway, self-gratification and slight impurities of motive are not what Roosevelt, Taft, and Lodge had in mind when they called him a dishonest opportunist. They meant that he deceived the public for his personal advantage. Surely the picture of the man as a whole does not sustain that interpretation of him nor make him out the man who put himself first and the task second.

Only a petty historian would poke around the words and deeds of statesmen with the sole object of picking up inconsistencies. For no man gets through life without them and the deeds of no man always match his words; and men who have to talk and act and almost think in public deserve considerate treatment. But the condition of mitigation must be that a man is ready to admit, at least to himself, that he was mistaken or has changed his mind. This was what Wilson could not or would not do. He has asked no mercy from posterity and so has been judged harshly, for of all characters the least likely to get sympathy is the righteous self-deceiver. The ability to obliterate from his mind, as he did in 1917, the thought that he had ever doubted the wickedness of Germany was part of a phenomenal power of self-deception, which he was driven to exercise in his search for a moral purpose.

All Wilson's acts had to be justified by a moral purpose. The supreme act of ordering blood to be shed needed more than justification; it had to be sanctified. So he had to convince himself that he was the leader of a crusade. It was, it must be assumed, a crusade that began in 1917. Although he referred to Germany's master plan, there is nothing in his war speeches to suggest that America was at last made free to join an existing crusade. He spoke as if Germany had shown her true colours only when she challenged American rights. Indeed, he never lost his distrust of Allied motives. So it was only when Germany challenged America, whose motives he knew to be pure and disinterested, that she revealed herself to him as truly wicked. The Allies did not, he believed, genuinely care about democracy and the right to self-government. He did: and he could proclaim his faith as they had not truly and sincerely done. In his mind it was then, and not before, that the war to rid the world of tyranny and injustice really began. What America touched she made holy.

The spirit must be nourished as must the flesh. The nutriment of the spirit is purpose: without purpose the spirit is killed by inanition: the essence of purpose is faith. So a man must believe in himself or die. Wilson could not believe in himself as a man who had made no answer to a noble call. He could not admit to his mind a picture of himself as one who hung back when good was arrayed against evil and, judging such questions by standards of self-interest, kept away from the battle. He could not join a crusade belatedly and take the place of a lieutenant.

Just as the body manufactures substances for its own needs, secretes them in the glands, and calls them up in the urgency of sudden action, so the mind in the urgency of self-justification will manufacture its own beliefs. As a man fights against the death of the flesh, so he fights against the death of the spirit. He will struggle as instinctively, as uncontrollably, and sometimes as irrationally against spiritual starvation as he will against physical. He will in the end believe what he has to believe in order to keep alive the spirit within him. If Wilson persuaded himself that there was no good in the war till he came into it, he was doing what many men have done before and since and what the needs of his own nature imperatively demanded.

But these mental processes do not take place without strain. This much more was added to the distress of his decision. Speaking of Lincoln's Gettysburg Address, Wilson once said he had noticed that great orations, when spoken under deep emotion, were simple in language.[139] His own style was often festooned in a manner that doubtless pleased an age accustomed to adornment and ashamed of bareness. But when he wrote his Message of 2 April to Congress, he was coming to the end of the time of agony in which his certitudes had been for a while dissolved. He had found for the first and perhaps the only time that acts could not always be determined by choice between good and evil or even between greater and lesser good. He had been given a sudden revelation of the tragedy at the fount of all human endeavour—which is that it is bad to fight but that only by fighting can the good be reached—and it caught at him for a moment as for all time it captured Lincoln, drained his words, and fined them to a great simplicity.

The hour was bigger even than he knew. It was not just the hour of committal of a great nation to a great task. It was the hour when America came of age. For a century and a half the new continent had nursed the thoughts of those who came from every country of the old world and brought with them, whether they knew and cared for it or not, bread ground in the mills of many hundred years. America had eaten of that bread. And now this child of Europe, heir to all the vast estates of Christendom, had stepped into his title and assumed his obligations. The burden was not to be put down after a year or a decade. The human mind was heaving itself, as it had done four hundred years before, into a new epoch. Men like children waking in a fright were running back to the notions that had mothered them or away to kiss new loyalties. They were turning to face each other in new arrays. The turmoil of the twentieth century had begun.

In language whose magnificence was for a generation unequalled and then was not surpassed, Wilson unfurled a creed for his time and for thereafter; and each sentence was a pennant and every word a blazoning and all of it a banner flown in a rushing mighty pentecostal wind.

But the right is more precious than peace, and we shall fight for the things which we have always carried nearest our hearts—for democracy, for the right of those who submit to authority to have a voice in their own governments, for the rights and liberties of small nations, for a universal dominion of right by such a concert of free peoples as shall bring peace and safety to all nations and make the world itself at last free. To such a task we can dedicate our lives and our fortunes, everything that we are and everything that we have, with the pride of those who know that the day has come when America is privileged to spend her blood and her might for the principles that gave her birth and happiness and the peace which she has treasured. God helping her, she can do no other.[140]

WOODROW WILSON

APRIL 1917–FEBRUARY 1924

CHRONOLOGICAL TABLE

1917	6 April	The resolution declaring a state of war between Germany and the United States is carried by a vote of 82 to 6 in the Senate and 373 to 50 in the House of Representatives
1918	8 January	Wilson's Address to Congress containing in the Fourteen Points the terms of 'a programme of the world's peace'
	6 October	Wilson receives the German Note accepting the Fourteen Points and requesting him to arrange an armistice
	11 November	The armistice signed
	4 December	He sails in the cruiser *George Washington* for Europe, the first President to leave the United States during his term of office
	14 December	He enters Paris and thereafter visits in triumph London and Rome
1919	18 January	First plenary session of the Peace Conference at Paris
	3 February	First meeting of the Commission on the League of Nations with Wilson in the chair
	14 February	He presents the Covenant to a plenary session of the Conference
	15 February	He leaves Paris on a visit to the United States
	26 February	Dinner party at the White House for Congressional leaders at which Wilson fails to secure informal approval of the Covenant
	14 March	He is back in Paris
	28 June	Signing of the Treaty of Versailles. The last meeting with Colonel House
	10 July	Wilson presents the Treaty and the Covenant within it to the Senate for its approval
	3 September	Refusing to compromise with the Senate, he sets out on a countrywide tour to win popular support for the Treaty and the Covenant
	26 September	He returns to Washington, cancelling the rest of the tour because of what was announced as a 'complete nervous collapse' but was in fact a stroke of the paralysis that

		struck again and irreparably at the White House five days later
	18 November	For the first time he leaves his bed for a brief period in a wheel-chair. He instructs the Democratic senators to vote against the Treaty with Senator Lodge's reservations
	19 November	The resolution before the Senate approving the Treaty with the reservations is defeated by 55 votes to 39; but for Wilson's instructions it would have been carried by 81 votes to 13. A resolution approving the Treaty without reservations is defeated by 53 votes to 38
1920	February	Wilson's condition improves; though he remains crippled, he is able to work at his desk. On 13 February he dismisses Lansing
	19 March	A resolution in the Senate approving the Treaty with revised reservations is carried—with the aid of 21 'disloyal' Democrats—by 49 votes to 35. Lacking the approval of the necessary two-thirds, the Treaty is finally rejected and returned to the President
	2 November	The Presidential Election which Wilson designated as a 'solemn referendum'. The Republicans win 404 votes in the electoral college against 127 and obtain 60·35 per cent of the popular vote
	December	Wilson is awarded the Nobel Peace Prize
1921	4 March	His term of office ends and he retires to a life of seclusion and ill-health in Washington
1922	10 April	Tumulty overreaches himself and is repudiated
1924	3 February	Wilson dies, aged 67

SOURCES

*The name or the abbreviation of it in capital letters at the beginning of
each item is the name used in the references*

I acknowledge with gratitude the use I have made of quotations from the sources
given below. In many cases I have benefited also from the studies contained in
the books from which the quotations are taken. It is difficult to pick out those from
which I have profited most except in the one case of Professor Link. It is not only
that his life of Wilson is an indispensable source which has saved everyone who now
writes on the subject an infinity of labour. Nor is it only because he is the greatest
of Wilsonian scholars. It is chiefly because of his unstinting generosity in helping
anyone who is really interested in Wilson and his period.

ANNIN. R. E. Annin, *Woodrow Wilson: A Character Study*, Dodds Mead, New York,
1925.

ASQUITH. The Earl of Oxford and Asquith, *Memories and Reflections*, vol. 2, Cassell,
London, 1928.

BAKER. R. S. Baker, *Woodrow Wilson Life and Letters*, 8 vols., Heinemann, London, 1928.

BAKER CHRONICLE. R. S. Baker, *American Chronicle*, Charles Scribner, New York, 1945.

BELL. H. C. F. Bell, *Woodrow Wilson and The People*, Doubleday, New York, 1945.

BERN. Count Bernstorff, *My Three Years in America*, Charles Scribner, New York, 1920.

BERTIE. Ed. Lady A. Gordon-Lennox, *The Diary of Lord Bertie of Thame 1914-1918*,
Hodder & Stoughton, London, 1924.

BIRNBAUM. K. E. Birnbaum, *Peace Moves and U-Boat Warfare*, Almquist & Wiksell,
Stockholm, 1958.

BRAGDON. H. W. Bragdon, *Woodrow Wilson: The Academic Years*, Belknap Press,
Harvard, 1967.

CAB. Cabinet Papers in the Public Record Office, London.

CECIL. Viscount Cecil, *A Great Experiment*, Jonathan Cape, London, 1941.

CHURCHILL. W. S. Churchill, *The World Crisis*, 6 vols., Thornton Butterworth, London,
1923.

DIGBY. M. Digby, *Horace Plunkett*, Basil Blackwell, Oxford, 1949.

DUGDALE. B. E. C. Dugdale, *Arthur James Balfour*, 2 vols., Hutchinson, London, 1936.

ELLIOT. M. A. Elliot, *My Aunt Louisa and Woodrow Wilson*, North Carolina U.P., 1944.

FISCHER. Fritz Fischer, *Germany's War Aims in the First World War*, Chatto & Windus,
London, 1967.

F.O. Foreign Office Papers in the Public Record Office, London.

FOWLER. W. B. Fowler, *British-American Relations 1917-18*, Princeton U.P., 1969.

FRUS. *Papers relating to the Foreign Relations of the United States*, Government Print-
ing Office, Washington. Supplements 1914, 1915, 1916, and 1917 (2 vols.) (1928 *et seq.*).
In the references the year is given only when it is not apparent from the text.

GEORGE.   A. L. and J. L. George, *Woodrow Wilson and Colonel House*, John Day, New York, 1956.

GERARD.   J. W. Gerard, *My Four Years in Germany*, Hodder & Stoughton, London, 1917.

GERSON.   L. L. Gerson, *Woodrow Wilson and the Rebirth of Poland*, Yale U.P., 1953.

GILBERT.   M. Gilbert, *Winston S. Churchill*, vol. 3, Heinemann, London, 1971.

GRAYSON.   Rear-Admiral C. T. Grayson, *Woodrow Wilson: An Intimate Memoir*, Holt Rinehart and Winston, New York, 1960.

GREGORY.   Ross Gregory, *Walter Hines Page*, Kentucky U.P., 1970.

GREW.   J. C. Grew, *Turbulent Era*, Hammond, London, 1953.

GREY.   Viscount Grey of Fallodon, *Twenty-Five Years 1892-1916*, vol. 2, Frederick O. Stokes, New York, 1925.

HALE.   W. B. Hale, *Woodrow Wilson*, Doubleday, New York, 1912.

HANKEY.   Lord Hankey, *The Supreme Command*, George Allen & Unwin, London, 1961.

HARBAUGH.   W. H. Harbaugh, *The Life and Times of Theodore Roosevelt*, Collier Books, New York, 1962.

HARDINGE.   *Old Diplomacy: the Reminiscences of Lord Hardinge of Penshurst*, John Murray, 1947.

HOUSE.   Charles Seymour, *The Intimate Papers of Colonel House*, Benn, London, 1926.

   House's diary is in Yale University Library. It has never been published in full. For extracts not in the *Intimate Papers* I have referred wherever possible to other works containing them, mainly Link; and where this is not possible, I have given the reference as *Diary*.

HOUSTON.   D. F. Houston, *Eight Years with Wilson's Cabinet 1913-1920*, 2 vols., Doubleday, New York, 1926.

JENKINS.   Roy Jenkins, *Asquith*, Collins, London, 1964.

JESSUP.   P. C. Jessup, *Elihu Root*, Dodd Mead, New York, 1938.

JOHNSON.   W. F. Johnson, *George Harvey*, Houghton Mifflin, Boston, 1929.

JONES.   Thomas Jones, *Lloyd George*, O.U.P., London, 1951.

KEYNES.   *The Collected Writings of John Maynard Keynes*, vol. xvi, Macmillan, London, 1971.

LANE.   Ed. A. W. Lane and L. H. Wall, *The Letters of Franklin K. Lane*, Houghton Mifflin, Boston, 1922.

LANSING.   *War Memoirs of Robert Lansing*, Rich & Cowan, London, 1935.

LINK.   A. S. Link, *Wilson*, 5 vols., Princeton U.P., 1947-1965.

Ll. G. I.   *War Memoirs of David Lloyd George*, Ivor Nicholson & Watson, London, 1933.

Ll. G. II.   D. Lloyd George, *The Truth about the Peace Treaties*, Gollancz, London, 1938.

LODGE.   H. C. Lodge, *The Senate and the League of Nations*, Charles Scribner, New York, 1925.

LOUIS.   W. R. Louis, *Great Britain and Germany's Lost Colonies*, O.U.P., London, 1967.

L & D.   C. J. Lowe and M. L. Dockrill, *The Mirage of Power*, Routledge & Kegan Paul, London, 1972.

LP.   *Foreign Relations of the United States: the Lansing Papers 1914-1920*, Dept. of State, Washington, Publication 1421, vol. 1.

McADOO.   E. W. McAdoo and M. Y. Gaffey, *The Woodrow Wilsons*, Macmillan, London, 1937.

McADOO Lrs.   Ed. E. W. McAdoo, *The Priceless Gift*, McGraw Hill, New York, 1962.

MARDER. A. J. Marder, *From the Dreadnought to Scapa Flow*, O.U.P., London, 1965.

MARTIN. L. W. Martin, *Peace without Victory*, Yale U.P., 1958.

MAY. E. R. May, *The World War and American Isolation*, Harvard U.P., 1959.

MILLIS. Walter Millis, *Road to War*, Faber & Faber, London, 1935.

MRS. W. *Memoirs of Mrs. Woodrow Wilson*, Putnam, New York, 1939.

OGD. *Official German Documents relating to the World War*, Carnegie Endowment of International Peace, O.U.P., London, 1923.

OSGOOD. R. E. Osgood, *Ideals and Self-Interest in America's Foreign Relations*, Chicago U.P., 1953.

PAGE. B. J. Hendrick, *The Life and Letters of Walter H. Page*, 3 vols., Heinemann, London, 1923–5.

PERCY. Eustace Percy, *Some Memories*, Eyre & Spottiswoode, London, 1958.

PP. Ed. R. S. Baker and W. E. Dodd, *Public Papers of Woodrow Wilson*, 6 vols., Harper, New York, 1927.

PWW. Ed. A. S. Link, *Papers of Woodrow Wilson*, vols. 1 to 12, Princeton U.P., 1966 et seq.

REID. E. G. Reid, *Woodrow Wilson*, O.U.P., London, 1934.

ROBBINS. Keith Robbins, *Sir Edward Grey*, Cassell, London, 1971.

ROOSEVELT. Ed. E. E. Morison, *The Letters of Theodore Roosevelt*, vols. 7 and 8, Harvard U.P., 1954.

ROSKILL. Stephen Roskill, *Hankey: Man of Secrets* (two vols.), vol. 1, Collins, 1970.

ROTHWELL. V. H. Rothwell, *British War Aims and Peace Diplomacy 1914–1918*, O.U.P., London, 1971.

S. R. Ed. S. Gwynne, *The Letters and Friendships of Sir Cecil Spring Rice* (two vols.), vol. 2, Constable, London, 1929.

SCOTT. Ed. J. B. Scott, *The Declaration of London 1909: Official Documents*, O.U.P., New York, 1919.

C. P. SCOTT. Ed. Trevor Wilson, *The Political Diaries of C. P. Scott 1911–1928*, Collins, London, 1970.

SEYMOUR. Charles Seymour, *American Diplomacy during the World War*, Johns Hopkins Press, 1934.

SINEY. M. C. Siney, *The Allied Blockade of Germany 1914–1916*, Michigan U.P., 1957.

SMITH. A. D. H. Smith, *Mr. House of Texas*, Funk & Wagnall, New York, 1940.

STEVENSON. Ed. A. J. P. Taylor, *Lloyd George: A Diary by Frances Stevenson*, Hutchinson, London, 1971.

TAYLOR. A. J. P. Taylor, *The Troublemakers*, Hamish Hamilton, London, 1957.

TREVELYAN. G. M. Trevelyan, *Grey of Fallodon*, Longmans, London, 1937.

TUCHMAN. B. W. Tuchman, *The Zimmermann Telegram*, Constable, London, 1959.

TUMULTY. J. P. Tumulty, *Woodrow Wilson as I Knew Him*, Heinemann, London, 1922.

VIERECK. G. S. Viereck, *The Strangest Friendship in History*, Liveright, New York, 1932.

WALEY. S. D. Waley, *Edwin Montagu*, Asia Publishing House, New York, 1934.

WATT. R. M. Watt, *The Kings Depart*, Weidenfeld & Nicolson, London, 1969.

WHITE. W. A. White, *Woodrow Wilson*, Ernest Benn, London, 1926.

WILLERT. Arthur Willert, *The Road to Safety*, Derek Verschoyle, London, 1952.

A number of other books which I have used less, but with no less gratitude, are noted in the references.

REFERENCES

page

PREFACE

vii   1   Churchill 3: 229

CHAPTER I

4   1   PWW 4: 472; *cf. also* 1: 273
     2   Ibid. 5: 719
     3   Ibid. 3: 466
     4   Ibid. 1: 604
5   5   Baker 1: 116
     6   PWW 2: 17
     7   Ibid. 2: 107
     8   Ibid. 2: 148
     9   Ibid. 2: 135
6   10   Ibid. 8: 162, 170
     11   Ibid. 2: 343
     12   Ibid. 2: 343
     13   Ibid. 2: 351
     14   Ibid. 2: 390
7   15   Ibid. 5: 139
     16   Ibid. 7: 161
     17   Ibid. 6: 409
     18   Ibid. 5: 625
8   19   Ibid. 6: 139
     20   Ibid. 6: 526
     21   Ibid. 6: 554
     22   Ibid. 8: 634
     23   Bragdon 230
     24   PWW 11: 349
9   25   Ibid. 11: 247
     26   Baker 2: 33
     27   PWW 10: 37
     28   Annin 337
     29   PWW 10: 31
10   30   Baker 2: 138
     31   Ibid. 2: 134
     32   Baker 1: 68
     33   Ibid. 1: 207
11   34   Houston 116
     35   PWW 1: 136
     36   Ibid. 3: 13
     37   Link 1: 94

page

     38   PWW 1: 163
12   39   Ibid. 1: 467
     40   Ibid. 6: 400
     41   Ibid. 6: 554
13   42   Ibid. 1: 338
     43   Baker 1: 38
     44   PWW 1: 658
     45   Ibid. 1: 443
     46   Ibid. 2: 146
     47   Ibid. 1: 448
     48   Ibid. 1: 700
14   49   Ibid. 1: 259
     50   Ibid. 1: 305
     51   Ibid. 1: 675
     52   Ibid. 3: 415
     53   Reid 27
     54   PWW 11: 206
     55   Ibid. 1: 209
15   56   Ibid. 1: 228
     57   Ll. G. I: 97
16   58   Bragdon 303
     59   PWW 3: 554
     60   Baker 1: 167
     61   PWW 2: 466
     62   Ibid. 2: 107
     63   Ibid. 2: 84
     64   Ibid. 2: 138
     65   Ibid. 4: 720
17   66   Ibid. 2: 468
     67   Ibid. 3: 323
     68   Ibid. 2: 485
18   69   Ibid. 2: 588
     70   Ibid. 2: 517
     71   Ibid. 3: 20, 109
     72   Ibid. 2: 435
     73   Ibid. 3: 235
19   74   Ibid. 3: 239
     75   Ibid. 4: 434
     76   Ibid. 8: 634
     77   Ibid. 3: 207
     78   Ibid. 4: 307
20   79   Ibid. 4: 429
     80   Ibid. 4: 431

20   81   Ibid. 2: 482

     82   Ibid. 4: 582

     83   Ibid. 3: 495

21   84   Ibid. 7: 572 (*Love's Labours Lost,*
         IV. iii)

     85   Ibid. 7: 467, 558; *cf. also* 7: 527,
         8: 460, 465

     86   Ibid. 11: 206

     87   Ibid. 7: 542

     88   Ibid. 11: 186

22   89   McAdoo 17

     90   Baker 2: 174

     91   PWW 6: 92

     92   Baker 2: 57

23   93   PWW 8: 496, 507, 508

     94   Baker 1: 267

     95   Elliot 200

     96   Ibid. 202

     97   PWW 3: 303

24   98   Ll. G. II: 228

     99   Reid 33, 64

   100   PWW 8: 472

   101   Baker 2: 53

   102   PWW 6: 41

   103   Ibid. 11: 174

   104   Ibid. 11: 136

   105   Ibid. 11: 163

   106   Ibid. 11: 175

   107   Ibid. 11: 240

   108   Ibid. 11: 503

25   109   Ibid. 11: 154

   110   Ibid. 4: 494

   111   Ibid. 6: 28; *cf. also* 4: 323 and
         7: 11

   112   Ibid. 7: 11

   113   Ibid. 4: 464

   114   Ibid. 4: 488

   115   Ibid. 4: 595

   116   Ibid. 4: 359

26   117   Ibid. 12: 191

   118   Bragdon 186

27   119   PWW 8: 51

   120   Ibid. 6: 55

   121   Baker 3: 61

   122   Ibid. 2: 204

   123   PWW 10: 525

   124   Baker 2: 281

   125   Ibid. 1: 51

28   126   PWW 9: 546

   127   Baker 2: 78, 80

   128   PWW 5: 41

   129   Ibid. 11: 157

   130   Ibid. 11: 177

   131   Ibid. 11: 214

29   132   Ibid. 11: 164

   133   Bragdon 334

   134   Ibid. 255

   135   Baker 2: 19

30   136   Daniel Halévy, *President Wilson,*
         John Lane, New York, 1919, p. 67

   137   Baker 2: 14

   138   PWW 1: 125

31   139   Ibid. 2: 499

   140   Ibid. 2: 70

   141   Bragdon 33

   142   PWW 2: 659

   143   Ibid. 8: 53

   144   Bragdon 153

   145   PWW 1: 278

32   146   Ibid. 11: 3

   147   Ibid. 10: 323; Reid 71

   148   Bragdon 229

   149   PWW 7: 202

   150   Ibid. 6: 61

33   151   Ibid. 6: 57

   152   Ibid. 6: 61

   153   Ibid. 2: 608

   154   Ibid. 3: 553

   155   Ibid. 3: 504

34   156   Ibid. 3: 417, 418

   157   Ibid. 6: 671

   158   Ibid. 4: 280

35   159   Ibid. 4: 237

   160   Ibid. 5: 389

   161   Ibid. 5: 395, 399

   162   Ibid. 10: 377

   163   Ibid. 10: 375

   164   Ibid. 1: 655

CHAPTER II

36   1   Bragdon 279

     2   Ibid. 305

37   3   Baker 2: 206

38   4   Ibid. 2: 251

     5   Bragdon 328

     6   Baker 2: 236

     7   Bragdon 324

     8   Ed. Link, *Woodrow Wilson: a Pro-
         file*, Hill & Wang, New York,
         1968, p. 48

39   9   Bragdon 331
     10   Baker 9: 314
     11   Bell 107
     12   Baker 2: 266
     13   Reid 108
40   14   McAdoo Lrs. 305
     15   Ibid. 308
     16   Elliott 267
42   17   Johnston 93
     18   Ibid. 420
     19   PWW 4: 438
43   20   S. E. Morison and H. S. Commager, *The Growth of the American Republic*, O.U.P., New York, 3rd edn., 1942, 2: 262
     21   'The Populist Platform of 1892' quoted in E. M. Hugh-Jones, *Woodrow Wilson and American Liberalism*, Hodder & Stoughton, London, 1947, p. 59
44   22   Morison and Commager, op. cit. 251
     23   Ibid. 261
     24   S.R. 197
46   25   PWW 11: 515
     26   Ibid. 12: 189
     27   Ibid. 12: 356
47   28   Baker 3: 9
     29   PWW 7: 177
     30   Baker 2: 197
     31   Ibid. 3: 4
48   32   Ibid. 3: 12
     33   Ibid. 3: 30
     34   Page 3: 12
49   35   Baker 3: 205
50   36   Link 1: 122
53   37   Baker 3: 23
     38   Ibid. 3: 42
54   39   Ibid. 1: xxxi
     40   Ibid. 2: 325
     41   Annin 391
55   42   Baker 3: 37
     43   Tumulty 45
56   44   Baker 3: 48
     45   Ibid. 3: 40
     46   Ibid. 3: 40
57   47   Ibid. 2: 341; Link 1: 83
     48   Baker 3: 50
60   49   Ibid. 3: 57
     50   Ibid. 3: 64
     51   Ibid. 3: 65

CHAPTER III

62   1   Johnston 164
     2   Baker 3: 53
     3   Tumulty 15
     4   Annin 72
     5   Hale 167
63   6   Baker 3: 98
     7   Link 1: 212
64   8   McAdoo 120
     9   Tumulty 22
     10   Link 1: 223
     11   McAdoo 160
65   12   Tumulty 70
     13   Link 1: 219
     14   Tumulty 62
66   15   Baker 3: 126
     16   Bragdon 394
     17   Baker 3: 192
     18   Hale 183
67   19   Tumulty 71
     20   Ibid. 75
     21   Link 3: 253
     22   Hale 197
     23   Link 1: 280
68   24   Baker 3: 196
69   25   Ibid. 3: 292
     26   Ibid. 3: 231
     27   Ibid. 3: 231
     28   Link 1: 446
     29   Baker 3: 196
     30   Link 1: 314
70   31   Baker 3: 196
     32   Link 1: 120
     33   Jessup 1: 236 and 2: 251
71   34   Baker 3: 232
72   35   Johnston 184
73   36   Tumulty 84
74   37   Link 1: 363
     38   Ibid. 1: 364
     39   Baker 3: 252
     40   Tumulty 37
     41   Ibid. 91
75   42   Link 1: 371
     43   Ibid. 1: 373
     44   Johnston 238
76   45   Link 1: 353
     46   Tumulty 95
77   47   Baker 3: 321
78   48   *D.N.A.B.* 18: 39
     49   Link 1: 433

78 50 J. C. Long, *Bryan the Great Com-
           moner*, Appleton, New York,
           1922, p. 247
79 51 Ibid. 243; Baker 3: 336
82 52 Tumulty 120
    53 Baker 3: 356
    54 Ibid. 3: 299
83 55 Ibid. 3: 355
84 56 Link 1: 398
    57 Baker 3: 357
85 58 Ibid. 3: 358
    59 Ibid. 3: 362
    60 Ibid. 3: 362
    61 Link 1: 513
86 62 Bell 77
    63 Arthur M. Schlesinger, Jr., *The
           Age of Roosevelt*, Heinemann,
           London, 1961, 3: 581
    64 Tumulty 17
    65 Annin 97
87 66 Bell 81

CHAPTER IV

88   1 Quoted in Bragdon 347
89   2 McAdoo 19
90   3 McAdoo Lrs. 271
     4 McAdoo 150
     5 Ibid. 114
91   6 Elliot 188
     7 McAdoo 45
     8 PWW 8: 13, 14; *cf. also* 9: 443
     9 McAdoo 80
    10 Elliot 195
    11 Ibid. 196
92 12 McAdoo 69, 104
93 13 Ibid. 167
94 14 Ibid. 82
    15 Tumulty 193
    16 McAdoo 127
    17 House 1: 119
    18 McAdoo 22
    19 Reid 66
95 20 White xiii
    21 Baker Chronicle 254
    22 Baker 1: 290
96 23 David Lawrence, *The True Story
           of Woodrow Wilson*, Hurst &
           Blackett, London, 1924, p. 127
    24 Baker 3: 304

97 25 House 1: 41
    26 George 93
    27 House 1: 47
98 28 Ibid. 1: 52
    29 Ibid. 1: 90
    30 Baker 3: 337
    31 House 1: 109
    32 PWW 11: 193
    33 Ibid. 1: 111
99 34 House 1: 119
    35 Ibid. 1: 115
    36 Tumulty 138
    37 McAdoo 208
    38 House 1: 119
    39 Ibid. 1: 118
100 40 Ibid. 1: 397
    41 Ibid. 2: 340
    42 Ibid. 1: 364
    43 Ibid. 1: 249
101 44 Ibid. 2: 107
    45 Ibid. 1: 130
    46 R. S. Baker, *Woodrow Wilson &
           World Settlement*, Heinemann,
           London, 1923, 1: xxx
    47 Digby 138
    48 House 1: 67
    49 Ll. G. II: 242
102 50 McAdoo 211
    51 Grayson 21
103 52 Baker 3: 458
    53 Link 2: 20
104 54 Baker 4: 38
105 55 Ibid. 4: 104
    56 Link 2: 79
    57 Baker 4: 232
106 58 Ibid. 5: 45
    59 This and the following Bryanisms
           are at Baker 4: 40-1
    60 Annin 164
    61 Baker 4: 45
107 62 Ibid. 4: 44
    63 Harbaugh 210
108 64 Baker 4: 30
109 65 W. A. Swanberg, *Citizen Hearst*,
           Bantam Books, New York, 1963,
           p. 162
110 66 S. E. Morison, *History of the United
           States*, O.U.P., London, 1927,
           2: 412. I am indebted to Professor
           Morison for permission to re-
           produce this fine piece of writing.

The other quotations are taken from the same volume, pp. 411–16

111   67   Harbaugh 103
     68   R. C. Bannister, *Ray Stannard Baker*, Yale U.P., 1966, pp. 71–2
112   69   This and following quotations are taken from W. K. Hancock, *Smuts: The Sanguine Years 1870–1919*, C.U.P., London, 1962, 89 et seq.
113   70   PWW 12: 18
115   71   Robbins 79
     72   Jones 27
     73   PWW 10: 397
116   74   PP 4: 8
     75   Jessup 2: 264
117   76   House 3: 234
119   77   Baker 4: 351
     78   PP 3: 49, 72
     79   *House Diary*, 30.10.13
     80   Baker 4: 286
120   81   Page 1: 187
     82   Baker 4: 290
     83   Page 1: 202
     84   Ibid. 1: 204
     85   PP 3: 111
121   86   Page 3: 109
     87   Baker 4: 310
     88   Link 2: 398
     89   Baker 4: 326
122   90   Ibid. 4: 347
     91   House 1: 299
     92   Baker 4: 266, 273
123   93   Ibid. 4: 305
     94   Jessup 2: 240
124   95   Ibid. 2: 255
125   96   Morley's *Life of Gladstone*, abridged edn., Hodder & Stoughton, London, p. 57
126   97   PP 3: 111
     98   Ibid. 3: 147
128   99   PWW 7: 344
    100   Ibid. 8: 607
    101   Ibid. 7: 81
    102   Ibid. 7: 359
129   103   Link 5: 96
    104   PWW 8: 277
    105   PP 3: 146
    106   Baker 3: 173
    107   PP 3: 95, 197, 203
    108   Ibid. 3: 322
    109   Bragdon 256
130   110   PP 3: 205
    111   Ibid. 3: 195
    112   Baker 3: 119
131   113   PP 3: 51

CHAPTER V

137   1   *Machiavelli: Discorsi XLI*, trans. C. E. Detmold, *The Prince and the Discourses*, Random House, New York, 1950, p. 528
139   2   Barbara W. Tuchman, *August 1914*, Constable, London, 1961, p. 132
     3   Ibid. 173
     4   Ibid. 313
140   5   House 1: 299
     6   Link 3: 50
     7   S.R. 223
     8   PP 3: 157
     9   Bern. 227
    10   House 2: 320
141   11   Ll. G. 1: 662
    12   Walter Lippmann, *U.S. Foreign Policy*, Hamish Hamilton, London, 1943: xvii
142   13   Quoted in G. P. Gooch, *Germany*, Scribners, New York, 1925, p. 112
    14   Gregory 61
    15   Baker 5: 290
143   16   Ibid. 5: 214
    17   House 1: 306
    18   Ibid. 1: 369
    19   PP 3: 250
    20   Baker 5: 2
    21   Link 3: 139
144   22   Ibid. 3: 55
    23   Ibid. 2: 8
145   24   *The Age of Roosevelt*, op. cit. 3: 223
    25   Link 3: 133
146   26   Gilbert 176
    27   Robert Rhodes James, *Rosebery*, Weidenfeld & Nicolson, London, 1963, p. 375
147   28   Viscount Samuel, *Memoirs*, Cresset Press, London, 1945, p. 90
    29   Grey 2: 268
    30   Trevelyan 48

147 31 Quoted in Robbins 72

32 Ibid. 32

33 Ibid. 55

148 34 Ibid. 154

35 Ibid. 154

36 *The Memoirs of Herbert Hoover, 1874-1920*, Hollis & Carter, London, 1952, p. 203; cited subsequently as *Hoover Memoirs*

37 F.O. 800. 241. 410

38 Page 1: 334

149 39 Baker 4: 33

40 Seymour 57

41 Baker 5: 169

42 House 1: 138

43 Page 2: 139

44 Ibid. 3: 22

45 Gregory 166

46 Grey 102

47 Bragdon 292, 406, 408

150 48 LP 700

49 *Hoover Memoirs*, op. cit. 204

50 Willert 57

51 House 2: 44

52 Ibid. 2: 234

151 53 Bern. 228

54 Willert 96

55 S.R. 214

56 Ibid. 245

57 F.O. 800. 84. 273

58 S.R. 245

152 59 F.O. 800. 84. 323

60 Ibid. 800. 85. 133

61 Ibid. 382. 12

62 Ibid. 371. 2795

63 S.R. 215, 435

64 Ibid. 211

65 Ibid. 202

66 F.O. 800. 94. 241; *cf. also* ibid. 800. 84. 266, 370, 379, 390

153 67 Ibid. 800. 84. 493

68 S.R. 212

69 F.O. 800. 84. 329

70 S.R. 239

71 F.O. 800. 241. 431

72 S.R. 245

73 F.O. 800. 241. 244

74 Ibid. 800. 84. 298

154 75 Willert 72

76 F.O. 800. 241. 476

77 Ibid. 800. 111. 390

78 S.R. 410

79 House 3: 28

155 80 S.R. 432

81 Percy 37

CHAPTER VI

156 1 R. W. Southern, *The Making of the Middle Ages*, Hutchinson, London, 1953, p. 16

157 2 Grey 107

160 3 *The Fox* (1811) Edw. 311; *Roscoe's Prize Cases, 1745-1857*, Stevens, London, 1905, 2: 61

4 *The Zamora*, 1916, 2 A.C. 77

5 FRUS 498

162 6 Quoted in 'Rights & Duties of Neutral States in Naval & Aerial War', prepared by the Research in International Law of the Harvard Law School, 1929, p. 397: subsequently cited as *Harvard Research*

163 7 *The Stigstad*, 1919, A.C. 279

8 Professor J. L. Brierley in *Law Quarterly Review*, vol. 51, p. 27

9 See FRUS, 1915, 139 for Sweden and 188 for Holland

164 10 Quoted in (1918) P.D. 211

11 Quoted in *Harvard Research*, op. cit. 400

12 Quoted in the *Cambridge Modern History*, C.U.P., London, 1903, 7: 330

166 13 Scott 2: 38

167 14 LP 268

15 FRUS, 1914, 216

16 Ibid. 218

17 Ibid. 220

168 18 Ibid. 232

19 Link 3: 110

20 S.R. 233

21 FRUS, 1914, 244

169 22 Ibid. 248

23 Ibid. 250

24 Ibid. 249

170 25 Ibid. 252

26 Page 3: 182

27 Ibid. 3: 187

28 Ibid. 1: 383

CHAPTER VII

176   1   Baker 5: 17
       2   LP 114
       3   FRUS 580
       4   LP 131
       5   Ibid. 140
178   6   F.O. 382. 1099. 15599
       7   Ibid. 371. 2786. 207558
179   8   Percy 23, 51; *cf. also* F.O. 800.
             95. 195
       9   Ibid. 382. 1099. 21163
      10   Hankey 359
180   11   Ibid. 96
      12   Ibid. 99
181   13   FRUS, 1916, 424
      14   Ibid. 458
182   15   CAB. 137. 37
183   16   FRUS 679
184   17   CAB. 37. 125. 32
185   18   Baker 5: 131
      19   FRUS 346
      20   Ibid. 375
      21   LP 259
186   22   S.R. 250
      23   CAB. 151. 31
      24   Link 3: 147
      25   Baker 5: 126
      26   Ibid. 5: 133
187   27   Ibid. 5: 131
      28   FRUS 682
      29   Ibid. 683
      30   F.O. 800. 85
188   31   S.R. 257
190   32   Birnbaum 35
      33   May 223
191   34   Marder 1: 363
      35   Churchill 2: 280
192   36   CAB. 41. 35. 30
      37   F.O. 372. 600
      38   Ibid. 500. 89. 18
      39   Ibid. 372. 588. 42063
      40   FRUS 274; CAB. 41. 35. 43
193   41   F.O. 368. 1183. 42873; 372. 600
      42   Ibid. 368. 1183. 44185
      43   Ibid. 372. 600
      44   Ibid. 368. 336
      45   Ibid. 372. 588. 43294
      46   Ibid. 372. 600
194   47   Ibid. 372. 600
      48   Ibid. 372. 601

      49   Ibid. 372. 601
      50   Ibid. 602. 69047
      51   Ibid. 601
      52   Ibid. 800. 94
      53   FRUS, 1915, P. 37; *cf. also* FRUS
             367
195   54   Ibid. 235
      55   PWW 1: 593
      56   FRUS, 1915, 142
      57   Ibid. 332
196   58   Lord Stowell in *The Jonge
             Margaretha* (1799) 1. C. Rob. 187
      59   FRUS 332
      60   Scott 155
197   61   *The Hakan* (1918) A.C. 150
198   62   CAB. 45. 35. 31
      63   FRUS 461
199   64   Gilbert 93
      65   FRUS 460
      66   Link 3: 314
200   67   FRUS 94
      68   Ibid. 96
      69   Link 3: 321
201   70   Baker 5: 253
      71   FRUS 106
      72   S.R. 255
      73   FRUS 99
202   74   CAB. 37. 124
      75   Hankey 368
      76   CAB. 37. 124
      77   Link 3: 336
203   78   Hankey 368
      79   FRUS 144
      80   Hansard H.C. 70. 600
      81   LP 270–3; FRUS 132
      82   Churchill 2: 294
204   83   FRUS 143
      84   LP 281
      85   Ibid. 278
      86   Ibid. 282
      87   Ibid. 285
205   88   FRUS 146
      89   LP 288
      90   FRUS 152
206   91   F.O. 382. 12. 228
      92   *The Stigstad*, 1917, A.C. 279 and
             Leonora, ibid. 974
207   93   FRUS 95, 102, 105
      94   Ibid. 110
      95   LP 361
      96   Ibid. 353; FRUS 107

208 97 FRUS 107
     98 Ibid. 111
     99 Ibid. 111
    100 Ibid. 119
209 101 Ibid. 119
    102 Hankey 366
    103 FRUS 126-30
    104 Ibid. 129
    105 Ibid. 128
    106 Ibid. 140
210 107 *Diaries & Letters of Marie Belloc
          Lowndes*, Chatto & Windus,
          London, 1971, p. 50
    108 FRUS 134
211 109 CAB. 37. 130. 34
    110 May 141
212 111 LP 368
    112 Ibid. 369
    113 Ibid. 379
213 114 Ibid. 11
    115 Ibid. 377
    116 Ibid. 375
    117 Ibid. 380
214 118 Ibid. 381
    119 Ibid. 388
    120 Ibid. 383
    121 Baker 5: 325
    122 House 1: 462
215 123 Baker 5: 326
    124 Jenkins 363
    125 Page 1: 436
216 126 *The Diaries of Sir Alexander
          Cadogan 1932-45*, Cassell,
          London, 1971

            CHAPTER VIII

217   1 House 1: 300
218   2 Link 2: 94
      3 Ibid. 2: 94
219   4 House 1: 253
      5 George 126
220   6 Ll. G. II: 245
      7 George 130
      8 House 1: 247
221   9 Page 1: 245
     10 House 1: 249
     11 Ibid. 1: 250
     12 Ibid. 1: 254
222 13 Ibid. 1: 259
     14 Baker 5: 39

     15 House 1: 265
     16 Ibid. 1: 268
     17 Baker 5: 40
223 18 Page 3: 118
     19 House 1: 268
     20 Ibid. 1: 267
     21 Ibid. 1: 270
     22 Ibid. 1: 274
     23 Ibid. 1: 275
224 24 Baker 5: 42
     25 House 1: 277
     26 Ibid. 1: 278
     27 Ibid. 1: 278
     28 Ibid. 1: 282
     29 Viereck 55
     30 House 1: 284
225 31 Page 1: 287
     32 Baker 4: 477
     33 McAdoo Lrs. 285, 283
     34 Ibid. 251
226 35 House 1: 285
     36 Ibid. 1: 298
     37 Link 2: 464
227 38 Ibid. 2: 465
     39 Baker 4: 139
     40 Ibid. 5: 138
     41 Ibid. 5: 142
228 42 Ibid. 5: 144
     43 Grayson 50
     44 Churchill 6: 222
229 45 Link 3: 198
230 46 F.O. 800. 84. 353
     47 House 1: 331
231 48 F.O. 800. 84. 274
     49 S.R. 226
     50 House 1: 334
232 51 Ibid. 1: 302
     52 Ibid. 1: 339
     53 Ibid. 1: 339
233 54 Link 3: 205
     55 House 1: 302
     56 Link 3: 206
     57 LP 10
     58 Link 3: 207
234 59 Page 1: 416
     60 Ibid. 1: 417
236 61 Baker 5: 286
     62 Ibid. 5: 42, 302
237 63 Gerard 191
     64 Bern. 136
     65 Gerard 17

238	66	Fischer 9
	67	Ll. G. I: 58
239	68	Stevenson 285
	69	Fischer 59
240	70	Camb. M.H. 147
	71	S.R. in vol. 1, p. 350
241	72	Marder 1: 120
	73	Watt 118
	74	Ibid. 118
	75	FRUS 93, 105
242	76	Grew 144
	77	May 107
	78	FRUS 104
	79	Fischer 103
244	80	Ibid. 125
245	81	Watt 118
	82	Fischer 186
	83	Link 3: 209
246	84	House 1: 345
	85	Link 3: 214
	86	House 1: 347
	87	F.O. 800. 84. 458
	88	Trevelyan 214
247	89	William Phillips, *Ventures in Diplomacy*, John Murray, London, 1925, p. 26
248	90	F.O. 800. 84. 481
	91	House 1: 349
	92	Link 3: 214
	93	Asquith 51
249	94	Trevelyan 315
	95	Link 3: 212
	96	House 1: 356
250	97	Ibid. 1: 357; F.O. 800. 85. 141
251	98	House 1: 353
	99	Baker 5: 302
	100	House 1: 363

CHAPTER IX

253	1	Baker 6: 50
	2	Mrs. W. 23
	3	Ibid. 64
254	4	PWW 11: 26
255	5	Ed. H. W. V. Temperley, *History of the Peace Conference of Paris*, Hodder & Stoughton, London, 1920, 1: 169
256	6	Ibid.
257	7	CAB. 42. 2. 5, p. 8
	8	Gilbert 332

	9	CAB. 42. 2. 5
	10	Asquith 65
	11	Ibid. 65
258	12	FRUS 385; Page 3: 239
259	13	Ll. G. I. 97, *cf. also* II. 765
	14	T. P. Conwell-Evans, *Foreign Policy from a Back Bench*, O.U.P., London, 1932, p. 106
260	15	Asquith 49
	16	Ll. G. I. 413, *cf. also* 431
	17	Asquith 57
	18	Ibid. 69
	19	Conwell-Evans, op. cit. 107
	20	Ibid. 108
261	21	Asquith 73; *cf. also* CAB. 37. 126. 27
	22	Asquith 69
	23	CAB. 42. 2. 14, p. 7
262	24	This and subsequent quotations on the topic are taken from Louis, pp. 37–43 and 61–5
263	25	CAB. 37. 126. 27
	26	Louis 75
264	27	F.O. 800. 85. 64, 70
	28	House 1: 368
265	29	Ibid. 1: 371
	30	Hankey 361
	31	House 1: 385
	32	Ibid. 1: 374
	33	Link 3: 219
266	34	Ibid. 3: 220
	35	House 1: 377
267	36	Hansard H.C. 70: 602
268	37	F.O. 800. 75
	38	House 1: 381
	39	Trevelyan 316
	40	F.O. 800. 85. 359
269	41	FRUS 9
	42	House 1: 382
	43	FRUS 15
	44	Baker 5: 312
	45	House 1: 383
270	46	Baker 5: 313
	47	House 1: 386
	48	Ibid. 1: 388
271	49	Baker 5: 314
	50	Ibid. 5: 313
	51	House 1: 395
	52	FRUS 17
	53	House 1: 420
	54	Ibid. 1: 428

272   55   Digby 180
      56   House 1: 370
      57   Ibid. 1: 375
      58   Ibid. 1: 380
273   59   Link 3: 218
      60   House 1: 375
      61   Ibid. 1: 388
      62   Ibid. 1: 403
274   63   Baker 5: 318
      64   Dugdale 1: 1
275   65   Dennis Judd, *Balfour & the British
           Empire*, Macmillan, London,
           1968, p. 75
      66   Dugdale 1: 415
276   67   House 1: 391
      68   Ibid. 1: 392
      69   Digby 189
      70   House 1: 441
      71   Ibid. 2: 118
      72   Ibid. 1: 400
      73   Grew 185
      74   House 1: 404
277   75   Ibid. 1: 407
      76   Link 3: 226
      77   House 1: 432
278   78   Baker 5: 318
      79   CAB. 130. 34
      80   House 1: 422
279   81   Trevelyan 319; F.O. 800. 95. 73
      82   F.O. 800. 58. 350
      83   Ibid. 800. 50. 108
      84   Ibid. 800. 95. 86
      85   Ibid. 800. 94. 88
280   86   House 2: 13
      87   Ibid. 1: 437, 441
      88   Ibid. 1: 439
      89   F.O. 800. 85. 222
281   90   Hankey 339
      91   House 1: 391
      92   Asquith 62
      93   Hankey 1: 779
      94   Ibid. 1: 794
      95   Ibid. 1: 794
282   96   Ibid. 1: 360; *cf. also* House 2: 126
      97   Baker 5: 315

CHAPTER X

285   1   FRUS 387
       2   Ibid. 389
287   3   Bern. 144

288   4   Ibid. 30
       5   Link 3: 380
       6   Baker 5: 333
       7   Tumulty 237
289   8   PP 3: 305
       9   Ibid. 3: 49
      10   Tumulty 234
      11   FRUS 392
      12   Baker 5: 332
      13   Bern. 144
290   14   FRUS 393; LP 395
291   15   Ibid. 393
      16   Ibid. 402
      17   Bern. 157
      18   Link 3: 385
      19   LP 404
292   20   Ibid. 411
      21   Baker 3: 242
      22   Ibid. 5: 333
294   23   House 1: 450
      24   FRUS 406, 415
      25   LP 416
      26   House 1: 454
295   27   CAB. 37. 130. 15
      28   Ibid. 37. 130. 25; Roskill 125
      29   LP 416
      30   F.O. 382. 12. 45
      31   Hankey 1: 375
296   32   FRUS 419
      33   Link 3: 405
297   34   S.R. 2: 271
      35   LP 441, 445
298   36   S.R. 2: 256
      37   Baker 5: 351
      38   House 2: 6
      39   Houston 139
      40   William G. McAdoo, *Crowded
           Years*, Jonathan Cape, London,
           1931, p. 334 (subsequently cited
           as W. G. McAdoo)
299   41   FRUS 407
      42   W. G. McAdoo 333
      43   Baker 5: 357
      44   Link 3: 422
300   45   Houston 124
      46   LP 399
301   47   House 1: 473; 2: 5
302   48   Ibid. 2: 120
      49   Mrs. W. 75
      50   Link 2: 456
303   51   Baker 4: 52

	52	Link 2: 453
	53	Ibid. 3: 428
304	54	W. G. McAdoo 338
	55	Lansing 102, 19
	56	Link 3: 427
	57	Page 3: 247
305	58	Lansing 21
	59	Robert Lansing, *The Peace Negotiations*, Houghton Mifflin, New York, 1921, p. 10
306	60	Baker Chronicle 283
	61	Link 2: 68
307	62	House 2: 416
	63	Ibid. 1: 131
309	64	FRUS 461
	65	Ibid. 463
	66	Ibid. 469
	67	Baker 5: 365
310	68	House 2: 17, 21
	69	Ibid. 2: 56
	70	Lansing 30
311	71	LP 456
	72	House 2: 16
	73	Ibid. 2: 16
312	74	LP 459
	75	Ibid. 463
	76	Baker 5: 367
	77	FRUS 480
313	78	Ibid. 646
	79	Ibid. 481
	80	Ibid. 461
314	81	Link 3: 449
	82	Bern. 155; Lansing 40
	83	House 2: 57
	84	Bern. 164
315	85	LP 466

CHAPTER XI

316	1	House 2: 11
	2	Ibid. 2: 63
317	3	Page 2: 25
	4	House 2: 59
	5	Ibid. 2: 61
	6	Baker 5: 371
	7	Ibid. 5: 374
318	8	Page 2: 99
	9	Baker 5: 372, 374
320	10	LP 468
	11	Link 3: 567
	12	Ibid. 3: 569

	13	House 2: 31
	14	Ibid. 2: 29
321	15	Link 3: 568
	16	Ibid. 3: 570
	17	Ibid. 3: 578
	18	FRUS 524-6
322	19	LP 471; Lansing 47
	20	Link 3: 578
	21	Ibid. 3: 571
323	22	Ibid. 3: 575
324	23	Bern. 179
325	24	FRUS 531
	25	Ibid. 533
	26	Baker 5: 373
	27	FRUS 548, 556
326	28	Ibid. 941
	29	Ibid. 539
327	30	LP 476
	31	Lansing 50; Bern. 192
328	32	Link 3: 657
	33	House 2: 38-40
329	34	Link 3: 659
	35	House 2: 84
	36	Link 3: 672; LP 432
	37	Ibid. 483
330	38	Ibid. 486
332	39	Baker 5: 375
	40	LP 470
333	41	Ibid. 485
334	42	FRUS 560
	43	Bern. 194
	44	FRUS 603
335	45	Link 3: 16
	46	Ibid. 3: 375
	47	Henry Cabot Lodge, *The Senate & the League of Nations*, Charles Scribner, New York, 1925, p. 26
	48	John A. Garraty, *Henry Cabot Lodge*, Knopf, New York, 1953, p. 395
	49	Ibid. 300
	50	Baker 5: 95, 335, 344; House 1: 443
336	51	B. 5. 372
	52	Roosevelt 402
	53	Ibid. 899
	54	Ibid. 859
	55	Ibid. 861
337	56	Ibid. 903
	57	Ibid. 922
	58	Harbaugh 448

337	59	Roosevelt 938
	60	Harbaugh 439
	61	Link 3: 586
	62	House 2: 71
338	63	Bern. 191
	64	Ibid. 184
339	65	FRUS, 1915, 447
340	66	Ibid. 337
	67	F.O. 382. 12. 45
	68	Ibid. 800. 85. 313
	69	FRUS 171
341	70	Ibid. 377
342	71	Page 2: 27
343	72	House 2: 66

CHAPTER XII

344	1	F.O. 800. 95. 213
347	2	House 1: 468
	3	Ibid. 1: 393
349	4	Waley 94
350	5	Link 3: 597
	6	F.O. 800. 95. 203
	7	FRUS 446
351	8	Ibid. 466
	9	F.O. 800. 75. 203
	10	FRUS 473
	11	Ibid. 479
352	12	Ibid. 502
	13	CAB. 37. 159. 18
353	14	Siney 128
	15	CAB. 37. 131. 5
	16	F.O. 800. 95. 202
	17	Ibid. 800. 110. 148
	18	CAB. 37. 131. 38
354	19	House 2: 58
	20	Link 3: 612
	21	Lansing 45
	22	Link 3: 612
355	23	CAB. 37. 132. 13
	24	Bern. 90
357	25	Page 2: 94
	26	House 2: 70
	27	Ibid. 2: 75
	28	Ibid. 2: 77
	29	FRUS 578
	30	Link 3: 683
358	31	Ibid. 3: 683
	32	House 2: 78
	33	Page 2: 117
	34	House 2: 18

359	35	PP 3: 250
	36	Smith 91–2
	37	Baker 5: 306
	38	Link 3: 593
	39	Ibid. 3: 592
360	40	PP 3: 406
	41	Bern. 209
361	42	Link 4: 31
	43	Annin 168
	44	*D.N.A.B.* 10: 439
	45	Link 4: 45
	46	*Boswell's Life of Johnson* (Bicentenary edn.), Sir Isaac Pitman and Sons, London, 1909, 1: 41
362	47	*House Diary* 31. 7. 1915
363	48	Mrs. W. 89
364	49	Ibid. 91
	50	Link 4: 7
	51	Ibid. 4: 7
	52	Ibid. 4: 42
365	53	Ibid. 4: 6
	54	Baker 6: 362
	55	Link 4: 32
	56	Mrs. W. 336
366	57	Ibid. 90–2
367	58	Bern. 191
	59	Link 4: 61
	60	LP 487
368	61	Link 4: 62
	62	LP 490
369	63	Ibid. 491; Lansing 147
	64	LP 493
370	65	Ibid. 496
	66	House 2: 105
	67	Bern. 215
	68	FRUS 623
371	69	Link 4: 63
	70	LP 498
	71	FRUS 639
372	72	LP 499
	73	Lansing 91
	74	LP 499
	75	Ibid. 503
	76	FRUS 647
	77	LP 505
373	78	Ibid. 506
	79	Ibid. 221
374	80	Link 4: 75
	81	LP 507
	82	Ibid. 505
	83	Ibid. 506

375   84   Ibid. 509
      85   FRUS 655
      86   LP 508
      87   Ibid. 511
376   88   Lansing 148
377   89   LP 13
      90   FRUS 43
      91   Ibid. 44
      92   LP 471
379   93   House Papers, Yale University
           Library, 2. 6. 15
      94   House 2: 87
380   95   Ibid. 2: 87
      96   FRUS 64
      97   Link 4: 102
      98   Robbins 336
381   99   House 2: 84
      100 Ibid. 2: 85
      101 LP 495
382   102 House 2: 58; Link 4: 103–4
      103 House Papers 13. 10. 15
383   104 House 2: 89
      105 Martin 101
      106 Baker 6: 128
      107 House 2: 98
384   108 Link 4: 106
      109 Ibid. 4: 102
385   110 House 2: 91
      111 Arthur S. Link, *Wilson the Diplomat*,
           Johns Hopkins Press, Baltimore,
           1957, p. 7
      112 Baker 5: 68
      113 Ibid. 5: 574
      114 Ibid. 6: 205
      115 Link 4: 107
386   116 House 2: 97
      117 Ibid. 2: 98
      118 Ibid. 2: 100
      119 Ibid. 2: 101
      120 Baker 6: 135
387   121 Link 4: 108
      122 House Papers 11. 11. 15
      123 House 2: 69
      124 Page 2: 40
388   125 House 2: 99
      126 Link 4: 108
      127 Digby 191
      128 Link 4: 110
      129 House Papers 10. 12. 15
389   130 Link 4: 66
      131 Ibid. 4: 111

390   132 House 2: 107
      133 Ibid. 2: 107
      134 LP 222
391   135 Baker 6: 138
      136 Ibid. 6: 139
      137 Link 4: 112

CHAPTER XIII

392   1   LP 6
393   2   House 2: 96; Link 4: 107; Millis 243
      3   *The Autobiography of Bertrand
          Russell*, George Allen & Unwin,
          London, 1967, 2: 44; *cf. also* 1: 57
394   4   Ibid. 2: 16–19
      5   Ibid. 2: 44
      6   Taylor 104; on E. D. Morel see
          103 et seq.
395   7   Quoted in Trevor Wilson, *The
          Downfall of the Liberal Party*,
          Collins, London, 1966, p. 66
      8   Trevelyan 326
      9   Gilbert 570
      10 Ibid. 756
396   11 Viscount Simon, *Retrospect*,
          Hutchinson, London, 1952,
          pp. 106–8
      12 F.O. 800. 86. 10
      13 House 2: 106
      14 Quoted in H. Montgomery Hyde,
          Lord Reading, Heinemann,
          London, 1967, p. 194; House
          2: 119
      15 Ibid. 2: 125, 133; *cf. also* F.O. 800.
          86. 77; and Edmund Ions, *James
          Bryce & American Democracy*,
          Macmillan, London, 1968, pp.
          256–7
      16 Trevelyan 322
      17 F.O. 800. 86. 79, 102
      18 Ibid. 800. 86. 79, 108, 499
397   19 LP 703
      20 House 2: 134
      21 Ibid. 2: 123
      22 Ibid. 2: 117
      23 Ibid. 2: 122
398   24 Ibid. 2: 125
      25 Ibid. 2: 122
      26 F.O. 800. 96. 55
      27 Baker 6: 141
      28 *Diary*, 10 Jan., p. 11

398   29 *Diary*, 10 Jan., p. 12
      30 Ibid. 12
399   31 House 2: 124
      32 Ibid. 2: 222
400   33 *Diary*, 15 Jan., p. 23
      34 House 2: 128
      35 Ibid. 2: 129
      36 *Diary*, 15 Jan., p. 24
401   37 F.O. 800. 96. 18; CAB. 42. 7. 8
      38 Rothwell 30
      39 House 2: 120
402   40 Link 4: 116
      41 House 2: 132
      42 Ibid. 2: 133
      43 Link 4: 115
403   44 PP 4: 25
      45 Ibid. 4: 71
404   46 Ibid. 4: 44
      47 Ibid. 4: 69
      48 OGD 1117
405   49 Tumulty 248
      50 LP 515
406   51 Ibid. 521; Lansing 151
      52 LP 524
407   53 OGD 1280; House 2: 138
      54 House 2: 207; *see also* FRUS 153
      55 Ibid. 148, 150; LP 29
408   56 FRUS 156
      57 Ibid. 160–2
409   58 S.R. 308
      59 House 2: 145
      60 Link 4: 93
      61 Ibid. 4: 93
410   62 FRUS 157
      63 LP 531
      64 Link 4: 96
      65 OGD 1286
411   66 F.O. 371. 600. 10 Aug.
      67 CAB. 37. 143. 34, p. 4
412   68 Ibid. 37. 143. 34, p. 10
      69 FRUS 611
413   70 LP 477
      71 House 2: 210
      72 R. H. Gibson and Maurice Prendergast, *The German Submarine War 1914–18*, Constable, London, 1931, p. 52; FRUS, 1915, 527–9
414   73 Admiralty 137, 1933, 135
      74 Link 3: 669; for Lansing's comment *see* LP 39

      75 Parliamentary Papers, vol. 184, p. 1
      76 CAB. 37. 142. 19 and 37. 143. 1
      77 FRUS, 1915, 576, 623, 650 and 1916, 253
      78 Ibid. 1915, 604
415   79 Ibid. 849
      80 LP 331
      81 F.O. 800. 88. 412
      82 Ibid. 800. 88. 410
      83 FRUS 850
      84 House 2: 211
416   85 Ibid. 2: 72
417   86 FRUS, 1916, 173
      87 Ibid. 196
418   88 Ibid. 250
      89 Ibid. 577
      90 LP 332
      91 Ibid. 334
      92 Ibid. 335
      93 Link 4: 144
419   94 Ibid. 4: 336
      95 FRUS 146
      96 F.O. 800. 85
      97 F.O. 352. 1099. 5778
      98 Ibid. 352. 1099. 8827
420   99 FRUS 150
    100 Ibid. 152
421 101 LP 337
    102 Link 4: 153
    103 LP 338
    104 Ibid. 339
422 105 House: 2: 140; Fischer 286
    106 Watt 120
    107 Fischer 177
    108 Ibid. 213
423 109 House 2: 142
424 110 Ibid. 2: 163
    111 Ibid. 2: 156
    112 Link 4: 125
    113 House 2: 163
    114 *Diary*, p. 79
426 115 LP 341
427 116 FRUS 167
    117 Ibid. 195–7
    118 Link 4: 159
    119 Link 4: 161
    120 LP 342
    121 Anderson Diary
428 122 Gregory 143
    123 Professor Link found a print in the Asquith Papers and has repro-

duced it at Link 4: 160; but a
search has not disclosed it in the
P.R.O. nor any sign of its preparation or subsequent discussion

124 CAB. 37. 142. 36
125 F.O. 800. 86. 64
126 Ibid. 800. 88. 461
127 FRUS 170
128 Link 4: 161
429 129 FRUS 211
130 Ibid. 244

CHAPTER XIV

431 1 Link 4: 129
2 LP 306
3 Ibid. 305
432 4 Page 3: 281
5 Link 4: 129
6 Waley 185
433 7 House 2: 171
8 Link 4: 124
9 *Diary*, pp. 78, 91
10 House 2: 174
434 11 Ibid. 2: 183; Link 4: 131
12 Page 3: 284
13 A. M. Gollin, *Proconsul in Politics*,
Anthony Blond, London, 1964,
p. 324
14 Page 3: 282
15 Link 4: 130
16 *Diary*, p. 66
435 17 House 2: 179
18 Ibid. 2: 181
19 Ibid. 2: 182
20 *Diary*, p. 74
436 21 Frances Lloyd George, *The Years
that are Past*, Hutchinson, London, 1967, 209
22 Stevenson 98
23 *Diary*, p. 79
437 24 House 2: 200; Grey 127
25 Digby 196
26 Page 2: 51
438 27 Gregory 154
440 28 Link 4: 171
441 29 FRUS 177
30 Link 4: 175
442 31 LP 533

443 32 OGD 1287
33 Ibid. 1128
34 Ibid. 1130
444 35 Link 4: 185
36 OGD 1142
37 FRUS 198
445 38 Ibid. 185
39 Link 4: 190
40 Ibid. 4: 191
446 41 Ibid. 4: 193
42 S.R. 316
43 OGD 1289
447 44 Lansing 112-15
448 45 LP 340
46 FRUS 204
449 47 LP 337
48 Ibid. 341
450 49 FRUS 183, 202
50 LP 348
51 Ibid. 349
451 52 Digby 196
53 Baker 6: 153
452 54 House 2: 199
55 F.O. 382. 1100. 44529
453 56 House 2: 202
57 Ibid. 2: 200
58 Ibid. 2: 220
59 Ibid. 2: 225
454 60 *Diary*, pp. 91, 93
61 CAB. 42. 9. 3
455 62 Link 4: 139
63 Roskill 245
64 Arnold Bennett, *Journals*, ed. F.
Swinnerton, Penguin, London,
1971, p. 397
456 65 Hankey 479
66 Link 4: 140
67 Hankey 480
68 CAB. 24. 2, G. 76
69 Link 4: 140
457 70 CAB. 42. 11. 6
458 71 Ll. G. I. 688
72 Hankey 480
73 Link 4: 140
74 CAB. 37. 145. 34
459 75 Hankey 483
76 Bertie 1: 334
77 Link 4: 136
78 Grey 2: 136
79 Smith 169
80 House 3: 155, 158, 169

459	81	Baker 7: 218
	82	Lodge 80
460	83	House 2: 256
	84	Ibid. 2: 257
	85	Keynes 178
461	86	Seymour 163
	87	Grey 2: 135
	88	House 2: 289
462	89	Digby 181
463	90	Ll. G. II. 245
	91	Digby 187
	92	Quoted in Millis 9
	93	Ll. G. II. 246
	94	Grey 2: 107
	95	House 2: 120
465	96	Baker 6: 129
	97	FRUS 110
466	98	Link 5: 141
	99	Ibid. 5: 142
	100	Ibid. 5: 142
	101	House 2: 92
467	102	Ed. E. C. Parr, *Lectures on Heroes*, Clarendon Press, Oxford, 1910, p. 200
	103	Annin 363
	104	Link 2: 81
	105	George 111
469	106	S.R. 366
	107	Bern. 107
	108	Page 2: 174
470	109	Ibid. 2: 222
	110	Baker 6: 426

CHAPTER XV

472	1	Link 3: 431
473	2	Tumulty 158
474	3	LP 537
	4	House 2: 226
	5	Link 4: 230
475	6	House 2: 222
	7	LP 539
	8	Link 4: 233
476	9	LP 540
	10	House 2: 231
477	11	OGD 971
	12	FRUS 225
478	13	Link 4: 243
	14	Ibid. 4: 244; House 2: 235
479	15	FRUS 227
	16	LP 546
	17	Ibid. 551
	18	Ibid. 549
	19	FRUS 232
480	20	Link 4: 252
	21	Ibid. 4: 255
	22	LP 555
	23	FRUS 252
481	24	Link 4: 273
	25	Ibid. 4: 268
	26	FRUS 253
482	27	LP 562
	28	FRUS 267
	29	Ibid. 257
	30	Ibid. 265
	31	House 2: 243
	32	FRUS 263
483	33	LP 565
	34	Ibid. 566
484	35	Baker Chronicle 282
	36	Ibid. 287
	37	Link 5: 18
	38	Tumulty 251
485	39	House 2: 278
	40	Link 5: 27
	41	House 2: 282
	42	Ibid. 2: 283
486	43	PP 4: 171; CAB. 37. 148. 31
	44	Baker 6: 212
487	45	House 2: 285
	46	Baker 6: 216
488	47	House 2: 286
	48	Link 5: 22
489	49	Ibid. 5: 22
	50	Ibid. 5: 23
	51	House 2: 296
	52	PP 4: 187
491	53	S.R. 347
	54	House 2: 229
	55	Ibid. 2: 300
	56	Link 5: 28
492	57	FRUS 272
	58	Roskill 274
493	59	CAB. 37. 148. 28; Link 5: 34
494	60	FRUS 42; F.O. 800. 86. 273
	61	House 2: 318
	62	F.O. 800. 109. 155
	63	S.R. 339
495	64	Link 4: 309
496	65	PP 3: 66
	66	Link 4: 318
497	67	House 2: 291

68 Ibid. 2: 304
69 Ibid. 2: 320
498 70 Link 5: 36
71 House 2: 323
72 Ibid. 2: 328
499 73 Houston 1: 322
500 74 Quoted in Max Beloff, *Imperial Sunset*, Methuen, London, 1969, 1: 253

CHAPTER XVI

501 1 House 2: 329
2 FRUS 769
502 3 Ibid. 779
4 Baker 6: 331
5 Willert 45
6 LP 421
7 PP 4: 282
8 F.O. 800. 96. 86 *passim*; Percy 142; Willert 75
503 9 F.O. 800. 86. 309
10 S.R. 344
11 F.O. 800. 86. 311
12 OGD 1295
13 House 2: 318
14 CAB. 37. 155. 20
15 Marder 2: 375–9
504 16 F.O. 382. 1099. 13353
17 FRUS 342
18 F.O. 382. 1099. 17418
19 FRUS 340
20 F.O. 382. 1099. 10308 and 16534
505 21 Ibid. 800. 100. 408
22 Page 3: 304
23 Dugdale 2: 187
24 Percy 37
25 F.O. 800. 96. 15
506 26 Ibid. 800. 96. 78
27 Ibid. 800. 105. 365
28 FRUS 361
29 CAB. 37. 149. 11
30 FRUS 413
507 31 Ibid. 329
32 F.O. 800. 372. 1099
33 FRUS 349
34 Ibid. 362
35 Ibid. 368
508 36 CAB. 37. 137. 28
509 37 Ibid. 37. 151. 32
510 38 FRUS 734

39 Ibid. 739
40 Ibid. 591
511 41 Ibid. 599
42 Ibid. 604
512 43 CAB. 37. 151. 32
44 FRUS, 626
513 45 Ibid. 339
46 Ibid. 352
47 Ibid. 411
48 Ibid. 421
49 Ibid. 422
50 Ibid. 455
51 Ibid. 420
514 52 Ibid. 436
515 53 CAB. 37. 157. 20
54 Cecil 42
55 FRUS, 1915, 206
56 Ibid. 1916, 510
516 57 Ibid. 505
58 Link 5: 67
517 59 F.O. 800. 86. 265
60 Link 5: 67
61 FRUS 412
62 Link 5: 68
63 FRUS 510
64 Link 5: 68
65 FRUS 462
518 66 House 2: 317
67 FRUS 477
519 68 LP 312
69 FRUS 425, 594, 689
70 CAB. 23. 1. 25, p. 54
71 FRUS, 1917, 997
72 Link 5: 74
73 LP 569
520 74 Ibid. 188
75 Ibid. 191
76 Ibid. 571
77 Ibid. 314
78 Ibid. 319
521 79 Gregory 177
80 Page 2: 185
81 Lansing 172
522 82 Page 2: 176; Lansing 167
83 Ibid. 171
523 84 F.O. 352. 1100. 189737
524 85 Page 2: 193
86 Link 5: 370
525 87 House 2: 348
526 88 Bern. 297
89 Baker 6: 250; Link 5: 64

527 90 S.R. 332
91 House 2: 361
92 Link 5: 94
528 93 Ibid. 5: 129
94 Ibid. 5: 129
529 95 House 2: 353
96 Ibid. 2: 379
97 Ibid. 2: 378
98 F.O. 800. 86. 361
530 99 Viereck 283
100 Baker 6: 290
101 Osgood 144
531 102 Ibid. 234
103 Ibid. 150
104 Baker 6: 275
105 House 2: 385
106 Baker 6: 296
107 Mrs. W. 136
532 108 Tumulty 217
109 Link 5: 157
110 Ibid. 5: 160
533 111 Ibid. 5: 42
112 Ibid. 5: 107
113 Ibid. 5: 149

CHAPTER XVII

535 1 J. W. Wheeler-Bennett, *Hindenburg: The Wooden Titan*, Macmillan, London, 1936, p. 5
536 2 House 2: 332
3 OGD 1161
537 4 Ibid. 1141
538 5 Ibid. 974
6 Ibid. 974
7 Link 5: 28
8 OGD 976
9 Bern. 279
10 OGD 981
11 Ibid. 981
12 Link 5: 196
539 13 Birnbaum 128
14 OGD 983
15 Bern. 283; House 2: 332
16 Ibid. 2: 334
17 OGD 983
18 Ibid. 984
540 19 Bern. 307; Gerard 293
20 Bern. 290
21 FRUS 55
22 Birnbaum 158

23 OGD 986
24 May 398
541 25 OGD 987; Birnbaum 159
26 Ibid. 165
27 Bern. 296; OGD 987; House 2: 334
28 May 299
542 29 OGD 989
30 Baker 6: 365
543 31 CAB. 37. 160. 15
32 Hankey 556
33 Roskill 312
544 34 Asquith 154
35 Hankey 557
35a Roskill 317
36 Ibid. 551
37 Ll. G. I. 856
545 38 Ibid. II. 31
39 CAB. 24. 2, G. 78; extensively quoted in Ll. G. II. 31–50
40 CAB. 24. 2, G. 76
41 Asquith 138
42 Ll. G. I. 833
43 Ibid. I. 877
44 Jenkins 416
546 45 Ll. G. I. 253; Baker 6: 357
46 Ll. G. I. 856
47 C. P. Scott 227
48 Stevenson 300
49 Jones 71
547 50 Marder 3. 2. 79
548 51 F.O. 382. 1100. 176387, 178020
52 Ibid. 382. 1100. 173266
53 House 2: 321
54 F.O. 371. 2795. 1763
549 55 Ibid. 371. 2795
56 Gregory 174
57 F.O. 371. 2796. 205593
58 S.R. 359
550 59 CAB. 37. 157, p. 4.
60 Link 5: 81
61 Keynes 197
551 62 Ibid. 201
63 Link 5: 182
64 Elie J. Bois, *Truth on the Tragedy of France*, Hodder & Stoughton, London, 1940, p. 214
65 Roskill 313
66 Hankey 557
552 67 *History of the Times* (1952), 339
68 Lord Newton, *Lord Lansdowne*, Macmillan, London, 1929, p. 455

	69	Ll. G. I. 862
533	70	Ibid. I. 904
	71	Rothwell 54
	72	CAB. 150. 16
	73	Ll. G. I. 873
	74	CAB. 37. 160. 22
	75	Ibid. 37. 160. 20; Trevelyan 322
554	76	CAB. 24. 2, p. 13, G. 76
	77	Asquith 147
	78	Ll. G. I. 891
	79	CAB. 37. 160. 30
555	80	Trevelyan 324
	81	F.O. 800. 108. 563
	82	Grey 2: 131
	83	F.O. 800. 96. 389
	84	Trevelyan 325
	85	Cecil 44
556	86	Stevenson 121
	87	Robbins 346
557	88	OGD 1172
558	89	House 1: 394
	90	F.O. 811. 111. 259
	91	Stephen Spender, *World within World*, Hamish Hamilton, London, 1951
	92	House 1: 463
	93	C. P. Scott 52; *cf. also* 48
	94	R. F. V. Houston, *Lives of the Lord Chancellors 1885–1940*, Clarendon Press, Oxford, 1964, p. 175
	95	House 1: 432
	96	F.O. 800. 108. 555
	97	Martin 68
559	98	F.O. 800. 108. 553
	99	Lord Parmoor, *A Retrospect*, Heinemann, London, 1936, p. 111
	100	Martin 103
	101	Ibid. 115
560	102	Link 5: 186
	103	Ibid. 5: 187
	104	FRUS 310
	105	Baker 6: 368
	106	House 2: 392
561	107	Ibid. 2: 393
	108	Link 5: 188
	109	Ibid. 5: 209
562	110	Ibid. 5: 189
	111	OGD 993; Bern. 305; LP 573
	112	Link 5: 194
	113	Seymour 186

CHAPTER XVIII

563	1	Watt 139
564	2	FRUS, 1916, 863
	3	Ibid. 1916, 71
	4	Link 5: 195
	5	LP 462; Baker 6: 343
565	6	Ibid. 6: 370
	7	Ibid. 6: 337
	8	Mrs. W. 145
	9	House 2: 395
	10	Baker 6: 380
566	11	House 2: 395
	12	Ibid. 2: 407
	13	Link 5: 199
	14	House 2: 397
	15	Lansing 178
	16	Link 5: 199
567	17	Baker 6: 390
	18	Link 5: 206
	19	Ibid. 5: 209
	20	Baker 6: 380
	21	Ibid. 6: 321
	22	FRUS 98
	23	Lansing 179
568	24	OGD 1000
	25	Ibid. 1075
	26	Ibid. 1053
569	27	Ibid. 1054
570	28	Ibid. 1057
	29	Ibid. 1063
	30	Ibid. 1066
	31	Ibid. 1064
	32	Ibid. 1060
	33	Ibid. 1066
571	34	Ibid. 423
	35	Ibid. 1066
	36	Fischer 315
	37	OGD 1060
	38	Ibid. 424
	39	Ibid. 991
	40	Ibid. 993; Bern. 305
	41	FRUS 312
	42	Ibid. 319
572	43	OGD 995; Bern. 307
	44	FRUS 700, 868
	45	OGD 997
573	46	Ibid. 1071
	47	Ibid. 1072
	48	Ibid. 996
	49	F.O. 800. 96. 378–82

574 50 OGD 998
51 FRUS 88
52 OGD 421, 790
53 Ibid. 1078
54 Ibid. 1066
55 Ibid. 1075
56 FRUS 93
575 57 Ibid. 92
58 Baker 6: 393
59 FRUS 95
576 60 Link 5: 217
61 FRUS 98
62 CAB. 161. 40
63 Ibid. 160. 44
577 64 Link 5: 217
65 House 2: 407
66 FRUS 98
67 Ibid. 103
578 68 House 2: 407
69 Link 5: 73
70 PP 2: 346
71 Ibid. 2: 381
72 Link 5: 73
73 House 2: 409
74 Page 2: 207
75 F.O. 371. 2806. 263429
579 76 Bertie 86
77 House 2: 411
580 78 Baker 6: 387
79 Link 5: 222
581 80 Lansing 187
582 81 Link 5: 225
82 Ibid. 5: 233, 332
83 Link 5: 223
584 84 Dugdale 172-4; S. H. Zebel, *Balfour*, C.U.P., London, 1973, p. 224
85 Ll. G. I. 999
86 W. S. Churchill, *Thoughts and Adventures*, Odhams, London, 1932, p. 195
585 87 Ll. G. I. 1105, 1106; FRUS 101
586 88 Link 5: 212
89 CAB. 42. 26. 2
90 Ibid. 23. 1. 2
91 For this and subsequent quotations *see* Crawford's memorandum printed in the Cabinet paper F.O. 371. 2800. 240887
587 92 Link 5: 204
588 93 House 2: 398

589 94 CAB. 23. 1. 41
95 Link 5: 231
96 Roskill 347
590 97 L & D 578
591 98 FRUS 123
99 Ibid. 6
592 100 John Grigg, *The Young Lloyd George*, Eyre, Methuen, London, 1973, p. 282
101 Fischer 317
102 FRUS 188
593 103 Bern. 320
104 OGD 1088
105 FRUS 112
106 Bern. 321
107 House 2: 416
108 OGD 1010
594 109 Bern. 325
110 OGD 1012

CHAPTER XIX

595 1 Hardinge 207
596 2 A. Zimmern, *The American Road to World Peace*, Dutton, New York, 1953, p. 77
597 3 PP 4. 405
598 4 Link 5: 226
5 Digby 204
599 6 Link 5: 269
7 White 478
8 Link 2: 142
600 9 Mrs. W. 148
10 House 2: 417
11 Link 5: 251
601 12 LP 575
13 Link 5: 251
14 Gerson 48
602 15 Stevenson 38
16 R. Lansing, *The Big Four and Others of the Peace Conference*, Houghton Mifflin, Boston, 1921, p. 210
17 Gerson 76
18 Ibid. 69
19 Mrs. W. 135
20 House 2: 419
21 Mrs. W. 151
22 House 2: 419
23 Ibid. 2: 419
24 Lansing 193

603	25	Seymour 194
	26	Lansing 194
	27	FRUS 24
	28	Page 312
	29	Lansing 195
	30	Link 5: 254
604	31	FRUS 25; PP 4: 407
606	32	Baker 6: 431
	33	Ibid. 6: 430
	34	Link 5: 271
	35	Hansard H.C. 90. 1209
	36	William St. Leger, ed. Moynihan, *People at War 1914–1918*, David and Charles, Newton Abbott, 1973, p. 52
	37	Julian Grenfell, '*Into Battle*', *Poems of Today*, Sidgwick and Jackson, London, 1924, p. 176
607	38	Quoted in Link 5: 274
	39	Link 5: 271
	40	Baker 6: 433
	41	LP 329
608	42	FRUS 82
	43	Link 5: 263
	44	Dean Acheson, *Present at the Creation*, Hamish Hamilton, London, 1970, p. 303
	45	S.R. 214
	46	FRUS 489
	47	Ibid. 509
	48	Ibid. 505
609	49	House 2: 429
	50	Ibid. 2: 400
610	51	Ibid. 2: 402
	52	Ibid. 2: 403
	53	Willert 64
	54	House 2: 403
	55	Ibid. 2: 411
611	56	Fowler 13
	57	Link 5: 254
	58	Ibid. 5: 280
	59	House 2: 422
	60	Ibid. 2: 423
	61	Link 5: 280
612	62	Fowler 15
613	63	Ibid. 16
	64	Link 5: 280
614	65	OGD 1013
	66	Link 5: 257
	67	Ibid. 5: 257
615	68	Ibid. 5: 257
	69	Ibid. 5: 258
	70	Ibid. 5: 259
616	71	House 2: 431
	72	Ibid. 2: 429
617	73	Link 5: 278
	74	Tuchman 136
	75	OGD 1047
	76	Baker 6: 443
	77	House 2: 433
	78	Lansing 210; Bern. 379
	79	FRUS 97
618	80	Ibid. 97
	81	Ibid. 102
	82	Houston 1: 227
	83	Lansing 211
619	84	OGD 1199
	85	Ibid. 1214
620	86	Ibid. 1201
	87	Ibid. 1205
	88	Birnbaum 283
621	89	OGD 1205
	90	Ibid. 1320
	91	May 414
622	92	Ottokar Czernin, *In the World War*, London, 1919, p. 118
	93	Ibid., p. 124
	94	OGD 349
	95	Ibid. 681
	96	FRUS 24
	97	Ibid. 27
	98	Ibid. 27
623	99	Gerson 70
	100	House 2: 434
	101	OGD 350
	102	Ibid. 410
	103	Ibid. 695
624	104	OGD 253, 273
	105	Ibid. 1021
	106	Ibid. 1027
	107	Ibid. 1045
625	108	Ibid. 1047
	109	Link 5: 284
	110	House 2: 434
626	111	Ibid. 2: 450
	112	*Thoughts and Adventures*, op. cit. 90
628	113	OGD 1217
	114	Ibid. 147
629	115	Hankey 2: 640
	116	OGD 1017
	117	LP 579; Link 5: 263
630	118	LP 581

630	119	LP 583
	120	Ibid. 582
	121	OGD 1218
631	122	Ibid. 1030
	123	Ibid. 1263
632	124	FRUS 92
	125	OGD 373
	126	Ibid. 1218
	127	Ibid. 1260
	128	Ibid. 1266
633	129	Ibid. 1265
	130	Ibid. 1267
	131	Ibid. 1268
634	132	Link 5: 248
	133	Watt 138
	134	OGD 345
635	135	Ibid. 125
	136	Ibid. 150

CHAPTER XX

636	1	Lansing 212
637	2	Lane 233
	3	House 2: 442
	4	Ibid. 2: 444
638	5	Lansing 219; LP 591
	6	Link 5: 297; Lane 233; Lansing 215
639	7	Baker 6: 460
	8	Link 5: 305
	9	Osgood 230
	10	PP 4: 425; FRUS 111
	11	Quoted from Rosenman in John Gunther, *Roosevelt in Retrospect*, Hamish Hamilton, London, 1950, p. 13
640	12	LP 19
	13	FRUS 104
	14	OGD 1322
	15	FRUS 112
	16	Ibid. 38
	17	Ibid. 40
	18	Ll. G. I. 985
641	19	FRUS 42
	20	Ibid. 129
	21	F.O. 371. 2803 (5 Dec.)
	22	FRUS 139
	23	OGD 1324; LP 603; FRUS 137
	24	Ibid. 55
642	25	OGD 1334, 1336
	26	Link 5: 293, 306
	27	FRUS 111
	28	Ibid. 124
	29	Link 5: 310
643	30	LP 610
	31	Ibid. 595
	32	H. Hoover, *The Ordeal of Woodrow Wilson*, McGraw Hill, New York, 1958, p. 7
644	33	S.R. 381
	34	Houston 235
	35	Lane 238
645	36	S.R. 379
	37	Link 5: 340
	38	Lane 239
646	39	CAB. 23. 1. 181
	40	Louis 79
	41	FRUS 493
647	42	Ibid. 119
	43	Ibid. 43
	44	LP 593
648	45	FRUS 152
	46	Ibid. 147
649	47	Page 3: 361
650	48	Tuchman 160
651	49	Ibid. 152
	50	Dugdale 2: 138
	51	FRUS 148
	52	Tuchman 165
652	53	PP 4: 438
	54	Lansing 227
653	55	Baker 6: 478
	56	Lansing 229
	57	Tuchman 177
	58	Ibid. 181
654	59	FRUS 158
	60	Lansing 231
	61	Fischer 84
656	62	J. Kerney, *The Political Education of Woodrow Wilson*, Century Co., New York, 1926, p. 142
657	63	PP 4: 435
	64	House 2: 460
	65	Houston 240
	66	Link 5: 362
	67	House 1: 210
	68	*D.N.A.B.* 18: 89
	69	Baker 7: 6
659	70	*The Ordeal of Woodrow Wilson*, op. cit. 6
	71	Mrs. W. 158
	72	PWW 8: 490

	73	Lane 175
660	74	Annin 214
	75	PP 4: 292
661	76	FRUS 520
	77	CAB. 23. 2. 95
	78	Keynes 224
	79	FRUS 516
	80	Link 5: 382
	81	FRUS 198
	82	Link 5: 324
	83	Ibid. 5: 346
662	84	LP 617
	85	Ibid. 623
	86	FRUS 197
663	87	PP 4: 292
	88	Link 5: 396
664	89	Lansing 233
	90	Link 5: 398
	91	House 2: 464
	92	Link 5: 397
	93	House 2: 454
665	94	Ll. G. I. 699
	95	LP 628; Lansing 286
	96	Link 5: 402
666	97	Ibid. 5: 405
	98	Houston 243
	99	Link 5: 405
	100	Ed. Cronon, *The Cabinet Diaries of Josephus Daniels 1913-1921*, Nebraska U.P., 1963, p. 118
	101	Link 5: 408
	102	Lansing 237
	103	House 2: 466
	104	Baker 6: 504
667	105	LP 360

	106	House 2: 467
	107	Ibid. 2: 469
	108	Link 5: 420
668	109	Houston 250
	110	George 190
	111	LP 638
669	112	Link 5: 423
	113	Millis 434
	114	PP 5: 6; Lansing 240
	115	S.R. 289
670	116	Baker 6: 511
	117	FRUS 199
	118	Baker 6: 515
	119	Millis 445
671	120	Lansing 243
	121	House 2: 473
	122	Tumulty 265
673	123	PWW 5: 356
674	124	FRUS 201
	125	Millis 452
676	126	Tuchman 180
677	127	Link 5: 419
	128	PWW 6: 663
678	129	Bragdon 404
681	130	Ll. G. I. 44
	131	Link 5: 414
683	132	PP 5: 47
684	133	Ibid. 5: 119
	134	Ibid. 5: 64
	135	Ibid. 5: 94
	136	Baker 7: 245
	137	Page 2: 214
685	138	Osgood 271
687	139	House 1: 124
688	140	PP 5: 16

INDEX

The larger subjects are in capitals and the larger headings under them in bold type.

WOODROW WILSON is in bold capitals, the larger headings under him in ordinary capitals, and the larger sub-headings under them in bold type. Note that the headings are confined to personal characteristics and general subjects; if the reference wanted is his connection with a specific subject, e.g. PRINCETON, it should be looked for under that subject.